The Arab Sprung

The Juliet Montague Book Collection

Part One of the Muslim Romance Trilogy

THE YEAR I LEARNED TO TEXT
Why Am I Having Sex with a Muslim in My Basement?

"If you want to be truly entertained by one of the most original writers in America today, *The Year I Learned to Text* is a must read. Ms. Montague brilliantly rivals Sarah Silverman's rhetorical disrespect for all things politically and religiously reverent—minus the gratuitous offensive verbiage." **Steven Emerson**, author of *American Jihad: The Terrorists Living Among Us*

"Ms. Montague cunningly spins one woman's appalling romantic tragedy into an enduring hilarious treasure." **Judy Carter**, humorist and author of *The Comedy Bible* and *The Message of You: Turn Your Life Story into a Money-Making Speaking Career*

Part Two of the Muslim Romance Trilogy

JIHAD HONEYMOON IN HOLLYWOOD
Not Without My Dogs

"Any Western woman considering an affair with a Muslim man must read this book—before it's too late. Juliet Montague is a crafty writer in her sensual frankness concerning the sexuality of a loving, post menopausal lady." **Abul Kasem**, Islam critic and the author of *Sex and Sexuality in Islam*

"Sharia law is coming—one American woman at a time! Juliet Montague laces her hilarious novel with the cruel insights of loving a Muslim man. I salute her candor. Pay sincere attention to her well written message." **Cassandra**, author of *Escape! From an Arab Marriage* and *Thirty-Three Secrets Arab Men Never Tell American Women*

"The *Fifty Shades of Grey* Trilogy is an unintentionally humorous lap cat compared to the Bengal cougar of this long-awaited sequel to *The Year I Learned to Text; Why Am I Having Sex with a Muslim in My Basement?* Juliet Montague continues to weave more colorful erotic tales in this intentionally funny, heartbreaking saga of love gone wrong." **C. Stephen Foster**, author of *Awakening the Actor Within*

The Arab Sprung

*While a Muslim Sleeps
in the
White House*

Juliet Montague

Banned-in-Indiana Publishing
Hollywood, California

Copyright © 2016 Juliet Montague

The moral right of the author has been asserted.

All rights reserved. No part of this publication may be reproduced, stored in a retrieval system, or transmitted, in any form or by any means, without the prior permission in writing of the publisher, nor be otherwise circulated in any form of binding or cover other than that in which it is published and without a similar condition including this condition being imposed on the subsequent purchaser.

Any resemblance to events, places, or persons living or dead, although probably true, is coincidental and the product of wishful thinking on behalf of the author.

Published by Banned-in-Indiana Publishing
Hollywood, California

Library of Congress Control Number: 2016950095
Juliet Montague, Los Angeles, CALIFORNIA

Print ISBN 978-0-692-69594-4

Typesetting services by BOOKOW.COM

Part Three of The Muslim Romance Trilogy is dedicated to my free-spirited bungalow buddy Beth, who never judged me. Sitting on my front porch, I sometimes hear her calling out to me from the walkway. May you rest in peace, Goth Girl.

THE MUSLIM ROMANCE TRILOGY

CAST OF CHARACTERS

JULIE	The Foolish Woman
ALI	The Muslim Misogynist
HOUND	The Faithful Shepherd Mix
BRUTE	The Snobbish Purebred Maltese
MORTICIA	The Cat
ALEXANDRA	The Model Daughter
RAE	The Omniscient Sister
TOMMY	The Nephew
CAPTAIN BRAINARD	CIA/Womanizer/Actor

And Introducing
MOTHER

THE HOLLYWOOD BUNGALOW RESIDENTS

Artemus	The Jewish Socialist Psycho
Bunny Brown	Original Resident, age 94
Elsa	Evil German Frau, age 92
Oscar	Bunny's lover, age 83
Kandi	Latina Transvestite
Marlene	Hollywood Historian Packrat
Michael	Resident Male Prostitute
Miranda (Randi)	Goth Girlfriend
The One-Legged Invalid	Le Miserable
Earl and Carl	The Newlyweds Next Door

COSTARS AND DAY PLAYERS

Adam Bender	Foot Fetish Internet Date
Ahmadinejad	The Crazy President of Iran
Ahmed	Liquor Store Indian Muslim
Akbar	Token Potential Black Lover
Allen Gainsborough	Husband No. 1; Father of Elizabeth
Avi	The Israeli Aviator
Barack Hussein Obama	Muslim President of America

Aisha	Muhammad's child bride
Barry	Neighbor with Garage
Bennie	Internet Bunny Killer
Benjamin	Hopefully, a Son-in-Law
Benayahu Ashkenazi	Masturbating Roofer
Beryl	Senior Female Advisor
Bill Nob	Talk Radio Spitting Host
Brandon	Surfer Dude
Brian	Husband No. 3; Father of Alexandra
Brian Ray Jenkins	Television Actor/Client
Bud Taylor	Vine Elementary School Teacher
Carrie Learned	Soap Opera Stage Manager
Cary Kowalski	Valentine's Day Massacre
Cesar	Another Really Bad Kisser
Christopher	Gay Realtor No. 1
Chuck Christensen	Radio Jock with Small Dick
Clark Ghabal	Superman
Clint Eastwood	Clint Eastwood
Cole	Crestline Mountain Neighbor
Dan	Crestline Peeping Tom
The DeCavalcantes	Mafia Investors
Doc	Husband No. 4
Dr. Hu	The Suicide Assistant
Dr. Wilson	Bob Hope Clinic Physician
Dutch	Another Ex-Boyfriend
Edwin	The Flasher Uncle
Elizabeth	The Uptight First Daughter
Gavin	Hero Husband with COPD
Ghali	Ali's Mentally Ill Brother
Glen	The Absent Son
Grant Sanchez	L.A. Loser and Scum
Hugo	The Hungarian Chef
Jack and Timothy	Cabin Rehab Crew
Jamila	Fellatio Instructor
Janet	Cellist and Brian Ray's Gal
Jaz	Medical Marijuana Moron
Jesus of Nazarene	Gracious Lord
Jim	The Hot Electrician
Joan and Bruce	Fair Weather Friends
John	Deaf Mini-Ranger
Kathleen	The Granddaughter
Kirstie Alley	Kirstie Alley

Koshy	The Christian Cunnilingus Pro
Leonard	The Pup Tent Philosopher
Magda	Drug Store Clerk
Manny	The Grandson
Marie	The Gold Digger Psychic
Maryanne	Passing Confidante
Mike Zamboni	Motorcycle Macho Man
Milton Billings	Husband No. 2; Father of Glen
Muhammad	Troublemaking Islamic Prophet
Pablo	Dancing Zorro Television Extra
Patti	Julie's Roommate Circa 1970
Peter (Pan)	Julie's High School Sweetheart
Rafael Ramirez	Relationship Guru/Lawyer
Robert & Ralph	The British Puffs
Samuel	Oktoberfest Slacker
Sarah & Sam	Co-Dependent Spouses
Sean Amir	The Beer Can Realtor
Siamanto Sam	The Angry Armenian
Spot	The Sister's Cat
Stanley Plotkin	The Horny Optometrist
Suicide Bombers	Too Many to List
Ted and Trudy	The Mountain Militia
Tina	The Brown Shirt Nazi
Tony	The Son-in-Law
Vince Vaughn	Vince Vaughn
Vivian and Charles	The Wannabee In-Laws
Wayne	District Attorney Investigator
Wilbur Shank	Reborn Mountain Felon

Manute Bowl: Julie, Jason, Jared, and Jonathan

Counter-Terrorism Squirrel Squad: Boris Badenov; Natasha Fatale; Rocket J. Squirrel; and Mr. Know-It All, Bullwinkle the Moose

The Fag Hag Heroes: Joel, Donovan, and Stephen

The Mountain Widows: Rory and Leighanne

Useful Middle Eastern and Islamic Terms

Allah	The god Muhammad dreamed up
Allahu Akbar	Our god is the Greatest
Burka	Full length rape guard
Beheading	The best way to kill anyone
FGM	Female Genital Mutilation
Ghusl	Ritual penis cleansing
Halal	Lawful
Haraam	Unlawful
Hijab	Modesty scarf to prevent lust
Jihad	An excuse to behead anyone
Infidel	Filthy dirty stinking non-believer
Inshalla	Blaming Allah for non-commitments
Kadija	Mo's first wife
Kafir, dhimmi	Non-Muslim, the unenlightened
Muhammad	Mo, the prophet ordained by Allah
Mussie	Modern derogatory term for Muslim
Mu'tah, sighe	Temporary marriage/prostitution
Sharia Law	Allah's Life Laws on Everything
Shawarma chicken	The only poultry Ali will eat
Ta'arouf	Phony Persian politeness
Tagwa	Good deeds and god-consciousness
Taqiyya, taqhiyeh, taqiya	Lies, lies, and more lies

Written on Location at

The Cahuenga Boulevard Bungalow, Hollywood, California
Le Petit Chateau d'Enchanté, Crestline, California

No animals were intentionally harmed during the writing of this trilogy

Acknowledgments

Writing is a lonely calling, for one must write alone. With gratitude I thank those of you who encouraged me to tell my stories, when others scoffed, and who left me in my loneliness to get the job done. You know who you are.

I am deeply indebted to Steve Passiouras at bookow.com, who took the pain out of formatting my books for CreateSpace and turned the daunting experience of publishing into pure joy.

Contents

Prologue
    Veterans Day, November 11, 2013   xvii

Chapter 1
    Ho-Ho-Ho; Christmas, 2010   1

Chapter 2
    The Summer of '66 and Great Expectations   4

Chapter 3
    Espionage and a Jew   15

Chapter 4
    1956, Women Without Men   23

Chapter 5
    Christmas Eve and Dirty Laundry   28

Chapter 6
    A Redneck Birthday and Sibling Rivalry Karaoke   37

Chapter 7
    Addiction Rewind and The Emperor's New Clothes   45

Chapter 8
    A New Beginning The Easy Way   53

Chapter 9
    Pub Crawl and The Big Dick   65

Chapter 10
    Westside Story and Te'Kila Shots   80

Chapter 11
    Too Sexy for My Shirt and The 80th Day   91

Chapter 12
  Pink Labia and The Cole Porter Song Book   105
Chapter 13
  Puttin' On The Big Girl Panties   116
Chapter 14
  Politics and Potty Training   127
Chapter 15
  Soft Water Salt and The Young Turks   135
Chapter 16
  Poisoned Arrows and Wine in a Box   152
Chapter 17
  The Camper Pee and Zorro   159
Chapter 18
  The Paramount Lot, Competition Zumba, and The Fable   166
Chapter 19
  Poster Beds and Hemingway on a Bun   180
Chapter 20
  Antipasto and The Shah of Iran   185
Chapter 21
  Circus Tents and Kissing Girls   193
Chapter 22
  The Long and Winding Road to Chaos   206
Chapter 23
  Go Ahead, Make My Day   210
Chapter 24
  Carrots for an Elephant and the Nurturing Gene   220
Chapter 25
  Empty Toilet Rolls and Naked on the Bed   226
Chapter 26
  Eleanor Roosevelt and A Guinness Moustache   234

Chapter 27
  The Writing Life, High Tide, and Audrey Hepburn   244
Chapter 28
  Mother's Day Regrets and Putting It All On My Tab   256
Chapter 29
  Seeing is Believing and Get Along Little Doggies   268
Chapter 30
  My Mother's Curse and It's a Dog's Life   284
Chapter 31
  The Prince of Polo and Jiggling Tin Cans   292
Chapter 32
  There's Always Hope   308
Chapter 33
  Handcuff Fantasies and Easy Check Out   333
Chapter 34
  Bowling For Lebowski   343
Chapter 35
  Noodling and Tom Sawyer   348
Chapter 36
  A Nip, a Tuck, and a Hand Job   359
Chapter 37
  Pride, Prejudice, and Pyramids   370
Chapter 38
  Never On Sunday and Breakup Breadsticks   381
Chapter 39
  Shaken, But Not Stirred   390
Chapter 40
  Green Boards and Hoping for a Miracle   418
Chapter 41
  Mikhail Baryshnikov and the Ugly Duckling   430

Chapter 42
    Dog Shit and Playing God   449

Chapter 43
    Crutches, a Stroller, and a Chair   465

Chapter 44
    DIY and Opportunity Knocks   481

Chapter 45
    Miss Manners, Drawing Blood, and Cruel Intentions   498

Chapter 46
    Honey, Don't You Have a Dream?   511

Chapter 47
    Cobwebs, Coconut Vodka, and Cocktails at Six   522

Chapter 48
    Looking For Closure in the Kimchi   544

Chapter 49
    Fan Letters and Tow Trucks   567

Chapter 50
    Potato Flakes and the Death of Butterflies   576

Epilogue   599

The Soundtrack   601

Juliet's Recommended Reading   604

About the Author   605

The Arab Sprung

Prologue

Veterans Day, November 11, 2013

Current Price of *Moving On*: $37,600

> Novel no. 1, $3,500
> Alcohol, $5,475
> Vent Decontamination, $300
> New Front Gate, $1,500
> Tankless Water Heater, $2,800
> One Pretentious Billboard, $4,200
> New Neck, $8,000
> Nicotine, $5,570
> Online Dating, $160
> Novel no. 2, $3,200
> Electronic Cigarettes and Nicotine Oil, $295
> Escape to Ireland, $2,200
> COCO Mademoiselle by Chanel, $175
> Reams of paper, ink, and highlighter, $225

Who is he carelessly fucking now? I ponder the null constantly recurring question.

You broke up with him before he officially broke up with you; remember?

And as I flip myself to one side and peak at the clock, I jerk the covers up and over my head. I am sure that right now in this pre-dawn moment, he is fucking no one, lest he has moved to another time zone, Afghanistan perhaps, as he had portended. It was not Ali's custom to be up and out and away from his mother before nine a.m.

Under the silently spinning, dust free—clean, clean, clean, you sad lonely woman—plastic palmed ceiling fan, where once he shamed me, in this room now chilled with the slightest hint of a California autumn, I awake still in darkness to what I hope to be the end of my international jet leg.

Always contemplating the current degree of my insanity, I tug the twisted, hot-flashed sheet tightly over my shoulder in the realization that, yes, foolish woman, even a trip to the Emerald Isle in search of a rugged potato farmer has failed to yield a diversion from your most intimate yearnings.

In that sweet, hot summer of 2010, did it truly take my very own personal Aladdin just a few days less than Mickey Rourke's 9½ *Weeks* to knock me from my imaginary tower of significance in his mystery life to a puddle of humiliation at his sandaled feet?

Just as the ghost of Emily Bronte's wild and cursed Cathy taunted Heathcliff from the fairy caves of Penistone Crag, I hear him whispering to me from beyond the draped sheers of the bedroom window, beyond the metal trellis twined with barren jasmine vines, beyond the bungalow walkway leading to the sleeping streets of Hollywood.

Perhaps it is from behind the dormant vegetable garden of Mr. and Mr. Gaylord, the tidy newly married neighbors, that my charming, black-eyed, chiseled chin Middle Eastern lover chastises me in a haunting whisper.

Julie, Julie, Julie,
Don't you miss me yet?

So today, the three-year anniversary marking the execution of a disastrous feckless relationship and the beginning of my sexual hiatus—time enough alone to vainly publish the first two volumes of the longest love letter ever written for the entire judgmental world to read—Ali has pierced the fourth wall of my pitiful life stage to thrill me, presumably posthumously, once again.

Tossing to find the perfect spot—the clock radio still quiet, the time five fifty-five—I pull the cool satin comforter up over my camisole-cupped breasts. Lying on my back, I settle in deeper. Bill Nob on the KFI early morning Los Angeles talk show would soon mumble out his fractured sarcastic version of the noxious news of the week, prattling on at the prescribed alarm time of six-thirty. No sense in starting my day yet, although two overstuffed suitcases urging my immediate procrastinated attention lay sprawled open on my living room floor, as my first day back on American soil was spent making a one hundred and eighty mile turnaround to my aunt and uncle's to fetch the one unconditional love of my life.

Ali is here beside me under the sheet asking me timidly in his culturally appropriate ta'arouf manner if *I am ready.*

And, of course, I am.

The pastel gold-framed watercolor of the resurrected Jesus watching over me, my legs open. I skim the toenails of my right foot under and across the top sheet, where it stops at the bump on the bed. Brute answers with a staccato snore and a robust spurt onto his blankie. The old Maltese with minimal teeth and dreadful morning breath, who has acquiesced to sleep on my bed one more time, wisely ignores such occasions of my lustful despair, and the seductive spell has been broken for only a shameful moment, as my hand furtively takes position.

I am so easy, a masturbatory slut. While I am battery poor, evidenced by my various solar-powered Victorian garden lights, flameless *LED* porch candles, and the Sony Walkman tape player, there is no need for the Energizer bunny in the bedroom.

I seem to regularly walk about with a sweet burning somewhere between the descending crux of the *V* and the very point at which my plush inner thighs begin. On mornings when he returns to me, I awake with a painful swelling that is only soothed by gently soothing fingertips through satin pajama bottoms. He's just taken a shower, dried himself with my rubber ducky bath towel and smells of his favorite blue Rainsoft water conditioner body wash. The long black hair swept about his neck glistens. Within a very short time, with his promise that he will enter me at the beginning of my climax, the gentle soothing fingers work themselves into a familiar frenzy as I turn my face to his, my eager thin walls painfully pulsating in the empty chamber, and beg for him to fill me.

But he never does. His arms never encircle me. His fingers never slip into the cotton cami to sweetly twist an erect nipple. His thigh never crosses over my tummy to trap me in place. But it is his right hand, delicate and light, that so cleverly parts the moist meaty folds to find the little man in the boat and bring him safely and exquisitely to shore. This is my fantasy of what never was, because I am the director and I call the shots.

I brought forth the morning's ablution with hysterical tears and the accompanying pitiful sob.

> *Ali, Ali, Ali,*
> *Don't you miss me yet?*

I am truly mad.

From the bedside radio Bill Nob *On The News* abruptly shakes my sensibilities as he reminds me once again that my inconsequential, small spoiled pouting life is truly not worthy of sympathy, empathy, or even a get well card. The result of Typhoon Haiyan crushing into the Philippines, the strongest tropical cyclone to ever make it to landfall, has left more than ten thousand dead and four million persons displaced. The people are seeking shelter in boats and in freight containers. Crazed survivors swarm the airport. Rotting bodies line the shores and fill the streets. All this mayhem while I lay sumptuously under a polyester faux-satin bedspread.

Looters have taken over and Mr. Nob votes vehemently for their immediate execution. "Shoot them on sight!" He's very good at ruling from his glass cage pulpit at the Clear Channel Studios in Burbank, just a hop, skip and jump, as the crow flies, from my bungalow on Cahuenga Boulevard to the other side of the Hollywood Hills.

My thoughts turn to my first self-publishing company, Xlibris, where my writing journey began, along with thirty-five hundred dollars, in the Midwest United States. From there it was quickly dropped into a cardboard office cubicle somewhere in the Philippines. Is my first Filipino grammar editor under water? I should have been kinder to her, after all. And is my first marketing advisor seeking shelter in a container? I should have stopped screaming at her each time she called with another scheme to get more money out of me. Making amends might be difficult, as all that ill-spent suspicious anger is water under the bridge now, so to speak.

I leap from the bed in disgust of my daily leisure routine, yet quickly return to my dry haven, but for the moist sheets, with a cup of java foamed with whipped hazelnut non-fat creamer and my Blackberry. Apparently, I am the only idiot in L.A. who still owns one.

The typhoon disaster story has now moved on to more frightening news of the morning.

Iran, it seems, is cultivating plutonium in some dark cave in the hope of removing all infidels from the planet. More frightening is the news that President Obama's approval rating is collapsing, which is frightening for Mrs. Obama, indeed. Mr. Nob repeated the presidential quote heard round the world regarding the implementation of *The Affordable Care Act*, "If you like your plan, you can keep it."

Government enforced healthcare at a somewhat surprising cost is being forced down America's throat; a sort of negative blow job for the tired, the poor, the huddled masses yearning to breathe free—and now anyone with a pre-existing condition. I have missed the regulatory coming out of Obamacare and its penalties on those who refuse to swallow. I am sixty-five and receive Medicare. Time will tell just how long I shall continue smiling like a Cheshire cat.

I receive a text from my good friend and creative guru, another married homosexual, Stephen. This town is rife with them. During my celibacy, I've become quite the sought-after Fag Hag.

> Monday, November 13, 2013; 7:25a STEPHEN: Remember, three pages a day!
> 7:26a   JULIE: Yes, of course. Thank you for the wakeup call.
> 7:26a   STEPHEN: What were you really doing?
> 7:27a   JULIE: Masturbating.

> 7:27a   STEPHEN: Well, cougar that should put you on the bestseller list right away!

As usual, my kitchen desk scowls at me through scribbled post-it notes, journals lined up against maize walls, diaries stacked like dead soldiers, mourned and not forgotten. I tire of the multiple three-ring binder research décor in my small living room, the pages of word-processed notes peering at me from the iron swirled cookbook stand on my kitchen counter. Where there should be a recipe for humble pie, instead there are merciless memories, ideas, quotes, and song lyrics waiting to be illegally unleashed onto a waiting world. And to my amazement, readers are awaiting the release of Part Three—and I haven't written one self-possessed, erotically stimulating, hysterical word.

A review of Part One on my Amazon Author's page:

> I started this book yesterday and am now TRYING to slow down, because I'm almost done. Jumped back on Amazon to order the next two and praying she is writing as we speak. I have had moments where I am pissed at her, but I love her honesty. This book will hold your attention and make u laugh. This woman did not get the memo that we're not supposed to let them know how crazy we are.
>
> Paige

For Paige and all the beautiful, emotionally starved, vulnerable, absolutely crazed women out there, Part Three of *The Muslim Romance Trilogy.*

Juliet

The Arab Sprung

The Unlicensed Musical . . .

Chapter 1

Ho-Ho-Ho; Christmas, 2010

> ♪ You like to think that you're immune to the stuff
> It's closer to the truth to say you can't get enough ♪
>
> *Addicted to Love*
> Robert Palmer (1949-2003)

THE honeymoon has ended and I'm in a downward spiral, drilling my way through the days in a functioning funk and drunk by five o'clock. How I am able to construct one grammatically correct sentence jam-packed with truth, humor, and clarity amazes me. Fuck it. Here we go.

Her concrete sidewalks stained with urine-infused, gun metal gray grunge and her asphalt streets bumped with pesky potholes, yet Hollywood remains the mecca where unrealistic dreams grow wings and take flight, where unexpected fairy tales do come true, and where love offered too quickly is to be questioned from the get-go. Guard your impetuous hearts, newcomers, for an imposter may snatch up your heart, the result a perilous misadventure into unrequited love, a misery that can last forever in a town void of beddable heterosexual Republicans.

Now in the second year of his reign, the War on Terror seemingly placed on the back burner, President Barack Hussein Obama's New America is taking shape. *Don't Ask; Don't Tell* is repealed; homosexuals may now openly join the military. No more Charlie Company; Steve Company will be sporting Government Issue Gay Pride uniforms by Abercrombie & Fitch.

The Dream Act is moving along. Will the children of good moral character, born too soon and carried over the border by wet parents, receive immunity from deportation? Thus, will a gay eighteen-year-old illegal alien get his stripes?

The first biracial American president promised to change the world, and the Middle East took note. Suddenly, all of Islam wants to be free. Muslim against Muslim! Shi'ite against Sunni! The Blue against the Gray! *The Arab Spring* arose from the sands of Tunisia and traveled into Algeria. At last President Ronald Reagan's democratic dream of all men choosing their own destiny had come alive, burning its way through the unplumbed desert.

Private Bowe Bergdahl's sympathetic walk away from his Afghanistan Army post into the arms of Jihadist soccer players culminates in his declaration that he has become a Warrior for Islam. His father immediately begins growing an Allah-approved beard.

At home we are at war with each other. The most divisive President ever to celebrate The Islamic Holy Days of Ramadan at the White House—on my tax dollar—has split the country into two groups: those who would proudly tell their grandchildren they had voted the first black man into the highest office—while polishing their **I'm Not a Racist** Obama campaign buttons—and those that had not voted *against* a race, but *for* a qualified man with the experience to do the job, even though they didn't like him or his bubbly brunette running mate all that much.

And the rain came down all over Hollywood. A full, non-stop week of rainfall set new records and busted a hole in my roof. Ali loves the rain. He is gone, sprung from my life forever, and I've sprung a leak.

Water found its way under the powder blue and salmon Spanish tiles and forced its way through a pinhole in the drop-down ceiling of the living room and onto my lovely hardwood floor. It is dripping steadily into a plastic bucket now. This expensive turn of events has disrupted my neatly out-of-control life and sent with it the chance to take on a new lover, a robust roofing contractor. I must replace the most perfect penis ever to fill my throbbing, thinning postmenopausal vaginal walls.

To quench this lustful famine, its graft must be of sturdy, noble, faithful flesh and wearing the correct condom, of course.

This time I would have no feelings for the beast. There would be no dopamine to mess up my mind. A trusted tangled tryst under sweating sheets is what I need, once I am convinced he won't be cheating on me. From my side of the bed, I have experienced unconditional love once in my lifetime, which is quite enough.

♪ What'll I do with just a photograph
To tell my troubles to?
When I'm alone with only dreams of you
That won't come true ♪

What'll I Do

Composed by Irving Berlin in 1924 and styled by Barbara Cook on her 1977 not-for-sale demo album *As of Today*, which was pirated from the Goodwill Store for less than two dollars and is continuously and illegally spinning on my Emerson turntable.

There would be no misguided passion, no rise of my serotonin levels to displace my common sense. Has my Islam-style husband Ali, with whom after a mere seventeen days of deserting me, I cut off all contact and communication, turned me into somewhat of a tart out to captivate the male population of the *hook up* generation?  Could I get it up to hook up without passion, void of chemical attraction to the man grunting on top of me? Is there anyone out there to oblige an aging romantic wrestling with the sudden deluge of cellulite, varicose veins, liver spots, and a broken heart that has come along for the ride? What has become of me?

And just how had this begun, the exploitation of my sexuality?

Chapter 2

The Summer of '66 and Great Expectations

♪ Hot town, summer in the city
Back of my neck getting dirty and gritty ♪

Summer in the City
The Lovin' Spoonful

It was the summer I graduated from high school in a valley below the San Bernardino National Forest, a valley where towels are placed on fiery Naugahyde seats before plopping bottoms in short-shorts and bare thighs upon them. Hope, my blonde, effervescent girlfriend, was babysitting the two toddlers of affluent parents—by Inland Empire standards—and had invited me to join her for a sun and swim overnighter. Dad and Stepmom were happy to see me go for twenty-four hours. I was, after all, to be in the safekeeping of the first daughter of an upstanding, middle class Mormon family of seven.

In a string-tied white bikini, Hope greeted me with an icy tumbler. "Thanks, but what's in it?"

"Something to get the party started," she flashed an oversized set of perfect white teeth. "The brats are at kiddie day camp until I pick them up at six. The pool, the bar, and the radio are ours for the entire afternoon," she cheered. Hope was a bubbly blonde with all the whistles: tall and thin, shocked blunt yellow hair, bright blue eyes, and a 1965 Volkswagen Beetle.

One year my senior, Hope was one of those "California Girls" the Beach Boys were singing about ♪ the cutest girls in the world ♪ and I wanted to be one too. One cannot rely on a high-school-homecoming-queen crown to keep the boys knocking at the door.

The local radio station beat out the best of the *Top 40*. We hung our elbows over the side of the pool, sipped our drinks, and splashed our legs up and down in the cool blue water—and that was as far in as we were going. I had spent the morning teasing my hair and gluing to my eyelids Twiggy-style eyelashes purchased at Woolworth's drug store. This was, unfortunately, my only resemblance to the British model known as "The Face of 1966."

Hope's fair arms, her swan neck, and cherub face were drenched in white creamy sunscreen, while I ignorantly allowed the noonday sun to further damage my olive skin. I would be Indian purple by July and spending large amounts of money for laser treatment on the boastful brown spots in my fifties.

The DJ on duty at the local station was Chuck Christensen, my escort the year before for the Miss 007 contest at the local ceremonial opening of *Thunderball* on the stage of a small, no cup-holder theatre in Riverside, another boiler-heat community. He opened his three hours of airtime with a Petula Clark British ditty.

♫ Didn't like you much when I first met you
Said you didn't want a friend or lover ♫

"Oh, listen! Chuck is playing my favorite song again." I scrambled from the pool to my assigned chaise lounge and nearly fell bottom first through the slats. ♫ I couldn't live without your love ♫ I sang along. "He plays it every Saturday at the beginning of his session just for me."

♫ Now I know you're really mine.
Gotta have you all the time ♫

"Have you gone on a date with him since the Double-0-Seven letdown?" my friend asked and began painting her nails with shocking-pink polish.

"It wasn't a date. He just took me to the theatre and introduced me on stage. There were a dozen other girls. He was really ticked off when I didn't receive enough votes from the audience to be KMEN's Miss 007. He told me I should've worn my hair down. And it wasn't a letdown. It was all just free publicity for the station. There wasn't any bread to win, anyway."

"Was Sean Connery there?" her blonde asked hopefully.

"In Riverside?"

"But you got to ride in a limo! Did he wear a tux?"

"Yeah. He's a really cool dude, a little like Rory Calhoun, the dark wavy hair and big brown eyes. He's tall. I was nervous. I don't remember much."

"Whatcha wear?"

"The black sateen sheath with those big white—those layered white chiffon bongo-player sleeves. No wonder I didn't win."

"'La Bamba,' babe. Hey, that's a bitchin' dress. Too bad we're not the same size."

"But he keeps calling. I talked to him once, but Dad always picks up the phone and says, 'she's not here.' My dad let me go to the contest with him, but he'd kill me if I actually went out with him. Chuck's twenty-five."

Blowing on her fingertips, Hope tiptoed over the blazing concrete to the poolside tiki bar and returned with fill-ups.

I clinked the contents. "I'm blitzed already, what with the sun and —what's in this?"

"Vodka and tonic water."

"Oh. I don't think I've ever had one of these."

"Julie, have you ever had a real drink? Maybe you shouldn't—"

"Hey, don't freak out, badass. A college boy tried to seduce me with Southern Comfort right out of the bottle, but he was a really bad kisser, so nothing happened. Is vodka in a Sloe Gin Fizz? I've thrown up plenty of those."

"You're drinking vodka, not gin, spaz."

"Far out. And now I'm having my second," I applauded.

The British serenade ended and Chuck mellowed out from inside the transistor, "That one was for you, Julie."

In time to the Beatle's "Paperback Writer" the whooping and knee slapping began.

"He said your name!"

I was on my third vodka when Hope began to tease me about my virgin status, while lathering up the insides of her taut golden thighs.

"My cherry has been popped," I reminisced.

"What? And you didn't tell me?"

"Junior year Peter was playing around. It made a mess in his dad's woody."

"Why didn't you ever, you know, do it?"

"I offered once after one green beer in a grape vineyard. We were necking and he got out to pee. When he came back, I was naked on the seat, covering myself with my arms, of course."

"Of course. Well, don't stop there."

"He stood at the window shouting, 'No, no! Not you. You're my princess.' So I got dressed while he ran around the car like a mad man."

"Well, finger diddling doesn't count. You've really got to let it go before you start junior college in the fall. You don't want to be caught inexperienced and scared out of your panties."

"I'm not dating anyone and Peter's not talking to me." I squirted onto my already suntanned calves streams of Coppertone QT, guaranteed to give me a tan indoors or out.

"Peter is an idiot, breaking up with you just 'cause you wanted to play the field— at the ripe old age of sixteen."

"It gets worse. Right there in the T-wing on my way to trig, he accused me of having sex with a football player. He heard some gossip at a party."

"Have you talked to him since?"

"No. He's really mad at me. He wouldn't walk with me at graduation like we planned. I went up to him. He huffed and rushed away. I had to walk with some pimply retard from the debate team."

"What a bummer. Well, I know someone who's just a teeny bit interested? Let's call him."

"Who? The DJ?" I looked down at my midriff bulge. Even at my fighting weight of one hundred and thirty pounds, the baby fat hung over my little boy shorts. The only way to make it disappear was to lie flat on my back, my arms thrust overhead in crucifix position.

"Call him! He obviously likes you."

Hope was an experienced child of God, apparently set free some time ago to conquer the panting masses. I was insecure, still heartbroken from the breakup with my high school sweetheart, detached from my divorced parents, and I had absolutely no idea what my responsibilities would entail when faced with an entirely naked adult penis. Not since the drive-by neighborhood pervert asked me for directions on my walk home from high school had I ever seen one out and straight up.

"Do you have the number? I'll call him," Hope rushed to the outdoor phone and pulled the cord to her chaise. "Come on, you've got to have his number."

The records kept spinning. The Supremes harmonized a warning.

♪ You can't hurry love
No, you just have to wait ♪

Vodka—my gateway drug to foolishness and shame—sent me to my purse where I wrestled out my compact mod address book, a birthday gift from my mother who had written her phone numbers in it.

"I'll do it." And I dialed with a trembling rubber finger the number Chuck had given me.

"KMEN."

"Hi, Chuck. It's Julie."

"Hey, chick. So cool to hear from you. What's up?" His voice sounded a bit different than on the air, his face a blur to me.

"What time do you get off?"

I suppose that would be up to me. On a vodka-high dare, I opened myself up to the inevitable.

"Three o'clock, the usual. What's up?" The big question to which I had no answer.

Hope chimed in, "Tell him you want to go to a motel."

My hand clasped over the black receiver, I whispered, "What?"

"Tell him you're a virgin and it's time," she whispered back.

"My girlfriend says to tell you I'm a virgin and it's time—and I've chosen you."

"Sure, kid. Give me an address. I'll pick you up."

In the bathroom mirror I watched myself pull the moist cotton madras halter up over my breasts and over my brunette flip-do. Stark white against my tanned chest, my offerings flopped back into place. I contemplated their future popularity. No man had ever seen them outside a bra before.

Not too big, just big enough. More than a handful, I guessed. *The better to tempt you with,* you infamous radio celebrity, you.

Yes, indeed, they were perky, yet soft, even lovely but for the largest and darkest areolas this side of Nigeria. I knew this to be a fact, because my fraternal step grandmother kept a large collection of *National Geographic* in plain sight, right there in her living room. I'd been shamefully thumbing through the pictures since I could sit up on my own.

My mother has pink nipples on soft beige proportioned areolas. From where had these the-natives-are-restless-tonight brown nips been generated? The next time I play canasta with my mother's mother, I'll ask her to bring one out at the kitchen table.

I pulled my white cotton panties up and hooked my white Playtex cotton bra in place. Hope opened the door and peaked in.

"Did you take your pill this morning?"

"What pill?"

"Well, just make sure he wears a rubber."

"He's supposed to put it on, right?" I was darned sure I wasn't going to be the one to do it.

"Maybe I'd better fix you another drink," Hope hurried away to the ringing of the phone.

In pistachio green pedal pushers and a matching crop top, I leaned into the mirror, frosted my pout with pink cotton candy, and gave myself a salute that my Marine drill sergeant father would be proud of.

At three-thirty he pulled up in front of the house and honked the horn.

Hope gave me a cheerleader hug at the front door and leaned in to whisper, "Just relax. Wow. Your first time and with a DJ."

A smoking exhaust pipe and thundering muffler awaited me at the curb. Chuck lit a cigarette and waived me to open the door. My vodka high down to a possible headache, once inside I was hit by the stench of a year's worth of Marlboro butts toppling from the ashtray and onto the floor, the scent of panting dog breath, presumably a St. Bernard, and the pungent onion-infused aftermath of tossed containers from the two fast food drive-thru restaurants within the city: McDonald's and Baker's. I was on my way to hell and damnation in a skuzz bucket.

The drive down E Street was silent, but for the tape deck unwinding a repeat of today's broadcast.

"I like to study my radio voice right after a show. You don't mind, do ya?" He flashed a wee grin, flicked a crust of sleep from inside the corner of his eye, leaned forward and turned up the volume.

"It's stuffy in here. Could you turn on the air?"

"Nah, it's not working."

I rolled down the window. Pushing my windblown hair out of my face, I snuck a peek at my chosen mate. He was good looking, but not dressed well. Those murky brown corduroy trousers could probably stand up on their own. Chuck was worn, torn, and disheveled. Hey, where'd the guy in the tuxedo go?

Passing the high school lawn, panic set in. Open the door and throw yourself out onto the asphalt. Peter's house is just two blocks away. You'll show up bruised and bloodied with gravel scrapes on your knees and elbows. He wouldn't turn away a lady in distress, would he?

We passed the original Golden Arches, its marquis boasting over a billion in sales; the Filet-O-Fish sandwich apparently a favorite of my summer romance. Making a left onto Rialto Avenue, Chuck placed a gentle hand on my covered knee. "You're gonna do fine." And then he winked at me decades before *Match.com* would urge him to do so.

He pulled into a blight-stricken parking lot, where young Negro men in white t-shirts hovered outside the liquor store door, perhaps to cool themselves with blasts of Freon each time a customer passed through. Chuck returned to the car with a small brown sack. At the end of the dreary drive down Waterman Avenue, a thoroughfare of used car lots, dairy cow pastures, and dry weedy fields running north and south the entire length of San Bernardino, he turned into a wide entrance leading to the welcomed foliage of a golf course under construction, where decades later in white bejeweled knee-high boots and wielding a nine iron, I would marry husband no. 4.

The road diverged into a stretch of potholed asphalt and too soon I was deposited into an olive green, Formica-infused seedy motel room with one metal sliding window above the carved Aztec-style wooden headboard. Through the grease streaks, one disturbing bullet hole, and a barbed wire fence was the view of a backhoe noisily moving dirt.

"Get yourself ready. I'll get some ice." He closed the door behind him, and as I turned to face the orange and green floral bedspread, everything turned an eerie white.

Billows of white sheer curtains tossed about my shoulders and played with my hair. From the air ducts floated a white fog scented with the sweetness of white rosebuds. The carpet was snow white with not a footprint to spoil its purity. The double bed was adorned in white tufted satin trimmed in white embroidered eyelet lace. Set on each puffed pillow was a chocolate kiss wrapped in foil and tied with a white ribbon.

There were no pictures hung on the freshly painted smooth white walls; large baroque mirrors flanked by golden cherubs dressed the room. A white velvet fainting couch filled the seating area. I might just need that, I thought.

Placed upon the white marble counter were two silver goblets and an intricately embossed ice bucket on a pedestal. Propped in the bucket was a bottle of chilled champagne.

I floated to the bathroom, undressed, and neatly stacked my clothes on the shelf of the stainless steel towel rack, my flip-flops placed next to the pearl white toilet. A wipe to the tush and bush with a soft white terrycloth towel, a bit more frost to the lips, a toss of the flip, and I made it under the slippery satin covers before he returned.

My eyes closed, the sheet over my nakedness, flat on my back, my arms locked down at my side, the jingle-jangle of ice into a plastic cup drew my attention.

Chuck tossed a key onto the console television and plopped down next to me. "I think you might need this, to relax you."

Though at age eighteen my feet had not yet been in the stirrups, the white blaze, the antiseptic aura, and the chill of stainless steel had all been scenarios of a gynecological wet dream. I opened my eyes to yellowed walls, a watercolor painting of geese by Howard Johnson, and a green shag carpet. In place of chilled champagne was a pocket-sized bottle of Ten High Bourbon Whiskey.

The white cotton sheet held tightly in my fist, I sat up, accepted the cup and gulped down the offering.

"Wow, not so fast. We've got half an hour."

Had he rented the room by the minute?

"Here, sip this one. I need to take a whiz."

The chocolates had disappeared.

Chuck left for the bathroom and I was pleased that he understood modern decency, that he should not undress in front of me, but return with a white towel about his privates. I would then invite him in under the covers. I did wish it weren't so bright in the room, but there were no drapes to pull shut at the window. Of course, there would be a ton of necking, sweating, sweet talk, all the usual passion pit foreplay to fog up the window.

The bourbon settled me in and I was ready. I mustn't forget that rubber thing in all the excitement.

Tightening the sheet to conceal my tummy, I cozied up in a Marilyn Monroe curl facing the bathroom door.

And out he came. Chuck's entire body was white with not a tuft of hair on it. Simply, he was a flash of white. The rubber was in place, all right. Trapped inside a thick white greased balloon, his proud mini-manhood was cocked, loaded, and pointing its little finger straight at me.

He wrenched the sheet away, crawled onto the bed and straddled me. There, he spread open my brown thighs, slid my knees up and pushed my ankles to my butt. *Hey, I only marched in drill team; I'm not a gymnast.* Gazing over my head and out the window—*Hey, Cassanova, I'm down here*—he kneed my legs further apart. *He is offended by my areolas, I just know it.* His hands balancing himself on either side of me

—without requesting that I *scoot down*—he wriggled his skinny, moist white dressed dick into my innocent, precious, unsuspecting vagina.

There was no pain. There was nothing. White silence. It may as well have been a lubricated cardboard Tampon. With his eyes shut, he gave it one rude shove, let out a whimper and jumped off the bed, taking his withered appendage with him.

He wasn't inside me long enough to have me write a review for the K/men 129 radio station fan club of which, apparently, I was now an official groupie. Another splash of Ten High into my Styrofoam cup, the final scene in a *Gunsmoke* rerun, and I was all grown up.

"There was no blood. I thought you were a virgin. Kind of took some of the fun out of it," he broadcast from behind the steering wheel of his disgusting imitation of an automobile.

I winced at his remark and made no explanation. The ride back to a deep cleansing in the chlorine-infused sacrificial swimming pool and loads more Vodka was the longest twenty minutes I would ever have to endure up Waterman Avenue, the weary pathway through my hometown, and where the black-and-white invisible boundary line began at Baseline Street, the street marking the Mormon Settlement of 1852.

"Hey, kid, you know I'm married, right?"

I flew open the side gate. Poolside I stripped down to my undies, jumped off holding my knees and landed one helluva cannon ball wedgie, its chilling spray a big surprise to Hope and her *Teen Life* magazine.

"How did it go? Tell me all about it."

I breast stroked up to the side of the pool. "When I can remember it in detail. Not now. Well, anyway, you can check that one off my to-do list."

"Ah, the first time is supposed to be the one time you remember forever. Not the second or the third, but the first time."

"What summer movies have you been watching? Where did you come up with that romantic slop?"

"Not good, huh? What a bummer. I think you lost an eyelash in that landing."

I swam over to the steps where Hope handed me a towel. "So, what's next on my list for this summer?"

"When I pick up the squabbling tow heads, you can learn how to change a diaper."

"They're not potty trained?"

"The boy's not, of course. Don't freak out. I'll be right here to make sure you do it right and not get a safety pin stuck in your throat."

"Haven't I seen enough pricks for one day?"

"You did it with your eyes open?"

This to-do would turn out to be a wise lesson learned. Over the next quarter of a century, I'd be changing thousands and thousands of those nasty wonderful white things.

Chapter 3

Espionage and a Jew

> ♪ She's all alone when she lowers her lamp.
> That's why the lady is a tramp ♪
>
> The Lady is a Tramp
> Rogers and Hart, *Babes in Arms*

That was Julie way back when, and for years to come I could take 'em and leave 'em. Four husbands and several ambiguous *lovers*—a word that has never quite fit the occasion—and not once had I turned into an emotional wreck wallowing in fits of grief and hysterical mourning; all this nonsense over a homegrown Islamic terrorist wannabe, who boasted of never paying his government-funded student loans. Whatever happened to the happy, mystical Muslims, as in the 1958 fantasy *The 7th Voyage of Sinbad*, a Middle Eastern Hollywood romp brimming with dancing girls, snake charmers, a shrunken princess, and a Cyclops?

Okay, so maybe back in the early 70s after our second make-up-to-break-up—and after I had married, given birth, and divorced—during the week of Peter's retreat from my sexually conflicting demands, I wrote suicide poems and drank sweet Spanada wine and put the needle back onto "Maybe I'm Amazed" over and over, while my toddler Elizabeth consoled me. I had my first lesson in learning the blues, but had no idea what the blues would look like in the twenty-first century. I called Peter just once that miserable week, but his mother told me that he refused to come to the phone. Paul had dedicated the song to his wife Linda, who had helped him get through the Beatle break-up.

> ♪ Maybe I'm afraid of the way you love me ♪

Yes, Peter was afraid, afraid of my frenetic writhing, which chafed his thighs and gut until his belly button caught fire. If only then I'd known where my clit was, we'd be celebrating our fortieth anniversary, living in a clapboard two-bedroom house with a new toilet still in its box in the living room and writing letters to our son serving time at Chino State Prison.

Okay, so thirty years after divorcing husband no. 1, I called him from an inspiring Amway rally to forgive him for his drug use, his cheating ways, for never paying child support and abandoning our little girl for eleven years. In a packed auditorium I had revisited my love of Jesus and wanted to be just like him, our Lord and Savior. Allen's wife answered the phone. Apparently, she gave him the tearful message, because our daughter Elizabeth caught up with me the next week to berate me for upsetting her runaway father's household.

But this break up with the Muslim manipulator was completely foreign to me. This wasn't your mother's old-fashioned broken heart to be dealt with internally, your head held high. File the divorce papers, buy a carton of cigarettes, fill the freezer with vodka, and paint the kitchen a bright yellow, a color he always hated. Here at the Hollywood Bungalows—twenty tiny vintage Spanish houses slid together with a shoehorn—to my neighbors' embarrassment, I was still screaming out his name, "Ali, Ali, Ali!" I was truly traumatized. More than a month ago, I had broken up with him once more and he has not responded to the email.

✳ ✳ ✳

"Julie? Julie? Hello? Anybody in there?" A male voice with a charming accent was calling out to me from the walkway.

Hound rounded the turn at the backdoor and scrambled down the stoop barking in his once-roused menacing manner. With keys in hand, I followed his lead to the back gate. Not one to short-change his twenty-two hours of sleep by foolishly traipsing out into a rainstorm, Brute stayed curled up under the kitchen table.

"Yes, yes. I'm here," I shouted through the pelting raindrops.

The roofer was here with a small crew, all dressed in yellow slickers.

"You must be making a fortune," I surmised as he pointed a serious finger at my roof.

"We're going to tarp your roof until the sun comes out."

And there he was, Benayahu Ashkenazi, the really hot Israeli with the really long oxymoron of a surname. With a name like that, you'd be foolish to start up any conversation, pro or con, about the Holocaust.

"How much is it going to cost me this time, Ben?"

We had been on a first-name basis since 2004 when he became the first man to tar up and hot mop the flat of my roof. The year I purchased the 1923 Spanish bungalow, the first rain to fall pooled alongside the air conditioning unit on the roof, tinkled into the little attic and onto the stackable washer/dryer in the living room closet. Benayahu showed up that evening wearing a ball cap over his dark curly head and carrying a very sexy flashlight. Realizing that he must be much younger than myself, I hadn't given a thought to flirting with this adorable, bedroom-eyed stranger with the tight butt, who had come to my rescue on a rainy chilly evening. Five years before my sexual awakening, I'd rather spend the evening rolling pastel yellow paint over the psychedelic orange bathroom, a cigarette dangling from my lips.

That was then; and this is now.

"I won't have an estimate until the roof is dry." Ben squinted and searched my face, as if to consider whether he should let me know I had spinach in between my teeth. "Your eyes have the most beautiful, subtle shade of green in them. What color is that? Hazel?"

"I'd like to think so, but my mom assures me they're brown," I blushed under my hoodie.

"No one's ever told you that? You're getting soaked. Go in and take a look. There's green in those eyes."

"You're flirting with me, right?" I dove headfirst right into another Middle Eastern hummus dip. "Aren't you married?"

"I'm divorced because I work too much, apparently. And, yes, I am flirting with you."

Perfect. I rushed into the house to begin my *Google* search on lovely Benayahu Ashkenazi and to phone Mom with the news that my eyes were hazel, not brown.

***

Captain Brainard stopped by to remind me why I was alone and cranky. Holding an umbrella over my head, I unlocked the swollen wooden gate and the counterspy Naval Intelligence officer working undercover as a self-absorbed, egotistical union actor, strutted up the porch stairs.

"Brett, why are you in your Navy whites? Wow, is this my Christmas present?"

"I had a soap audition as a pilot. I'm soaking wet. Let's go inside," he directed me, tipped his cap and led me through the door.

"An officer and a gentleman. You are my Christmas present."

Passing by little Brute, Brainard stooped to waken Hound from his nap. "Ole boy, give me a handshake." Hound jumped to attention at the masculine voice and sat up on his hind legs, one large tan and gold paw outstretched.

"Wait just a second, hot shot. You're telling me there's a casting director still in town during the holidays?" I was suspicious.

"Yeah, sure. *General Hospital* never sleeps. Hey, you need to get a new guy, a regular American guy, not the 'dogs are of the devil' chicken shit Muslim. Hound is starving for male attention."

"Are you offering yourself up?"

"Hell, no. You know I only do teeny chicks under twenty-five with firm tits that I can swoop up and carry out of the factory."

"Debra Winger and beer commercial models with no common sense. Want something to drink?" I asked from the kitchen sink.

"How 'bout a beer?"

"No beer. I only keep straight alcohol and one bottle of wine at a time in the house."

"Just ice water then."

Taking the twelve-cube tray from the freezer, I twisted it lightly to crack out the ice.

"You have purified water, right?"

"You know I do. It's part of the soft water system. I use it to fill the ice tray, too." I took the glass to him, aware of my burgeoning size and his judgmental glance. "Okay, asshole, I quit smoking, but I'm about to start again."

"Men don't like women who smoke, except after sex. You need to get to the gym. Gotta show you this girl."

"Please don't pull out your phone and show me any more young girls touting their pussies," I scowled. Brainard, handsome and in great shape, picked up lonely young women late at night, when he'd had more than enough to drink and, apparently, so had they. He took them home to enjoy what he describes as *banging them*. His top choice of foreplay techniques is popping Viagra.

"You're going on fifty, darling. How do you do it? Let me guess. The first thing you tell them is 'I'm a pilot'?" I landed on the love seat in disgust. He was safely seated on the floor next to Hound.

"Well, I'm not going to tell them I'm an actor, not in this town."

"Do you tell them you're a spy?"

"Only when the Navy pilot plug doesn't work."

"That's not wise, Brett."

"I never see them again, except when they send me texts with porno shots." He picked up the glass and moved to the chair. "You've had no contact and he's not contacted you."

"Well, you're the one with the capability to know if I did or if he did. Correct, no contact. None whatsoever."

"Good girl. Have you gone through your Squirrel money yet?"

I had betrayed my lover for a wire transfer from the enemy, enough to pay off all my credit cards. "I need a new gate. I'll use the balance for that."

"I could use your help again." Brainard reached down to snatch Brute from the floor.

"Don't use the dogs to talk me into anything. My counterspy career was a one-summer fling, a one-lover episode. I'm not proud of it. I wouldn't even know what I'm supposed to do, to ask, to say—"

"Just keep your eyes open. This town is bulging with Middle Eastern men that wanna get laid and talk your ear off."

"Whoa! I'm too out of shape to be a seductress. I'm not an exotic nude dancer turned spy like Mata Hari and I don't relish being executed by a firing squad." I leaned in to hear more.

"Don't be so quick to put yourself down, number one. Number two; you may find dissidents that are on the brink of defecting. You can influence them to do so. Can I have some more water?"

"Get it yourself."

From the kitchen sink, Brainard explained that the department had a great concern with Israeli nationals that may be recruiting American Jews to leak secret information.

"What sort of information would an American Jew have to offer, anyway?" I picked up the fluff-moppet Maltese and stole him to the loveseat.

"You'll have to ask Jonathan Pollard. He gave thousands of classified documents to his Israeli handlers. He won't be released from prison until 2015, after a thirty-year sentence."

"And he was a computer geek? No, wait. Were there computers thirty years ago?"

"Nah, a civilian intelligence analyst for the Navy."

"Maybe I should be spying on you."

Brainard took his glass to the kitchen counter. "Just let me know if you meet up with anyone that seems suspicious. Don't worry, I'm not asking you to attend a mosque—or a synagogue."

"And no more hidden cameras in my basement until I drop ten pounds."

I kept the info on Ben the Israeli roofer to myself. My *Google* search had been promising. His contractor's license was current with no bad reviews or citations. In public records, I found that Ben, and Ben alone —along with the Bank of America—owns a three-bedroom, two-bath home in Toluca Lake, a charming white neighborhood tucked above Universal City on the north side of the Hollywood Hills, where children can still be found playing in the street after dark.

A stone's throw away from Ben's eight hundred thousand dollar fixer-upper languishes the Bob Hope eight-bedroom, five-acre estate. Republican Bob passed away at the one hundred mark in 2003, excusing himself from the currently acceptable Hollywood climate of blackballing conservatives and the hypocrisy of having to write politically correct jokes about another zombie Democrat in the White House.

His wife for over sixty years, at the age of one hundred Delores Hope is still kicking. I wonder what she's up to these days behind that long garden wall. Maybe she's tapping her ball into the cup on the green of her one-hole, three-par golf course; that is, if she's not stroking laps in the indoor or the outdoor pool. A vocalist before marrying Mr. Hope, perhaps she's collaborating on another Christmas album, while my eighty-two year old mother skillfully rearranges another drawer once again, discarding nothing.

On the main street in Toluca Lake is America's first Bob's Big Boy—no relation to Mr. Hope—a restaurant where roller skating waitresses are no more. Lining the street is a playhouse flanked by dog groomers galore, upscale gift shops, quaint eateries and ostentatious wine bars, the Cinema Secrets Beauty Supply, a tiny bookstore tucked inside an eclectic t-shirt shop, and the snootiest 7-Eleven in Los Angeles County.

Yes, Benayahu Ashkenazi, I could live there with you. We'll invite Delores for Friday night Shabbat dinner. I'll learn how to make fresh water gefilte fish. But first I've got to find out if you're a good kisser.

***

Christmas Eve, another familial drudgery, has me phoning Mother again to agree on a precise time for her pick up in San Bernardino, the city I escaped from at age fifty-five, in order to make the drive backwards to Rae's trendy condo in Glendale by three o'clock. Rae swears she is the only non-Armenian that lives in that city. The sojourn to Mother's Spanish inheritance on a once posh street is a one hundred and fifty mile turnaround of which I am pleased to endure, if only Mother could bring her selfish self to appreciate my offer. The 210 Freeway is a safer place without my octogenarian mother behind a wheel that she cannot see over.

My having a cabin just fifteen minutes up a mountain road from her house in the valley has not cured Mother's me-me ways. Disturbingly, she has declined visits from me when I am staying at the cabin, romantically dubbed Le Petit Chateau d'Enchanté. She too owns a cabin in the same woods from which, by way of the tangerine 1970s rotary phone, she has broken many of our lunch dates last minute. However, Mother has no qualms about requesting that I return from Hollywood to accompany her to the symphony—to which she continues to purchase season tickets for two—within twenty-four hours of my magic wand—*bibbidi-bobbidi-boo*—long and bumpy drive back home.

My sister Rae, who is omniscient and will not be questioned, states that Mom has dementia; I think Mom is just mean.

Chapter 4

1956, Women Without Men

Within minutes following an autumn cloudburst, the threatening gray aura having moved east into the desert, the mountains looming above the San Bernardino basin sparkled an emerald green in the sunlight. The ardent cleansing cast off leaves from the towering maple trees. In the crisp breeze, the leaves found their way to the gutters. Their snapped twigs as rudders, crimson and brown, they floated away and became miniature sailboats in the running water lapping the cement curbs. And on the little street that wound its way from the elementary school passed the community plunge, now shuttered and locked until school would let out again in June, two little girls, the younger fair with golden braids and the older still brown from the summer's sun, spilled out the front door of their little pink house.

The silent neighborhood of many little pastel post-war houses—but for a retired colonel's large and white three-bedroom on the corner—jingled with the laughter of two sisters allowed outside on this Saturday morning, the sun peeping its way through the trees lining the sidewalks. Carefully tugged into yellow slickers and red plastic boots, the sisters waded into the rushing gutter and placed popsicle sticks gently on the backs of the larger leaves, each hoping that their sailboat would reach the cross street before the other's.

From inside the living room, their young mother peered protectively through the glass at their playfulness. She wiped her floured hands on her apron and pulled the drapes fully open, their leafy design of green, red, and brown woven into brash brocade mimicking the fall scene outside. Wearing black winged prescription glasses, her face clean but for her Ponds, eyeing herself in the beveled mirror over the dining table, the lady of the house tightened her deep mahogany ponytail and took the four steps across the living room carpet and out onto the cement slab at the front porch, delicately stepping over the deserted game of jacks.

Leaning over the white wooden railing, she spoke loudly, but kindly. "Stay close to the curb and don't go any further than the pool and stay on our side of the street."

Orders received, Julie and Rae continued to scamper along behind their Thumbelina rafts, assisting them when they landed onto small mud islands of debris.

"Smell how clean it is," Julie articulated. Julie had entered third grade this fall. Her sister was new to kindergarten life.

Spinning in her rain boots, Julie took it all in. "The mountains are so green. Look how close they are."

Rae quietly fumbled her way alongside her tiny ship to catch it before the current rushing from the top of the street sent it cascading passed the community pool gates. Her plump cherubic legs couldn't keep up.

"Can't go any more," she complained, her pink lips set in indignation. Rae about-faced and stomped back through the gutter and up the driveway.

"Don't go in," Julie pleaded to her baby sister. "There's lots more leaves coming by."

Hoisted up and into her mother's arms, Rae refused the invitation. "I'm cold."

"Five more minutes, Julie. I don't want you catching cold. And leave your boots on the porch."

"But, Mom, it smells so good outside. Why don't you come out, too? Then Rae will stay. Please?" Julie clasped her hands together in a hopeful plea, but kept silent when the front door slammed shut. Her head bowed, she stepped into the gutter once more and with the tips of her red boots kicked at the mud.

The ten-twenty city bus rattled down the street and began to slow as it passed the yellow curb, its glass and metal door whooshing open, but no one was there to get on. Julie waved him on from the driveway. The blue and white bus was a source of adventure and the only way to get to town ever since the lime green Chevy convertible's clutch had ceased to function.

The wife, her career Marine sergeant serving overseas, had tired of stopping the rusty old car in the middle of the road to manually jerk the transmission back into place. As she disappeared under the hood, her high-heeled feet dangling, her antics entertained the girls. A source of amazement it was for them to see that Mom, as delicate and pretty as she was, knew anything at all about a car's operating parts, especially when out of necessity she had begun her driving career only that spring.

The ragtop no longer would cooperate and was stuck in the open-breeze position. Thus, their only transportation was locked in the single car garage until the man of the house could send enough money to cover repairs or until he returned.

The city bus trip was a delightful jaunt through the densely populated neighborhood, each modest house stamped with a green lawn and a driveway leading to a garage, where inside fathers fiddled with go carts and cycles and popped chilled bottles of beer from a fridge smudged with Valvoline fingerprints.

Each stop along the way brought on board another person to whom the children were not to speak. Their mother was careful to guard them from strangers, especially those that didn't own their own car, but most were elderly white women no longer able to drive and the occasional black or brown lady returning home from her housecleaning duties, presumably from a large house like the colonel's. The children never had seen a school chum board the city bus.

In their go-to-town best, the three would take in a movie at the Ritz Theatre or sit on shocking pink spinning stools at Woolworth's stainless steel counter, where the waitresses wore white pique uniforms and hairnets over their chignons, and where the sisters would order chicken salad sandwiches on wheat toast. A stroll into Harris' Department Store for wishful window-shopping filled the wait time until the next bus came to take them home.

Hopeful that her mother might agree to a trip downtown today, Julie turned quickly into the driveway, up onto the porch and strode through the front door and onto the tweed carpeting.

"Mommy, let's dress up and go to town today. Another bus comes right after noon." As the muddied little boots hit the kitchen linoleum, her mother slammed a spatula into the bubbling skillet filled with floured chicken parts.

"You walked right through the living room, didn't you?"

Julie's answer was a quick look back to the front door and then down to her feet.

"You're so stupid. Stupid. Stupid." She lunged at the child, her lips so taut that wrinkles as deep as sidewalk seams burst onto her beautiful face. Her forehead veins popping, she jerked Julie around the neck and swung her into a breakfast nook chair. "So you think you're going downtown, huh? We'll see about that."

From the bathroom doorway, Rae tiptoed on socked feet along creaking oak floorboards into the bedroom.

Julie knew to stay still and quiet, waiting for the storm to pass.

"Rae! Get out of your room and bring me a hanger now!"

Down the short hall in the shared bedroom, the five-year-old slunk from her twin bed and went to the closet. Skidding into the kitchen holding a metal hanger, she saw her sister on the floor, her mother kicking her.

"Give me that. Where the hell is your father, huh? He's off screwing slant-eyed whores on an island in the Pacific, that's where. And where am I? Stuck in this tract house with no money, no car, and two whining brats."

Rae, now included in the melee, dropped the hanger and began to cry.

Nightfall came early, and from their bedroom, two little girls hungry for love and fried chicken, snuck slowly into the light of the kitchen, where their mother was dishing out plates of boiled, unbuttered green squash and a ration of crusty poultry. Each took their seat and ate in silence.

"Why aren't you eating your squash, Julie?"

Rae smiled up over her cleaned plate.

The established punishment for not eating what is placed before you was isolation and lights out in the pink-on-black tiled kitchen. The squash must be eaten. There are slant-eyed children going to bed hungry all over the world.

And as Julie sat in the dark slumped over chicken bones and cold green squash—jealous of the two who sat in front of the console beyond the kitchen wall watching their favorite Saturday night show—a little mouse crawled on all fours to the kitchen table and stole away the squash, bunching it into a paper napkin, making it to the trashcan and back to the couch before the theme song *"When You Wish Upon a Star"* finished.

The sibling rivalry continued at bedtime.

"First one to sleep is a princess," Julie whispered.

"I'm asleep," Rae mumbled from the nearby bed.

"No, you're not or you wouldn't be talking. You're lying. Start now. Ready, set, go. First one to sleep is a princess."

The orange Tabby Cat-With-No-Tail, the stray cat Rae had *crossed her heart and hoped to die* followed her the two blocks home from school, kneaded himself into his final position and let out a goodnight meow. Neither sister said another word.

Chapter 5

Christmas Eve and Dirty Laundry

♪ Let's be jolly
Deck the halls with boughs of holly ♪

Rockin' Around the Christmas Tree
Brenda Lee, Thirteen Years Old, 1958

Mom hibernates in chosen alienation from old friends, family, and new neighbors in her inherited Spanish three-bedroom on a once posh avenue that has been taken over by neighborhood tenants who park their commercial vehicles on the street. Christmas of 2010 would be no different. This snobbish retreat from socialization, infrequently interrupted by attempted visits from her two brothers, is easily booby trapped by the monthly San Bernardino County retiree's luncheon held one mile from her house at the country club and by any man willing to knock at her spider-webbed door, including my fourth ex-husband, erroneously known as *Doc*, who attends the same tedious luncheon where he still calls her *Mom*.

"Now, besides their auto glass business, they have a gardening business. I'm explaining to you the renters across the street. Yes, I'm sitting at the kitchen table and I can see what's going on. Is it still raining there?"

"Yes, it's non-stop. I'll leave for your house within a half hour."

"The daughter is pregnant and the boyfriend is living there now. He's the one with the white truck and the lawnmowers."

"Mom, are they messy? Is the neighborhood under threat of blight? Do you want me to find the number for your Code Enforcement officer?" I popped a Nicorette from an open packet and began chewing feverishly. To avenge the sociopath who had withered my tempestuous spine is the only motivation I have going for me: to become unstoppable, healthy, lithe, and inspirational; to clean up my act and be the change in the world we all want there to be. So grand a gesture, but I am gaining weight from not smoking faster than I lost it from fornicating feverishly in my basement.

"No. I can find the number myself. There's still 9-1-1, isn't there? Come on, Julie, I'm not dead yet. And their lawn looks like an advertisement for *Better Homes and Gardens*. By the way, I have magazines that I've saved for you. I cut out the ads that Alexandra's in. The articles in Cosmo are something else."

"Mom, I already have every magazine Alex is in, but I don't read them. Just how many different ways are there to lick the nipples of a hairy, selfish, domineering boyfriend anyway?"

"Get with it, Julie. Have you called him yet?"

My big mistake was letting mom in on the play-by-play of the last few months, sans the counterspy escapade, when no one else would any longer listen to my unrequited love saga.

"Why would I do that?"

"To see if he'll come back."

"If I called him, he'd come back," I said with certainty. "After all, what does he have to lose, one more condom?"

"Come on, if he hasn't returned on his own by now, he's moved on, dear."

I could see through the phone her red cherry lips pursed over a set of venomous fangs. "I don't want him back, Mom."

"What in the world would you do with him anyway? A man taking up space in your tiny house."

"Spend luscious lazy hours just watching him sleep, I suppose."

"Whatever."

"Precisely." I shook the fantasy off my shoulders and began again. "I'm ready to go. Presents wrapped and in the car. The dogs fed. I'll be there within two hours."

"You're going to leave those dogs locked up in the house all day?"

"I leave the backdoor open. They'll be fine. I'll lay towels down."

If she had read my first novel, Mother would know this already.

"Well, that doesn't sound very safe. Hey, listen, I'm not letting you drive all this way on Christmas Eve in the rain." The poison was spewing from my landline, oozing green and ghoulish through the LCD screen and onto my cheek.

"And you're not driving yourself to Rae's either, right?"

"Don't you love it? The neighbors across the street have invited me for margaritas." The lie scale was beginning to creep up.

"The neighbors with the trucks in the street?" I pictured them standing wet in the street waving sombreros, begging her on over.

"Yes. They speak English as a second language. I'm perfectly fine. I didn't buy a lot of presents, anyway. You and Rae can come over some other time for our special gift opening. We can get together on my birthday."

She was refusing a ride to Christmas Eve dinner and yet expecting us to drive on over seventy-hours later at the Queen's request. Shame on demands made by anyone born during the week of Christmas, but for the Son of God, of course, who simply demands that we believe in him.

"Let's get with it, Julie. I am not spending the night and I wouldn't want anyone to drive me both ways in one day."

My sister Rae has a guest toothbrush in an en suite guest bedroom. The bathroom is stocked with dependable senior diapers. Ever since the chintz sitting room chair was discovered less than dry after Mom's last visit, Rae is taking no chances.

"You know you can always spend the night or even a few days, Mom."

"Oh, no. Get real. I have too much going on. And I have my cat."

That cat, had it followed Rae home? Rae is still punishing herself for bringing that kitten to Mom. Whatever gentle, adoring pet he may have inspired to be, Mother has raised him to be a feral, clawing, antisocial snob. There is nowhere in her house that one can sit down without getting up with mange hairs flying from the seat of their pants.

"This is crazy—" Oops, wrong thing for me to say.

"You're the crazy one. Carrying on with a boy that no one ever met, writing your book, embarrassing our family, and driving around wasting gas on auditions for jobs you never get. And when was the last time you sold a house? Get with it, Julie. Who do you think you are? Rita Hayworth?"

"How did Rita Hayworth get into this conversation?"

"Back in the forties she married a Muslim prince who cheated on her, of course, and when she left him and took their daughter, he offered her one million dollars to raise the child as a Muslim."

"Did she?"

"Heavens, no. She had her own money. She was a star."

"It's Christmas Eve, Mom. Rae is expecting you. Alex and Tommy are looking forward to seeing their grandma. Don't make me come over there to a locked front door again."

"Why can't you have a good job like your sister?"

"I realize you never believed it, but I was an Official Certified Court Reporter for twenty years at the courthouse just ten blocks from your house."

"And why in your novel did you change everyone's name but mine? It was very confusing. You kept calling me *Mother*."

"Because that's your name. I'm coming to get you right now."

"If you do, I won't come out. I'll lock the door."

God, let me fall asleep at the age of eighty-two, never to wake again.

"All right, Mother. Have it your way."

Rae has out done herself, as is the usual. Her hope was to begin the evening's gluttonous affair with cocktails and hors-d'oeuvres served on the grand patio. My front porch is decorated with a small round glass table and four white plastic chairs; Rae's entertainment arena is an outdoor living room warmed by a cast iron baroque fire pit. The only misstep in this *House Beautiful* setting is the street below lined with parked cars where a kidney-shaped, glistening pastel blue pool should be. There are so many colorful pillows carefully placed on the couches, one cannot sit down without knocking one to the polished cement. Party lights laced through large potted trees and meticulously draped about the perimeters of two sun umbrellas set the stage for a spectacular evening, a very wet evening that kept us inside. As the rain beat down, I would not talk about politics, my regret at choosing love of country over raw, undulating sex, my weight, my bereft heart, or my no-smoking Nicorette gum chewing—as Rae leaned out her sliding patio door to light up one cigarette after another.

Gone were the days when the children sat for hours ripping the ribbons off of carefully wrapped, excruciatingly selected, expensive and highly desired electronic gadgets, name-brand jeans, and the obligatory new batch of pajamas and underwear. I had surprised Alex four years ago on her twenty-first Christmas with diamond earrings, after trading in her father's engagement ring sweetly given to me twenty-seven years before. I was out of surprises and out of jewelry.

We exchanged gifts of an amusing nature. Rae was thrilled with a Lazy Susan Scrabble game, including a competitive-edge hourglass timer. Tommy was pleased with a twenty-five dollar gift card for gasoline. Alexandra approved of another year's membership at 24 Hour Fitness. ♪ All I want for Christmas is you ♪ I opined silently while ripping into a box of flannel pajamas.

I was drunk by five o'clock and the rain came down all over Southern California. It is estimated that enough water poured from the streets of Los Angeles into the Pacific Ocean to supply well over one hundred and thirty thousand homes for a year. My uninhibited melancholy thoughts turned again to Ali. I know he is happy tonight, because he loves the rain.

Alexandra surprised us with the news that she had turned in her leased BMW and purchased a new Toyota Hybrid Prius. I silently hoped the bumper of her eco-friendly, battery-operated car would not have the Obama *Hope and Change* sticker on it, which all hybrids seem to have as a stock item straight from the factory.

The kids presented to their moms identical gifts wrapped in silver foil, a silver frame with their faces in it.

The gift opening followed with prime rib, Yorkshire pudding, garlic mashed potatoes, and creamed spinach. The cousins are concerned about my bashed offer to taxi grandma in to Christmas Eve dinner. Alex calls her at six o'clock and passes the cell phone around, the speaker on.

Two rum and Cokes in, Mother is over the top with charity and charm. We should have called before five.

"Oh, your aunt always puts on such a fancy feast. Too bad I can't be there."

"Grandma, we would have driven out to get you. My car gets over fifty miles to the gallon and it's only an hour drive from Rae's," Alex resurrected the offer that had been laid forth to Mother by each one of us, each invitation only to be axed by a vicious and haunting vainglory.

"Your mother said it was almost two hours, dear. Besides, I've been invited by my neighbors—"

"Well, from Mom's in Hollywood, sometimes it can be. But from here at Rae's—"

"Come on, Alex, let's get with it. I don't want you driving all over the state on slick roads to please me."

"What neighbors? Grandma, Alex and I will come and get you right now. You can wake up here Christmas morning."

"But then where would you sleep, Tommy?"

"The couch. The guest room is yours. Why are you so stubborn?"

"I'm not. I'm just too busy. There's always so much to do."

"I'm arranging a book signing for mom at a fabulous hotel bar. Would you like me to bring you in for that?" Alex suggested.

"She's going to gloat over that book? You know she calls me *Mother* all the way through it. I'd be too embarrassed."

"I'm sure there's a *Mom* in there as well, Grandma."

My sister poured herself another glass of champagne and waved the phone away.

"Tommy, it's just not the same without your dad, Julie's children and my two great grandchildren there. We need to have a family reunion. I'll get started on the invitations tonight."

Mother does not tolerate her two brothers. Rae has been estranged for the second year from her husband of thirty years. I have been divorced from husband no. 4 since 1997. My two oldest children do not include me on their guest list. No one but the four of us in *the family* has spoken civilly to Mother in the last five years. No one but the four of us has even sent her a Hallmark card. The New American Family has been perfected.

"I'm looking forward to my birthday on the 27th. What time should I expect you?"

Rae grabbed the phone. "Merry Christmas, Mother."

✳ ✳ ✳

Christmas morning, in my red velvet and musty fur Santa hat, I arrive at Alexandra's townhouse to cheerfully deliver the perfectly sized microwave, a gift I have perilously searched for, ending up at a Sears outpost in Van Nuys of *The Valley*. This gift I had saved for our private Christmas morning. Jiggling a red umbrella over my head and balancing the hefty scarlet foil box, I have to call up to her from the porch to get her to open the front door of her vintage townhouse. I have the key, but I am wary of entering. At twenty-five, she's continued dating a metrosexual—a straight and stylish urban man—of the same age, a young man whose parents, to my limited information, are from old and new money. Benjamin apparently celebrates Easter, Mother's Day, Independence Day, Halloween, and the usual Hallmark card occasions, because Alex has been celebrating these occasions with him and not with her dysfunctional mother, who lives alone with two abandoned, leftover dogs in a miniature petting zoo on a noisy, dirty street three miles away. Heaven knows what type of Christmas present the relationship-thief may have brought to her last night.

"Is he here?"

"No. Why would you think that?" she scowled. Alex applauds as she plugs in the cord behind the small microwave. "Oh, thanks, Mom. It fits perfectly on the counter."

"Are you going to see Benjamin today?" I have not yet met him.

"No. He's with his parents in Hawaii through New Year's."

She would be mine for just a little while longer.

"I had to call the roof contractor. The rain's done a job on the Spanish tile. His name is Benjamin, too."

"Why do I need this information, Mom?"

"In case I start sleeping with him. I don't want to confuse you or the reader."

Having been given the news that her community laundry room is not functioning, somehow I leave without milk and cookies, but with two weeks' weight of dirty laundry to be washed, dried, and folded: ten pairs of black jeans, twelve Minnie Mouse brassieres, twenty thongs in black and flesh, five striped t-shirts, eight pairs of black spandex running shorts, six spaghetti strapped black camisoles, a stained blueberry cotton terry robe, and so many pairs of athletic socks I dare to count them.

Don't all international models use a wash-dry-fold service? Apparently, they do.

While the majority of Hollywood toasted the birth of Jesus with the late morning exchange of bodily fluids and a champagne brunch, I celebrated by sorting the blacks from the whites, the evil from the good.

The first load in, I begin sipping *Christmas Day Alone* vanilla rum while in the basement wrapping gifts for my grandchildren. I shall see them later this week when I take them to see *West Side Story* at the Pantages Theatre, just six blocks from my house and ninety miles worth of driving for their mother.

The stuffed Santa is glaring at me. "Why didn't you put me on the porch this year?" he asks through stitched lips framed with white polyester fur.

"It's still raining. I didn't put out the poinsettia flag either, so you've got company."

"It's lonely down here. I miss the scent of candles and cuming."

"Yeah, Santa, me too."

The truth is I couldn't bear to go down to the basement. I had enjoyed my holiday ritual of shopping for a tree with Alex, tying it to her car, and pine-needling it all over the hardwood floor of her apartment, but I had lost the excitement of pulling out my own cherished storage box of Christmas decorations. I couldn't roust out the jolly to make dozens of frosted sugar cookies and deliver them with a bogus smile under a red and white fur hat. I had lost the childish thrill of hanging velvet stockings from the fireplace screen, because I didn't believe in Santa Claus anymore. I'd hung one lousy wreath on the front door, and the exercise had me crying like a banshee before I started up the wooden stairs with that one red velvet-bowed plastic green circle. Continuing to tempt my sense of reality, the dangerous scent of him still mystically clinging to the Persian runner in the underground room, I knew he was never coming down those steps again.

I move the first load to the dryer, start up the washer again, and sit at the computer and gaze at my December 25th inbox. The new arrivals are scant. I am relieved that realtors, casting directors, my agent, and Nigerian scammers are quiet today, but saddened that there is not a response from Ali to my breakup email of November 4th; perhaps just some little note to let me know he'd gotten it.

Merry Christmas, you unclean Infidel bitch.

My daughter Elizabeth, the mother of my two teenaged grandchildren, has sent me an email. Subject: Manny's Christmas Present. There is an attachment. I open it. My grandson, age sixteen, who has violated several Health and Safety Code sections in his effort to recreationally self-medicate himself and others as treatment for the traumatizing effects of puberty, apparently has been forgiven. He has been awarded a bright red four-wheel drive Jeep, a gift from his parents and his paternal grandmother. I summarize that *Tough Love* has not made its way east to the dry lands of Cherry Valley, an outpost destination thirty miles west of Palm Springs. I raised Elizabeth there, a horse property community, but never meant for her to actually stay there.

After an hour and a half, the clothes in the dryer are still heavy and wet.

Not unaware of the circumstances that may cause a dryer not to dry, I use the long pointed brush, the big bristle brush, the small vacuum nozzle, and a lot of fist thumping. I am outside at the vent behind the trashcans on all fours shoving the big pointed brush up into the plastic coil. Nothing comes out. I am inside the dryer shoving the long pointed brush down into the lint trap. In and out she goes. I have successfully dislodged one miserable, itsy bitsy lint ball, just enough to stuff a baby's belly button.

Chapter 6

A Redneck Birthday and Sibling Rivalry Karaoke

> ♪ Happy Birthday to You
> Happy Birthday to You
> Happy Birthday, Dear Mother ♪
>
> *Happy Birthday To You*
> Patty and Mildred Hill, 1893
> The singular lyric that can be included legally
> without penalty or imprisonment in this novel

By December 27th, two frustrating days later and a hundred and one pushes to the dryer button, Alexandra's fashionable laundry is dry, although a tad wrinkled. It is folded and stacked into two mesh stand-alone net baskets. The Maytag repairman has been called and the sun is out.

I deliver the bounty of my labors and receive a curt *thank you*. Alex, our designated driver, and I take off for Glendale to pick up my sister. We are on this turn-around trip to San Bernardino to celebrate Mom's eighty-second birthday and a belated Christmas gathering. Mom's favorite date, her grandson, has wiggled his way out of this one by taking off on a ski trip, *ski trip* being my sister Rae's secret code for winter *rehab*, which will become interchangeable with *surfin' safari*, her secret code for summer *rehab*. The destination for girls' night out is The Ye Olde Lamplighter Bar and Restaurant for karaoke and old school, redneck people watching.

We pull up into her driveway and carry our packages to a dark front porch. Not one light shines from inside her house. Rae knocks and calls out to her.

"You'd better not be hiding in there," Rae bitterly warns. Stooped over and adorned in metallic polyester, Mom finally comes to the door. From three feet away, I can smell the deathly scent of her unwashed, yet perfectly placed silver hair. She guards the entrance and begins the visit with a few formal announcements.

"I'm saving on the electric bill. I have nothing to serve you. No champagne, no snacks. So let's hurry through the presents, because we have reservations in one hour."

Shocked, my sister and I began biting our nails. No alcohol? Where are the teeny pink frozen shrimp, the deviled eggs, and taquitos? How could Mom unexpectedly put an end to the expected? As distasteful as her traditional treats are, they are part of the ritualistic visit to her stately living room. All she had to do was thaw out everything in her freezer.

After being routinely seated, we exhale and begin the birthday gift opening and the Christmas present exchange.

"Damn it, I shouldn't have worn black. What was I thinking?" Rae dismays as she heads to the kitchen to look for cat hair removal tape. Mother lives for her weekly visit to the downtown dollar store, but there's not one ninety-nine cent lint roller in the house.

Mom rips through her gift bags like a cherished five-year-old. Oohs, aahs, and over-the-top gratitude spill forth over a year's supply of Almond Roca, orange-flavored tea, a box of See's chocolates, enough specialty boxes of liquor to see her through the tepid winter, a set of food storage containers—which she will never use and will regift to one of us next year—and a silver-framed picture of the grandkids.

"Remember last year when I told you—if you even remember—that I said I was going to give you—"

What? My memory perked.

Excited, Rae spoke up, "I remember something said at your timeshare by the pool over drinks and frozen shrimp."

My hazel eyes roll secretly to my sister's blue eyes. Hers roll back. It was in Palm Springs that Mother had mentioned gifting to us a bit of our inheritance without her ever dying.

"I think it was Mother's Day and you gave us each a card with a twenty in it," Rae gently reproached.

"Nope. You forgot! So you can forget it!" Mother reaches furtively under the coffee table and brings out two identical gold boxes. My heart stops. Visions danced in my head of a new air conditioning unit, a professional paint job to the wooden trim on the outside of my bungalow, or an adventure to parts unknown.

Mother soon turned off all the lights and rushed us out into the dark for the ten-minute drive to dinner.

"Don't you want to leave the porch light on, Grandma?" Alex timidly asked and hooked into Mother's arm to lead her through the darkness.

"I can find my way to unlock the door in your headlights, dear."

We left in Alex's Prius; the two sisters now wearing identical brassy, rhinestone-studded bracelets. But much like the seven-year-old girl who was surprised by and forever grateful to her grandparents on that Christmas Day long, long ago, I will not give up hope that the green Schwinn bicycle will be wheeled through that front door once again.

The *no smoking ban* is statewide, but the news has not reached the long polished mahogany bar of the old school 40th street hideaway; the glass ashtrays are full and fuming.

Thirty years ago, as a court reporter assigned to superior court, I came here for long two martini lunches with groups of sheriffs, bailiffs, and defense attorneys waiting for the jury verdict to be called in. Mom and I have enjoyed carafes of wine here over great conversations, when she was still sane. I've taken a date or two here, when I didn't want to date them anymore. This is where you can still order a grand, steamy baked potato with all the fixings brought to your table in a wooden Lazy Susan spinning with butter, sour cream, orange cheddar cheese sauce, and tiny chopped green onions.

The stools are toppled with the weight of boorish hangovers; each seat taken by a robust and rotund truck driver, or his equivalent, his belly proudly strapped with leather through a silver buckle wrestling with a muffin-top spill over. I enter in long flowing layers in order to conceal my no-more-rigorous intercourse bulges hoping for a nudge from the peanut gallery. As is the usual, time stops when Alexandra enters. These men have not had a five-foot-eleven, lithe brunette angel in their midst since—well, they never have.

At the booth, the four of us scoot into the red faux leather seats and Mother begins her irritating whisper under the mic'd bravado of the bartender's karaoke serenade.

"Now, tonight is my treat," Mom threatened.

"What? Speak up," I begged.

"Mom's hearing is going. Probably from driving up and down the mountain," Alex informed the group. Always leave it to your children to diagnose your social skills, your disabilities, and your mental health.

"Say that again, Mom, so Julie can hear you," Rae teased. "Better yet, let her borrow your hearing aids."

"What?" Mom speculated, suspicious of our every move.

"I think she said that tonight was her treat," Alexandra confirmed.

"Tonight is the weekly special. Rib eye steaks and my favorite, prime rib, all for under ten dollars," Mom whispered and tilted her coquet head to study the bruisers at the bar. "Why don't men buy ladies drinks anymore?"

"That was last night, Mom," I warned her.

"They were buying drinks last night? Were you here last night?"

"No. The special was last night."

"Don't tell me what day it is. Tonight is the special. And until seven, drinks are three dollars."

Mom has not found her way to the Lamplighter since the 210 Freeway finally reached San Bernardino in 2007. Rather than actually driving up Sierra Way to the 40th Street hot spot, she chooses to daydream about attacking a bleeding slab of meat while foraging through the ads in the hometown newspaper, like a scientist searching for a cure for cancer.

"Ah ha! I have a coupon," and Mom unleashed the cure from her purse, a small perfectly dissected black and white newspaper ad from the *San Bernardino Sun*.

"Mom, let me see that. I can't read it. It's too dark in here. Julie, did you bring your readers?"

I hadn't. Rae passed the coupon to Alex, who at twenty-five still has her sight, even in the blackout outskirts of upper San Bernardino.

With a wink to Rae, Alex hands the coupon back to Mom. "Reads like a special to me, Grandma."

The dark, friendly gathering spot began to crowd with large ladies in rock 'n' roll t-shirts and their matching pony tailed mechanics. By seven o'clock, the gray-haired widows and their walker-friendly beaus, who scored the large booth in the corner, would be sufficiently buzzed. If I were scouting for a porn shoot location, this would be the perfect venue.

Rae and I are on our second Cuba Libres, when Alex brings the songbook to the table.

"It's one dollar a song. Here's the paper and pencils." Alex passes the book between the sisters. Mom, sipping her second glass of red, slaps down a cache of one-dollar bills bunched inside a rubber band and insists that we girls get up there and sing. Karaoke is my territory, but now single and rum instilled, Rae makes a play for a duet.

"'The Lady is a Tramp' is not a duet, Rae."

"It is now! But you start." And soon I was competing with my sister, who deposited a speaking line here and there.

♪ I get too hungry for dinner at eight
I love the theatre and never come late ♪

Julie, you're hogging the mic

♪ I'd never bother with people I'd hate ♪

That's why my sister is a tramp!

"Are they singing the right words, Alex?"
"Mom is. She knows that song like the back of her hand."

♪ I don't like crap games with barons and earls ♪

*She won't go to San Bernardino
in ermine and pearls*

♫ Won't dish the dirt with the rest of the girls ♫

That's why my sister is a tramp!

"What was that all about?" I inquired during our embarrassing walk back to the table.

"Can't you take a joke?" was all I was going to get.

Alex easily outdid the sibling-rivalry fiasco with her sober, pouting rendition of "Bette Davis Eyes." It was the second time this evening the belly-up-to-the-bar boys lifted their heads away from their shot glasses. I returned to the pulpit with a sad country song guaranteed to churn my melancholy inebriated heart: "Shut Up and Drive"

♪ I'm the voice you never listen to
And I had to break your heart to make you see
That he's the one who will be missing you
And you'll only miss the man
That you wanted him to be ♪

Chely Wright wrote the lyrics and sang the song, but I'm sure she's not the only woman out there living it. I left the stage with moisture filling my eyes and headed straight for the cowgirl's room to catch any foolish tears.

Rae orders a carafe of cabernet and two more rum and Cokes. It's rib eye steaks, salads with chunky bleu cheese dressing, and baked potatoes piled with the works all around. Mom orders her prime rib along with a take-home box. And don't forget the garlic toast. We went for it. The young tattooed waitress giddied about the bar letting everyone know, as Mom had hinted voraciously, that it was the silver-haired petite lady's birthday. Mom was on her throne.

"Who are you waving at, Mom?" Rae leaned in to ask.

"The only decent looking man at the bar."

"He's barely forty. Let Julie wave at him," Rae admonished.

"I heard that. Just so you know, I've set my new appropriate age minimum at fifty-one."

"That's my dad's age."

"Exactly, Alex."

I leaned into Mom. "Mother, what color are my eyes?"

"Brown. Oh, they're dancing," Mom spoke with white dressing gurgling from her teeth. "What is that?"

"Line dancing, Mom," I informed her.

"But it's women dancing alone. What fun is that?"

"What did she say?" Maybe it was true; I was losing my hearing in a room mumbling with background conversations and a gentleman belting out "Achy Breaky Heart."

"Mom, I heard grandma perfectly. She said it isn't any fun dancing without a man," Alex stated flatly. "You need to have your ears checked."

Mother is static on the point that doing anything without a man is a worthless and most embarrassing endeavor. I do suppose that includes climax by masturbation, a subject she has skirted many a time.

> "Mom, what's an orgasm?" I asked timidly
> with my first child in my arms.
> "You'll have one when you're in love."

Mother, circa 1969

> "Mom, do you masturbate?"
> "Do I what? Wait, I need to put my hearing aids in."

Mother, circa 2009

> "Mom, have you ever had an orgasm?"
> "Don't tell me what I have and haven't had!"

Mother, circa 2010

Sparkling with one candle, the cake arrives along with the booming voices of the drunken throng and we three sing along.

Swallowing back sour cream and chives, I dutifully finish up the chocolate birthday cake. If I fail to eat my share, there will be hell to pay. According to Mother's lifelong harangue, if I don't eat up, the Chinese children will continue to starve to death and I will be left alone in the dark until every scrap is choked down.

Tonight the only one that choked was Mom when she asked for the bill, was told her coupon was only good last night, and that the cake was not free.

Chapter 7

Addiction Rewind and The Emperor's New Clothes

> Art that rewards its creator long after the
> average person would quit is admired,
> but is rarely encouraged.
>
> Srinivas Rao, Author
> *The Art of Being Unmistakable*

After loads of alcohol and a big meal, the Nicorette gum is not working. My sister lights up in the front seat and Alex asks her for a cigarette. It's a long painful ride back to Rae's in Glendale, as the smoke puffed out the windows gusts into the backseat of the Prius. I try desperately to catch a nicotine rush with my tongue.

"Is that bothering you, sis?" Rae asks politely with no intention of putting the thing out.

"No, it's okay," I reassure her, my now snobbish anti-smoker posture secure.

"I'm so proud of you, Mom," Alex encourages me, her left hand dangling a Virginia Slims menthol out her open window.

In the dark, I am desperate to break open another child-protected seal of crutch gum. I can't do it. I didn't prepare a medicinal baggie of opened, loose pieces of the damned things. I didn't bring a toothpick or a pocketknife. I didn't plan well.

"Anybody have a metal nail file?"

"A what?" Rae answers and lights up again.

Thwarting a return to an addiction takes planning and forethought. I had been too busy folding thongs and sorting socks to think ahead.

Let me out! Let me run alongside the car! My toes cringe and my arms begin to quake. After letting Rae off in Glendale, we finally reach Alexandra's street and the privacy and security of my own car, where I am doomed to fail. I head up and over to Vine Street and straight into the parking lot of CVS Pharmacy, Liquor, Photo and Beauty—and it's closed?

Not to be dissuaded, I pull out and make a left and then a quick right into the dregs of the 7-Eleven, where the undesirable night owls gather for hot dogs, a slice of pepperoni pizza, or a blowjob from a transvestite. My bladder about to burst, sober and twitching, I opt for a pack of Benson & Hedges Light, but I am told there are no *lights*. The Federal Drug Administration has stuck its controlling protective hand into our shameful habits again. Cigarettes may no longer be marked as *mild, low tar, or light*. After all, they all cause wrinkles, yellowed teeth, and bad breathe.

"Menthol or Luxury?" the Indian clerk asks.

And I choose *Luxury*.

The Jehovah's Witnesses have ended their nightly meeting at the neighborhood Kingdom Hall, so I luck into an all-day parking spot. I turn off the engine and I can hear Brute yipping from the front porch steps. My key pinched tightly between my fingers, I walk to my gate and quickly get inside, locking the gate behind me. I truly enjoy my neighborhood, but I'm not an idiot. After licking the end out of the bottle of vanilla vodka and passionately sucking the filters of four delectable cancer sticks, I cried myself to sleep again. The dogs were glad to have me home.

* * *

The Los Angeles Department of Water and Power gas meter reader awoke me at half passed seven. I need a full, uninterrupted ten hours of sleep to perspire the alcohol from my brain and body, and now I'm going to be hung over all damned day. Tapping a stick along my wrought iron fence, he called out to me again. My eyes sunk into crackling craters, I rushed to the bathroom sink, brushed my teeth and hair, and pelted my sockets with Visine to get the red out. Unlocking both gates, I greeted him flirtatiously in my robe and slippers.

"Come on in." I'm a glutton for men in uniform.

"Good morning, ma'am," he smiled and moved the trashcan away from the meter behind the screen and under the house. Brute and Hound wagged their trusting tails in unison at the kitchen door.

"Even though I was wrinkled, overweight, and aging, he always made me feel as though I were desirable. Too much of a complainer, I was. If only I'd kept my mouth shut, he would still visit me. I'd have one more good reason to get up every day—other than your enticing monthly visit," I thought.

"What color are my eyes?"

"Brown? See you next month, ma'am."

Refilling the dogs' water bowl, I slapped my head at the scant thought that an innocently attractive, thirty-something city employee in blue shirt and pants would give me a second look. I was too soon becoming my mother. Currently, the only difference between our nonsensical vanities was the fact that I did not voice my stupidity. I wrote it down in black and white, while Mother embarrassingly flaunted it in the open for everyone to see and hear.

My kitchen butcher-block table is stacked with shiny colorful paperbacks, bookmarks, and postcards. Marketing self-published work can eat you alive and give you plenty to do other than writing another self-indulgent *roman à clef*, a non-fiction novel in which real people and events appear with invented names, with the exception of *Mother*.

My diaries and research binders are all lined up. I will begin writing what has now become Part Two in a hopeful trilogy, *Jihad Honeymoon in Hollywood; Not Without My Dogs*. Soon to be available on line in paperback, hardback, and *Kindle*: Part One, *The Year I Learned to Text; Why Am I having Sex with a Muslim in My Basement?*

I shall have a book signing thanks to my daughter's enthusiasm. Alex is my biggest fan and the only family member that has actually read the entire book.

"Mom, I loved it! Move to your cabin and just write!"
"Sis, I glanced through it. That's the way books are read."
"Julie, It was too confusing. Why did you name me *Mother*?"

My daughter Elizabeth has made it clear through her intimating silence that she has no desire to understand or encourage my endeavors.

My AWOL son Glen is completely out of the loop, except for an occasional drink & dial communication with his sister Alex, who immediately hangs up.

I remind myself that I am writing for myself with the hope that full disclosure of my shameful behavior will aid women in making better decisions before tossing their hearts, their bodies, and their reputations straight into the toilet. Bolstered by this self-effacing ideology, I begin to procrastinate in the best ways I know how.

I move the stove out from the wall and clean behind it. I pull out the fridge and mop and shine the tile under it. I vacuum out the fireplace and find little funny berries resembling seedpods. Where do they come from? What are they? And there's always my real estate hobby to take me off course.

Smoking my new best friends, The Multiple Listing Service supplies me with enough local expired property listings to fill a week's worth of postcard addressing. I like to use a lovely roller pen. It's so much more personal than printed labels. In the past, this exercise has proven to be a highly successful waste of time. One hundred postcards touting my willingness to put up with a client's tantrums, one hundred postage stamps, and I know the result will be one phone call asking me to come on over and tell a prospective seller how little their house is really worth and leave without a listing contract.

The Maytag appliance repairman is here. He's young, tall, blond, and extremely undesirable. And because I am still in my bathrobe and slippers, he mistakes me for a sixty-two year old grandmother and not the vixen I have become. We are undoubtedly on the same page as far as the viability of any house call hanky-panky.

He shakes his Russian head, "No fix."

"I have wet sheets in there, buster. And the dryer is still under warranty."

"You need vent cleaner service man."

Another possible mating opportunity may be coming my way.

Within twenty-four hours the Air System Decontamination Team, an offshoot contractor of Sears and Roebuck Home Services, will be invading my space. This time I shall be dressed to impress and camera ready. The sun is out, but ♪ Hallelujah, it's raining men, Amen ♪

My seduction plan has been foiled again. The early morning basal cell freeze appointment with the young Persian-Jew dermatologist has left the pre-cancerous spot on the bridge of my nose a weeping red boil. There is nothing I can do to hide it. Dr. Gorgeous has given me explicit instructions *not to touch it*, and I honor each phrase that delightful young man bestows upon me.

Adorned in stained gray sweats to compliment the ooze thingy on my nose, I am excited to open the gate for my visitors.

"Do your dogs bite, ma'am?"

"No. They love men. They're starved for male attention."

Whoopee! There are two men in uniform in my house! I am my mother.

"We need to get into the attic," the better looking of the jump-suited duo demands.

"That's odd. Most men head straight for the basement." Hold me back. "The dryer vent is under the house. Why do you need to get in the attic?"

"You have a basement?"

> Alone in a big city, a single woman over sixty, unable to dry her sheets, has been found raped, pilfered, and wrapped from head to toe in duct tape.
>
> The one identifying mark is a crusted basal cell carcinoma on the bridge of her nose. A DWP gas meter reader found her mummified body under her small bungalow. It is estimated she had been dead for a month.

Up and over the stackable washer and dryer in the living room closet my two killers climb to the attic crawl space. I return to my desk and the bleakness of a blank Microsoft Word page. Chanting, "I'm a writer, I'm a writer, I'm a writer," I listen to the sound of padded knees crawling over my head. I type. Chapter One of my second novel, *Jihad Honeymoon in Hollywood*, has come to life.

> Monday, August 9, 2010; 7:35p HUSBAND: Get ready for me, Darling. Be there within the hour.
>
> An unexpected sizzling August heat wave set into motion a sudden hush stifling the usual hustle and bustle of the dirty streets of Hollywood.

"Excuse me, Ma'am? Have you been coughing and sneezing?" the hot guy inquires of me.

I look up over my reading glasses and point to the *Magic Carpet* couple on the cover of Part One of *The Muslim Romance Trilogy*.

"No, but he sure has."

"Who, ma'am?"

"The cute little Aladdin guy on the front of the book. And I change the filter over my head two times a year, so don't try to sell me one."

"Well, the vents and coils are old and have come apart in some areas up there. We can replace all with brand new for thirty-five hundred, including an upgrade on the filter."

"It's been a bad year. No money. Can't you mend it?" It was the end of Christmas month and I was broke.

"Yes, but it will only last four or five years, ma'am."

"Hell, I may die tomorrow. How much to duct tape it together?"

By your sixtieth year you've put on a new roof, repainted the house, purchased new appliances, and paid off your car. I'll be damned if I want to scrimp and save to do it all over again in twenty years. But the fear of entropy of my personal space will have me borrowing on my home to make it last as long as I do. Just who can afford to live passed eighty? My mother.

Financially endowed, Mother continues to threaten us with life beyond one hundred years, so I can't understand why she refuses to replace the faucet at her kitchen sink. She's been washing her dishes in cold water ever since the hot water handle stiffened and stuck ten years ago. A child of The Depression Era, she also catches the decade-long drip from her bathroom faucet into a plastic pitcher, and when it is filled, she dumps the water into her bathtub. By evening there's a tepid wading pool awaiting her, where once a month without fail she washes her hair.

Mom has never taken a shower because she practices hydrophobia and is mortified by the rush of wasted water flowing over her feet and down the drain. As water is measured at one cubic feet per second, which she has read equals 7.4805 gallons, Mom touts that my failure while in the shower to return her phone call within thirty seconds is indicative of my spendthrift personality. She is never giving me an advance on my inheritance because I would spend it.

"Three hundred. Two hundred for the air vent cleaning and one hundred to unclog the dryer vent." His good looks were fading.

"When did you go under the house?"

"We don't need to. We'll suck it from outside at the flap."

What is the going rate for a blowjob in Central Hollywood?

From the truck at the curb, my two new boyfriends, now in erotic HAZMAT suits and synthetic rubber gloves, rolled into the house a large metal box on wheels. Soon the whir of dust mites and plastic debris being vacuumed out of my air vents and into the box through an eight-inch hose brought me into the bedroom to investigate.

Knocking on his helmet, I sweetly demanded, "Hey, I'd like to see what nasty little buggers are going into that box." I wanted to be sure I was getting my money's worth of allergens captured and removed.

"Can't let you see it, ma'am. There's a black plastic bag inside. The box is taken to an environmental site, opened, and the bag is hermetically sealed and disposed of."

I wondered if NASA was involved?

"Well, then, how do I know you're not just blowing hot air?"

"We're not blowing, ma'am. We're sucking. You're very wise to have this done. You're one of few to understand the need for this procedure. Clean air may even cure that thing on your nose."

I should be puffing with pride that a senior citizen alone in a big city in a six-hundred and forty square foot house has made the intelligent decision to protect her health and the health of her two dogs—and certainly the health of any future suitors. But I was feeling more like that old Emperor and his new clothes, a tale by Hans Christian Andersen, which somehow has been kept neatly in the cobwebs of my aging mind.

A vain fashionable Emperor hires two weavers to sew for him a new wardrobe; a wardrobe they tell him is only visible to those of excellent breeding and high intelligence. When the suit is finished, the swindlers mime dressing him and he, not wanting to appear unworthy, also pretends to dress. Flaunting his "new clothes" before his subjects and his ministers, fearing they will appear stupid, they also feign delight over the invisible clothes.

The pretense is broken when a child on the parade route shouts out, "But he isn't wearing anything at all!" The townspeople then join in the proclamation that the Emperor is, indeed, naked, as he gallantly continues the procession through the streets.

I gallantly wrote out a check for three hundred dollars to Air System Decontamination: the check seen by all; the dust mites invisible to those unworthy of seeing them.

I didn't get the maddening news that the dryer still did not dry until New Year's Eve morning. When promising myself to awake in 2011 with a vibrant attitude wrapped in freshly laundered, four-hundred count Egyptian cotton sheets, I stripped the bed and, unfortunately, I washed them.

Chapter 8

A New Beginning The Easy Way

♪ Tell Saint Peter at the Golden Gate that you hate to make him wait, but you got to have another cigarette ♪

Smoke, Smoke, Smoke (That Cigarette)
Merle Travis and Tex Williams, 1947

New Year's Eve morning, my head stuck under the house and my flannel Frosty The Snowman pajama-bottomed ass bobbing up and down, I revisited the Battle of the Dryer Vent.

"Hey, watcha doing in there?" came from outside the gates. It was my wild and free, charmingly unconventional Goth neighbor Miranda.

I would not bore her with the details of my home repair crisis. The monetary curse of homeownership is as foreign to her as is the necessity of paying parking tickets, evidenced by the stash of little white and red envelopes strewn all over the back seat of her car. Randi has not paid rent since taking residence in the courtyard more than fifteen years ago —apparently a trade for past bi-sexual lesbian services rendered, a tad of house painting, and unfinished tile work—which is how the more-than-not unemployed studio set painter can afford to drive a bright red, high performance Mini Cooper.

"What I'm doing is cursing violently into this long plastic tubing."

Gripping the trashcan handle, I pulled myself up and tiptoed higher to see over my fence. She, too, was in pajama bottoms, black with a skull and crossbones pattern.

"Unlock the gates. I've got something we both need."

The boys needed a trip to the grass, so I grabbed the gate keys, two plastic bags, and signaled for them to follow. Bending down to give Hound a tummy scratch, Randi held out a paperback.

"We're both going to quit smoking! I just finished reading it."

"*The Easy Way*? And how drunk were you this time when you dyed your hair?"

Randi's thick wild red mane is now feathered with shades of purple, green, and black, a complement to her twelve ear piercings, two nipple rings, and silver tongue ball. I worry that she will be found in her bungalow consumed by heavy metal poisoning; her overweight pet rat having eaten her two tarantulas, and the cat, having eaten all three, mewing at Randi's side.

"Julie, that's why I love you. You just say it."

"To you maybe. But never to my own kids—or my grandkids."

"I'm serious about this book. This guy hypnotized me. 'You no longer want a cigarette.' But he won't let you stop smoking until you finish the entire book," she urged me.

"But I can smell tobacco on your breath," I leaned away to prove the point. I was hurt. Randi had taken the time to read this guy's how-to, but had not mentioned my book and I'd sold it to her for the discounted price of ten bucks. This would be a repetitive and disheartening realization in my new writer's life.

"I'm not finished yet. I haven't read the author's bio. Besides, it's New Year's Eve." Filling ashtrays to disgusting levels, Randi and I have spent many an evening on my porch dissecting the mysterious Muslim's behavior and my sexual awakening at the age of sixty. "Are you going anywhere tonight?"

"But of course. The limo arrives at seven."

"It's a date then. I'll order some booze and cigarettes from Bogie's."

"No more smoking in the house. I just blew two hundred bucks on vent decontamination."

"You're so funny. I'll be at your front gate at five."

"Don't forget the Cheetos."

The ninety-two year old ethnically pure German Holocaust survivor stopped by to let me know the vile creatures had dropped a few loads in front of her bungalow.

"I'm valking to Dollar Store. You have twenty minutes to remove the filth!" A widow for over a quarter century, Elsa is horny as hell; thus I forgive her short temper and animal cruelty, but I'm calling PETA the next time she hoses down the dogs. Why can't she be sweet and peaceful, like the ninety-year old, silver-haired lady in bungalow 1238? Bunny just lies there in her reclining hospital bed hooked up to a feeding tube watching *Lifetime* movies and Jerry Springer while her Korean caretaker sucks on brown noodles all day. A visit from Brute is the highlight of her palpable existence. She gets off petting his tummy.

In front of Elsa's little house, this year's Code Enforcement nomination for demolition, I was certain that she had run out of home repair cash long ago. Studying the peeling paint and the tree roots turning over her front steps, I foresaw my timely suicide performed neatly on clean sheets with the help of pharmaceuticals at the age of eighty, when I too would run out of money, while Mother at ninety-nine would still be kicking and screaming.

When the grass in the walkway would grow out of control, a neighbor would search me out to find me in my final sleep. I am in charge of collecting five dollars each month from the twenty residents and paying the monthly gardener bill for The Hollywood Bungalows. I will be missed.

Looking down at my boyfriends, I caught myself. "Don't worry. I'm not leaving you yet. I'll wait." I bagged up the poop and the three of us strolled back to the side gate and into the house.

My favorite sheets in the dryer, I pushed the start button one more time. I could see a flame through the crack, but there was no heat in the drum. I called the Air System Decontamination Team. A sultry female voice picked up. They were cheating on me already. I let her have it.

"You fucking morons, my dryer is still cold and my sheets are wet! What did my hundred bucks get me, you swindlers of murky practices? I want you over here and under my fucking house right now. Oh, this is Julie in Hollywood. You know my number!"

The recorded message told me that the office was closed and would reopen on Monday, January 3rd.

My Tuscany-style one-bedroom/one-bath villa is equipped with an outdoor pullout clothesline on which I pin two moist sheets and two pillowcases. The favored sheets droop in a slight breeze as they hang heavy between the bougainvillea trunk rising up at the lattice fence and the flowered tree found on the Caribbean island of Puerto Rico, the Allamanda Carthica, commonly known in my back garden as the Golden Trumpet tree. Her scent is tropical, a delicate fruity mystery of delight which pours into the open window at twilight. Years ago, the she-he Kandi, a native of Guatemala and the owner of a white whimsical bungalow trimmed in Royal Caribbean blue at the far end of the walkway, forcibly presented to me an infant plant with yellow buds as a neighborhood friendship offering. The bush has spiraled with continuous aspiration, against my will and constant trimming, to the top of my roof and beyond. Her trunk is strong and able to bear the weight of today's errant-dryer angst.

I redressed the bed with a set of thinned yellow cotton sheets from the pine hope chest, the same strategically boiled sheets that Ali had jumped from with the accusation that spiders had attacked him, immediately breaking out in a nasty rash. It was the first time he had been treated with Calamine lotion, an American medicinal tradition.

I sat on the edge of the bed and tried to remember. Hey, I wrote a novel so I wouldn't have to remember and so I would never forget. From *The Year I Learned to Text*:

> "Wait, I'll get the Calamine lotion," I assured him and took off naked in the light of the bedroom to fetch the cure for poison ivy and the temporary relief of pain and itching.
>
> "Something bit me. You have spiders," he accused me.
>
> We sat on the side of the bed and I coated his arms in pink lotion. I sat completely naked, while Ali, of course, sat covered up in his undershorts, checkered in black and red.
>
> He looked so vulnerable and sweet and unreasonably upset.
>
> "I haven't seen a spider since last spring. Besides, I let off an insect bomb in here not too long ago. Maybe it's your fear of intimacy

rising to the surface," I said as I blew on his arms and the lotion crusted over his mini rash.

"Intimacy? Having a climax is your responsibility. It's not natural for a man to have to do something, babe."

I had to let go of the love-hate addiction to this manipulator, but the *fix* was not easily available. The fix could not be found on every street corner. Yes, everywhere I looked—the produce section of Von's, the Sunday Farmer's Market, the do-it-yourself carwash on Santa Monica Boulevard—there were young men with arrogant five o'clock shadows and carefully tousled dark hair, but none with the black eyes of a heartless marauder and none that looked back at me. I seemed safe from repeating the dysfunctional, addictive cycle of giving sex in the whimsy of receiving love.

But cigarettes are easily available. CVS, Rite Aid, the drive-thru Smoke Shack, the seedy liquor store on Vine where the unwashed clerk Ahmed from Bangladesh is a permanent fixture, the degrading 7-Eleven —are all within a short obsessive *Lady Sings the Blues* heroin-withdrawal crawl. I had just spent two hundred dollars to sanitize my air ducts. I had to quit smelling up the house.

The pillows fluffed, the bedchamber prepared for my possible pass out at midnight, I curled up on the loveseat, my ashtray and cigarettes on the TV tray, and opened the pages of *The Easy Way To Quit Smoking*. Brute and Hound left their feeding bowls and fell together into a long nap.

A cold wind banged incessantly at my front door, the French door lites pinging with each gust. Spellbound, I ignored the unusual weather while turning one page after another, lighting one cigarette after another. At the end of the afternoon, I was hypnotized and mad as hell. There will be no deprivation, no moping about, and no more bumping into walls. There will be nothing to be depressed about. I am free!

It all began with that first nasty cigarette. It made you nauseous because it was full of poison. Our wonderful bodies rejected it and screamed out *don't suck this thing!* That one cigarette set up the horrors of the nicotine cycle of pain.

When was that first cigarette? Other than dad's second-hand smoke, which I inhaled in 1948 on the ride home in my mother's arms from the maternity ward, there was the forced inhalation of an entire Lucky Strike when my father caught me lighting up my first cigarette on the toilet of our World War II tract home. I was nine years old and nauseous for a week.

Ah-ha! My senior year Easter week spent at San Clemente pier, where I spent lazy days soaking up ultraviolet rays in a red and white polka dot two-piece and looking cool as I lit up Tareytons in the ocean breeze. Eighteen and legally free to destruct, I returned home still a virgin dying for a smoke. When Dad and Stepmother, both chain smokers, found the makeshift tin ashtray under my bed—this will happen if you don't clean your room when told—my father nearly gave me a black eye. Stepmother, however, conceived her own evil plan: rain, sleet or snow, *let her smoke outside.* She was on track to my eventual expulsion from the maple furniture and braided rug, death-trap asylum.

By the end of my first and last semester at San Bernardino Valley College, I was a full-fledged nicotine user. Everyone smoked and they smoked everywhere: in the cafeteria, in the gym, in the lecture hall. My lunch was simple: a Tab and two Tareytons. Weighing in at a seductive one hundred and thirty-three pounds, I easily bummed the two Tareytons. I would not accept any other brand, because *I would rather fight than switch.*

Over the years there have been nicotine breaks, because there's nothing more unappealing than a bloated pregnant woman blowing smoke.

Mysteriously, the habit subsided for decades, except for an occasional sneak behind the barn or a roll in the hay between husbands with a fellow smoker. Alone in an empty nest and free to make my own choices, am I destined to continue the self-sabotage?

Randi knocked at the gate at six o'clock, not five o'clock, which gave me time to change out of the pajamas and into blue jeans, my *Dogs Rule* t-shirt and some holiday sparkle.

"I've got to get this damned gate fixed." I struggled with the lock through my black satin elbow-length gloves.

"The wood's still swelled up from the rain," Randi assured me. "Wow, fancy bracelets. Did Bogie's deliver on time?"

"Yes, sweetheart." A bottle of Grey Goose, two packs of cigarettes, and a bountiful bag of Cheetos had been delivered along with the bill for fifty-two bucks plus delivery charge plus tip. Randi has good taste, but no clue, and she's worth every penny I have to unload for an evening of non-judgmental girl talk.

"I forgot to order tonic. Do you have any?"

"No. When have we ever mixed?"

The evening turned tepid. The wind satiated, she left Hollywood quietly. We set up fort on the front porch overlooking the city lights; the city lights being the headlights of traffic rattling through the Media District. I lit candles while Randi turned my Mexican tile kitchen counter into a bar.

"You don't have any ice," she shouted over Michael Buble's suggestion that his returned cheating lover should cry him a river.

"Yes, I do. It's the little white plastic thing in the freezer," I shouted back. "Crack the cubes out, fill it back up and it'll be frozen in no time. Oh, and use the filtered water fountain thingy."

She set the bowl of crunchy processed orange carnage on the table, slid me a cold tumbler, and flopped down across from me.

"I've got to get you some new music. Jesus, all you listen to is sad, moody love songs."

"I can put on *Cher*."

"Oh, God. It's the same thing only faster." Randi pulled the gold paper string and flipped open a box of Marlboros. "Did you read the book?"

"Yes. I'm excited. He's so right. The first cigarette was the trigger to all this unhappiness." I borrowed the lighter and lit my Virginia Slim. "I haven't read his bio yet, so I guess I'm free to light up, huh?"

All the way through Ella Fitzgerald's greatest hits and the entire *Saturday Night Fever* album, we smoke and we drink. The Cheeto bowl is refilled twice. My black satin fingers are now a dusty orange. Bungalow neighbors waive us a *Happy New Year* on their way in and out of the early twentieth century mews. Street side, the wide sidewalk is alive with the chatter of passerby club goers speaking into their phones, planning their evening meet-ups on Sunset Boulevard and beyond.

"I need to get that old rickety gate fixed."

"You need to get your old rickety heart fixed first." Randi softened. "It's time to move on."

"It hasn't been eighty days yet. On the eightieth day of no see, no hear, no touchy, I'm gonna know he's just not that into me. Until then —" But I knew I would never make contact again. How could I and not tell him the truth, a truth I could not share with my only BFF.

> Yes, I turned you in to the FBI, and the FBI turned you in to Intel, and Intel counter-intelligence turned you in to Hezbollah and to the Los Angeles Chapter of Hamas, and nobody wanted you because you're nuts. And I received enough money in my espionage squirrel account to pay off my charge cards, to publish a novel about us, and to get a new gate.

"I never saw that asshole, but if I ever do, I'm runnin' him over with my car."

"I don't think that the Mini's gonna hurt much."

"I'll borrow a van from the *Dexter* set."

"You've been getting a lot of painting work on that show?"

"Hell, yeah. Blood splattered walls have to be repainted."

"You read my book, huh?"

"I lived your book, remember? You've been crying at your mailbox for over a year."

"And I never even had the thrill of throwin' his clothes in the street, 'cause he never left anything in my house."

"Julie, ya gotta watch out for the man who doesn't care enough to ask any questions, never has you meet any of his friends or family, and never admits to anything. This guy has many secrets…and you're one of 'em."

"Ya know, his first kiss was like that first cigarette, the one cigarette we shouldn't smoke. I shoulda spit it out and mooshed it under my boot."

"But then ya wouldn't know the rest—the restlessness of being without it. Ya woulda missed the misery that makes you the woman you are today, for sure."

"One kiss. One cigarette. I had to have more and more and more."

"Yeah, you were addicted. That's it. And now you're left with a need that only more of the same can fix. You didn't love him, Julie. You loved his dick."

Pushing my plastic chair out, wobbling to and fro, I stood and lifted my glass in a toast to my beloved French Quarter style, ornate streetlights, their stately glow a torturous reminder that I had been gas-lighted by a manipulator who had at one time turned me into a woman doubting her own sanity. "Shit. There's a bulb out. Now I'm going to have to spend hours on the phone calling street services."

"Who?" Randi stood to join me in my salute, spilling her drink into the Cheetos.

"I loved his dick! May his dick rot inside the asshole of a transvestite hooker." I was on a roll of some kind.

"We need to find you a new dicky-wicky and quick."

♫ We're off to see the wizard ♫

♫ The wonderful wizard of cock ♫

We fell back into our chairs and caught our breath. Two cell phones sounded the jingle jangle of a text message.

> Saturday, December 31, 2011; 11:57pm WAYNE: I just finished your book. What were you thinking? I would have slashed his tires somewhere before Chapter 3.
> 11:57p JULIE: I nvr knw whr his car was pkd.
> 11:58p WAYNE: Is that court reporter shorthand?
> 11:58p JULIE: No, I'm drnk.

Wayne is a steadfast friend and my intercourse interloper of over twenty-five years. He's the guy you only fuck when you're passed out. His well-intentioned willy is uncomfortably bulbous and floppy, and his teeth—well, you've heard the radio ads for a certain dentist.

> You drive a Porsche; you own a great house;
> and you're teeth look like that? Shame on you!

He is a never-married criminal investigator, assigned to the San Bernardino County District Attorney's office, and a blonde gold digger's benefactor of three thousand dollars a month towards her living expenses in exchange for one fuzzy pink nightie choreographed fuck within twenty-four hours of the rent's due date. He will not heed my subtle warning that, perhaps, she's just not that into him and may be getting off elsewhere the other days of the month and that an investigation of his own may be prudent. I've offered him one flannel pajama go round per month for just five hundred, but he knows I'm kidding.

"Who's texting you?"

"The married guy," Randi declared.

Ah, another married guy. Using no names, Randi always refers to her latest conqueror as *the married guy*, not to be confused with *last month's married guy* or the-guy-who-doesn't-really-love-his-dominatrix-wife *married guy*.

"He's meeting me at the garage in the afternoon."

"Ah, jeez, New Year's Day? The same routine?"

Randi's rendezvous with the Italian-American father of three is at her male friend's raunchy apartment garage in Culver City. There the hopeful mistress and the cheating scum park their cars in the alley and she gives gratuitous, spine tingling head inside a cobwebbed, dark and dank, hoarder's stink hole.

"My friend's promised to move the lawnmowers over, so we can use the mattress. The married guy is tired of rubbing his butt up against a termite-infested two by four."

"So you're gonna have intercourse tomorrow, not just you licking the Popsicle and the married guy doing nothing?"

"I told him I can't have kids, but he's paranoid."

"What? Why can't you have kids?"

"Too many abortions. Oh, and a hysterectomy. Have you ever had one?"

"An abortion? A hysterectomy? No, but God did grant me a miscarriage once."

"He complained about getting splinters."

"Randi, what goes around, comes around. Just warnin' ya."

"Come on, you've never done a married guy?"

"My mother uses that term."

"What term?"

"*Come on.* It's irritating. No, I've never knowingly done a married guy. Well, not after the Jewish optometrist episode way back in the 70s, but he started and finished outside, not inside, so that really doesn't count. There was the DJ who let me know he was married right after he stuck his itty bitty into me. There was my fourth and last legal husband, Doc, who feigned being divorced during our courtship and remarried another foolish believer exactly six months after I filed the divorce papers. *Beware the man who can't live alone.* During my career as a court stenographer there were many a lawyer, a cop, or a judge who invited me to an intimate lunch, but I always insisted on a note from the wife. I was hungry for twenty years."

"Why are we talkin' about men anyway?"

"Want to talk about my duct cleaning?"

"No. What's that crusty thing on your nose?" Randi asked while flicking the ashes off her cigarette.

The vodka was working its magic. "I thought I could love him into being civilized, reciprocal, faithful, devoted, truthful—"

"Stop sounding like a babbling idiot. You thought you could tame him, change him."

"And maybe, just maybe, change the whole goddamned Muslim world too."

"Have another drink."

"He came back, though, didn't he? I'd break up with him and he'd come back. He always came back."

The neighborhood sounded off a new beginning with illegal fireworks, shotgun fire, and car horns honking. Hound scrambled from his sleep to bay in celebration. Little Brute hightailed it to his hiding place under the bed. From the porch we sorta kinda *oohed* and *aahed* at the fireworks over the Hollywood Bowl. We were too drunk to care.

In the Mediterranean port of Alexandria, Egypt, an Islamic suicide bomber took out twenty-one Christians at a New Year's Mass. The survivors rushed into the streets and beat up Muslims passing by. The riot police fired rubber bullets and tear gas to disperse them. How can you tell an Egyptian Christian from an Egyptian Muslim? The Muslims carry signs that say: *Death to America.*

I lifted the weight of a tired wooden Persian blue gate, a gate that he had walked through many a time, and I missed him. Stumbling onto the sidewalk, my friend pulled me into her.

"Julie, he came back to finish the job. He came back to convert you."

In a drunken stupor, my author was happy; Randi had read my first book.

Chapter 9

Pub Crawl and The Big Dick

> ♪ Since my man and I ain't together,
> Keeps raining all the time ♪
>
> *Stormy Weather*
> Harold Arlen and Ted Koehler
> Lena Horne, Songstress, 1917-2010

Rae parked her silver Mercedes convertible in the ArcLight Cinema parking structure. I locked the front door and left the back door open. On the front porch I ruffled two sets of pouting ears and said my goodbye. "No fighting over food while I'm gone."

Years ago I had given up on the separate dog bowls theory. Hound would end up eating small dog specialty mush, which showed up within twenty-four hours as vile slush. Nipping at Hound, little Brute would violently snatch dry kibble away to secret brown hard tidbits under my bed, where they eventually rested untouched to gather moss. The solution is one big bowl filled daily with nutritious *aging dog* medium kibble pebbles of vegetable, protein, fat, and fiber guaranteed to keep them alive, with no guarantee they would ever again be capable of chasing fire trucks and squirrels.

My head still throbbing from last night's New Year's Eve indulgence, in a black herringbone cape and swinging a cautious umbrella, I walked the few blocks up to Sunset Boulevard and met Rae at the ticket counter inside the grand lobby.

"Two tickets for *Blue Valentine*," she requested of the young man.

Disappointed at the display of seat selections, I huffed, "I should have reserved my favorite seats. Looks like we're going to be rubbing elbows today."

"Let's take the aisle seat in case we have to pee," Rae set her index finger at the end of aisle *N*. "We have enough time before the show for a cocktail."

"I'll use my member number and see if I have enough points for free popcorn." I leaned into the counter and waited for the answer. "Oh, and we're both seniors."

"No discounts on holidays, but it looks like you have just enough points," the young man shared. "Don't forget to give them your number at the concession stand."

"You and your popcorn," Rae sighed.

It was one-thirty in the afternoon, but what the heck, one *hair of the dog* might do me some good. "Okay, but remember, they won't let us in after it starts."

The ArcLight Cinema multiplex is a glamorous adult experience boasting fourteen stadium-seating theatres, a Hollywood history bookstore and gift shop, a full-service bar, a restaurant with secluded booths and table-clothed tables for six, and a patio for people watching and cigarette smoking.

Looming over the Sunset Boulevard sidewalk, the Cinerama Dome, originally built for three-projection screenings, is historically preserved so that I can show it off to visitors as one of my very few childhood memories. Apparently, Daddy was somewhat of a movie buff. The desk Marine broke his weekend tradition of slouching in the recliner in front of the TV console draining cans of Falstaff—or drowning his sorrows in Elvis Presley's "Heartbreak Hotel" single that had followed us from house to house for years—and drove the four of us one hundred and fifty miles away from the desert training base. On the interstate, we passed through our hometown where the grandparents lived, Daddy growling at the two young girls in the backseat to stop signaling at the truck drivers to honk their horns, while Mother finger waived a flirt at eighteen-wheelers rumbling by our two-toned Ford Fairlane. We were off to the foreign land of Hollywood to see the premier of *It's a Mad,*

Mad, Mad World at the newly constructed Cinerama Dome. More remarkable is that he drove us in once again to enjoy *How The West Was Won*. Rae and I were scurried passed the snack bar on both occasions. And if this excursion has been mentioned before in either Part One or Part Two, strolling down memory lane is always exhilarating.

The complex is also a taunting sense memory for me and my first inclination that, perhaps, Ali did not use deodorant: my first date with Ali, where he seduced me with a guiding hand to my back, a barrel of buttered popcorn, a diet Coke, and an unexpected jolt to my unconscious libido.

Once upon a time, Prince Ali, having hacked his way through the brier patch thicket of late afternoon traffic, showed up to our first meeting in the ArcLight courtyard fifteen minutes late to deliver the fateful kiss that would break the spell of this sleeping beauty. Not following the fairy tale format, in the back row—with no one behind to see—after I refused his offer of a relaxing kiss, he chose a surprise hand drop to his corduroy crotch and erect manhood to get my attention and to shake me back to life. And I haven't had a good night's sleep since.

"Here," Rae handed me a dry and dirty martini. "Head out to the patio."

Shuffling through her oversized posh gold bag, Rae brought out a hard pack of menthols and a lighter. "Is there an ashtray on another table?"

"I don't see one." I had left my cigarettes back at the scene of the crime, my front porch. My mouth foul from the end-of-the-year tobacco marathon, I would feign continued abstinence.

"Well, I guess the ashes are going on the pavement," Rae shrugged as she lit up.

Coifed in salon-perfected golden blonde bubbled layers, tiny silver birds floating in silver hoops dangling from her ears, my sister is the fashion headliner of our twosome. We both shop discount, but she has the patience and talent for buying the best and buying it cheap. She always finds the good stuff, but it's gotta hurt stuffing a size nine-and-a-half into those narrow shimmering leather stiletto ankle boots. I go for the comfort and not the glory. Today I am wearing black flat-soled faux leather boots; my straight-legged blue jeans tucked inside. Suffering from New Year's Eve regret, my unwashed hair is hidden under my black ragamuffin Notting Hill cap, purchased in London seventeen years ago.

I do my budget best to keep up with Rae; consequently, I've been dying my own hair a raspberry mink, a concoction of various shades of mahogany, chestnut, and chocolate, since Clairol came in a box. Put me between my polished sister and Alexandra, the Oscar de la Renta runway model, and I am the frump.

Rae is Mother's favorite blue-eyed blonde who married late, birthed one time in her mid-thirties, and stayed married to the same guy for thirty years, while I jumped for the first guy that bought me a three-dollar cheeseburger at The Curve Inn pool and dart bar, and I've kept on jumping like the bouncing ball on the roulette wheel hoping to land on the green double zero and cash in, which I never have.

After a quarter century of never hanging out as giggling, tell-all-secrets sisters, but for the relegated family celebrations and babysitting trade-offs of the cousins born six months apart, suddenly last year we found ourselves divorced at the same time. Since abandoning her cherished foreclosed California Bungalow and moving into her leased entertainment suite in Glendale, a short drive to Hollywood, Rae has nominated me as her fair weather buddy, a title I accept with gratitude and open arms. I have brought the umbrella just in case the clouds break open into a familiar, full-scale sibling storm.

A waiter in a red button-down military coat whizzed up to the table offering a red tin ashtray. This is why I spend the senior discounted twelve dollars to see a midday feature: customer service.

"No smoking, ma'am."

"But we're outside, sir," Rae retorts and inhales ferociously, letting out an anti-establishment fog.

"There's a no smoking city ordinance that covers the entire complex. I'm sorry, but you have to put that out."

"Is there any place that's fun anymore?" Pseudo-liberals are a funny lot; they like very much making laws, but don't seem to want to follow them.

"There's always my front porch," I suggest, but foresaw many a half-smoked cigarette stomped out on the sidewalks of today's after-movie bar crawl down Hollywood Boulevard.

"Drink up. Bathroom?"

I fingered out my two olives and followed her gilded Inspector Clouseau trench coat through the restaurant, passed the ticket counters, passed the espresso kiosk, passed the legendry black and white screen icon photos, and up three stairs into the bathroom, where cruise ship sized wooden slatted doors hide each toilet inside a claustrophobic nightmare water closet. Never come in here after two martinis. You will never find your way out. One martini is fine. A test run into the ladies' room before cocktails is suggested.

Rounding the dark uphill runway, we flashed the usher our tickets. Entering from the bottom of the stadium, a stoic sea of semi-lit faces, like the snapshot of a celebrity memorial held in the grandstands of the Rose Bowl, confronted us. Thank goodness for reserved seating.

A free tub of buttered popcorn is balanced on my knee. I tip the rim towards her, but Rae waives it off with a flinch of disgust. This is my indulgence and she will have no part of it. As I cover my lap with the necessary abundance of recyclable khaki napkins, I sneak a peek at the handholding lovers cooing off my right shoulder. Their hands move to each other's knee as the coming attractions end too soon. Lately, that's the best part about coming to the movies; you get to see all the good parts of bad films without having to pay twelve dollars to watch the entire self-indulgent creative production.

Blue Valentine is Rae's pick and I can tell within the first fifteen minutes that I'm going to be watching it with my eyes closed. Ryan Gosling in a constant five o'clock shadow is a charismatic slacker. His wife, Michelle Williams, a registered nurse, has tired of putting out to a part-time house painter. They have mistakenly brought a young innocent female child into their failed marriage, a child who thinks of her daddy as a playmate, while mom fries up bacon in the pan, washes out forty-four pairs of socks, hangs them on the line and greases the car—all before taking the kid to school on her way to work.

The camera lens is way too close on this shot. What was the director thinking? The entire screen is bulging with Ryan Gosling's face bobbing up and down between two white thighs. I can see his nose hairs waving back and forth. Where was the script supervisor in this scene, huh? Where's the continuity? Shouldn't his lips be slathered with offensive moisture? Simultaneously, I wonder how Randi is doing in the garage.

I'm already half way through the barrel. The napkins are greased up, even if Michelle Williams is not—maybe she is still mourning the drug overdose death of her baby daddy, Heath Ledger—and the two boyfriends to my right are cuddling up and I can't see their hands. I'll have to step over Rae to excuse myself. I'll say I have to pee. She won't believe me. She'll sneak me the evil eye. I shall endure another half an hour of two losers never finishing a sentence. Good God, is this tribute to love gone wrong in America ever going to end?

"Whew, I thought it was never going to end. What kind of ending was that anyway?" I mumbled as we took the lighted stairs out of Cinema no. 5.

"I loved it." Great, another topic we cannot discuss along with politics, religion, and my sordid, non-existent Muslim love life.

As planned, we ventured up Vine Street and crossed at the light onto the north side of Hollywood Boulevard. We giggled as we passed under the marquis of Déjà Vu Showgirls boasting *100s of Beautiful Girls & 3 Ugly Ones.* Careful not to step on the stars, I jumped over gossip columnist Hedda Hopper.

"Wouldn't she, a Republican, be shocked to know that her star is right in front of the nudie show?" I noted. Rae ignored me.

The *Walk of Fame* begins at Capitol Records on Vine Street, backtracks to the Pantages Theatre and continues on both sides of Hollywood Boulevard to front Grauman's Chinese Theatre and the Kodak Theatre, the venue of the Academy Awards. The chamber of commerce receives today thirty thousand dollars from the recipient entertainer or a benefactor for each pink terrazzo star rimmed with brass and inlaid into a charcoal terrazzo sidewalk. These stars are the keenest attraction for the star-struck, bringing thousands of tourists each year to trample upon them.

Keeping the brass emblems spit-clean—a television with rabbit ears, a phonograph record, a classic film camera, a radio microphone, or a comedy/tragedy mask—is the resident one-legged sixty-something crabby man, John Peterson. If I only had one leg to stand on, I am sure I would be crabby too. Weathered and appearing to be a homeless schizophrenic, you will find him dutifully removing with a moist workshop rag the grime, gung, and Sharpie graffiti. He began his second career when a few shopkeepers began paying him to polish the stars in front of their storefronts. The Hollywood Entertainment District is now his official employer. Be careful not to step on a freshly *Brasso*-buffed star or John just may trip you with his crutches, which are always at his side.

Skipping along, I looked forward and then back, flipping myself in order to read the names of the movie stars, radio personalities, and recording artists, as each one sits three feet apart facing in opposing directions.

"Oh, oh. Grace Kelley is inlaid in front of a hot dog stand!"

"How much farther?" Rae dismayed. Those scrunched toes must be feeling the burn.

Three blocks later we reached our destination and disappointment set in. The tattoo parlors, the sex shops, the bong and hookah galleries, and the Hollywood Suit Outlet—where you get three suits, three shirts, and three ties for under three hundred bucks—are all open, but the famous Musso and Frank's, where Charlie Chaplin dined in the carved wooden corner booth by the front window, is closed. Shrimp Louie salad and fifteen-dollar martinis are scratched off the itinerary.

"I need a drink," Rae urged us along the boulevard and through the maze of holiday tourists, their cameras at the ready to paparazzi Brad and Angie. They, too, would be disappointed. The *Ugly American* in Bermuda shorts and Hawaiian shirts is no less abundant here than in Paris, London, or Rome. Obviously, the unsuspecting visitors rushing into souvenir shops for a Rolling Stones zip-up hoodie had packed their bags in Michigan for a warm Christmas getaway.

I jumped over the stars imbedded in the sidewalk. "Step on a star and you won't go far!"

"Don't you mean, step on a crack and you'll break your mother's back?" Rae corrected my attempt at rudimentary rhyming 101.

"By the way Mom hunches over, I'd say we've stepped on a shit load of cracks. Look! The Pig 'N Whistle's open."

The cloud covered sun slipped away behind the Roosevelt Hotel's rooftop Tropicana pool and bar. We crossed the boulevard at Las Palmas and the sisters found one empty table at the Pig 'N Whistle, Hollywood Boulevard's meager attempt at mirroring an English pub.

"The only item resembling anything British on this menu is the fish and chips," I commented over a glass of house chardonnay.

"Just so you know, this place opened its doors in 1927 with fanciful hand-carved wood décor and traditional American fare. It was an instant favorite with the movie colony as well as the locals." Rae just knows everything. "Yes, I'll have another, thank you. The Egyptian Theatre being next door, it was a pre-premiere hot spot for household names like Cary Grant, Jane Wyman or Walter Pidgeon. Celebs could often be spotted dining here."

"No, I'm fine, thank you." The waitress rushed off to the bar. "Well, we're not likely to see any of them here tonight."

Now on her second gin and tonic, Rae continued on her historical foodie adventure.

"The Pig 'N Whistle closed for a time in the fifties and became a clothing store, but, alas, was restored to its former elegance by restaurateurs Breed and Hajjar in early 2001."

"Sorry, I have to take this. It's my neighbor Randi." The place was abuzz with the rattle of utensils to plates and high-pitched conversation. "Yes, speak up, honey."

"He didn't show up. I sat on that stinky mattress in a red teddy for hours waiting for him."

"Who's Teddy? He didn't show? He's Italian and not a Muslim, right?"

"Yes. No. He called just now and mumbled something about New Year's Day and the kids and—"

"He wants to have more kids now? He's married, Randi. At least he has an excuse for not showing up. I'm out with my sister. Go home and we'll talk tomorrow. Chin up, okay?"

"Piss on him. Piss on all of them."

"Please what? Randi?" Randi hung up and Rae continued.

"The original restaurant featured a stenciled Italian Renaissance dining hall and a balcony for private parties."

"Yes, please, another wine," I answered. The waitress hurried away to the bar. "Do you remember when Dad took us all to the Cinerama Dome?"

"If it was before I started menstruating, I don't remember much if anything of our idyllic childhood."

"Oh, okay. Maybe we should order something to eat?"

"The California Nachos sound yummy." Rae turned the menu to my side of the table.

"Fried wonton chips, melted cheddar and Jack cheese, pico de gallo—Rae, how do you retain all this trivia?"

"It's on the back of the menu."

My tummy full—Rae had turned up her nose at the nacho order and decided on another gin and tonic instead—I paid the bill and we precariously strolled out of the historic monument and headed away from the dense populace of the Hollywood and Highland complex, where fake, unlicensed Spidermen and Batmen forcibly pose for pictures with you—at five dollars a snap.

I turned us into a souvenir store where I found a fabulous pair of black and silver sparkling Michael Jackson—may he rest in peace—replica gloves.

"Whatever are you planning to do with those?" Rae condemned my purchase.

"Liven up the bowling league. We start up again next week. I'll cut off the fingers."

A Metro bus stopped every ten minutes at every bench along our trek, but Rae declined the idea of riding along the boulevard with maids, nannies, and shop clerks returning home.

"Remember when we used to take the city bus downtown with Mom?"

"I don't remember anything before the age of twelve."

"Yes, you do. Woolworth's Drugstore and chicken salad sandwiches on wheat toast?"

"Ham salad. I always had a ham salad sandwich on white toast." She was adamant.

Well, I'll be damned if I'm going back and edit that story to fit her memory. It's my memory and I'm sticking to it.

"You're an idiot, jaywalking on Hollywood Boulevard!" Rae shamed me as she crossed through traffic to catch up with me at the Mexican bar for a margarita or two.

When we reached the Frolic Room Bar, the infamous narrow dive beside the Pantages Theatre, *West Side Story* ticket holders were lined up at the bar. Years ago, the bar connected to the theatre lobby adjacent, but the entrance is now sealed and a fancy computerized jukebox blocks the phantom doorway. The wall opposite the long bar stretches out a mural of caricatures of Einstein, Freud, Groucho, and Satchmo enjoying an evening of mayhem and mischief at gala tables, much like one thinks of in a post World War II dinner theatre.

"Do you suppose those fellas ever really had a drink in here?" the gay married tall one asks Rae.

"Well, we're here, aren't we?" She accepted their offer of a second margarita served in a tall glass without salt. The two thirty-something males shared with us that they had been married during "a legal window," that they lived in Palm Springs, and that we should exchange numbers. We all pulled out our phones to add new contacts. *Feeling no pain*—Dad's phrase remembered fondly, at least by me—we accepted two tequila shots from the lovely couple before they hurried off to their seats. Warming up my voice for tomorrow's Pantages Theatre family Christmas present, I sent them off with my rendition of "Tonight."

♪ Tonight, tonight, won't be just any night. Tonight there will be—♪

"Stop it."

Without jaywalking, we crossed at the green light over to the auspicious W Hotel for eighteen-dollar martinis.

"Please take that hat off. You look like a homeless person." I oblige her and shake, rattle, and fluff my head. "Christ. Please put it back on." Towering over me in a flash of glint, Rae opened the glass doors and we made our 2011 grand entrance into the *living room* of the hotel.

Following the 97th annual Tournament of Roses Parade through Pasadena, the annual New Year's Day Rose Bowl football hoopla had come to an end, sending pigskin enthusiasts to continue celebrating the Texas Christian University Horned Frogs' win over the Wisconsin Badgers. At the bottom of the red carpeted grand white staircase trimmed with glistening acrylic glass sheets and stainless steel railings, Rae and I found a winning fan nestled among red pillows on a white leather couch.

"Did you say 'Horned Dogs'?" I leaned in over Rae's lap to hear the muffled flamboyant conversation she was having with Mr. *Decent-Looking*, a gray-haired man dressed in a white suit, white loafers, and a red and blue striped tie.

"My hometown Horned Frogs took the Rose Bowl trophy home today," Mr. *Southern Drawl* clarified. "I'm guessing you're not a football fan, Miss."

"And she can't hear. So you live in Texas and you came all this way for the parade and the game?" Rae asked.

"I'm an alumni of TCU. A group of us came out together." This guy is money, unless he hooked up with a really great Rose Bowl group room rate.

"Where's your cowboy hat?" I was suspicious already.

"In the car. Have you two been to the Rose Parade?"

"Not together," Rae answered for us. "My ex-husband and I used to get up early in the morning and be at the beginning of the parade route when the flowers were still being fastidiously placed onto floats, and we always had seating at—"

"I lied to my parents in 1969 and told them I was going, but I ended up learning *69* in a motel room with a Navy Seal and watching the parade on television. It was a horrid experience."

"Julie, that's the last time anyone did *69,*" Rae faced me.

"When was what?" I whispered back to her.

"1969."

"You stole that from Carrie Bradshaw."

"You're the writer. You stole it."

"Do you come to Hollywood often?" I inquired of the man I hoped would spoil us with an elegant dining experience and fine wine at Delphine, the upscale brasserie here at the hotel.

"Nope, ya all. This is my first time. I suppose I could have just as well stayed in Pasadena, but didn't want to miss the opportunity of meeting Hollywood natives. Do you gals live here?"

"She does," Rae hitchhiked a finger across her chest at me.

"Julie, is it? If you don't mind my asking, but are you a Scientologist?"

"Hell, no. I'm a Protestant."

"Well, it sounds like a difficult religion, just by the name of it."

A man alone in Tinsel Town staying at the posh Hollywood-inspired W Hotel stirred up an irrepressible, absurd idea that a man in his sixties did not have a hooker arriving soon. But if not, it's a well-known fact that a decent looking grandfather with any spending money prefers bimbos and blondes. Rae jumped on that fact.

Lifting her tattooed eyebrows—in her teens she had mistakenly shaved the hefty lot, only to have them never return—Rae proceeded with zest, dignifying her blonde thoughts, "Will you be going out with your friends later to play tourist?"

I was pleased that my sister was flirting. Finally, I'm not the only sister seeking recognition and, just perhaps, a bit of romance, after three gin and tonics and four or five shots of tequila. But who is counting?

"Nah, most of them have crashed for the night." His blue-gray eyes looked up to the top of the winding staircase. "I tried to get a few fellas to share a taxi down Sunset Boulevard, but no takers."

The waitress finally stopped by in a short black skirt, stilettos, and a tightly tucked white tailored shirt. "Drinks?"

Rae glanced at me. "I think we'd better stick to chardonnay."

I nodded in agreement that, yes, sticking to white wine would sober us up right away. Mr. *Mighty Friendly* ordered himself another Drambuie on ice.

After sharing information on their mutual six-figure careers and the weather, I attempt to insert my commercial acting fame, my love of reading to the kids at Vine School, and the upcoming release of my first novel—all of which are diluted by my sister's explicit diatribe on the architecture of the hotel.

"The fifteen-story hotel opened just last January and hosts a three-hundred room hotel and a separate condominium tower. It's all conventional glass, aluminum, and architectural precast. And the approach is a shot of glamour: the red carpet made of terrazzo. The wall facing what the *W* likes to refer to as 'the living room' has a retractable screen for showing movies. It's, oh, so Hollywood."

"I've always wanted to visit the Whiskey A Go-Go," he timidly admitted. Rae placed her hand on his white knee.

"You know, it's been an anchor on the Sunset Strip since 1964. All of the great ones have played there. The Doors, Janis Joplin, Hendrix, Zeppelin. It has live music every night. All the up and coming bands play there. It was even inducted into the Rock'n'Roll Hall of Fame. It's historic," Rae finishes breathless.

"Who did you see there?" I interrupt the candor.

"Janis Joplin."

"But you were just a kid then."

"You tell your stories and I'll tell mine."

Yes, switching to wine is a good choice.

"Well, it's getting late," Mr. *Southern Gentleman* interjects.

"Let me see here," Rae instructs, pulls out her phone, and leaves us for the Internet. "Okay, a show starts in forty-five minutes and the price is eighteen dollars at the door. So you, sir, are going to the *A Go Go*. My treat."

Returning from the restroom, where I realized the degree of my sobriety when I waived my hand under the soap dispenser for three minutes with no result, I scour the lounge, but it is baron of a lonely man whom I can quickly kidnap to change this threesome into a double date. And in this urchin cap, I am surely not tempting anyone.

Before I can ask Mr. *Cattle Rancher* for a copy of his driver's license, the valet pulls up with a four-door midsize rental.

"Please don't tell me you paid the tab," I hiss into Rae's collar.

"He's our out-of-town guest." Rae jumps in the back seat on the driver's side and signals me to get in front. Isn't Mr. *Texas Oil Baron* her catch of the day?

"Don't you want to sit in front?"
"No. Hey, mind if I smoke back here?"
"Sure, doll, anything ya'll want."

The car hung a right up Argyle traversing the eastside of the hotel, then a right onto Sunset at Nickelodeon Studios. Rae rolled down her window and brought in the noise of passing vehicles trolling the late evening for an In-N-Out burger or a fifty-dollar hooker. The brake lights blinked as the signals turned yellow to red to green; the flow of cars on the boulevard had become a bumper crop. We were heading through Central Hollywood to West Hollywood, passed the Laugh Factory and the Comedy Store. But before we left my neighborhood, Mr. *Armchair Quarterback* began talking from behind his cheap rented wheel.

"My wife's in the hotel room. She's mad. No, we're not staying at that hotel. It's too expensive. I have a girlfriend and my wife knows, but she doesn't care. Why? 'Cause I make a lot of money and have a big dick." I glance back at Rae, who is enjoying her smoke through the open window, oblivious to the scene beginning to play out in the front seat.

We come to a red light at Cherokee, just down from the post office and in front of the Catholic Church and just before the Crossroads of the World business center, when Mr. *Cowboy-Goes-to-Hollywood* begins massaging my thigh. I turn to Rae with a wide-eyed silent "Let's get the hell out of here," and I jump from the car to the curb. I wait there spellbound waiting for her to follow me when the light turns green; the passenger door still pushed open. I can see her leaning over his shoulder into the front seat as they slowly continue through the intersection.

What could they possibly be talking about in there?

> *My sister becomes hysterical over the tiniest thing.*
> *Here's my card. Call me later. I'd better go with her*
> *or she'll tell Mother.*

In those fretful few seconds, I fear that she has not yet learned the joy of self-effacement, whereas I have become an expert in the art.

The traffic bumper to bumper, the car pulls to the curb, instituting a rash of horn honking. Rae rushes through the standstill headlights and onto the opposite sidewalk and I follow, swinging my umbrella as an oar to push me faster and faster. But she's flying down the street away from me, her gold raincoat my only landmark. How does she do that in those spiked little boots? Suddenly in front of the Cat and Fiddle Irish pub patio entrance, she spins around and stops, opening up a storm cloud.

I stop in my tracks to open the umbrella before continuing on to her.

"You think you're better than me, don't you?" greeted me. Even with a helicopter hovering over my head, I heard that one.

"You're going to get soaked. Get under here."

Rae twirled on her masochistic little booties and burst through the downpour, stopping to shout out to me, "You left me! Not cool."

"Why did you stay in the car? Rae, when a cop ducks, his partner ducks. He doesn't stop to ask questions."

I held the umbrella high to tuck us both under.

"It's only ten-thirty and I'm going home with shame on my soul. That's why I hate booze, no matter who."

I didn't understand what she was trying to say or how to respond, but I do know that sometimes silence is golden, especially between sisters.

Chapter 10

Westside Story and Te'Kila Shots

♪ The blues they send to meet me
won't defeat me ♪

Raindrops Keep Falling on My Head
Burt Bacharach and Hal David, Composers

THE following afternoon, my mouth stinging with blue peppermint antiseptic, my hair washed and free of the *grandma is smoking again* aroma, I welcome my two teenage grandkids, their travel-weary mother, and Aunt Alexandra onto the porch and out of the continuing unusual deluge.

"We're both parked in one-hour, Mother," Alex informs me of the impossible parking situation; a situation, which to my way of thinking, happily keeps most visitors away. "Elizabeth found a place across the street for her hay-hauling truck." Will wonders ever cease?

"It's Sunday, honey. No parking restrictions on the block, so it doesn't matter. Come in."

In my endeavor to enhance familial bonding by introducing the grandchildren to the arts, I have invited everyone to share with me the foreign experience of a true Broadway musical, *West Side Story*, the first musical to enrapture my soul, to stir up adolescent longings of unfulfilled love—at that time being Little Joe Cartwright of *Bonanza*—and to set me on a course to star in every high school musical production San Bernardino High School had to offer. There had been just one: *High Spirits*, in which I co-starred as the deceased wife of a husband who was glad to be rid of me, but was charmed by my ghostly return in twinkle dusted blue chiffon flying through his living room. Of course, I sang during flight. The trainer for Mary Martin of *Peter Pan* fame protected my vagina for future use by securing stacks of Tampons on the strap seat of the harness, and with the yank of a pulley contraption sent me, arms outstretched, smack into the set designer's fireplace mantle. By show time, I had mastered *Flying by Foy*.

"Well, at least your nasty sidewalk is getting a bath," Elizabeth scoffs at my choice to live on a dirty street in a city of debauchery. "I need to use the bathroom," and she scoots by me and through the bedroom to my Windex and paper towel wiped-down bathroom.

Infectious cleaning tip: install a paper towel holder in your bathroom.

Go-Green conservationists will be breaking down my door soon in violation of the *one paper towel holder per household* rule, but there is never a stray hair left behind in my pedestal sink.

"Grandma, are you still smoking?" Manny accuses and sniffs the walls of my living room, as the dogs beg for his male attention. He has grown taller in his sixteenth year; his mannerisms consistent with the cocky posture of his father, a trait I do not find cohesive in a high school boy. "I smell smoke."

"Not to worry. The fire station is one block away," I amuse him.

The windows had been closed for several days due to the intermittent rain. Like so many attempted promises, I had breached the *smoking in the house* ban and am now being harassed for it by a troubled teen.

"I cannot tell a lie. So don't ask me again," is my retort to a child I rarely interact with and whose opinion of my failures is as important to me as the price of KY Jelly; never used and never needed.

"It's really bad for the dogs," Kathleen chimes in, echoing her mother's recurring criticism of my intolerable habit.

"They're going to live on long after I succumb to lung cancer, and then Alex is taking them back." My response brings out a sly understanding smile from Aunt Alex, the original mother of our two pets and also an occasional *only when I drink* smoker. I check my purse for the small tin of half-opened Nicorette packages. I would need them, to be sure, with no explanation necessary as to why grandma has taken up the chew.

There are only four seats available in my living room: two on the love seat, one on the upholstered chair at the vintage writing table, and one on the dogs' bed, if you can coax them into scooting over just a bit.

The five of us stand in the round on an edgy precipice, the covered wagons circled, having nothing to say that will not upset the other.

"How do you live in this cracker box?" Elizabeth broke the unspoken rules of visitation to share her admiration of my charming bungalow. "You certainly won't be forcing us to play musical chairs in here."

Beyond the metal arches twined with bougainvillea, the fuchsia and orange petals washed by the release of nature's pent up tears, and beyond the coral wall, the traffic splashes its way up and down the boulevard. And in the distorted thin glass panes of the preserved wooden French window panes beginning at the wood floor and stretching to the vaulted ceiling, I see myself overlooking a shimmering rectangular blue pool lit with candles from inside floating skulls. At the end of the diving board, a black vulture is perched atop a scowling jack-o-lantern. The night of my annual Halloween celebration has begun.

Prior to the grandchildren beginning school and before their parents accustomed them to judging harshly adult behaviors that might not mirror the perfection of their own four-squared household unit, our interactions had been unrestrained and pure joy. Perhaps having my own six-year-old daughter in tow confused the grandmother role a tad, but all in all things had gone well.

Welcoming my guests, orange and black lights led the way to the poolside patio strung with skeletons and white billowy cobwebs stretched out between black and orange wrapped posts. Red apples bobbed in the steel tub and a lineup of white plastic chairs was set-aside in anticipation of the traditional game of *musical chairs*. The competition would be fierce.

The costumes varied from the innocence of Lucille Ball in polka dots hand-in-hand with her Desi to horrifying zombies, their ripped white shirts covered in blood. As Elvira switched "Monster Mash" on and off at the tape recorder, drunken gaiety assured that the most timid of partygoers would fight to the death for the last chair, mercilessly tossing teeny-tiny goblins onto the concrete. No one would tease me about my low cut Vampira gown and Draconian black wig or the blood curdled at the corner of my mouth. It was expected of me. It was fun to come to crazy Grandma's house. And her fourth husband was a child himself, throwing Grandma in the pool to alert the guests that it was time to leave, that another Halloween treat had come to an end.

The sprawling pool house of the '90s sold to purchase another, which was later sold and left behind, my Halloween decorations are now minimized into one long plastic box and a witch's cauldron filled to the brim with tangled orange and black lights, recirculated spider webs, tape cassettes of spooky sounds and The Mistress of the Dark's *Revenge of the Monsters* cassette starring Bobby "Boris" Pickett. Down the wooden stairs and into the infamous basement, my Ruby the Fortune Teller costume is hung with care; Spidey, the Velcro monkey, and Victor the Vulture are always at the ready to charm even the most jaded computer-game barraged, technically advanced five-year-old trick-or-treater.

Held in check by years of holding back my opinions or knee jerk reactions, my filter as fine as cheesecloth, I restrain myself and do not comment on the noticeable fact that both my daughter and granddaughter have continued dying their natural chestnut hair an American Indian coal black. Kathleen, a recent graduate of cosmetology school, has framed her face with two foolish purple streaks. I bite my tongue.

"Grandma, where's the cat?" Kathleen asks.

"Mom had her put to sleep," Alex informs her captured audience.

"Yes, but only after dear Morticia was mauled by a possum and put on life support for almost five days," I fill in the blanks. I wasn't going down for that one. "Well, let's get going. The show starts in half an hour."

"Do you have a plan?" Alex speaks sharply to me. It is apparent that I have mistakenly taken my younger daughter away on this Sunday from a better place, where better people gather, where unhappily married jealous sisters and their unsophisticated brood are not allowed. "We can't walk the six blocks. It's raining."

I had taken this one out of the country, away from the farm, where she spent her first years toddling about the lawn collecting brown slithering snails and squeezing newborn kittens until their eyes popped. The self-centered realm of fantasy and red carpet premieres have, sadly, set a bit of a snoot on her cosmetically turned up nose, while road trips with her father to the Ozarks of Missouri for semi-annual family reunions will, hopefully, bend it back into shape.

I checked my wallet for cash. "We can all fit into your car and I'll pay the twelve dollars to park next to the theatre."

One block south in front of the Armenian middle school, all umbrellas collapsed and dripping onto the floorboards, the family slid into the politically correct protection of a black fuel-efficient automobile; the engine so quiet that I have listed *being run down by a Prius* on the top of my expected causes of death.

"You drive a Prius now? What happened to the Beemer?" the strangers inquire in great surprise.

"The lease was up on the gas hog. I'm buying this one," Alex answers. It is the dream of parents that their child will someday drive a car better than their own and let you sit in the front seat.

"What does 'Prius' mean anyway?" Manny asked out of sheer boredom.

"I believe from the Latin 'to come before.' Toyota began production on the hybrid electrical car even before the mass hysteria of social pressure to buy one," I spit out. I must stop midnight madness *Googling*.

"Are you still driving your cute little Scion?" Kathleen flatters her.

"Yes. She's happily parked right in front of my gate."

"What does 'Scion' mean anyway?" Manny inquired, always trying to trip up his grandmother.

"Descendant. Apparently, the Toyota Corporation feels that this model is so owner-friendly that it becomes a part of your family, an heir, which means I'm leaving everything to my car."

Restless, Manny jiggles his feet up under the front passenger seat to test my patience. "What's this play about anyway?"

"Do I look like a walking *Wikipedia*?" It was taking forever to swim silently upstream the six blocks to Hollywood and Vine.

"Well, you're the writer, Mother," Elizabeth chides in disapproval from the back seat.

"Inspired by Shakespeare's *Romeo and Juliet*, without the poison, originally set in 1950s New York, it's about two teenage gangs—the *Sharks*, a Puerto Rican gang, and the *Jets*, a Caucasian gang. White Tony falls for brown Maria—although, I've always thought of Maria, played by Natalie Wood in the movie version, as a wop. It was written, choreographed, and produced by three homosexuals, so who knows who's supposed to be what exactly."

"Grandma, what's a wop?"

"An Italian, Manny. Like your other grandma."

"Mother, you're such a racist."

"Elizabeth," I thought, "you have absolutely no sense of humor."

"Kids, the music will have you dancing in the aisles and the lyrics will make you laugh, cry—"

"Please don't cry tonight, Mom," Alex shuddered, acknowledging my frail unspeakable condition.

Throwing my head back and crossing my hands over my heart, I assure her in song that I will not embarrass her tonight with any foolish romantic nonsense. ♪ Gee, Officer Krupke, we're down on our knees, 'cause no one wants a fella with a social disease. Tonight, tonight, won't be just any night ♪

♪ Tonight there will be no morning star ♪ Alex finished the stanza.

"How do you know all the words anyway?" Manny foolishly asked.

"When I was a kid, Mom woke me up with Broadway tunes on the stereo. Then she had me on stage at the age of seven as Jill—of *Jack and Jill*—in a Christmastime production of *Babes in Toyland*."

"I was the Sugarplum Fairy," I remembered.

"And a village wench serving lemonade on a silver tray."

"That's right. In Act One Alex and I both sang the big ensemble number. ♪ Le-mo-nade. Let's have a lemonade ♪

A court reporter on her fourth husband by day; a dancing fool by night; however did I find the time or the strength? My multi-tasking days of singing while sashaying are, perhaps, forever behind me. I can still chase a tennis ball, however, my mouth wide open.

"During my lifetime, your grandmother has been a nurse in the South Pacific, a nun in war torn Austria, and a jealous fox hunter on a Georgia plantation," Alex summarized.

"We took you kids to see Grandma in *South Pacific*. You were too young to remember," Elizabeth explains. "While I'm still trying to forget the embarrassing pointed bra under the tight khaki t-shirt thing."

Maybe she does have a sense of humor. Dry, very dry.

The grand foyer of the Pantages Theatre is in glorious 1930 splendor. I pity the employee who will be polishing the golden handrails lining the two sets of opulent carpeted staircases in the morning. No one dresses for the theatre anymore. Yes, there are a few stragglers left lagging behind the New Hollywood Chic; the season ticket holders circa 1955 bumping stooped shoulders with each other at the bar in black tie and after-five. The majority of visitors to this elaborate setting of shimmering candelabras and gilded statues have lazily dressed in disrespect or they have simply missed the exit off the Interstate 5 freeway to a Dodger Stadium home game. My entourage is dressed appropriately all in black; a dry run for my funeral.

From the orchestra pit, the overture begins and I find myself mouthing the Sondheim lyrics. ♫ I like to be in America; Okay by me in America; Everything free in America; For a small fee in America! ♫ Hollywood had not censored, modified, nor condemned the soundtrack—not yet.

The two teens sitting behind us, Alex, Elizabeth, and I side by side on the aisle, I hold my breath as the curtains, fingered by a mysterious puppet master, float up and the magic begins. By intermission I am in musical culture shock hell.

Waiting in line at the ladies room, chomping on a Nicorette, hoping the nicotine will hit my craving veins immediately, I apologize. "The obscene gestures were not in the original choreography, girls."

"Very Michael Jackson," Alex comments. "The crotch grab move."

"Why are they sometimes speaking in Spanish, Grandma?"

"Why are they singing in Spanish, Kathleen? Political correctness in this town makes my heart ache. I'm so glad I know the lyrics. Oh, no, they can't take that away from me. You can't mock the obvious anymore. Oh, no! You can't even smoke in this town! And where are the shiny members only hoodlum jackets? At eighty-five dollars a seat, they couldn't afford them? All the gang members are in Banana Republic checkered shirts."

"You moved here," Elizabeth taunts me.

"Look at those vintage mirrors," Alex changes the subject and with bursting bladders, we hide behind stall doors.

We catch up with Manny at our seats. He leans over and whispers to me. "Grandma, all the dancers are homos."

"Shhh."

"Grandma, can I have a piece of your gum?"

"No."

Into my palm, I stifle a weep when Maria laments her bad relationship choice in Spanish while her best friend Anita insists that she *stick with her own kind.* And in my head, I translate my bad relationship choice into English.

> ♪ I have a love, and it's all that I have.
> Right or wrong, what else can I do?
> I love him; I'm his and everything he is
> I am, too ♪

Lyrics by Stephen Sondheim

By the time Maria is slumped over Tony's dead body, my muffled sobs become uncontrollable as I remember that somewhere there was a place for us: under my house on a flowered bedspread over a carpeted concrete floor inside a mystical nomadic Persian's tasseled canopy tent.

Leaving the car in the lot, I lead the disgruntled pack of theatre critics through another downpour to *Te'kila*, an indoor-outdoor Mexican restaurant four stoplights west on Hollywood Boulevard. One block over the stars in the sidewalk, Manny moves on ahead of us at the frenetic urging of a slick looking Arab waving a flyer. The cheap marquis bulbs suddenly come to life at Déjà Vu Showgirls.

"Hey, Osama, he's only sixteen," I shout.

"Hey, lady, he can come in, if you do."

"Where's Homeland Security? I'm calling a cop. I'm calling immigration." I slide under the awning and into the disgusting enclave, where posters surround me of the painted faces of painfully buxom women posed to look as though they had just experienced yet another vaginal ejaculation. "Manny, don't get any closer to that door!"

"Mom, calm down or you'll be the one getting arrested." Elizabeth rushes up to join me. "Manny, put your tongue back in your mouth."

"Nothing I haven't seen before."

"Mom, is there anything else we should avoid on our walk?"

"No, Elizabeth, except for head shops and the L. Ron Hubbard Life Exhibit building."

"L. Ron Hubbard?"

"Those f-ing Scientologists are buying up the historic buildings of Hollywood, but have to be hog-tied to follow the rules of preservation. They'd like to turn all these beautiful old buildings into heliports for their Thetan spaceship landings with Tom Cruise as the pilot. Keep Manny curbside. He's ripe for cult counseling."

"Do you serve pitchers of Margaritas?" I asked the striking tattooed waitress.

"Sure thing. Strawberry? Melon?"

"Do I look like a woman that drinks fruit? Just the regular kind and salt the rims, please."

"How many salted rims, ma'am?"

Raising her hand, Elizabeth summoned, "Well, I'd like a strawberry and my daughter a virgin."

The hot, smoldering erotic summer following her high school graduation in the desert having come and gone, instinctively I squint the evil eye, one eyebrow lifted in an accusatory arch, in my granddaughter's direction.

"What, Gramma?"

"Don't worry, Mother," Elizabeth insisted. "I put her on the pill her junior year. There won't be any shotgun weddings resulting in unwanted children."

"What? I never said I didn't want you. Abortions were legal in 1969 —I think."

"That's enough," Alex sent us back to our corners.

"I want a Coke," demanded Manny.

"I'm not drinking. Just water with lemon, please."

"Our designated driver and family referee is not drinking, so bring me shots of tequila," I resolutely change the order. "One after the other."

Carna Asada cheesy fries, a taco plate, a tray of hot saucy chicken wings, and three shots later, the conversation twists between the historic California rainfall to Alexandra's latest commercial to the theatrical exploits of the male singer/dancers, who have turned my street-wise rough and tumble *Jets* into flamboyant sissies.

"♫ When you're a Jet, you're a Jet all the way, from your first cigarette to your last dyin' day ♫ How could they sing that with their little pinkies pointing up? So disappointing."

"Okay, Mom," Elizabeth mounted her tree-hugging high horse. "You don't want to see them on stage or married."

"Whoa! I don't want to see *them* cast as Rambo and then acting like Boy George is all."

"Mom has lots of gay friends," Alexandra called out strike three from behind home plate.

"And eons of black ones, I'm sure."

I want to push my chair back, slam down my napkin and flee, but it's raining again and I'm more mature than that. Instead I sucked it up and thought, "How does being the proud mother of mixed heritage children turn a corn-fed country girl into a race-card carrying liberal?"

"Well, Maria was hot," Manny chimed in.

"The end was so sad, Grandma. Do you think Maria killed herself after Tony died?" Kathleen mourned.

♫ I have a love and he's all that I have,
Right or wrong, I will be true ♫

"My God, you're not going to start crying again," Alexandra reprimanded me.

Elizabeth sets down her chicken bone. "We agreed not to mention it, but we all saw you crying during the show."

"Mom, you're sixty-two years old. Please get over it," Alex sympathized with reservation.

"No! I'm not getting 'over it.' I'm not allowed? Oh, no, no! Falling in love is not a specialty granted to only those of a certain age, girls, and I'll never be too old to forget what it feels like."

"But in case you ever do, you've written the whole mess down, apparently," my 1969 mistake mumbled.

"Her novel is really very good, Elizabeth."

"I don't want to hear anything about it, Alexandra."

"Gramma, what's that thing on your nose?"

"The beginning of the end, Manny."

When will these twelve days of Christmas be over and I can go loudly and shamefully back to my grieving without spending any more money foolishly in my sullied attempts to forgive and to forget?

Alex pulled up next to my Scion where we scrambled out into the rain. She said her rushed *good-bye* from the front seat and the Prius silently sped away into oncoming headlights showering their way through the flooded streets.

"Don't you want to come in and use the bathroom?" I asked with concern.

"No, we're good," was their unified response.

"Wait, your gifts." Manny waited at the gate while I scurried into the house and brought out two large plastic bags tied with ribbon.

"Thanks, Gramma," and he brushed a smooth cheek against mine.

From across the street, truck lights swung a *U* and the back door of the cab flew open. He and the bags jumped in.

The family dynamics revisited, now let's start turning some pages. After all, *girls just wanna have fun*.

Chapter 11

Too Sexy for My Shirt and The 80th Day

♪ I've hungered for your touch
a long lonely time ♪

Unchained Melody
Alex North, Hy Zaret

Monday morning presented itself with plenty of excuses for a pity party, but I would put away my ultimate personal degradation and drunken remorse for a few more days.

Stepping out onto the sidewalk, brush and paint can in hand, I happily set forth to fulfill my self-imposed duty of covering up this weekend's gratuitous graffiti offering on the phone company box, a tall metal eyesore imbedded into the cement with two locked doors, something of a wire locker, outside my front gate. Since my first scream of horror heard round the block, I've been repainting the box cherry-orange to match my six-foot stucco wall that protects me from wild dogs, the occasional raging schizophrenic, and the solicitous Jehovah Witnesses, who also travel in packs. It's okay to toss the *Watch Tower* magazine over the gate; I know the end is near and it's pleasing to read that others are preparing also.

My little Scion is there, her coat spotted from more than enough days of rain, but apparently not enough to wash her streak and muddle free. She's parked in an all-day parking zone. Why is there on my front window tucked under a windshield wiper blade a fresh and dry ticket from the City of Los Angeles citing a violation for *no tabs*, which after careful investigation leads me to believe that the officer meant to write *no tags*. A thief in the night has removed the registration sticker from my rear license plate.

While bald, seventy-year-old Jerry *Moonbeam* Brown, another zombie Democrat who rose from the dead, is inaugurated as the Governor of California for the third time, I spend the day chasing the bureaucracy down with a photocopy of my DMV registration taped to the front and back windows of my car while tongue thrusting mint-flavored Nicorette into my gums. And while the Governor's female opponent opines the one hundred and sixty million dollar price of her lost campaign, I pout over being forced to pay a twenty-five dollar fine for someone else's thievery. The price of righteousness is relative. I am notified that I must pass a *smog check* before they will reissue my tags. I spend another hour and a half lined up at Arman's *Smog Check* gas station behind three other unhappy campers who also had their *tabs* stolen today. We share our citations. Yes, the same parking enforcement official has had a very busy day.

Total damages for the day: ninety-five dollars and another hole in my already punctured heart put there by the once trusted and revered parking enforcement officer of the day. I suspect that it is not only actors and writers who receive residual income from a job well done.

I arrived home a law-abiding citizen and noticed that the blue tarp had been removed from my roof. I sent out a text to Benayahu, my prospective lover and roofing contractor.

> JULIE: The sun is drying the roof. What's your estimate?
> BEN: I will know better after I will remove some tile over the leaking area. Could be 1300 to 1800 aprox, but I will do the best I can for u.
> JULIE: Thank u. I'm going out now to find a very rich, very old man to marry and to pay your bill.
> BEN: LOL, u r so cute. Should I open my eyes for you? LOL

Remembering that English is Ben's second language, I am cautious in my criticism, but I am wary of the one too many bullshit Laugh Out Loud acronyms.

JULIE: Yes! I prefer old men around 45.

Playing hard to get has never been my forte. Being playful is very sexy.

BEN: Ok. And sexy guy as well.
JULIE: I'll be the judge of that.

Whoa, Julie, tighten up the clapper bells on your inner belly dancer. He's the mirror image of the man that got away, but for his successful entrepreneurship, his belief in the defensive bombing of the Gaza Strip, and his smiling display of big white teeth, all in perfect order; not a brown one in the bunch. Julie, get out of the Middle East. There's plenty of oil there, but none of it free for the taking.

As Persian princes are close to my heart, it is upsetting to learn that Ali-Reza Pahlavi, age forty-five and a descendant of the very handsome Mohammed Reza Pahlavi, who in his attempt to modernize Iran was overthrown by the Islamic Revolution in 1979, took his own life in his Boston apartment. He was unmarried. Perhaps he was heartbroken over the breakup with an American woman who had become sick and tired of Shawarma chicken.

* * *

Ben's crew arrived in the morning. Tat-tat-tat, the roof was repaired and new Spanish clay tiles placed in wet cement. Ben arrives and shows me cell phone pictures of the *before* roof, climbs up the tall leaning ladder perched on the side of the house and returns with *after* pics. On my porch I greet Ashkenazi, his cap removed, presumably in reverence to my austere presence in Lycra and a ripped t-shirt sporting my latest cause: *Careful or You'll End Up in My Next Novel.* This warning does not bring forth any comment at all, because Ben is, after all, after only one thing. I write a check for seventeen hundred dollars and offer him a beer served in a freezer frosty mug.

"You look very sexy today," he winces in the sunlight of my porch. Appearing playful in a ripped t-shirt gets them every time. Being a man, the sighting of fat upper arms dangling with old age creping crinkles and spotted with precancerous moles is vicariously dismissed in the anticipation of sexual conquest without commitment, because she's going to be extremely grateful and dead soon anyway.

"I didn't know I'd be seeing you today," I feign embarrassment for my at-home fashion glitch.

"I'd like to take you out for a nice dinner this week. Would Tuesday work?"

"I have bowling league on Tuesday," I admit to my weekly gluttony of pizza and beer. Ben does not inquire of my bowling average. He doesn't want to know a thing about it.

"So let's try to meet on Monday—or Wednesday? You look very sexy today." He already said that. English is his second language. His come-on phraseology diminutive.

"Do you have children, Ben? I have three, all on their own."

"No. I live by myself, too."

Bizarre sex can be had in either house, day or night.

"And you cook and juggle, too?"

He doesn't get my irony at all. I could probably say just about anything and still get the same reaction.

"You're so cute," he injects into my lonely, wanton veins.

"Looking at you is a bit like looking into a mirror," I test his English.

"You are welcome," he laughs. "Thank you for the compliment."

Brute waddled out to our conversation, his tail between his legs.

"He's depressed. He was up for a part in a movie, but they booked a poodle instead."

"Oh." Ben is not the least bit interested in asking what that is all about. Ben wants just one thing. Beware of men who don't ask questions.

He left for the Burbank Airport, where his company has been contracted to install new roofs on several hangars. "Be safe, Ben. Don't get too close to the edge."

"You are so sweet. I will call you over the weekend."

And in Islamabad, Pakistan, a governor who opposed the blasphemy law of death to anyone insulting the Muslim faith was shot and killed. I should be next.

After showing returning client Mr. Mitchell, Attorney at Law, the foreclosed investment possibility at the end of the bungalow walkway, to which he and his wife turned up their combined snobbish noses, I packed up and took off for my dear mountain getaway with a promise to *the writer* to throw down a few pages in book two. I am getting away from one-hour parking signs, corrupt parking cops, brown gurgling human feces dressing the sidewalk, abundant Obama bumper stickers, and the fear that if Ali did call, I would let him back in.

The ninety-minute drive east on the 210 Freeway is unremarkable. The fifteen-minute drive up the winding highway to Crestline is, as always, a welcome reprieve from honking maniacs and speeding double decker tour buses. The tire chains are confined to the back cargo area of the hatchback and the California Highway Patrol has not set up a *chain-up* or *turn-around, you idiot* station. Whew, smooth sailing so far for this fair-weather nature lover. The sun is out and not a cloud in the sky.

Reaching Top Town, braking at the stop sign and the timberline, suddenly I've reached a land of four seasons in Southern California: the San Bernardino National Forest. The main road is clear, but the festive, hard-packed remains of a white Christmas borders it. Robust men in puffed ski jackets, some with mountain man beards, lean against the railing outside the Rim of the World Sports Bar, their breath articulating for me the immediate change in temperature. Or is it the *no-smoking inside* ordinance inflicted upon them after a laborious day of chopping wood, shooting bear, mending fallen power lines, or collecting cans along the roadside that has brought them out in the cold?

The dogs, their chops set in adventure mode, peer from the backseat as I am forced to park at the bottom of my neighbor Cole's cleared driveway, my driveway a winter wonderland photo op. I inch the back door open into the snow bank and Hound and Brute bound onto the fresh softness of the storm's gift of white fluff. Together we forge up the street passing my massive gray and white river rock stonewall to the six-foot berm shoved forth to the front of my driveway by the steadfast transportation department snow plow. Up, in and over wet snow, in the last light of day, I trudge in my Hollywood sunshine Payless *Champion* brand tennis shoes through the mountain of snow to the buried stairs leading to the landing. The dormant climbing rose bush trailing the iron arch droops from the weight of the recent storm. "Don't worry," I think. "Spring will bring new buds." At the end of the untouched frosty walkway, I unlock the swelled crimson front door.

The dogs make yellow snow before traipsing through the living room, where they shake off, and immediately curl up on the plaid blanket in Hound's king size straw basket bed. While the boys fight over territorial rights, at the wall I set the thermostat to sixty-eight degrees and the heater switches on. Brute bows out of the growling match and slinks across the wood floor to his assigned poufy *little doggie* donut bed. The French wall sconce porch lights and the three-light lamppost in the driveway automatically sense approaching darkness and in unison shed light over the deeply powdered landscape, which strikes me as an excellent space for angel making. But I have work to do.

In mountain woman rip-off *Uggs*, I retrace my steps across the landing, down the twelve steps, clenching the wrought iron railing, and bound into the snow in the drive. I open the door to the *build-up*, mountain speak for the basement under the front deck, where the forced-air heater, hot water heater, and gardening tools are easily accessed. Under the aluminum wrapped heating vents I have safely stacked over fifty photo albums overflowing with the faces of children in all stages of life, obscure ex-husbands and the resultant honeymoons to hell. Secure in plastic boxes, they sit on tarps and very expensive yards of concrete laid by the local beer guzzling Mexican tradesmen. For weeks after the job was done, I came upon littered beer cans in the forest foliage, which I gathered and simply threw down the embankment into my neighbor's yard across the street.

I will busy my last days by tearing never-to-be-forgotten faces out of those albums, separating them into guilt-ridden bundles for appropriate gift-giving from a tired old scoundrel of a woman, who has been crossed off everyone's Christmas list. I have, perhaps, twenty years to redeem myself.

I bring out the snow shovel, put on the gloves, and begin digging out a small section to back the Scion into. Across the street in his cleared driveway, from the bed of his pickup truck Wilbur Shank, the ex-meth addict and reborn Christian handyman, chats with me through his restored teeth. Giant, tattoo-sleeved Wilbur lives with his wife, their teenage son, and a black dog that runs rabid back and forth from a tether linked between two century old trees in their front yard of rock, dirt, and a collection of tin cans stuffed into dozens of blue plastic recycling bags. Because these unattractive bags have been in his yard for over a year now, I assume he's wisely waiting for the price of tin to skyrocket.

"You should have waited a week to come up," Wilbur advises. "When the snow melts, you might find more cans in your downslope."

"If I do, they're all yours, Wilbur. Whenever are you going to redeem all those cans?"

"I'm waiting another twenty years."

Rounding the corner, my hero neighbor, sporting three half fingers on each of his sturdy hands, shows up carrying a shovel. Cole and I dig and toss snow for over an hour as the sun slips behind the white tipped forest and Wilbur, languishing against his tailgate, picks at his new set of enamel with a flossing pocketknife.

A space cleared, it now looks like I can wedge the Scion into my driveway. I drive in reverse up the hill and back in. We need two more feet. As we throw snow over our shoulders, I share with Cole my new fascination with the Jewish womanizing roofer. "No, he has no idea how old I am. Don't worry. I'm wary. Very wary."

"Is it possible for you to get out of the Middle East?"

"They're drawn to my dark hair and my—"

"And your dark brown eyes peering seductively from inside a burka."

"Apparently, you haven't heard. They're hazel."

In the dark, we congratulate each other's efforts with hugs all around. Wilbur waves us goodnight. Obviously, the tailgate party has been canceled. Cole returns to his football game saved by TIVO. I clear the ping pong table of six inches of the stuff and head into the cabin for my first rum and Coke.

Once inside again, I am pleased. Le Petit Chateau d'Enchanté is small and tidy and easily kept clean. The hand painted sign in the kitchen reads: *Crestline, My Little Piece of Paradise.* Keeping clear of black bear toilet paper holders and horned-deer towel bars, I have chosen neutral colors and a French country feel influenced by a poster of the Eiffel Tower, a fringed fainting couch, a striped satin settee with a carved lion's head at the end of each arm, and a cream wrought iron toilet paper holder that resembles the gates of Versailles. There is a simple tweed couch, which pulls out into a comfortable double bed for overnight guests. It's just comfortable enough for a one-night visit. Under the kitchen window in the dining room—the space allocated as such by a round pine pedestal table and four pine swivel chairs—is a built-in storage bench for guest linens and bed pillows. Red tasseled pillows tossed on the couch add a splash of color.

The gray stone fireplace separating the wooden counter galley kitchen from the living room spirals through the ceiling up through the floor of the bedroom loft and crashes between two skylights and through the roof. The wood floors are stained a creamy white. The pine ceiling is crossed with white beams. Knotty pine panels the walls. Cut into every wall are white French windows and doors to bring the forest in. Off the living room is the terrace for morning coffee. There from my heart-shaped padded chair, I cannot see the poor deranged dog across the street, but I can hear him yelping for attention.

Off the kitchen through the back door is a patio with a table for six for summer bar-b-ques. A three-foot curved black and gray river rock wall separates the patio floor from the steep incline, which rises to a *V* ending at the Dogwood tree at the redwood fence. A green umbrella shades the table for noonday toasted cheese sandwiches. A gift from my sister from her *now-divorced*, foreclosed Craftsman collection, the periwinkle glass-topped table invites me to write.

Above the patio is a backyard terrace laid with red brick—an easy, but sweaty job I remember starting and finishing in one afternoon—where a chaise awaits to lazy away an afternoon with a raspberry iced tea and a good book. Towering trees spot the terrace, their trunks begging for the ropes of a stripped canvas hammock to be fastened. I don't like hammocks; they're deathtraps. A brick bordered pathway laced with a carpet of spewing vinca catches the rain and melting snow and spirals the water down and around to a hole under the fence. Where there had been nothing but large rocks, debris, and truckloads of sandy soil, I've shoveled, wheel barrowed, and with the brick-laying skills of Wilbur and his salty-dog father, I have transformed the small, steep yard rising up and away from the cabin. There's a lot of gold in that hill.

When I first met my chateau in the winter of 2009, the buildup of erosion from years and years of neglect had deposited four feet of dirt and pebbles, which blocked the back door and buried the concrete patio floor and its river rock wall. Opening the backdoor to the inside, I was stopped by what appeared to be a massive mudslide, the week's snowfall adding another two feet, like a chocolate cake topped with white icing. "It's been eight years since I've seen anybody out there with a broom," Cole had welcomed me from his deck over my head, as I shoveled out a walking tunnel to discover what I would be buying and what I'd be getting myself into. The clearing, planting, scrubbing, painting, furnishing, lighting, and plumbing now all behind me—would I someday make this my permanent home?

Two rum and diet Cokes and a romantic comedy in the player, I receive a call from Benjamin. The connection is broken immediately, so I call him back from the cabin landline.

"Hi, I'm at my cabin. Cell phone reception not good here."

"Uh, who is this?"

Hey, stupid, it's the lady you just called.

"Julie. The roof you just fixed."

"Oh, didn't recognize the number."

"I'm at my cabin," I repeat. Now, the information that *I have a cabin* is usually greeted with speculation. Is it a big cabin? Is it close to skiing? Can we have sex there?

"You're in a cabin. I must go with you. I snowboard and ski."

My cabin is an hour's drive to the ski resorts, but not to bust Ben's opportunistic bubble, I simply agree to dinner on Monday night at eight. He will pick me up at my house in Hollywood.

After stoking the fire, I mix my third rum and Coca Cola. I toast to us. Tonight is an historic event, for it is the eightieth day.

The psychologists have spoken: after eighty days of no contact, the no vasopressin, nonbonding male is *just not that into you*. But you, the bonded, trusting, vulnerable, lovesick postmenopausal, retired counterspy will now continue to gain weight, indulge in excessive alcohol use, smoke 'til your fingernails are stained yellow, chew nicotine replacement gum until your gums bleed, disrupt your familial relationships, and cry like a baby every time someone sings "The Way You Look Tonight," which you just keep rewinding on the tape player. This self-effacing mourning procedure can last up to two years for most healthy females. However, if you continue to write embarrassingly honest novels about your foolishness, we guaranty that you will never get over it.

The requisite eighty days have passed since I had last seen him, touched him, spoken to him, received an email or text from him, which means that Ali is not returning. I won't have the chance to tell him how miserable I am without him. He already knows anyway. Yet the dream he had so eloquently escorted me into of a fairy tale coming true still breathes within me: the Persian Prince will return, changed, kind and true, as a Republican Reborn Christian, of course.

But this time there will be no more sucker releases of oxytocin to my brain to decrease my mental processes and impair my memory; just wet, sloppy, hard, nasty intercourse. There will be no more addictive dopamine injections; the poison of romantic love with its grandiose highs leading to its eventual lows of lethargy, despondency, and depression. I am now an honorary burned bitch. And if I've written this before, I am writing it again to implant it solidly into my subconscious, delirious brain.

After clipping the fingers and thumbs off the Michael Jackson bowling gloves, stitching all ten wounds tediously with the needle and thread I have brought along, and realizing I only bowl with my right hand, I celebrate my pity party by typing at the speed of one-hundred words per minute a manifesto of sorts.

> I have been legally married four times, and when those marriages ended, I was upset and sad that they ended, but none of them were anything like this "romance." Was I still the same person?

No, I had changed over the years, but what was so different this time around? Why couldn't I have a few drinks and hiccup the husband away, as I had done so easily before? Why couldn't I move on with my life? What did the sociopath do to me or give to me that no one else had before?

None of my husbands came close to giving me the excitement and wonderful feelings that Ali had given to me. No one had caused me to be physically ill, frightened, sexually heightened, and devastated.

When I should have been glad to wisely kick him good-bye, I found myself praying for his safety, his happiness, and, of course, that my God would send him back home to me; but, alas, Allah is in charge of the situation.

Why would I want this tyrant to return? Because he gave me something I so desperately needed: acceptance and the feeling of being loved—until he turned on me.

He created the little world we lived in, a magical world where for a time I was utterly beautiful, young again, and wanted—and all without Ali ever actually saying an encouraging word of commitment, unless being married "Islam-style" is a promise of fidelity, which it is not. There were a few precious moments that I projected as favorable. "You don't need to fix up; I like you just the way you are," he had said, when actually he was just hungry and in a hurry to get to Zankou Chicken for grease and garlic-laced Tahini sauce.

I loved his childlike aura, because then I too could be childlike.

I loved his quietness, because then I too could be quiet and not feel as if I must entertain him.

I loved his rare moments of silliness, because then I too could be silly and appreciated for it.

He got me. He knew how to spin me.

He got me from the minute he said, "Sorry I'm late."

He continued to be late, but never again said he was sorry.

Nothing was real. While I was having a deeply moving relationship, it was not the same relationship he was having. While I experienced great joy, he felt nothing.

Ali stole precious time from me. I wasted hours of my life nervously waiting for his selfish, narcissistic tight ass to show up. After arriving two or three hours late, he reveled in admitting to his tardiness, explaining that I should have no expectations, that he was immune from any and all hysterical accusations; thus approving his own bad behavior and precluding any recourse on my part.

Ali uncovered my deepest needs and showed me how to feel good about myself. And if a con artist can bring out the best in me, there's got to be someone out there for whom I can peel off the armor once again. But this time, he is going to know how to love and he is going to fall in love with me first before I fall blindly in love with him.

Spinning from much too much drink, before shutting down the Mac —and not having written one eloquently, splendidly slanderous word in the second novel—I check into the cruelties of the day and find the world is collapsing, while I dribble over what should be an insignificant ruffle in my romantic life. I have signed on to the Internet with the password given to me by the funny little man whose cabin sits uphill from my bedroom windows, which are never draped. He's unessential to my story, but I can't help but wonder why there is a telescope perched on his back deck aiming downhill.

U.S. Representative Gabrielle Giffords and eighteen others were shot in a supermarket parking lot in Tucson, Arizona. Six people died, including a nine-year-old girl. Jared Lee Loughner drew a pistol and shot Mrs. Giffords in the head. Loughner, a deeply troubled paranoid schizophrenic, was arrested at the scene.

In the bathroom magnifying mirror, I spy the encroaching gray hairs weaving in and out of my dark brows. Spindly little buggers, they steal beneath the good hairs and artfully dodge from the tweezers. Mistakenly yanking out two good ones, I decide this job would be better done during the sober daytime hours of ten to two.

After scrubbing my thin skin of the evils of our world in the clawfoot tub, I patted Hound *sweet dreams* and carried Brute up the tight steep stairs. Placing him picture perfect upon his drool blanket, his rear legs splayed out tempting me to pinch them, I crawl next to him onto the pine sleigh bed and tuck myself in under the second-hand Tommy Hilfiger duck cloth duvet.

Unable to control myself, I reach over and pinch one of his itsy bitsy pads. "This little piggy went to market." This act of selfish intimacy, tipping on the edge of animal cruelty, brought out a mini growl, yet he stayed put. We've done this one before. Pinching the next, I continued my night-night *Mother Goose* serenade, "This little piggy stayed home. This little piggy had none. And this little piggy went—"

Brute repelled from my overt advances with another muted Maltese growl and a violent paw jerk. I held on tight and wiggled, "'Wee, wee, wee, all the way home.'"

The trees looming outside the windows cried for all of us, the melting snow shed from their boughs by a rustling breeze. As I snuggled down for a long winter's nap, I resolved that it was time to put an end to my babbling and to begin an earnest search for an appropriate lusty replacement and have a little fun before a stray bullet brought an immediate end to my foolishness.

Sunday, I awoke in a *Casey Kasem* time warp. Listening to familiar music through the clock radio's distorted mountain reception, I hummed along in half sleep to a replay of a 1970s *American Top 40*: "The Long and Winding Road," Paul McCartney; "He Ain't Heavy; He's My Brother," The Hollies; "Bridge Over Troubled Waters," Simon and Garfunkel. Ah, 1970, when I played *This Little Piggy* with the pink toes of my first little baby girl. Through the static, I could understand every word.

I attend the little Presbyterian Church, the white church with blue shutters and a steeple, where when you open the door, *there's all the people*. Today the icicles spearing from the pitched roof's fascia board add a foreboding storybook charm to the little house of worship. Did Hansel and Gretel ever come out of there and find their way home?

It's brisk inside. I can smell the gasp of the heaters churning on. An artificial Christmas tree strung with hand carved miniature nativity characters and tiny red glass balls stands cockeyed in front of a choir loft where a choir should be. In contrast a fresh pine bough drapes the pulpit. The congregation is sparse. The fear of early morning black ice has kept the righteous at home in front of a roaring fire. Not so righteous and in dire need of a good smacking, I sneak into the last pew, pull off my mittens, and grab the hymnal in the slot before me. Is it the simple hymns of my youth clumsily plunked out by the white-haired, rosy-cheeked organist, or the sermon on forgiveness, or the fact that the soft-spoken handsome pastor is married that has me crying in the pew? Or, perhaps, it is the call to prayer for the fourteen decapitated bodies found in Acapulco, a resort city of Mexico, and the dismay of realizing that my international time-share vacation possibilities are dwindling.

Immediately following a lonely and quiet two-and-a-half mile walk around the lake in sloshy snow—the dogs too weary to make the trek and the batteries in my Walkman dead—I head back to my never-land utopia. The Air System Contamination Team will return in the morning and I have a date with Ben, who thinks I'm sweet. At the bottom of the hill, I deliberately and in bad form jump on the freeway without visiting my mother. She has not picked up the phone and she probably wouldn't come to the door anyway.

Chapter 12

Pink Labia and The Cole Porter Song Book

> ♪ Matchmaker, Matchmaker
> Make me a match
> Find me a find
> Catch me a catch ♪
>
> *Fiddler on the Roof*
> Jerry Bock and Sheldon Harnick

In anticipation of a hot dryer, I stripped the bed, remade it—a woman's boudoir must always appear inviting—and started up the washer. The *team* arrived in coveralls and spent one hour under the house straightening, connecting, and sucking out the dryer vent. The retrieved problem was a compilation of Hound's hairs and lint bombs trapped in a swooped down loop. Before writing a check for another two hundred dollars, I forced the hostages to stay put on my loveseat until the sheets dried to a burning ember.

While they waited, I entertained them with DVD's of my national commercials: the wise woman sipping coffee in an Adirondack chair for Prudential Insurance and Investments; the ER nurse rushing a man with clogged arteries on a gurney from an ambulance for Trilipix; and the loving, playful wife eating muffins off trees for Little Debbie's Cupcakes. When they begged for more, I put in the one episode of *General Hospital* in which I play a hospitalized patient for one minute and fifty seconds. When the sheets dried in record time, I had four extra hands to fold them.

"Call us immediately if there's any more trouble," the better-looking one humors me.

"You know I will."

"And, ma'am, that thing on your nose is looking much better."

"Thanks. I have a date tonight."

Randi rushed up before I could lock the gate.

"Who was that?" she asked.

"Masters and Johnson. They fixed my vent."

"Oh. I need to show you something." Randi always has something bizarre to share with me. Maybe her rats bore fruit over the weekend and she'll want me to keep her company in front of Pavilion's with a box of teeny rodents to give away. Maybe her tarantulas sprouted wings and are flying all over inside her bungalow. Maybe *the married guy* is handcuffed to her bed.

"What's up? I have a date to prepare for," which to my way of thinking will take the rest of the morning and well into late afternoon. "Mani-Pedi, liposuction, and a facelift."

"I finally did it. Always wanted to. Come on, you'll be the first to see." She blew by me and I caught a whiff.

"You've been drinking before noon again."

"Sure, sure. No work today and bunion surgery in an hour. Come on."

Alongside my bed, before I could stop her, Randi wriggled down her black leggings, exposing precisely waxed pubes. She fell back onto the bed, her rusty curls fanned out behind her, the leggings pushed down puffing up her pale freckled thighs. Flat on her back, she reaches into her privates with both hands and shows off rosy lips.

I winced and closed my eyes. "Whoa! What the hell am I supposed to see?"

"I had my pussy pierced. I put in a barbell."

I backed away and into the living room. "Oh, no. I don't want to see it. I believe you."

"I'll take a picture and email it to you."

"No, no. Please don't." Shocked, mortified, and disgusted, yet my heart is warmed by the intimacy of a lifelong dream shared by my free-spirited bungalow mate, who truly believes that her Republican neighbor will not cast judgment on her distasteful life choices.

"How could you do that to yourself? What the fuck is wrong with you?"

"It's just through the hood, not the clit."

I protectively cupped my crotch. "Oh, Randi, that makes all the difference in the world."

"It does. I won't get off every time I sit down."

Her tongue ball, multiple earrings, and nipple rings work as excellent lightning rods already, but I ask, "Aren't you afraid you'll be shocked during an electrical storm?"

She struggled into her pants and headed for the front door.

Admitting that I may have sneaked a peek, I whispered to her, as if dogs' ears may be burning, "Your labia majora is still pink. Mine's turned a dark gray."

"They have dye for that," Randi assured me with a nonchalant wave of her hand. "I'll get you some. You have a date? With a man?"

"Well, I'll be the judge of that."

"Try to give him some slack. Life is too short."

"He's from Israel. Who's driving you to the doctor?"

"An ex. We had an abortion together. He owes me," Randi surmised and turned the lock on the gate. "And you, my dear friend, need to get out of the Middle East."

※ ※ ※

Gazing at the finished product in the magnifying mirror, I dabbed on just a touch more concealer to the side of my nose. Benayahu Ashkenazi is on his way. The multi-layers of the raspberry mink, mahogany brown, and Egyptian plum crowning glory frame my face; the bangs just long enough to diffuse the deep thought crevice between my eyebrows, their field clear of telltale springy coarse white strands. Perhaps, that's been the problem all along: I think too much.

A bit nervous, I pass the waiting time sipping a vodka tonic and reviewing the unlicensed Islamic Encyclopedia, which is chock full of damning information: *Thirty-Two Secrets Arab Men Never Tell American Women; A Dissection of How Muslims Treat Women and Infidels,* by her nom de plum, Cassandra. My Jewish date arriving soon, I should really be reading the wisdom given to Moses directly from God, *The Tora*: the rules for Zionists wooing fragile American Christian women.

The cell sounds. It's Brett Brainard.

"Anything going on? Are you out there?"

"I'm out there. I have a date with an Israeli roofing contractor."

"The Gaza Strip is heating up again and if you don't know what that's all about, *Google* it. Go in tonight. See what you can find out," he gasped rapid fire. I truly believe he has Attention Deficit Disorder or he's high on Viagra.

"The only thing I'm going into tonight is my Spanx."

After taking pictures of myself in the bathroom mirror as a remembrance of my first *post-Ali* date, I open the gate and the roofer rushes at me with a hug. His scent is musky sweet; his face smoothed by a recent shave.

As I lock up, Ben rushes ahead of me crossing the street to a glistening pearl Porsche Carrera convertible, top up. He jumps in while I struggle with a locked door at the curb.

"Are the seats warm enough? I like the way you look tonight. I like the way you touched my sleeve. My wife didn't appreciate me and jealous, so I divorced her. It's a lease. My accountant says it's the best way to expense it. Do you know how much Worker's Comp Insurance I have to pay a year?"

"You're just telling me all this so I'll understand why you're taking me to a cheap restaurant."

"No, no. I like good food, nice things."

"How do you keep that adorable accent after being in America for twenty-four years? Watch the Israeli cable channel?"

"Do I have an accent?"

We headed west, an exciting change from heading six blocks east to Ali's favorite Middle Eastern dive, Zankou Chicken on Sunset and Normandy. My date seemed eager to be an open book, another nice change. At age sixteen, Ben came to America for a year as an exchange student. He returned to Tel Aviv to do his military service in the Israeli Defense Forces, mandatory for both men and women. His mother resides in Tel Aviv, as well as all of his five siblings. He visits his family every other spring. He has long lashes, dark eyes, a dimple winks on and off in his strong chin. His black hair is cut close to stifle the tight curls. There's a tuft of black fur at each wrist, his arms covered by a long-sleeved gray sweater. Is gray the favorite shade of fashion for Middle Eastern men? Ali wore a similar sweater.

We agree on Italian. He is looking forward to a veal chop.

"Your name, Benay—what does it mean?"

"Ben-a-ya-hu, but you can call me Ben. In Hebrew it means 'God has built.' My surname Ashkenazi is symbolic of the Holocaust. Our family lost more than their share."

God has built a man with large feet and hands.

On 3rd Street, passing La Cienga Boulevard and the posh Beverly Center, California's premier fashion destination in West Hollywood, the first in the line of cars, we come to a red light in front of Cedars Sinai hospital. I can't help myself; my inner child exploding with joy, I open the door and run wild in knee-high leather around the Porsche waving my arms over my head shouting, "Look at me! I'm passed La Cienega!"

"What was that?"

"A Chinese fire drill in honor of my first date west of Cahuenga Boulevard," I announce and buckle up.

"What are you going to do for an encore when we get close to Rodeo Drive?"

"You're taking me to Beverly Hills? The town? Armani, Ferragamo, Versace, and my dentist?"

"You're cute, sweet, and funny. You should be a comedian."

I already am and I'm never directing you to my YouTube channel.

I take his free hand and hold it between my two hands and examine it as I would a diamond tennis bracelet given too soon, distrusting its authenticity, suspecting that the jewels are nothing but rhinestones. His hand is beautiful, without wrinkles, popping veins or moles, and the nail beds are pristine. Ali's hands were small and delicate. This hand is strong. Little black hairs lay flat on its back. I turn to him, "You have lovely, large hands."

"You know what they say. Big hands, big feet—"

"Big heart?" The inner child drops her defenses and dumps out her expectations in a one hundred and fifty thousand dollar automobile.

"I believe the saying is 'big hands, big feet, big dick.'"

Whoa. Did he actually wink at me?

I'm in control. I'll drive this thing. I will negotiate the terms of this relationship, as long as I don't drink too much.

From Wilshire Boulevard to North Canon Drive, Ben wheels the sports car to the curb in front of Caffé Roma, an Italian restaurant for the trés chic, I suppose, because the valet at the kiosk on the sidewalk is wearing a white shirt, a black vest, and a bowtie, not a black t-shirt and running shoes.

Ben jumps out of the car and around the back to the driveway behind us. I wait. Either the valet will open this door or Ben will open this door. How long should a lady stay inside a low-level vehicle with massive, heavy doors under the assumption that a gentleman will open it for her, take her hand, and ease her up and out of it?

In the rearview side mirror I can see Ben standing three car lengths behind me. Is this a Gaza Strip standoff? The valet has not rushed over to take the keys from him or rushed to my door to end my embarrassment. Is there a cultural gap here, a long-standing Jewish tradition of celebrating women's independence, or simply the ignorance of an egotistical maniac? No wonder his wife divorced him. Ben may have stated that he divorced her, but do I look like an idiot?

I decide that I've been patient long enough and scrape the hell out of the bottom of the door, sort of an antipasto appetizer before the main course. Now I have two men scrambling to get me out of my seat. "Oops. I didn't know the curb was so high."

Ben rushes ahead of me to the glass entrance of the subdued palazzo. There is no hand to the small of my back. He doesn't turn around and offer his once beautiful hand, a hand that now even in the dim light of evening I can see is more ape-like than it was in the darkness of the car.

A model-actress-hostess guides us to a table for four in this bright, white laminate garden-style open room. Is it my imagination, or is Benayahu flirting with her? For a weeknight, the place is bustling, but what do I know? The tables are scattered catawampus and so close together, the diners may as well be sitting at one long picnic table under a grape arbor sharing plates of cantaloupe wrapped in prosciutto and passing carafes of vino.

"See the distinguished gray-haired man over there? He plays a doctor on a soap opera," he points with a nod of his head. "No, over there, with that big group."

"I recognize him, but I'm bad with names."

"Don't stare. I used to date the actress that plays his daughter on the show," he gloats. "My ex-wife is a model. I know what I want. Have you decided?"

I want a taxi and I have the number on my cell phone.

"May I have a glass of chianti? I love red wine with my bread."

"I usually don't drink. I don't like to be out of control, but one glass won't be a problem."

I'm in Tuscany with a teetotaling control freak.

The menu is overpriced and limited. Currently weighing in at one hundred and sixty-two, my returning girth hidden under the drape of a flowing black sheet, I am careful not to order anything that may give my eating habits or my bulges away. "The arugula and shrimp salad sounds good. I'll share."

"Yes, and light. But Jews don't eat shellfish."

A model-actress-waitress whizzes up without a script, a pen, or props.

"I'll have the veal chop with Portobello mushrooms and she'll have the arugula with shrimp. Oh, and two glasses of the house Chianti." The waitress whizzes off. Our order rehearsed and memorized, she is completely off book.

"Isn't veal a baby cow?" I ask showing off my gastric sophistication.

"Yes, best when slaughtered before a month old."

"I'll stick to the shrimp salad."

"Maybe we should ask how old the shrimp were when they caught them in a net and took them away from their mothers."

To this I have no response, but am fearful I may be dining with a crazy-maker.

His eyes wander about the noisy room—perhaps he is in search for another celebrity sighting—but under the table his leg is inching its way between my knee-high boots. Ben's affect has suddenly changed from a comfortable place to Neil Diamond trying to hit a high note. He's actually squirming in his seat. I think I'll bring him back by throwing a wrench.

"I'm a Republican," I alerted him. This information usually sends men, women, and children scurrying in fear to the nearest Democratic fundraiser.

"Me, too. I love Bush and Reagan. I can't stand Obama and Clinton was a rogue."

"Well, that's a relief," I exhale and we reach out for the other's hand.

Halfway through his glass of wine he begins, "I'm lonely and in need of female friendship."

As I dip dainty pieces of bread into the oil and vinegar, I am all ears, heaving breasts, and throbbing vagina. The man owns his own company, owns a house, and drives a Porsche. In celebration, my mother will soon be thawing taquitos and deviled eggs resembling baby chicks to be served on cut glass plates at the engagement party.

"I need a very sexual woman, a woman who understands the concept of 'no rules,' a companion that I can count on to be there when I need her."

Is he talking chains, handcuffs, and servitude?

"Would this woman be invited to your home?"

"I have a very nice house in Toluca Lake. She can visit me there and I at her home. I have a swimming pool and I enjoy barbequing."

"I have a barbeque. Toluca Lake? Have you ever seen Delores Hope walking around—or being wheeled around?"

"Who?"

I tried to gaze into his eyes, but they continued to jerk back and forth in the oddest manner. "Once a week, you said?"

"Yes, I usually have a barbeque on Sunday."

"No. I mean would this wildly sexual woman be requested once a week?"

"Twice a week at my request."

He shoots a look at my chest, which from my downward view appear only slightly larger than the growing expanse of my waistline. Is he envisioning me naked to determine whether I am worthy of this conversation? I'm already worried about what I'm going to look like in a swimsuit come June. Put the bread down.

Why can't I blindly fall without first having the *The Rules* run across a screen right in front of my face with a bouncing ball pointing out the disastrous consequences of the proposed relationship? Why can't they just shut up and surprise me?

"Lamb chop shish kebab is my specialty."

"Baby sheep? Don't you like anything old?"

"I like older women. They are experienced, open, not afraid."

I'm sitting here shaking in my boots, buster. I'm the girl who cries when I'm flipped over and slapped on the butt.

"And comfortable having lots of sex."

I'm not in shock. I've been here before. Perhaps dating men who were born the year I voted for Governor Reagan is senseless, but lamb chop shish kebabs by the pool is tempting. I will pretend it's chicken.

Homeward bound, Ben sings along to the music surrounding us.

♪ You'd be so easy to love. We'd be so great at the game ♪ "Do you like sports?"

I flash a grin. "As long as I get a hot dog and beer."

"Last week Obama signed thirty-five new acts into law while on vacation in Hawaii. He needs to be stripped of pens."

"Do you think Donald Trump is really considering running against him in the next election?"

"Donald has been quoted as saying that no one respects America anymore and that in ten years China will overtake us easily. He's right, but the GOP needs a black Jewish woman to run. That would be a slam-dunk. Do you like basketball?"

"Three pointers from the free-throw line. But I can't stand the baggy hoodlum shorts."

♪ Back stairs and love affairs ♪ he continued to interest me with his knowledge of pre-war Broadway musical theatre lyrics lilting from his surround sound. Then it was my turn.

♫ Birds do it, bees do it, even educated fleas do it. Let's do it—♪

♫ Let's fall in love ♫ We finished together.

It is rare that lovers finish together, D.H. Lawrence stressed in *Lady Chatterley's Lover*. And I'm sure that I shall not breach Mr. Lawrence's sentiment nor will I upset the neighbors by serenading them with a cosmic climax in two-part harmony any time soon, unless there is mutual masturbation involved.

"Ben, how did you become a fan of Cole Porter?"

"My grandmother loved the flaming fag."

Ben found a parking space and asked if he could come in to use the bathroom. "You should have gone at the restaurant," I tease. This time, he opened my door and walked me to the gate, crossing a quiet late-night boulevard, a securing hand to my back. I should not have let him in.

Making out on the miniature loveseat, Benayahu swoons at my kissing ability. I swoon right back. The dogs don't move a canine muscle; they so understand when to lay low. In the darkness of my living room, our lips and tongues slobber away. Our arms wrapped around each other, there are tender kisses to necks, cheeks, eyelids, and even foreheads. The heat is rising, but I will hold back the fire. This is not going to the bed. I'm cinched into full-body Spanx armor, which takes a tire iron to get out of. And in the blink of my eye, before I can shout *Golda Meir*, Ben has his cock out and is stroking it up and down in a frenzied fervor.

Stunned, I shove him and he lands bottom down on the floor.

"What the hell are you doing?" I ask to the tune of *Like a Virgin*, kissed for the very first time.

"I need a lot of stimulation, especially oral," he calmly instructs me, his hairy hand milking away, his eyes jerking uncontrollably side to side in his egotistical head.

"Stop fiddling with that. Put that away." *That* is an engorged wrinkled trunk, with additional plumage, of some bluish-gray shade, a disgusting turgid presentation of man's decline into savagery. "It's our first date, you asshole, and I haven't even learned how to pickle gefilte fish, and now this? I should have left you on the roof where you belong."

Similarly aroused by the virulent scent of the forthcoming spill of bodily fluid, Hound bares his teeth and in one giant leap from his bed lands smack dab on Ben's lascivious lap. The old Queensland Hound shepherd hasn't moved that fast since Alexandra surprised him with a baby brother. Years ago, Hound took one frightened look at fluffy white, arrogant Brute and skidded out the backdoor. He slept in the garage for two days.

"Don't you dare lick that," I command and pull him away by the collar.

Backing out the door, the fiddler zipping up and in a hurry to go, Ben dismissed himself with a few last words. "We can be friends."

I shouted out to him from the gate. "You're a Jew. Aren't you supposed to be circumcised?"

For fifteen minutes, I brushed Mr. Ashkenazi's saliva off my teeth, my tongue, my gums, and my dangling uvula, the gag reflex almost sending me to the toilet. I am anxious for morning to come when I will ask Randi if this is the norm for first dates in the new and exciting 21st Century.

Chapter 13

Puttin' On The Big Girl Panties

♫ Sittin' here, eaten' my heart out waitin'
Waitin' for some lover to call ♫

Hot Stuff
Fahey, Bellotte, Blanchard, Faltermeyer,
Forsey, Gallifent, and Kenny
(How many songwriters does it take to screw in a light bulb?)

THE sun's illumination of the stained glass window in my en suite bathroom alerted me to a new day, a day I choose to ignore for just one more cuddle up moment, both hands safely outside the covers. Brute lay still on his blankie, securely tucked behind shammed pillows protecting him from an accidental midnight thud to the hardwood floor.

The clock radio came on with KFI 640 talk show host Bill Nob sputtering and spitting out the news.

> Iran has captured a fifty-five-year old American woman found at the Armenian/Iran border wearing concealed spy equipment and a microphone stuck in her teeth. There is much worldwide speculation as to her reason for filming border crossings and guard posts.

I yawn. The poor thing is simply looking for her lost mojo, her young Iranian boyfriend.

When the aroma of automatically timed morning coffee sent me to the kitchen, with a Nicorette stuffed behind a lower molar, using the house phone, I woke up *The Lightening Rod* and regurgitated last night's folly.

"This is not the first time a man flattered you by workin' the wiener," Randi reminds me.

"Oh, yes, cocky Adam, the Rasputin haired, foot fetish guy. You really did read my book."

"Julie, things have gotten out of hand. If you give the slightest hint that you may be up for it—well, anything goes. No one *necks* anymore. *Making out* in the Urban Dictionary is limited to preteens only. After the age of thirteen, it's nothing or all the damned way. Except when it's a blowjob, 'cause they're usually done after that, anyway."

"No more *petting* either, I suppose? Benayahu didn't even try to touch my breasts. There was no attempt to grease up the machine."

"He's been taught he doesn't have to. That's your responsibility."

Touch yourself. It is exciting for me.

Ali, the winter of 2009

"Blowjobs on the first date? Randi, just who is this bitch out there screwing up romance for the rest of us?"

"Well, don't point the finger at me. I never go on first dates."

"Let's make a wanted poster, *Dead or Alive,* with the reward of a plugged nickel to the man who brings her in."

"We should end up with a mob posse. Anyway, from what you've described, would you ever want that particular dong inside you?"

"Yuck, no. I've been spoiled by the perfect pink, blue-veined seven-inch, baldhead penis. I need to find its replacement, an exact replica, before my aging walls crumble."

"The paint job still looks sweet," she assured me with her union painter's perspective.

"Not those walls, my vaginal walls. They pulsate inside an empty chamber, while I cry out his name."

"All right. That's it. Get dressed and fixed up."

"I'm staying in my pajamas and writing all day," I promised myself.

"I'll be finished feeding crickets to the tarantulas in—"

"Whoa. How did the surgery go?"

"I'm high on pain killers. Can't feel a thing. Meet me in front in an hour."

Good God, another shower. The house phone rings while I'm toweling off, rubbing the elbows excessively. Dry, wrinkled elbows are a glaring sign of old age, along with liver spots and skin tags. Note: begin the exfoliating regime at the onset of puberty.

"Yes, Brainard, I'm here. Don't hang up," I speak over my answerphone greeting.

"So did you interrogate the roofer?"

After spitting out a G-Rated version of last night's dog and pony show, Brett laid into me like a pimp short on cash.

"That's all you got? He's a Republican who likes Cole Porter? No pillow talk? You turned off the Israeli?"

"Brainard, I'm still chemically addicted to the Muslim. I go for a few days and then pop! His scent is back. I worry about him. I yearn for him."

"I wish someone loved me like that."

"That's never gonna happen, Captain. There is one thing. Ben is not circumcised."

"You told me you didn't have sex with him."

"He gave me a preview."

"Julie, Jewish males from the Former Soviet Union were never circumcised due to the communist prohibition of any Jewish religious practices. He may be lying to you about being directly from Israel."

"At this point, it doesn't really matter. I don't think he's inviting me to his mid-life bris anytime soon. If he's a Russian spy, then put Natasha, Boris, Rocky, and Bullwinkle on his tail. I have a date with a hood-ringed tarantula wrangler in twenty minutes and I haven't even creamed my thighs yet."

"Ya hoodwinked me there. Who's the lucky guy?"

"No guy. Randi is taking me on a surprise outing to help me forget, I suppose."

"How is the wild thing?"

"She's never having sex with you."

"Just keep your eyes and ears open. Things are going down."

But I am not, not on an anteater's head when I prefer a firemen's helmet.

* * *

Dressed entirely in black from the sheer Madonna headscarf securing her purple-red unruly mop to the black thigh-high orthopedic boot, Randi limps on crutches down the walkway.

"How are you going to drive with that?" I exclaim as she bounds down two steps and onto the sidewalk.

"It's on my left foot and don't ask me where we're going. I'm driving."

"You're on medication; you're wearing a cast; and the Mini Cooper has a clutch. I'd better drive."

"What? And lose your parking place?" She had me there.

Inside the tiny sports machine, surrounded by red-piped black leather still smelling new, Randi opened the glove box and rifled through a collection of tampons, condoms, disposable pink razors, and Bic lighters. Tossing a few parking tickets to the floor, she wrestled out a travel size bottle of blue mint Listerine. Does anyone keep gloves in there anymore?

"Well, you're prepared."

"A girl has to be," she said and threw back a gulp. "I keep an overnight bag in the trunk."

"I keep snow chains and a water bowl for the dogs in my trunk."

"Things are about to change, Julie. Snap in your belt and hold on."

The passenger safety belt was a single strap, but the driver's belt was a double stitched racing harness. Slipping the straps over her head, she double clicks, switches on the ignition, pushes a button and the engine purrs.

Blocked at both ends by giant SUV's, after shifting from reverse to first gear a half dozen times, all the while cursing anyone who would drive such atrocities and the children they harbored inside them, Randi gradually made her way out of the parking space and bolted into traffic rushing from the intersection behind us. Never more than a half a car length behind, swerving in and out, she flew out of first gear, then to second, then to third, and ignored the red light at Santa Monica. Charging in front of a thundering garbage truck, she took the corner on two wheels, geared down to second, and started all over again. Always in bumper-to-bumper traffic, I couldn't see how she would ever need a fourth gear, but she had five of them on the floor.

"Wouldn't it be better for the car and your foot if you just stayed in second and sort of cruised along rather than slamming on your brakes at stoplights?" I suggested.

"Now what fun would that be? Relax."

Gripping the panic handle above my right arm, I held on for dear life as Randi whizzed our way west on Santa Monica Boulevard. I hadn't experienced motion sickness since last being stopped at the top of a Ferris wheel—and there's even a song about it. Unfortunately, it didn't happen at Palisades Park, but at the nasty, dusty San Bernardino National Orange Show, when they were still squeezing crates and crates of oranges inside a grand exhibit hall and when I last saw my date for the day escaping the violent return of my mustard-dipped corndog and frothed Orange Julius. I have not eaten yet today, so the damage to her Mini Cooper authorized floor mat should be minimal.

"Please slow down. I'm going to be sick."

"We're almost there. Roll down the window."

Looking down, I can't figure out the door lock from the window button. Looking up, I see just ahead what is a Hollywood rarity, a storefront set back, almost hidden from the street and sidewalk behind tall reeds and a cluster of palm fronds, short enough to trim without climbing a ladder. Randi jerks a right into another rarity; the shop has its own parking lot for customers without a push-the-button ticket gate or a strong-arm attendant eager to take your keys and your cash. It is my experience that only chain drug stores and chain grocery stores have free parking lots in this town. Wherever I am, I'm coming back soon just to park my car.

"We're here!" Randi cheers as she limps out of the car. She reaches back behind her seat for the crutches and is immediately at my side to help the old lady up and out. Still reeling from the ride, I approach a tinted double glass door and am struck breathless by the neon sign above it.

"Oh, no. I can't go in there. Jeez," I implore her.

"Yes, you can. You're a big girl."

Jutting up from behind her bobbing head is a black tower boldly displaying another neon designation for sex gone mad: *The Pleasure Chest.*

"No, actually, I'm not," I tell her as I pivot to head back to the car.

"You come back here. You want a replacement for the penis that got away?" she roared and stomped her crutches in challenge. She has the keys. I can catch a bus.

"Not that kind. I don't even own a vibrator. My fingers and the fantasy get me off every damned time. In three minutes flat," I assured her.

Standing close, she held my hand. "So tell me your fantasy."

"His long black hair spins around his head and he stares at me as if I'm the most beautiful woman in the world."

"You are the most beautiful woman in the world to me. So that part's not a fantasy." And the strangest girl I would ever know balanced her underarms on a pair of crutches and hugged me. "He's not there to fill you anymore, Julie. Just for fun, let's see if you can pick him out of the bunch. Hell, there's gotta be at least one pink, blue veined seven-incher in there."

Now I was laughing. I pulled my big girl panties out of my crack and strode right into a sex shop in broad daylight on Santa Monica Boulevard.

The aisles are wide and brightly lit. A swath gaze about the large room calms my apprehension. Upon stainless steel and glass shelving are colorful displays of how-to books, boxed bachelorette gag items, some very interesting edible panties stretched onto half mannequins, their stubbed legs sitting in a row. Placed neatly like tiny plastic soldiers is an abundance of boxed scented vaginal lubricants with names like *Super Slide*. Dangling from one wall is the expected choice of materials in handcuffs, but I cannot tell without reading the tags whether they are edible. A pair of black licorice cuffs would be fun. There are the typical red fluffy fur crotchless panties, red brassieres with cutouts for nipples, and sexually significant board games. I'm in *Toys R Us* for the big kids.

A thin blonde buxom tranny is at a glass counter. Wearing a nice wig, a conservative shade of lipstick, with the usual animated female gestures, in complimentary conversation, she greets Randi by name. Apparently, Randi visits *The Pleasure Chest* with the same regularity that I visit CVS Pharmacy, Rite Aid, and the do-it-yourself car wash. Straightening a display of feathered boas, a large black woman in skintight leopard and an armored bustier stops her labor of love and rushes to welcome us. The *hi-how-are-you's-and-why-do-u-have-that-thing-on-your foot* completed, Randi introduces her sheepish sidekick.

"Jamila, this is my neighbor Julie. She's an actor, a writer, a realtor, and a damned good gardener. And she reads to kids, too." Then my friend added a cover. "She's come to do kinky research for her next novel."

"Can I be in your book?" the blonde hovering at the counter asks.

"Honey, you can read to me any time," Jamila sizzles. "Just kidding! You should see your face, girl. I've got to teach a class in five. There's another one right after. Why don't you two sit in?"

"First, I'm taking Julie to the upper level to find the perfect slipper to fit her broken hearted foot," Randi blew my cover.

"Well, as long your clit's not broken, right? Two ladies and two broken feet in one day, however did that happen?"

"I left the ball too late, apparently." I contemplated, "But shouldn't it be the other way around?"

"Oh, girlfriend, I get it. *The perfect foot to fit your glass slipper*. I've never heard it put quite that way before, but we've got 'em all, all shapes and sizes. You go with Randi and slip your sweet little white foot into a few—or imagine slipping in a few. Either way, you'll find just the right fit."

"What's the class about?" I ask.

"Hands and mouth-on instruction for improving oral sex, blowjobs, the usual. You should see your face, girl! Don't worry. I demonstrate using bananas covered with colorful condoms. Go to the front desk upstairs and sign up for *Suck it, Lick it, Love it: Tips for Better Sex*. There's no charge."

I followed Gimpy up a short set of stairs to another well-lit arena into a wonderland of willies. Surrounding us in what Randi nicknames *The Fun Chamber* are larger-than-life erect phalluses skyrocketing from platforms. Modeled in plastic, rubber, and glass in a rainbow of colors, the permanently excited shafts are given names.

"Look. Here's the *Doc Johnson* for just forty-nine bucks in black, beige, and a fleshy pink."

"No, Randi. His was longer than that," I insist and move on to an overly realistic dildo that squirts. "Oh, my. Whatever do you refill it with when it's empty?"

"An exhausting supply of vaginal lubricant."

"Are the balls attached to keep it from going all the way in?" I was full of questions, when an Asian man approached.

"Hello. My wife sent me to bring home an American dick. A seven-incher with blue veins."

"Follow us. We're looking for the perfect replacement, too," Randi whispered to the tiny man. Feeling my discomfort, she turned to me.

"Don't worry. This isn't the kind of place where the guy's going to jack off onto the linoleum floor."

We passed by the spiked strap-on belts, the limp rubber *packers* for female transvestites, and the double dildos for the excruciatingly experimental. Into another aisle, there encased in its own glass box, perched on a single black marble stand, a single light beaming down on its perfect glans, spiraled the pink, blue veined vibrating marvel, the perfect fit.

"One hundred and seventy-nine dollars? I could slather up a Persian cucumber for less than fifty cents," I blurt out. Perhaps my love affair had truly come to its budgetary end.

"Do you think she'll like this one?" the frightened little man asked.

"Oh, hell, yes. She'll be in heaven. She'll lose herself. You'll never get her back," I confirmed.

"Well worth the money, then," he replied and in haste left us to find the floor clerk.

Giving the fertile farmland of dildos one last second look, I mentioned to Randi, "There's nothing here that resembles last night's fiddler on the roof."

"That's where they hide them."

"Where?"

"On the roof, where they belong."

Leading me quickly passed the horse masks, studded collars, nine-tail whips and floggers, Randi patiently settled us into the vibrator section.

"Say, you didn't have to run me passed the costumes. I was a very sexy Bat Woman in the early 90s," I cock-a-doodle-doo.

"Let's see how open you are to finding your G-Spot, Superhero."

Unable to place them in my hand, I gazed wearily at the wide selection: Vibratex Snugglepuss, an over-under-in stimulator; Decadence G-Spot for under eighteen dollars that tickled my fancy; the Mood Frisky and the Cute Toyfriend.

I whispered to my walking sexual encyclopedia, "I don't need a vibrator. I need a boyfriend, not a toyfriend."

"I get ya," she sighed and then surprised me with a revelation. "I have over a dozen of these things and it still takes me hours to get off."

"I'll print up the picture of Ali for you. It may do the trick."

She pulled her eyebrows together in a grimace, locked her eyes shut, and shook her head vehemently. "I need to get that image out of my head: the two of us beating off to the fantasy of a terrorist that looks like Aladdin, his hair spinning around his head. I suppose you throw a camel or two into the mix?"

"Not always," I assured her.

The tranny appeared out of nowhere and slid in between us, her large manicured hands flying in all directions. "Jamila has ordered me to sign you up for a class. There's several going on before lunchtime, which is perfect because I would never advise eating before any of these demonstrations. We've had a few newbies just lose it completely. What a mess."

My stomach already doing flips, I unfortunately inquired as to the available classes.

"There's Tristan's *Anal Pleasure 101*, a very funny, educational mini-seminar on the myths of anal sex and anatomy, the G-Spot and the prostate—oh, that gives me goose bumps—basic preparation and hygiene, of course. She'll walk you through the use of lubes, toys, and safe sex. It's basically anal penetration for beginners."

"Randi, if you're going to make me take a class, I think I'll stick to the prophylactic fruit instruction."

"I'm not making you do anything, but you'll hurt my feelings if you don't sit in on just one."

"As long as I don't have to sit on one."

"Oh, she's gonna do great! See, she has a sense of humor. Oh, too funny," and Tranny wiggled off in her leopard skin stiletto short boots.

When we sneak into the small gathering place behind black metal room dividers, both male and female voyeurs are in a state of heightened awareness. Her students on the edge of their metal chairs, Jamila, standing proud, is charged and gregarious as she professionally slips a bright green cellophane-like rubber over the outside of a good sized banana.

"Why doesn't she peel it first?" I whisper into Randi's shoulder.

"Shhh," a finger pokes me from behind.

Fifteen minutes into it, the lovely and entertaining Jamila talks a good game, but she's not sucking, licking, or loving it. This blowjob class is like learning to drive a car without ever touching the steering wheel.

"Why doesn't she put her mouth on it?" I whisper into Randi's shoulder.

"Shhh," a fist pokes me from behind. I turn to face an angry aging black man. "You should be listenin' and takin' notes. None of you's women know a thing about cocks."

"Herman, you're welcome to sit in on my class, but please do it silently," Jamila interrupted what seemed to be the beginning of his routine tirade. Herman flopped back into his chair, happy to have had his say.

"This little maneuver will really get his attention, ladies and gentlemen. Flick, flick, flick," Jamila demonstrated with her forefinger.

"Shouldn't she use her tongue?" I whispered into Randi's armpit as I slunk further down into my seat.

"Shhh," a hand turned me around.

"It's a fact that you women don't know nothin' about it and should be driven straight to this class and be tied to a chair. I'm offerin' up my big long dick as a lab rat and my wife's gonna be the first one I'm dragging through that door."

"Herman, please stop interrupting the class."

"I'll be turnin' queer if'n I don't get a decent blowjob before I die."

"Wow, has he got an axe to grind," I whispered into Randi's elbow as I sank lower in my seat.

I returned home with a complimentary *Fit For Fun* condom, a small container of *Bodyglide* lubricant, and a friendship card with one long-stemmed rose embossed upon it; the sentiment *I love the way you smell.*

Chapter 14

Politics and Potty Training

Once again, Tuesday night bowling league began at Pinz in Sherman Oaks on Ventura Boulevard, a challenging drive up the Hollywood Freeway. Fifteen minutes before nine p.m., I picked up the assignment sheet at the desk and trotted over to lane no. 21. Jared and Jonathan were laced up and dressed in our red and black Manute Bowl team shirts; their balls spit-shined and glistening on the ball return.

Setting my rather grimy blue ball down next to theirs, I teased Daddy Jonathan. "You've just had your second son and your wife is still letting you bowl?"

"Keep that down. My wife is Chinese. We're only allowed one."

"Did Jason call in sick?" I asked. Jason is my rebound thirty-something pretend lover. He is a wild, tattooed, unemployed actor, and he reeks of tobacco smoke. I can't wait to smell him.

"Nah, he's still in the parking lot," Jared criticized.

"What's he doing in the parking lot?" I returned a suspicious glare and put on my new sparkling glove.

"Is that for luck?" was Jared's answer.

"I thought we could use a little more pizzazz—or at least I could."

"Isn't Jason's pouting, swearing, and kicking the ball return enough?"

"Hey, he only does that when he doesn't roll the third strike," I defended my anti-establishment narcissist. "He hates missing out on a turkey."

The opposing team prepared for tonight's joust, ordered a pitcher of ale from the wandering wench, and sitting boy-girl-boy-girl, they joined in the wait for Jason, bowler no. 1 on the scoreboard. The music videos began and practice balls rolled. At nine-fifteen, the announcer pronounced league play to begin.

Strutting through the upper level in a white wife beater t-shirt and ripped-knee blue jeans, patting shoulders and whispering sweet nothings into the ivory necks of fair maidens as he passed through, Manute Bowl's star and confrontational monarch entered lane no. 21 holding a slice of pizza he'd pilfered along the way.

"Sorry to keep you all waiting," Jason mumbled through the pepperoni and fumbled out of his boots and into his shoes. He removed a mangled team shirt out of his ball bag and unhappily buttoned it on.

"You're up," Jared said. "You might want to get your ball out of the bag."

"Sure, sure. But first I have to give our mascot a hug."

Flattered, I melted into him. It felt good, but his scent was strange and unexpected, evidence of my friend's new sport. Jason had deluged us with news of his prideful intolerance for alcohol, refusing to partake any longer of even an offered lager. This holier-than-though path had become yet another grandiose ideology he chose to bang out from his mighty keyboard at the computerized scoreboard pulpit, along with political rhetoric concerning the evils of capitalism and the reciprocity of the new world order.

My lips at his ear, I accused, "Have you been smoking a joint?"

"Ya gonna call a cop, grandma?" And he pushed me away.

"Come on, Jason. Let's bowl," Jonathan pleaded. "I've got a tired wife and two babies at home. I need to be out of here by eleven."

Tonight Jason continued his ranting. Over the rumble of the alley and the constant thumping of the 80s music, I really couldn't hear much of what he said, except for his purposeful insult that I was a Republican and wouldn't understand any of it anyway and that Obama had personally extended his unemployment insurance. Jason's protestations were lost on us; we were simply trying to pick up our spares.

"Why are you chewing gum?" Jason asks me as I approach the ball return. "You know that's not a good idea on the lanes."

"I quit smoking last year. You forgot. I'm chewing Nicorette."

"My old man died of lung cancer. It's the government's plan to kill us all with our own weaknesses. They control the tobacco industry," he continued his harangue and followed behind me on my approach to pick up the seven pin I had left sitting all alone in the left corner. I overshot my mark, the second arrow on the lane, and the ball dumped short into the gutter. My head hung, I turned and almost stepped on Jason's feet.

"Should I ask the front desk to bring out the bumper guards for you?"

At the end of the final frame, Jason was heading into a perfect game, but threw it away with a *7-10* split, an almost impossible pickup. My glove and the baby powder dusting to my fingertips put us just a few pins ahead of the heavily handicapped competition; they were given a hundred and seventy pins at the start of each game. Jared and Jonathan rolled along, enjoying their beers over talk of changing their television editing careers to becoming producers of their own silly sitcoms. Manute Bowl took two out of three.

We packed up our balls, stowed our smelly socks and shoes, and left Jason pouting, swearing, and kicking the ball return. He would remain in the alley wagering with other sore losers until closing. He would not report his winnings to the State of California.

Driving home, I exit the Hollywood Freeway at Vine Street. Passing the Capitol Records building, the parking lot flagmen darting in and out of the street, the young and restless lined up for two blocks behind a bouncer's rope in front of Avalon, I kept one eye out for a man in a soft grey long-sleeved t-shirt, his black hair dancing just at the nape of his neck. Alexandra assures me that once you stop looking for him, he will appear out of nowhere. She insists that I keep looking.

Nearing midnight, I cheered to find that the dear Lord had saved me an all-day parking space on my side of the street. I must be doing something right. Before I clicked on the car alarm, little Brute welcomed me with an irritating high-pitched shriek from the front porch. One of us still has excellent hearing.

Still in my bowling shirt, I invite the dogs into the walkway to empty their bladders for the night. As we wander in the black shadows into the courtyard of little houses, Randi's bungalow is dark behind her rickety wooden fence. Inside the old German Frau's living room, the big screen still flickers. She's probably fallen asleep again on the couch. A few porch lights are on where cats perch in hope of a late-night snack. Morticia passed away last September and I wonder if anyone here remembers her, my wildly opinionated gray cat. Knowing that your pet will die before you, why do we so freely take on a predetermined heartache?

She ran free for seventeen years—old house to new house, old city to new city, old dog to new dog—and in spiteful defiance stayed away days at a time, always to return. I miss combing out her matted hair while she hissed at me, always with that ungrateful look in her green eyes, as if she were going to give me a clawed *what for* at any moment.

Strung on the upper branches of the tree outside my bedroom window are tiny white lights. They illuminate the beginning of the walkway and are timed to turn off at midnight. I replace them year after year. I hurried the boys home just as they twinkled us a goodnight.

I can't sleep. I toss and turn with ideas for the second book I'm supposed to be writing. I contemplate what I will do if he returns, what I will do if he never does. My decision to reach for the *Bodyglide* on the nightstand begins innocently with just a squirt to the fingers and a gentle massage to ease me to sleep. The headlights of a car cast a sudden light onto my pastel Jesus and in shame I jerk my hand away. But he's already here. He can't stay away. I cannot turn him away. He's sweet and young and mild and mine. I smell him, feel him, and talk to him. Our lovemaking is urgent, moist, and frenetic. He whispers *touch yourself, touch yourself, touch yourself.* Lingering is not a possibility. The climax comes too fast.

"Oh, Jesus, forgive me. When will this end?"

"Nevah. You veel have vis fantasy forevah."

"Great! Now I'm talking with God," I laugh maniacally, the usual tears running down into my mouth. I sit up and beat the bedcovers. "Why don't you come back so I can shriek at you? How dare you leave me!"

"There eez to be no contact, dahlink."

"Natasha?"

"Yes, dahlink. Stop zee melodrama," a cartoon-like Pottsylvania accent implores me. "Vee are all in zee bathroom blushing."

I never close the bathroom door, but right now it's shut and the light is on inside. I hear water running.

"It must be crowded in there. Is Bullwinkle in the tub?"

"Excellent espionage conclusion," Rocket J. Squirrel called out.

"I'm getting up," I muster.

"No, no. Don't ya get up, Julie," a large moose grumbled. "You'll wake up and we won't be able to visit."

"You've got an odd assortment of lipsticks, dahlink. All bad," Natasha let me know.

"The good one's in my purse," I retort and fall back into my pillow. "You're not here to perform a celebrity makeover, are you?"

"You're a celebrity now? Dahlink, when was zee last time you were on zee red carpet?"

"I think that was in 2009, when Alexandra let her mom tag along," recounted Mr. Know-It-All, Bullwinkle the Moose.

"Ah, yes, Alexandra's premiere een zee Big Apple. None of your own?"

"What's this about? Why are you here?"

"The Counter-Terrorism Squirrel Squad eez checking een, that's all."

"The Fearless Leader sent us to cheer you up!"

"Thank you, Bullwinkle, but I'm not spying on anyone anymore."

"Well, you've gotten too chubby to vee of any use. Vee do have our standards."

"Thanks, Natasha. How are you handling your break up with Boris?"

"I took zee short fatty back."

"You tired of crying yourself to sleep?"

"I couldn't replace zee little sheet, okay? But you can. You can do eet. Ve're—vat do you say—rooting for you."

"Yay, Julie!" Rocky applauded.

"Where have you all been assigned? Certainly not my bathroom."

"We've been carrying out our covert surveillance duties from inside a hall closet in the oval office. Boris drilled a peep hole and we take pictures from there," Rocky explained.

"What kind of pictures? Obama finally sinking his sixth putt on a portable green?"

"The President praying on a yoga mat during early morning meetings with administrative operatives. His knees really get a work out. It hurts to watch him," Bullwinkle moaned.

"His prayer buddies include: Arif Alikhan, Assistant Secretary of Homeland Security; Mohammed Elibiary, a member of the Homeland Security Advisory Council; Rashad Hussain, the—"

I reached for my diary and pen. "Wait, slow down, Rocky. I'm writing it down."

"Een zee dark? No need, our leetle historian. Eet's all over the Internet, dahlink."

"I've been trying not to *Google*. Just gets me in hot water."

"Shall I continue?" Rocket J. Squirrel cleared his throat. "Rashad Hussain, the U.S. special envoy to the Organization of the Islamic Conference; Salam al-Marayati, co-founder of the Muslim Public Affairs Council; Imam Mohamed Magid, President of the Islamic Society of North America; and—"

"Do they sleep at the White House?" I questioned.

"Well, they do seem to always be in their pajamas," Mr. Know-it-all confirmed.

"—and Eboo Patel, a member of President Obama's Advisory Council on Faith-Based Neighborhood Partnerships. An interesting note on Alikhan; he's Obama's Muslim link to the Arab Spring revolutions currently unfolding in the Middle East."

"What's his senior advisor Valerie Jarrett doing during all this genuflecting?"

"Brewing tea, humming the call to prayer, and pulling the strings on Obama's pajama bottoms."

"Is the President still smoking?" I asked, hungry for fellow-addict news.

"Shhh, you leetle squirrel. That's classified," Natasha muffled Rocky's answer.

"There's gonna come a man soon, the brother of Dudley Do-Right," Bullwinkle informed me.

"Is his last name Do-Right?"

"No, stupeed. He's a lawyer and Superman all wrapped up een one big handsome galoot," Natasha reported and seemed to lick her lips.

"Where do I look for Clark Kent?"

"He weel find you, dahlink. Get back on Match.com."

"He's on an online dating service? How much is he going to cost me?"

"Use what's left in your Squirrel account, dahlink. Rocky, hand Bullwinkle a towel quickly!" The vision of a moose dripping all over my bathroom floor had me in a tizzy.

"Guys, please use the paper towels to wipe up any hair."

"Gosh, Julie, I don't shed until spring," Bullwinkle assured me from behind the door.

"I'm not assigned to spy on this Do-Right character, correct?"

"No, I'll do the spying. Besides, you can't fit into any of your low cut evening gowns. Such a shame. Go back to sleep now, dahlink. Talk to you at the next debriefing."

* * *

Early the next morning, groggy from an overdose of REM sleep, I trudged cheerfully down Cahuenga Boulevard and over to Vine Elementary School. Up the multi-colored tiled stairs and to the tall periwinkle blue steel door, I skip. Pushing the security button, I wait for the door to magically unlock with a buzz. Is there someone in the office who actually screens who it is that wants inside? Am I on television? There is no camera; just a little metal box with a button to push. I've been coming here as a Screen Actors Guild BookPal for three years now and today is the first time I've asked myself these questions. Although I am unfamiliar in my bad-hair-day urchin cap, they've let me in again.

Inside Bud Taylor's kindergarten room, arranged on an industrial-style carpet of colored squares, my young fans jump off their assigned color and surround me. A sea of beautiful little faces glow to find that over the long holiday vacation Grandma Julie did not forgot them; she came back. Only my dogs are this thrilled to see me.

Mr. Taylor, humongous and in a child's blue plastic chair, adoringly leads the applause, because he'll be able to take a long overdue potty break. Shaking clinging arms from my thighs, this moment is the best part of my week. English their second language and not a fair head in the bunch; these children are, hopefully, California's future taxpayers. I may appear to be a lighthearted, fractured fairy tale Mother Goose, but I have ulterior motives. These children of illegal immigrants must be educated, taught to love the hand that feeds them, and become Republicans or we are doomed.

Mr. Taylor hands me a shiny pastel book suitable for five year olds. On the cover is a chubby yellow duckling in a large white diaper and his friend, a pink piggy toddler. Turning the pages of this not-so-subtle tale, I am quite shocked to see little piggy behind a closed bathroom door keeping his guest waiting while he reads a book on the potty, his cute cotton little boy shorts dangling around his four-toed feet. Tired of waiting outside the bathroom door, little yellow ducky opens the bathroom door to witness pink piggy's expert use of the toilet. Soared by peer pressure, little yellow ducky removes her diaper and also uses the toilet. No more diaper for ducky. She is a happy duck. The kids are happy for chubby ducky. Mr. Taylor returns from his sojourn. Sniffing the air, he cruelly chastises the sweet kids with "Some of you need to listen to your bodies."

Next week: *Little Ducky Slips on a Condom.*

Late afternoon I forced myself into a quick shower, begrudgingly forced myself into a rehab makeover, and dressed in beige toned "nice casual," as ordered by Central Casting. I left a perfect parking spot and took off to a restaurant in North Hollywood for a night shoot on *Desperate Housewives.* A storytelling of the evening is a waste of time, ink, and paper, unless you like tales of cold pizza and my own shoes becoming too tight.

These are the days of my life.

Chapter 15

Soft Water Salt and The Young Turks

On January 14, 2011, the government of Tunisia was overthrown and I had not *officially* smoked a cigarette for three months. On January 25th, 2011, thousands of Egyptians would gather in Cairo at Tahrir Square demanding the resignation of President Hosni Mubarak, an ally of the United States. With his blessings, President Obama had let the genie out of the bottle.

Apparently, Benayahu was letting his genie out too. He sent me a text explaining the needs of sexually active, perverted forty-year-old uncircumcised Jewish males, along with an invite to play tennis. My right knee has been giving me trouble, so I declined the invitational.

Back on Match.com, PlentyofFish.com, and a *dot com* for the elderly, I was busy deleting frothing fan mail from several twenty-something males, when I was beckoned by a *flirt* from a gold chain laced, salt and peppered hunk. My profile pictures—not one showing anything below my décolletage—were at least three years old, taken once upon a time when I was free of fear, self-doubt, and self-loathing. To the unsuspecting stranger, my smile promised a sweet, vulnerable woman with a playful spirit and soft heart. My current heart was not yet incurably hardened, but somewhat the consistency of Swiss cheese, dotted with wise bullet holes into which true love might find its way in.

In an online response to Mr. Hunk's flattering introduction, in which I commented negatively on his posting of an inappropriate picture shot in a motel room in his tighty-whities, he chastised me for being a prude. I gave him my home number. As I began my morning writing ordeal and sipping my second cup of coffee, he called.

"Hey, vees is Sam from Match," he whipped at me the catch phrase he has undoubtedly resonated on many telephonic occasions.

Of course, Sam is on his crackling cell phone. Doesn't anyone but me have a landline anymore?

Wise beyond my All-American Girl years in recognizing an accent resonating from somewhere deep in a Transcaucasia valley, or the gas station on Santa Monica, or the carwash on Vine, I asked politely, "Is English your second language, Sam? And is 'Sam' your real name?"

Proudly he strutted, "I am Armenian. My true name is Siamanto."

"Well, that's the sexiest name ever, other than Giovanni, of course."

"Please just call me *Sam*. Your profile name *Romantic Fool*. What eez your true name?"

"Julie. Back in the day, when American mothers named their children to fit in, not to celebrate a particular gene pool or a cultural diversity, the choices were simple: Linda, Kathleen, Debbie, Victoria, Julie —Juliet was way off the grid."

"Off the *grid*?" Siamanto italicized, his dialect beginning to match my own.

"Not important. Just testing your English skills."

"I've been in America for twenty-eight years, honey. I do fine," Sam retorted giving me a *what for*. I purred. I liked him already.

Inside her bungalow, stuck on all fours upon a sticky tarantula-breeding mat, I could hear Randi shouting to me.

Get out of the Middle East. Run.

"Well, your very slight accent is adorable, but are we going to be able to communicate?" I asked.

"Vat is there to communicate? Boy meets girl; girl meets boy. Eet's been happening everywhere for thousands of years."

"What else do you do other than meet girls?" I hinted at my disenchantment with Sam, who had meticulously plucked little ole me from hundreds, if not thousands, of *girls* eager to find love on the Internet.

"I run companies, take houseboat trips, and drink a lot of beer."

"Yes, I enjoyed your pictures of bikini clad ladies barfing off the side of a ski boat."

"You funny. Those are my daughter's friends. Seasick."

"How many children do you have? I have three grown kids and two dogs," I spewed out my unsolicited autobiography.

"Let's meet and see if we can stand each other, okay? We talk then. I am free later today."

Wow! How easy was that? Two days ago I had renewed my subscription and *poof*, just like that, a commanding, arrogant man of *zee* world is coming my way.

"You aren't a lawyer then?" I inquired.

"No. I have no degrees. I don't need them."

"Well, I need to go to the bank and then to OSH hardware to pick up two forty-pound bags of salt for my soft water thingy," I shared my exciting day to come.

"Let me help you with those. Leave them in your car. I can meet at your house, okay? Text me your address."

Rinsing the lunch dishes through the cold water at her sink, I could hear my mother muttering, "Don't let him know where you live. Don't be so available, stupid."

Texting him my address, he also now has my cell phone number.

I showered, shaved my legs, slipped into my terrycloth robe, and in the magnifying mirror, I shaved again with a highly sensitive triple blade. As I pumped out the foamy turquoise Gillette *SatinCare* with a Touch of Olay shave gel, I wondered how, if ever again I were to cohabitate with a man, I would be able to hide the interesting fact that now in my 60s, I no longer have to shave under my arms, which gives me more time to shave my face.

Dressed in my usual black Lycra over-the-knee bun huggers—of late the only pants that are sure to fit—and an extra-large *five-for-twenty* Hollywood souvenir t-shirt, I took the dogs out into the courtyard for their morning dump. The mail had arrived early to the little blue metal box secured to my wrought iron fence in the walkway. As on every occasion that I humbly discover a surprise in the box, I loudly announced the arrival of another residual check. Of course, I sound as if I'm sharing the news with my pets, but I'm not.

"Oh, look," I exclaim as I tear open the envelope from my agent. "The *Little Debbie* spot has earned your little old mama more residual cash!"

Current total payout to little old mama for sweetly biting into a blueberry muffin over and over again in the middle of a peach orchard under a blazing California desert sun: twenty-one thousand dollars.

I finished my neighborhood gloating ritual with, "A man is coming over today. Don't everyone get all excited. I'm trying not to."

The mews was quiet but for the violent rattle of a cane to torn, yellowed Venetian blinds inside the crumbling bungalow across from my bedroom windows. Shouting his usual platitude of obscenities at me—and to anyone else that dares to pass by before noon—the one-legged curmudgeon surely is applauding my good fortune. I had envisioned my ornery neighbor to be a Vietnam War tragedy until Randi gave me the rundown; he actually lost his leg in a drug deal gone bad twenty years ago. That's when I stopped bringing him a bucket of Colonel Sander's *Extra Crispy* on Veteran's Day. If he continues this raucous unfriendly behavior, my delivery of frosted Valentine's Day cookies will also come to a stop.

Before driving to Wells Fargo and to salt pickup, my *Googling* fingers found their investigative way to Armenia, a country hot in the summer and cold in the winter, a country with mountains and green valleys bordered by Turkey, Georgia, and Iran. It is a democracy and the first state in the entire world to adopt Christianity as its official religion. Sam is a Christian who drinks beer. So far so good.

Scrolling down the *Wikipedia* article, I came to a link to *Armenian Genocide*; a holocaust of its very own?

Interest in my new friend's culture lead me to discover that the Jewish people of Europe, a hugely justifiable chip on their weary shoulders, are not the only victims of a crazed ideology desiring ultimate power through so-called *ethnic cleansing*.

Unfortunately for most of us growing up in the 50s and 60s, the cruel reality of genocide was not on the curriculum. My fourth year of grade school history was spent entirely on the good works of Father Junipero Serra, who rambled through California up and down the El

Camino Real—*The Royal Road*—building missions with free redskin labor, while converting the Native American Indians to Christianity. I don't remember mention of one Indian being raped and pilfered and left to die along the trail or of one Jew being stripped naked and incinerated in a gas oven. I had an idyllic childhood education.

Once ruled by Muslim Turks, Persians, Greeks, Romans, Byzantines, Arabs, and Mongols, the horrific tale of *The Armenian Genocide* begins in World War I when the ruling Muslim Turks took the side of Germany, Austria, and Hungary. Under the guise of impending world war, every rifle and pistol was forcibly seized from the Armenians.

Because our elementary school education did not alert us to either the Jewish or the Armenian tragedy, here directly from *Wikipedia,* the Free Encyclopedia, is a recap—just in case you are about to have an Armenian man carry bags of salt into your basement.

> **The Genocide Begins**
>
> At this time, about forty thousand Armenian men were serving in the Turkish Army. In the fall and winter of 1914, all of their weapons were confiscated and they were put into slave labor battalions building roads or were used as human pack animals. Under the brutal work conditions they suffered a very high death rate. Those who survived would soon be shot outright. For the time had come to move against the Armenians.
>
> The decision to annihilate the entire population came directly from the ruling triumvirate of ultra-nationalist *Young Turks.*

Author's Note: *Young Turks* should not to be confused with the song title of the same name released in 1981 on Rod Stewart's album *Tonight I'm Yours.* "Young hearts be free tonight" is the way I remember the lyric. Apparently, Mr. Stewart enjoyed the same jolly elementary school history lessons that I had, although his studies may have taken him on a Merry-Old-England colonization and imperialism extravaganza.

> The actual extermination orders were transmitted in coded telegrams to all provincial governors throughout Turkey. Armed

roundups began on the evening of April 24, 1915, as three-hundred Armenian political leaders, educators, writers, clergy and dignitaries in Constantinople (present day Istanbul) were taken from their homes, briefly jailed and tortured, then hanged or shot.

Next, there were mass arrests of Armenian men throughout the country by Turkish soldiers, police agents and bands of Turkish volunteers. The men were tied together with ropes in small groups then taken to the outskirts of their town and shot dead or bayoneted by death squads. Local Turks and Kurds armed with knives and sticks often joined in on the killing.

Then it was the turn for the Armenian women, children, and the elderly. On very short notice, they were ordered to pack a few belongings and be ready to leave home, under the pretext that they were being relocated to a non-military zone for their own safety. They were actually being taken on death marches heading south toward the Syrian Desert.

Muslim Turks, who assumed instant ownership of everything, quickly occupied most of the homes and villages left behind by the rousted Armenians. In many cases, local Turks who took them from their families spared young Armenian children from deportation. The children were coerced into denouncing Christianity and becoming Muslims, and were then given new Turkish names. For Armenian boys the forced conversion meant they each had to endure painful circumcision as required by Islamic custom.

Author's Note: It's one thing to have the foreskin lopped off at the age of eight days during a celebratory bagel and lox bris; but at thirteen, when the hormonal juices are flowing? That's just cruel, although the result a more attractive male genitalia.

> Turkish gendarmes escorted individual caravans consisting of thousands of deported Armenians. These guards allowed roving government units of hardened criminals known as the 'Special Organization' to attack the defenseless people, killing anyone they pleased. They also encouraged Kurdish bandits to raid the

caravans and steal anything they wanted. In addition, an extraordinary amount of sexual abuse and rape of girls and young women occurred at the hands of the Special Organization and Kurdish bandits. Most of the attractive young females were kidnapped for a life of involuntary servitude.

The death marches during the Armenian Genocide, involving over a million Armenians, covered hundreds of miles and lasted months. Indirect routes through mountains and wilderness areas were deliberately chosen in order to prolong the ordeal and to keep the caravans away from Turkish villages.

Food supplies being carried by the people quickly ran out and they were usually denied further food or water. Anyone stopping to rest or lagging behind the caravan was mercilessly beaten until they rejoined the march. If they couldn't continue, they were shot. A common practice was to force all of the people in the caravan to remove every stitch of clothing and have them resume the march in the nude under the scorching sun until they dropped dead by the roadside from exhaustion and dehydration.

Author's Note: And from embarrassment.

An estimated seventy percent of the Armenians on these marches perished, especially children and the elderly. Those who survived the ordeal were herded into the desert without a drop of water, thrown off cliffs, burned alive, or drowned in rivers.

Author's Note: And you thought Hitler was innovative.

During the Armenian Genocide, the Turkish countryside became littered with decomposing corpses. At one point, Mehmed Talaat responded to the problem by sending a coded message to all provincial leaders: "I have been advised that in certain areas unburied corpses are still to be seen. I ask you to issue the strictest instructions so that the corpses and their debris in your vilayet are buried."

But his instructions were generally ignored. Those involved in the mass murder showed little interest in stopping to dig graves. The roadside corpses and emaciated deportees were a shocking sight to foreigners working in Turkey. Eyewitnesses included German government liaisons, American missionaries, and U.S. diplomats stationed in the country.

Author's Note: And who will be our eyewitness?
Coming soon to a town near you: The Muslim Caliphate.

Western Response

During the Armenian Genocide, the Christian missionaries serving in the Empire were often threatened with death and were unable to help the people.

Author's Note: Chickens, you should be ashamed!

Diplomats from the still neutral United States communicated their blunt assessments of the ongoing government actions. U.S. ambassador to Turkey, Henry Morgenthau, reported to Washington: "When the Turkish authorities gave the orders for these deportations, they were merely giving the death warrant to a whole race."

Wikipedia, The Free Encyclopedia

Author's Note: And you don't think this can happen in America?
Astounded by this newly acquired *Wikipedia* information, I sank into my office chair. My afternoon rendezvous may not be too keen on Muslims. I set about to steal all things Islam from my living room, my koffice, and my bedroom. The magic carpet couple's flight over the Hollywood sign might send poor Sam into a tizzy, so I stashed the books. There was nothing conspicuous in my bathroom, unless one considers Marilyn Monroe's first nude pose hung high above the toilet as *conspicuous*. I hid the triple-blade razor in the nail polish bin inside my grandmother's white glass-paned cupboard and took a deep breath. No

matter what Sam may present himself as—overpowering, womanizing, and cheap—my empathy for him and his people would carry me forth into our burgeoning relationship with soft kid gloves, non-judgmental fortitude, and a throbbing clitoris.

Still gloating over the ease at which I had snagged a date for this afternoon, I drove to the bank to make the deposit, not at the ATM, but at the teller's window, where serendipity found me opposite a young woman in a black suit, her nametag identifying her as Vartouhi Kardashian.

"You look lovely today, Miss Kardashian. Are you related?"

"Heavens, no," she scowled.

I opened my political-asylum arms, flag unfurled, "Welcome to America!"

"Thank you, but I was born here," she replied with perfect Southern California ease.

"It's from my talent agency. When will it be good?" I asked the Armenian teller, her jet-black, heavily lined eyes investigating the check. "I've deposited checks from *my agent* many times. Surely it's all good."

"Only six hundred of the total will be available in twenty-four hours," she courteously explained through her boldly lined red pout.

Scanning the busy area beyond the bullet-proof-glass, I realized what I had not taken note of before my recent Armenian education: Wells Fargo just below the famous corner of Hollywood & Vine was full of them, dark-haired men and women with facial hair in black, ill-fitting pinstriped suits. In the 1970's Armenians fleeing persecution in the Middle East reached sixty thousand plus, most landing in Glendale, California. These were their darling grandchildren, third generation cultural remnants. I wanted to hug them all.

"How old do I look today?" It was important to know right now. A genocide survivor's grandson was coming to inspect me within an hour.

The lovely Armenian teller answered, "Forty-two?"

"Wait. Can you ask him?" I spied an older banker-type strolling behind the glass. The teller reached for his sleeve and pulled him to the window.

"How old does she look today?"

"Forty-eight?" he answered with a bit of a twinkle in his left eye.

"I'll take that one! And may I have forty dollars in cash? I need to buy salt and alcohol."

"Are you making margaritas?" she asked.

"No, the salt pebbles won't stay on the rim."

Trader Joe's is next door to Wells Fargo, a skip and a jump really. I decided on a six-pack of European beer, two bottles of two-buck Chuck Pinot Grigio, and, to be on the safe side, a bag of pita chips and a container of eggplant hummus. The urge to please a total stranger quickly passed as I waited in line. I took my place in line again carrying a large tray of California Rolls, my kind of sushi. I was not in the mood for harem faire just yet. If this blind date blossomed, I might never taste of green wasabi paste again.

OSH, or *Orchard Supply Hardware* as we information overloaded do-it-yourselfers are aware is its true label, was busy with homosexual partners of both genders selecting paint colors, the perfect yellow climbing rose, and it wasn't even spring. The downpour having passed through, Hollywood weather any time of the year is perfect for planting and living on the streets.

OSH is rainbow heaven; whereas Home Depot across the street is a disgusting hellhole filled with Mexican day-workers crowding the driveway entrances with catcalls and lewd whistling as every car driven by a woman passes through. I am safe here from any and all undesired flirtation.

At the checkout register I gave the Hispanic gal the ticket for soft water salt pellets.

"You peek them up outside," she warned me.

"Yes, I know, and a guy puts the bags in my car. Been there, done that. But this time I have someone to take the bags out of my car, the ancestor of a survivor of the Armenian Genocide!"

"I can check to see if we have a store in Glendale, if you'd rather go there," she snapped.

"Glendale is coming to Hollywood, senorita," I snapped back. "Olé!"

The wine chilled, the beer cold, the sushi rolls set on a serving platter in the fridge—and I still comfortably in my errand-running outfit—

Siamanto began a parking-while-texting exchange. Freshly lip-glossed, I answered his confusion with a text message that probably needed editing: *It's after 5:00. Find a parking space in one-hour and you'll be good all night.*

I stood on my porch to watch an irritated cream-colored elephant of a Cadillac Escalade, trimmed out in Egyptian gold, fight its way into a parking space across the street.

The January sun nodded off and the streetlights came alive. Wearing a chocolate brown wife-beater tucked into dress jeans, my Armenian hero forced his way through rush hour traffic to my gate. In the lights of oncoming cars, I could see the blaze of gold chains. Nestled into his hairy chest dangled a large jeweled crucifix.

"Hi. Are you for me?" I smiled and stepped down to open Sam into my life. Soon to be sixty-three, I would, perhaps, settle again. However, a crucifix is a sacrifice I'll make any day over the tacky 14-carat gold Superman *S* emblem my fourth husband wore, with absolutely nothing to back it up.

And from miles away, my mother had her say, "Beggars can't be choosers."

"Let's get the salt," he commanded.

"My car's right there," I pointed. "It can wait."

Leaving a trail of sweet, but spicy vanilla sawdust in the air, Sam plopped himself down in a plastic porch chair and lit a cherry cigarillo. "Do you mind if I smoke?"

"No. Go ahead. I quit some ninety days ago," I remembered, the blur of a few slipups forgotten. "You're very handsome, just like your pictures."

"I don't smoke cigarettes, just these Armenian miniature cigars," he assured me, without assuring me that I, too, had passed the viewing muster.

"Smells good." I was suddenly itching for a cigar of my own. "I'll get you an ashtray." My cravings triggered, I rushed to the kitchen for the Hollywood souvenir ashtray where I keep the Nicorettes, quickly gnawed a crutch gum, and emptied the remaining Nicorette packets into a drawer. I returned with the ashtray to my captive audience, a wad of nicotine gum wedged between my teeth and gum, its calming relief winding its way to my brain. Tails wagging in anticipation, two dogs trailed behind me.

Hound rambled sixty-five pounds of German shepherd loyalty on over to the intruder, who pushed back deeper into his chair. "Does he bite?"

"Goodness, no. Not usually."

Hound sat sweetly, his caramel eyes begging for male attention, and welcomed Sam with a gigantic outstretched paw, his one self-taught trick; the *roll over and play dead* trick I forced upon him never mastered.

"He wants you to shake his hand," I pointed out the obvious.

"Oh, okay. Nice to meet ya," he bonded with the old traitor. "His face looks as if he's wearing a mask."

"Yep. We should have named him Zorro," I smiled.

"He might just have some *Gampr* in him," Sam informed us.

"Ga-what?"

"Nomadic shepherd of ancient Armenia. Many Armenian's rescue them and bring them into the United States. What's that?"

"That's little Brute from the Island of Malta, Italy. I rescued him from a pet store in Dana Point. He's shy," I covered for the snooty Maltese who was not coming out from under my chair.

"The indigenous Gampr survived through many wars, including the Turkish regime of the Ottoman Empire," Siamanto orated.

"Wow, you do speak a mean English."

"And your president has failed to fulfill his campaign promises to recognize the Armenian Genocide at the hands of the Turks," he continued.

"Hey, he's not *my* president." I ran my hands through my hair. "I didn't vote for him. I'm a Republican."

"That is good. I apologize. I get excited over some things. Not much, but some. That man is always on the side of Islam," Sam calmed and finished with a whisper. "Because he is Muslim."

Whoa! I'd found my soul mate. But would he be a good kisser?

"All these decorations on the patio walls, are you Mexican?"

"No, no. Irish-French-English. These are pottery pieces from trips to Baja, Puerto Vallarta, Mazatlan—you know, a colorful ceramic iguana here and there. The house is Spanish architecture, 1923."

"Oh. Armenians don't decorate with Mexican trinkets; only Armenian pottery and Armenian ceramic bowls."

"Oh, okay. Would you like something to drink? Beer, wine?"

"Wine sounds good."

I rushed to the kitchen to open the Pinot Grigio. I returned to find Randi leaning on her crutches in the walkway interviewing my guest from beyond the porch wall.

"How do you know Julie?"

"Match. I just met her," he confessed.

"We're a pretty tight group here, so don't mess up," she chastised my perfect stranger.

"Hi, want to join us for a drink?" I broke in.

"Nah, I've gotta feed my *tarantulas*," she threatened and swung on home.

In friendship, we clinked our wine glasses. "Genatset."

"Cheers?"

"Bottoms up," he answered.

"Do you ever go to the Armenian church around the corner? I've always wanted to go to a wedding there. I can hear the dance music from my kitchen and the trees in the outdoor areas are always lit up and—"

"No, I go to Saint Mary's Armenian Church in Glendale. I do much business there."

"My sister lives in Glendale."

"Is she Armenian?"

Sam begins the first-date soliloquy. I pretend to be an earnest listener, filing each distasteful tidbit of information in the *Out Box*. I should have let him put the salt away before having to endure the dating game once more.

Sam's wife of twenty-five years divorced him because he cheated on her, but he cheated on her only because she didn't like having sex. *Do you like having sex? You look nervous. How about a neck and shoulder massage?*

> "It's natural to cheat. Sex doesn't mean anything to a man, as long as you don't have feelings for the other woman—or you don't get caught," I heard Ali remind me from the living room, where once he shared his universal truism just before I followed him to bed.
>
> But that was years ago, when I foolishly thought I could change a heart.

Sam and his understanding ex-wife still live together in a spacious marble and stucco tract home in a gated community somewhere in the hills of Glendale. *You're so tense. Relax.* All the children, the children's spouses, and the grandchildren live there also. The wife doesn't take lovers, because she doesn't like sex, but Sam is allowed to take as many lovers as he wants, as long as he doesn't bring them home, because Sam likes lots of sex all the time. *Do you like having sex?*

The family income from their real estate investment firm and the car wash empire would suffer if he moved to his own place, so finding a lover with her own digs is preferred. *Does that feel good? How 'bout a kiss?*

While Sam worked on my perceived nervousness, Michael, the gay boy prostitute currently renting the bungalow owned by the head bartender at the Viper Room, innocently called out from the walkway.

"Hey, is that Ali?" Everyone here wants there to be a happy ending.

"No, Michael. This is Sam," I cheerfully introduced the most recent massage therapist to come through my warped gate.

"Don't do anything I wouldn't do," and with that Michael enthusiastically gave us his approval to snort cocaine, ingest methamphetamines, shoot up heroin, and engage in sodomy as he lightheartedly skipped on his way.

Sam insisted on continuing with his loosen-her-up hand job.

"Stand up so I can get to your lower back and hips," he ordered and continued the standard Middle Eastern foreplay, which in my experience happens only once in the relationship, like that one moment of exhilaration the first kiss brings, promising more to come.

Our lips suddenly face to face, I didn't turn away from his eager attempt to kiss me. The chemistry I was longing for just might be in his kiss.

It doesn't happen so much to any of us and I'm not forgetting the magic any time soon. To want to kiss another person until your lips swell? To cuddle up under a lover's bare arm glistening with afterglow and to lose yourself in the smell of him?

> Stop it, Julie. Was there truly any cuddling, but for your idolizing arm over Ali's chest, trapping him in a post-coital nanosecond before he skedaddled up the basement stairs to the bathroom sink?

Yes, there was one remarkable moment.

> Remarkably, he spooned us and we closed our eyes in an attempt to nap, and soon he arose behind me and asked gently, "Are you ready again?" And I was. I always was.

The Year I Learned to Text

I curse him to fall in love as I did and have nothing come back. I curse him to have his heart broken and to never recover. But his heart can't be broken for it is incapable of love. Allah is a selfish god.

I lingered, hoping Sam's tongue would stop darting against my teeth. Sitting him abruptly back down, I insulted him. "Sam, your wife doesn't like sex because she can't get passed the bad tongue action. And, no, I'm not teaching anyone how to kiss. Would you like a California Roll?"

"I don't eat Asian food. We don't eat Asian food. It is important to keep our Armenian culture. We will never let it slip away! We eat only Armenian food. We dance only Armenian dance. We speak only Armenian. It's difficult for me to text in English. I have to use Armenian alphabet translator."

"Well, you certainly are excited about your heritage. Then why do you want to have sex with an American woman?"

"Because you have no hair on your face. Now let's get the salt." I like a man who believes in hard work before lying down for the night. It wouldn't be the first time I had taught a man how to kiss properly and probably would not be the last.

With a forty-pound bag over his muscular shoulder, gentleman Sam watched me lift the door in the floor of my walk-in closet.

"What's down there?"

"It's best to go down backwards. Let me go first to turn on the light," I cautioned him.

Ever so gently, Sam maneuvered the wooden steps down into the bowels of the bungalow.

Setting the bag on the carpet as if it were a bag of down feathers, Muscle Sam climbed up again and returned with the second bag. Taking in the unexpected, he reveled at the secret space.

"Way cool," he complimented the set up: a sewing machine, clothing racks, boxes of holiday decorations, and a small television for slipping in a VHS. "You have a video player. I love porn. Do you like porn? I have a great collection."

We were suddenly startled to glance upon a large colorful poster advertising in bold **The Year I Learned to Text** with the italicized subtitle bursting into the room like a colossal billboard under flood lights, *Why Am I Having Sex with a Muslim in My Basement?*

"Why is who having sex with a Muslim in a basement?" he asked.

"Oh, that." I fumbled. "It's a novel written by Juliet Montague. I'm her—I'm her publicist. Book signing coming up!"

Now even I was confused.

"Juliet, Julie? What's your last name?"

"My maiden name?"

"I doubt if you were ever a maiden."

"Your English is very good, good use of words. Let me help you pour the salt into the thingy there." Yes, put more salt into the Armenian Genocide wound, you culturally starved American. When was the last time I had *Googled* the American Revolution, barbequed an Oscar Mayer wiener, said the Pledge of Allegiance under God, or listened to Johnny Cash? When was the last time I had danced *The Mashed Potato*?

"No, honey. I've got it," he politely said and dumped forty more pounds of salt into the water softener thingy.

Saved by the sound of a text message, I hightailed my ass up the wooden ladder. Before I took three steps and without so much as an impromptu, "Give it to me, baby," tongue-thruster Sam surprised me from behind. With his hands cupping my underwire bra, and his thumbs flicking at my nipples, he took a quick nip at my left cheek with his large white teeth.

Obviously, the news that perhaps it was *I* who had tasted of a Muslim morsel opened Gentleman Sam up to the idea that I am easy prey. Would a proud and sensitive Armenian male, whose grandmother was raped by a marauding throng of Young Turks and left to die along the side of the road, put a Christian woman willing to have sex with a Muslim man in the same category as the justifiably raped gangbang chick?

"You bit my butt!" I shrieked and climbed hand over hand to the bedroom floor, where on my knees I grabbed my cell phone off the linen chest. Randi was exactly on point.

Get out of the Middle East. And right now!

Chapter 16

Poisoned Arrows and Wine in a Box

Sam was gaining on me when the doorbell chimed. At the top of the basement stairs, Hound cut him off with a big grin and a handshake. I scrambled to my feet and headed to the porch.

"What are you doing here?"

"Just checking in."

The front gate still unlocked, as Brainard opened it, Sam escaped leaving skid marks across Cahuenga Boulevard.

"Hound! You stay put." I caught him by the collar as we both headed down the front steps. "Remember the Holocaust!" I shouted at the man running to his Escalade.

"Get a driveway!" Sam commanded from across the street.

"Who's getting away now?" Brainard accused me from inside a camouflage flack jacket.

"A judgmental Armenian with cultural issues." I took in the landscape and the boots on the ground. "Are we at war?"

"Not officially. I had an audition as a soldier in a mini-series."

"Doesn't the CIA pay you enough?"

"I love being an actor, the entire casting process: the adrenaline rush, the anticipation of a callback, the exhilaration of a booking. Then there's always the humiliation of a rejection," Brainard laughed and strolled into the living room. "And you got made, by the way."

"I didn't get laid," I corrected him.

"Not laid. *Made.* Maybe you should have your hearing tested. A field operative reported that you bought pita chips and hummus this afternoon," he pontificated.

"This is how my taxes are being spent? Bad intelligence? I put the chips and dip back and decided on California Rolls instead."

"She missed that. Any left?"

"I'm saving them for my pity party later tonight," my tummy growled.

"Did you turn him off too? You are aware of the Armenian Power Gang of Glendale and the Medicaid fraud, the stealing of social security numbers, right?"

"The what? I thought Armenians were the good guys," I sadly replied and slumped into the loveseat.

"The feds are rounding them all up, but we could still use more leads."

"Tell me again exactly who it is that you work for?"

"The citizens of these United States, chickie."

The house began to tremble and the boys rushed to the porch to have a look-see.

"Why are there helicopters over my head?"

"Ah, there's a crowd lined up at the Palladium. Surveillance. Just a precaution. Crowd control," he pompously explained.

"Because Lawrence Welk and his Champagne Music Makers are performing tonight?"

"God, sometimes I forget just how old you are. Nah, just some violent alternative band drawing every dreg of humanity out from under a rock."

"Brainard, are you a cop or a spy?" I asked, my wine clock alarm buzzing. "Or are you just a *man*?"

"I'm here for you, baby," he said and walked out to wrestle with Hound. "Oh, and after reading your book, it's hard for me to look at you in the same way."

"The intimate details?"

Brainard lingered at Hound's bequest, the two of them in man-on-dog heaven. "You're starved for attention, huh, boy."

"Me, too."

"You don't seem concerned about the possibility that a Fatwa will be ordered by some raghead Iman ordering a *YouTube* video of your head on a platter?"

"Wait, wait. You bought my book?" Excitedly, I began counting literary fans on my left hand.

"The e-book is now on my phone. I had to check it for any leaks."

"You'll have to wait for Part Two of the trilogy to charge me with treason," I said while easing him out the gate. California Rolls, wasabi, and a cheap bottle of Pinot Grigio were shouting my name in unison from inside the fridge.

"You're not really going to write another book."

"Get out. You sound like my mother."

* * *

Later in the week, I meet Alexandra for a random lunch. I feel comfortable spilling my absurd dating tales about a roofer's hand job and an Armenian's chains, for I am *moving on*, the prescription she has urged me to fill. I ramble on non-stop about auditions, extra work, worries over my weight, and the current size of Hound's fecal matter. She laughs along with me.

"Hey, that's okay, Mom. Then you don't have to do it."

"What? Pick up poop?"

Suddenly, I feel uncomfortable having shared in humorous fashion my misadventures along the treacherous trail to the perfect foot. From her unexpected response, I am taken aback by the idea that my precious little girl has potentially been in a similar predicament, a predicament that did not include picking up poop, because she doesn't have a dog.

I've brought with me her order of Amway's *Artistry* facial toner and the very popular *no more wrinkles* wrinkle spray, a must-have for globe-trotting models. She will treat me to lunch in exchange for the thirty-two dollar delivery.

From her townhouse, we begin our walk up to Beverly Boulevard to the Milk Shop, a glass and steel deli for the pretentious, pious, and pitifully thin. Knowing that I am not to embarrass my daughter on her own turf by wearing a ripped out t-shirt and Lycra, I am scratching, perspiring, and wriggling in a proper tailored shirt and khaki pants. I have just left an audition for yet another pharmaceutical as *the hero woman*.

Yes, ladies, the actress in the migraine/osteoporosis/diabetes commercial is a fake. She does not have a headache, a brittle bone, or hyperglycemia. And her husband gets it up just fine without a pill. She's a fucking liar. But you will rush to your doctor to insist that he prescribe whatever *the hero woman* is taking.

"Mommy, I made a lot of money last year." Terrific, but she never calls me *Mommy* unless she needs me to do something for her. "My tax man says I'm screwed and that I need to come up with another eleven-thousand to pay the IRS by April 15th."

"Okay. The toner and wrinkle spray are gifts. Lunch is on me."

Still making our way under a bright sun in the stately Hasidic Jew neighborhood of West Hollywood, I looked down at her twelve hundred dollar Christian Louboutin leather boots and her neatly tucked two hundred dollar black jeans, and before I could foolishly offer her eleven thousand dollars of her speculative inheritance from my Individual Retirement Account, her phone sounded. The conversation was once giddy and then hush-hush, Alex's boyfriend on the other end.

"Well, how is he? And when do I get to meet him?"

"He's so sweet, mom. He's at the family cabin working on his music. He says that if he needed that kind of money, his parents would simply write him a check," she burst forth with a poisonous, unfathomable pride, its toxic arrow piercing my heart.

And then she drew back her unconscionable bow and let go of another. "It's all right, Mom. You've never had any real money, so you don't understand."

Choking back the tears that welled up like discouraged, forgotten dreams, my hands and teeth clenched, I wanted to slap her. But I chose to tighten my lip and admit defeat. "At this age I can't take that much money out of my savings."

And without a soft touch to my disgraced shoulders, drawing her flowing mink and butternut waves into a chignon on the top of her head, she mitigated her shallow intentions. "Please don't take it personally."

And it was then that I knew I had lost her.

Mamas, don't let your daughters grow up to be international models and television guest stars. Don't bring them to New York City or Hollywood. Let 'em be hairdressers and such; then they will always show up for Thanksgiving, their tattooed mechanic in tow.

Spooning tomato bisque soup passed my stiff upper lip, I listened while Alexandra assuaged my sorrows. "Benjamin is a college graduate. He's really smart. He says that some day he's going to take care of me, that I won't have to live under such pressure."

> Whoa, Ms. Pressure Cooker, before you boil over. While you don't have one itsy-bitsy illegal pet turtle to worry about, at about your age, I was sloshing a toddler's dirty brown cloth diaper in toilet water, tiptoeing over an alcoholic husband passed out on the living room carpet, and trying my damnedest to raise an unhappy five-year-old daughter who never liked me. I had freely traded my unappreciated independence for the unknown: a *stay-at-home-mother* sentence I had given myself, handed down in the spirit of age-old feminine ignorance—from my own pulpit. Bang that gavel! For ten years I operated on a twenty-five dollar weekly allowance of fear, intimidation, and betrayal. My stalwart decision to stick it out was never a decision. I swallowed hard; I had nowhere else to go.

And while I raged silently, Alexandra found probable cause to write me a fix-it ticket.

"And Mom, Rae and I are concerned and we love you, but if you ever let that Euro-trash Persian back into your life, we will have you 5150-d."

And never take your daughters to work with you where they can pick up the courtroom lingo for a seventy-two-hour commitment to a psych ward for the *crazy one on the loose.*

"You're not taking care of yourself. It's obvious you're drinking too much. You need to get to the gym. They have Pilates, kickboxing, treadmills, machines, a sauna, a lap pool. Don't let him do this to you."

And never buy a lifetime family membership to 24 Hour Fitness.

"Honestly, I don't know why you don't just move to the mountains and write your second novel there. And please try not to be so intimate in your writing. It's embarrassing. Leave me out of it—along with your politics."

> Blindly, we mommies get so excited
> when our child says their first precious word.

"You told me you very much liked my novel. I'm sorry that I have embarrassed you, but I wrote the intimate truth in the hope women could be saved from their own vulnerable selves."

"You sound like a crazy lady."

"I need to warn them. The Muslims are coming. The Muslims are coming."

"Mom? Mom, I'm proud of you and I'm working on a venue for the book signing, but just don't *talk about it* anymore. And please get your hearing checked out."

> Get this woman out of Hollywood. Send her to the redneck forest where she belongs.
> Nobody likes me. Everybody hates me.
> Think I'll go eat worms.

The short three-mile drive home was grueling. With no cigarettes, no alcohol, and not one Euro-trash Persian to look forward to, instead of pressing full throttle home to change and robustly hitting the god damned gym, I swerved erratically into the CVS parking lot. I'm in luck. White wine in an elegant cardboard box on sale for just four dollars; mini-sized caramel ice cream cups, two for the price of one; and jars of salted peanuts at a twenty-five percent discount.

By midnight, now unblocked and back into her second novel of unrequited love, shame, and bondage—*Jihad Honeymoon in Hollywood*—our writer sat slumped over her desk, two empty ice cream cups tossed in the trash, another glass of wine and a bowl of peanuts at her side. In an inebriated haze, her gums stinging with chewed nicotine, she continued to save the women of the world by penning self-indulgent, mournful monologues until *she* would *get over it*.

During the day, she fooled the neighbors, a few human contacts here and there, her dogs, but not herself. After another night of indulgence, she woke to brush extraordinarily her coated teeth; then went back to rest on her duvet, an ice cold wash cloth covering her glazed, swollen eyes. The Maltese followed her back to bed, where with one hand she tickled his tummy. Already after 8 o'clock, when the world outside was up and busy with assigned chores, she had none; only those that she gave herself; those that if remained unfinished by the cocktail hour would not affect anyone. There was always tomorrow.

And today the promise was made again: no booze; no cigarettes. And the empty longing began after the caffeine of her morning coffee had lost its power. Exercise and a walk with the dogs, smelling the roses, so to speak, she skipped to music from her headphones, not caring what the passerby may think.

Even before nightfall, the craving began. And she filled it with food. She found one lonely beer in the fridge. It tasted good. She chewed Nicorette gum, sloshed the brown liquid down slowly, and once again began to cry.

CHAPTER 17

The Camper Pee and Zorro

> ♪ I'm in the mood for love
> Simply because you're near me ♪
>
> *I'm in the Mood for Love*
> Jimmy McHugh and Dorothy Fields, 1937

Six hours later in an early morning fog, I reread my pitiful masterpiece and holding the key down, turned the words a light blue and hit *delete*. Good God, how much longer must you submit your readers to such bullshit? Until you *get over it*.

I returned to bed with an ice cold wash cloth over my swollen eyes and tickled Brute's tummy while I waited for the coffee to drip. Before passing out last night, I had neglected to prepare the coffeemaker and set the timer.

My morning scratch, Bill Nob *On The News*, alerted me to an interesting question regarding a suicide bombing in a Russian airport, where the thirty-something Arab's head was found. "Does the head get blown away on impact? Or does it fall off when the body explodes and there's no neck to hold it on?"

It was time to shine: Call time for *Desperate Housewives* nine a.m. As I tossed skirts and shirts onto the bed, I found myself swearing. Preparing the requested wardrobe—a chore that should have been done last night—for a day on set as a background actor is always a maddening chore; but in my morning-after nauseous state, it was off the chart. "Wear one outfit and bring two more. No black, no red, no white. The actors will be wearing shades of green, so don't bring any green," rung in my ears like a threat from the National Republican Party.

Do you want four more years of Obama?
Contribute now or forever hold your peace.

One chiding from a wardrobe lady could mean I'd never work again.

"I can't fucking button anything and I'll be damned if I'm going to be stuck in that corset all day!" I bellowed a temper-tantrum at little Brute, buried somewhere under a free-for-all of cotton, knits, and polyester.

Yes, the *corset curse* is selectively put on ladies who have traded in sex and cigarettes for ice cream, peanuts, and wine-in-a-box. A one-piece boned and beige contraption that slips on like a wet bathing suit, under the crotch are three small metal hooks-and-eyes. If you undo them to pee, you will be in a panic when the assistant director bangs on the porta potty to ask what's taking you so long in there. My hooks are always safely in place while I do the *camper pee* pull with my right hand and the toilet paper grab with my left. There are times when the teeth come into play. If you can stretch the crotch over and under your bum securely, wiping is less stressful.

Choosing a camel pencil skirt, a burgundy surplice-wrap sleeveless top, and a navy blue long-sleeved flowing cover up, I wiggled the corset up. Up and over the corset, the pantyhose punishment came next. And, yes, they come down before sitting on the toilet, way down to make room for the camper pee slide to the right. (Lefties do the opposite.) Now perspiring, I dressed my Mae West body—always hoping that someone will come on over and see me sometime—zipped up my tan boots, and prayed that I would pass through the wardrobe-check parade without having to change into either of my other two outfits; both belonging to a much slimmer gal, whom I missed very much.

Foolish was I to have altered my favorite clothes to fit the nuanced body of a woman in love. Ali found me at one hundred seventy-three pounds and left me at one hundred fifty-five. He always said he liked me a bit chunkier; more to shake, rattle, and roll, I suppose. I was inching my way to pleasing him again.

My location instructions found me at the Burbank Town Center Mall parking structure, where a white van collected the background artists. Next stop the parking lot of Henry's Farmers Market next to a CVS

Pharmacy. After waiting in a long line for my voucher, which must be signed off at the end of the shoot in the same long line, I was directed to another long line for wardrobe inspection. My wardrobe bag over one arm and my stomach clenched under the strain of girdled meaty flesh, the handsome feminine guy waived me on with a toss of his hand and a "Terrific!" Whew, I made it through.

After dropping off my garment bag on the back of a white plastic chair under the canvas tent at extra's *holding*, so named because background extras are held there against their will until told to *head to set*, I searched out the coffee wagon.

A selection of sweet flavored creamers were set out along the side of the caterer's truck, and it was there that Pablo approached me and offered to share his three-egg omelet filled dry with teeny crumbles of ham. Pablo and I had first brushed shoulders a few weeks ago at the Shakey's Pizza Parlor location shoot. Apparently, our faces had not made it to the little screen, so there was no chance that an avid *Desperate Housewives* fan would recognize us; thus we had been booked again.

"Can't we go back to the omelet man and beg for a little cheese?" I teased him.

Pablo is tall, in great shape, a Latino with Mayan features, who enjoys talking, talking about Pablo. Naturally, his hair is thick and dark and delicious. He's the perfect specimen of the forty-something male who, due to the actions of others, just missed success. Pablo has slept through his life embracing sideswipes with fortune. He is a dancer, a choreographer, an actor, and an entrepreneur. He shares an eight-hundred-dollar a month apartment with an older woman who is, of course, just a friend, a friend who works from noon to midnight at a drug rehabilitation center.

"My apartment is nearby," he graciously informs me in his quaint Guatemalan accent.

"Any cheese over there?"

"You like to hide your sexuality behind your humor," he psychoanalyses my dietetic desires.

"Is that so?"

"Today you are mine, Chiquita."

"Well, I'm not going anywhere."

"The last time we met our fingers and toes were frozen."

Yes, it had been a cloudy cold evening when first we met and I never thought about you ever again.

"We should play together later this afternoon. They are shooting only two scenes today. We should be wrapped by noon."

The prospect of *playing* with the ladies' man of lower Burbank flipped a bit of the switch, but then I remembered I was wearing a bulletproof vest.

"Come dance with me," he coaxed and steered me onto the asphalt dance floor. "I sing, too."

In a Dean Martin clutch, Pablo wooed me with Latin rhythms.

♫ Come sway with me ♫

"Nice voice, sir."

His hips urging me, Pablo did the dirty, scrunching his pelvis into my armored pubic bone. "Don't be shy. The morning is young."

In a parking lot outside a farmers market, the morning clouds parted and a ray of sunshine danced on our samba. Pablo pulled me in and twirled me out, all the while chanting his list of accomplishments, in between a deep throated chorus of "Come Fly With Me." He has been in this movie and that for many years, as an extra of course. He's been an alien on *Star Trek*. It is then I notice he has interesting ears; the round ones that stick out just a bit, like that of a Down syndrome child. His almond-shaped dark eyes are filmy and empty. He sends all his money to his long-suffering elderly Madre in South America. He bemoans Hollywood, how he has been used and abused. He cannot sleep, he says.

When the assistant director chooses a dozen extras to follow him into the market, excluding the samba dancers, hand in hand we hurry through the doors of CVS. Inside Pablo purchases two boxes of sleeping pill capsules. Buy two; fifty-percent off the second box. I am out of toothpaste. At the checkout counter, Pablo offers to buy my toothpaste, so that later in the relationship I will be obligated to buy new tires for his car, which I assume is a beat up Toyota Corolla four-door. But he is so charming, so very animated, so demanding to watch, I allow Pablo to include the toothpaste and puzzle at how easily I have become indebted to him.

The production assistant does not see us as a shopping couple; we are called into the market separately. Inside I am flabbergasted at the bounty set before me. Rows of wooden tray kiosks toppled with the greens, oranges, reds, and purples of nature's very best. In this open barn without rising shelves to spoil the view, from the cheese and knockwurst case, Pablo waves and whispers with a wink to me across the aisle, "Last shot of the day and then you are all mine." I must tell Alexandra that my hearing is excellent, if not clairvoyant.

I'm blown away by the selection of bread in glass cases. Marcia Cross as Bree Van de Camp is somewhere behind me pushing a shopping cart, but I'm not allowed to look that way, so I have no idea what the plot is, what this scene is all about, or what the actors are saying.

"Reset. Back to one," an assistant director calls out and I walk back six steps. Pablo is waving again, but I can't make out what he is saying. The reading of lips is a skill I picked up in the courtroom, but not from twenty feet away.

"Background action," the A.D. calls out and I walk forward six steps along the bakery aisle until I hear *cut*. Pablo is waiving. There's something magical about unexpected attention. The layers we cover ourselves in slowly fall away and we're waving back.

The A.D. repeats again and again *reset, back to one, background action*, and in less than an hour we are wrapped and lined up again to have our vouchers signed, assuring that the correct amount of wages will be paid.

His apartment at the end of a long second floor terrace is red and green and ethnic. Dark furniture and patterned rugs; a sheepskin drapes the brown leather couch. The sweet smell of lavender catches me off guard. She must use a plug-in. The windows are spotless, although trimmed in dreadful rusted aluminum. The white walls seem to be freshly painted. An oil painting in sky blues and olive greens of a wooden sailboat nestled in a peaceful inlet along a stonewall is centered over the bricked fireplace. His home is clean, calm, and non-threatening. There is not one *Hustler* magazine on the marble coffee table.

"Make yourself at home. I'll go get out of this extra wardrobe!" He raises his arms in anticipation and disappears down a hallway.

"May I use the bathroom?" I ask after him.

"Sure. I'll be right out," he assures me and then stops before turning into a doorway. "Hey, do you like Johnny Depp?"

"But of course."

The armored crotch tugged to the right, I relieve myself. The bathroom is beige on beige, but for the white sink cabinet. We are synchronized: the beige walls, the beige toilet, and my beige corset. The closed shower curtain of cascading autumn flowers on beige gives not a hint of alarm. I choose not to open it; the sight of dripped and caked shampoo on the faucet may turn me off.

Reaching across with my left hand, the toilet paper holder to my right is empty. Where is the toilet paper? It's behind me on the lid. Not letting go of the corset crotch, I twist and clumsily grab at the spool, sending it unraveling toward the bathroom door. It's now a shake and run to fetch the damned thing. Holding the tissue spool in my left hand, using my front teeth I unwrap the sheets one by one. This is undoubtedly a deleted scene from *Eyes Wide Shut.*

I enter the living room to find Zorro, complete with cape, eye mask, toreador pants, leather gloves, and knee high laced up boots. The ruffled shirt is amazing.

"Do you tango?" Zorro asks and draws a dramatically wild *Z* across the air.

"But of course," I answer.

To the tune of "Have You Ever Loved a Woman," his hand cups my tightened waist and dips me to the floor, nearly breaking my back. Immediately, he swooshes me into his arms and then releases me into a throw. I counter. He passes and kneels before me, his gloved hand reaching out to me. I twirl and land on his thigh. Our faces on point, our eyes connect, our lips tremble.

♪ You've gotta breathe her, really taste her . . . ♪

"Pablo, isn't that the theme song from the movie *Don Juan DeMarco* in which Johnny Depp's character really believes he's Don Juan, the world's greatest lover?"

"Does it *really* matter?"

He pulls away and as if I am a feather, he swoops me up and into his arms, the ruffles on his shirt tickling my chin.

"Can you keep the mask on? Let me pretend you're my lost lover and you shall love as you have never loved before. Why, you'll see your unborn children in my eyes."

"Of course. I will give you fantasy wings so that you may fly."

"Sounds good, Pablo."

Fully aware of the underwear curse, I point to the sword he has leaned against the front door. "You may be needing that." And he carries me to the bed.

Who needs a Persian charmer, when one can have all this—and a full days' union wages for four hours of work too?

At the lineup in the parking lot of CVS, he passes by me, as if I'm just a woman he used to know, and rushes to have his voucher signed off. Pablo unmasked maneuvers his way to the front of the line and climbs into a van, the only van, and I wait for it to return empty fifteen minutes later. Deposited at the parking garage, I am not disappointed, yet surprised that Pablo has not waited for me there. I smile a mischievous smile and hang my garment bag on the inside of my little Scion, which begs to be washed. From inside I am enchanted to see a large *Z* fingered into the dust of the windshield. Romance with a non-union extra in a moldy ghetto apartment somewhere in Burbank will have to wait until another day.

Home again, I watch myself in the mirror of my sliding closet doors. Shooing away my canine groupies, I slice off my corset unleashing my deserted sexuality, which beyond the additional fold in my stomach is getting harder and harder to find and to shave. Yep, I got a lot, a lot of what I got, and what I got's all mine. Come up and see me sometime.

Chapter 18

The Paramount Lot, Competition Zumba, and The Fable

♩ The headaches, the heartaches. . . ♩

There's No Business Like Show Business
Irving Berlin

My radio clock alarm began another day on Cahuenga Boulevard. I covered my head and slept until eight o'clock through the fumbling and the mumbling and the incessant reminders that I need to replace my mattress with a Sleep Number adjustable bed and treat my hair loss with Regenixs.

> Get up, you shameful alcoholic. At nine o'clock sharp, the flamboyant manager of Overpriced Homes Realty has ordered all salespersons to attend a mini-seminar on foreclosure and short sale stats. That means *you*.
>
> You can have your bagel and cream cheese there. Following the meeting, you have the Tuesday Brokers' Caravan, which will have you jumping in and out of your embarrassingly dirty car and in and out of newly listed million dollar mansions throughout Hancock Park to see just how the other half lives. At noon you have a *meetup* doubles match with a female Korean sex therapist at the Plummers Park tennis courts. And don't forget your *Groupon* fifty-percent-off Zumba class at two o'clock on Hollywood Boulevard. Oh, and tonight is bowling league.

> The President, whom I begrudgingly admit voting for, is destroying our country and you can do nothing to stop it, so busy yourself with mundane chores and unimportant appointments. Islamic extremism heralded by The Muslim Brotherhood wins over dictatorships—the intent to Islam-a-size the entire world—while camels and heavily bearded virile men with whips run through the streets of Cairo. I just threw that in lest you've lost your feel-good morning twitching fantasy. But because you have slept through my six-thirty wakeup radio talk show, you do not—I repeat—you do not have time to scratch it. Now get in the shower.

My wet head wrapped movie-star style in a lavender towel; I dripped all the way to the cell phone still plugged into the charger on the nightstand.

"Can you make an interview at Paramount today?" Kristin calls from the Sandi Alessi extras casting line.

"What time?"

"Ten-fifteen. A photo still, SAG rate, a murder victim to hang from a clothesline as part of *The Girl with the Dragon Tattoo*. You were picture-picked because of your 1950's shorter hairstyle."

Realizing that I had not updated my pictures at Sandi Alessi since 2006, I informed Kristin, "My hair is almost to my shoulders."

"They can fix it." The casting office was not losing face or a commission because of the current length of my hair.

Tiptoeing through the back door and straight to the bagel basket, I glanced over my sunglasses into the crowded room. The real estate office was spotted like a poorly-bred, aggressive Dalmatian: agents in black suits and white shirts leaned forward from their office chairs spellbound at the news that sales volume was up, but prices down, prepared to leap teeth bared onto the leg of every downtrodden underwater homeowner within a five-minute drive of Hancock Park.

An unknown agent, an effeminate young Asian man with slicked-back hair, had taken over my desk. I leaned against the wall balancing my coffee and creamed bagel. Graph after graph slid by from the projector as the manager in supervisorial red bowtie read to us the words we could see for ourselves. I escaped to the bathroom to tidy up and paper towel the cream cheese from my teeth. In my all black winter outfit complete with a string of pearls, known only to me as my Hasidic Jew Open House Costume, I snuck out the back door and hurried away passed the Mercedes, the Jaguar, and the Range Rover in the *Only For Successful Realtors* parking lot to my nifty Scion parked two blocks away. The reality is that most the realtors at OPH Realty lease their cars, do not own property, and live in rented apartments provided by stupefied boastful parents living in Hoboken, New Jersey, who wait in hopeful ignorance for their child to become a highly paid television star on Bravo's *Million Dollar Listing*.

Entering the Lemon Grove @ Van Ness parking garage across from my assigned entry gate at Paramount Studios, I handed the man in the window seven dollars cash in return for a teeny paper receipt which must be returned stamped by production in order for me to receive the seven dollars cash back upon my exit. The very top of the garage is reserved for background actors, so up and round and up and round I go, my tires making that eerie screeching sound at each turn, until the car is out of the shade and into the blazing sun of January in Los Angeles, while Chicago is under snow and more on the way.

From the open level I can see to the east what a young Alexandra and I had coined as *The Emerald City* during our bygone days of long drives together into the city, when the sighting of the skyscraping silhouette of downtown told us we were almost there and brought an end to the *how many more miles* whining question.

The jolly guard at the Lemon Grove entrance returns my driver's license and sends me through the turnstile with a map. From the *You Are Here* he has penned a squiggly line through the entire width of the lot to Stage 25. I turn to question why I have reported here, to the far east side of the sixty five acres, when it is apparent that Stage 25 is on the west side, the proper parking lot being on Gower Street. I swallow my boorish inquisition; I am just an extra who knows her place in the Hollywood caste system. The guard kindly wishes me a *good day on set*.

In my buckled knee high boots and long black knit pencil skirt, I wander through memory lane at a calm pace. The sun is beating down and I don't want to be seen perspiring at the interview. I've been on this lot many times before. I know the way, which is a great feeling, and paying no attention to the lot map in my hand, I take a wrong turn. The whir of a skill saw and the clean scent of sawdust alerts me to be mindful of my steps as I pass quickly by craftsmen scurrying in and out of the woodworking mill to a pallet of new wood delivered by fork lift.

Ah, there they are: Stage 4, Stage 2, Stage 1, where *Nip/Tuck* came alive: the weird television series about two sexually active plastic surgeons and their sexually active patients, and where I was treated to increased union wages as Jacqueline Bisset's stand-in for the entirety of Season 4. As a stand-in, I was part of *Team Two* and part of the crew, a moderately huge step up from a non-distinguishable background actor. I was not filmed, but took Ms. Bisset's position in front of the camera while the gaffers, grips, and best boys erected walls and placed the lighting for *Team One,* the actors, before they were called in for rehearsal. If her wardrobe for the scene was royal blue, they dressed me in a royal blue t-shirt. If she was to straddle a man on a bed, I was to straddle the man's stand-in, always a pillow between our privates.

Those were the good times, times before I was turned into a slobbering tearful sex addict in need of a fix, times when my one compelling desire was to earn enough wages to qualify for my health insurance—not to yearn for the spotting of a shaggy Persian slut slowly cruising by my front gate in a black SUV impatiently looking for a parking place.

Jacqui liked me being her stand-in; we are brunettes of the same age, if not of the same weight. One morning over coffee and red vines at the crafty cart, she shared with me the crushing decision to end her eleven-year relationship with a much younger man because he would not marry her. Two bites into the vine, red dye on her teeth, she began to cry. I guess there is not a Hollywood cast system protocol for female frailty and certainly not a posted sign: *Don't Cry in Front of your Stand-in.*

Passing through New York Street, which is a cluster of facades replicating an older Brooklyn-type neighborhood, a set painter on a yellow ladder is freshening the red on a store front door. Otherwise, today the street is a ghost town.

It was from that very stoop Beryl, one of my very few senior cohorts, walked with me nonchalantly around the corner on "background, action." Over and over again we mimicked two older women strolling the street deep in silent *mouthed* conversation until from some mysterious place we heard "reset." In winter hat and mittens, I huddled in that doorway to stay out of the early morning cold and smelled sausages broiling on a stainless steel barbeque at craft services just around the corner, hidden from the cameras. I pretended to window-shop on this little make-believe street in my black and white herringbone cape, a favorite piece among the wardrobe czars. I ran and stumbled in a herd of teachers along the pavement fronting the school steps. We chased Chris as in *Everybody Hates Chris,* while the real Chris Rock looked on.

Right on time I stand in the outer doorway of Stage 25 on Avenue C and wait for the red light to turn off, signaling that the camera has stopped rolling and that I may enter. A sound studio is an ominous soundproof garage or more precisely a hangar, where entire homes, neighborhoods, hospitals, and cities are built within the four walls. I won't pretend to be an expert on making one's perilous way through the dark maze, but be careful to watch for dangling ropes, cords and wires, duffle bags, gaffer tape, and just about anything else you can trip on. It is here on Stage 25 that Kelsey Grammar had double luck with *Cheers* and then *Frasier,* where Lucille Ball took another stab without Desi as a widow on *The Lucy Show.*

A young man named Allen comes to my aid, studies me, and leads me to a golf cart.

"Are you Hasidic?" he asks kindly.

"No, I had a real estate meeting this morning."

"Oh." Allen is an assistant director, maybe a 2nd, 3rd, or 4th A.D. in the production system pecking order. Probably not an A.D. at all, but a production assistant, a P.A., because he is the one sent to pick up a loathsome background actor. He is heavy on the pedal. Wow, this is more fun than the Snow White ride at Disneyland. The old broad beams, her bouncing curls flying away from her face, as she is royally driven and delivered to base camp for her interview as a murder victim sprawled over a clothesline in *The Girl with the Dragon Tattoo.*

Base camp is set up—the wardrobe wagon, the honeywagon, so called due to the honey-colored excrement that is removed when emptying the holding tanks, the makeup and hair wagon, the privileged star wagons, and the production office—in front of the water tank tower rising over the lot. The tower is painted with the recognizable Paramount Studios mountain and stars emblem, and I wonder if it has been erected there for historic atmosphere or actually filled with emergency water. Paramount Studios is a small city with its own power generators, a fire department, police department, and medic station, so why not its own independent water storage?

My arrival stymies a bit of my Hollywood starlet buzz. After not being able to find my name, another male P.A. shakes his head in disbelief, finally checks me off a list, and tosses me a union voucher for the interview. Because an interview takes up my valuable time as an actor, I will receive thirty-eight dollars just for showing up.

"Are you Jewish? Can you take off your wig for the interview?"

"No, I'm Protestant. Baptist, actually. And I'm not wearing a wig. I had a realtor meeting this morning."

"Sorry. I was told to look for a brunette woman with a short 50s hairdo. Your clothes remind me of my girlfriend's mom and she always wears a wig."

"Whatever for? Does she have cancer?"

"No, it's the Hasidic Jew culture. Hair is sexual, so they believe it should be covered up," he stuttered.

"Well, that explains the funny hairdos on a few of my realtor associates, but does not explain why the Muslims hate the Jews."

"They do?" he quizzed.

"According to Islam, Jews are the reason for all evil in the world. But seems to me the two have a lot in common."

"Oh, I get it. The head scarf verses the wig thing."

"Yes, that hijab thing. And, of course, impudent machismo men," I dared to lay the sexist card on the table. Will his girlfriend's father ever really let him marry her? I think not, not until he owns a car dealership in Beverly Hills.

After my querulous pass by the sign-up sheet guy, a rather touchy-feely circle of creative types surrounds me.

The young pierced and purple braided one asks the important question of the day. "Are you Jewish?"

"No, actually, I'm a writer and the author of *The Year I Learned to Text* and—" I belched out in totally inappropriate speak.

"You look familiar," a fairy dusted man in a khaki cotton suit surmised and squinted at me.

"Yes, and your hair's too long," the third in the artistically frantic trio despaired.

"I'm familiar because I've worked on this lot many, many times. I practically have a postal address on New York Street. Or you may have caught one of my daring commercials: Andrionik chair lady, caring emergency room nurse, muffin mooching mischief maker, basement boozer—"

"Oh, sure, okay," the khaki man cut me off. "She has to be nondescript and you're a football field away from that. Where is the other lady?"

Jumping out of her golf cart seat is Lady no. 2. She is about my age, smaller build, and much shorter hair. When is my competition ever not of a smaller build?

Standing in the sun outside the production trailer, the interview begins.

"Are either one of you squeamish about portraying a woman brutally beaten, raped, and left to die with her arms draped over a clothesline?"

We answer in unison, one for all and all for one: Hell no! It would be cool to be forever implanted in a ghastly scene and to have our picture posted on the police *murder victim board* to be reviewed over and over again during the movie.

No. 2 and I hug and jump in the air and almost kiss each other on the mouth.

"Is the fact you will be heavily smeared with blood going to be a problem for either one of you?"

Hell, no!

Not having familiarity whatsoever with this *book-to-movie*, I apparently ask the stupidest question ever posed on the warm asphalt of Paramount Studios. "Is this the reenactment of a real murder?"

Laughter is let go all around. "Hell no! And you're already dead before the movie even starts."

The girl with the purple braids makes the decision to let me go. "We're going with shorter hair."

No. 2 almost kissed Ms. Braids on the mouth and, of course, immediately shunned me, the loser of the day.

No more windswept golf cart runs down memory lane for me. Half way across the lot on my way to the Lemon Grove parking lot, I remember my seven-dollar receipt. Hoofing it back to the gentile P.A., irrationally dating a Hasidic Jew Princess, for a red stamped validation is humbling at the very least. At the very most, I may have burned an additional twenty-five calories.

Skipping the tennis doubles meetup and an unwanted sex therapy session, I headed north on the 101 to Studio City and the Sandy Alessi Extras Casting office on Ventura Boulevard. There I smiled at a chubby tattooed fella behind the camera and left a ten-dollar bill on the counter. Net income for the day: $28 minus three quarters for the parking meter.

Heading back to the car, I stopped to glance into a pet store window. I can see some sort of hay material piled along the glass, but no puppies.

"Don't buy a dog from this store," a female voice violently warned me. I turned around to find a redhead in a flounced white shirt and alligator boots reprimanding my innocent window-shopping.

"Bad puppy mill puppies, perhaps?"

"The breeders practice forced caged breeding," she huffed.

The picture inside my head was hedonistic: little fluffy paws pushing down on little fluffy ears, little fluffy thighs pulsating against little fluffy rear ends, little fluffy growls whispering sweet fluffy nothings. Brute would be in unneutered heaven.

"Do they have forced senior citizen caged breeding as well?"

"What's wrong with you? This is serious."

I'm horny as hell, lonely, forsaken, and lovesick. "I was just thinking of my little Maltese, Brute. My daughter purchased him from a pet store; donation nine-hundred dollars."

"He's the product of forced copulation," she hammered at me, her tie-dyed peasant skirt flirting with danger. "He's most assuredly anti-social, violent, and distrustful."

"No, actually, he's a better person than you are right now."

And I made it to the car before the meter flicked over to *violation*.

The phone sounded and Mom was on the other end.

"Julie, you won't believe my water bill for last month."

"Well, give me a try."

"Three hundred and eight dollars."

"For the house?" I exclaimed.

"No, for the cabin. And I haven't been up there for months."

"Mom, you may have a leak."

"What? No, I am not going to wear those senior diapers. I'm fine with paper towels."

"What are we talking about? Do you have your hearing aids in?"

"Just a minute."

I'm sitting in my car watching the meter flick to a bright, beeping red. "Mom? Mom?"

"I should put my aids in, but the batteries aren't any good."

Slowly and loudly, I offer my unsolicited advice, "Call the water company and have them meet you at the cabin."

"I don't know anyone at the water company."

"I'm not accusing you of anything. Calm down. Call them to complain about the bill, that you need help finding the problem, the reason for the high bill. They should come out."

"I don't want anyone coming inside the cabin."

"I can't promise I can come up this week. I won't know if I'm free until the night before when my agent or call-in service notifies me—"

"What are you talking about? I can take care of my own stuff. Don't you worry about it. Don't you worry about me!"

"I'm getting off the phone now. I have to get to my Zumba class."

"Who? I haven't had anyone named Lou at the cabin. The last man there was the German brick mason. He was married, so I stopped seeing him."

I made a mad dash into the house and changed into Lycra, a ripped t-shirt and tennis shoes and trotted my fat ass up Cahuenga to Hollywood Boulevard west to the hidden doorway of the Stella Adler Studio of Acting, just passed the Snow White diner and just before the famous corner of Hollywood and Highland. Almost a mile-and-a-half under my belt, I climbed the stairs to the dance studio, where from behind a wooden counter, a lovely muscle-bound ballet dancer took my discount coupon and my fifteen dollars. I signed a no-lawsuit waiver and entered a torture chamber. There, I took in my young, deliciously thin, exuberant, confident classmates. I made the ridiculous decision to keep up with them at any cost.

The South American beat tossed me from knee to knee, as I swayed and jumped at every slap of the drum.

"Please do the class at your own pace," the tribal leader advised, which simply gave me license to protest by belligerently bouncing all over the goddamned wood floor. After a long, grueling fifteen minutes, my hair was stuck to my neck like honey on a spoon. My headscarf was saturated and the sweat streamed into my mascara-laden lashes. My reflection in the ghastly wall-to-wall mirror of shame was that of an overweight, over-aged woman out of her element and in a losing competition with the Rockettes at Radio City Music Hall. While I endeavored to revive seventy-eight-year-old Chita Rivera's role in *Westside Story*, my legs trembled, my knees ached, and my eyes burned. The flab under my arms wriggled and waggled, but kept perfect time to the music. I kept dancing until the last encouraging words from the slave master were spoken.

"See you all next week."

I walked all the way home, my tail between my legs, my right knee throbbing, and my ego crushed. Perhaps low-impact aerobics, such as scuba diving and darts, would be a better choice for a woman whose heart and mind are still in their forties, while her sixty-two-year-old body refuses to keep up.

At bowling league I complained about and used my Zumba abused knee as a cover for my rotten scores. I also used bad boy Jason to exonerate my dating foul ups.

"So the Jew wanted you to rush at him for oral?"

"He hinted at that."

"Would you do that thang, if—"

"Well, when I care about someone, yes. I'm not afraid of the snake."

"He was inappropriate, totally. It takes me three dates to get to breast suckling," Jason shared and leaned in to hear more. "So you're telling me about this guy in gold chains and a wife beater shirt, and you don't like him just because he's Armenian?"

"No, not at all," I attempt to clarify.

"You are such a racist, Julie. Get over yourself."

Jared steps into the conversation. "What guy with gold chains and a wife beater shirt? Are you dating an Armenian?"

"Why is it when you say it, it's not a racist comment, but when I say it, I'm arrested?"

I ordered hot dogs and fries all around and Jason helped himself. The protein must have kicked in, because in the last game he just missed a perfect three hundred score by one strike.

Almost at the stroke of midnight, as I turned the key in the old wooden gate, Jason sent me a text.

> Tuesday, February 8, 2011; 11:58p JASON: Thank you for the wiener. I owe u one.

And if he thinks I will ever respond to that, he is mistaken.

As I toss and turn, my mind scripts on the ceiling another thought, a joke perhaps, What did Allah say to the last successful Muslim suicide bomber? "I apologize, but we've just run out of virgins." Not very original, but I laugh. And then my hand finds its place inside my satin pajama bottoms, my stomach warm and trembling. Ali is next to me, his nakedness crawling about me, his voice soft and relaxing, which is obviously a distortion of our reality. Allah continued.

> "But shrouded shyly in the corner is a lusty romantic, our Julie. She's plump, but proud, and in no way a virgin. Be sweet to her. She loved a Muslim brother unconditionally. She will make a good wife for you here in the Garden of Everlasting Bliss."

***

Sony Studios in Culver City takes up the entire southeast corner of Washington Boulevard at Overland Avenue. My right knee now swollen into the size of a cantaloupe, I am driving over there today; call time four-thirty. After the gas man shrugged at the discovery of a leak under the house and the termite man shrugged at the discovery of a few termites—"If I see one, you can bet there's thousands"—I took off to never-never-land to play pretend on a short-lived episodic titled *Mad Love*. My instructions from the Central Casting info line: eveningwear, no black, no red, no white; enter at the Overland gate. Exhausted from homeownership and packed again into the corset, I am sent by wardrobe to change in the extras changing tent, and there I meet a very quiet, dismal woman wearing an unattractive *Brady Bunch* wig, which she continually pulls down around her ears.

I've been very good at not blurting out my Muslim romance miseries to strangers, neighbors, gas company employees, or termite inspectors. But for some ungodly reason, I am sitting in holding, pinched into high heels provided by wardrobe, spilling my guts to this timid woman. After reciting to her the entirety of *The Year I Learned to Text; Why Am I Having Sex with a Muslim in My Basement?* I headed full speed into the unwritten, but diary-riddled, Part Two.

"He said he couldn't love me. That he's only to love Allah."

"That is not true. I am an Iranian Muslim and I will tell you an Islamic fable and you will listen."

I'm kind of figuring that if she's sat in silent repose listening to my pathetic tale and she's doing extra work on a sitcom in an evil Western Civilization motion picture and television studio, where the background actors are going to be dancing at a party, that she's probably a moderate, Americanized Muslim, if not a total apostate.

"I'm all ears, honey," I let her know and kick off my shoes under the table.

"A man goes to Allah and asks, 'How can I please you?' And Allah answers, 'Be good to your wife.' The man returns to Allah and asks again, 'How can I please you, oh Great One?' And Allah answers, 'Be good to your wife.' Not believing that simply being good to his wife will get him into Paradise, he returns to Allah and asks him again, 'How can I please you, Master?' And Allah responds, 'Be good to your wife and you will greatly please me.'"

Her telling of the fable started the tears and it seemed I could not stop, even with two dozen men and women dressed in dark suits and satins staring at me.

"You need to see a psychiatrist, preferably a Muslim Iranian of good moral standing. You have been damaged. The man is a fraud. He may not be a Muslim at all. We do not marry more than one wife. We do not allow sex with children. He is a crazy-maker who has damaged you. How you—or any woman—can give their bodies and their hearts without total commitment is what causes all of this pain."

"Please give me your number so that I can invite you to my book signing. It would mean a lot to me. Leave that uncomfortable wig at home and wear a hijab." I pulled out a pen and small glittered notebook. "There will be plenty of wine and food."

"If I leave my house without my husband or an uncle, except to work, I will be placed in a pit and stoned. And we do not drink of wine."

"Then bring them, too. I'd love to meet them."

"I'm not allowed to go to evil infidel gatherings and my husband wouldn't be caught dead at one."

✱ ✱ ✱

The estimate for the termite tenting is a neat and tidy two thousand. The plumber will send me a bill for the new gas line. Next door, Barry's roommate, Hugo the Hungarian French chef-to-be, has requested my presence for some kind of boiled chicken in a pot. Randi has turned in her crutches for a quart of gin. And Mr. Song, the conscientious Korean wrought iron man, is designing for the entrance of the bungalow a stately eight-foot tall front gate infused with ivy filigree. To be welded across the top in letters ten-inches high, the two halves coming together to form a half-moon, at my front porch table, we excitedly sketch the unauthorized and copyright infringed pièce de résistance.

HOLLYWOOD

For fifteen hundred dollars, sober or blissfully high, I'll know exactly where I am.

Chapter 19

Poster Beds and Hemingway on a Bun

Investigator Wayne called in with Blondie news.

"She's pissed because I only gave her five thousand towards her new van. But she'd just spent fifteen hundred on a new king size canopy bed for the two of them," he reported.

"The two of them?" I quizzed.

"She sleeps with the kid. Another great way to keep me out of her bed."

"Isn't the *kid* a menstruating teen by now?"

"Hold on a second. The hotline is ringing."

I pictured his obsessively tidy office at the District Attorney's office in downtown San Bernardino. There are no post-its, paper scraps, nor framed pictures of dead parents on his desk; there is a half-eaten bagel, a candy bar wrapper, and a can of diet Coke.

"Sorry about that. Investigations heating up here at murder central."

"And here I am missing out on all the gory courtroom testimony at three dollars a page," I reminisced, my right wrist beginning to throb.

"She also wants a ring and a big house."

"You should call her Christian-morality bluff and marry her. But I warn you that if you do, the sex will go from once a month at your place to zero in your new prestigious million-dollar digs."

"She's the best, most exciting sex I've ever had."

"Thanks, Wayne."

"So what's up with you?"

"Writing book two and stupidly meeting some old Englishman who found me floundering on a free dating site, *Plenty of Fish*," I moaned.

"After seeing him online naked but for a whirling red cape and a pair of Superman undershorts, I actually agreed to a date," I winced.

"Is he taking you to dinner?"

"I'm meeting him for lunch at Venice Beach today. Let's hope he leaves the underwear at home." I glanced up at the clock. "And I'm going to be late."

"Wait. Am I in the second book?"

"Of course."

"Why? My classic wardrobe and bad teeth?"

"No, I am not mentioning your tube socks again. You're in the novel because your monthly affair with a sociopathic whore, who has lived off the kindness of sexual partners for years, is far more interesting than my tedious, tiniest stabs at finding myself another bad boy."

The Santa Monica Freeway is Saturday silent. I left the grunge of my beloved Hollywood and landed on the blue and salty shores of the Pacific Ocean in just twenty minutes. Where have all the commuters gone to that so choke up the lanes from Monday to Friday? Turning into a residential area, I find them, their automobiles lined up neck to neck on the street. I ease my handy compact car into a crevice. I refuse to pay fifteen dollars to park at the Venice Beach boardwalk to meet a man who honestly believes posting ludicrous pictures will tempt me. No, I usually let the perverts come straight to my front porch, which saves me wear and tear on my car, gas money, and time ill spent.

The Armenian posted an underwear picture. I have a dreadful habit of repeating the same mistakes. It's like when I buy a new lipstick. It always looks brownish-burgundy in the store, be it the Macy's counter or the CVS cosmetics aisle, but mysteriously the shade ends up orange on my lips, and I will buy the same damned stick over and over again. Why doesn't a Calvin Klein underwear model send me a photo? So I can make the same mistake—over and over and over.

Strolling an enjoyable ten-blocks on Ocean Front Walk which fronts shops on one side and the sand, bikeways, and grassy knolls on the other —you can't see the waves hit the sand unless you walk up and over— I pass unnoticed through the bohemian characters on my timid way to the Sidewalk Café. Dressed to meld into the hippie atmosphere, my hand-painted gray and lavender long cotton vest wisps about my tall boots. It's a twinge chilly today; a refreshing change in temperature and a chance to wear another flab-forgiving outfit.

The tourist shops are open to the air; their steel doors will be brought down and locked in place at closing time. T-shirts, string-tied cotton shorts, and sweat pants, all labeled *Venice Beach,* swing clothes-pinned from ropes in the gentle breeze. Calling out to me from across the paddleball courts crowded with unconventional locals who have come to people watch when they are the people being watched, a thin bald man in yoga diapers invites me to come on in for a medical marijuana card. I continue on my way.

At the café, colorful bikes are lined up like kiosks of seasonal fruit ripe for the taking. Under the red and white striped awning in a lineup of hungry tourists, I spy an older man with neatly-groomed gray hair peering at me over prescription lenses that have turned dark in the sun. Through yellow teeth outlined in brown, Jaz calls out to me. He has a giant long lensed camera dangling from his neck.

"Sorry I'm late. I stopped to renew my medical marijuana card," I joked.

The venue is a loud greasy spoon with exemplary architecture. The patio for people watching is the clamored-for spot, but we are seated inside where sculpted towering columns support a domed ceiling. Over our red and white checked tablecloth, Jaz is eager to order. On the plastic menu, I find the *Hemingway* advertised as "An author's delight! A choice filet mignon written on a toasted bun with lettuce, tomato and onion and served with steak fries, $16.95." I order it to feed my writer and my already disappointed research scientist, who searches for a cure for the broken heart by putting another foot under the microscope.

Over the excessive chatter and utensil to plate clatter, my blind date breaks forth in excited conversation. His thick lenses now cleared, I can see his blue-gray intense stare.

"I have one, too," he proudly announces and pulls from a pocket in his worn gray corduroy pants a neat brown wallet. He fingers through credit cards and pulls out a green plastic card.

"I was kidding, Jaz," I let him down.

"Oh."

"So what is so painful that you need medication?"

"Arthritis, two hip surgeries, a knee surgery, and backaches," he proudly announces.

I could still be home in the basement with a wheezing, sneezing Iranian hypochondriac if only I'd known this was going to be my future.

"So you just kind of sit around and light up to ease the pain?" I comforted him.

"I mix it with tobacco. I'm growing my own in the backyard. It's allowed—I mean it's legal. Harvest soon. The government has a handbook on how to grow your own."

"It's always nice to know where my tax dollars go, Jaz."

His lovely English accent accounted for; I'm feeling the pain. "Oh, waitress!"

Feeling my pain, she returned spit-spot with plenty of celery and green olives in a spicy vodka Bloody Mary.

Jaz droned on about his ex-wife who liked to go braless, his LSD experiences, and his slobbering Bull Dog. Through the window, I watch a street performer in leotards break empty bottles of beer and wine into a metal trash can and then place the shards into a pyramid in front of a wooden chair. He is mic'd and asks the crowd to gather in closer, so he will not get fined for crowding the sidewalk. He steps up and onto the chair and removes his beach thongs.

"I'm sorry. What were you saying?" I ask as two bare feet bound into a pile of glass. The crowd disperses. He gathers a few coins and walks away triumphantly unscathed.

"So you're retired too?"

"Not exactly," I answer.

I have a job: the get-over-it career, and Jaz is not helping me one bit. "I'm a retired court stenographer, dabble as a realtor, do some background work, and occasionally book a commercial."

"I'm on Social Security Disability and I get some alimony from my ex," he proudly announces.

Jaz drops his doggie bag into his car in the fifteen-dollar parking lot and invites me to go with him to deliver the half-eaten burger to his

Bull Dog. I decline. He points to the back seat of his rusty sedan. "I cleaned out the back in case we wanted to neck."

He walks me to my car, which of course is lost somewhere in a maze of twisting, turning little streets.

"I like you," he proudly announces at the end of our little blue Scion hunt.

Of course you do. Although my right knee is inflamed, I am young, vibrant, and sexy; fun and funny. I glow when my Persian lover is inside of me and my body is flawless as he pulls away to gaze at me for just a moment and to proudly announce that he's going to buy me a Jaguar. And in the midst of my delicious delusion, I let the frog kiss me. I am pressed into marijuana-tobacco-burger breath. No lips, no tongue, just a hollow pit of brown and yellow.

I hightail it to Ocean Park Boulevard and the El Torito restaurant east of 26th Street, where in front of a big screen, I peacefully sip a Grand Marnier margarita with a salted rim and watch Mexican soccer players bang the ball off their heads. I can almost smell the sweat pouring from their testosterone bulging balls.

I raise my glass to Natasha, who signals Rocky to fly down from the ceiling fan. "You said to watch for Superman."

"Dahlink, he von't be vearing a costume. And pleeese stop dating men who impudently flaunt der own fables."

Chapter 20

Antipasto and The Shah of Iran

> ♩ When the moon hits your eye
> Like a big pizza pie ♩
>
> *That's Amore*
> Henry Warren and Jack Brooks

It is February and time to put Cupid out. Unfurled from the bungalow flagpole, a manly pink cherub holding a red bow and arrow invites dark chocolates, wine by a roaring fire, and presents wrapped and tied with curled red and pink ribbon. The most miserably romantic day of the year found me alone at my cabin sweeping pine needles off the deck while I waited for Mother's call. I had driven up to look for the leak. The morning was brisk, but no need for gloves.

Not having brought the laptop, suddenly novel ideas for *Jihad Honeymoon* spontaneously popped into my head, one following the other. The wish that Ali would linger with me by a crackling fire to watch the gentle white downfall paint snowdrifts on the windowsill was never granted; the daydream of the two of us wrapped in lovers' slumber in the loft sleigh bed never came true; the promised silver Jaguar convertible wrapped in a red bow never arrived. But with a clickity-click to the keyboard I could make it all come true. I tossed the broom aside and grabbing a notepad quickly scratched my fantasies into life. A writer must write down her thoughts before they are consumed by short-term memory loss—or a phone call from her agent letting her know she is *on hold* for an Advil pain reliever national commercial. I need to book it in order to qualify for my health insurance before the first of June.

"The man from the water company shut off the water to my toilet, so there's no need for you to come over," Mom called in from the tangerine rotary phone at her cabin in the Valley of the Moon, an undesirable neighborhood east of the lake, up the mountain, and down to Grandmother's house we go.

"Well, I'm here, so let's celebrate Valentine's Day together," I offered with enthusiasm. I was ninety-miles from civilization and three miles from Mother's rustic, charming Pinocchio of a mountain cabin. How hard was she going to make this?

"Hey, listen, the day is getting away from me. I really need to get home before dark."

Home is twenty minutes back down the hill, where the sink faucets in both bathrooms have leaked for years. Her vicious roommate of a cat has a constant water supply. No worries there.

"It's noon. I'm sure we can do lunch and get you back to your car in time," I urged her.

"Don't you love it? The handle was stuck. Three hundred dollars worth of water right down the drain."

"I'll treat."

"You have to laugh. Keep your sense of humor," she babbled on.

"I'll be over in fifteen minutes."

Mom was outside on her flaking redwood porch. As she clutched the railing and maneuvered her stooped shrinking body down the three creaky stairs, I went around and opened the passenger door.

"Did you notice that the tree trunk is pushing into the roof?" she asked, her silver head cocked in a threatening gesture.

"It's been growing into the roof for some time now."

"Well, I had a man come by to give me an estimate on removing it, but he just laughed. 'Let your kids worry about. Why spend a thousand dollars to remove it when you'll be dead and gone by the time it pushes the house over?'"

"And you agreed, of course," I countered.

"Oh, don't you love it? You two will have so much to do after I'm gone."

My sister and I do not agree on much, if anything, but arson is the one option that holds us together.

Taking the Rim of the World Highway, which slides with centrifugal force along the edge of the mountain, to The Original Cottage Family Restaurant induced Mother to a state of paranoia.

"Where are you going?" she frantically questioned me one mile into the four-mile drive.

"An Italian restaurant in Rim Forest."

"Where's Rim Forest? Why are we going to Rim Forest?"

"You've owned your cabin since my son was a year old, Mother. He'll be forty this year. You drive up the mountain from your house all the time. Don't tell me you've never driven beyond the Crestline turnoff before?"

"My husbands always drove."

"You haven't had a husband for twenty years."

The vast valley below beckoned the car to miss a turn at high speed and catapult head down, down, down to its demise, but I hung on tight, resigned to finish out this venomous Valentine's Day.

"They won't have fish and chips," she pouted.

"They have red wine, Mother. All is well."

I ordered the antipasto salad and Mother ordered a large pepperoni pizza.

"Please, please bring garlic bread and a carafe of your finest, cheap house cabernet ASAP," I pleaded with the robust woman in a ruffled apron splattered with marinara sauce.

"We have a burgundy, okay?"

"So how have you been? What have you been up to?" she began her sly inquisition into what she believes to be my sordid, clandestine, sixty-two year old life.

"Writing the second book, auditioning, reading to the kids, taking care of the dogs." Do not tell her anything about Jewish dates, Armenian dates, English dates, or Middle Eastern dried fruits and dates.

"I know you'll be interested in this." She unsnapped her clutch and tossed a neatly excised newspaper article on the table. "I know you're too young to remember, but the same thing that's happening in Egypt today

—you remember that Edgar and I visited the pyramids at Giza during one of our trips—happened exactly thirty-two years ago in Iran."

Traveling the world with her last husband, I doubt she ever got off the tour bus.

"What happened exactly thirty-two years ago that I don't remember?"

"The Shah—he was so handsome—was thrown out by rioters and the Ayatollah-Whatever took over and all the women had to hide themselves under scarves."

"Hijabs. I do remember. I remember a handsome prince who liked America, but at the time I was, what, thirty, a mother of two young—"

"And you never read the newspaper or watched the news. When you're my age, you'll start paying attention."

She's adamant that when I get to be her age, I'll not be able to do anything but stare at the television and read the local newspaper from front to back, from front-page headlines to obituaries to *letters to the editor*, and just like her I will clip every coupon. She is so wrong. I'll have *Facebook*, *Twitter*, and the Internet. I'll still walk—or ride my Buzzaround Electric Scooter—to Trader Joe's for California Rolls, CVS for rum, and to Wells Fargo to count my money from the fire insurance payouts.

"Well, I know about the Shah of Iran and the takeover now. I've made it my life's work to know, apparently," I gasped in personal horror at the amount of research that was piled in paper stacks and pressed into three-ring binders all over my living room, kitchen, and hidden under my bed. Why make literary use of any of it, when it's obvious I can fill an entire three-book anthology with entertaining stories about my Mother.

"We mustn't get all worked up about it. All that nonsense in the Midwest—"

"The Middle East."

"Yes. All that nonsense over there will never get here. I lived through the fear of Stalin, Hitler, Khruskhev, and that Cuba thing." She shook her crooked finger at me. "And the president is just one man. He doesn't run the country."

"Japan attacked Pearl Harbor, Mother. Mo Hassan, a Pakistani Muslim TV producer concerned about the negative portrayal of Muslims in the media, beheaded his wife Taliban style two years ago. So they're here."

"What's in your salad?"

"He was convicted of 2nd degree murder last week. Roasted peppers, artichoke hearts," I forked my way through the bounty. "Gorgonzola, Provolone, and cheddar cheese; sundried tomatoes, onions, mushrooms, and black olives. Want some?"

"No, you go ahead."

She was not going to offer me a piece of that pizza. She would have two bites out of one piece and box the rest.

"Are you going to eat all that garlic bread?"

"No, please have some," I offered, knowing my taste buds were going to slap me later that night when the cupboard was empty.

"You've gained some weight. You really ought to try and stay trim in case he comes back," she advised and poured us each a splash more wine. "Oh, how exciting. You have a message."

I dug the phone out of my purse. "Yes. A *Happy Valentine's Day*."

"From who?"

"Just my roofing contractor. He probably sends them out en masse to all his customers." I gulped down a forkful of Gorgonzola and chased it with purple water.

"That's nice," she smiled, her lipstick now merged with the tomato paste on her teeth.

"I've been re-reading your book. Breaking dates and all the rest of it was just his way of trying to get rid of you."

"Thanks, Mom. Happy Valentine's Day to me." My phone rang out its cell phone jingle. "Why do you always want to upset me with what I already know?"

"Who is it?"

"It's Wayne."

"Oh, how is he? Say hello for me."

"I'm not picking it up. I'll call him back later," I said, making a wise decision.

"I don't know why you two just don't get married and be done with it."

"You don't want me to marry Ali, Mother."

"Wayne, the District Attorney. You've known each other for years and he's such a nice young man."

"He's an investigator, not a D.A., and he's having the best sex he's ever had, apparently. And he's not so young anymore."

"With who?"

"A blonde time bomb for three-thousand dollars a tick," I winked.

"Girls these days. They'll never get a husband that way."

Rolling my eyes is a bad habit. They will surely get stuck in that position one day.

I received another text and tossed the phone back into my purse.

"Who is it this time?"

"Another *Happy V Day* from a nice old man who helped me find my car the other day," I cast off Mr. Marijuana with a *delete*.

"Go ahead and call him, if you want, but he won't come back."

"Who won't come back?"

"The young Muslim fellow."

"Why do we always have this conversation? Believe it: if I called him, he'd come back. Is that what you want?"

"I hate to see you alone. Oh, how exciting! You have another one of those text messages."

The texter was Siamonto, the angry Armenian. This is why you do not delete names from your contact list—not ever—unless ordered to do so by the CIA. This wise practice prevents you from foolishly texting back an unknown number with *who in the hell is this?* beginning an entire unwanted conversation with someone you never wanted back into your life. "Just another *Happy Valentine's Day* message. It's from a car wash I visited once."

"That's odd, isn't it?"

"Great marketing, don't you think?"

The phone alerted me again. I answered. "Shucks. Well, thanks for letting me know."

Mother was gnawing tidily on a crusty edge, so I filled her in automatically. "That was my agency. The client has taken me off *hold* for an Advil spot. I didn't book the job."

Her lips pursed onto the rim of her glass, she sipped; her nose so deep into the wine she appeared to have suddenly become a burgeoning sommelier. She didn't comprehend what I was telling her and she had no desire to. If my phone conversation didn't involve a man, it wasn't worth discussing. She did have a great need to comment, however, from left field.

"You're retired. I don't get it—all this folly you waste your money and time on. Why don't you move into your cabin and enjoy yourself, take a break. You're always so nervous. Get with it, Julie. You need to take time out, to rest."

Perhaps her trivialized opinion was not as deep into left field as I hoped. Alexandra was calling and I answered it before shrieking across the table at who comes across to the unsuspecting public as a petite, innocent silver-haired grandmother day-tripping out of the assisted-living home for a special occasion luncheon with her vile, elder abusing daughter.

"Happy V Day, Mommy. We're on our way back from a long weekend in Palm Springs. I figured you'd be alone and want a call."

"Who is it?" Mom sneered and snatched up the last piece of bread.

"I'm not alone, Alex. Mom and I are having Italian up on the mountain. Would you like to speak to her?"

"I'm losing you. Get a new phone, Mom." And Alex and the official *WE* were gone.

"Well, Mother, the new *WE* spent the weekend in the desert."

"We who?"

"Alexandra and the boyfriend, Benjamin," I muttered. "She's in love."

"Well, let's hope he is. Have you met him yet?"

"No. Maybe that's why it's hard for me to get excited about the whole thing."

"That reminds me. When we get back to the cabin, I have a stack of *Cosmopolitan* magazines I want you to have. They're full of information on how to be sexy."

"Thanks, but no." She has offered up her collection of glossy subscriptions on several occasions. "Really, Mother, just how many ways are there to perform fellatio, anyway?"

"Perform what, dear?"

"Oh, miss? May we have a box, please?"

On February 15th, 2011, in Benghazi, Libya, protests broke out against the Muammar Gaddafi regime, an uprising that would begin the Libyan civil war.

Chapter 21

Circus Tents and Kissing Girls

♪ But if you'll hold me tight,
All the way home I'll be warm ♪

Let It Snow
Sammy Cahn and Jule Styne

Too soon it was that we returned to the mountains. This forced evacuation would be put to good use; this time I would seclude myself in the petit chateau to thump, thump, thump on the keyboard, only taking sprinting breaks to pee, bartend, and open the door for the dogs.

The gas company lady in black braids arrived at dawn's light to turn off the gas under the house and at the water heater in the basement. She is followed by the exterminator's truck, double-parked on the busy boulevard between two orange cones in front of the bungalow, which is now covered with a big blue and orange circus tent. Why is it embarrassing to have one's house fumigated? At the ungodly hour of seven a.m., the dogs and I snuck through the flapping tarp over the front door and took off in a car filled with refrigerator perishables and the contents of my entire medicine chest, all packed air-tight into NASA-grade nylon polymer bags provided by a Filipino gentlemen in a blue jumpsuit.

"You can leave that on the porch. It should be fine," he had said, but I would have to be gone three nights and I might get a headache, leg cramps, a cold sore, or even a sty.

"Never know what I might be needing," I had answered while rescuing the Cupid flag from any unforeseen dangers.

Upon awakening this Friday morning, the bungalow residents would be brewing with gossip as to the shame perpetrated on their proud, private neighborhood by the house in front, the Republican's house, facing the boulevard for all to see, which obviously is swarming with disgusting teeny-tiny wood guzzling critters—or worse.

"It's those filthy dogs," the German Frau would conclude. "They bring in everything."

"Whatever it is they are trying to kill, none of it better escape under my house." Artemus, the porch voyeur, would roll his first sweet cigarette of the day and shake his finger at the tarpaulin abomination erected on the other side of the fence.

"She seemed so neat and clean. How could this happen?" Marlene, the self-declared Hollywood Historian, would shake her head in disbelief. She appreciates the care I take to show off my home in its entire bohemian splendor, cracked façade to boot. She's the first in the mews to pay up her share of the monthly gardener bill. Unfortunately, I have had to anonymously call Code Enforcement over the years to report her packrat haven porch—decorated with the decade's collection of the *L.A. Times,* each and every FedEx cardboard box ever delivered, and weaved baskets for every holiday season stuffed with paper sacks—as a fire begging to blaze.

"It's so boldly striped! It's so fashionable," Kandi, our resident transsexual lovely, would exalt the happening as she passes by on her bicycle, the ribbons from her handlebars streaming alongside her.

The ripped blinds in the window across the walkway would rattle violently and the panes shake with the clanging of a cane. "Get that fucking hose off my sidewalk!" the one-legged man would shout. "Are you trying to fucking gas me?"

"Have another beer, asshole," Michael would recommend as he skipped on by. "It's so pretty! It's so pretty!"

"Hey, fella, did she leave any vodka in the freezer?" Miranda in her bathrobe would inquire of a man in a blue jumpsuit.

"She took everything from her icebox," he would answer.

"Shit," she would stomp with her good foot and limp back to her little house to order a shipment of liquor and cigarettes from Bogie's. By noon *The Married Guy* would cancel their bungalow tryst.

There was a long weekend ahead.

While everyone on the "We're so glad you broke up with the Muslim" advisory council is busy with his or her sanctimonious life, I am happily alone again with my dogs. These two are the precious, faithful, and easygoing voyeurs of my life. They have not yet groomed one opinion between them as to my morality or lack of it. Hound's black nose is pressed against the backseat window as the freeway sound barriers and landscaped exits fly by. Curled up in his blankie, Brute has made himself a hiding place on the floorboard. I'm chewing a Nicorette and switching the radio to KFRG, K-Frog country 95.1, now that the reception from the Inland Empire country station is clear. There has not been a complaint barked, nor has anyone asked me, "Are we there yet?"

An unfamiliar song has me singing along with a country gal.

♪ Driving through town—something—you're comin' back—you're gonna love me forever, according to the song, according to *The Best Song Ever*! Whoa-oh! ♪ The song said we'd always be together, such a perfect fairy tale.

♪ According to the song, according to the *The Best Song Ever!* ♪

Half way up the mountain, drifting fog hit me like a cream pie smack at my face. I switched on the headlights and leaned into the wheel to get my bearings. Even though daylight, the winding road before me was mysteriously gone from view. From the safety of sunshine and balmy breezes to a nail-biting mountain journey in less than ninety minutes, that's the way we roll. We are fog avengers. Nothing can stop us from reaching our destination at the top of this hill.

"Hey, Hound, want to get out and lead the way?" I teased. Hearing his name called out, he moved his gangly sixty-some pounds and neatly placed his paws between the front seats, his snout nudging my shoulder. "Whoa, fella. I was just kidding."

Before I was in tune to the turns in this road, when my first winter experience on this mountain found me and my two young children in a long, wooden station wagon on a cold foggy night, the tire chains rattling uncomfortably on four inches of packed snow hiding the evil black ice below, I let my six-year-old daughter out onto the highway to show me the way home. Did I really do that? Well, I'm not admitting it here.

The highway markings dividing the road were not reflecting in the daylight haze. A queue of headlights followed the little Scion in and out of curves in the blind faith that she could safely lead them home. I caught up with the rear lights of a pickup truck and stayed close behind all the way to Top Town, leaving the cloud layer behind to spook the mountainside.

The day finished in due time with six pages struggled through and six inches of snow on the ground. I followed the dogs out and wondered at the sight before me. The white evergreen fir trees were now perfect for next year's Christmas card picture, but I had quit mailing out yearly Happy Holiday notices to people I hadn't spoken to all year. I clicked away on the Blackberry and sent to *Facebook* a picture of Hound spraying yellow into a snowdrift.

Three bourbons and a cheesy tuna salad chased by an entire bag of tortilla chips later, I craved a cigarette—a white wonderful stick that burns sensually at the end of it as you puff nonchalantly—and I was going to have one. Snow continued to fall and I needed to get to the gas station before closing time. This is not L.A; this is Crestline, where the 24-Hour Laundromat closes at ten.

In boots and gloves, I headed for the trunk of my car, and after fumbling rusted chains from a metal box, I neatly splayed each one out along a front tire. The idea of lying on my back in icy snow to hook chains under, behind, and around to the front wheels of my car, which was a dozen feet away from the street and a half a foot deep in the stuff, was short-lived. The snowplow had not come by yet. Chains would not get my front-wheel drive little Scion up the big hill to the main highway without mayhem. I would surely lose momentum, slide backwards into a parked car, sounding the car's alarm; the Mounties would be called, and I'd spend the night in the county drunk tank in Twin Peaks. I was saved from this embarrassment when Cole bounced by in his Jeep heading for his driveway.

From the edge of my driveway I pounced, "Stop!" He did.

"You're not going to ask me to put on those chains for you right now, are you?" he hoped.

"Do you have any smokes?"

"I thought you quit."

"I can't think. I can't write," I demanded. "I can't get any bigger!"

"I've got a stash of Marlboro Reds."

"You know I only smoke Virginia Slims."

"Beggars can't be choosers, you sniveling nicotine addict. Give me a minute and I'll toss a pack down into your backyard."

Soon it was there. Alongside the redwood fence, an icy red and white box sparkled in the light of the Snow Moon. I carry it gently to the patio table.

Ceremoniously, I remove my glove and pull the gold cellophane chain to unleash the luxuriously thin plastic film from the box. I tap the box upside down onto the glass table, where I had wiped off the snow and placed a glass ashtray. I wondered if the Marlborough Man taps his box before opening it. Then I right the box, cock back the lid, and tapping it against my palm loose a golden filtered cigarette from the crowd of twenty. My thumb and forefinger gingerly remove it safely and place it between my lips. I should have stopped there.

Using a long fireplace match fired up at the gas stove, I lit the end of the first cigarette and lightly inhaled. The nauseous rush instantly settled the creeping, crawling, restless gnawing. My mind opened; it was free. Not free of thoughts, experiences, feelings, but free to think of them, write of them, grasp each tingling sensation and expose them audaciously. Or so I thought. This one cigarette will begin the chain of addictive response; *I'll have just one . . .* and then another after another after another. Just as Ali's first gentle touch to my back guiding me to the popcorn counter began an unhealthy belief in me that *happily ever after* romantic expectations wouldn't hurt me, I craved another. It was good to be home.

The Blackberry sang out. Paranoid that the world was, indeed, watching, could it be calling with warnings on the health hazards of smoking? Wayne must be up late and alone.

"I'm in Mammoth. It was an uneventful drive, even though I'm driving another new Porsche," he bragged humbly.

"Nothing better to do after a day on the slopes than to check in with the President of the Crestline Lonely Hearts Club?"

"You're at the cabin. Good for you. Just wanted to thank you for the birthday card, the *Happy 100th*."

"Sorry, I couldn't find the correct age. Hallmark doesn't put out uneven numbers."

"So how are you? Honestly."

"I have thoughts of suicide, drunk or sober. I cry uncontrollably. I was just about to have another sobbing bout and huddle up with the dogs."

"And I have rescued you. It sounds like you're smoking again."

"You can hear me exhale?" I mushed out the butt. "What has he done to me?"

"Drug addicts go through withdrawal but survive. What doesn't kill you—and this will not—makes you stronger. Don't give him the satisfaction of giving up."

"Are you talking about smoking, drinking, or Ali?"

"You know what I'm talking about. Smoke all you want, but absolutely *no* contact. And remember what our Lord and Savior Obama has spoken, 'Never be at war against the Muslims.' It might have been *with the Muslims*, but—"

"Oh, no, I won't contact him. I just come onto these melancholy moments brought on by a song or a ghostly sensation. He did make me so happy, as is the way of the charming sociopath," I shared in cathartic madness. My phone tucked under my chin, I snapped out more ice from the tray. "I need to put the phone down for just a second."

A fresh bourbon and seven in hand, "Okay, I'm back."

"He certainly fits the bullet list, especially the pitiful hypochondriac routine. Oh, heck, it could be worse. He could have lured you off to a cave in Afghanistan."

"Nah, I'm not that foolish," I hoped.

"I'm reading the new Tom Clancy novel. It's a real page-turner. Muslims are the villains."

"I want to read that."

"Nine-hundred and fifty pages. Started it last night and already halfway through. It's a fictionalized hunt for Bin Laden."

"There's a theory brewing by Muslims themselves that the terrorists, because of the 'no sex until married' are frustrated men in their twenties and thirties, and that the promise of virgins as a reward is too irresistible. Not to mention they are all unemployed sociopaths," I emptied an interesting tidbit from my *Googled* brain.

"In the book, the Bin Laden character is a horn dog, hires big-money hookers."

"Sounds a bit close to home, doesn't it?" I reminded him.

"Oh, stop. Blondie is not a hooker," he demanded. "I like your proposed theory, but I wouldn't want seventy-two virgins. I want women who *know* what to do." And he's paying her three thousand dollars a month to keep up the continuing education courses.

"Does the writer actually call him *Osama Bin Laden*? Or is it just obvious who the characters are?"

"He's *The Emir*, but the characterization is obvious. A very bad man, he had one hooker killed because she asked too many questions."

"I've been chastised for the same thing," I remembered.

"Did you hear that the Muslim guy who ran down his daughter in the parking lot of an Arizona welfare department was finally convicted?"

"The young Iraqi girl who'd assimilated into American culture and refused to hook up into an arranged marriage?" I remembered seeing a picture of her seductive face, her eyes lined in charcoal pencil, and her dark hair razor cut on an angle sweeping about her chin. "Did daddy use the *Honor Killing* defense?"

"Heavens, no. He wasn't tried in a Sharia Law court, where the jury would have applauded."

♪ I want to live in America ♪ I sang out angrily. "Where religious freedom reigns supreme."

"The D.A. used it and set a precedent, but didn't get the result they hoped for. The defense argued that dad meant to just spit on his daughter's female companion and accidentally ran over the two women. The jury came back with second degree murder."

"I'm setting the phone down. I need another drink."

"By all means."

As I twisted a few ice cubes out and into my highball tumbler, I clenched my teeth. *Honor Killings* are a way of life in the Middle East, and although when Islamic immigrants take the oath to become American citizens—additional ingredients in the grand *melting pot*—and swear to leave the laws they were under and to abide by our laws, they cling to their medieval culture like strung-out heroin addicts cling to their drug dealer; their goal to entrench us all into their violent dysfunctional deception.

"So the asshole is cashing in on his American citizenship bennies. Can't deport him, so we get to feed, house, and nurse him through dementia," I shook my head.

"You're gonna love this tidbit. Dad was at the welfare department to sign up for food stamps."

"Perfect. Par for the course."

"I still think *you-know-who* is a deep cover plant of some sort," Wayne said. I lit up, the plume of smoke rising to the still fan blades above me. I switched the fanlight on and opened the back door.

"I agree. But the truth is they all are. It's their mission to kill all infidels, to infiltrate our government and our universities, and to *marry* —and I use that word loosely—our women and have children who instantly become cash cow welfare recipients. Ali is very proud that he never paid one cent of his student loans after graduating from UCLA." I stopped. I had so much more to say, but would keep my short-lived escapade as a non-official asset an intelligence fantasy. Natasha was never out of earshot.

"If and when he reads your so-called novel—"

"Don't even go there, Wayne. He's not going to kill me. I didn't mean that much to him. However, let's just hope his mother doesn't read it," I contemplated. "She might just want to avenge her son's honor."

"You need to go back to American men. Time to circle the wagons."

"I totally agree. However, my sick Middle Eastern adventure has made me smarter, wiser, more loving, and less tolerant. And much more sexual," I beamed.

"How much more sexual, my little pussycat?"

"Free, wild, completely abandoned! Because I adored him," I stifled a swell up. "Now I'm going to cry. You see, when I was with him, I was twenty-five and lived in a tent with fringed silk drapes and a camel tied up outside, and the world just went away."

"You go sleep now, Scheherazade."

"Yep, it's midnight at the oasis."

"Time to put that old camel to bed and turn out the lights on another Arabian Night."

By Sunday morning of the weekend, I was out of cigarettes and alcohol. I tromped out to put the chains on. The snow on the road had been shaved down to a powdered ice pond; the berm left across the driveway by the snowplow a crusty three feet high and three feet deep. My car parked aiming into the street, I shoveled ferociously for an hour.

Cole found me in feminine distress cursing behind the wheel in the *little car that would* on the steep curve heading up to the highway.

"Stop spinning your wheels. You're sparking," he shouted out to me from inside his Jeep.

Upon male inspection, he decided I had put the chains on correctly, except for a minor mishap; I had wrapped them around the axle. Together on our knees in the street we removed them. My neighbor with three fingers clipped above the knuckle of each hand is more helpful than my four anatomically correct husbands had ever been. He guided me as I backed the car into the driveway and kindly drove me into town for provisions: rum, caffeine-free diet Coke, and two packs of Virginia Slims. I tossed him two packs of Marlboro Red as I climbed down from his cab.

Muslim Somali pirates now killing Americans on their hijacked yacht off the coast of East Africa, I am now geared up and fueled to continue writing blasphemous Islamic trivia into my second novel, for historical purposes only of course. Collecting further fearful diatribe for the book I shall write after that, which I am writing now, is slowing me down.

Writing this paragraph now, I am as confused as you may be. A writer writing a novel about a writer and events occurring in the past while the heroine is writing another novel is just cause to pour myself straight rum on the rocks and to light up another cigarette.

On the Internet, using my neighbor Peeping Tom's password, I hooked up again with good old Ahmadinejad, the current President of Iran. In celebrating the 32nd anniversary of the overthrow of the Shah, he spoke of a New Middle East spiraling out of the desert stirred up by the Egyptian revolution and hurried along by the coming of the 12th Imam, like the weekend's snowfall, a few months too late for Christmas. Whipping up a frenzy of sorts, he spoke of Mahdi, the Shi'ite Imam who disappeared as a five-year-old in the 10th Century and who is, as promised, on his way back. I suppose the wagering on the race between the return of Jesus versus the return of the 12th Imam is a never-ending blind act of faith. Will Jesus beat Mahdi to the finish line? And who shall be left at the finish line to take another selfie for their *Facebook* page or to collect their winnings?

> "The final move has begun. We are in the middle of a world revolution managed by this dear 12th Imam.
>
> A great awakening is unfolding.
>
> "Come and take away the Zionist regime which is the source of all crimes. . . take it away and liberate the region. Free the region and give it to the people and take this regime, which is the child of Satan, out."

The *Zionists* are the Jews and the *child of Satan* is the tyrannical, good-old United States of America. A chill runs down my spine, knowing that when once asked by students to define what is the most beautiful for a Muslim on earth, Ahmadinejad answered, "To kill and be killed," which is certainly a bit to the left of "an eye for an eye" and a world away from "turning the other cheek."

* * *

Returning to Hollywood on Monday, we waited nervously in the car for five minutes in front of the Armenian school, and then at the magic hour of one o'clock, the end of today's street cleaning, I pulled up smack dab in front of the house and three bulging bladders jumped out. The dogs rushed to the courtyard, as I unlocked the new gate and sprinted to the toilet.

When I returned to collect the dogs, my fellow advantageous valets—Randi, Artemus, Marlene, Michael, Hugo the Hungarian, old humbug Oscar, and the one-legged charmer—were pulling their cars systematically curbside into the Monday afternoon lineup, each bumper stationed a responsible and courteous two-foot distance apart, one behind the other. We are all professional parallel parkers. Uninvited guests who selfishly park leaving half a car length behind them receive a ticket replicating a Parking Enforcement violation with the heading *You Park Like an Asshole*. Sliding these bogus tickets under a windshield wiper is a bit of a thrill-seeking maneuver, one you don't want to get caught doing, especially when the violator is a tattooed weight-lifter returning from 24 Hour Fitness.

The circus tent is gone, my plants crushed, my outdoor lights mangled, and there is no hot water. A gas company guy is banging on the gate.

"You don't have a driveway," he advises me. At the gas meter behind the trashcans and under the house, he reaches in and turns something on. I lead him to the basement to ignite the hot water tank. "You're all set." And he is gone.

Randi is excited about the news: Julie's smoking again. We rendezvous on my porch at sundown. I had declined many invitations for cocktail hour on the porch since our New Year's Eve bash. Nicorette and vodka just don't seem to mix very well.

"Don't be so hard on yourself. You cleaned out your lungs for almost four months!" Randi rallied.

"But for a few slips, yes. I guess some of us are just inclined to the evil of enchanting, dare-devil tobacco use," I surmised after two vodka tonics.

"I have news. I start at Universal Mini this weekend."

"Uh, is that a new TV series?"

"No, silly, I was laid off again. Set painting is way too competitive, so I'm going to try car sales."

"I love houses, so I sell houses. You love your Mini Cooper, so why not sell them? Here's hoping you sell more Minis than I've sold houses," I shrugged.

"Commission only, like twenty-five percent of the dealership's profit on each car I sell—plus some kind of desk rent."

"Are you sure it's not a real estate office disguised as a car lot?"

The evening was delightful. My crazy friend, a cool breeze tossing the Cupid flag over the crushed bougainvillea, two faithful dogs at my feet—could it get any better?

"Call the cops! Call the cops!" a young man in great distress shouted to us from the bungalow walkway. "I don't have a phone! Can you call them for me?"

Randi leaned over the porch wall. "Are you hurt? What's the matter?"

"The woman in the back house, she pulled a knife on me when I didn't pay. *He—He* pulled a knife!" He was frantic.

"Slow down, sonny," Randi placated the kid. "How could you not know Kandi is a tranny?"

"Her—his pictures on the internet. So beautiful," he sulked.

"Let's see: huge perky tits, a small tight ass, a beautiful face made up like a circus performer, long flowing black hair, and no body fat whatsoever? Sounds like a tranny to me," she chuckled, embarrassing the would-be John.

"She pulled her cock out and shoved it at me," he said while simulating the action with his hand. "I told her no, no, and she wanted seventy-five bucks anyway."

"It's been tough for her since the cops shut down her trap house," Randi sympathized

"Her what?" I asked.

"Her crack cocaine business. I try to keep you as oblivious as I can."

"Thanks."

"You don't want us to call the cops, kid. You were soliciting her for prostitution."

"I know what that means!" I said triumphantly.

"No, no! I'm not a catcher! It was an Internet date, honest," he pleaded.

"She's probably great at blowjobs," I shouted after him.

"Keep running and don't come back here," Randi advised.

With his tail between his knees and seventy-five bucks still in his pocket, the dissatisfied Romeo left the block party.

"So now I understand why very strange men pass through here day and night. I should call the police," my conservative homeowner spoke.

"Live and let live, Julie. And live every day like it's your last, I say."

"What kind of man wants a transvestite?"

"A man who doesn't want to admit to himself he's gay."

"Oh."

As I lit another Virginia Slim, Hound, sprawled out in comfy pose, set both golden paws over his nose. I didn't misunderstand the position.

"Hey, Mr. Judgmental, give it a rest. Live and let live!"

"Have you ever kissed a girl?" Randi surprised me with the question.

"Sixth grade, I had a bit of a romance with a girl with premature tits, but it was short lived."

"My first sexual romance was with a woman. We worked at McDonald's together," Randi shared with her friend who she knew would not judge her. Hound, however, moved from under my chair to cower in the corner.

Returning from the kitchen with our third vodkas, I insisted, "Well, Miss Filet of Fish, don't stop there."

"She was something. She taught me about how my body works. She was the best."

"Go on. Don't start crying on me. What happens next?"

"She fuckin' cheated on me with the fry cook."

"Male or female?"

"A greasy Mexican guy. That's when I got myself wired into the groupie thing. Marilyn Manson was next. Me and Marilyn and all the girls. He liked to watch."

"Okay, slut. I have to go to bed now."

My call time for a movie shoot in Malibu: six a.m.

Chapter 22

The Long and Winding Road to Chaos

> ♪ Over, sideways, and under
> On a magic carpet ride ♪
>
> *A Whole New World*
> Alan Menken and Tim Rice

After hitting the sheets just before midnight, I awoke at four a.m. to become camera ready for a background booking on a movie titled *Welcome to People*. Upon its release, the movie would be titled *People Like Us*. Neither title would be awarded an Oscar.

Running late, just after five a.m. I took a barren and wide-open Sunset Boulevard all the way west to the assigned location, a restaurant on Pacific Coast Highway in Malibu. I spent the day pretending to eat shellfish at a long wooden table lined with a half dozen bikers. Long ponytails, tattooed sleeves, and the very sexy smell of wind-slapped leather whipped an exhausting fourteen-hour day into a short-lived erotic moment. When wrapped early evening, I unwisely took the same route home on *The Boulevard of Broken Dreams,* which passes through Pacific Palisades, upper Santa Monica, the residential glamour of Brentwood and Bel Air, the Sunset Strip with its comedy clubs, infamous nightclubs, and state of the art edgy hotels. Two hours of bumper-to-bumper traffic later, it was ten o'clock when I returned to the urban delight of Central Hollywood and the perfect parking place awaiting me in front of my house, presumably because no other car had been able to fit into it.

Hanging my wardrobe of the day on the crowded pole beyond the door in the floor of the walk-in closet, I smelled rain. Ali liked the rain. Ali talked all the time about liking the rain. Why do I smell rain? When I last looked, there wasn't a cloud in the sky.

Then I heard the sound of running water. After checking the faucets and jiggling the toilet handle, I opened the door in the floor and from the darkness below came the sound of rushing water raging into an obstacle and splashing into more water. Back pedaling down the ladder, I reached over and switched on the light in the ceiling. Holy Shit. My basement was flooded.

The hot water heater was belching out a violent stream from a copper valve on top. Keeping my slippers on, I waded into a foot of water sloshing from all sides and from under the stairs. There was only one thing to do. So I started to cry.

My sanity returned in a matter of moments and I high-tailed it outside to the water turn-off thingy under the garden hose spigot. In a bit of hysterics, I called the gas company hotline and a sympathetic single grandmother immediately sent out a grumpy old man in a blue shirt.

"Well, they just blow sometimes," he assured me, both of us calf-high in murky cold water. "It's a good thing you had your wits about you and turned off the water to the house, otherwise, the tank just keeps filling up and spitting it out."

"What a fucking coincidence, sir. The gas company turns the gas back on, lights the pilot, and within twenty-four hours it blows a gasket!"

"It's not my job to replace the valve for you, so you'll have to call a plumber. I can come back tomorrow to see if it's possible to light the thing, when it's dry and all."

"My children's keepsakes are in those bottom drawers," I whined. "My son's Billy Bean doll, his original Gizmo creature from *Gremlins*, a stuffed collectible Chubaka—I took him at four in the morning to see the very first *Star Wars* when he was just a little guy—a baby doll that cries just exactly like Alexandra did when she was a baby, my daughter Elizabeth's report cards and her poetry." I knelt down in front of a clear plastic drawer in prayer and wriggled it out into the wading pool far enough to stick my hand inside.

"Well, looks like you'd better be gettin' those upstairs right quick," he suggested and left me there in the basement.

Water dripping onto the oak floors as I went, I scurried flooded plastic drawer after plastic drawer, drenched cardboard box after cardboard box, moist bag after moist bag up the basement stairs to the front porch. My high school scrapbooks were soaked through. The bottom of the zipped plastic wardrobe closet was floating in the tide. The bottom of each winter coat, formal gown, and unprotected costume was now stained with a water line. Anything on the floor was submerged in dirty brown water. I had no idea that the wall-to-wall cream carpet was so filthy.

Santa Claus, Victor the Vulture, Spidey—everyone needed to go upstairs. The red-topped Tupperware storage boxes protecting Valentine's Day, St. Patrick's Day, Easter, the 4th of July, Halloween, Thanksgiving, Christmas, and every glossy magazine Alexandra's face was ever in. Everything needed to get out of the moisture and onto the porch.

My feet are numb and the carpet sludgy beneath them. The Persian runner, its weight now resembling a small child in my arms, is lifted and taken out to drip its tears over the porch wall. When the sun comes up, everyone passing by will think I'm having a yard sale.

This is my Noah's Ark. Two by two, up the wooden rungs to the new land go the treasured moments of my life.

My suspicious insurance company recommended a restoration water and mold removal company. The soft water crew arrived at noon to carry the water treatment apparatus up and outside, after scooping out the dry salt pellets into buckets, of course. Two nice men in brown jumpsuits arrived at noon. They kindly and without complaint dismantled the two metal collapsible wardrobes, gently moved the sewing machine table and chair up to the living room, yanked up the wet carpet and dragged the beast out to their truck. With a very long hose, they sucked the basement dry. They left me with instructions to keep the door shut, not to enter the basement for seventy-two hours to allow the wind machine to do its magic.

On closer inspection of the damage scattered all over my front porch, by late afternoon carefully selected moist paper memories were spinning wildly as they dried in the gust of a wind machine under the house. This turned out to be an efficient cure. The dolls were hand washed and dried.

In the days that followed the flood, I treated the legs of the antique table and chair with lemon oil. Outside in the warm sun, I emptied, cleansed, and re-organized each drawer, each container, and replaced any cardboard boxes with burp-top plastic tubs. The restoration team returned to take away the wind machine. The day before new cream carpet was installed, I repainted the walls. With the help of my neighborhood wood mill and my trusty drill, I replaced the two bottom rungs of the basement ladder. This particular week would have been an awfully good time for Aladdin to show up, Brainard's *no contact* orders be damned, my assumption being that Ali would be the number one person who would want the basement brought back to its original grandeur.

The soft water crew returned the salt tank to the basement, removed the water heater and replaced it with a compact tankless water heating system bolted to the outside of the house. The crew graciously moved the furniture back down and reassembled the garment racks. Along with the check for twenty-eight hundred, each left with their very own autographed copy of *The Year I Learned to Text; Why Am I Having Sex with a Muslim in My Basement?* I felt it was the least I could do.

I spent Day no. 4 of chaos gingerly hauling all of my crap back down the basement stairs. I hadn't bathed since the morning of my drive to Malibu by way of *The Boulevard of Broken Dreams*. Setting Santa in his place, I caught a whiff of fresh paint, new carpet, the crotch of my bike shorts, and my underarms.

His scent had been erased. It was gone forever.

Chapter 23

Go Ahead, Make My Day

THE month of March is full of promise because I will put another candle on my birthday cake and St. Patrick will surely send me a frisky leprechaun to tickle me with his sparkling green shillelagh. A new flag will fly. The pink cupid shall be packed away until next Valentine's Day in exchange for the lucky green shamrock.

Bill Nob *On the News* clamored out more Muslim mania.

> The supposedly Lone Wolf Jihadist suspect in the slaying of two U.S. airmen at the Frankfurt, Germany, airport has confessed to targeting our American military members. He aimed at them, to be sure. German federal prosecutors have gone so far as to say that there is suspicion that Islamism may have motivated the shooter. And Julie, this does not mean that all Muslims are bad.

I threw the covers off in excitement. Today I have a callback audition for a national union scale commercial paying time-and-a-half for a seven-day shoot, plus the residual income that twenty-two months of airtime will produce. I shall once again be *the hero woman*, this time spouting the benefits of Spiriva, a COPD—chronic obstructive pulmonary disease—medication.

Copied and pasted from the L.A. Casting audition ticket, here is the role description:

> Real to slight character looking, interesting face.
> Caucasian with dark hair. No blondes or redheads please.

A likable, relatable, intelligent woman with a few
wrinkles and maybe a touch of gray in her hair.
Lives life to the fullest and exudes confidence.
Great actress, great with lots of dialogue.

And, of course, smokes like a chimney and drinks like a fish.

Having mouthed, written one hundred times in cursive, and memorized the heavy thirty-second script, the *sides* for Spi-ree-va, *the once daily inhaler*, until my lips were trembling and my throat dry, sitting on the edge of the bed, I slid blue jeaned calves into my tall black boots, slipped into an XL navy blue tailored shirt, and kissed the dogs good-bye.

This is the way it works: be prepared for the initial audition; be doubly prepared for the callback, where the director, the money people, and the creative advertising executives will be in *the room* to judge you, while nibbling on their catered lunch of kale and cucumber salad. Drive safely and park as close to the casting office as possible. You will never be able to park in the parking lot of the casting office, however. You are only an auditioning actor and not given such privileges until you book the job and instantaneously become the treasured *talent*.

Once in the casting office: fill out completely the sign-in sheet; glance at the posted *story board* and do not be dismayed that the actor you are reading for is characterized in cartoon form as a much younger, much thinner woman, not resembling you one tiny bit; and do not be intimidated by other actresses who have known each other since being background actors on *Welcome Back Kotter*, who look exactly like the cartoon character on the story board, have never given birth, are still a size 6, and whose husbands are dentists or plastic surgeons, and whose parents have died on time, leaving them a legacy. Extra tip: do not talk with them, to them, or at them, and do not let them talk to you. Their instinct is to derail you from your purpose and to fill your head with self-doubts: Why am I not a size 6? Why didn't I marry a dentist? Why is my mother still alive?

Be outside *the room* when they call you. Do not be in the bathroom or on the phone. Smile graciously at all times and at everyone, including the Ritalin-inspired, six-year-old ballerina, who is throwing a tantrum because her mother will not buy her another soda from the vending machine. There are secret cameras recording your every move. These moves are shown on wide screens behind secreted doorways in secret rooms.

Once in *the room*, the camera operator, who has no decision over whether you will be booked or not, unless he insists on sharing anecdotes as to your inability to show up on time, will ask you to *slate*.

Of course, being a fan of *The Muslim Romance Trilogy*, you already know what slating entails. But in case you have picked up Part Three at a garage sale, it will be explained to the boredom of everyone else.

The *slate* is very simply the only chance you're going to get to tell everyone your name. There is no need to say "Hello, there, I'm John Aren't-I-Cool," while slapping a high-five into the air. Just say your name as a grand statement of who the hell you are. This name should be the same name as on your union card, not necessarily on your birth certificate.

Parked on Sycamore in all-day parking in front of a stately 1920's two-story duplex, I carefully walk the block and a half, passing by the grand parking lot of *Petco*, a full-service, elaborate store catering to all our furry friends. Passing the chandeliers shimmering in the *Lamps Plus* showroom window, I enter through the glass door of 200 S. La Brea decorated with the familiar taped sign:

> Actors, do not park in the Petco parking lot.
> You will be towed.

Note to greenhorn actors: I've just saved you a frantic run to your car parked in the Petco lot, after which you would return to your audition nervous, sweating, and late; or the panic attack when not finding your car in the Petco lot, taxi fair to the tow yard, and the towing fee of around one-hundred and fifty. And this book, jammed pack with information, cost you less than twenty-five bucks.

Once up the two flights of stairs, I scan the chalkboard listing today's casting sessions, the name of the product to be advertised, and the room number in which I will be auditioning. After a long wait outside *the room*, the casting director—who, by the way, must please his clients and answer all their demands—makes an announcement. The first four ladies called in will be reading as *the hero woman*; the next bunch of crackers will not be required to do any line reading, as one of them will be cast as *the silent wife* of *the hero husband* with COPD. In the Screen Actors Guild commercial world, talk or no talk, the pay is the same.

"Also, the actors chosen will be working with an elephant. Is that okay with everyone?"

Typically, *that actress* speaks up. "Oh, my god. My dissertation was on elephants! I would be thrilled," she exclaims and stampedes to the front of the herd.

I am not on the list of the first four. I fold up my *sides* and stuff it into my purse with a silent slam; hours of numbing memorization wasted, never to return.

I'm inside. The room is dark, but for the reflection of laptop screens onto faces, faces which will not be introduced. These faces will be watching my performance on their individual unforgiving screen. They sometimes never look up. The casting assistant is standing at a raised computer desk behind the camera. I glance a subtle *hello* at a silver-haired heavyset gal at the end of the couch. My eyes scan three men dressed in casual button-down shirts. I stop at the third man and we lock eyes. We know each other. Forgetting the Golden Rule of auditioning, Do Not Speak Unless Spoken To, regrettably, I become *that actress*.

"The Prudential insurance job?" I inquire.

"No. US Bank?" he fishes.

"No? Gosh. Let me think. San Bernardino High School, class of 1966?" I stumble, admitting my true age and increasing his by ten years.

"You can be a wife, huh?" he teases me.

"Yes, sir. Many times."

The casting assistant stands behind the camera and fires it at me, "Slate."

My hands gathered in silent prayer over my muffin top, I say my full Screen Actors Guild name, nothing more.

"Thanks, Julie," the familiar face dismisses me.

I am not booking this job.

Disgruntled, disappointed and deflated, I head for the 7-Eleven on Vine Street for cigarettes, where a delivery truck beats me into the only parking space. I continue through the lot and back onto Vine to Fountain to El Centro to the Gower Gulch strip mall and Rite Aid. I need cigarettes, wine, and a tube of bright red lipstick. I'm booked as a secretary for the newly founded Federal Bureau of Investigation in Clint Eastwood's time-period biopic of J. Edgar Hoover, titled *J. Edgar*, starring Leonardo DiCaprio.

My character has been previously fitted at Western Costume into vintage attire: a tight-fitting long black wool pencil skirt, a matronly pleated blouson beige silk shirt, and black thick-heeled shoes, which are longer than my feet. I assume as a secretary I will be seated during the scene, so the loose shoes do not concern me. My instructions for tomorrow's shoot at Warner Brothers are: arrive with only moisturizer on face, hair in sponge rollers, flesh-colored body-control undies, black stockings with seams, and a tube of red lipstick. Having worked previously on several period costume films, my collection of seamed stockings has saved me from investing another ten dollars. Black stockings with seams ☑ Beige corset ☑ Sponge rollers ☑ Virginia Slims, one huge bottle of Gallo Family Moscato, and a tube of cheap red lipstick ☑ ☑ ☑

Call time: eleven a.m. tomorrow at Warner Brothers, giving me plenty of time to get myself blitzed, moribund, and totally psychotic.

In order to bolster my depression and to send it spiraling into familiar sadistic territory, I've dug into my VHS collection and shoved in the animated musical, *Aladdin*. I haven't been able to walk over to the Goodwill donation center with this videotape, my only chance to spend the night with a fairy tale Arab.

A movie and dinner in the great American TV tray tradition, by nine o'clock I've devoured an entire wok full of stir-fried bok choy, leafy baby spinach, pared white onions, and bean sprouts—topped ruefully with salted peanuts. Jasmine learns that her singing prince is really a street beggar, but loves him anyway. And now the après-dinner cigarette, heaven to behold, which leads to more cigarettes, an abundance of wine, and the eventual sputum cough up, the violent teeth brushing, and the fully clothed walk of shame to my bed.

And, of course, the resultant dreams of my visit to the Kasbah ensue. I spend the night in and out of consciousness on and off a flying carpet, my heart breaking for Princess Jasmine, who has been introduced to a whole new world of sex with nine-year-old children, female genital mutilation, and a husband who stops kissing her, but brings home three more wives.

By loving Aladdin unconditionally and accepting their differences, she has upset her father. "Oh, Daddy, when he wants me, he has such a wild look in his black eyes. I can't help myself."

Wielding a hatchet, Dad chases her around the minaret shouting "Honor, honor, where is your honor?"

And there is nothing I can do to save her.

Warner Brothers sprawls in a mini-city configuration from the L .A River basin to Barham Boulevard, which changes to Olive Avenue fronting the barricaded studio lot and its thirty-five sound stages. Cahuenga Boulevard follows alongside the Hollywood Freeway and ends at Barham, which loops east and slightly north and onto Olive. Today I have a stress-free, no freeway fifteen-minute commute to my destination at the parking lot for Gate no. 2 check-in on Olive Avenue. Looking like Aunt Jemima, my hair in pink rollers and wrapped in a silk polka dot scarf, in comfy suede booties and blue jeans, I take the long walk to the wardrobe trailer for background extras appearing in *J. Edgar*. After a cruel visit to the makeup trailer, I hide out in the *holding* tent, along with a half dozen other women who now resemble Joan Crawford in a very bad wig. Before them are paper coffee cups, each stained with red lip impressions.

I am called to set. Leaving the secretary pool behind, I am *the chosen one*. Inside the sound studio, I am asked to wait in a folding chair, along with a dozen young men, all in dark brown double-breasted suits and all brunets with no facial hair and hairstyles trimmed severely above the ear. The darkness of the sound studio changes to light at the entrance of the set, an erected office building hallway, where crew and camera back in and back out.

"They're shooting an FBI hallway scene with DiCaprio," a nice young man in a brown double-breasted suit whispers to me. "They'll move to the interior office pretty soon."

This is the on-site *man-in-the-know*, typically the non-union extra who somehow got ahold of the day's script, along with the privileged call sheet—with absolutely everyone's name, number and email on it—and is dating the perky production assistant, who has gotten him this union background gig by confiscating the one remaining union voucher.

"Thanks for the info," I whisper back.

"They're not giving out any more union vouchers on this production," he advises me.

"That's okay, sonny, I'm good," I assure him. "Are they giving out any lines?" was all I really wanted to know, my union voucher safely tucked away in my purse.

The perky production assistant led us through the empty hallway to set. Placed into the dark interior office lined with dark wooden desks, each with a black rotary phone and dangling receiver, pad and pencil, I was left to stand in a doorway, while the supposed *agents* were each assigned one of eight desks. The desks flanked the aisle through which a blonde female stand-in moved toward a cluster of wooden file cabinets with cute little cubbies for three-by-five inch cards; apparently, the cubbies holding secret information relating to all things criminal.

The camera crew is at the end of the aisle hidden behind the file cabinets. I am asked to carry and deliver an important letter-sized dark brown leather folder to the agent at desk no. 3 on the right. I am to lean next to the agent, open the folder and point with my right hand to a blank piece of paper. He will sign the blank paper and I will close the folder and clutch it to my breast and head to the glass door to the left rear. I will open the glass door and close it behind me.

"When the actress starts down the aisle, you will counter her on your way to desk no. 3. Do not look at her, okay?"

I do not believe that the soft-spoken assistant director is chiding me, nor that the actress has told him that background actors are not to make eye contact with her. The scene is set in a busy office, where employees are in and out frequently, employees who pass each other on a daily basis. Attempting to get *screen time* by lingering starry eyed at a movie star on her way down an aisle will get you blacklisted, especially if you are a staunch Republican.

"Of course. I understand," I agreed.

The stand-ins, *Team Two*, in their places, the agents at their desks, and I standing to the side, a male stand-in at my back, we do a run-through without the actors, *Team One*, for the camera blocking. Walking deliberately to desk no. 3, I curl my toes to keep my shoes from slipping away from me. The linoleum is slick and the shoes can be heard sliding across the floor. As I close it, the glass door rattles.

"Remove your shoes. The camera can't see your feet. And don't close the door all the way. The shot ends as you open it. Got it?"

"Yes, sir. Thank you."

There is an off-limits area somewhere inside the vast sound stage called *video village*, where the director, the producers, and anyone important sit in black director chairs—usually with their names embossed on the back—and watch the filming. In front of the video screen, copious notes are taken, creative changes discussed, excuses aired, and hair pulled out when the voices of highly paid talent are drowned out by the skid of rubber heels across a floor, followed by the high-pitched slam of a clattering glass door.

Team One, the *real* actors, is called onto set. The stand-ins rush out to use the bathroom, answer their phone messages, or to scope out the latest goodie crafty has cooked up. A makeup artist comes out of nowhere to freshen my lips by dipping a disposable lipstick brush into a palette of colors, one of which has been lifted from my own tube.

Feeling a hot breath at my neck, I turn just slightly to find the lead actor in likewise cruel makeup, slicked back hair, and a wool-weave camel suit. At the moment I start across to enter the aisle, he will follow me, as his stand-in did, and turn the opposite direction into the library. Flushed, I quickly turn away, but he leans in to console my nervousness.

"I'm right behind you," he began. "And I can't move until you do, so listen up. The director is overly quiet sometimes."

And through the glass door the director enters. Holy shit. It's my ten-year-old girl's wet dream, Rowdy, the dusty chapped cowboy. In a soft blue, worn zipped sweatshirt over a baby blue chambray shirt and loose cotton knit gray sweats, my first black-and-white television idol, stops to chat with the female lead, who is standing at the top of the aisle. My teenage girl's *spaghetti western* man-with-no-name heartthrob is on his way down the aisle and is coming towards me. I move back to make room for *Play Misty for Me* to pass, and my stockinged foot lands on my costar's shiny brown shoe. He steadies me with a hand to my elbow.

"How's my secretary today?" the director speaks directly to me, his piercing blue eyes locking mine in a momentary daze.

They are never as tall as you thought they would be. *They* look different in person. A few inches above me, his gently worn and wrinkled face is close enough to begin a kiss when I answer, "Ready to go to work, sir."

Go ahead and say it! Go ahead, Dirty Harry, say it once for me! But he moved along to make someone else's day.

I heard each subtle "Action, let's go again, and that's enough" whispered from behind the file cabinets, and I only stepped on J. Edgar's foot one more time, so he could steady me.

After only three takes, while the camera setup was reversed for the next shot, we were sent back to holding and snacks in the big tent.

I used the break to check for phone messages outside Stage 16—rather than rushing to the abandoned typing pool to gloat over my celebrity encounters with a boastful glazed donut between my teeth.

The first voicemail is from a wardrobe lady letting me know she has emailed me the time and place for *my fitting* and to respond to the email, so she will know I received it. My agency had not called to tell me I had booked anything and wardrobe ladies do not call from Central Casting. Could it be? Had the aggressive chatter of *that actress* I had become for one teeny-tiny regrettable moment not ended my career? Has Hollywood forgiven me?

The phone was silently vibrating. It is my agent. Not one of the assistants, but it's my actual *agent*. I'm in more trouble than I thought.

"Julie, you booked!" He was gaily ecstatic. "I wanted to be the one to tell you."

"The time-and-a-half elephant spot?"

"You weren't even put on hold. No such nonsense for my favorite actor."

This was news to me, the *favorite actor* bit.

"Thank you. I think I've worked with the director before," I winced. "Do you know who it is, the director?"

"Not his name, but the casting assistant asked me to let you know that after you left the room, the director figured out who you were. You were his Little Debbie wife."

"Really?"

"Yes, the Little Debbie Million Smile campaign? Muffins in trees, was it?"

"No—yes. You mean the casting director asked you to let me know how I know the director?"

Whew, saved by the one mysteriously recurring jutting black whisker on my chinny-chin-chin.

"Yes. Same casting director, same director, and same role."

"The smiling, submitting, non-sexual, unemployed wife."

"Type casting, my dear. Type casting."

Chapter 24

Carrots for an Elephant and the Nurturing Gene

> ♪ Yes, it's gonna take a miracle
> To make me love someone new
> 'Cause I'm crazy for you ♪
>
> *It's Gonna Take a Miracle*
> Teddy Randazzo, Bob Weinstein, Lou Stallman

MOTHER scolds me for not having a daily newspaper to read from cover to cover, but I have Bill Nob *On The News* to shock me awake every morning. And when that is not enough to turn my stomach, I turn on the Mac and am instantly confronted with *Yahoo! News*. Again, I am not disappointed.

As the President and First Lady may need it in the future, the Obama administration drops the defense of the Federal anti-gay marriage law, Defense of Marriage Act or DOMA, passed by Congress fifteen years ago, stating that *Same Sex Marriage* is legally indefensible. After that mouthful of news, I light a delicious morning smoke, chase it with creamed coffee and picture Mom's small town newspaper pelted onto her porch, the front page headline boldly scribed: *Queers Go Wild!*

In Lubbock, Texas, of all places, a Saudi Arabian college student is charged with the attempted use of a weapon of mass destruction. His foiled plan was to hide bomb materials inside dolls and baby carriages to blow up dams, nuclear plants, and the Dallas home of former President George W. Bush, thus perhaps vindicating George's accusation that Arabs hold weapons of mass destruction.

In Tripoli, Libya's leader Muammar Gaddafi fights back protestors by firing at them from helicopters and warplanes. Charlie Sheen's outrageous ranting gets his show *Two And a Half Men* cancelled; but he's still *winning*. Mother will be in tears; it's her favorite show. But she won't know until her paper is delivered tomorrow morning, and I am not going to be the first one to tell her.

I've been selectively passing out bookmarks for *The Year I Learned to Text; Why Am I Having Sex With a Muslim in My Basement?*—currently abbreviated fittingly as *TYILTT*—sending out en masse email advertisements by way of blind copy, so as not to offend, and discovering to my dismay that Muslim bashing is not yet popular. My marketing has been broached with negative comments such as: That's not very nice; Muslims aren't allowed to have sex; That's not very nice; You are a racist; Remove me from your email list. I take it all in stride, because I'm going to get paid time-and-a-half to play with an endangered species and the doomsayers are not.

* * *

"Why are you calling so early? What's wrong?" Mom gasped in drama queen delight. "Has something happened to your sister?"

"Not that I know of—"

"She hasn't returned my calls for weeks. You know how I worry."

"She's the one who works. I'm sure she's fine," I apologized for my sister. After answering phone calls and emails during her work day, Rae is not up to returning Mother's pitiful, guilt inspiring voice mails, until she's two vodka martinis into the cocktail hour, and then she blissfully forgets her favorite-daughter duties.

"Yes, she has a lot of responsibility," Mother bragged.

"Try calling her at the office. She's given you that number over and over again."

"I wouldn't want her to lose her job spending time on the phone with me," she gallantly disagreed. "I understand that she makes very good money, but do you know what it is exactly she does there?"

"Something extremely important for which they pay her a lot of money."

"Oh, okay. Why are you calling so early?"

Oh, how I'm dying to ruin her day with a *Two and a Half Men* spoiler.

"Well, Mother, you're always suspicious that I'm doing *something*, but not telling you about it, so I'm calling to let you know I'll be in Perris today—"

"I've always stressed that you must do your traveling before it's too late. Is your passport current?"

"Not that Paris. Perris, California."

"Why, when there are so many wonderful places in the world, would you want to go there?" she asked.

She forgets. Although she has seen all the pictures, she forgets that I've traveled to Milan and Venice and Rome, to Japan, to London, and to Paris twice.

"I'm going there to meet an elephant named Rosie, my costar in a commercial I'm shooting this week," I explained. There was a lull on the other end, so I continued my enthusiasm. "Rosie is not the elephant in the movie *Water For Elephants*, but her friend Tai played the part of *Rosie* in the movie."

"Well, you have a nice day, dear."

"I should be done by late afternoon. Perris is on Interstate 215, so I thought I'd drive north and take you out to dinner?"

"Oh, not today. I want to be home when your sister calls."

***

"I'll be back before dark," I promised my canine brood staring at me from their living room bed. "Brute, you follow Hound out that kitchen door. I don't want to come home to another damp yellowed bath rug, understand?" Brute cowered down into a shaggy clump up against Hound's back. Hound quickly nipped him off. "Don't look so sad. Don't I always come back?"

After a smooth hour-and-a-half freeway drive, I reached the *Have Trunk Will Travel* Ranch and my costars for the shoot: one hefty round-faced, fifty-something giant of a husband and a heavily wrinkled charming Asian elephant. The trainer joins us for a meet-and-greet, introducing us to his playful herd behind steel poled fencing, as the five gray ladies, averaging eight-feet tall, toss a log to and fro with their trunks. The grounds are impeccably clean, continuously raked clean, evidenced by the tidy crisscrossing lines in the hard-packed dirt. The scent in the air is of open fields, alfalfa, and hay. There is not one green gastric dump circled with flies; not one soiled bathroom rug to wash out. I could live here.

Rosie is brought out—no chained feet, no ringleader hooking her trunk—to familiarize herself with us. Basically, she has simply lumbered on over to get a whiff of two more strangers. Funny, she's not as tall as I thought she would be. Our job is to remain calm, not appear frightened, and to cozy up. Rosie sits down on her back legs, and I'm looking into the kindest eyes that have ever looked down on me. My nurturing gene takes over and I'm stroking leathery ears and tickling a hairy chin.

Feeding Rosie another carrot from a wheelbarrow of carrots, always aware of four giant feet next to my booted toes, I begin a conversation with my husband.

"Gavin, I suddenly feel petite."

"That's maybe the answer to self love," he whispers from the other side of Rosie's trunk, which has curled about my hand.

"What do you mean?" I ask.

"Hanging out with others heavier and more wrinkled than yourself."

With a scrunched up face, I held my nose and blurted out, "Did you just fart?"

"Nah, that was the elephant."

As promised, I returned home before dark. Brute and Hound scampered to the front porch with eager *she came back* barks. I reached out my hands to comfort them and was rejected. "Ah, so you smell a wild animal, huh?" I unlocked the front door to sniff a Brute boo-boo. He instantly hid under the bed.

Tomorrow is wardrobe-fitting day, for which I will receive a minimum of two hours pay at union scale. I mixed myself a vodka tonic, lit a cigarette, and went hunting on the Internet Movie Data Base to get a feel for my new chubby hubby. Using the IMDB site, one can search for names, movies, and television shows. As is the industry tradition of discounting commercial work, Gavin's only credit is his twenty-five year marriage to a television sitcom star, a thin wisp of a redhead. My chin in my hand, I think tomorrow my nurturing gene will be stretched to include a man who may need a bit of pumping up.

In between each change of *costume*—pastel tailored shirts and khaki pants, because that's how creative advertising executives believe that women all across America dress inside their homes on lazy Sunday mornings—I am brought before the director, the producer, and the clients, commonly referred to as *the money*. No one speaks directly to me, but discuss the clothing options in whispered discontent, as the wardrobe lady signals me to shirk away for another selection.

Gavin passes by me in a plaid shirt cruelly tucked into khaki pants on his way to the lion's den.

"Hey, do you think they'll give us lunch?" he asks.

"No feeding is required for a union wardrobe fitting—and you know it," I teased. "You look great in that shirt." My nurturing had begun.

♫ I'm too sexy for my shirt ♫ he laughed and sashayed around the corner to the wardrobe arena to change into another *look*.

The *committee* orders in couscous and pita bread, trays of Middle Eastern vegetable fare, and with its mouth full continues to wave me off with stained paper napkins again and again. At the end of the day, they agree on the blue shirt, my blue shirt, the same one I wore to the audition and the same one I wore previously in the *Little Debbie* commercial. The director shoots me a friendly wink and a teeny smile. Today, unlike the dopamine-consumed, oxytocin dribbling, love-drugged thinner me of a few years ago, the new alcohol soaked, vaginally vacant me is sucked up tight inside the cursed corset so that I can button the damned shirt. The wardrobe crew completes a billable day, keeps my stretched shirt for the shoot, and I can't wait to get home and get the body armor off.

"Wait up," Gavin hails me from the curb as I am tossing my garment bag into the backseat of the car.

"What's up?" I ask, realizing I should have used the restroom one more time before my rush-hour drive home.

"Traffic is thick. Why don't we have a pre-shoot drink and wait for it to thin out?"

"Should we call the wife first?"

Stumped, Gavin leaned his back against the car door, his arms folded. "Some days I just wonder what it would be like to be single."

"After twenty-five years, is it?"

"Ah, ha, you've done your IMDB homework, have you?"

"Just like to know who I'm working with. Single? At our age there's no one left, Gavin. Be happy with what you have. Be happy with your wife."

The conversation drifted into the familiar territory of the married man who hasn't had sex for a decade, a man who has lost attraction for his wife. I knew that part was a lie, that the truth was his lovely wife was no longer attracted to him.

"First thing tomorrow, we both need to go on a diet and start training for the L.A. Marathon, but tonight . . . tonight text her on your way home to be . . . to *be naked on the bed*," and my eyes welled up in delicious memory of a time when stretch marks, skin tags, and varicose veins had been erased by such a request. "It worked on me," I smiled. True to form, I stopped the foolish release of a melancholy tear with a serious joke. "Oh, and changing the toilet paper without being asked is a turn on."

"She'll think I've gone crazy," he laughed.

"I've had my once-in-a-lifetime great romance. Things, feelings, butterflies, they all happened to me. I'll never forget and I'll never regret allowing it to happen to me. Your wife may just be your once-in-a-lifetime great romance. Now, go home, grab ahold of the trust hormone, the love molecule—"

"What's that?"

"Oxytocin, the love drug. Go and be good to her."

He reached for me with a thankful hug.

This nurturing business is exhausting.

Chapter 25

Empty Toilet Rolls and Naked on the Bed

Bill Nob *On The News* and his morning crew are right on time this sunny morning with more good news.

A 9.0 magnitude undersea earthquake—♫ *under the sea, under the sea* ♫ That's what comes from having two daughters who grew up on Disney animated musicals.

I rolled over and smiled. "Oh, Bill, we all know you forced your kids to watch *The Little Mermaid* with you, when they wanted to watch *MTV* music videos."

Okay, let's start again. A 9.0 magnitude undersea earthquake off the Pacific Coast of Tohoku, Japan, powered up a gigantic tsunami with waves reaching up to one hundred and thirty-three feet crashing six miles inland and hitting nuclear reactors. This is the worst thing to happen to Japan since World War II, when we dropped the first atomic bomb on them. Japanese earthquake and tsunami, with two you get—

"Nothing extra, Bill. Not even an egg roll."

I doubt there'll be the United States standard looting of abandoned property. The Japanese have too much honor for that. Doesn't Japan have an Earthquake Early Warning system? Oh, eight-second warning, huh? That's not enough time to find the family dog. Well, they're estimating over ten thousand dead and thousands missing. And, Julie, you're only missing one loser and nobody cares. That's the news. We're done.

While the Coast Guard kept watch for an aftershock to hit the multi-million dollar beach homes of Malibu and while Gavin was on set delivering his lines as the Spiriva *hero husband* at Raleigh Studios in Manhattan Beach, I kept busy with my routine.

I walked down to Vine Elementary School for nourishing applause from enamored children, the innocent fans of Grandma Julie; children who had no idea I was hung over, that my coughing was not from a cold, and who had all begun to look like my greatest fear: the bastardized half-breed children of one errant Persian infiltrating the Latina population of Hollywood. I yearned to take them all home with me and to call their irresponsible father with scathing threats to turn him in to the Department of Child Support Services.

Instead I called my daughter Elizabeth, who today is forty-two years old. "I'm sorry I can't drive out for lunch today. Did you get my card?"

Elizabeth was busy at her register with customers. "Hold on, I have to put the phone down," she quickly said. I heard the sound of the cash drawer close.

"The business is doing well?" I continued.

"Bustling," she huffed. "Thank you for the card and the check."

"Wow, somebody stressed out?"

"Oh, Mother, sometimes I just want to be single again. When the kids are finally grown and out of the house—"

"Whoa. Have I lost track again or aren't the *kids* almost nineteen and seventeen? You can stay the course for another year. There's nobody else out there, anyway. Take it from your well-worn mother," I tried.

"I don't want to date anyone, Mother. You know I don't like talking about my marriage with you. I'm just having a bad day. Sometimes I just want a lousy job as a waitress, live in a crummy apartment, and be left alone," she shared, an anomaly.

"Spark it up. Text him this afternoon with *be naked on the bed*. It worked on me," I offered.

"Why would I wanna do that? Sex is not the problem. I just want him to change the toilet paper roll without being asked. How hard is that? Why am I the only one that sees an empty roll and replaces it?"

Having been married four times, I had plenty of explanations, but advising her to take her chosen role seriously as mother, cook, businesswoman, breadwinner, bottle washer, and sex goddess was akin to my own mother's mantra of *You've made your bed, now lie in it*, so I left it alone.

"You're very lucky to be surrounded by a family that loves you. Cash that check and you two go out for a fancy dinner tonight, okay?"

"We never go out without the kids."

Bingo.

Keeping my appointment, I walked up to Wells Fargo, where I caused Viktor, the Armenian guard of my IRA account, to wince in pain once more when I moved another chunk of my life's savings out and into the checking account to cover my expenses. This is truly the *year of the house*. At this rate, in ten years I will be out of cash, the house will still need painting, the roof and the air conditioner replacing, and the Scion on its last tires.

For some odd reason, I thought about egg rolls all day and returned from another walk down Vine to Pavilions and Panda Express with a twelve hundred calorie Styrofoam take-out box oozing with noodles, orange chicken, and two vegetable egg rolls—a bottle of white wine in a paper bag tucked under my arm. I have a seven a.m. call time tomorrow and I want to be sure I pass out by nine p.m.

It's calming to know where you're going. I've worked at Raleigh Studios in Manhattan Beach as an extra on many a television series. Except for one stint as a juror on *Boston Legal*—my lengthy camera time prompting friends and family to call during the airing to inquire whether William Shatner was nice in person—today I would not be a deliberately camera-fuzzed, non-distinguishable woman in the background. Today I would be *naked on the bed* for all to see, so to speak.

Talent is to park in the tiered parking garage along with the makeup artists, the hair police, the production assistants, the crew, the cameramen, and the director. The clients are delivered to set in a limousine. Rosie is delivered in her silver trailer, her trainers at the wheel of a silver truck driven in from Perris.

Rosie swung her tail as I passed by a loosened bail of alfalfa and into a cavernous sound stage, a bustling city at work. Neatly displayed on foldout tables are designer fabric choices for the drapes, pillows, and rugs of the *hero family's* living room and raised billiard room, which have been built and dressed midway between the viewing section and a virtual home accessory store. I suddenly have the urge to go shopping for non-distinguishable lamps, pillows, side chairs, coffee table books, and knitted throws—the background actors hired by the set design team.

The clients lounge in black leather couches placed in a *U* formation, each bobblehead dangerously sipping hot coffee over the computers on their laps. There are long tables set up to accommodate the thinkers, the shakers, and the troublemakers.

And as always, there are plenty of things to trip over: electrical cords, metal tripod lighting stands, and my own nervous feet.

A man representing himself as the legal arm of the production team shoves at me a threatening sheet of paper disguised as a welcome memo.

The commercial shoot Warning Sheet prepared by a humorous production company assistant; the grammar corrected for easier reading:

Welcome to the Spiriva commercial shoot

1. Do not attempt to get a photo of or with the elephant. Autographs are also frowned upon.

2. The elephant (hereafter referred to as Rosie) will have a holding area in the corner of the stage, behind the sets. Please leave her be.

3. Once the elephant is on set, ALL WORK MUST CEASE, unless approval is given by the trainers. Please go through the first AD and/or trainers prior to moving about the set when Rosie is out. Generally, we will bring her in for a line-up and take her away while we light and set. Then she'll come back to shoot.

4. Let's endeavor to work quietly and minimize banging and crashing, especially behind the sets where she is resting.

5. As ever, no food or drinks around the set area.
6. No pets. While few, if any, crew members would ever bring a pet to set, some "others" have been known to.
7. We will have American Humane Society representatives on set.
8. Rosie will live in her trailer outside the stage for the duration of the shoot. Please observe the same respect and quiet there as well.
9. The set floors have been designed for easy cleanup, should something bad happen.
10. The Puppeteers are not as sensitive; however, please be kind to them, and no autographs!

Thank you in advance for your assistance.

Gavin has been here since six-thirty this morning and all day yesterday. Rosie, representing the weight of C.O.P.D. upon my husband's rotund chest, will be making another appearance today. Watching Gavin and the director bobbing their heads together in huddle formation and coming up for air in gusts of laughter, I surmise that they have had plenty of time for male bonding and that Gavin is sufficiently pumped up. Neither one acknowledges me as the 2nd A.D. scoots me off to hair and makeup and wardrobe.

After arguing unsuccessfully with the *Dragon Lady*—the same evil hair stylist from the *Little Debbie* shoot—I now look nothing like the woman who auditioned for this role. My makeup is barely there and my hair has been meticulously flattened against my head. I have been transformed into the smiling, submitting, non-sexual, unemployed wife.

Waiting to be brought to set, I hide out in my trailer biting a bagel slathered with blueberry cream cheese and watching reruns of *Home and Garden TV*—just because I can. I have promised myself the return of the cable box, but not until after the release of Part Two, which is coming along in wild uncontrollable spurts between bougainvillea trimming, dog walking, auditioning, lookie-loo-homebuyer time wasting, and nose hair plucking. I have brought along a few dozen bookmarks to pass out.

Realizing I am actually not being paid to stare at a television, I mosey into the stage to catch the action. Gavin is lying on the living room couch delivering his lines for the one-hundredth time.

"Be conversational," the director shouts out from his chair alongside the camera. The *suits* whisper, the makeup artist powders Gavin's forehead, the caterer passes out multi-colored Jell-O shooters topped with whipped cream and shaved almonds.

"Take a break, Gavin. Let's get Julie in place and shoot her before lunch."

I am quickly lip-glossed and hurried under the lights and into the living room for a few *Lucy* double-take looks at my *Desi,* who is not on the couch, and a few more eye-roll looks at the elephant, that is also not in the room. I have nothing to interact with or to play to but empty furniture. Careful to stand straight and clench my midriff bulge pinched inside the corset, I use my instincts.

"There's an elephant sitting on your husband's stomach, Julie!" the director roars at me.

I try again, again, and again.

"Oh, fuck it. Let's go to lunch."

I'm not going to be passing out any bookmarks on this set.

I ate alone in my trailer. Gavin ate with *The Money,* the producers, and his new best friend, the director.

I have not a scene with Rosie in the flesh—she will be magically implanted into the living room set postproduction—but right now she is stationed just below the raised billiard room set, her rear end facing my barstool at the end of the pool table. The camera and director stationed at the opposite end of the table, Rosie teeters back and forth from one foot to the other, as my husband walks around the pool table eyeing his shot at the eight ball. This is my cue to smile adoringly at him as I gently turn the pages of my non-distinguishable magazine.

"Action," whispers the director, and Rosie lifts her tail and secretly releases a disgusting, guttural scent, which wafts its way to my adoring face. My smile quickly fades to curdled pursed lips, my nose scrunches up in a snarl, and my eyes wince in a flinch.

"Cut. Smile, Julie. You love this man, got it?"

"Got it."

"Go again. Action."

Gavin bends down and lines up his shot. I turn a page and look up adoringly at my husband. Rosie restlessly shifts from side to side and lets out a warning bellow, her trunk tossed over her head before releasing another stream of silent death.

"Just keep rolling. Action. Hell, Julie, what kind of a smile was that?"

"I'm trying to smile, but Rosie keeps farting, thus the smirk," I explained and waved the aroma away from my face.

"Can someone stop the elephant from passing gas? We're trying to shoot a commercial here," he rattled. "All we need is for you to smile with wifely charm at your husband who is playing pool, lining up the cue ball with the eight ball," the exasperated director restated as he had again and again. "Do you think you could do that just once?"

"Oh, my God. She did it again," I answered timidly.

"Put a cork in it! Take a break, everybody."

I waived at the assistant director in charge of my whereabouts, but he was on the phone as I flew by. Knowing that at any moment the director would be expecting me back on my barstool, I hightailed it to my trailer outside the studio and into the bathroom for a camper pee quickie. When I entered the sound studio, it was apparent from all the mayhem that I had been missed.

The director was shouting. "Where is Julie?" The wardrobe lady rushed at me from behind to hand press my shirt while the makeup czar skipped alongside waving a lip brush in the air.

The legal arm guy whispered into his phone as I passed by, "We're giving the use of the wife a second thought."

My stomach flipped and I tripped on the stairs before taking my place at the end of the pool table. I knew my goose was cooked; my absence for five minutes now the only elephant in the room.

"Julie, you're killing me," was the last direction I would get.

The ride home was a bumper-to-bumper, three-smokes and sour milk pity party inside a car that reeked of the nasty, shameful smell of burnt Virginia Slims. Chugging along at five miles per hour, there was plenty of time to listen to sad love songs and yearn for him, he who had said, "I like you the way you look. You don't have to put makeup on for me."

I had triumphantly reached my revenge best: overweight, addicted, and flatulence intolerant. Within a few days I would also be cut and strewn to the floor of the editing room as odoriferous outtake waste from a commercial that would run nationwide for twenty-two months, where an overweight, barely breathing *hero* would stroll through his bachelor pad and shoot pool while a sweet old Asian elephant rambled faithfully behind him. Gavin would soon begin depositing his residual checks, while I would continue counting my wasted regrets, as thousands of bodies float back onto the devastated shores of an island in the Pacific.

CHAPTER 26

Eleanor Roosevelt and A Guinness Moustache

♪ And when Irish eyes are smiling
Sure, they steal your heart away ♪

When Irish Eyes Are Smiling
Chauncy Olcott, Ernest R. Ball, and George Graff Jr.

Spinning in a whirlwind of excitement, Randi surprised me at the gate with a bottle of red wine and a collection of mail tucked under one arm.

"I sold another car today, and when the guy came back to pick it up—all washed and waxed—he brought me your favorite, pinot noir! It's French, right?"

"You really get away with playing salesperson in that outfit?" I chastised her belly busting, low-cut Marilyn Manson t-shirt and black and white, thigh-busting skull and crossbones leggings. "Why in the hell are you wearing that?"

"Having a bad day?" she comforted me.

"I still have a love hangover, my kids hate me, and I'm *not working in this town again*," I laughed, reciting the legendary phrase.

"Hollywood got to ya today, huh? Let's go inside and kick the dogs," Randi teased as the beasts scampered onto the front steps.

"This is good stuff," I praised my glass of wine, spinning the liquid and watching it leave a shade of crimson on the inside of the glass. "Stick your nose all the way down into the glass and take a sniff first," I instructed her as we both lit up our accompanying cigarettes.

"It smells like smoke."

"Good enough!"

"So now all your kids hate you? I thought it was just two out of three," she began our counseling session.

"Well, I haven't heard from Alexandra in weeks. I stopped texting her, so I wouldn't feel bad when she doesn't text me back. Apparently, I'm supposed to check her *Facebook* page to see what she's up to. No pictures of her new boyfriend as yet. My son Glen has deserted me and now has been officially disinherited. My oldest, Elizabeth, is tricky. I always say the wrong thing to her—to all of them, I suppose."

"As in 'why in the hell are you wearing *that*?'" She swung her crossbones up and onto the glass table, jiggling the wine bottle.

"Point taken. Why are you wearing that?"

"It's Hollywood, baby. The customers have dreadlocks, arm-sleeve tattoos, and chains hanging from their leathers. I fit right in. And they all have money, usually from their parents. Go figure."

"Thanks for bringing in the mail. What prompted that?"

"Because you can see your mailbox from the street and there was a Netflix red envelope sticking out. Didn't want your movie to get stolen."

"No television, no cable, just the perversion of a no-commercial movie every other night until I get the second book out," I squirmed in my plastic chair, knowing that writing instead of talking is what I should be doing right now. "Besides, I like being able to pause and tinkle."

"Have you thought about sending Part One to him?"

"If I had an address—no, no, heavens no."

"If it becomes a best seller, you think he'll sue you?" she asked with wide eyes.

"I'll swear that I just made him up. Anyway, the best defense to a defamation of character case is *the truth*. Besides, what would be his damages? What's he going to sue me for? That because of the popularity of my books, he can't hook up anymore? Women don't believe his lies anymore? How much money is that worth?" I quizzed.

"What about all the Muslim stuff? Aren't you worried about a rock being thrown through your bedroom window?"

"*Hollywood Woman Stoned By Mullahs.* Great headline. Free advertising. I can only hope."

Randi stood in grand pause and raised her glass. "His attorney will examine you and bring you to tears. And you'll finally answer 'Sir, the plaintiff is a handsome young man, much younger than I. Any woman would be thrilled to have even a moment of his attention. But, sadly, I just made the hero up. He was never real.'

"And then Ali will rise up in front of the judge and jury, his arms outstretched to you and plead, 'Julie, Julie, don't you remember? We had a spiritual connection. I miss you. Don't you miss me?' The gavel will bang and the judge will dismiss the case. The jurors leave dumbfounded and pissed that they don't get to hear the end—"

"Well, that doesn't make any sense," I shook my head.

"No, but it's a good movie ending."

Watching my friend, with her broad, big-toothed grin and mild temperament, she resembles a caring and giving spirit, beaming with loves lost and friends gained, a flaming liberal always willing to listen to the other side, which means the wine is working on me.

"You look like Eleanor Roosevelt tonight," I said.

"That dyke? She might not like the comparison. I used to be a stripper, you know."

"No, I missed that. Go ahead. I'm all ears," I said and settled back with another cigarette.

"Yeah, I was a stripper. No pole, though. They forgot to build it into the stage floor. My floor work was hot, but I refused to grind on the laps of the gross pigs that came in. Two hundred bucks a night and that was three years ago."

"We're in a recession, so it might be less than that now. Why did you quit?"

"I was fired for getting fat."

"Sue the bastards!"

* * *

St. Patrick's Day, I visited the basement to fetch the shamrock dotted leprechaun flag and the Irish Pub wench costume, a cotton cream ruffled peasant top attached to an ankle-length velvet skirt. Tired of being a recluse in a neighborhood lined with restaurants that I pass by, but rarely go inside, I will strut up to the Hollywood Boulevard festivities in my green suede boots and sidle up to a hot plate of corned beef and cabbage. Maybe I would strike up a flirtatious conversation with a fellow brisket lover, who through splendid and garrulous persuasion would turn out to be the perfect foot to fit my glass slipper, which today will be disguised as the *Erin go Braugh* dancing boot. Clutching the see-through plastic garment bag, I trotted upstairs to prepare for my holiday.

Years ago I began my once-a-year career as a "Danny Boy" crooner, fetching dollar bills into my bosom from raucous fans belching from too many green beers. *Have Karaoke Machine; Will Sing.* Have family and friends; always have an audience, just in case the bawdy brigade fails to show up. I memorized five of the most popular ditties on the sing-along tape, and when prompted I would sing them over and over again. There was not a dry eye in the place, when I hit the high note.
♪ And I'll be HERE in sunshine or in shadow ♪

Perhaps this evening I'll hook up with a folk band strummin' out the cords of "Toora Loora Loora," I imagined while snuggling mee arms into the bouffant sleeves. So far so good. I haven't worn the "I'll Take You Home Again, Kathleen" costume since arriving in Hollywood, eight years ago. I shook out the shocking red Maureen O'Hara wig. It still fits. Well, I haven't grown a fat head. Surely, I thought, as I laced meeself up in the cinched burgundy cummerbund, a costume that came in a plastic bag labeled *fits most* would certainly be forgiving. As I tugged and struggled, I caught a horrifying glimpse of myself in the mirror. There in the sliding glass closet door was an old lady in a red wig looking back at me and the reflection of Natasha sprawled like a mischievous black cat across my bed.

"You're not going out een zat getup, are you, dahlink? Think again. Dun't embarrass yourself."

"I can't get the cummerbund to meet in the middle, so no, I'm not," I admitted defeat and let the air out.

"You could alvays try it with that evil corset of yours, but after a few beers, you veel be camper peeing all over Hollywood."

"I suppose you want to borrow it and strut your lithe self all over town."

"You know no one sees me but you. So vat vould bee zee point?"

I snatched the wig off and tossed it at Natasha. Am I ready to kiss *Kathleen* a fond farewell and to bag her up as a donation to The Goodwill? Are my *When Irish Eyes Are Smiling* vanity days behind me? Staring at myself, I am devastated. So this is what getting old is all about: having to admit it, do it gracefully—and stop playing dress up?

"Before you heet me with that lovely Irish walking stick, let me say that your green jacket, a pair of skinny jeans, and the green boots will do nicely. You always look good in that. And you can wear that silly hat with the sparkly shamrock pin on it."

"You certainly go in and out of that Transylvania accent quickly," I said and rummaged through the closet for the green jacket, circa 1992. Whew, it still fit, as long as I don't try to button it. "Where's the rest of the team tonight?"

"The Counter-Terrorism Squirrel Squad is een Islamabad, Pakistan, searching for Osama Bin Laden," she posed and stretched out a glamorous hand. "May I borrow a nail file, dahlink? I've broken one of my claws."

"They're on assignment without you, Julia Child?"

"I vouldn't geet within five yards of that voomanizing, greasy old Islamic fart. Besides, zee agency would have me marry him to get information, and I don't sleep around," she emphatically brushed her black hair out of one eye. "Why you call me *Julia Child*? I don't cook. I haven't heated up a can of borsch for over fifty years."

"Julia was a bit of a top secret spy in World War II. It is said that it was during her time with Secret Intelligence, now known as the C.I.A., that she gleaned her discipline and organizational skills."

"I'll be darned."

"What's the plan when they find him?"

"To keel him."

Dazzled by the unexpected window display of St. Paddy's Day t-shirts, cups, caps, and shot glasses, I turned my green boots into the shelter of Urban Outfitters up the sidewalk from the Jack in the Box at Sunset and Ivar. Upon my inspection, I found in fancy lettering that the celebration items designated all Irishmen as out-of-control Gaelic alcoholics with cute sayings such as: *IRISH I were DRUNK; Leprechaun Piss;* and *Downward Facing Upchuck*. I protested by leaving empty handed.

Would they dare to defame the Holy Days of Ramadan by displaying a t-shirt depicting a thin, bony Muslim Terrorist strapped with explosives above the caption: *Fasting Fanatic*? If, indeed, the religion of peace expects everyone to become part of the cult, they have really got to—as Mother would say—get with it and "keep their sense of humor."

Hollywood Boulevard is Tinsel Town's poorly executed improvisation of St. Patrick's Day. The only thing reminiscent of snakes being run out of Ireland is a young girl slithering along the sidewalk in tiny green sequined shorts with mock shamrock tattoos stuck onto her cheeks at both ends. At Dillon's, the tourists in splashes of green are lined up two by two from the doorway back up Vine Street passed the Capitol Records building. There might be corned beef and cabbage inside the Irish pub, bagpipes, and a folk band, but standing in line was not how I wanted to spend the evening.

It was chilly and getting colder when, after asking at one restaurant after another—including the Pig and Whistle—if they were serving corned beef and cabbage, I was directed to The Cat and Fiddle, a fine and dandy English pub on Sunset Boulevard, just a short walk down the less traveled street of Shraeder and across from the Hollywood Athletic Club, once a health club, nightclub, and event space. I hoofed my way on down the empty sidewalk, warming my rusty pipes with a verse or two of "My Wild Irish Rose" on the chance there would be a string trio in need of a vocalist.

At the entrance of the courtyard, a young man in a green bowler is manning a rope tethered between two towering grandfather trees.

"Five dollar cover charge, ma'am," he insists.

"In honor of the Irish religious holiday?"

"Yes, ma'am."

Ignoring his security guard attitude, I investigate the festivities. The outside seating is crowded with good looking young men gathered at mix 'n match wooden tables chatting it up over pitchers of beer. This is Hollywood. Call me a homophobe, but groups of handsome men in designer skinny jeans dining together is a bit of a clue that I'm not finding that pot of gold here.

"Uh, let me see if I have enough. You know, I don't walk around with cash on me, sir," I stupidly explain while rummaging through my green suede cross-body mini bag. "Ah, here you are: four dollars and four quarters." I'm thinkin' that if he calls me *ma'am* one more time, I'm calling St. Patrick himself to rough up the bugger.

"I can't take change, ma'am."

Oh, if only I were Catholic, I'd have more pull with the saints.

"My quarters are not good here? Bollocks, sonny. Unhook that rope." He has my Irish dander up.

"If I let you by, ma'am, do you promise to change your quarters for a dollar bill and bring it right back to me?"

A line of hungry revelers is forming behind me, but I'm not through yet. I live alone. At least tonight I have someone to talk to.

"Why won't you take the quarters? Has there been a rise in counterfeit George Washingtons?"

"Just following orders from the manager, ma'am."

"Cross my heart and hope to die, I'll be back straightaway," I promised and wished I'd brought my shillelagh along. As a mother, I have dished out needed punishment with a sturdy wooden spoon, but this prat needs a walking stick shellacking.

"And, ma'am, no celebrity sightings allowed. Please do not ask Morrissey—or anyone else—for a selfie. He'd like his privacy tonight," he instructed.

"Who?"

"Moz, ma'am."

"I don't know who the hell you're talking about, sonny," I admitted.

"The singer/songwriter, ma'am."

"The Who?" I am so out of the loop, so lost in the sixties. They say that your choice in music is set in stone by the time you're sixteen;

memories of long car rides with your feet on the dashboard, the forty-fives spinning into the wee morning hours of the pajama party; your first school dance and the boy that slow danced with both arms around your waist.

"No, The Smiths."

"Whatever," I blow him off and step across into the golden rope fun zone.

The courtyard is lit with strung lights from tree to tree, but they are white, not green. The heat lamps have not yet been ignited. The tiered stone fountain flows with clear water. If I had my say, green food coloring would have been a nice touch. The wait staff wears black with one string of plastic green beads, something left over from Mardi Gras.

There is not an open table outside, so I wander under the black oval awning and inside. There's a big screen TV over the shellacked bar, a futbol game the entertainment. The fireplace is lifeless. There is no music, just the sound of a lonely woman asking for a single table in a roomful of talkative traveling companions, back-slapping best buddies, and presumably the entire Cat and Fiddle Dart Board Club.

A waitress with one arm in a sling seats me at a wooden table for four smack dab in the aisle next to a row of booths bulging with shaggy haired, five o'clock shadow faces bellowing in laughter at the slightest chance to do so. I sip my Guinness, the malt leaving a frothy moustache on my lip, as darts whizz behind my head.

The plate arrives and it is sparse, the mash potatoes wet, the cabbage comes without carrots, and I have to ask for bread. The young men wander from the booth to the bar, bringing back pitchers of foamy brown beer, all the while intently studying their I-Phones, perhaps in the hope that *she* is on her way.

One man wears a Kelly green t-shirt with *IRISH I were DRUNK* across the front in celebration of the Irish Holy Holiday. Urban Outfitters must be ecstatic over its one sale of the day. He is typical with his brown eyes and fluttering dark lashes, a mop of brown hair, a dimple in his chin. Would I see him here? I must keep looking, looking in the oddest of places. Would he saunter through the door in his shiny running pants, his untethered tool leading the way, accompanied by a caravan of swarthy Muslims insisting on Halal corned beef? Would he be wearing the soft, long-sleeved gray t-shirt? Would he recognize me in this muslin urchin hat? And I wondered if there might be marketing success for a soft and gray long-sleeved t-shirt sporting the phrase *Do I Look Hungry?* celebrating the sun-up-to-sun-down fasting he so adamantly refused to break, and I chuckle.

"You have a pretty laugh," comes from the booth close by.

"Why, thank you," I chuckle again.

"I like your hat. Are you Irish?" asks the brunet young man with dark eyes.

"My grandfather swore he was—each time he poured himself another glass of whiskey."

"Oh, you're funny, too. Enjoy your dinner, lassie," he said and went back eagerly to search the screen on his phone, his fingers racing.

Under my jacket is a green t-shirt with *Kiss Me I'm Irish* across the chest. Noticing there are no potential leprechauns over the age of forty, I pull the jacket tighter. There is no reason to have anyone read my tits. I won't be meeting the perfect foot tonight, nor will I stumble upon the allusive pot of gold at the end of this rainbow.

Suddenly an older man, attractive but a bit worn and glum, as if the weight of the entire world sat upon his very own shoulders, pulled a chair out at my table.

"May I sit for just a moment?" he kindly inquired in the Queen's English.

Hells bells, you sure can. A St. Paddy's Day miracle had found its way to me. Must be my hat.

"If you like," I answer.

"You're the only patron sitting alone. I'd just like to say that I do think that it's possible to go through life and never fall in love or find someone who loves you," he said quietly, rose from the chair and went on his way.

There was a hush in the room that followed *Mr. Gloom and Doom* out. I ordered another Guinness to give me time to take in his sordid words of wisdom. Had he really thought that I had never fallen in love?

That no one had ever loved me? Did I really appear to be that lonely? It must be the hat.

The young man leaned across the aisle to gasp in a whisper, "Wasn't that Moz?"

"Who? He didn't give his name."

"You should have asked for a selfie."

The waitress traded my four quarters for a green back, which I slapped into the Royal Guard's hand on my way out.

Now after nine o'clock, the streets are beginning to fill with green out-of-control merrymakers. It is time for *Kathleen* to sashay on home.

I poured myself a Jack Daniel's, lit a cigarette, and went onto Alexandra's *Facebook* page to *catch up* with her.

> If you see a lady in a red wig and a green dress with
> green boots—that's my mom. Be nice to her and
> she might sing you an Irish song.

I don't comment on the post. Let the legend live on.

Chapter 27

The Writing Life, High Tide, and Audrey Hepburn

Obviously, there is no outline utilized in my writing; simply, rambling glimpses into the passing slices of a life. Inching my procrastinating writer's way through Part Two of *The Muslim Romance Trilogy*, I flick the pages of my diaries forward through eventful remembrances, to auditions lost, to jobs won, to real estate clients disappeared, and to some extremely needy text messages recorded in shameful detail. For Julie's sake, I could redact a few of the, oh-so-painful-to-read epics fingered from her texting gun, but to do so would be dishonest. The following text to Ali written in October 2010, as she desperately reaches out to him, is one such pitiful example.

> 8:00p   JULIE: I love you, even though in Islamic law we are not married. But I don't need to be married. Been there. All I need is fidelity, trust, and your address.

Always throw a bit of humor into the nail-biting pleasure of hanging oneself.

> 8:02p   JULIE: I want to give you a place to love. If I am just a place among other places, you do not deserve my passion. It is time for you to promise your fidelity and to speak your heart.

Well, that bit of nonsense should have the guy in tears for fear of losing her.

Oops, here comes his immediate reply scribbled across the bottom of one diary page and feverishly completed on the next. Deciphering the scrawled handwriting, it is obvious I was a bit tipsy, when in court stenographer fashion I had copied our texting conversations verbatim from phone to paper.

> 8:04p ALI: Islamic law? There are no rules. No such thing exists. No oppression. Complete freedom. That's the point.

Hell, his bald-faced lies have got to stay in the story. They are in essence the caveat to the throughline of the entire unfathomable fairy tale, along with Julie's drinking and smoking, and the musings of that wise old cat of hers.

Each night, turning off the tap of memories, regrettable moments, and scenes yet to be written is frequently a toss-and-turn task. Lights out, but the faucet continues to drip, drip, and drip some more. Sleep comes and too soon the radio alarm begins a new day.

Film legend Elizabeth Taylor, the woman with purple eyes, passed away this morning at the age of seventy-nine of congestive heart failure. In my early morning grog, I wept. *She's with him*, I thought. No more gorging on comfort food; no more smoking; no more taking of too much drink. She's found peace now; the nagging, empty hole is filled, for she is with Richard. The two wild lovers made raucous celebrity history in the 60s and 70s by divorcing their spouses, marrying, divorcing, marrying again and divorcing—all in between tempestuous, sexually stimulating fistfights and drunken punches.

A few days later, less than twenty civilian fans, including my girlfriend Beryl, gathered on a walkway behind a white picket fence at Forest Lawn to pay their respects. This minimalistic mourning crowd was so exceptional, KTLA news interviewed the funeral goers, who, in their worn tweeds and second-hand store woolens, all looked like last minute *rush call* non-distinguishable extras hired by Central Casting to high tail it over to the lawn of the mortuary.

Would it be only in death that I would be with him once again? Would he pass away years after my hopeful assent to meet up with me in my promised heaven and not the paradise he had been promised? Would he be terribly upset to pass through the pearly gates and find at the end of the white cloud runway just one old lady reaching out her withered hand to him?

This morning my right ear is mushed into the side of a gentle pillow encased in lavender sateen. The soft whir of cars scurrying in intermittent whooshes from the stoplight at Fountain in their repetitive attempt to beat the red light at Santa Monica Boulevard has become to me the blissful sound one hears when pressing an ear to a conch seashell. Outside my windows, the engines roar and lap the shores like giant waves. I could be sleeping in a beach house, its porch steps the walkway through the sand to the breakers. Here I have seaside sounds as the sea gulls flap and soar, circle and screech from rooftop to rooftop. I've spotted a group of them outside the bedroom window overhead in the distance heading west, perhaps taking the day off from city scrapping to visit the ocean and to fish for seafood in the tipping waves; that is, if the Pacific is not too cold for their citified beaks.

Bill Nob coughs up more bad news, Mr. Coffee begins his automatic drip, and Hound turns over on his bed to curl up for another dream. Brute does not stir. The repeat, repeat, and repeat of too many mornings just like the one before.

The throbbing is worse when after I return from the morning void. It's a bouncer today. Men have boners and ladies have bouncers, I smile. I don't really want to do this. It's becoming quite a bit of a chore. But if I don't answer this irritating call, it will ring all day long. I know who it is on the other end. I'm going to answer it and be polite, but I won't be buying anything. The covers, the sheet, and the stillness wrap me up into the tiniest bundle. Hugging my knees, rocking myself, I want it to go away. Oh, Jesus, my pastel savior on the wall, make it stop. I playfully toggle my feet back and forth. Because when I do answer it, he's here again just for a moment and then off he goes to wherever lost lovers hide away. At the end I always cry, calling out his name, *Ali, Ali, Ali*. How did such a bad lover end up with so many accolades for just showing up to stretch out alongside me, shake out his hair, and wink the dimple in his chin, while I do all the work?

Well, I don't have all day to linger. On my back is the quickest and most natural way to get this done. As long as I don't cup my writhing gut, the revolting growing girth will not be a stumbling block on the very short trip to tantalizing. Fingers on the trigger, thumb on the handle, the imagined cock and balls at aim, what begins as a nasty, embarrassing activity arcs into the innocent splendor of indescribable phantom fireworks. There's the split second of the hopeful swell surging into a high tide; that's when I can feel him heavy on me, his sweet warm breathe going in and out bringing me back to life, while promising to buy me a Jaguar. No, I'd never been this saucy before, not ever. He gave this fantasy to me. Sue the bastard.

Funny thing about short-term memory loss, by this afternoon I won't remember what I had for breakfast, but at midnight I'll try to sleep, remembering every word he ever said to me.

* * *

Rae and Alexandra have cooked up a celebration for my 63rd birthday. For twenty-six years, my nephew Tommy and I have shared our special day. Not as potentially disabling as being born on Christmas Eve, but devastating nonetheless, he has on a few occasions escaped this family tradition by way of spring snowboarding excursions; but, alas, this March the snow is melting, it's far too warm to fire up the snow-making machines, and he's under firm orders to drive the seventy-five miles from his apartment to fetch his grandmother. Glendale, here we come.

"Everyone's read Mom's novel, right?" Alex inquired as she turned the pages of my first novel placed on her lap. The captive audience answered with mumbling, eye rolling, and my sister quickly explaining that today the true reader actually finger scans through the pages. "Well, I'm in charge of the upcoming book signing and I think she should read aloud a few tidbits, and I've found a great excerpt that I'd like to share," Alexandra began the afternoon festivities.

"I'll go outside and check on the—" Rae jumped from her mid-century modern, textile couch. With a pleading gaze, Alex gently reached for Rae's arm.

"Please, sit. Everyone be quiet. We're having a reading here of my mother's very first novel. Stop cringing, Tommy."

"Let me freshen up everyone's champagne," Rae made a beeline to her stainless steel refrigerator at the far end of the loft-style living area.

Mother loves the bubbly. When she actually gets into a welcoming carriage, she brings along a gifted bottle from our last visit, chilled for months because she refuses to learn how to pop the cork. Once the cherished bottle is empty, we can begin the margarita blending.

I helped myself to a paper plate of strange looking delectable dips and a handful of Ritz crackers. I sat back in silent embarrassment as proud Alex began to read.

> Twelve months later, I woke today, this Sunday morning, to a strange May 22, for outside the—

"Shouldn't that be *May 22nd*? Sounds better," Rae interrupted.

"You're spoiling the cadence of the piece, Rae. Please no interruptions until the end and then we can discuss."

"Actually, I agree," I said. "It's my first attempt . . ."

> For outside the bedroom window there was the cold of January, gray clouds filling up the sky. Mom called last night to alert me

"She's speaking of grandma here," Alex clarified.

"I want to know why I wasn't given a name in that book," Mother blurts out in her irritating whisper from behind fluted crystal, her lower lip unable to contain the fullness of her drink. "Mother this, Mother that. Mother, Mother, everywhere."

"Somebody hand her a napkin." Alex instructed. "Moving on."

> —to alert me there were forecasts of snow in the mountains again. The breeze looked chilly that tossed and churned the jasmine still spilling over the metal arch and over the gate—

"Mom, I really think you meant *fence* and not gate here."

> —into the walkway. And on this cozy stay-in-bed Sunday, until Open House signs must be put out, I conjured him up, as I often do; and he was boldly entering me and changing me forever.
>
> My fantasy so perfected, I came wonderfully, the soothing electric burn—

"Wow," the cousin jerked.
"Where are you going?" his cousin asked.
"Wow. I'm going out to the deck for a cigarette," Tommy almost made it to a full stand.
"No, you're not. It took my mom a year to write this and you can give it your attention for two minutes. Sit down."
She cleared her throat and smoothed down the page.

> I came wonderfully, the soothing electric burn shooting into the inner and uppers of my thighs—

"I don't get it," Mother stepped into the pre-discussion.
Rae mumbled, "Exactly what we've suspicioned all these years."

> —the joy of calling out his name, and the immediate spew of childlike tears that seem to go on forever. The kind of crying that turns to bubbling bawling hiccup sobbing; so many tears and snot, I am sure the neighbor from his—

"You never told me you had a male neighbor," Mother accused me from the other side of the glass coffee table. "Is he single?"
"You've had two glasses of champagne, Mom. Why don't you visit the little girls' room?" Rae suggested again, having insulted Mother upon her arrival with the same shrugged-off suggestion. Sitting in thin cream polyester pants upon a fabric dining room chair, she waived off Rae's fearful gesture, as she continued to feign genuine interest in the reading.
"Come on, Julie," Mother snidely postured. "What's he like?"
"He's fat, ornery, and hasn't washed his sandaled feet since he moved in next door four years ago," I cleared up Mother's inquisition as to why I was not dating Artemus, the chain-smoking psycho.

"Well, it's your novel. Apparently, you can sleep with whomever you want to in it, but *Mother* doesn't have a computer, so Internet dating for me—"

Alex closed her eyes and shook her head. "Continuing on."

> I am sure the neighbor, from his little porch, where he sits and rolls his own cigarettes with sweet paper, can hear my foghorn blows into the tissues. For you see, I am writing this now so I shall never forget—

"Oh, you'll forget. I try to imagine your father's kiss and all I get is the smell of tobacco and bourbon," Mother reminisced.

"When was the last time you kissed him?" Alex wondered aloud.

"A few months before we separated. You girls were—well, let's get with it. It was a long time ago."

"Forty-six years and two more husbands to go," Rae filled in the blanks.

"Well, I never knew my grandpa at all," Tommy summed up in one sentence the history of a fractured family.

"Such a shame, Tommy. You look so much like him," Mother smiled in a way only the matriarch lauding over her male possession could. "You know, after we separated, your mother stayed with me and Julie chose to live with your grandpa."

Rae winced. "*Chose* may be the wrong word. No. Wait! You *chose* your boyfriend over my sister and threw her out the house on the very first day of high school—" She turned the attention onto me. "Wasn't it?"

"Yes."

"Your dad only let you live with him to spite me."

"Hey, I only met him once, when I was ten, I think," Alex mentioned and found her place on the page.

> —so the feeling will never go away. What a magical gift I have given myself to take into my last lonely twenty years. And I can hardly see the words as I type them onto the laptop, my eyes blurred and joyously continuing to tear. I do see through the

opened Priscilla curtains the couple, who have been together yet another year; the new neighbor and his visiting aunt, all heading to the Farmers Market on Selma. They are bundled up against the cold wind and impending storm when only last year, the days and nights were warm.

"Honesty to the Nth Degree. Can't you just hear her voice?" Alex cheered. "If I weren't your daughter and didn't already have a free copy, I'd order it on *Amazon*."

"Well, not to be critical, but it sure sounds like the ending to a *Sex and the City* episode, very Carrie Bradshaw," Rae criticized.

Alex rushed to my defense. "Hardly. Carrie Bradshaw had sex for six seasons and never even took her tube top off."

"Who's Carrie Bradshaw?" Mother leaned in, a moist triangle forming at her crotch. I motioned to Rae just as the champagne's residual urine ran down Mother's pant leg forming a tidy pool at her feet.

"Don't argue. Get in the bathroom. I'll get you a pair of my stretch pants," Rae proceeded toward the matriarch, her unwashed silver hair shaking with incontinent denial. Tommy vanished as Rae lead Mother to the bathroom door, then hurried upstairs to search for a tiny pair of leggings.

Alone at last, Alex's exuberance still aglow, she asked, "How is Part Two coming along?"

"It's getting close, but I feel another book coming."

"A trilogy!"

Mother emerged from the living room toilet, a towel wrapped about her bottom. "Tell me you're not going to write a third."

"There must be resolve and closure. I shall keep writing until the heroine is free at last."

Tommy leaned in from the deck, his Marlboro pointed at me. "Aren't you afraid the Muslim terrorists will come after you?"

"Stop writing because I'm *terrified* and let them win? That's what terrorism is. Evil deeds and threats to scare us into obedience, to stop us from thinking, speaking, living! And to never get on a plane again!"

"Here, Mom. Put these on," Rae burst into the room tossing something black wrapped over a bright white plastic diaper at Mother and proceeded to fetch a bucket of soapy water and a thick towel.

Emerging again from the bathroom in see-thru tights under her sequined cowl-neck tunic, a freshly applied Cheshire cat smirk on her face, Mother crept fully stooped across the floor to pounce upon unsuspecting Alex for a private *what's new?* Spying the adult diaper tossed to the bathroom floor, my sister raced Mother to the couch and threw down the terry-cloth towel, almost knocking the frail, tiny woman to the living room floor.

Unfettered by all the excitement, her interrogation began. "Well, I understand you have a new boyfriend."

"Yes, Benjamin. He's great."

"What does he do, dear?" Mother continued over the crunch of ice spinning in the blender.

"Does everyone want salt on the rim?" I called out from the kitchen.

"He quit his job to work on his music. He's a musician, singer and songwriter," Alex explained.

"How does he live? How does he earn any money?"

"He's receiving royalties from a song he wrote five years ago and he does get a monthly check from a family trust."

"Yes, salt for me," Mother responded, assuring there would be something to rub in the wound.

"He's a college graduate," Alex polished the new beau's credits.

"And you're not. What does his family think of you, dear?"

"They're great. I'm the daughter they never had. Just the two boys."

"So you've met them," Mother stated, her jealousy budding, while mine began to spiral out of control.

"Oh, we spend every other weekend at their house."

Hurriedly, I sat down an icy margarita in front of Mother. It was time to change the subject. Alexandra was well aware of my disapproval of the sleeping arrangements granted to her and the boyfriend by parents of sons, parents who couldn't imagine my stomach flips after receiving the news that they allowed my precious daughter to sleep in their son's childhood bedroom, as if they were man and wife.

"I'm seeing someone, I think," I interjected loudly and plopped down on the couch in the nick of time. "He's way too young, a realtor, and cheap. Forty-three, never married, no kids."

"The typical L.A. loser," Alex summed him up in record time.

"You bet your life," I humored her. My eyebrows twitching in a Groucho Marks' double take, I just needed a cigar and a rubber duck. "But he's awfully cute."

"Good God," Rae moaned from inside the refrigerator door.

"I heard that," I shouted across the room.

"And don't forget that anyone under fifty who wants to date you has serious mental and social issues," Alex continued.

"Who's buried in Grant's tomb?" I asked her to diffuse the attack.

"Rae, do you need any help?" Alex leapt from the sofa leaving a sag in the cushion. I scooted in closer to the towel.

"You've never mentioned him to me," Mother insinuated an obvious lapse in my promised communication.

"Nothing to mention. I met him at a Tuesday broker's open house in Hollywood. He's Hispanic, charming, looks Italian, and has a very proper English first name, Grant. Grant Sanchez."

"Way too much information, Julie. You're going to be repeating it to her for the next six months," Rae warned from the kitchen sink.

"Well, has he taken you out?" Mother sneered, her head nodding skeptically side to side.

"That's just the trouble. He calls and texts, of course, with way too many *LOLs* and happy faces. We'll set up a time and then he cancels with excuses ranging from office duties to boxing matches to sports bar hockey games. He showed up just once carrying a six-pack of beer with two bottles missing, and we just sat on the porch," I recounted our dating history realizing she had heard only every other word.

"You haven't let him in the house, have you?"

"He used the bathroom. He hasn't made a move on me, just bums cigarettes."

"Hey, I thought you quit smoking," Rae bobbed her head up from the oven door and waived a baked potato stabbed with a fork. "Twenty minutes to dinner."

"Shit. Yes, I'm smoking again and I'm going outside to have one right now. Anyone want to join me? And don't forget your drinks."

Suddenly, Mother was left alone and the four of us lit up in unison at the outdoor patio table.

"Well, Mom, if you're going to smoke, restrict yourself to just five a day," my daughter advised me. "Do the *Audrey Hepburn Five*: one with coffee in the morning, one after lunch, one after dinner, and two for boredom."

"Which one of the *five* are you smoking now?" I asked.

"Boredom no. 1."

"Well, I can quit anytime," Rae tossed in her familiar mantra and drew in a puff.

"Oh, and I booked a *Blackberry* phone commercial for Great Britain shooting in Griffith Park," I tossed my good news into the lull of conversation. "And I have a Blackberry!"

"Soon to be extinct," Tommy assured me.

"Sounds like a buyout," Alex pointed out.

"Yes, just a four-hundred dollar job with no residuals to run only in Britain. Something about how a mother in England receives a text implying her daughter's engagement displayed as an etching on a tree trunk in Sherwood Forest sent all the way from a beach on the California coast."

"Well, that was a mouthful. Once again, art imitates wishful thinking," Rae mused, because she can get away with it, when I can't.

"I used your expectant *I smell cookies* pondering expression at the auditions," I said, flaring my nostrils and gazing expectantly into nothingness.

"It works every time," Alex acknowledged.

Rae surprised me with a white t-shirt stamped with a color copy of my novel's jacket across the chest. Printed on the back were cartoon-like steps leading to the basement. In her way, she had acknowledged my effort.

After a scrumptious dinner, a frosted cake and the simultaneous candle blowout, we all made sure Mother used the bathroom before she and Tommy began the long ride back to San Bernardino. Tommy left with a wisp of a woman, three gasoline gift cards, sincere thanks, and a pair of urine-soaked double-knit slacks in a plastic bag.

Chapter 28

Mother's Day Regrets and Putting It All On My Tab

In my attempt to reunite the shrinking family, I foolishly invited the entire clan to meet up at Le Petit Chateau d'Enchanté for a Mother's Day barbeque, discounting the forecast of a late spring timberline snowfall. My invitation was immediately vetoed. My daughter Elizabeth was not speaking to my mother; my son Glen was not speaking to anyone; Alexandra was on the verge of exiling herself from our dysfunctional family; Mother announced she would be at her Palm Springs timeshare, a sure bet for clear skies and sunny weather, and that she wanted us all there for *her* special day. Pleased with the news that our fragile, incontinent, contemptuous mother was still driving herself forty-five miles on the freeway into the desert, Rae, Tommy, and I agreed. We were always willing to give her a second chance at kindness. There were no other RSVPs to her formal snail mail invitations. Alexandra flew north to Oregon with her boyfriend Benjamin to spend a Mother's Day week alongside the Pacific Ocean at what she coined *the family cabin*, undoubtedly a formidable compound able to comfortably house father and mother, two sons and their plus-ones, and extended family members.

Sunday morning, I left Hollywood in anticipation of Mother's fluffy scrambled eggs, an entire pound of bacon burnt to perfection, and fresh orange juice doused with champagne. Two hours later, as I pecked at my one-hundred mile ride breakfast of donuts and coffee, the smell of bacon coming only from the patio slab next door, I imagined Alex surrounded by generations of well-to-do aunts and uncles, educated successful cousins, and revered philanthropic grandparents. They gathered politely and playfully, never speaking of politics or religion, at a polished grand dining room table set with heirloom china and cloth napkins. No one would become boisterous from drinking too much fine wine. A walk along the beach or, perhaps, a civil game of croquet would follow dessert. There in the piety of the perfected legacy—a marriage of over thirty years bringing forth two male children, one an artistic homosexual and one a soft-spoken musician, who turned down law school in favor of trust fund freedom and entrepreneurship—Alexandra will be cherished unconditionally as their only hope for a respectable society wedding.

Saddened by the recurring realization that I had not given my three children the stability of a safe haven to return to—one child per husband will undoubtedly reek that seemingly unforgivable result—I looked around the patio table at my sister, my nephew, and Mother, a smear of chocolate frosting at the corner of her mouth. Mother had enjoyed the solidarity of a home to return to. Grandmother and grandfather had given us all a long table to gather for Easters, Thanksgivings, and Christmases to cherish. And as I grew as an adult and mother, over a game of three-deck Canasta at the kitchen table, my widowed Grandmother had shared her wisdom: *Grandpa strayed, but I stayed, and now I have it all.* Unfortunately she *had it all* for only three more years. Upon her mother's death, Mother left her third husband and moved in.

Killing two birds with one stone, I left early as planned, heading west on the 10 Freeway, to meet up with Elizabeth and my granddaughter Kathleen in Beaumont at a community center turned theatre for the local talent revival of Rodgers and Hammerstein's musical comedy, *I Love You, You're Perfect, Now Change!* This tribute to those who have loved and lost proved to be the perfect outlet for my unstable emotional condition on this Mother's Day. As I laughed and cried, cried and laughed, my two hosts looked away perplexed, shaking their heads in mystified disapproval.

During intermission, I shook off the romantic memories churned by the too familiar mating game boxing match playing out before me on stage and ditched inside a bathroom stall to blow my nose, reappearing stoic and unmoved.

"Thank you so much for this unexpected treat. I've never seen this musical before," I showered Elizabeth with smiling pleasantries at the punch and cookie table.

"You've really got to rein it in, Mom," she hissed, her bedside manner showing. Oh, how I did want to talk with her about my unrequited love exploits and the residual misery and shame, if even to find the funny in it, but she has made it clear that she is off limits as a confidante, understanding daughter, or a non-judgmental sounding board. I do understand her disapprovals of me stemming from my short-lived marriage to Alex's father, a man eleven years my junior. Apparently, Elizabeth as a teenager was forced to do her dusting and vacuuming chores around Brian's feet as he watched late-afternoon reruns of *The Three Stooges* before my arrival home from the courthouse carrying under my arm a demanding infant rescued from the daycare. Ever since Elizabeth called me a racist because I did not vote for Barack Obama, I've suspected an increasing disdain for anything I might do or say. I would not be passing out any bookmarks here at the community center.

A reprise of "Tonight I Will Be Loved" started up the waterworks, proving once again that I was not yet ready for prime time. Sitting through dinner at Chili's, there was no talk of politics or religion. I didn't become boisterous from my one glass of Gallo cabernet.

At the stoplight waiting to turn left onto the 10 Freeway, I turned my silent phone back on. During the musical, I had received several texts wishing me a *Happy Mother's Day*. The list was daunting: Wayne, my friend the investigator; Brainard, the Navel Intelligence womanizing counterspy; Benayahu, the prick-pelting Israeli roofer; Sam, the chain-rattling angry Armenian; Grant the L.A. loser poster child; and my son Glen.

My little boy, I loved him so. His early years of yellow curls and baby blue dancing eyes; the way he chowed down on scrambled eggs with grated cheese in his high chair; the way he taunted his sister Elizabeth by ripping off the heads of her dolls, while I continued to patch up his beloved Billy Beans cloth doll; and the daily frantic search for his security blanket, *his blankie.*

Home to Hollywood by ten-thirty, I wheeled into Pavilion's on Vine and returned home with Jim Beam bourbon, cigarettes at seven dollars a pack, and a Red Box DVD, *Public Enemies* starring Johnny Depp, the star of the upcoming book-to-movie *Sex with a Muslim in My Basement*, a more marketable title, the producers would conclude.

I crawled into bed after midnight conflicted over the ramifications of having returned my son's text with a simple *Thank You*, as I had done with the other text messages. I was uncomfortable to the point of fear with actually calling him, talking to him over the phone. Knowing that my *Thank You* would be the end of the texting exchange, surmising that Glen had been urged by his wife to at least text me today, I tucked Hound in and gave Brute one final squeeze to his backside and turned off the world and my growing cache of regrets.

* * *

Seal Team Six, accompanied by a military working dog named *Cairo*, completes mission *Operation Neptune Spear*—named after the three prongs of the trident representing the operational capacity of SEALs on sea, air, and land—killing Osama Bin Laden at his compound in Bilal Town, Abbottabad, Pakistan. Like a Rose Bowl football fanatic who has never carried pigskin into the end zone, President Obama cheers in the White House Situation Room. The media reports that Bin Laden's body is later dumped into the sea off an aircraft carrier. But can you kill an ideology? Obama's plan for a Muslim Brotherhood takeover of the Middle East has just begun.

In his *I killed Bin Laden* speech to the nation he reaffirmed "that the United States is not and never will be at war with Islam."

This bit of presidential grandstanding overshadowed my book launch to be held outside the Sofitel Hotel at the Stone Rose Bar patio, a snobbish venue complete with private tented couch arenas, procured by Alexandra through her Hollywood connections and the fact she had begun working there as a hostess to supplement her model/actor income. I have agreed to fund the event, allowing one glass of house wine per guest. After that, they are on their own. The venue belongs to Juliet Montague from six to nine tonight. The young and hip Hollywood crowd will not begin their industry networking, general debauchery, and non-emotional hookups until well after ten o'clock.

With my friend Beryl's help, at the valet entrance, I lugged from my car a box of forty paperbacks and twenty black-on-gray *The Year I Learned to Text* t-shirts scented with COCO by Chanel. Standing at the entranceway on Beverly and La Cienega, I found myself on the corner of *What are you doing here?* and *Who do you think you are?*

"I'm so excited for you. You did it. You wrote a book!" she shivered in delight and set about arranging the display of books and shirts on a portable plastic table supplied by the management. I nervously unhinged the tripod and taped the cardboard poster to it.

"Well, sweetie, let's hope someone shows up, drinks one free twelve-dollar glass of merlot, and slaps down a twenty for a signed copy. Each book cost me eleven dollars, not to mention the cost of publishing. Oh, and let's not forget, a year of my life," I shuddered.

"Oh, how cute. The *Magic Carpet Couple* icon is embossed on the front. They smell good, too. How much are you asking for the t-shirts?"

"I'm giving one away to everyone who promises to wear it."

Who am I to expect a throng of progressive well-wishers to leave their homes, drive through West Hollywood traffic, pay a valet fifteen dollars to park their cars, and spend twenty bucks for a novel about a charming sociopathic Islamist bedding a foolish Republican—for one free glass of wine and an offensive t-shirt?

Ali, in explaining away his absences, his tardiness, his little white lies, had urged me to not expect anything from anyone. I shook the déjà vu off.

"The cardboard blue box has dollar bills in it, just in case someone buys a book and needs change. Will you be the cashier while I schmooze?"

"Yes, of course. You know I love to hide behind the scenes."

"And you don't drink, so I'm twelve dollars ahead already."

"Not to be negative," Beryl swallowed in her inimitable passive-aggressive way. "But if someone has a glass of wine and buys a book, aren't you in the red three dollars?"

"You're forgetting to add in the wait staff tip."

"Oh, okay."

A petite, befuddled jolly bundle of a woman, Beryl is my senior partner in crime. Sadly surprised, I notice that my waistline is catching up to hers at a reckless pace. A confused agnostic liberal born and raised in Texas, having graduated with a degree in Dramatic Arts more than four decades ago, she has yet to fulfill her dream of being a *working actor*, her short stint on *Ozzie and Harriet* a faded memory. Early on in my Hollywood adventure, in vain the daring duo took turns driving while the other dove to the curb to hand deliver our headshots and resumes to well-known theatrical agencies in our hope to land representation for television and movies. Steel trimmed glass doors were routinely slammed shut; receptionists violently slid and locked their glass cages; and janitors, afraid of losing their vocation, waived our attempts off with a wet mop.

I pay to attend her gratis stage play performances; she pays to attend my gratis stand-up performances; she drives me to and from drive-thru surgical procedures; I drive her in mild hysterics to search for her lost parked car. Beryl is always the first to praise me when I luck into a commercial booking. Her adult children feel she should be on medication. I just feel she should write her own story, which she never will.

A cooling breeze rustles the canvas umbrellas as I greet Alexandra. "Thank you for doing this."

"I'm so proud of you," she beamed and squeezed my hand. "Hi, Beryl. Thank you for helping out. Have you read it yet?"

"I was privileged to read the initial manuscript. Such a divine love story," Beryl swooned, gripping a paperback to her swelled breasts.

"Beryl's a bit of a romantic," I smiled, squelching the oblivious comment. And I wondered if Beryl had just *scanned* through my novel reading only the nauseously erotic sections, skipping entirely any and all blasphemous references to the evil of Islam.

"Maybe he'll show up," the beacon of love eternal spoke.

"I didn't post fliers at Zankou Chicken—or at the Vermont Mosque —so I think not. I did, however, drop a few off at the real estate office, the Indian gas station minimart, a few synagogues in and around Hancock Park, and the Déjà Vu strip club."

Keep looking for him, I reminded myself. If you stop, he'll show up in a tuxedo holding the hand of an unsuspecting, naïve young Latina and I'll be shattered.

"Oh, Mom. It was just so hard to watch what you let happen—what you let happen to the smartest woman I know."

The guests arrived in a swarm: standing five-feet tall, my humorously gay playwright Stephen, who quickly took over Beryl's duties when she became flustered in attempting to make change for two ten-dollar bills; two unrecognizable bookers from my talent agency, who would go Dutch on one book; my sister dressed to the nines eager to share her expert opinion of my writing; my token Black Haitian voodoo doll, a sales agent from OPH Realty disguised as the temptress out for a night of salsa dancing; the smug, overtly Democratic married couple, the wife having already ordered on Amazon.com the hardcover now tucked under her arm; the Manute Bowl cheering squad, who remarked in unison *you never told us you were writing a novel*; Mr. Taylor without his kindergarten class, who remarked that *I didn't know you smoked;* and one doe-eyed, handsome, curly-haired Benjamin the songwriter, dressed in skinny jeans and a buttoned up cotton check shirt as the boyfriend, who looked mysteriously like my third husband, Alexandra's father.

Sitting at a round wooden table, I waited nonchalantly for a line to form, the book buyers eager for a personal note on the title page from the author. The frenzy came in spurts. Pen in hand, I carefully inked out my hope for each reader:

> *May you experience the joy of unconditional*
> *love at least one miserable day of your life.*
>
> *J. Montague*

"I don't get it," Mr. Taylor quizzed.

"Read the book. You'll *get it,*" Stephen assured him.

Alexandra sidled up alongside me. "Grandma just left a really strange message. Cryptic, actually." She fiddled with her phone and I listened to Mother drool on.

"Hi, honey. I had no alcohol in the house and no way to go get any since I crashed the Camaro—I haven't bought a new car yet. I almost was going to scream in the front yard, but then remembered the fancy bottle of rum you gave me at Christmas and where I'd hidden it. So, I'm okay now. I want to talk to you about asking you to do something for me—but I don't want to say now."

"Good grief," was my reaction and handed Alex her phone.
"What do you think she wants to ask me?"
"Heavens, I don't know and she's probably forgotten already."
The voodoo doll approached the table with my book and a let down. "Osama Bin Laden's former African mistress and sex slave just released her memoir, you know, now that he's supposedly dead."
My competition in the *sex with a Muslim* genre is getting fierce.
Then came the ostentatious jab from my longtime frenemy Democrat, who has continually ridiculed my taste in politics, as she abruptly dropped the book onto the table.
"I scanned through it," she complimented my effort. "You really must be careful what you say about particular government officials."
More often than not mistaken for a dyke-style lesbian, Stephen came to the rescue. In rumpled khakis and an oversized corduroy jacket, he seemed to leap across the table bearing his protective teeth, stopping short of an artistic attack. "And just how many novels have you written, lady?"
"Well, none yet. I have plans for an explicit restaurant guide of Los Angeles," she calmly flaunted. "As a retired television news anchor, I feel I can—"
As her arrogance droned on, Alexandra slid away to the safety of a canvas couch under a tent and the warmth of her lover's hand.
To my embarrassment, in a subdued manner, the assigned model-thin waitress alerted the guests, one by one, that a second glass was not included in the Juliet Montague event package and that a credit card was mandatory to open up their own tab. They lingered, ordering more wine.
The fire pit is gassed up, the steel propane heaters turned on, and those little strung lights bob overhead. The L.A. loser, Grant Sanchez,

did not show up, although in text messages always stamped with ☺, he had feigned great interest in schmoozing with my friends and family, while whispering disgusting suggestions in my ear; the main subject surely to be *when can we blow this place?* In my cell phone contacts, I changed his name from *Grant* to *Scum,* as a subtle reminder not to answer any further communication.

Alexandra's proposed *author reading* was whisked away by intellectual grouping, the mini throng having its own ideologies, bravados, and trite commentary to discuss—none of which had absolutely anything to do with the content of my work. But for the occasional whisper "Aren't you afraid of retaliation?" to which I replied, "Bin Laden's dead," no one seemed interested enough in the theme of my novel to chat me up about it. After all, all that Muslim crap—female genital mutilation, the cruelties of Sharia Law, sex with nine-year-old girls, and the threat of world domination—was thousands of miles away from our safe haven called *America.*

The perceived chaos of having each guest pay for his or her own libations sent me to chase down the waitress.

"Just put everything on my tab," I feverishly instructed her. I looked out to see the patio groupings beginning to comingle with a bevy of casual partygoers. "Do your best to make sure they're here for the book signing."

"Sure thing. The blonde by the fire pit ordered a tray of hummus and pita chips. The heavy fella is just drinking coke, but he's on his third." She began rattling off a culinary list of appetizers ordered by the three men in bowling shirts.

"Okay, okay."

"And the short lady in the corduroy jacket ordered another Shirley Temple."

"Stephen, yes. That's fine. And bring me a bourbon and seven."

"Your choice of bourbon?"

"The cheapest you've got."

I found comfort at the round table with my two creative groupies.

"Get used to it," Stephen advised.

"What? Paying for my own books—and the care and feeding of my loyal fans?"

"You sold five books!" Beryl enthusiastically reported. "That's—that's—one hundred dollars. I haven't figured out the profit margin. I didn't bring a calculator."

"No, Julie," Stephen leaned in closer. "Get used to your friends and family discounting your creative spirit. They are obligated by some universal logistics to totally fuck you up."

"My sister wrote me an email telling me that she was actually reading the book and that *this stuff is golden*."

"Okay, sure. But what did she *really* mean by that, huh?"

"Alexandra isn't like that," Beryl infused. "She believes in you."

I patted Beryl's hand. "Thanks, Stephen."

"I didn't grow up in Texas—queer, abnormally short, and a dreamer—without having to overcome that sad, little fact."

"You're from Texas, too?" Beryl enthused. "I'm from Texas."

"Will you sign my book?" the assigned waitress stood over me, her face flickering in the firelight.

"You bought a book?" I replied, astounded.

"Yes. Yes, she did," Stephen proudly acknowledged.

"I think it's totally cool that you actually wrote a book," she confirmed.

And while I wrote my satirical *hope* for this young lady on the title page, I couldn't help but think that maybe my faithful fan, my daughter, had tipped her a twenty.

There would be several more book signings at which I would supply the wine, the fruit, the cheese and crackers, and the books. I contracted with bookstores at a seventy-thirty split on each sale. *Book Soup* on Sunset Boulevard in West Hollywood even put the book in the window in the local authors display. I would continue to be in the *red*.

In my mountain resort village of Crestline, McCabe's granted me two hours at a *Meet the Author* night, a night I shared with a darling lady pushing her cookbook, ceviche dip, and homemade aprons. McCabe's bookstore is classic homespun Christmas card. Two holly and red berry plaid tufted high back chairs frame the miniature stone fireplace, where the house cat curls up on the hearth warming its toes. An antique footstool is host to a children's hand-painted pottery tea set. In every nick and cranny of the little store are shelves for books, their spines of many colors enchanting the small space.

Up a tight flight of wooden stairs is the children's corner, where after being read a fairy tale or two, cotton gingham pillows are tossed on the floor for napping. Also upstairs is an intensive collection of *how to books:* how to knit and how to sew; how to build a tree house out of driftwood; how to harvest homegrown fruit, vegetables, and various categories of marijuana.

Rae supported my continuing endeavor by lending me a fashionable black dress—and black full length Spanx—complimented by strappy black low heeled shoes. She kindly brought Mother along, who insisted on spending the evening outside on a wooden bench sipping chardonnay.

"I've already met the author," she explained.

Rae excused herself early on, leaving with a thirty-five dollar apron and an incontinent passenger strapped into a car seat protected by a stack of bathroom towels.

That night I sold eight paperbacks to eight strangers. The writing world dictates that to write is not enough; to publish is not enough; that marketing is the real work, for only when you're truly *out there* have you accomplished the goal. I disagree. If I can touch just one person, have one person realize they are not alone, that we're all a bit screwed up, then I have accomplished the goal.

Soon after the McCabe's *Meet the Author,* on a turn-around summer weekend, I found an envelope tucked under the cabin door. Inside the envelope I found a note asking me if I were *the* Juliet Montague, because a mother and daughter had read a wonderful book that described this exact cabin, and could we all meet up? I had touched someone. We've been meeting up now for several years.

With my first book out there, the second moving along, and my Juliet Montague, LLC—a limited liability corporation—credit card on fire, breaking another promise to myself, I call home the cable box. It's time to end the Netflix *movie and alcohol* highball habit and get to the real addiction: *Home and Garden TV*. I tell ya, I can sit for hours on my ass watching brain dead couples in Alabama restore a farmhouse, while the paint on the wooden window trim of the Hollywood bungalow peels before my glazed eyes.

Chapter 29

Seeing is Believing and Get Along Little Doggies

One of two hundred postcards sent out to the surrounding neighborhood promising homeowners their chance to meet the Hollywood Realtor Gal gleaned one appointment close by on Las Palmas and Willoughby, so I took the opportunity to walk off a few calories. The young, vibrant, Hispanic mother of three, born and raised in Los Angeles, now married to an Italian restaurateur, was not interested in putting her mother's duplex on the market, but needed a realtor to investigate income property possibilities in the surrounding areas while she returned to the pizza parlor in New Jersey.

There are time-wasting buyers who bleed you dry. There are buyers who lie, cheat, burn up your gasoline and steal your thunder. There are buyers who haven't prepared their taxes for five years, have a foreclosure in their history, and a FICO score of fifty-five. And then there are buyers who hand you their impressive bank statements and credit scores, along with a pre-approval letter from their lender. These buyers give you a reason to rise and shine, to wash your hair and swing out the gate to spend your day previewing properties. These are the DeCavalcantes.

When husband and wife returned late summer to view the selected properties, their four-year-old daughter and her car seat joined us on the bumpy Scion tour through Los Feliz, Silver Lake, and Echo Park, where two-bedroom/one bathroom fixers were in abundance. In between the unrestrained, precocious child's hunger complaints and the continual kicking of her rhinestone studded cowboy boots to the back of my seat, we stopped, unlocked, and viewed more than twenty homes in the trendy outskirts of downtown Los Angeles. Cash offers were written simultaneously on two properties; both offers to purchase were unanswered.

"It's a hot market. You have competition for every decent property out there, and you aren't going to close a deal by pissing off the sellers with a ridiculously low offer, even when it's all cash," I explained in street-wise realtor-ease.

My expert real estate advice was proven to the wide-eyed DeCavalcantes, when the very next morning we pulled up to a house just listed for sale the night before, only to meet the happy buyers conducting their home inspection with an unshaven, overworked contractor wrapped in a tool belt and wielding a laptop computer.

"Please take a look at the two bedroom on La Mirada just east of Vine. It's clean, slightly renovated, has a front yard, and a shared driveway. Asking price is three hundred and fifty, well below your budget," I urged again, the DeCavalcantes having pooh-poohed the Central Hollywood property in email correspondence.

"That's the house on La Mirada alongside the pawnshop parking lot on Vine, right? Vine is a busy commercial street. I know, I know, the walk score is almost a hundred, but will I be able to get a renter in there for two-thousand a month?" Mrs. D, the leader of the pack, needed assurance from me.

As a realtor, I cannot really promise anything, but I can give my honest opinion, leaving out any potential unknown disclosures.

"Look, I live right around the corner from La Mirada on Cahuenga. Hollywood is undergoing a facelift; redevelopment is taking place here. There's big money, glass towers, high-end retail coming in. Who knows what the future may bring to this neighborhood."

The DeCavalcantes offered full price, and by the end of their California summer vacation, a dozen more ride-alongs, just in case the deal fell through, and a dozen more Kid's Meal boxes strewn to the floor mats of my car, escrow closed on the house around the corner. Being neighborly and a sucker for customer service, I took on the responsibility of watching the empty house and making sure the handyman, the termite man, and the air conditioning man had access to do their dirty work. Back East, the DeCavalcantes returned to rolling out fresh dough for the Mafia and leased the nine-hundred square foot Spanish stucco for twenty-three hundred a month to a friend of a friend, not securing my services as the listing agent on the rental.

Three years later, a development company would purchase the pawnshop corner for just over six million and begin clandestine negotiations for off-market procurement of the first five homes on La Mirada to complete the project. The DeCavalcantes would sell the rental at a four hundred thousand dollar profit. I would not receive a thank you note.

***

Not everyone or everything that winds up in Hollywood is a fake, or so I hoped until I found myself booked as a union background actor for three weeks, Monday through Friday, on a movie shooting at a zoo, some thirty miles north in Thousand Oaks. Travel expense would be added to the paychecks at sixty cents per mile. This rare opportunity would bring into my jumbled schedule twenty-one days of consistency, twenty-one days without parking restrictions. I would be gone each day before parking enforcement began its cruel, inhuman tire marking and home in time to grab the last all-night parking space in the *one hour only* from eight a.m. to six p.m., Monday through Saturday, lineup in front of the Armenian school.

I pay special attention to Hound and Brute this first morning. They are used to sleeping in until full bladders pull them from dream-filled lingering. After my shower, a towel wrapped on my head and in my bathrobe and slippers, I woke them today in the black crispness of predawn and led them outside to the walkway, the cast iron antique street lamp showing us the way. Two annoyed, groggy sleepyheads did their morning voids, leaving frothy puddles in the frosty grass. The backdoor would remain open for them to take the three stairs off the concrete stoop down to the brick pathway through the south garden. From there, they will race to the front porch stairs to spend their day bathing in the sun, as they bark ferociously at every passing leashed dog, in their continual vigil, awaiting the sweet sound of my four-cylinder car to return.

Leaving them special doggie snacks inside and outside, an extra water bowl, and a vigorous *be good* ear ruffling, after which Brute in disapproval of my attention dove through the bed skirt to his blankie under the bed, I locked the front door behind me.

The moon still watching over the boulevard and the sun catching a few more winks before rising, wrapped in my self-sewn quarter century old Herringbone cape, I was in my usual tardy rush to the car, my garment bag weighted with footwear selections and summer pastel clothing choices.

"You're up early this morning," I remark as Randi hurries by in fatigue greens and a camouflage helmet, juggling a tool in one hand and a rug in the other. "What's with the hatchet?"

"I've been up all night. I chopped down the jungle of bamboo outside the kitchen window to let light in."

"And the throw rug you're tossing up and down?" I asked as Randi hurled dust and debris onto the sidewalk in front of my house. "And please don't tell me the bamboo has been discreetly dumped on the corner."

"Someone needing firewood will pick it up as soon as the sun comes up, Miss Neighborhood Watch," she fired back.

"Randi, the wood is probably green and wet. Who would burn that? And when was the last time you saw smoke coming from a chimney around here?" I pointed out, as I shivered in the dark. "Haven't you heard? The Air Quality police have banned the use of wood-burning fireplaces to protect us from soot pollution, unprotected sex triggered by the blue flames of an erotic roaring fire, and the eventual demise of Santa Claus."

"What side of the bed did you wake up on this morning?"

"The lonely side, as always."

I've never made mad, wanton hardwood-floor love in front of the bungalow's hearth. My fireplace hasn't seen a log of wood since being condemned by the chimney repair guy, who estimated the rehab at a hefty two thousand dollars. I passed on the reconstruction and have made do by placing a wrought iron, tea light candle motive inside on the log grate, its flickering lights an inexpensive ambiance fix, on the few occasions I've been inspired to light them. The flue, which does not have an open or close hatch, is stuffed securely with crunched and balled aluminum foil, which prevents the invasion of windblown wayward palm tree orange balls into my living room. The hearth screen, a charming, hand-painted metal floral find from the household décor section of Ross Dress for Less, has no screen.

"Have you no respect for the homeless and their knack for recycling?" she bombarded my unsympathetic nature. I pictured a shopping cart toppled with stalks of green bamboo bumping along the sidewalks of Hollywood heading east to a freeway underpass in downtown Los Angeles and Skid Row, an area of some fifty-four blocks of unbridled stench, where the dazed resident homeless junkies gathered in anticipation of a moist bonfire.

"What are you saying, Randi? That the street people keep the streets tidy?"

"No. I'm just covering my ass for dumping a dozen armloads of bamboo on the corner. Married guy is coming over to spend the whole day," she excitedly reports.

"At dawn?"

"By eight or nine. The wife is taking the kids to visit her sister in Palm Springs. As soon as they leave, he'll be heading this way."

"Disgraceful. When the cat's away, the mice will play," I dismayed in a half whisper.

"I heard that," she smiled. "So I'm cleaning. I want everything to be perfect."

"Is there a bubble bath on the program?" I inquired as I judged her current bamboo thrashing style: no makeup, grunge hair, and a foul odor that even her vodka breath did not disguise.

"Oh, God. I need to get in the tub for vaginal sludge sterilization."

"Well, have fun, Cinderella," I reluctantly encouraged her already spun out of control hopeful, foolish heart.

I'd had a disgraceful love, too, and I hadn't needed much encouragement. I remember those exciting gushes of promiscuous energy ignited by a sordid text message—*be naked on the bed*—that sent me in a wild scurry to the nail spa for freshly painted red toenails, to CVS for wine and his Kit Kat candy bars, and to the tub for the bridal bubble bath soak, only to vanquish into a pitifully disappointed damsel in distress, when Prince Charming showed up three hours late to the ball.

The thirty-mile freeway drive ended and I was treated to a winding two-lane country road laced with white polyurethane fencing, where well- bred chestnut horses trapped inside them grazed in a chilly fog rising from the tall spring grasses. Grand gated driveways lead to sprawling ranch style homes in the distance. The morning freeze would not thaw until after lunch.

Spotting two long white school buses, I pulled into a clearing, the assigned parking lot, which was empty. Not seeing anyone manning the buses nor a production assistant waving me over to check in, suspicious, I called the Rich King Casting information line and punched in the digits assigned to today's shoot. As I sat in my car at seven-fifteen, the recorded line informed me that my *call time* had been changed— no doubt by some nefarious production assistant in the middle of the night—to eight-thirty. Having worked on movies for over ten years, the fact that I had ignorantly not called the info line before going to bed, had not called the info line before leaping into the shower at five a .m., and had not called the info line before hurling the little Scion onto the 101 Freeway at dawn, found me slapping the side of my head with frozen fingers.

As I waited for civilization to join up with me, Bill Nob *On The News* kept me entertained. Through careful translation of Mr. Nob's mangling of the English language, the gist of the mornings report: The body builder, actor, and former Governor of California, Arnold Schwarzenegger, and his wife Maria Shriver of the Kennedy clan have separated just because Arnold fathered a child, now a bastard of fourteen, with *the help*, a woman whose obese breasts were certainly the catalyst of his long-term finagling. The *End of the World*, as predicted by Minister Harold Camping to occur within the coming month, will have true believers swept up to heaven while everyone else descends into hell. Perhaps the Schwarzeneggers should wait a few weeks before hassling with all that unnecessary divorce court paperwork.

Mother called, but I let it go to voicemail, to enjoy later over hot coffee.

By eight-fifteen the parking lot was overloaded with rows of inexpensive cars, their drivers queued up in obedient position for check-in by the exuberant production assistant nicely warmed up in leather gloves and a ski jacket. Like cattle blindly heading for the slaughter house, their garment bags swinging in time to the *get along, little doggies* continual shout out from an impatient wrangler, two hundred men, women, and children boarded two buses bound for a destination unknown.

Two bends in the dirt road later, passing a dilapidated farmhouse and the rusted metal remnants of a time gone by; the herd was deposited in front of a white canvas circus tent. The production assistant snapped his whip and bellowed out instructions to grab some breakfast, head to wardrobe, hair and makeup, and to use the porta potties ASAP. The first scene for today is at the giraffe meadow in forty-five minutes.

Rows and rows of fold out tables with fold out chairs crammed side by side soon became a lively prison dining hall, all the inmates happy to be here, the aroma of sizzling bacon beckoning the break of their overnight fast. Heaters hummed; electricity supplied by two noisy generators, their thick yellow cables slinking under the canvas to the outside.

The caste system is enforced with boldly labeled placards stretched between poles: the left side of the hall for UNION and the right side for NON-UNION. The best part of this division is that the non-union children and their tag-along parents will not be breaking bread with me. I also am pleased that the non-union men, who may be sleeping in their cars until tomorrow's call time, will not be accessible to me, at least during meals and down time; thus, I won't be tempted to take a young, dark-eyed charmer home with me. A location shoot is never the arena for trying on a perfect foot, unless, of course, a robust cameraman in his cargo pants-with-many-pockets lifts an eyebrow my way.

Inside my trusty-dusty extra work *carry-on*—with its pockets full of pens, little writing pads, a lipstick and powder compact, a small hairbrush, and my cell phone turned to *all alerts off*—I have wisely stashed twenty-five bookmarks. As I gazed about the vast barn stuffed with performers shoveling in free food as fast as their breathing talents would allow, it seemed that with careful genetic decoding, I should be able to find at least twenty-five zoo goers who would not be offended by my offer of a *free* bookmark, its title taking a gentle poke at one particular male Muslim manipulator.

The icy politically incorrect climate was slowly heating up, but wasn't quite the scorcher it would become in another three years, when even the mainstream media would no longer be able to bury the news of another beheading by Muslims claiming to be fighting for Allah; videos of same provided by ISIL, the newly founded Islamic State. Today I would wait to alienate myself as the Republican who has a bone to pick with the Religion of Peace. Nobody likes a hate monger. I would be spending three long, chilly, windy weeks with my fellow movie-star-wannabes. I would wait to drop the information bomb when and if I felt safe that I had chosen wisely my future Juliet fans, fans that were open to learning how one woman could be so stupid.

Halfway through hair and makeup, wardrobe pleased with my cream cargo pedal pushers, orange sherbet linen boxy hoodie, and beige Velcro walking shoes, a megaphone turned the crowd's attention to the front of the tent. Omelet chefs stopped flipping, stylists stopped curling, and even the children stopped running around the tables. I whirled around in the makeup chair, the blush brush skimming pink powder across my nose, to spot a candidate for my pulsating glass slipper: a dark haired replica of a handsome middle-aged take-charge man. Is this the Superman I have been waiting for? I quickly pulled my tongue back into my mouth and settled into my caste position as *extra*, discarding the lofty idea that this robust, newly divorced Hollywood Icon would notice me. The director himself has come to welcome us all to *We Bought a Zoo*.

The ultimate in brazen creative genius—well, he did graduate high school at the age of fifteen—Mr. *Almost Famous*, showered his captured audience with compliments not yet earned and bestowed upon us a short synopsis of his project starring—drum roll—Matt Damon, Scarlet Johansson, and Thomas Haden Church. We would be the throng of excited well-wishers who have come over hill and dale for opening day at the rehabilitated zoo, the last scene in the movie. His hope is that we would all become *family* by the end of the next three weeks. I doubted that his intent was to invite us all home for a barbeque. He then invited the children to come forward to meet the monkey.

Today is chimpanzee day, a chance to pet a vicious animal on a leash. During the next three weeks, always during my first rushed cup of coffee, we would be treated to peacock day, zebra day, lion cub day, cheetah day, and gigantic tortoise day—thankfully all tethered by the on-location animal trainer. Only one tyrannical six-year-old was scratched, but the medic came to her rescue with ointment and a pink rainbow sucker. Not one elephant showed up.

The movie is based on the true story of a recent widower who, in a heroic attempt to begin life anew, buys a rundown wild animal zoo, his young son and daughter in tow. True to Hollywood lore endings, the family of three, after struggles, misgivings, and the eventual economic crisis, fall in love with the animals, the head keeper Scarlet, and with each other.

Checking my phone messages, I sadly heard that Randi had not been given the love she yearned for.

> "She made him go with her. He passed by on the Hollywood Freeway and snuck me a text message: Sorry, I'm in the car with family. Married Guy is a fucking fake. Blowjobs in a garage he can fit in, but an entire day at the Goth Girl's? Never going to happen."

This too shall pass, I believed, and replied to her as such by way of text message. However, I have not been Randi's exemplar of the *move on and get over it* feminist zealot.

Mother's message was entertaining.

> "I don't know if I told you, but I bought a car, so you don't have to worry about me anymore. The nice man from Crest Chevrolet where I buy all my cars, as your grandfather did, picked me up and drove me to the dealership. Did you know they have free donuts

and coffee in the waiting room? Being an old lady has its rewards. Keep me in the loop. No need to call back."

To keep up with my new work schedule, getting to bed sober before ten p.m. has saved me from late-night, loathsome intoxicated hours spent alone in mourning while listening to sad, painfully pitiful Charles Aznavour love songs on my VocoPro tape deck. Lyrics such as these could coax even Maria Shriver into making the mistake of typing up a foolish *come on home, Arnold* text message.

> ♪ There's no other world that is worth passing through
> After holding you, after kissing you,
> After loving you ♪

After Loving You
Charles Aznavour

Smacking the *rewind* button with my bitter finger brought out the worst in me. "Shame on you for leaving me. How dare you."

My work-a-day schedule also saved me from ever again waking hung over and disgusted to find a Trojan *Ultra Thin* lubricated condom slipped over a good-sized green Persian cucumber sitting on the Bible next to my bed; obviously, something my oversexed, drunken libido thought might be a helluva great idea at the time, just before she passed out for the night.

Each new shivering, wind-chilling day, the horde of extras in their *Ugly American Tourist* shorts and summer vacation Hawaiian shirts would be placed as voyeurs outside the fenced-in wild animals of the day, while Matt and Scarlet dilly-dally about in form-fitting forest green uniforms. In this movie, the background actors are the ultimate in *background actors*. We are never close enough to the action to hear one heart-pounding, tear-jerking, mesmerizing line. However, the director gives a very young blonde in Ellie Mae Clampett short shorts and boob-busting checkered shirt, tied just below her bra, a line. Well, he's got to have noticed *her*. She deserves the credit that would run at the end of the long list, long after moviegoers had scurried out of their seats in the darkness: *The Girl with the Frozen Nipples—Ellie Mae from Rich King Casting.*

Leaning against a tree at the monkey house, I comment on the landscaping with my husband of the day. "These gorgeous purple flowers are blooming everywhere at my feet. Along pathways, trimming the swan pond, bordering the sickly lion's homestead. They're thriving. Blooming more and more each day. I guess they don't mind the cold."

"The purple flowers are following you. Look a little closer," my paunchy better half said. "They're sneaking up on you day by day."

My eyebrows pinched in a quizzical glare, I bent over and squinted into the greenery. "Oh, no. The flowers are in a basket with a wire hook." I spun around in horror, horror that my need for reading glasses was also sneaking up on me.

"All the plants are put to bed in a greenhouse and trucked back in each morning. This entire set is a relaxed reproduction by 20th Century Fox of Benjamin Mee's zoo in England, the Dartmoor Zoological Park."

"Well, hunky husband, you've done your homework."

"It's always fun to know the history of a film. And by the way, the wife died of a brain tumor a few months into owning the zoo, not before. And Fox spent over a million dollars to have these hidden hills come alive, to make it a zoo."

"It's all fake?" I was mystified and saddened. After working on movie sets for over ten years, I still believed. "Well, I'll be damned."

"That's why they shoot one selected animal reserve a day. The animals are shot as background and then taken away, back to their owners."

"Well, I'll be damned." Next he was going to tell me there was no Easter Bunny.

"They just called lunch. Let's get out of the cold. Tri Tip, au gratin potatoes, and a smorgasbord of vegetables, bread, and fruit await us."

"That's for real, right?" I hoped.

"For real."

Into the second week, a topic tossed around the feeding trough was the amount of waste carelessly thrown away into large metal trashcans.

"These Hollywood types are the first to gloat about their charity endeavors, while they throw out enough food to feed a small country."

"And there's no recycling containers. So far today I've gone through three heavy-duty paper plates, three plastic forks, three coffee cups, three wooden stir sticks, two Dixie cups, four paper towels, and my share of single ply toilet paper."

"Some people pile up their plates as if it's their last meal, just to throw half of it away."

"Well, we're not allowed to smoke anywhere on the grounds, not even in the porta potties, so maybe the smokers are simply trying to gorge away their nervousness."

"Well, that never works," I advised, looking forward to the cigarettes left in my car. "And before heading out, I'll be taking two Ziploc baggies home."

"What Ziploc bags?"

"I didn't see any food storage bags for the taking."

"The two Ziploc bags I brought with me." I pointed to my carry-on. "Stuffed with meat for my dogs." I would do my part to stop the sinister waste of perfectly good food when children in China are starving. Mother would be proud of me.

Upon arriving home to my lonely salivating canines, my first chore was to fill two empty bowls with roasted pork chop, sliced chicken breast, Tri Tip tidbits, and a morsel of dilled salmon, to which Brute snorted a decisive dislike for fish of any kind.

This evening my second chore is to deal with the fact I have a call-back audition tomorrow morning for *Aricept,* a pharmaceutical used in the treatment of all stages of Alzheimer's disease, formally known as *dementia. Aricept* is advertised as a helpful aid in managing memory loss, reasoning, thinking, judgment, and the onslaught of irritating behaviors, such as refusing to turn on the lights in a dark house. Mother will get a kick out of seeing me in a commercial swooning over an old lady, who, as a caring daughter, I am elated that she has begun taking the drug.

My mother refuses to take any medication. She has been prescribed a heart medication, a once-a-day teeny white pill that she chops in half, so that she can brag to her doctor that she only needs half as much as the next old lady, by golly.

But I digress.

It is a matter of reputation, honor, responsibility, and utmost integrity to show up tomorrow at eight-thirty to catch a bus that will take me again to the zoo—and to show up for the callback. Always following the motto *to live your life, so that you have no need to lie*, I pour myself a strong one and light up. Pondering the situation has me at my wit's end. If I don't show up for the callback, my talent agency will surely rebuke me for having taken the job as an extra on a movie, for they will not be receiving a percentage of my pay and will lose any possible commission from the commercial, if I were chosen, which I have no chance of booking if I don't show up. If I don't show up for the movie, Rich King Casting will blackball me from ever working as a background actor again.

Realizing I had been playing Russian Roulette for the last few weeks —having not booked out from my agency for fear of hearing again the shaming bellow that *real actors do not do extra work*—I poured another and carried the highball from little room to little room contemplating my dilemma. After leaving message after message on the Rich King Casting info line begging permission and forgiveness, I stumbled into the shower to remove the real dust and grime from the fake zoo, to wash my hair, and to shave my legs; my underarms having been bald for quite sometime now.

I was inspecting my jawline and my upper lip in the magnifying mirror—I was good on that stubborn jutting hair on my chinny-chin-chin for another few days—when I spied a long black hair wound over my left breast. I swooshed it away, as I do all hairs that fall from my head; eventual baldness on the list of things to come. It stuck in place. I waived the end of it to toss it into the open toilet, but it didn't budge. I tugged at it and a pinch came from under my arm. I followed the dark wisp across my breast and up into my armpit. I stood there astonished. How long was this hair last October? And why doesn't the hair on my head grow this fast?

Is this why he didn't want to see me anymore; one long hair that had begun to grow and curl before his very eyes? Had I lain sprawled in ecstasy under his magnificent spell, my arms thrust over the pillow, one armpit boasting a disgusting display of meticulous hygienic endeavors gone unattended?

Finding my one pair of reading glasses on the kitchen desk, I snuck naked passed the living room windows and back into the bathroom. Tweezers at the ready and 1.5 lenses to show me the way, I clenched my teeth, aimed, and pulled. After estimating the Rapunzel drape at twelve humiliating inches, I wrapped her around a finger and then pushed her gently into a window envelope. She sits peacefully now in my desk drawer next to my retired court reporter *COPY* stamp. May they rest in peace.

Having made the decision to face the consequences and to make the *Aricept* callback at ten a.m., I am awakened at seven a.m. by the ringing of my landline.

Rich King is gracious, especially for an older gay man awakening to hear an extra's frantic messages. "It's okay. You're all just a blur in the background. No continuity to worry about. Good luck today."

"Thank you, sir. I can be up there by noon today."

"No, dear. You missed your call time. Go book that commercial and be on set tomorrow."

"Thank you so much, sir," and I gently put the phone in its cradle.

I entered the audition room with my soul cleansed and with the lightheartedness of a believer once again, until I was brought down to earth by a forty-something cougar of a director, who seemed to not be getting any young stuff at the moment.

"Go ahead. Do the line, honey."

"I want to give to the woman who always gave to me."

What woman would that be? My deceased, chain-smoking grandma who took me in when my parents split up my teenage home; the sweet woman who coined enduring phrases such as 'really and truly'; the woman who made sure I had a proper dress for the homecoming dance and never mentioned my virginity or lack of it? That woman?

"We brought you back in because of your smile and you're not giving us that smile. You're using way too much technique, sweetie. We just need a real person. Try again, please," she coaxed impatiently.

Steadying myself, my head reeling with too many corrections, somewhere through my line, I found Alexandra's *I smell cookies* smile.

"I want to give to the woman who always gave to me."

"That was not the smile, dear. Where did you leave it? Can't you find it? And you pushed that line. Don't you love your mother?"

Returning to set bright and early the next day, I was hurt to learn that my familiar husband had been given away to another woman during my absence. According to my new balding, yet much younger husband of the day, I had missed cougar day.

"No, I didn't," I corrected him.

Finally came the day to shoot the last outdoor scene consisting of the walk to the entrance, the rush to the gate, a parade through the zoo, to a grand finale in the grassy bowl, a band whooping up the crowd. Build it and they will come. I continued to hide from the cold wind under my herringbone cape until forced to stuff it behind a wandering bush before the call to *action*.

As the scriptwriter has written, a gigantic tree fell during last night's storm and is now blocking the dirt pathway leading to the entrance, but here we come, extra after extra in the shivering wind, down the road to the fallen tree. There on the sturdy branches of the tree to pull us one-by-one up and over and to set us down on the other side stood Matt, Scarlet, and Thomas Haden Church.

Out of the camera's eye was a perfectly good open field to walk through, but *reset, back to one* we returned to the start of the dusty path, as the icy wind cut through our linen and cotton shirts. The sun was fading when the last walk up the tree trunk was filmed.

During the usual daily rush to have vouchers signed in the UNION and NON-UNION lines, I stayed at the table gathering my things into the carry-on.

Who would be the lucky winners of my bookmark giveaway? The lesbian who was living in her car, because her partner ran off with their savings, along with a dyke truck driver from Georgia? The young brunette who actually believed that blowing the wardrobe guy in the men's changing tent would get her a line? The retired teacher who worked as the on-set babysitter for the mongrels and was still wearing an Obama *Hope and Change* button? The innocent, impetuous blue-eyed college girl who had given her phone number early on, against my solid advice, to charming Mustafa, the Muslim Non-Union guy, who spent his breakfast and lunch texting her from the other side of the room?

I caught up with college girl on the final bus ride back to our cars.

"I've written a book about my love affair with a Muslim man. I'd like you to read it before you get hurt."

She snatched the bookmark from my outstretched hand. After reading the title, she smiled. "I believe there's good in everyone. You just have to look closely to find it sometimes."

The Giant Dollar store was still open when I returned to Vine Street in Hollywood. I left with three pairs of cheaters: 1.5, 2.0, and a 2.5— just to be sure I could see clearly.

CHAPTER 30

My Mother's Curse and It's a Dog's Life

THE prophesied *End of the World* failed to take me away and it's a good thing, because at exactly the time it was to occur I was in the middle of changing the bed sheets. If I had been raptured, my unmade bed left behind, the shame of it would haunt me forever in heaven.

We never made it to Yemen for our honeymoon; we never left Hollywood. In this year of 2011, the brothers Kouachi, funded by Al-Qaeda, have left their birthplace in France to travel to the Yemen Jihadi training grounds. This military training will prepare them for the 2015 slaughter of an even dozen at the *Charlie Hebdo* satirical magazine offices in Paris in payback for publishing cartoons of Muhammad, the Pedophile of Peace. Their hope, as always, to be martyrs for Allah, the inspired French gendarmes would gun them down a few days later, granting them their wish. This rash of violence carried out in balaclavas and brandishing Kalashnikovs, while hatefully shouting *Allahu Akbar*, will spurn the lefty French to blast their protest in lights: *Paris IS Charlie*. President Obama will couch his conciliatory speech to the masses in the continuing concept that although the evil brothers were both Muslim, their atrocities have absolutely nothing to do with Islam. When world leaders hook arms in solidarity in opposition to the Muslim violence, President Obama will not be there to march with them through the streets of Paris.

Renewing his status as a licensed *exhibition animal* by the Department of Agriculture, after having his home inspected by an obese, unhappy woman in a jungle safari uniform—who upset us both by pointing out his girth, as he waddled across the kitchen floor—Brute accepted a three-day union walk-on role in a movie titled *My Mother's Curse*. I was booked as Brute's dog walker. The title apropos, we looked forward each day to spending quality time together on the hillside streets of Angelino Heights, a neighborhood overlooking downtown Los Angeles, a strip of restored Victorian homes and smooth sidewalks bordered by century-old trees, the backdrop for the San Francisco scene. Hound would fritter away the three days unfettered by the missing high-pitched chaotic barking of his ferocious companion.

Brute being the only cuddle bunny in the cast, he enjoyed mingling with the extras in holding, a spattering of lawn behind a crumbling, unkempt piece of architecture down the street from the location set, where the action was. A nifty woman of eighty-seven, a retired grade school teacher who takes a city bus to set, allowed him to rest on her lap, because she worried that the ground was too cold for him, that he appeared uncomfortable, and to pick sticky thorns out of his paws.

Young men in casual clothes gathered on the wooden back porch of the house to discuss their booming acting careers, their art, their half-written scripts, their black box theatrical experiences, and to boast of celebrity sightings on their last movie or television show. An African-American couple prepare for their stroll down the sidewalk by bouncing a pink rubber baby doll on their laps and then tucking it gingerly under a blanket in a stroller. I pulled out my sparkling mini-notebook and jotted down exactly what I just wrote and came to this conclusion.

I'm not finding the perfect foot here.

On the third day of filming, I bring along in my carry-on bag a pair of tweezers, Brute's bacon-flavored treats to appease the little movie star, his blankie, and his hairbrush.

We settled on a brick planter in the warm sun a short distance from the action. On my lap and angry that I am grooming snarls out from between his legs, I accustomed Brute to the goings-on that he would soon be a part of.

"Here come the actors again," I whispered into one pink earlobe. "They always look so different, don't they? So much smaller in person."

Barbra Streisand and Seth Rogan, as mother and son, pull up in a dusty red hatchback along the curb across from a two-story Victorian. On the passenger side, Barbra pulls down the visor, says a few words, and then exits the vehicle, crosses in front of the car and heads across the street. This is day no. 3 at this location and Brute and I have not yet been called to embrace the movie screen. Several extras have been placed in the scene as *strolling neighbors* on the opposite side of the street, but the majority of the background natives are growing restless as they concur that Babs and Seth should know their lines by now. This scene has been shot under silver light screens as many times as Ms. Streisand has performed her signature song, *People*.

Her wardrobe is travel savvy, a navy blue knit unstructured long sweater jacket over a lighter blue flared and forgiving blouse. Navy blue knit slacks tickle at her low-heeled black strappy shoes, as she leaves the car to head across the street. Her blonde hair is down, banged, and bouncing at her shoulders. We see the hair and makeup duo rushing to primp, powder, and perfect the star before she returns to the car, a female director soothing the actress and helping her into the passenger seat before the camera begins to roll again. From my one block away view, Barbra is a petite, yet voluptuous woman, who in her late sixties has also been cursed with the post-menopause midriff bulge, her muffin top concealed under flowing layers.

Following lunch break in the backyard holding area, where Brute enjoyed a feast of roast chicken pieces tossed to him in the grass, he began walking sheepishly, each paw set down gingerly in a protective gate. The charming great grandmother whisked him into her lap to pluck out thorns, but it was too late. Brute and I were called to set.

Hiding behind a large tree next to the sidewalk, I cradled my buddy tummy up football style and picked away at his paws. Too soon it would be time for him to prance by the red car for his close up; his trainer in khaki pants at the other end of the leash.

I've never let up on theatrical training for Brute. We've been taking walks with the *background action* command in play for a few years now. At a stop, he readies himself, always turning his head up to me in anticipation of the command followed by a swift tug to his collar. I don't know if he really gets it, but, as we know, he's always looking for ways to please me, especially when surrounded by a crew of thirty, two large outdoor lighting screens, and a big fat camera pointing his way. I hoped that today would be no different.

Babs was nowhere to be seen, but Seth stood next to me.

"What kind of dog is he?" Seth made small talk, his affable onscreen manner now close up in *3D*. A mass of curly brown hair, an unshaven light brown scruff, his brown eyes highlighted by clear rimmed glasses, he stood slightly above me in a blue and white checkered short sleeved shirt, the ribbing of an olive green t-shirt peaking from the button-down collar. There is a softness about him assuring me that, perhaps, man boobs were hiding under there.

Now, I'm not supposed to fraternize with the stars in any way, but he had initiated the conversation.

"He's a Maltese," I answered. "An Italian stallion from the Island of Malta."

"Is his name *Romeo*?" he chuckled.

"Nah. This is Brute, named for his vicious temperament."

"He seems pretty docile to me," Seth swooned and gently scratched the top of Brute's white and pink head. "Yeah, sweet guy. Et tu, Brute?"

"Clever. I never thought of that, Caesar."

Do you want to come home with me and be my son?

"Barbra's a dog fan. She always has her pooch with her. She's an animal activist, actually."

> *And an abortion-for-all activist, a gay rights activist, and a bleeding heart liberal, who I hoped would be a background-actors-are-people-too activist.*

"Gosh, I hope she doesn't poo-poo my using a dog to book a job," I winced.

"Ah, I don't think she would."

"He keeps getting little thorns in his feet from the grass," I explained, and like a mother ape, I continued the lice removal routine. "All clear, I think," I exhaled and set Brute gently on the sidewalk, where he limped away in slow motion the length of his leash, tilting his head back to me.

Suddenly in a burst of navy blue, Babs was heading towards us, her hands fisted at her round hips, which tapered to painfully skinny thighs. In a soft-spoken authoritative manner, she chastised me. "Is that dog limping?"

My jaw dropped and nothing came out. As the *not-so-Funny Girl* got closer, my eyes widening in surprise, I listened for the roar of the Animal Control sirens coming to take me away. Before I could stumble through my *thorns in the paw* explanation, the makeup and hair brigade spun her away in a hair-brushing and lip-glossing frenzy, saving the day. Seth walked to the car and before he got into his seat, he turned and gave us a gentle *thumb up*.

My Mother's Curse released in December 2012 as *Guilt Trip* and did not receive rave reviews or awards. Brute received a butter-fingered standing ovation by two old high school friends, when on the silver screen, appearing larger than life, he scampered by that red car in high gear, his ears flying, his trainer having to skip to keep up. Shushed by the rude, scowling couple behind us, I pulled Leighanne back into her seat. I couldn't have been prouder of that belligerent, trusting little dog.

Few things ever change at the Hollywood Bungalows. My three trash cans are wheeled out to the sidewalk—along with dozens more—each and every Thursday evening to be pinched, mauled, and emptied into gargantuan smelly trucks by the manual hydraulics of the claws of life each and every Friday morning, except on holidays; the Monday and Tuesday street cleaning fire drills come and they go, except on holidays; the mailman delivers Monday through Saturday, except on holidays; the Vine School children eagerly greet me each week, except on holidays; auditions are, as usual, sparse and far between, even on holidays; Manute Bowl meets every Tuesday night, with or without me; I dye my hair chocolate/burgundy once a month; I treat myself to a mani-pedi at the Korean nail salon once a month; the dogs visit the Korean groomer once a month; I prune the bougainvillea, the jasmine, and the yellow trumpets once a month; the gardener shows up to mow the walkway every other Wednesday; buckled into a rope, Gerardo in spiked boots trims the fronds and debris from my one palm tree, which grows taller each year, once a year.

The one thing that has changed is Hound's bathroom habits. At the first worry over the smell of urine in the house, I blamed Brute, but couldn't find a puddle anywhere; not on the bathroom rug, not under the bed, not on his blankie. Sitting on the loveseat, the light from the kitchen lead me to glistening ripples in the hardwood floor up against the white baseboards under the cherry wood writing desk. Crawling on all fours, I pulled the chair away and slid my hand under the desk. My hand to my nose, I was furious. How long had this been going on?

"Which one of you is peeing in this corner?" I demanded, my index finger pointing frantically at my once perfect flooring. "The oak floor is bumpy and saturated! Who is too lazy to go out the back door?"

More afraid of slipping in the dark on late-night urges than I was of a possible rob-and-rape, I'd taken to leaving the backdoor open twenty-four hours a day. Voiding on my beautiful floor was certainly avoidable.

Neither dog raised a paw. I would have to be vigilant to spot the culprit in the act.

The spoiler alert on the who-done-it showed up that night. Unable to sleep, after a bit of tossing, turning, and handwriting the next chapter of *Jihad Honeymoon in Hollywood* on my pillow—specious plots and grandiose ideas that would be lost to me in the morning—I can see in the dimly lit living room Hound's form struggle to rise up from his bed. Clumsily, his legs trip over the wooden floor, where he wriggles under the small desk and almost collapses against the wall.

"Don't you dare!" I scramble over Brute, hit the floor in my bare feet running and swing the desk chair away. Too late, I grab him by the collar and haul his half-breed German shepherd ass through the kitchen and down the back stairs. The saddest, mortified black and gold eyes beseech me. *I can't control myself* is what they say. *Please still love me* is what they plead. Sitting together in the cool air at the bottom of the stairs, we commiserate; Hound in embarrassed silence, his master babbling on, her arm gently around his neck, pulling him in tighter.

"You're getting to that age, I suppose. You know, I've never had a dog live so long. What are you now, going on seventeen? My first dog, Tippy, was only a few months old when he went around the Thanksgiving table and said his last good-byes before curling up in his bed. That was in Twentynine Palms, when we lived in the desert. There were dogs—I vaguely remember a Toy Collie and a pink poodle—that came in and out of my life inconsequentially. Then there was a big black furry dog that found his way to us at the farmhouse in Cherry Valley. He liked to visit the neighbor just one street over behind the horse stall. That man was so upset when he sped his white pickup into our dirt driveway with that dead dog in the bed of his truck. Before I could stop them, little Glen and Elizabeth rushed out to see what was up. The dog had fallen asleep in the sun up against a rear wheel of his parked truck, I guess. And then there was sweet rusty Pomeranian Charlotte, the mother of just one runt puppy. Elizabeth was a fan of the book *Charlotte's Web*, the story of life on a farm and a spider that befriends a baby pig named *Wilbur*, so we named the runt *Wilbur*. We left for the day on a family outing and somehow the pup was locked inside the garage and was dead when we returned. It was very hot inside is all I could reason. The car-chasing shaggy poodle, dear Champ, finally got hit on the noggin and decided to live next door with the old lady on her farm. I suppose scruffy Champ lost his memory in the accident.

"Ah, I remember the handsome mountain wolf Husky that my little boy loved so much. They were inseparable. Do you know that that dog saved his life? Yep. Glen was just three years old when he wandered away from our cabin in the woods. I was so frantic; I didn't notice that Sheba too was gone. Night fell and it was only when the firemen spotted a dog running up to the road and back down the slope again and again —barking, barking, barking—that they were able to rescue the little whippersnapper. Imagine piling your tricycle on top of your red wagon and climbing over the play yard barrier to visit the little girl next door? They found little Glen dangling from a tree trunk some thirty feet above the rocky creek below. Some time later, when we had moved into town and started the paving company, the wolf came in from the snowstorm, rested his head on my lap, and went to sleep. The vet said later that

Sheba probably had some kind of brain trauma or tumor or something. Glen's dad went out into the snowstorm, and with his yellow bobtail tractor, he dug a grave into the soil and slid the sweet dog into it. She's buried where the skate park is now. The snow went on and on that winter.

"Then there was that precious puppy I bought for Alexandra when we lived in Highland, our first dog to be rescued from a pet store. I wasn't raised with dogs sleeping in the house. So while Alex was on a road trip to Missouri with her father, at bedtime I put the puppy all comfy in the garage. The next day the poor little thing was gone. Well, I don't have to tell you how ashamed I was over that one. Then one day we were at a PetsMart adoption day and Alex and I brought you home. You were eight months old, full grown really. You were never any trouble. Never chewed up a thing or made any messes. You know, in dog years my mother is younger than you and she's incontinent. Apparently, she doesn't know when she's going to pee. I give you credit, because at least you're embarrassed about it. Is that what's going on? You don't know until it's too late?"

His eyes searched mine. He placed his head on my knees. In retrospect, I had noticed Hound drinking an excessive amount of water during our late-evening *Home and Garden* TV down time.

"Well, this is what we're going to do. I will force myself to take both of you out into the walkway—in my bathrobe—just before we turn the lights out. Also, no water after nine o'clock, does that sound like a good idea?"

Together we wiped up the baseboards and floor, dried the wood with old towels from the hair-dying and dog-washing basket, and rubbed Murphy's Oil into the oak. I placed one thick Clairol-stained towel under the writing desk, just in case.

As Hound circled down onto his bed in front of the fireplace hearth, I realized that time was, indeed, marching on.

CHAPTER 31

The Prince of Polo and Jiggling Tin Cans

"Mommy, it's finally happened." Alexandra surprised me with an actual phone call.

Voice-to-voice communication had become a rarity between us; the sometimes rude, brusque text message had taken over, short-handing the art of intimate conversation into abrupt, disjointed notes, which needed careful scrutiny in their translation and in deciphering their actual emotional intent. Without a GPS application on the cell phone, one never knows where the texter—an unrecognizable urban term to *spellcheck*—is positioned in the world when she is typing out curt responses to her aging single mother who suffers from Post Traumatic Stress Syndrome after being put through the texting ringer by a sociopathic charmer. This woman lives alone, sometimes not seeing another human being until it's time to move her car, with two leftover dogs in a one-bedroom/one-bath money pit in an unforgiving town that believes anyone who calls themselves a grandmother should have stark white thinning hair, popping varicose veins, and walk with a cane.

She's called me *Mommy*, which always spells *trouble*; trouble that I relish getting into.

She's at an audition at Warner Brothers and has forgotten to bring a black bikini, as requested in the casting notice? Would I rush to her townhouse and deliver said bikini to gate no. 4 on Barham, a ten-mile tour through West Hollywood, her chaotic bedroom drawers, over the Hollywood hills to Burbank, and a forty-five minute memory to treasure?

She's headed for a go-see in downtown Los Angeles and has left her model's look book on the runway booker's desk at her agency on Sunset

Strip and would I fetch it and catch up with her within the next half an hour? Mother's coming!

She's grown breasts and will never work again? Has the genetic mother's curse finally caught up to her?

"What's happened, honey?" I inquire nonchalantly. Try to stay calm and don't blurt out an *I-am-my-mother* response. Do not let the word *pregnant* form on your lips. "Where are you? Do you need me to—"

"I'm fine. Am I talking loud enough? Can you hear me?" Alexandra's concern for my auditory senses is excruciating.

"I hear you just fine."

"Okay. Remember when I was twenty-four and having body issues and worried that I'd wind up being a waitress serving cocktails to ex-boyfriend celebrities?"

Ah, the art of conversation. No one is going to type out a text message that long.

"And I told you not to worry, because at the magic age of twenty-five you'd be able to work in alcohol and tobacco commercials, opening up a new pot of gold?"

"Good memory, Mom."

I remembered the conversation almost verbatim, because I had written that exact luncheon scene in Part One of *The Muslim Romance Trilogy*.

The *coming of age* moments: Drive at age sixteen; smoke and vote and go to war at age eighteen; consume alcohol at age twenty-one; shoot glamorous Courvoisier cognac ads at age twenty-five; have sex with a thirty-eight year old Muslim terrorist in your basement at age sixty. Before you know it, you're collecting Social Security benefits at age sixty-two and carrying a Medicare card in your wallet at age sixty-five.

"You booked an Anheuser Busch spot? You get to play with the Clydesdales?"

"No. I'm at the Santa Barbara polo grounds in Carpenteria serving cocktails to royalty," she hinted and I took the bait.

Whew, no bun in the oven.

"Prince is performing *Little Red Corvette*?"

"No. The Duke and Duchess of Cambridge, William and Kate. Kate's even lovelier in person," she swooned.

"Which one's on a horse?"

"Prince William, of course. It's so cool. All the ladies are in hats. Royal Salute Whiskey booked a few of us as servers. I'm making six hundred for eight hours, minus twenty percent agency commission, plus twenty for gas. Less than I'm worth as a model; more than I make as an assistant manager at the Stone Rose bar."

"A helluva lot more than you'd ever make flipping burgers back in the Inland Empire," I thought. Don't say it; simply bask in the glow. "You're doing great."

"I'm working Monday too. And hopefully Tuesday and Thursday."

"As a cocktail waitress at the polo field?"

"No, as a model. I'm getting out of debt. I can feel it happening."

"You're building a career that can take you into old age."

Alexandra will be booking all the pharmaceutical jobs: the frightened Cialis wife of a four-and-a-half hour penis erection; the embarrassed victim of an overactive bladder; the pool hustling wife of a C.O.P.D incapacitated husband who spends too much time with his elephant.

"Benjamin leaves for a tour with his band on Wednesday, so if you feel like feeding me? A movie? Tennis? I might be available," she made my day.

"I get you all to myself? Unemployment check hopefully on its way."

"Ha. Get a zero percent credit card. I need new school clothes," she teased.

"No joke, really. The Spiriva elephant commercial is running without me in it, and there will be no extra work again until September."

"Go sell a house, Mom."

A few blocks from my home, I spotted a *for sale* sign at the once dilapidated semi-Victorian charmer on the corner of Wilcox Place and Lexington, just above the Honda dealership on Santa Monica Boulevard. A developer purchased the uninhabitable, moldy house six months ago for three hundred and seventy five. Serving *floor-time* at Over-Priced

Homes Realty, hoping for a spotting of the newly wed Royal Couple, who it has been advertised will be visiting Hancock Park today, I searched the Multiple Listing Service hoping to find an open house scheduled for the Wilcox Place property. There was none listed for the following Sunday. The real estate company sign at the gated property was not familiar, perhaps an independent broker.

This property is in my hood. I should be selling it. Next option is to offer my services as an open house host and to bring the listing agent a buyer, going outside the rules of real estate, holding an open house not listed by Over-Priced Homes Realty. The listing price: six hundred and twenty-five thousand. The listing agent: Sean Amir.

"Sean Amir here."

With just two words spoken, along with the surname, I knew with whom I would be dealing with. This is L.A., the melting pot of California.

"Oh, I like your accent. You must be from Alabama," I teased, foolishly jumping with flirtatious charm into another Middle Eastern tahini hummus dip.

"No, I'm Persian."

And I'm in trouble.

I gave him my name, office, and my license number. "I'm calling about Wilcox. I notice that you haven't had an open house yet, and as a homeowner in the neighborhood, I think I should host an open for you one Sunday," I belched out a mouthful, my hand sweating all over my cell phone.

"Can you hold?" he stated very matter of fact, out of time and bothered.

"Yes, sir."

The property listing on the MLS does not have a picture of the listing agent, but somehow I was intrigued with the voice, a déjà vu melody that pulled me in seductively, after just a few words.

"I used to work at OPH. But we can break the rules, can't we?" Mr. Amir exhaled into the phone. His breath was sweet.

"Yes, as long as the commission goes to OPH in escrow."

"Of course. I'm not your typical Persian."

"Mr. Amir, are you saying that you don't lie every time you open your mouth?"

"You can call me Sean," he insisted. Suddenly, we were sparring and teasing, and I'm finding him wonderful and gregarious and—thirty-five? I can see the dimple in his chin opening and closing as he plays with me. "You sound—now I'm going to get in trouble if I put your age . . . well, at forty?" he asks.

"We may never meet, so I'm not admitting to anything."

We bounce back and forth with well-rehearsed sexual innuendoes while he looks me up on the OPH website. "Nice picture. I'll bump your age up to fifty. Fifty's good, very sexy."

"How many wives do you have, Sean, which I'm sure is not your given name." I'm guessing Samir, but we can't have another Sam in this novel.

"Me? None. I don't plan on getting married for a long time."

And like Ali's stated manifesto, the fortieth year beckons the year of manhood and marriage.

For ten minutes I enjoyed the attention of a man whose face was unknown to me, whose scent was unknown to me, whose age was not forthcoming. Hadn't I grown, matured, and become self-aware as the reinstated woman who knew it all, the woman who could no longer be fooled by a charismatic smooth talker? Hadn't the very best teacher lessoned me in all things unscrupulous?

"Okay, what's your real name, Sean?" I delved.

"Sharir, but it's too sexy for real estate."

"Actually, Chérif is even hotter."

He fell out of laughter and into an inquisitive mode. "So you're familiar with Persians?"

"Yes. I let one break my heart. He's forty-one now. Please tell me you're forty-two," I lifted the conversation into an information finding first date. After all, he was out there somewhere staring at my headshot gathering information as to my age, the color of my eyes, and the likelihood of my eventual demise beneath his humping hairy chest. "Before I admit to anything, you go first. How old are you, Sean?"

"Not anywhere near forty-two." Not answering my forthright question with a straightforward answer, he threw a curve ball into home plate from left field, "Honestly, I don't have to lie."

Why would anyone say that without being provoked? Perhaps they feel the need to cover their next unnecessary false statement. If you're going to lie, please make it enticing. Tell me you drive a sleek black Maserati, live alone in a mansion in the Hollywood Hills, and that your fantasy is to enslave a woman in her sixties, a woman with a fetish for glass slippers with two mortgages you'd like to pay off, so that the two of you can travel to exotic ports of call, while she collects the rents, and I'll believe you. There is always the hope that my past experience with a pathological liar would not shadow a new friendship.

Sean has been in the United States for fifteen years; the code for the lockbox at Wilcox Place: *12345*. Outside of that information, I know nothing more about Sean Amir. The Duke and Duchess did not come into the office looking to invest in a piece of Los Angeles. I assumed the newlyweds already had plenty of Hancock Park mini-mansions at their disposal.

Alexandra's photo shoot has been canceled and she's asked me to meet her right away to see Woody Allen's *Midnight in Paris*. Leaving the cleaning bucket and ladder, and a *see ya later* to the smudge on the ceiling, I hastily fix my face, climb into Lycra and sandals, toss a white floppy over my dirty hair and hightail it to the ArcLight Cinema.

Sharing popcorn from a cardboard box on my lap, we are taken through warm golden hues into a tourist's landscape of all things Parisian. As the hero, an unhappy screenwriter with dreams of becoming a novelist, finds himself in a nostalgic time-travel fantasy, I too drift back in time. Taking brief peeks at my daughter's lovely profile, I am back to our week in Paris, when a lonely twenty-year-old model on assignment invited her mother to join her. The year was 2005, a decade after my fourth and last divorce and before I knew the misery of breaking my own heart.

Surprising me at my deplaning in the De Gaulle Airport, her arms waving in a spirited welcome, much as the small child who had greeted me enthusiastically upon my return to her daycare at the end of each work day, we were taxied to downtown to the one-bedroom apartment at 17 Boulevarde Arago on the Rive Gauche, the Paris of Hemingway, F. Scott Fitzgerald, Colette, and Gertrude Stein.

As serendipity would have it, I had met a young lady at the patio of a small hotel on Venice Beach, where the dogs and I were staying while my new hardwood floors were being installed, sanded, stained, and sealed, a duration of four days. The young lady owned and rented out an apartment in Paris. I had taken her information that day, and now Alexandra would be moving out of her assigned *models' apartment* she shared with various characters of interest and into the Arago space in the 13th Arrondisemont near the Gobelins metro station. We would be roommates for a week in the one-bedroom furnished apartment on the third floor before her time in Paris came to an end.

Spiraling above the Café Premiere, its patio covered in a red canvas awning, and a magasin de fruit et legumes next door, which also carried a fine selection of wine, the apartment building was a delight, although there was no elevator to assist us in dragging two overly crammed weighty suitcases up three flights of a worn, courtesan red carpeted winding staircase. The key not found under the doormat welcoming us *Bonjour,* we panicked for a short time until, as promised, the Filipino cleaning man opened the door from inside where he was finishing up, the last tenants having just vacated.

Once inside, I danced around the gay apartment with its ornate wooden moldings and polished trims, the white walls cluttered with wrought iron madness, brassy antiques, cut glass, impressionistic prints by Monet, and bookshelves bursting with color. From the French windows beyond the scrolled iron window guard was a view to the window boxes of more apartments, the copper rooftops of Paris, and the quiet street below.

Each day there were baguettes to choose wisely from the boulangeri, red wine to enjoy slowly on the Avenue des Champs-Élysée, and tightly woven streets to get lost in. We spent a day at the zoo with Alex's Parisian friends, gave out candies—until we ran out—to Halloween trick-or-treaters from the front step of a small chalet, and took in a violent American movie with French subtitles at La Cinématèque Française, where I discovered that buttered popcorn in France tasted all the better when shared with your charming daughter, who seemed to have perfected her Audrey Hepburn flair.

Having honeymooned in *The City of Light* many years before, nothing struck me as nouveau, but for the stunning display of sparkle strung massively on the Eiffel Tower, to which the citizenry complained was a nuisance that enticed tourists to stay out past a decent bedtime.

A fond memory of that week was tasting of my first dandelion tossed into a crisp salad prepared by the hostess of a cottage, the location of a magazine shoot to which we took train and a long walk, where Alex in watermelon red silk flew from a twisted rope suspended from a crossbeam in the patio ceiling. At least, that is the way I remember it. My camcorder chronicling my surprise at finding my daughter had come to fetch me from the airport, our talkative taxi journey into Paris, and our luggage travails was stolen the first day from a changing room at *H&M*, where I had struggled with the minuteness of European sized blouses and in my despair had left the movie camera on a shelf.

"We were there," Alex whispered and squeezed my hand, bringing me back to the screen and the lights of the tower reflecting in the River Seine. Sensing my faraway lapse, she asked secretively, "Are you okay?"

"Comme ci, comme ça, ma petite."

The end of July slowly heated up into August. This year was taking its sweet time.

While cleaning, sweeping, and beating the cobwebs away from the prickly holly bushes, the final coup de gras a power hose blasting to the sludge from the sidewalks, in preparation for show time at 1157 Wilcox Place, I socialize with homeless Leonard, who lives across the street in a pup tent in the backyard. He complains that he must live with dopers and drunkards until he can get his life back together; but until he can forget or forgive the woman in his life, an alcoholic living in Springfield, Missouri, he is emotionally unable to take a real job. He tells me proudly he once had a construction company back east, but, hell, how did he know Bin Laden was going to blow up the Twin Towers and the bond company would no longer issue insurance for projects?

Leaning on my rake, he rants. "There will be no more white people left in forty years, because we quit having kids and the Mexicans and the Blacks just keep having them. Thank goodness for free Planned Parenthood abortions or they'd be running us over right now. But it isn't the black folks' fault that their families fell apart, because the government welfare departments wouldn't help ya if daddy lived in the house, so out the daddies went." I concur, having worked as a budget clerk at the San Bernardino County Welfare Department in my early years, where the minimum requirement for government assistance was having a child without a father, which, of course, is physically impossible.

As he holds the black leaf bag open for me, he becomes nervously paranoid and whispers that the landlord will suspect that he is being paid for helping me and that the landlord will want a piece of the action. I cool everyone's suspicions on the spot.

"I'm *allowing* you to hold the bag, pal," I shouted to the unseemly group of onlookers across the street. "You seem to like the company."

"Yeah. It's nice to get away from the weirdoes over there," he whispered. And I was glibly enjoying the company of a fifty-something Caucasian lunatic.

"I like your shirt, Lennie." *Freedom Is Not Free.* A large red and white *stars and stripes* dressed his chest. "Are you a Republican? I am."

He backs away taking my rake with him. "Nah, not me. I'm a liberal."

"Well, if a liberal heard you talking that way, disparaging the minorities, he'd burn the flag right off your nipples."

As I lock up and return the keys to the lock box, Leonard sheepishly pushes his stolen jiggling grocery cart by.

"I was waiting for you to leave, so you wouldn't see this, but you seem to never be leaving."

"It's okay, Leonard. I used to go canning as a kid." I remembered when my uncle Edwin and I would excitedly search through pine needles down the steep sides of mountain roads for bottles and cans to turn into coins for the penny arcade games.

"Yeah, but I'm not a kid anymore."

"And you're a conservative."

"Shhh, don't want them to hear that." And he was off behind the rattle of glass and tin to metal on his way to the Las Palmas recyclables redemption center.

Packing the mighty Scion with the broom, dustpan, rake, hose, Windex, and paper towels, across the street I spotted a dark, dangerously thin woman in a long blonde wig with blue glitter tentacles for nails, her hands on her sparkling gold lamé hips, propositioning an old African-American man in a wheel chair. Only one block north of Santa Monica Boulevard's Theatre Row, Lord, what a difference one block makes. I am never going to sell this thing.

At the bungalow, I put the open house signs in the car for tomorrow. If I do it later, my nails will still be in that crucial place of *almost dry*. I grab cranberry red for the toenails and the neutral boring beige for the fingernails. I rip off the tennis shoes and the socks and realize I must wash my feet and calves of the mud that has splashed up from the sidewalk outside the historical 1923 two-story, which has recently been updated inside to resemble a stark Korea Town condo, minus the pungent, unappealing scent of spicy cabbage kimchi steeping on the stove. I am never going to sell this thing.

At the strip mall at Melrose and Arden, I languish in the burgundy leather lounger at the nail parlor. I am calm in the quiet of women who speak minimal English, who keep their eyes lowered. My feet relaxing in the warm swirling water, what drifts me off into a realm of peace is the elevator music of violins and other instruments I cannot name. Each sorrowful melody captures a glimpse of a familiar love song, but somehow that familiarity floats to the yellow and pink trimmed ceiling in a haze of symphonic creativity, never finishing the refrain. Pulling at my heartstrings, the orchestration takes me back to a time when a text would flutter my heart, wet my bike shorts, and send me into a delicious dither.

I like it when you get ready for me.

There were so few tender moments—moments that moved me; moments that meant nothing to him—it's difficult to cull another quote. In retrospect, I should not have been so harsh as to his tardiness. The poor guy drove a large SUV and had to hunt for a scarce accommodating parking space to come to me, which is somewhat akin, to my way of thinking, to Sleeping Beauty's prince, machete in hand, clawing his way through the forest of trees, the thorns and bramble to get to me.

♪ The world will always welcome lovers, *As Time Goes* ♪ but the music wafts off into some unrecognizable chorus, and I finish the song under my breath with one tear leaking out the inner corner of my eye and onto my cheek. *As time goes by* will I ever stop crying in the nail parlor?

"Excuse me, miss. I've changed my mind. I want the red for my fingernails, too." He would like that, I reminisced, lifting my baseball cap and shaking out my hair, now grown longer and fuller. He would like that, even though I was still cutting a thin layer of bangs, when he preferred to see them grown out into a cascade, making it easier to slip under a hijab, I imagine. When would I stop considering the desires of someone who never stopped to consider mine?

And as the petite Korean young beauty, massaged my calves with cherry-scented thick cream, my bike shorts seemed to tighten at my crotch and there was moistness there.

Late into the night I did my homework and printed up comparable properties in the area along with the open house handouts of the MLS listing for Wilcox Place, my face and information across the top. Sunday early morning, I picked up a tray of cookies at Subway on Vine. For only five dollars, you get a fresh and warm selection of chocolate chip, ginger, and sugar cookies in a round plastic tray. Sunday is a great day to give up my parking space, run errands, and park again, as there are no restrictions within the two blocks of my street; Sunday being the parking enforcement Gestapo's one holy day of rest.

Dressed for real estate success, at eleven I met Alexandra at the ArcLight Cinemas to enjoy an apropos cinematic delight, *Crazy, Stupid Love*. I then rushed to place the open house signs at the corners of cross streets bordering Wilcox Place, signs that bravely displayed my name as an agent for OPH Realty hosting an open house for another broker's listing from two to five p.m.

Being careful not to chip my celebratory polished red nails, as I opened the lockbox to Wilcox Place, I said good-bye to Ali one more time. I miss him. I miss the game. Another unexpected tear surprised me and streaked down my cheek and into my mouth, where I licked the salt and smiled. Today would have been our first wedding anniversary.

***

"Fucking wow," Sean fell exhausted into my pillow, his greasy slick-back fallen from grace, his sweating forehead almost landing a head bump on my already irritated psyche. All of that trumped up, orchestrated thigh massaging, succulent toe kissing, and now this? Rolling onto his back, exposing the culprit, he moaned in mindless afterglow, "*That* was hot."

"You're not serious," I underestimated his completely out-of-touch machismo. Hasn't anyone previously remarked on the languid, dangling repulsive girth he hides under white terrycloth boxer shorts until it's too late to turn back? Why do I have to be the one to burst his overly-wanked bubble?

"You forced me to jack that thing off while you were dry humping my belly button."

"It wouldn't go in anywhere else. And I didn't force you to do anything."

"Maybe not. But if I hadn't, you'd still be trying to stick that under inflated piggly wiggly into me. That thing is missing parts, buster."

"I've got a beer can dick, lady," he triumphed over my unsympathetic and unkind words. "You just didn't turn me on."

"Okay, now you're just being mean. You were supposed to help me get over the bad Persian, not encourage me to run back to him. And why aren't you wearing a Yamaka? Not a Yamaka day? Don't you believe in your religion? Jeez."

There was no *head* to lead the way. The size of a *Colt 45* malt liquor aluminum can, the massive jiggling gel of pink skin appeared as though the top had been stomped by a motorcycle boot and made ready for the recycling bin. Sean's maker had given him a wide one, but then lopped the top off. Who was walking around with the other half?

"Don't you get it, that if a normal sized condom is drooping three inches beyond the end of that thing—void of any fulfillment—that you may not be normal? You should warn people. Hasn't anyone ever told you?"

"Told me what?"

"That your schlong has no head on it. How do you pee?" I tossed the open box of condoms at him, a box Ali had left in the basement. This encounter was an experiment, really. Had it been the swirling black hair, the penetrating black eyes, and the perfect pink penis that had brought about my unexplainable sexual arousal at the age of sixty? Or had it simply been the perfectly fitted *THINTENSITY* latex with *UltraSmooth* lubricant secreting the mystifying deceit of a Trojan horse?

"Read the instructions, pervert. 'No. 2, place the condom on the head of the erect penis.' I repeat, 'the *head* of the *erect* penis.' Look at the diagrams. Look at how tightly it fits over this anatomically correct penis. Now look at yours. There's at least three inches of latex swinging in the breeze off that thing."

"Because I'm not erect anymore."

"Sean, you were never erect. And what was all the biting about? And there's no semen in the tip of that condom. Does this room look like a junior high school sex education class to you?"

How hard is this? Why can't I find a normal sized foot?

"It'll be better next time," he glumly chattered away as I led him to the door.

"And what's that stuff in your hair?"

"It's *VO5* Conditioning Hairdressing."

Wiping the grease from my fingers onto my lavender bathrobe, I sealed the deal. "There isn't going to be a *next time*, Sean. But this evening will be immortalized."

"Be what?"

"Be commemorated in print. I'm not a realtor, Sean. I'm a writer. Instead of a siren red linen dress, I should have been wearing my favorite

Flash Dance, ripped out t-shirt posting a warning: *Be Careful or You'll End Up in My Novel."*

Hours before, Sean had snuck into the open house as I was entertaining a crowd of house hunters mucking it up around the gourmet granite kitchen island: Lennie from the pup tent across the street, a jolly black comedienne, and her box platinum blonde, Botox-abusing mother. As they ate my cookies, the three bemoaned the sad fact that not one of them could afford a six hundred thousand dollar house and that they would not be *movin' on up* in the near future.

Looking like a character from *The Godfather*, a short and stout Al Pacino strolled surreptitiously through the front door and quietly up the stairs to the second story. In a striped shirt tucked bravely into black dress slacks over spit-shined shoes, he coyly returned to peer from the foyer entrance. His arms crossed at his chest, one heel at the baseboard, he leaned into the wall and shot me a sly white-toothed smile and complimented my red linen dress.

"Now that's how a sexy, successful realtor should always dress."

"Thank you. To be honest, I wasn't sure I could still get into it," I pathetically discounted myself. I was up ten pounds since Ali's departure, but I had another three years to totally glutton myself up another fifteen meaty pounds by way of McDonald's cheeseburgers, Panda Express orange chicken, Bacardi rum, Sobieski vodka, and Jim Beam bourbon before the red dress would be retired and folded neatly into the *I Wish* Tupperware storage box.

He ran chubby fingers through his dark slicked back hair and sauntered up to me. "After you close up, why don't we discuss my offer on this fine redo over dinner?" His pleasant scent was that of an expectant lover, sweet soap and steamy shower and aftershave.

Putting the voice and amusing flirtation together, I responded, "Only if you're paying."

Over vodka pink pasta and delicate red wine, Sean amazed me with his exotic history. He arrived in America from Paris at the age of sixteen speaking Farsi and French. His parents are immigrant Persian Jews, having fled Iran from what he coined *the crazy Muslims* in 1979, the year he was born. Devouring American soap operas and Saturday morning cartoons, just two years later, after graduating from Beverly Hills High, he spoke English fluently. Dropping out of college at the end of his sophomore year, he dove into the business of real estate tycoon, opening his own brokerage at the age of twenty-five. He lives with his parents, an engineer and a chemist, in a two-bedroom apartment in Westwood. I was impressed, although greatly disappointed in his living arrangements.

Sitting in the patio of Fabiolus Cucina, I snuck glimpses at *our* table. We had shared one utterly insignificant night of silly conversation over a messy meatball sandwich, because the pompous, obsessive-compulsive, hypochondriac Persian Muslim with a questionable sprained ankle refused to order anything he would need to eat with a fork, the utensils obviously having been washed by dirty Italian infidel hands. This young powerhouse treating me to a nice dinner certainly appeared unafraid of the flatware and had even placed the white cloth napkin on his lap without being told. When would I stop with the déjà vu torture over *the crazy Muslim*?

We flirted through the topics of property values, foreclosures, and the length of time it takes to close a short sale.

"You owe me a back rub for letting you do the open today," he smiled his handsome boyish grin, while I tried to do the math in my relaxed Chianti brain.

"You're thirty-two?"

"That's a good age, don't you think?" he winked and kissed my hand.

Summer days can sometimes be too long, when the sun does not set until after eight o'clock. By six-thirty that evening—following his massage instructions of placing my hands to his back/neck/shoulders, arms /wrists /hands/fingers, thighs/calves/ankles, and feet/toes only, in order to enhance and enlighten the senses—my bi-lateral carpal tunnel pain was at a fever pitch. By seven-fifteen, standing at my bedside, I was stripped down to my black overly-stretched onesie, my torso bent over Sean's face, his head drooped over the edge of my bed, his quiet and peaceful sex secreted inside what oddly resembled a giant baby diaper.

"What is that, a bathing suit?" he commented on my Spanx. "Take it off."

And in the cascading summer's light of my bedroom, I did. Skipping quickly through Sean's reciprocal pre-coitus therapy, attempting in vain to keep the sheet wrapped tightly about my abundant and stretch-marked gut, I rushed, clitoris thumping, into unknown territory, when he announced that he was *ready*.

In a symbolic gesture to shame my whoring ways, Natasha strolled out of the walk-in closet in Red Carpet elegance. In over-the-elbow black satin gloves, she hurriedly flipped Marilyn Monroe's face and red glittered lips to the wall, protecting the immortal queen of sorrow from another bit of rambunctious nonsense and sordid tragedy. She didn't rush the Jesus pastel into the living room, because we both know he's got his eye on every sparrow, no matter where you try to hide. The living room was already crowded, anyway, with two dogs, their paws placed over their innocent ears, whimpering behind the loveseat.

Sean and I parted as friends, at his insistence. Would I do another open house for him? Hell, no. I'm never going to sell that place.

I digested the realization that in this demeaning escapade, perhaps, I had hit the bottom of the boyfriend barrel. Looking for love in all the wrong places and out of alcohol, I called Randi for the number of Bogie's liquor store.

"Don't go so fast," she implored. "How was your day? What have you been up to?"

"Alex and I took in a romantic comedy and I did an open house on Wilcox Place for a thirty-two year old Persian Jew, who wooed me with sourdough and pesto dipping oil, so, of course, I brought him home."

"Good for you. How was it?"

"Bad for both of us."

"I thought we agreed you'd stay out of the Middle East."

"I'm never going to sell that thing."

Frantic for a nightcap, I ordered cheap five-dollar chardonnay for ten dollars plus a five-dollar delivery charge—plus a three-dollar tip. I put today's antics away as a momentary lapse in discretion. My rock bottom was looming on the horizon.

Chapter 32

There's Always Hope

♪ Let's go surfin' now
Everybody's learnin' how ♪

Surfin' Safari
The Beach Boys

A television pilot titled *Revenge* is shooting at Culver City Studios and I am booked as a senator's wife visiting the Hamptons. By the time I am through hair and makeup, the crew has renamed me *Elizabeth Dole*. Apparently, Senator Dole's wife is so charming that over red vines and colored M&Ms at the craft table, she is invited by a trim, handsome man booked as a senator to engage in freakish sex play in the very near future at his single-wide trailer in the Santa Monica woods, where she will choke him until he asphyxiates into an orgasmic coma of some type. I wait until day no. 2 to decline his invitation, giving me a stimulating total of twenty hours on set of tantalizing, tempting male attention and one sensuous foot massage to soothe my high-heeled pinched toes. All this and SAG union pay, too. These are the days of my life.

KFI radio talk show host, Lisa Ann Walter, a bawdy, outspoken conservative comedian, recounts the tragedy of the Egyptian father and his two-year-old daughter found dead in his car at the end of an *Amber Alert*, a nationwide manhunt for a kidnapped child. The father's brother speaks out to a television reporter that he's proud that his brother has taught the American court system a lesson in justice after not giving custody of the toddler to the estranged father, but to the child's American mother. After the fatal shooting and suicide, his brother claims, "My brother is in a better place."

Ms. Walter finishes the disturbing tale with an aside, when boldly on the air, Lisa points out what is obviously missing from the news report. "He's got to be a Muslim. Just saying."

Naturally, finding a not-so-politically correct radio celebrity who may be in tune to a scorned lover's warning that *The Muslims Are Coming and They Do Want to Kill You*, I immediately mail to her in care of Clear Channel in Burbank a copy of my first novel. Two years later, I will meet up with Ms. Lisa Ann Walter at a charity event and present her with Part Two, after which to my surprise and thunderous applause, she mentions my books on her Sunday late afternoon *local author* segment. This does not cause my Amazon.com book sales to soar, but I beam in solitude at my kitchen table.

Three months after the alleged assassination of Osama bin Laden—the American president having set a precedent by publicly naming Navy SEAL Team Six as the shooters—a Chinook helicopter built in the 1960's transporting members of SEAL Team 6, an Army National Guard aircrew, several support personnel, and eight Afghan commandos is ambushed and gunned down by Taliban insurgents in Afghanistan. On August 9th, the cremated remains of thirty fallen American heroes, of which twenty-two were Navy Seals, touched down on American soil at Dover Air Force Base. President Obama spent five hours there visiting with family members whose sons, fathers, and husbands died in the deadliest single incident in the tenth year of war in Afghanistan.

Between August 20th and August 28th, the Battle of Tripoli occurs in Libya. This is not to be confused with the very first theatre the United States Marine Corps entered into in the Middle East to overthrow the Muslim Pasha of Tripoli in 1805. Apparently, Islam was a problem way back when. This *Battle of Tripoli* is a private civil war—perhaps with a nudge from the Obama administration—the rebel forces capturing and gaining control of the city and overthrowing the government under

Muammar Gaddafi. By October Gaddafi will be captured and killed by rebels in the city of Sirte and the 2011 Libyan Civil War will officially end.

Stateside, another civil war was brewing.

Alexandra has tired of her roommate, a long-time female friend who monopolizes the living room television. Breaking up with a roommate is somewhat like the end of a marriage, when two miserable people are forced by economics to sleep in the same bed, although in this case separate rooms, their legs protectively thrust to opposite sides, their icy feet dangling cautiously outside the covers, an accidental graze of rump to rump sending nauseous shivers up their spines.

Alex has availed my services as a realtor to search out one-bedroom apartments in her neighborhood and within her price range. This daunting futile exercise will over time result in sending her into a non-committal domestic relationship with the unsuspecting boyfriend, relocating his two roommates, upsetting her mother's morality code, and leaving her long-standing roommate to hold the bag and the keys to a lovely two-bedroom townhouse, which she cannot afford on her own.

At her Prius door following another disappointing apartment viewing, Alex opened up to me, a rare happening, because she knows that anything she tells me, I can use later.

"I've asked Benjamin to get a job. I'm tired of being the only one with daily commitments, while he's free to do whatever he wants." It appeared that my daughter's upbringing and respect for hard work had caught up to the relationship, even though they were not sharing expenses in a domicile arrangement. "His dad wants him to go to law school. He has to start doing something."

I am not commenting, because I know that anything I say, she can use later.

"Beach condo week is coming up in September. Why don't you two stay over a few days? Ben and I can get to know each other, and you can show him your childhood sand crab hunting spots."

The implications of a few days with a male stranger in a one-bedroom /one-bath oceanfront timeshare overlooking the Amtrak train tracks and the Pacific Coast Highway would necessarily include mandatory makeup before breakfast, my best walking-on-eggshells behavior, and no underpanties hung to dry over the showerhead.

"Where are we going to sleep?"

"He can sleep on the living room pull out, and you and I can bunk together."

"If we can't sleep together, we're not coming."

Unfortunately for my children, I have standards and requirements, if not for myself, but for their wellbeing. Without an engagement ring on her finger, I was sticking to them. I was uncomfortable with the thought of walking into the living room of my beach condo to find my sand crab poking little girl wrapped naked in a semen smothered sheet snuggling under the hairy armpit of a satiated young male, because I certainly would not be giving them my precious private bedroom.

The pending ruckus was settled when good news came in a few weeks later.

"I booked *Charlie's Angels* shooting in Miami, Florida. So I won't be coming to the beach, anyway. " A revival of the popular television threesome of the 70s was underway with my daughter costarring as a model who runs an illegal Green Card factory using models as bait in an episode titled "Runway Angels." Although art does imitate life, she would not be playing a cocktail waitress. "And I'll be in Palm Springs with Benjamin for my birthday."

Alligators eat their young. Simply a notation.

Cousin Tommy was once again unavailable for pool time or dolphin sightings at Dana Point. My grandchildren were spending the end of summer with their grandfather, my first ex-husband who had abandoned their mother when she was six months old and who did not reappear until she was, unfortunately, in her very impressionable eleventh year. *C'est la vie* and so it goes. So much for children keeping you company in your old age, unless, of course, you are able to tempt them with plane tickets and a fishing boat off the coast of Oregon. *C'est la vie* and so it goes.

It would just be sister Rae and I carbohydrate pounding and alcohol abusing at San Juan Capistrano Beach for the week, my twentieth year at the repeat vacation rendezvous, the one place I had held onto, the one safe haven for Alex to return to. Bonfires on the sand, chasing the errant ping pong ball down the concrete stairway, pleading with the dry cleaner clerk for wire hangers for marshmallow roasting, walks to the ranger station and the tide pool exhibit, dangling cocktail-size hot dogs tied to sewing thread for crab catching at the marina, a bicycle ride to the San Clemente pier, and watching the sun set into the Pacific from the patio deck—all these summer week happenings would go on hell or high water, with or without children, with a slight urging from early morning Bloody Mary injections.

Loving my dogs as I do—shamefully, on occasion more than my own children—the guaranteed true-blue constants in my life are my first priority when planning a trip away. I lingered momentarily as I foraged the bathroom for deep tanning lotion and sunscreen. What would it be like to be absolutely free? What would it be like after forty-two years of husbands, children, and pets to be able to instantaneously, on the insidious spur-of-the-moment, throw together a getaway bag, turn on the house alarm, and lock the door behind me with no one to worry about, with no one and nothing awaiting my return?

I enlisted my neighbor Marlene, the Hollywood historian, PETA rep, and bungalow pack rat, as the beach week canine caretaker in exchange for Netflix mail delivered movies, cable TV, the use of my Internet password, a freezer brimming with her favorite coffee ice cream, and sixty dollars in cash. She would bring Hound and little Brute out into the walkway early each morning, again at noon, and just before bedtime at ten, when the back door would be locked up for the night. The water bowl was to be emptied and not refilled until after their morning voids.

Randi's hot water heater had rusted out months ago. Free rent with the responsibility of property upkeep, the hot water heater left unrepaired, Randi began showering up the street at the gym, 24 Hour Fitness, while the red Mini Cooper was spotted on the street wearing an expensive new black leather bra. Therefore, she had been eager to dog sit, to snooze from midnight to noon in the luxury of my bed linens, and to shower ad nauseam for seven days. I had bolted, my hands held high in defense mode, at her suggestion of a tarantula and rodent move-in, along with my anticipation of the scent of blowjob remnants jolting my olfactory senses upon my return. I did, however, give her permission to use the shower at Marlene's discretion, paper towels and Clorox spray bleach conveniently placed alongside the bathtub under the pedestal sink.

"Get out of that suitcase," I insisted, and Brute cocked his faithful shaggy head, his wet black nose twitching in pitiful reply. Hound hovered in repose close to the open suitcase, one graceful paw resting on my satin pajama bottoms, his sad yellow and black eyes breaking my heart with his plea, *please don't leave us again.*

Leaving the Hollywood Freeway where the grandeur of the downtown Los Angeles skyscrapers ends and the gray industrial portal begins, I merged onto the 5 Freeway heading south to the farthest point of the Southern California Riviera: the marina at Dana Point, the gentle surfing cove of Doheny State Beach, the pebbled, seaweed strewn sand of San Juan Capistrano Beach. The back seats of the Scion hatchback pulled down flat into cargo mode, a large cardboard box hastily jammed with condiments from the refrigerator and dried staples from the kitchen cabinets shifted unsteadily on the folded orange beach chair placed on top of the carry-on size rolling suitcase. The worn canvas beach bag stuffed with towels, swimsuits, oils and creams leaned against a clear garment bag jammed with cotton skirts, cotton tees, and flip-flops. Secured behind the passenger seat, snug and safe sat the laptop bag, my promise to write each morning before dawn.

There were no sand pails, no plastic shovels, and no sand sifter, for there would be no more sand castles dug in the sand, the surf filling the moat. There was no beach Velcro glove to toss a Velcro ball, no spool of black thread to tie onto little hot dogs to tempt crabs, and no child's sand chair. None of these bits and pieces of childhood summers had been necessary for many years, yet as I drove away, I felt an emptiness, as if I had left something behind.

After a five-cigarette Friday afternoon free-for-all, unless you pay to use a toll road, in and out of four heavily congested start-and-stop lanes —while the carpool lane lay temptingly empty, I exited at Pacific Coast

Highway and headed for Ralph's grocery store on Golden Lantern above the Dana Point Marina. At the stoplight on the hill, I relished my first ocean sighting of the week and was immediately chastised by the honking of an irritated horn behind me when I failed to rush into a left turn when the light changed to green. I suppose if you are blessed to live by the water as a normal course, staring sublimely at a sailboat, a mere white dot on a blue canvas, returning to shore after a day of chasing wind is no longer a thrill and certainly not enough of an enchantment to stop the flow of traffic.

Parked in the Ralph's strip mall, my first regimen is to rent the traditional summer vacation videos: *The Blob* starring Steve McQueen, the original black and white *Invasion of the Body Snatchers* starring Kevin McCarthy, *Gidget Goes Hawaiian* starring Deborah Wally and James Darren, and *Beach Blanket Bingo* starring Annette Funicello and Frankie Avalon.

My heart sank. In place of the video shack is a *Nothing Over $5* women's clothing store, with nothing in sight over a size two in cruel Chinese sizing. Have I been away that long? Could missing one year away from my beach condo in exchange for an Hawaiian Island paradise, where I had cried myself to sleep over the end of the Middle Eastern affair, erase away twenty years of blissful familiarity? I shook my disappointment off and walked cheerfully into the dry cleaners.

"It's so nice to see you're still here," I commented to the little Asian man at the counter. "The video store is gone."

"Nobody rent movies anymore. Everyone still clean clothes. You want clean clothes?"

"No, but might I buy a few wire hangers from you, sir?" I asked, my eyelashes batting uncontrollably, a wide smile on my hopeful face, while I rummaged through my straw bag for my Marilyn Monroe wallet.

"No one want wire hanger. Everyone want fancy cloth hanger. Why you want wire hanger?" The little man backed away, bumping into an automated rack of plastic wrapped shirts, suits, and questionable eveningwear. Becoming overtly suspicious of this senior citizen, who was innocently contemplating a marshmallow catching fire over the roar of a circular concrete pit, her toes immersed in the sand, he reached for a silent bell under the counter. My court reported dry cleaner kidnapping and murder case of 1987 jumped forefront in my beachcomber brain.

"No, no. I'm not going to hurt you. Whoa, get your hand off that buzzer. This is not a stick up, sir! I'm not going to kidnap you, rape you, strangle you in a motel room, and then pee on you in the bathtub. Please, I just need coat hangers to roast hot dogs and marshmallows," I assured him, the fear of a police siren screeching to a halt in the parking lot swiftly putting an end to my week at the beach.

Shaken and disoriented by my tirade, Charlie Chan tossed papered wire hangers one after the other onto and over the pink linoleum counter. I backed out of the doorway clutching my loot.

I locked into the car a half dozen wire hangers, their necks ready to be untangled, and walked through the automated glass doors of the grocery store.

I whizzed by the ice cream, the onion soup mix dip and sour cream, the potato chips, and the sweet and sour Gummy Bears in the candy aisle. My lithe little girl who had tossed her week's dietary plan into the carts of long ago was no longer leading the way. Snapping my fingers in the air, I remembered to grab a bag of jumbo marshmallows, a package of eight kosher all meat wieners, and a cellophane bag of a dozen hot dog buns, still, after all these years, wondering what I'm expected to do with the other four buns. I'm not Jewish; a Hebrew National just tastes better. The Jews know their meat, except, of course, Sean Amir.

Exiting the Ralph's check out, the debit card swiped, I skipped behind a grocery cart of brown paper sacks clattering with bottles of rum and diet Coke, vodka and diet tonic water, a bag of limes, two T-bone steaks for the barbeque, a cheap jug of red wine, gigantic potatoes to microwave, a tub of sour cream, green onions to chop into chives, and a few packages of ready mix washed greens—dressing, cranberries and croutons included. The creamery butter from my fridge was softening nicely in a box in the back of my car. In my summer vacation excitement, I did not forget the firewood stationed at the end of the checkout aisle.

The spring of my divorce from Alexandra's father, a much younger man with a much younger economic ability, now being free to build my debt-to-income ratio without answering to anyone, I had purchased the timeshare after a long and patronizing, attacking, insinuating, frightening, admonishing, grueling and threatening sales pitch followed by a tour of the nearby restaurants and shops at the exclusive Dana Point Marina. The salesman promising a fleet of wealthy yachtsman lined up to invite us aboard, I had signed away twelve thousand dollars plus interest for a once-a-year, week-long oceanfront getaway with a maintenance fee of five hundred dollars to be paid each and every year. This fee would reach the eight hundred dollar mark by 2014.

The next step on the agenda is to check in at reception, a foyer dressed in blue and seashell pearl, before emptying the contents of my car onto the wobbly luggage cart in the covered parking garage and forging my way into the elevator. Without Alexandra's set of little helping hands to steer the cart forward in her haste to put the groceries away and her swimsuit on, the cart veered right to left on the third floor, striking the walls of the open air hallway. I needn't have missed her childish summer vacation enthusiasm, which had awakened me early each foggy coastal morning and kept me moving quickly to keep up with her antics; very soon she would join in on the ritual vacation by telephone and I would revisit my role as the model's personal assistant.

Rae would be coming down early the next morning. I had the evening to myself. There was alcohol in the freezer and a terrace to smoke on while I sadly and pitifully watched the sunset turn from a wafting yellow to a pink slam dunk into the Pacific Ocean; not the perfect arrangement for a woman, who two summers ago had spent her vacation week almost entirely alone with her laptop, her cell phone, and her weakness for one AWOL Persian womanizer who had consistently used the Islamic food and sex fast of Ramadan to abandon her. In her monotonous misery over the boy, her common sense dissipated by drink and delirium, she had loaded the relationship gun with nonsensical ammunition and shot herself in the foot once again.

I poured myself my first rum and coke of beach week, and from the desktop of the MacBook I double clicked the *TYILTT* pdf file, searched for the words *Pacific Coast Highway*, and soon was reliving the beginning of one of many unsuccessful and disgraceful texting tirades from 2009.

An excerpt from *The Year I Learned to Text:*

> 9:52p JULIE: I am open to a good talk, if you are. I am at 34630 Pacific Coast Highway. I am looking at our moon and listening to the surf hit the sand.
> 9:54p ALI: How late will you be up? I want to call you after I'm done with this work. Eleven is okay?
> 10:06p JULIE: A man, not a boy, would have been in his car by now.
> 10:09p JULIE: Waiting for Ali. When does it ever end?

I had cut my vacation short that summer to return to Hollywood in great anticipation of our date for a Thursday night long ago, a date that never happened. That bastard.

I had protected myself from any chance dalliance into the dangerous realm of drunk-texting the wannabe terrorist. His phone number was not on my cell, my address book was void of any reference, and I was under strict orders from the CIA and the FBI, by way of Brainard, my salacious undercover case officer for the National Clandestine Service, to have absolutely no contact. I was free to drink myself under the glass top coffee table assured that no amount of idiocy would seduce me into the self-indulgence of finger thumping through the night. My hand stealthily attached to the television remote, I scanned through the movies of the evening and wished I'd stopped at the Ralph's freezer to pick up at least one pint of Ben & Jerry's Cherry Garcia.

I did not write one word in Part II, *Jihad Honeymoon in Hollywood*. And because my sister would be my scrutinizing cellmate for the remainder of the week, the artist in me would be squelched, my private hours of creation hovered over, and my writing life discredited. It was to be beachfront frolic all the way, baby!

As I iced up my final nightcap, the rum bottle appearing embarrassingly half empty—or is that half full—I remembered one of my *not so killer* jokes created while under the influence of my own undoing.

I have to stop drunk-texting him. There ought to be a law against it. Drunk driving is so passé. When was the last time you heard of anyone running into a pole and breaking up with her boyfriend at the very same time?

Rae arrived in her Mercedes convertible, the top down and her blonde hair in beach-breeze mode. Forever the perfect guest, she presented me with a chilled Rubbermaid pitcher of Margarita mix for undercover prohibited poolside refreshment.

"It's been in the trunk for almost two hours. Traffic was hell all the damn way. We need to add ice," she began her impeccable instructions which would continue for six more days.

"I'll do that while you change."

"Yes, we're missing the best rays from ten to two. Shit, it's noon already."

Competing with the lingering summer sun, the condo pool rules beat down on us from the placard over the hot tub: no alcohol, no glass, no pets, no running, no diapers, and no one who has had diarrhea in the last five days. From behind tempered glass walls framing the seaweed and pebbled beach view a four-lane highway and two train tracks beyond, two sisters in one-piece tummy-tightening *Miracle Suits* sunned on towel-draped loungers in a Southern California heat wave.

"No, really. I'm telling you, he wore boxer shorts that could have been terry cloth diapers," I chuckled, realizing my attempt to entertain my sister with my dubious sexual conquests was merely setting me up to succumb to a minor superficial irony—my pitiful self.

"Please keep this shit to yourself," she instructed me, her wide-brimmed straw hat cocked ever so precisely. "Nobody wants to hear it."

Nobody else was around to hear it, although a relentless heat had hit the coast. The families had vacated, returning their children to schools around the world. Except for a saucy couple applying oil to each other's thighs a long-range Frisbee toss away, we had the pool and two hot tubs to ourselves.

After feasting at our upstairs patio table from a tray of fresh cold prawns on ice—another host gift driven two hours in the trunk of her car— Rae and I emerged from the third floor kitchenette with another plastic pitcher and again set up camp by the pool.

Sticking to our pact not to let Mother know of our whereabouts, we would let her calls go to voice mail, vowing to return them when the sound of the surf hitting the sand was silenced by the closing of the bathroom door. We were on a *sneak away*. I received my first call from Mother at two in the afternoon, during her second cocktail hour. Seeing that it was Mother, I let it go to voice mail and left it there.

"We're both on the verge of having our jowls erased and our necks tightened, right?" I opened up the discussion of age-defying cosmetic surgery.

"Several gals at work have had remarkable success with a doctor in Santa Clarita," Rae began a diatribe regarding her non-debatable expertly researched opinion and her predetermined decision, and nothing I could do or say was going to change her mind. "I've made an appointment."

"Well, today I have a bit of a surprise for you, an actual *Lifestyle Lift* infomercial model is arriving. An old girlfriend from high school is coming to share her neck surgery experience," I gloated in anticipation of Hope's visit this afternoon. "I mean, she's as old as we are and looks fabulous." The golden California girl of my virgin youth was in residence close by, a married mother of three grown sons living the coastal life in the hills of Laguna Beach.

"Lifestyle Lift?" Rae spit out her high-priced tequila, covering her mouth in a gasp. "I've heard and *Googled* nothing but bad reviews, lawsuits, and stories of victims with nerve damage. I don't need to meet a bitch plugging a malpractice suit waiting to happen." The tequila was working its personality enhancing trickery, freeing limit-setting inhibitions. The relentless sun baked through her straw hat and fair skin, burning away her forced façade of social appropriateness. I slipped into my protective *walking on eggshells* jeweled flip-flops, their soles wearing thin.

"She's coming as a friend, not a salesperson. We reconnected on *classmates.com*, when she wrote to me apologizing for being a total shit way back when," I attempted to soothe the beast emerging from the lounger before the innocent kitten arrived at our poolside lion's den.

"Please call her off or I may lose the shrimp."

As I remember it, with a slight question mark as to its accuracy, when I've had hot summer sun tequila arousal, I've let loose by watching hours and hours of continuous *Lifetime* movies, stuffing my gut with cheese melted over tortilla chips and black beans, or foolishly venturing out in public to perform karaoke in the wrong key. And if there's a swimming pool nearby, I might have been freed up enough to belly flop unabashedly amidst public scrutiny at my inebriated splashing antics. Perhaps my sister needs a lesson on the correct behavior of a drunk and debilitated disaster. Being mean, nasty, and belittling is not on the wine list. That's Mother's particular talent.

Yes, Hope, one of the Beach Boys' "California Girls" we had all wanted to be, contacted me to apologize for mysteriously dumping me as a bridesmaid from her first wedding back in 1969. After her rushed in-and-out visit to borrow my veiled pillbox bridal hat and my white train car overnight bag, finding me grotesquely pregnant with baby no. 1, she had conveniently lost contact for forty years.

I answered back on *classmates.com* demanding the return of my now vintage 60s fashion items she had stolen from me. She apologized with some self-serving mumbo jumbo about how *she is a much different person now*, and crushing my hope to regain my first wedding memorabilia, alluded to the irresponsible fact that she had absolutely no idea where the items were. Through *Facebook* friends she had learned that I was an actor living in Hollywood, who had written a sexy book about love gone wrong, and wanted to reconnect.

After meeting up with Hope and her third husband of over twenty years at their million dollar home, where for the last twenty years she had spent her days mothering her sons, decorating, furnishing, redecorating and refurnishing, my thoughts as to her past perception of loyalty were piqued. How could such a lovely, fit woman tie herself up into a marriage with an overweight, commandeering bore, who assuaged my negative opinion of him by entertaining us with an immense wit? Taking Hope in, her three young boys in tow, he had supplied to her more than a veiled pillbox hat and train car overnight bag. Hope had not been in the work force since leaving her employment at Disneyland, the happiest place on earth, where *cast members* are expected to remain younger than springtime and where Snow White never ages.

"Oh, my god. Tell me that's not her," Rae wrapped her hands around her knees and sank deep into her towel, the plastic straps of the chaise groaning under her pinched buttocks.

Striding unmistakably down the concrete ramp, a trim blonde gracefully lifted her hand and waved to us from the far end of the pool.

"Bo Derek has arrived and she's not even wearing a cover up," Rae fluttered her eyelashes over her baby blues, which in the sunlight seemed to be churning into emerald green.

"Sure she is, see the little bow tied around her neck?"

"Let's give her a *10.*"

"Cheer up. Maybe she brought cute little Arthur with her."

"That is an entirely different movie."

My sister is a walking *Wikipedia* when it comes to movies, the stars that star in them, and all things trivialized by Hollywood. She also has a more techy phone than I do and is able to *Google* such information faster than I can take a potty break.

In slow motion, a tall, fair and comely woman tied ever so gently into a white bikini blazed a sultry trail through a maze of blue umbrellas, glass tables and patio chairs, a flounce of sheer elegance billowing behind her taut, thirty-year-old neck.

I took off around the pool to greet her.

After snacking on chips and salsa and a bottle or two of chardonnay, the *Lifestyle Lift* information packet spread out on the coffee table inside the condo, Rae lamented in no uncertain terms that the same procedure would not reveal the same results because our skin was not the same as our guest's, that the doctors performing said mini-surgery were all quacks, and that Hope could peddle her wares elsewhere. At five that afternoon, it was lights out for Rae, who silently stumbled down the hallway slamming my bedroom door behind her, not to return from self-exile until late the next morning.

Stunned by the outburst and hasty departure, Hope and I moved the conversation to the terrace, where I could inhale a needed bit of nicotine.

Hope was eager to talk about her family and I sat back and listened.

Watching her smooth neck, free of any excess wobbling skin, her jawline smooth, I thought how kind, patient, and noble this woman is, this sweet lovely woman who cherishes her sons, her grandchildren, but not so much her husband. We mothers seem to do a lot of juggling, balancing our stifled sex drives with mortgages to pay and school clothes to buy; we do a bit of horse trading for our children.

"We were wild that summer in Carpenteria," Hope changed the subject to my final self-absorbed vacation way back when, my last shout out before leaving my stepmother's stifling maple furniture coffin and stepping onto the city bus with my few possessions. Slung over my escaping shoulder sacked in a stolen pillow case had been five dresses, one pair of sensible shoes, one pair of rockin' *Go-Go* boots, a clock radio, and enough underwear to last through my new workaday week until I could zero in on a Laundromat in walking distance from the little duplex I had rented for eighty-five dollars a month with my first paycheck.

"Correction. You were wild. I was just along for the ride," as it seemed to my memory I always was.

"A ride in a prop plane with two strange boys we picked up on State Street in Santa Barbara," she remembered and let go a hearty laugh, a laugh I had not yet seen on her all day.

"We were kidnapped over the Pacific ocean. While you were necking with the good looking one in the passenger seats, I was crying in the copilot's seat."

"Hey, he was letting you fly the plane. From my VW to their VW to an air strip and a hole in a chain link fence to an actual cute little airplane! And then we landed in a field running distance to a pink motel?" Hope restyled the event.

"Wasn't it us that were staying in a pink motel and we ended up in an apartment somewhere in Santa Barbara?" I corrected her.

"All I really remember is that they let us go after we gave them our drivers licenses and promised to come back in the morning to get them."

"And we secretly spent the next day back in San Bernardino at the DMV getting new ones," I came to the end of the adventure.

"Whew. Nothing really happened." There was no disappointment in her voice, but a relief.

"It was a different time and we had no fear. The term *serial killer* was not yet in our vocabulary."

"Gosh, *rape* wasn't exactly a household word either."

"And who had ever heard of a *pedophile*?"

We fell silent in an unspoken grateful prayer; somehow throughout our coming-of-age dalliances, we had been spared. "Hey, you never told me about, you know, that day with the disc jockey."

"You'll have to read all my novels. I'll be sure to put it in there somewhere."

Suddenly that evening, just as the sun set over the marina, the lights went out from Arizona to Mexico. Not one streetlight was controlling traffic on the California coast. The air conditioning came to a sweltering halt. Hope left with my free advice to *stick with it*—there's no one else out there anyway—in complete blackness to drive the ten miles home. And while Rae would never admit to or apologize for her rudeness to our guest, an embarrassed technician waving his wire cutters as he clung foolishly to the top of a power pole somewhere in Arizona let out a big *oops,* initiating the Great Blackout of 2011.

Not wanting to awake the sun-soaked green-eyed monster, I took her place on the sleeper couch, the lulling sound of crashing waves interrupted by the roar of an Amtrak diesel locomotive on its run south to San Diego or north to Santa Barbara and through the living room. Whether or not the railroad crossings had been affected by the blackout had me tossing and turning for hours deciding whether or not to get up, get dressed, and park my car with its lights beaming onto the nearest crossing, a vigilante maneuver. When it came to me that the Pacific *Surfliner* quit running after midnight, I fell asleep.

After more sun and swim, the following evening a distress call came in.

"Mommy, I've booked a shampoo commercial shooting in Singapore and I need my passport."

"Where's Singapore? You're in Miami without your papers? Don't get too tan."

Rae's attention turned abruptly from her turn at the Scrabble board. "Is that Alex?"

"Very funny. Mommy, I need it by Tuesday afternoon. Do you still have my key?"

"Of course. It's been on my keychain for five years."

"Can you go to my apartment and FedEx it to me?"

"Where is it?" I pictured the monolith of strewn clothing, drawers half closed bursting with beige and black thongs, and a closet exploding with designer dresses, coats, shoes, and purses—a stylish black vortex of unending shopping.

"Top drawer of the nightstand on the right side of my bed."

"I'll get it in the morning—early."

"Thanks, Mommy. I'll text you my hotel address."

"Okay."

"Oh, and heads up. Grandma knows you're at the beach."

"How does she know that?" Wide-eyed, I glared at my sister.

"She called in hysterics because you weren't answering your home phone, so I told her you two were at the condo. Love you."

"Tell me you're not going to rush back to L.A.," Rae shook her head and fished through her tiles. "What are you, her personal assistant? You're always pampering her."

"And you don't pamper your son?" People who live in glass houses should keep their opinions to themselves, I thought, but was afraid to speak out loud. Many, many things are best left unsaid, especially when you're stuck in a one-bedroom beach condo with a seemingly functional, yet easily angered, sister who just plopped down a double-word score beginning with an *X*.

"I'll go at dawn. There shouldn't be any traffic. When I return, we'll bike to the pier," I coaxed her, switching an icy out-of-bounds topic into a wind-in-your-hair, sun and sea five-mile divergence down the Pacific Coast Highway.

"Not until after I'm fortified with hollandaise sauce dripping over soft boiled eggs and ham, vodka, and V8 juice."

"Great. I'll be back in time for Eggs Benedict at the marina. We can order one huge plate and share."

"You know I don't share."

The sun was up when I parked outside the 1920 two-story townhouse. Once inside Alex's upstairs bedroom, her roommate's bedroom door shut tight, my phone rang from inside my purse.

"Are you there?" Alex asked.

"Yes, I'm in your room." I tiptoed around the bed to the designated nightstand and fished through the thongs. "Got it."

"Go to the closet. Can you see the blue bag?"

"No, but I see an expensive leather jacket with a price tag still on it," I whispered.

"You don't need to whisper. She's in England."

"Oh."

"Do you see the blue bag?" she insisted.

"Hey, I'm not mailing purses or clothing."

"I'll pay you back."

"I'm on vacation. It's inconvenient."

"Never mind. Can you go downstairs to my desk?"

After writing a check to the Internal Revenue Service and signing it, I placed it in the envelope with the corresponding paperwork. I would need to buy a stamp immediately. I then signed the back of a pricy residual check and made out the deposit slip. I would need to swing by Bank of America ASAP. Taking the car keys from the drawer, I moved her car to the non-street cleaning side of the street, while Alexandra instructed me during each one-handed turn of the wheel on how to start, maneuver, and stop a hybrid, while I held the phone to my ear, because I had no idea how to put it on speaker.

I arrived in the historical town of San Juan Capistrano, which sits two miles north of Capo Beach, just before eight a.m. It is said that wayward psychic swallows return to the mission at San Juan Capistrano every year at the same time, but I doubt they have ever shown up this early in the morning. Finding nothing open, I sat at an outdoor table at a coffee shop, which was not as yet open, waiting for the FedEx doors to unlock. Forty-nine dollars and one stamp later, the nice FedEx man at the counter aimed me toward a Bank of America a few blocks up the street, where I was the first customer in line to make a deposit at the teller window.

Rae was still sleeping off her wine and big win from last night's Scrabble tournament, so I made coffee and took my cigarettes and cup onto the terrace. The beach parking lot across the street and beyond the chain link fence separating it from the railroad tracks was alive with day campers in different sorts of colorful cottons cranking up their trailer awnings over fold-out picnic tables and covering them with checkered cloth. Rollerblades, bikes, and early morning kites dressed my canvas. The surfers like rolling specks of Thumbelina Lilly pads rose and fell at Doheny cove.

Coffee cup in hand, Rae joined me in robe and slippers and coke bottle glasses. She has admonished me that although a laser has corrected my nearsightedness to 20/20—I can see the cellulite on her thigh from twenty feet away, but not that day-old dried booger up my own nose—her astigmatism is not a candidate for corrective surgery. It saddens me to watch her continue to saline drench those pesky little discs and place them over her corneas morning after morning after morning. And I'm sure it pisses her off no end that I don't have to do that anymore.

"Change of plan. We're driving to Salt Creek beach today. There we can lunch from the snack bar and sneak into the ritzy Ritz Carlton overhead for a cocktail," she licked her lips in anticipation. "So dress appropriately."

"White sands, a blue ocean, and spoiled young men?" My plans for a no makeup bike ride were tossed. I jumped up and headed to the bathroom mirror to speed through the beauty routine. "Beat you to the Benz!"

"Top down, baby."

It's a steep rocky walk from the one-dollar-an-hour self-parking to the sand at Salt Creek. My right knee spasms as I carefully step my protective way down. Following my sister, I trudge along carrying my orange beach chair and orange canvas beach bag heavy with towels, Banana Boat Tropical tanning spray, sunglass readers, and the cell phone. For beach reading I've brought along my friend C. Stephen Foster's newly released *Awakening the Actor Within*, a workbook geared to discovering your personal vein of gold, which I would soon discover by following the absinthe-soaked, shamefully psychotic Irish literary giant Oscar Wilde's advice to *be yourself; everyone else is taken*, and *Water for Elephants*, my interest in performing with endangered species having been piqued. What I do not have is a pair of binoculars, which I soon realize could certainly have been put to good use.

Rae sets up camp by fanning out the bright towels at an angle to the flapping shore for the perfect ultraviolet ray reception. The heat wave has migrated the immodest, arrogant, and vain flesh of youth, which to my inner calendar should be back in school taunting aging teachers and not us. There they are jubilantly frothing in and out of the sea, each leaping bounce into a wave loosening their miniscule bikini tops, while the boys of this endless summer straddle their boards contemplating the next ride and make bets on which bubbly young lady will lose her top first. So it is before noon that I am made aware once again of my loose and laboriously horrid aging skin, which startles me each morning upon removing my upper arms from under the sheet.

"It's the movie set for *Gidget*," I reluctantly remark as my elbows hold my miraculously girdled torso up to span the foreground. Pastel surfboards planted in the soft deep sand like popsicle sticks; rainbow shades of beach bags and terrycloth towels; firm breasts swell against skimpy chards of fabric; the gleam of tanned oiled vertebrae blind me.

"Yes, school must still be out for Orange County," Rae surmised. "Or they're playing hooky on the old ladies' time."

"Excuse me? Playing hockey?"

"Enjoy the view and the silence, yee old deaf one. I'll go check out the snack bar and see what's cooking." Throwing on a stylish cover up, Rae prattled off barefoot in the deep pure white sand of Salt Creek.

Before me, an arm's length away, plops a young man. He has the entire shoreline of the Pacific Ocean, but has chosen to tease my barren womb with the seductive sprawling of his presence. A head of thick dark, ink blue hair shakes out salt water and wet sand, which lands playfully upon my painted toenails. In sustained slow motion, he stretches out like a cat into the sand onto his oiled, preposterously sumptuous golden brown back. His fingertips graze my ankle.

"Oh, sorry, ma'am," he speaks and languishes there at my feet, his royal blue eyes opened wide, his full lashes brushing his virile arched and impeccably woven brows. He's brute handsome, even as I view him upside down. Soft black hairs circle his nipples, alert and stalwart, not yet warmed by the sun after his swim. The silky strands continue and tempt my eyes down to the navel and down again to that seductive dip of the two shallow grooves of Aphrodite's Saddle, the Adonis belt, descending from the iliac crest to the pubis, secreted just below the knot of string strapped through his board shorts resting there about his thin hips.

"Say, shouldn't you be in school?" I slam on the brakes to counteract the impending head-on collision of my foolishness with twenty-five years to life for child molestation, if he'd have me. He flipped over to face me.

"Nah, I'm over eighteen, but the kids are out because of the suspected terrorism plot they think caused the blackout." He was sitting up now cross-legged, the white lining of his suit securing a fine fleshy presentation slipped generously onto his thigh. When I was twelve I wore a pink two-piece swimsuit with little boy shorts, which had no lining. It wasn't until the very end of that summer at the community pool I was informed by a six-year-old rumormonger why it was the boys gathered about as I sat on the edge kicking my feet. Perhaps I should tell this fellow to be more careful when he sits that way, but I was enjoying the view, the sun, and the titillating tremble of my clitoris.

"I'm on vacation. I'm out of the news loop, I guess," I commented, realizing that I hadn't even turned on a radio since arriving. "But the blackout was a few days ago."

"Yeah. Maybe they're just playing hooky, 'cause it's so hot."

"Playing what?" Kids today, they all mumble.

"Say, you wouldn't have a few bucks for lunch, would ya?" Adonis played his card and I trumped.

"Nah, no bucks at all, sonny."

And my summer romance wandered off down to the water's edge.

"Can't leave you alone for five minutes. Who was that hunk?" Rae asked and set about arranging her towel just so.

"A very good looking con artist."

"Ah, the laws of attraction. You attract what you wish for," she touted.

"I have an electromagnetic field surrounding me, which attracts only manipulators, losers, and sociopaths. But I'm on to it."

"An old woman sees a young man on the beach and fantasizes about humping him. Your daughter wrote a poem about that."

"Yes, Elizabeth won an award for that poem. She was in high school when I brought home a strapping much younger man and married him, Alexandra's father."

"Ah, the catalyst for the poem. Art does imitate life. Well, at least you're not *that* old yet."

"True. The dirty old lady in her poem wears gloves to the beach and I'm not," I said and looked at my large, ruddy hands.

"Not yet you're not."

"Maybe I should."

"What you should do is put that poem in your next book. Ask Elizabeth."

"Yes, I will."

"That way you'll be sure to have something interesting in it."

The snack bar opened for lunch and two ladies in swimsuits beneath fashionable cover ups waited for their order: cheeseburgers, fries, and diet Cokes. The showgirl revue had moved from the surf to the wooden picnic tables. Not one bouncing bikini breast or string cinched cherub butt was respectfully covered up. Obviously, there are no local laws in force to squelch the lack of pubescent decency at the snack shack.

Settling at a table etched with various crudities, I scoured the bevy of banal beauties and their nonchalant counterparts; the males having absolutely no timidity as they fondled necks, rubbed shoulders, and placed fingertips down the back of stretched triangles. I wouldn't be surprised if nibbling French fries from inside a bikini top was on the menu.

As a young mother, I had adored watching little girls in little swimsuits, wet sand stuck to their ruffled bottoms; the innocent years before they become body conscious, before they start pulling up straps and pulling down bottoms to cover their cheeks, before someone like me, stuffed with piety and jealousy, stifles their self-assurance. Apparently, no one in this devil's playground has been stifled in the least.

Rae set down our feast. "Watcha thinkin' about?"

"I should be at Vine School reading to my kids. School is back in."

"What does all that volunteering get you? Are you looking to get a job with the school district?"

"Heavens, no. Those days with the kids are my best days. I look forward to them. I miss them. I miss my dogs."

"I commend you; you haven't mentioned the wayward terrorist, which I'm sure you miss also. Well, you'll be back soon enough. Don't weep."

After spilling Thousand Island dressing down the front of my cover up, I vetoed the Ritz Carlton cocktail. We reached the timeshare in time to unravel and shower and to tune into *Jeopardy*, the intellectually stimulating know-it-all game show, to happily compete for insensitive Alex Trebeck's affections, because at a very handsome seventy-one, the host of the show knows all the questions to all the answers. The categories tonight were exhausting, but as we drank chilled chardonnay, they seemed to simplify. Rae screeched out all the questions along with the contestants, so I couldn't ever tell whether her response was the correct one. The game was more enjoyable to watch at home alone, where my lack of spontaneous knowledge of junk trivia was kept to myself.

When *The Wheel of Fortune* began spinning and Vanna White began turning a few vowels, Rae switched off the television.

"Don't forget to follow up with Elizabeth on using her poem."

"I left her a message and I just sent her an email," I answered.

"After three glasses of wine? Not very smart."

"Here, you look at it."

There I was on the sand and I saw him. Don't worry, I didn't go near the guy, but I thought of your poem and will check with you later if you will allow me to include it in my next novel, with credit to you as the author, of course. You will then be published. So true; so beautiful; so true of my sadness.

Love,
Mom

"Which sadness are you referring to?"
"Ali, of course."
"Would she know who that is? Has she even read your book?" she cornered me.
"We've never really discussed it. It's one of *those* subjects, but Alex has probably filled her in."
"Good luck with that."

My writing life was never discussed with daughter Elizabeth. My feeling has always been that as far as she is concerned, I should be filling my final days making cookies, trays of them, although deliveries of these various cookies have not been requested by her for years and years, holiday after holiday. Her final answer to my request to make good use of her excellent poetry would come by way of an email, just as I was about to send the manuscript of *Jihad Honeymoon in Hollywood* to my publisher.

Picking up my phone, I asked Rae, "Hey, did you get a call from Mother?"

"No. It's been rather quiet."

"I think maybe we'd better listen to this," I said and held the phone between us car to car.

"God. Give me that. Don't you know how to put it on speaker?" Rae grabbed my phone, pushed something and set the phone down on the coffee table. Mother's cocktail hour diversion entertained us for an exhausting thirty seconds.

"Hey, listen, I know you're not home, because I've called your house over and over again. I think I'm leaving this message on your other phone. I got worried, so I called Alexandra, who also doesn't answer my calls.

Because Rae is busy at work, I didn't want to bother her. Just want you to know that I can't make it to the beach. Come on, there's too much to do here. I'm finally getting to the paperwork in your grandfather's desk and I've lived here for over twenty years. Don't you just love it?

Let's get real, I have doctor appointments and, if you remember, the pet motel has banned my cat and I'm not speaking to my neighbor, so I have no one to watch him.

Whatever. No need to return my call. Keep me posted."

Alexandra arrived safely in China, her passport in hand. At the end of the week, the unused firewood, wire hangers, marshmallows and four hot dog buns were left intact for the cleaning staff. Mother never called again. I left for Hollywood and the comfort of my dogs, a naked pierced Goth Girl in my shower, and a *Lifestyle Lift* consultation appointment imbedded in my calendar. There was still hope for me.

CHAPTER 33

Handcuff Fantasies and Easy Check Out

BILL Nob *On The News* woke me at the usual hour of six-thirty, along with a banging at the metal gate and the ringing of my doorbell. Who would be up at this hour?

"Oh, okay," I drooled and rolled over. Bill continued.

> Thousands of Egyptians are gathering in Tahrir Square, Cairo, where there's only one bathroom. The men are lined up back to back in front of a single porta potty. And near Beverly Hills, a Muslim-American has handcuffed himself to the doors of the Bank of America building on Wilshire, south of Burton Way. It's been reported that he's threatened to use his cell phone to detonate a bomb in retaliation of B of A's refusal to fund his fledgling manufacturing endeavor to mass produce long-sleeved, soft cotton men's t-shirts in gray only with the logo *Fasting Fanatic.*"

The knocking continued outside, but after tying one on last night, my head ducks under the covers for another forty winks.

"Wake up, Julie. It sounds like our boy. He is requesting that his wife, 'the nicest Republican he knows' be brought to the scene. That just might be the FBI at your gate."

"Bill, I'd better shower."

"Let the men in black know you're getting ready for your close up."

"Will do."

Sirens blaring, the black sedan raced through the streets. I continued to apply powder from my compact.

"You're gonna be great," Bill assured me from the radio speakers.

"Thanks, Bill. It was so nice of the men in suits here to give me forty-five minutes to become presentable."

"Right this way, ma'am," the officer in LAPD blue officially greeted me and lead me through a groggy early morning gathering of fire trucks, ambulances, cameras, the Channel 5 news van, and craft services offering hot coffee.

"What do you want me to say to him? 'Where's my Tupperware?'"

"No, ma'am. Just try to talk him down."

"He's on the roof?"

"Just a matter of speech, ma'am."

And there he was in his Adidas running pants and long-sleeved, soft cotton gray t-shirt, his black hair long and wispy. He was fashionable in an Allah-approved Jihad beard, one wrist handcuffed to a steel door handle.

"Hello, Ali. You've drawn quite a crowd. The City had to bring in porta potties," I shouted through the bullhorn.

"You look really nice, darling. I always liked that red dress," he shouted back through a wheeze and smiled that half smile, hiding away the little brown tooth.

"It's a little too tight."

"You always dress appropriately. Most girls dress too provocatively. But soon that will all be over," he sweet-talked me and blew into the sleeve of his shirt.

"Over? There aren't enough burkas to go around, pal, and you can't kill everyone, dear. In fact, the FBI said you'd probably just blow the glass doors up, and yourself, of course."

"You're still my wife, Julie. I never said 'I divorce thee' three times. I may have mumbled it under my breath once or twice, but—"

"Shhh. What do I have to say to get you to put your phone down and go get a bite, huh? The FBI promised me we could have one more greasy dinner at Zankou Chicken, if you were a good boy. Why don't we do that?"

"Wake up, Julie, before there's garlic sauce running down your neck and shawarma chicken grease all over your fingers."

"Bill, I'll do anything for my country."

"Did you ever write that screenplay about us? Did you get Johnny Depp to play me?" He hadn't forgotten our pillow talk.

"Nah, I was too busy crying and masturbating and Johnny was too busy doing voiceover work in a cartoon."

I stayed back, where the officials had stationed me. My senses were dull at this distance; I couldn't smell him, that musty scent that comes from laboring in the summer sun sweating over the keys of a cell phone only a man persistently three hours late to a moist tryst in my basement could thrill me with. I could, sadly, still hear him through his continuing nasal congestion.

"You know, I haven't had sex with anyone since I last saw you."

"And the sand dunes never blow. I do have a few questions I need you to answer truthfully before you blow yourself up."

"Of course, darling. I am a Muslim. I cannot tell a lie."

"Why haven't you called me?"

"You blocked my number."

"Okay. Do you ever eat American haraam beef?"

"Only at Del Taco, but it's mostly filler."

"Why did you stop kissing me?"

"I was not worthy."

"Good answer. Why did you not desire to touch my private parts?"

"Because they're icky, Julie. Just plain—ewwwe—icky."

Hung over once more from gluttonous indulgence, a nicotine overload, Jim Beam Red Stag bourbon whiskey, and a nightmare that had me driving around in an unmarked government town car in an ill-fitting red linen dress, Sunday morning I awoke to the déjà vu sense memory of soiled teenage tampons left on the floor of a stadium restroom after the football homecoming game. Upon further sniffing, I also inhaled the fragrant essence of vomit. I had neither miraculously reinstated my menstrual period nor propelled chips and salsa onto the living room floor, but upon inspection, I found that Hound had.

Together we sloshed and scooped and disposed of the slimy regurgitated muck, shined the floor with Murphy's Oil, and commiserated. To cleanse our souls, we thought it best to attend church, so I turned on the television. Brute curled up close to Hound, who trembled in an aftermath of weakness. I admitted openly the reasons for my morning sickness and swore to the boys that I would clean up my act. I had responsibilities: small children to inspire, homebuyers to comfort; casting directors to swoon; and an aging dog to comfort. So it was in robe and slippers, bolstered with coffee and cream, we tuned in to Joel Osteen, the smiling televangelist.

> "If you're still upset over the same things you were five years ago, it's time to grow up! Stop falling for the same temptations, stop arguing over the same thing."

Wow, Joel's hair is hot.

> "Never ask God to change anyone until you ask him to change you first."

Only he's not asking for change; he's asking for dollars. Okay, Joel, no money for you. *Lifestyle Lift* here I come.

Filled with the aftermath of joy only small faces and amazed eyes can bring, I drove away from Vine Elementary School and headed south to the Wilshire Corridor into Beverly Hills and parked the Scion in the eight-dollars-an-hour parking structure next to a Rolls Royce *Ghost* under Larry Flynt's *Hustler* building and found the elevator to the eighth floor. From the walls in the blue-gray carpeted hallway leading from the reception area to the consult chamber, a portrait of Hope's angelic face smiled larger than life at me, five feet by five feet to be exact, encouraging me to "Do it for yourself!"

"We'll be taking some *before* pictures today. Is that all right with you?" the charming overtly Caucasian surgeon urged me on through his sales pitch. "You're an excellent candidate. We'll diminish the marionette lines and tighten up the neck a bit. The less-invasive facelift procedure requires only local anesthesia and a shorter recovery time than the typical face lift."

"What are marionette lines?" Had I been walking around with noticeable strings?

"The drooping lines about the mouth. Also referred to as *disappointment* lines."

If I had never had any expectations, I would never have been disappointed, Ali had assured me. Had Ali's teachings been sincere when he urged me in his arrogance to have no expectations as to his arrival times, as he had resigned himself to having no expectations from the world?

> "I am not boasting. I am very, very intelligent. I am teaching you.
> In years to come you will remember how much I taught you."
>
> Ali, *Jihad Honeymoon in Hollywood*

"Well, Doctor, can't I just lift them by smiling ad nauseum from now on?" I suggested.

"The damage is done. But after the procedure, when we'll make a small incision under the chin and in front of the earlobes and tie a knot behind them, I certainly can prescribe laughter as being the best medicine."

"Just a few nips and tucks, huh?"

Running his finger down my patient information form, he instructed, "You'll have to quit smoking pre-surgery for two weeks and no alcohol for at least one week. And for a better recovery, don't smoke two weeks post surgery."

"When should I stop having sex?" I quizzed, always hoping that the chance of a low-impact aerobic activity lay forth on the barren horizon.

"I suggest replacing the alcohol and tobacco with rigorous exercise. Losing a few pounds before the lift is always a good idea."

Having been illuminated by the good doctor as to my impending obesity, I jogged back down the hallway with uplifting strident steps, my right knee clicking at each lurch, to the reception area and threw down my charge card.

Having all of October before the pre-surgery weeks of abstinence would kick in, I stopped at CVS Pharmacy, my home away from home. My cart full of the necessities, while standing in the usual line in front of the registers, Magda in her buxom burgundy CVS logo polo shirt waived me over to a peculiar kiosk with the even more peculiar title of "Easy Checkout."

"It's easy. I'll show you how," she coaxed me. "You simply find the bar code, pass the bar code over the light, and slip the merchandise into the bag. It's all totaled up for you here. You can use cash, one bill at a time, or your debit or credit card. Don't forget to put your ExtraCare card number in or just wave the card over—"

"Whoa, Magda. Unless you're going to go behind the counter and bring me three packs of Virginia Slims, I have to wait in line anyway."

Wasn't I doing enough already? I'm the one who has to select the wine, the rum, the bourbon, the vodka, the no-caffeine diet soda, the toilet paper, the paper towels, the lipstick, the mascara, and the tobacco, and then commandeer the machine by swiping my card and pushing one button after another before I am allowed the opportunity to pay the bill.

"Oh, I see you have alcohol in your cart. You'll have to check out at the register," Magda shamed me and pointed me to the back of the line to join the other addicts.

* * *

In this novel there are neither chase scenes nor special effects and no one gives birth, gets married, or wins an Oscar. Into my eighties, I shall be forced to write many novels to get all of that stuff in. Rape will also be an interesting subject; not physical rape, of course, but a new term, "rape by fraud," the manipulation of lies and deceit to bring forth consent for sex. But haven't I written enough on that subject already?

However, there will be political exile, pain, drought, and shameful antics for you to shake your judgmental fist at. To ensure the shameful antics will continue I have once again updated my profile and pictures on plentyoffish.com, the no-charge Internet dating site. Go ahead and say it, "You get what you pay for." Remember the shoe-fetish, masturbating actor, introduced in Part One, whose only sustaining grace was that he lived in the same apartment house where Sal Mineo was bludgeoned to death by a homophobic? He is still on Plenty of Fish.

The first candidate for pre-surgery sex and continuing into post, my hope being to fulfill the *Lifestyle Lift* prescription for weight loss through wet, sticky, rigorous activity is Cesar. Cesar is a fifty-something Guatemalan house painter living in the outpost of Van Nuys in an apartment over a garage, an apartment I happily would never visit. Over a crackling cell phone line, he reminded me again and again in his incompetent use of the English language that the correct pronunciation of his name was not like the salad dressing, but more accurately spewed as *Say-Zar*.

Say-Zar treated me to the El Torito taco and karaoke night in Burbank. His competitor, candidate no. 2, a twenty-seven year old recovering alcoholic and pre-med student, Brandon, whom I had not yet met, entertained me by text message in between salsa dances and my Margarita inspired rendition of Frank Sinatra's "Lady is a Tramp," chosen because Frank and I sing in the same key.

BRANDON: Hey, what's up?
JULIE: I'm on a date.
BRANDON: Tell him you only like sex with surfer boys.

Now I realize it is highly impolite to text while on a date with someone who is trying so very hard to win you over with an extra basket of tortilla chips. However, Cesar's come-hither dance steps were totally unnerving and not getting him the results he so desired, and if he didn't stop licking my neck, I was going to samba right out to my car, which I soon did. At my car door I let him kiss me—to get that delving chore out of the way—in order to discern his acceptability as a lover, sexual intercourse being the one vice left for me before the prescribed cessation of smoking and drinking crept up on my calendar.

When the bite to my lower lip drew blood, Cesar was immediately dropped from the list of possible coitus candidates.

A few days later I met up with young Brandon on the patio of the Coffee Bean on Sunset and Argyle. This being our first face-to-face, I was thrilled that the weather had turned chilly and I was able to entice him in full cover up, from thigh-high boots to cowl neck sweater and a flowing duster. This get-up is designed to tempt and tantalize while hiding each and every flaw.

A bit rugged and unsettling, my second candidate is tall and muscular, his physique hidden beneath a burly wool Pendleton shirt. His blond shaggy thick mat of hair springs and juts from dark roots. Brandon is handsome, articulate, and obviously just a little crazy, because he's bombarded me with unsolicited attention endlessly on plentyoffish.com, complimented me endlessly through email and text, all the while knowing I'm older than his own mother, who he describes as "bitchin," apparently a term of art still uttered by wave riders who are stoked on anything. He doesn't offer to buy me a coffee or a sweet, but continues to dunk a crusty chocolate croissant into his hot chocolate as we exchange the first date mutual memoirs.

"Why doesn't your son want a relationship with you? Is it a trust issue?"

"What? Sorry." Lost in the depths of the deep blue sea pigmentation of his iris, I had drifted away to hang ten over the bow of my sinking ship, the familial satire embarrassing me. Here I was sitting across from my nephew Tommy, a young man of the same age and, perhaps, of similar ailments, including the residual effects of one too many a wipeout.

"You were talking about the estrangement with your son."

"That's a long word."

"I'm an alcoholic, not an idiot."

"Why he is not speaking to me? Oh, might be the time I backed the station wagon out of the driveway with the kid sitting on the luggage rack in his car seat."

"What? How old was he?"

"Three or four months old."

"How would he even remember that?"

"His big sister probably told him. The raging slap incident as he threw a tantrum while I drove down a one-way street the wrong way? My sweet affair with the young golf pro? He was just jealous. Taking his car away the third time he came home drunk and violently broke all the geese in my farmhouse kitchen? Believing that it was me who coerced him into dressing as a woman for Halloween, when it was his own hilarious idea? Oh, and divorcing his playmate, my third husband? Yes, his sister probably filled him in on all of it. She's never liked me much."

"Why not?"

"Might be the slam of her head into the handle of the fridge door when she was five."

"Is she disabled from that?"

"Nah, just irritated."

"Wow, I'm not sure I want to have children."

"Besides the one glaring fact that it won't be you going through the rigors of a ghastly birthing, it's easy enough. You simply change their diapers, keep them clean—and without scrutiny or blame remove the white slithering lice from their hair—buy them more than you can afford, and hope that they don't kill you in your sleep."

"Want to work out some of your issues with me?"

"As long as you don't tell my children. I don't think they can take much more."

The sun went down and Hollywood moonbeams streamed into the sky over the ArcLight Cinema Complex, where another red carpet was unrolled. Brandon and I continued our meet-and-greet on my chenille loveseat, which is really a "big chair" in correct decorator vernacular, its seating capacity one-and-a-half persons. The dogs padded away to prepare themselves for the humiliation that was sure to follow.

"My father is a urologist, so I understand the care and nurturing a woman your age deserves, her tender spots, her motivations."

♪ Tonight you're mine completely.
You give your love so sweetly ♪

He also knows the correct, enticing words to say to a woman down on her luck, but does he carry in his wallet the correct condom: Trojan latex, *THINTENSITY*, with *UltraSmooth* lubricant?

"I want a lasting relationship, but I never spend the night."

"Why not?"

"It's a man thing. And I won't move in."

♪ Tonight the light of love is in your eyes ♪

Necking away my brown spots and marionette lines with his sandpaper stubble, he was cautious not to encroach upon my foolishly unfettered flirtation too quickly. Throbbing in sober anticipation, I, however, took the reins and pulled the horse into the barn.

♪ But will you love me tomorrow? ♪

A frenetic rumble, the dressed penis suitable, a replacement foot perhaps, he jumps out and off of me grumbling that he cannot cum. "I never had any problems when I was drunk."

And what sensible young man would attempt sexual contact with a sixty-three-year-old woman without being drunk?

Scrambling for his shoes, shirt, and pants, he runs to the front door, proving once again that you can lead a horse to water, but you can't make him drink. My flabby underarms reaching out from the twisted sheet, I attempt to seduce him back into bed with the tried and true harrowing female whine, "Hey, wait, I can."

"Zat was nauseating to watch, dahlink." Casting a femme fatale figure in a sculpted purple dress, my Pottsylvania nemesis once again brought me back down to booty call reality.

"I dried up pretty fast."

"And here is zee culprit," Natasha orated and tossed a red and white package onto the bed. I reached for my readers and gasped.

"Trojan latex *non-lubricated*?" I was horrified. "Natasha, when does Superman show up?"

"Ven you renew your subscription to Match.com."

"Are you a shareholder?"

"You geet vat you pay for, dahlink."

Chapter 34

Bowling For Lebowski

> ♪ We're never gonna survive
> unless we get a little crazy ♪
>
> *Crazy*
> Seal, the soon-to-be ex Mr. Heidi Klum

THE no alcohol ban in force, chewing nicotine gum, my right knee secured inside a Velcro brace, at a quarter to nine I reluctantly arrived at Pinz for the weekly Tuesday night bowling league extravaganza. Jason, no longer deemed a suitable candidate for replacement sex—best not to dip your finger in the league oil—has shaved off his beard and I compliment his new look.

"You did it just for me, huh?" I get big laughs all around the ball return, my Manute Bowl teammates Jared and Jonathan always ready to poke fun at the starry-eyed couple and their romantic squabbles.

"Right, I shaved off my cool, month-old beard for the old lady."

"Jason, there's no need to get snide before we even get our shoes on," Jonathan came to my rescue.

Yet I persist. "Why the teeny bits of band aid on your face? Did you cut yourself shaving?"

"I'm removing brown spots with apple vinegar, an experiment. You should try it."

Then I make the mistake of asking him his political theories, always interesting and an easy way to get his goat, on the Occupy Wall Street protestors causing a bit of a ruckus in New York City.

"They are as the protestors of old; they are righteous."

"I read they were leaving a mess all over Zuccotti Park."

"Where? It's a worldwide movement against social and economic inequality spanning the globe."

"Well, I heard that claiming no jobs in sight, the 99% gang are protesting having to repay their huge student loans. I think we should do as Russia and China, educate for free those that show promise, to help the country." That bit of liberal thinking should calm the anti-consumerist.

"Julie, you're up," Jared hastened me to the ball return.

Shouting at me as I readied myself to release the ball, "What the hell do you know about Russia and China? Damn this country. We need to change the world!" Jason continued his philosophical tirade. I left three pins and failed to pick up my spare.

"Ignore him, Julie, before he starts his own religion, just to piss you off," Jared consoled my open frame.

Jason was on a roll, his third straight whiskey urging him on—I had errantly chosen the wrong Tuesday night to stop drinking—when he started in on his agenda topic of a so-called resource based economy, which only a forty-year-old unemployed actor would rally round.

"The earth is abundant. We don't need money or credit or barter. We as a global people will no longer be indebted or in servitude. But you're too selfish and too stupid to ever understand that," Jason continued. Biting down on my Nicorette, I realized that I had errantly chosen the wrong Tuesday night to stop smoking.

What I did understand from his "the earth is abundant speech" was that in a Resource Based Economy, all goods and services would be available for free. How Jason pays his bills or his child support is apparently a result of resource economy, where money grows on trees.

At the end of the second game, Jared ordered chicken strips and fries, while I ordered fried zucchini with dipping sauces: marinara and ranch. We split the tab. Jason helped himself to his global share of both offerings.

"How are we going to get the barren Middle East to join in?" I threw a wrench into his philosophy.

"There you go again, putting down the Arabs."

"Is that all you got out of reading my novel?"

"I didn't read that racist piece of shit."

Hovering delicately over the zucchini, Jonathan whispered into Jason, "Hey, I come here for one peaceful night away from the nursery, not to listen to you two fight. Fuckin' roll, man."

Jared joined us at the chicken strips. "Thanks. I'm starving," he salivated and tried to slip a ten to Jonathan, who waived him off.

"You paid for the drinks, pal."

"All of them?"

"Personally, I think our country is turning out a bunch of wusses who decry that we have no enemies, just friends we haven't apologized to, just friends we haven't hugged enough," I blurted out, but no one took heed of my regurgitated *Facebook* brainwashing.

Returning to the marinara sauce after a lucky strike, a Justin Timberlake music video booming from the overhead screen, Jonathan turns Jason's new topic of the upcoming end of the world due to Global Warming to celebrity bashing. "Julie, what do you think of Justin Timberlake?"

"He's gay and should stop acting as if he's not?"

"Who the fuck cares if he's gay, straight, or bisexual. He has more talent in his little finger than you do."

I had apparently struck a homophobic nerve.

"Yeah, well, you know, that's just, like, your opinion, man," Jared tried his best to dislodge Jason's bullet from my trembling bowling arm. "Don't ya think, maybe, Julio Iglesias is gay, Jason?"

Jason came out of nowhere with more fun facts about Manute Bowl's only female teammate. "Julie is thirty years behind in technology and is still using a nine-pound ball."

"Ah, geez, Jason," Jared commiserates. "Lay off her."

"I can handle this, Jared. Hey, asshole, I'm on *Facebook*. I have a cell phone—"

"A Blackberry."

"This is a league game, man. Be cool," Jonathon reminded us.

"And I have Internet access," I proudly interjected.

"This will not stand, ya know, this aggression will not stand, man," Jared pointed out.

"My dear Julie, your stupidity is what is ruining this world," and he's screaming at me. There is no longer any chance for a laugh; he has it in for me tonight.

The boom of balls hitting the wood ceased. The video screens went blank and the music died. The waitresses stopped in their tracks. Trays of pepperoni pizza slices and orange Blue Moon beers were set quietly on the counter. The pinball machine blinked off and the pool cues were set aside. All this quiet to be able to hear what Julie was going to say next.

And that's when I realized that I didn't belong here, that I tired of keeping my prejudices, my politics, and my heartbreaks all hidden away like the varicose veins and the knee brace under my pull up Lycra pants. And the half-hour drive to Sherman Oaks every Tuesday evening was exhausting.

I sat down on the plastic bench, yanked off my shoes and my stinky socks, walked barefoot to the ball return and grabbed my ball, which slipped out of my powdered fingers and rolled all the way passed aisle no. 22 before it landed at the foot of Jeff Bridges, who graciously rolled it on back. It seems that we're always doing a movie together, Jeff and I. First there was *Seabiscuit*, then *Stick It*, and now the remake of *The Big Lebowski*.

I slipped into my flip-flops, zipped up my bag, threw my purse strap over my head, and headed for the door. But first I stopped to glance at Jared and Jonathan, while Jason from the loud speaker at the front desk continued to embellish his opinions as to my ignorance. When he finally took a breath, I got the last word.

"Sticks and stones may break my bones, but names will never hurt me. Nice bowling with you guys. Good-bye."

Jared pleaded with Jason to put the microphone down and apologize. As I pushed open the glass doors, the bewildered Pinz night manager was hot on my heels. "Wait! Don't go," he pleaded. "Hey, you know, he's got emotional problems, man."

In the car I switched from talk radio to the easy jazz station and scarface Seal sang to me.

♪ We're never gonna survive unless we get a little crazy ♪

So crazy Julie, the bitch who struck down Manute Bowl, pulled out onto Ventura Boulevard with a resolute smirk on her face; I wasn't gonna take it no more. I was on a roll.

Chapter 35

Noodling and Tom Sawyer

Wiggling my arm into the zippered plastic wardrobe, I retired my monogrammed Manute Bowl shirt. I crammed the boxy red and black cotton shirt next to the green velveteen Irish Pub wench. I wouldn't need either of them any time soon, but I refuse to admit defeat. The time would come to let them go.

Leaving the basement and turning off the light, I caught myself on the stairs. Had it been one year since last we touched? Three hundred and sixty-five days without the exhilaration of neurotransmitters messing up my brain. Fifty-two weeks without touching him, smelling him, loving him. My exotic affair with flying carpets and magic lamps had been put away along with Ruby the Fortune Teller, that Halloween one year ago. I rushed up the stairs and threw myself on the mercy of my two best friends, who had no idea why I was crying.

"Wake up, Julie. I've been up since five a.m. Time to begin another day."

"Holy shit. Okay." It was six-thirty once again.

> Bill Nob *On The News:* All you Hollywood Democrats, unless you've plunked down plenty of cash—five thousand to thirty-eight thousand—to attend the Obama fundraiser tonight at the home of Melanie Griffin and Señor Antonio Banderas in Hancock Park, keep your Prius in the garage; the streets will be closed—again. It's to be a very sexy event, as the President will be walking through a pathway of rose petals before begging for more money for his 2012 campaign.

While the President leaves Los Angeles with another million dollars and a doggie bag from Roscoe's House of Chicken and Waffles, I have been forced, due to an oversight in budget planning spanning almost a decade, to become a landlord. My cabin is now rented fully furnished from spoons to sheets, from tables to toiletries, from videos to vacuums. I took the rum and vodka home with me.

Enjoying my rum and Coke, and taking a writing break before tearing my hair out, I pick up the landline when candidate no. 3, my new sight-unseen soul mate from Match.com, calls again from a very long, long distance number. Avi, an adorable fifty-something originally from Israel, is a private pilot for an undisclosed entity. One can put just about anything on a dating site profile. He has begun *love bombing* me by phone three to four times a day from various phone numbers; however, his accent stumps me.

"I'm sorry, Avi. I didn't understand you."

"I am telling you joke of camel condom."

As thick as his accent is, I realize that I may be having phone sex and not even know it.

"I apologize. You speak so beautifully, but I just can't understand you."

"I speak Hebrew, French, English, and German."

"And apparently, all at once. Tell me again about your son?"

"He stay with housekeeper in our house in Sherman Oaks. He is seventeen. I been to house in Switzerland where they hid."

"Who hid where?"

"My parents escaped the Holocaust to Palestine, then to relations in New York City. I have no grandparents, uncles, aunts. All killed. When you with me you wear jeans and t-shirt and we go to beach."

Whew, no bikini requirement.

"I must go to Sweden until late November for trip and simulation certificate renew. Think about what kind of chocolate you want me bring back."

"Well, okay."

"Will you be good girl until I come back?"

I've never even been in the same room with you, but I vow to you, you hunk of a macho pig pilot, my chastity and fidelity.

"Sure, Avi. See you soon."

My mountaineer fan club, having digested *The Year I Learned to Text* in one gasping mouthful and always eager to hear more, Trudy, of Trudy and Ted, has invited me to spend the weekend in Crestline at their guest cottage, just a turn in the road passed Le Petit Chateau d'Enchanté. Daughter Kylie, who devoured my first book while screaming and stomping her feet, would join us at Oktoberfest to be celebrated Sunday afternoon at the San Moritz Lodge on the south side of the lake. With the promise of beer, bratwurst, and an oompah Bavarian-style band, I loaded the dogs in the car. In no time at all, I spotted the American flag waving over the road. We had reached the old wooden bridge, which takes you over a stream onto their property and two identical small houses in a clearing. The Scion rumbled over the gravel to a stop, and two fun-lovin' salts of the earth rushed hand in hand to open my door. The dogs peed and I hugged. My bags put in the guesthouse, we gathered at the main house around the raised kitchen table. Brute and Hound found the cats' food and all was well.

"We have rum for you," Trudy seemed nervously pleased with her selection.

"Thank you. That's so nice of you, but why *rum* exactly?" I hadn't the heart to inform this gregarious gracious new friend that I was trying to quit drinking or at least cut back until after my neck job. Information on my impending nip and tuck would not be let out of the bag to anyone, in case the knife slipped and I became a recluse hidden away behind Spanish walls draped with bougainvillea vines never to reveal my disfigurement.

"That's what she drinks in the novel, white rum and diet Coke."

"Oh, sure, of course."

"It is *you* in the book, isn't it?"

"As I've stated before, Trudy, it's a fantasy and I'm stickin' to it."

"I'm not a reader, so I have no idea what she drinks," Ted, who melted me with his huggable Teddy Bear composure, countered. "But I can make a Cuber liberal as strong as you like."

"I think you mean Cuba libre, like to free the communists."

"Nice to know. It's Mexican, huh?"

Seated at the table, the wood protected by a fruit-inspired plastic tablecloth, I sipped my expertly mixed rum and diet Coke and found it interesting that my portrayal of the foolish heroine and her bad habits had been so indelibly etched as to establish forever my taste in spirits.

Trudy busied herself with the peeling of carrots, a slicer in one hand and a glass of cabernet in the other. Ted reclined in his worn saddle brown recliner and I joined three well-fed cats on the quilt covered couch to watch *Hillbilly Handfishin.'*

Trudy's newest yard sale find peered at me from the wall high above the black bear lamp, a mountain cabin necessity found on every pine side table from Crestline to Big Bear City.

"Nice buck, Trudy. Great pair of horns," I complimented the tacky head.

"Don't you make her watch that. You saved it from last week. You can watch it anytime," Trudy suggested over the iron skillet spitting bacon grease from meticulously sliced red potatoes.

"Oh, no, it's okay. I'd love to watch it," I teased the Teddy Bear, who jumped up and brought me another rum and Coke.

In a murky river, two braless spindly blonde girls in tank tops and blue jeans stood waist deep in the muck. Two grungy hillbilly types waded in after them.

"There's not going to be any sexual plundering, is there?" I asked, my hands over my eyes.

"No. They're going to learn how to *noodle*," Teddy Bear assured me.

"Catch big, juicy fish with their hands," Trudy explained, as she wiped her hands on her apron.

"How big are these fish?"

"Monsters," Teddy growled. "Monster catfish of Oklahoma."

The fish were biting, biting the girls. The brown water splashed with scrambling arms, kicking legs, jiggling décolletage, and swarming whiskered fish. The men wrangled with enthusiasm, encouraging the girls to *get 'em!*

"They use their hands and feet as bait," Ted clarified. "It gets real exciting when they corner a big one."

"Can I have another one of these?"

"Comin' right up," Ted obliged.

"Oh my god. She's underwater."

By the time one of the screaming girls caught a fifty-pound blue and kissed it to prove her worthiness as a brave noodler, Trudy called us to the table.

"Turn that off, Ted, please." Ted commandeered the remote and joined us. "He's got at least three episodes calling his name."

"Teddy, Teddy, Teddy," I echoed.

Buttered bread, fresh broccoli drenched in butter and almonds, carrots swimming in maple syrup, fried red potatoes, and baked ribs in a glass casserole dish fresh from the oven took up all the counter space in potluck fashion.

"Help yourself. White wine or red? We don't always eat this way, but we can go off the wagon for company."

My plate filled to the top Army mess style, I sat on a stool opposite the cook and the bartender.

"We moved our Obama picture into my office, so not to upset you," Teddy alerted me. "We knew you wouldn't want him watching you get sloshed on Bacardi."

My mouth full of carrots, the syrup dressing my chin, I sat dumbfounded and off balance. These were my mountain folks, my country cousins, my redneck Republicans. I was safe here, safe to spout and spill and belch out my conservatism without retribution. Ted has an arsenal of weapons in the hall closet and a two years' supply of freeze dried emergency survival food in sealed plastic tubs stacked to the ceiling in the second bedroom of the guest cottage. They own an eighteen-wheeler on consignment hauling beer from Tennessee to Missouri. The license plate frame on his four-wheel drive reads, "Don't Tread On Me." Had I drawn the wrong conclusion? Am I stuck on the mountain with no place else to go?

Trudy's poker face broke and she couldn't hold the giggles in any longer. She grabbed a paper towel from the spool on the table.

"Don't choke. I get it, you devil," I snorted. "You got me."

"Trudy read a few parts to me. You moving Jesus from your bedroom wall every time that Mussie showed up, that was worth turning off the TV for," Teddy Bear confessed.

The laughter began and we couldn't shut it down.

"Let me help you, Trudy," I insisted as I viewed the aftermath of our delectable smorgasbord. I also viewed the aftermath of, perhaps, breakfast and lunch dishes piled high in the one-basin stainless steel sink. "Can these go in the dishwasher?"

"Nah, the dishwasher doesn't work. I keep pots and pans in there."

"Kylie can't make the Oktoberfest, so we have an extra ticket, if you know of anyone that drinks beer."

"Thanks, Ted. I'll think on it."

Ma and Pa Kettle go to bed early. Alone in the cottage at nine o'clock, the dogs wondering where the heck we are, I bundled up, the evening now beginning to chill, and we ventured out to drive the mile-and-a-half up and down the road for smokes, a night cap, and a fill up. At the Valero station, the only lights on Lake Drive still burning, gruff and always irritated Koshy, the manager, is stacking propane tanks into the storage unit. I am familiar with Koshy only as the nice looking man behind the counter who grumbles while handing me cute little airplane bottles of liquor, packs of cigarettes, and five-dollar *SuperLotto* Quick Picks.

Twenty dollars of gas in the tank, I rolled the rear window down just a teensy bit. "You two watch for serial killers. I'll be right back." Two forlorn faces followed me across the well-lit lot.

Tonight Koshy seems shorter, as I pass by him into the convenience store, very conveniently located at one of the only two gas stations in Crestline. The other station is at the unattractive 7-Eleven, where pizza slices are warmed under a light for days at a time. The station sits on an oily dark corner across from the lake, like the foreboding set of a horror movie in which every drunken teenage girl is eventually raped and disemboweled. There you might still find a telephone booth, the receiver dangling from the last unanswered call for help. The 7-Eleven does not offer spirits and I don't carry a gun, which is why I frequent the Valero station, which carries a sophisticated selection of spirits and where the concrete drive appears to be steam cleaned on a daily basis.

Together alone in the store, I notice how full Koshy's lips are, how his broad shoulders strain under that tight fitting button-down shirt, how his skin is light—no black hairs on his hands—and how he looms over me from the other side of the counter.

"Koshy, are you on a box?" I ask as I slide my debit card.

"The platform behind the register is raised to intimidate," he grumbled.

"Oh. Well, it's working," I smiled, my alcohol level just tipsy enough to investigate this man, who is obviously Middle Eastern—he's managing a gas station, after all—and who is, to my mountain knowledge, the only Middle Eastern person working in the San Bernardino National Forest.

"And may I have a Quick Pick? Let's do five."

"You don't have your own lucky numbers?"

"Nah. The fear of choosing six special numbers and then not betting them, only to find my numbers won someone else millions of dollars, would be a bit unsettling. I'll let the lottery computer pick 'em."

"You feel lucky tonight, huh?" he let go a sneak peek of his smile.

"Nice teeth. You sure keep this place tidy," I rushed through the compliments and continued my interview. "Do you live in Crestline?"

"Just up the street on Outpost. I rent a friend's cabin there."

"I'm single. Are you single?"

Well, maybe my level of tipsy was leaning toward drunk and disorderly, but I sure was having fun.

"Yes, I'm single. Why do you ask?" The smile on Candidate no. 4 collapsed entirely.

"I'm up just for the weekend, staying with friends, and we're all going to the Oktoberfest tomorrow afternoon. The senior citizen club is putting it on. Bratwurst, sauerkraut, and brown beer. We can do the chicken dance together. Wanna go?"

"I can't. I have to work."

"I see," I silenced, my lips pursed into a flirtatious little pout. I was jumping into muddy waters here, trying to cajole a Muslim into flapping his arms like chicken wings while biting down on haraam pork. I wasn't giving up on this big fish. If he'd let me tackle him, I'd give him a big wet kiss.

From my white tiled shower ninety miles away, I could hear Randi singing her favorite song.

♪ Get out of the Middle East ♪

I rushed back into the bayou, using my flaying arms as bait. "Can't you get someone—I know you have other employees. Maybe one of them could—"

"I would not be welcome there. The people in this town do not like me. They've broken windows, scrawled evil words on the doors. I am an American citizen now for fourteen years. The Muslim terrorists attack on 9/11 and now I am lumped with them."

The floodgates opened and I didn't back away. The interview was not over.

"I am from Homs Province, Syria. I am Christian Orthodox. I attend the St. Ephraim Orthodox Church in Burbank with my cousins. I am not one of those lying deceivers who come here not to assimilate or work or to be Americans, but to force their Sharia laws, their evil god, and their barbarism down our throats."

"Koshy, you're trembling. Is there a chair? Please sit down."

As much as I wanted to console him with my own Islamophobia, this was not the time to share with him my extensive knowledge of American Muslims, having had sex with one in my basement. My instincts told me that such interesting and vital information might be a complete turn off at this juncture in our relationship.

I walked behind the register and holding his hand, I suggested, "You should wear a cross at that big, brave chest of yours. Do you have a honkin' jaw-dropping crucifix? You know, one with Jesus strapped on it?"

"Yes, I do," he shyly answered.

"I'll pick you up here at two tomorrow. Wear it."

Candidate No. 4 has no idea what bratwurst does to me.

As the sun set over the timberline, from Koshy's porch swing we watched it all go down, while puffing on heated tobacco marinated in cherry juice from an intricately carved, ornate glass-bowl hookah or "argilah" as Koshy insists is the correct Syrian term, which at first disgust I declined. However, Koshy having obliterated the chicken dance to please me, tit for tat, I was forced by good manners to put my Virginia Slims away in favor of a puff or two or three from the water pipe he had so ritualistically prepared. The moon worked its way into view. The conversation international in scope, Koshy instructed me on the politics of Christian Syrians and the fear of foreigners being implicit in protests against their government. The lamb stew finished off and on our third shot glass of Ouzo, a Greek anise-flavored liqueur that will knock your socks off, I began another lesson.

"So what did you learn today at Oktoberfest, Koshy?"

"The chicken dance?"

"Besides that."

"That there are some very nice people here."

"You can kiss me now."

I had found a friend with excellent attributes: an educated Islamophobe with a worldly knowledge of alcohol who managed a liquor store. How lucky I was.

However, he had to be the worst kisser in any of my novels. My kissing lesson sent us straight to the low couches, the majlis, of the living room where Koshy lit the fire. In this dark room drenched in heavy fringed tapestries and warmed by wall-to-wall Persian rugs, it was apparent his desire to assimilate had not reached as far as American cabin decor. There wasn't one black bear lamp in the place.

At just forty-one, a professional at cunnilingus, relentlessly Koshy devoured me. I clenched my eyelids, my fists and my inner thighs until from out of a mystic fog rising from the rug Ali's face floated above me, but I couldn't keep it there. I dodged my head side to side, but Koshy kept lifting up, his lips drooled with pent up vaginal saliva, and blocked my view. Bearing down was no use; my lover kept slipping away. Each forced unfinished orgasm presented a singular bleep until I wilted, begging him to stop.

"One more orgasm and I'm moving in," I complimented his technique. No need to discount his attempts, but alone with my fantasy, I just do it better. "My cabin is rented."

Who is this wanton naked creature, this Julie, who so carelessly within five hours of a first date allows another human being, a Middle Eastern man to boot, to see her exactly as she is? This ribald tour into hedonism has got to stop. But what if Rae is right, as she always is, and the surgery goes badly? If she's ever to find that perfect glass slipper, Julie had best get in as much obscene indulgence as is offered before her face is altered into such a gruesome manner no man will ever offer her a hit off his hookah.

"Do I have to put that on?" he pleaded as I dangled a Trojan *Ultra-Smooth*.

On further inspection, I could understand his quandary. It was so white and so very little, how could it do any harm? I would just be trying it on for size, like so many others.

Well, fair is fair. If he puts it on, he could have a go.

Funny, even when there is no magic, no dopamine rush, no pulsating grind, I expect there to be a bit of a crush, a tad of sexual chemistry pulsating in the stale air. Having intimacies without lust was the hardest thing I'd ever do.

Stoking the dying embers, Koshy spoke, perhaps to undermine the non-occasion. "A woman of your age is exactly what I need until I marry."

"Balderdash."

"What are you saying?"

"Rubbish, hogwash, baloney. We just had intercourse and that's what you have to say to me? Do you really think that a woman of a certain age," I took in a dramatic breathe, "no longer has feelings?"

"Please don't cry."

Koshy and I are still friends. He mail-ordered a virgin bride his parents arranged for him from Homs Province before the bombings and the civil war began. They now have a child. His foot fit perfectly into her inexperienced, fertile glass slipper.

***

Trudy shouted out from her front door, "Get over here. Bacon and eggs!"

"We'll be right there."

Bloated after a hearty breakfast, I needed the two-and-a-half mile walk around the lake to break it loose. I'd been eating and drinking for three days. "Anyone want to take a walk?"

"By the way, when did you get home last night?" Teddy asked.

"Ah, Ted, don't pry. Besides, anything she does of interest will end up in her next novel."

CHAPTER 36

A Nip, a Tuck, and a Hand Job

♪ I should be over it now I know.
It doesn't matter much how old I grow,
I hate to see October go ♪

I Hate to See October Go
Johnny Mercer and Barry Manilow

Halloween Day I brought up from the basement Ruby the Fortune Teller and her entourage. After judging the annual Vine School costume contest, I stopped at CVS for the usual addictive supplies, along with a bag of Snickers and a small bag of kettle corn candy for Ruby. The front porch previously prepared with the traditional cobwebs draped about the black metal chandelier, its candles lit, Victor the Vulture placed ominously on the baker's rack, I switched the tried-and-true portable tape player on, sending frightening sounds of screaming ghosts and rattling chains into the night air.

"I'm going to shut both doors to keep you safe," I assured the boys, Hound being forever the watchdog that could still outrun me. "I don't want you two attacking any undocumented little monsters tonight." *Attack* may not be the correct word; *licking* might work better here.

Swinging my bejeweled hips to "The Monster Mash," I opened the gate at five o'clock. When the witching hour of six o'clock brought complete darkness and the ghoulish vintage streetlights switched on, the expected smattering of trick-or-treaters began to arrive. Ruby stepped down from her perch and offered a plastic pumpkin of treats to five Latino goblins, a folkloric weeping five-year-old bride in a wedding dress streaked with blood, and a horrifying trio of teenage transvestites, who cleaned me out. Randi in my lavender bathrobe, the scent of day-old vodka and cigarettes oozing from her unwashed hair, came by around seven o'clock. Finding I had no more Snickers, she tried for a cigarette, but I hadn't any. I invited her in for a molded skeleton plastic cup of wine.

"I can't. I'm waiting for *Married Guy*."

"It's Halloween night and he's got kids and you need a shower. He's not coming."

"I know," and she disappeared into the darkness of the walkway.

At eight o'clock I locked up.

In my black wig and red lipstick, I visited social media to soothe my sudden bout of loneliness, which in doing so just made me feel worse, of course. Alex and Benjamin had quickly posted the happy happenstances of their very personal Halloween on *Facebook*, but never showed up for a palm reading or a candy bar. Watching my vintage videotape of *Invasion of the Body Snatchers,* I tried to stay awake, finishing up a bottle of pinot noir and the entire bag of kettle corn, fearful that if I did fall asleep, I would awake with no human feelings, no worries, and no money problems.

"According to his various phone numbers, Avi the Aviator, the misunderstood Israeli, is calling from all over the world day and night," I informed Brainard, who had called in early this morning to check on my dating schedule, to update me on his sexual prowess, and to inspire me with his expertise on the Queen's Muslim population.

"Britain will suspend immigration now that the Muslims are breeding out of control," he continued.

"Nothing I can do about it on my end. Maybe if the parliament makes it a crime to have four wives and multiple girlfriends—"

"Is it parliament that makes laws over there?"

"Hell if I know. You're the unofficial asset. Or is that *case officer*? I'm retired. Aren't you supposed to know all that shit?"

"Just keep a list of Avi's phone numbers. Has he said anything worth repeating?" Brainard hammered at me in his earnest hope of hatching a conspiracy or, at least, catching a conspirator, a homegrown terrorist, or a day player role on *Criminal Minds*.

"If he said anything subversive, I didn't understand it. Oh, and I slept with a Syrian, who after two Ouzos shared the belief of his countrymen that Bin Laden is not dead, but living in the White House."

"Good work, Mata Hari."

"Yeah, just shoot me. He's a Christian from Homs."

"Nothing there. They're on our side. A recruit asset, perhaps?"

"Sorry, Brainard, but I'm not recruiting anyone to recruit assets in Syria. Truthfully, I tire of the entire mess. I've even turned off the *Yahoo! News* constantly bombarding me on my computer. The emails are upsetting enough. I'm helpless to stop what's coming. You sleep with him, but I warn you he's a bad kisser."

"Which reminds me. Did I tell you about the eighteen-year-old virgin who is seriously thinking of giving it up to me?"

"No, but you're going to. I'll set the phone down."

* * *

The day had finally arrived. Hope was on her way from Laguna Beach with an overnight bag in her Mercedes to take me to the knife at the *Hustler* building on Wilshire. We were on a clandestine mission when all hell broke loose.

"Shit. It's my extra work call-in service with a text. I'm booked with my Scion on a night shoot in Pasadena." It had been months since I'd been called to work and I'd forgotten to book out.

"Can't you just tell them you're busy?" Hope naively asked.

"What? And never work in this town again?"

I wrote back with an excuse sure to warm the hearts of the liberal casting community.

> JULIE: I'm in the emergency room. Can't make it. I was on my way to Skid Row to feed the poor at an early Thanksgiving dinner, when I was hit by a city bus under a freeway overpass.

"Who's texting you now?"
"It's Alex."

> ALEX: Mommy, could you maybe pick me up from the airport? Benjamin ended up having to work tonight.

"Good news. Alex's boyfriend has a job, I think, and she wants me to pick her up from the airport."

> JULIE: Well, I've been caught. I cannot tell a lie. Surgery within the hour today. My friend Hope, driver and nurse.
>
> ALEX: How are you paying for it?

"Christ, she didn't even ask what kind of surgery and she wants to know how I'm paying for it," I raged. "I could be on my way to a full-blown hysterectomy for all she knows."

"How *are* you paying for it? Are you using their no-interest deal?"

"The same way I paid for her childhood braces—twice—her nose, her *Invisalign* mouth piece, and her Screen Actors Guild membership. I charged it."

> ALEX: And what surgery?
>
> JULIE: Lifestyle Lift of neck and jowls. They agreed to accept my last child as payment.
>
> ALEX: I'm too busy working. They can't have me. I will pray for a safe and quick surgery and recovery.
>
> JULIE: Thank you. U know I love picking u up. Sorry.

"Didn't you let anyone know?"

"My agent thinks I'm away on a week's vacation. I told my Goth friend Randi, when she showed up for her shower this morning."

The examination chair in the consultation office is also the surgery chair. For eight thousand dollars I don't even get to lie down? A silver tray of syringes is rolled on over. I hate needles. I'm the biggest chicken ever, ever. "The anesthesia must be injected," he says.

"Can I squeeze your hand?" I ask the assistant, whom I've been told is not a registered nurse, even though her name is Teresa. Included in the price is a burning laser treatment to remove brown spots and I'm not getting anything but local anesthesia. When is he going to stop? Pricks here and there and here again. I'm awake and although a band of gauze has been strapped over my eyes, I can see my reflection in the window.

Where is Hope? She's been banished to the waiting room. I'm alone with an overly cheerful car salesman who is nipping, tucking, and slashing, I suppose. I'm in an interesting fuzz. I can't feel anything, but I can hear every pull to my skin, every request from the doctor to the assistant, and I can see from the corner of my eye a needle pulling thread. What if I were to jerk? How can he trust me to stay still? Is he an idiot? What is the thing he's waving in front of my face? Shit, that really burns. *Stop! Please stop!*

I am wrapped at the neck in soft cotton and gauze and sent home, where I sleep sitting up in bed. Hope enjoys snacks and wine and watches television before joining me, little Brute snuggling between us. The painkillers began to wear off around midnight.

"Get this thing off me!" I cry out, my hands gripping the noose tightening about my neck. "Please make it stop."

From somewhere in the dark a soft voice spoke. "I'll get you another pill. Stay calm and don't touch that. You're going to be okay. You're going to be young again."

By ten the next morning we are at *Lifestyle Lift* for the physician's follow up. We wait an absurd two hours to be called in. Hope complains for me.

"Yes, that's me on the wall. Now get her in there. She needs to be lying down!"

Teresa removes the bandages from my neck and gently applies ointment and wraps me in gauze again. The overly cheerful doctor whizzes in and out, but never inspects his work under the wraps. I sleep on the ride home. Hope returns home to her husband and her charmed life of trade-offs.

On day no. 3, I unwrap to find stitches in front of my ears, behind my ears, and beneath my chin. My skin has formed gruesome bubbles between each stitch, and upon close inspection through my readers, it looks like my left ear lobe has been sewn to my cheek. I nap off my fears and in early evening I call Hope, who bolsters me with praise and the promise that I'm going to look just wonderful. Then I call Bogie's Liquor for wine and cigarettes. Upon their arrival, I settle into my desk chair and post my Vicodin-chardonnay cocktail good-bye letter to all the fish, from Beverly Hills to downtown L.A., from Hollywood to Burbank, young and old.

> Nice knowing you all, but you take up way too much of my precious time. None of the men who write to me really want a true romance or a relationship. And I've been told more than once that the "three dates before sex rule" is soooo old school. I think they just like the idea of dating ladies on the screen while they drink beer, belch, and jack off.
>
> So it's a sweet farewell to all you men who think you look like Antonio Banderas, dance like John Travolta, and kiss like Johnny Depp. I do not belong on this site, but thank you for some excellent fodder for my next novel. You may just find yourselves in my books. Available now! *The Year I Learned to Text; Why Am I Having Sex with a Muslim in My Basement?* Soon to be released: *Jihad Honeymoon in Hollywood; Not Without My Dogs*

The eighteen-year-old degenerate who sent me a simple *Wanna Fuck?* received a personal note:

> I hope you rot in hell after being crushed by a city bus against a freeway underpass which decapitates your teeny tiny dick.

Day no. 4 of my recuperation, the phone call of concern came in, Alexandra, I assume, having spread the news.

"When were you going to tell me? What if you died?" my daughter Elizabeth shrieked at me from ninety miles away.

"Never, actually, unless you were going to take me, pick up my medications, spend the night, and return me to the doctor the next day."

"You're just like your mother."

And that's when I hung up.

Alexandra must have told them, but neither Rae nor Mother had called. Were they respecting my privacy and honoring my desire to be left alone? This question was soon answered when Mother left a cryptic message on my landline answering machine.

> "I have tickets to a concert for Saturday night and if you don't call me back by six o'clock this evening, I'm inviting someone else."

Apparently, neither Rae nor Alexandra have shared their hysterical prophecy of my anticipated disfigurement with Mother, because no one wants to be on the phone with her for that long and no one wants to use that ticket. I had to call her back and break it to her gently that I would not be joining her in San Bernardino to escort her to the symphony this weekend. Just having had cosmetic surgery is the best excuse I've had in years not to attend a stodgy cultural event, which would have me twitching uncontrollably in my front row seat.

"It's only been a few days and I'm still a bit groggy, but I look fabulous!" No need to share the nerve damage to my neck, which was causing me concern. I pressed the small round pink ice pack against the burn.

"Oh, I wish I had done that when I was your age. It's too late now."

"It's never too late, Mom. They'll just charge you more."

"Why would it cost me more than it did you?"

"Because they charge by the wrinkle."

It seems my entire address book knows of my surgery, as friends and lovers come out of the woodwork by way of coincidental phone messages inviting me out, just when I was laying low. Cesar invites me to karaoke. Brandon invites me to a booty call. Koshy invites me to church. My neighbor Hugo invites me to taste his newest Cordon Bleu culinary school recipe he has painstakingly prepared for Barry's fiftieth birthday. Bud Taylor is worried as to why I hadn't been in to read this week. My agent wants me back to work for an audition on Monday. Avi is back in town. I called just two of them back and went to sleep.

Brainard came by with a get-well card and parked himself on the bed. He talked incessantly, but through my haze his well-meaning buzz diminished as I fell back into a drug-induced prescribed coma.

Beryl, bless her heart, came by with peeled orange slices, which I like to call *citrus smiles*, and a pint of Cherry Garcia. We watched a movie, but I couldn't tell you what it was about. She rambled on for hours about the memoirs, the screenplays, and the political thrillers she would never write.

Neither Rae nor Alexandra called or came by.

I am not ready to present the newly refreshed face and neck at the office yet and I don't have a FAX machine; so it is that in a white chiffon scarf draped over my head under a white poplin sun hat and crisscrossed about my neck, I walk to FedEx on Vine to put out a brewing real estate fire, which, of course, will go nowhere. I am not to drive an automobile for another twenty-four hours. I shop at Trader Joe's, Rite Aid, and CVS. No one cares that I wear no makeup. I communicate from behind large tortoise shell sunglasses, which I never take off.

A few days before Thanksgiving, Alexandra let me know that she would be driving the sisters into San Bernardino to pick up grandmother for the forced familial holiday, apparently in reparation for leaving me during the upcoming two weeks of Christmas for a private house on a beach in Hawaii with the boyfriend and his family.

The event had been well planned in advance, the reservations made at the hilltop Castaways, the only restaurant within five miles of Mother's house serving a digestible smorgasbord of gargantuan proportion, where finding the traditional turkey, dressing, mashed potatoes and gravy amongst the shrimp on ice and carved prime rib takes some doing.

Thanksgiving Day is to be my reveal.

The stitches having been removed by the good doctor, I shower for the first time in more than a week. I apply makeup gently and style my hair so that it covers the finite incision in front of my ears and wrap the long flowing white chiffon scarf around my neck to hide the bruising and the stitches under my chin. Studying my new face in the mirror, I am intrigued. The brown spots have faded, the marionette lines have vanished, but my smile seems tight about my teeth and my dimples have almost disappeared. Chin down; I'm ready for my close up.

Should we really expect compliments and a standing ovation from blood relatives? Is there jealousy in the air? Do I look so disfigured that no one wants to speak of it? What have I done to myself? No validation from my loved ones? They're kind. They're polite. The most important topic of Mother's conversation is the cost of such an extravagant culinary display, alluding to her annual suggestion that she could have made us a traditional dinner at home, although her oven has been inoperable for years, as she skirts around the subject of Tommy's disappearance. I drink too much wine and gulp down too much food, adding to the post-surgery constipation. I haven't had a bowel movement since going under the knife.

I am deposited back to the bungalow by eight o'clock. And though doggie bags are not allowed at the Castaway smorgasbord, I have brought home a large zip lock of treats for my best friends. Brute and Hound are outspoken in their thankfulness. "So thoughtful of you. By the way, you look great."

"Turkey, shrimp, and prime rib. Thank you for the compliment."

With their compliment in mind, when Avi called, I invited him over ASAP. His son is spending the day with his mother. At least that's what I think he said.

I changed into soft gray velour sweats and a coordinating cable knit sweater, and placed the chiffon scarf around my neck. The lights dimmed, a nice bottle of Pinot Noir unscrewed on the kitchen counter, braless and going commando, I unlocked the gate.

He's double take, blush-to-my-cheeks handsome. Up the tile stairs he saunters, workin' that pilot jacket of French lamb leather. He drives forward in a pair of tailored polished khakis, his crotch leading the way, an impression flouting the natural curve of the zipper. By the time he settles next to me on the big chair, I am putty in his sensual hands.

Maybe it was the Thanksgiving meltdown, the long ride home holding in a fart while lushes second-hand smoke wafted into the backseat, or the vodka tonic I had refilled twice in my kitchen. Maybe it was his dark eyes, the eyelashes like the hairs of a mink coat, the shock of chocolate waves he masterfully shook away from his tan forehead, the sultry way he was speaking to me, telling me how lovely I am. At least that's what I think he said.

Facing the dark television screen, my neck so tight I fear it will rip if I move too quickly, he began caressing my thigh, his hand easily making its way to the *V* in my sweatpants; his other hand clutching the arm of the chair. They met there, his strong large hand and my beating heart. Like a magician's sleight of hand, Avi was inside, inside silently untethering my lips, massaging the meaty folds, pulling up anchor and gently swirling the little man in the boat. I would go on here, but how many times is it necessary to describe the details of a climax? The final spasm and the convulsing were kept under control and quite subdued to protect the delicate nerves of my smooth neck and my reputation.

"Avi, that . . . was . . . perfect," I moaned through a quick moment of unconsciousness.

"It is you that was perfect."

My ovaries awakened, I slowly turned my head for our first kiss. My eyes open in the sultry dreamscape, my lips aroused and receptive, the testosterone in my saliva eager to mix with his; I was almost there when he jerked his head away and stood up.

"I don't kiss. I've never kissed anyone. I've never kissed my parents, my ex-wife, or my son."

I understood each Hebrew-French-German abuse of the English language. I've just met the ultimate whore-Madonna complex man.

"Come on, baby, I've got more for you." Standing, he held out his hand to lead me to the bed. "Can I wash my hand first?"

Not his hands, but his hand. Repeat of Muslim ghusl? (I've given you a list of Middle Eastern terms. Probably time to review it.)

I stood up, not to follow him. "Avi, in place of kisses, what are you offering me?" I asked over the sound of water running in my bathroom sink.

I couldn't think of one thrilling thing that would replace kissing, except for his immediate departure.

"Intense intercourse, world travel, orgasms until you beg me to stop, financial stability, a faithful companion for life—"

A life without kisses.

"You know, I think I've had this offer before," I said and took his clean hand. "Besides, I'm really supposed to stay out of the Middle East. Now come with me."

As he droned on, I led his virile French lamb jacket out the front door, down the steps, and straight out the *Hollywood* gate; the permanent bulge in his pants preceding him. Two mystified canines followed me onto the porch. The infrequent chance at male bonding ripped from their lives, they huddled close to sit with me on the step.

As I kissed both dogs on the lips over and over, I could hear Avi continue to mutter as he crossed the street to his Lincoln Navigator, "Jewels, furs, a house on the beach, and a Jaguar convertible." At least I think that's what he said.

I hollered over the lull in late-night traffic, "Hey, you, you didn't bring me chocolates!" Always get the last word in.

Score. After just one week of swelling, pain, and eight thousand dollars, my *Lifestyle Lift* had paid off. With a new confidence, the maturity to trust my gut feelings—and act on them without reservation—powered with the knowledge that I could not change anyone, I swore off all men; thus, over the course of her remaining lifespan, possibly saving a dozen or more lost souls from the agony to be perpetrated upon them by a sixty-three-year-old woman, who drinks like a fish and smokes like a chimney.

I may never own a beach house, dress in Ermine and pearls, or drive a Jaguar, but I will always be able to buy my own box of chocolates.

CHAPTER 37

Pride, Prejudice, and Pyramids

♪ Sharif don't like it ♪

Rockin' the Kasbah
The Clash, *1983*
Politically Incorrect and ahead of their time

DURING Rae's four-day Thanksgiving holiday from her six-figure stressful executive responsibilities, she surprises me with an invite to the ArcLight Cinema and Clint Eastwood's *J. Edgar*, showing at two o'clock. Lavender and olive green at the eyes, the boots zipped over black jeans, I cleverly hide the scars, which I have been promised will sink unnoticeably into my skin in no time, under a beige and gold threaded infinity scarf wound about my head and neck and topped with a cream knit French beret. Appearing somewhat like a costume designer's nightmare of *Fatima Goes Burlesque*, I meet up with my generous sister in the lobby, where she has tickets in hand.

"Put this in your purse," she indicates and hands me a bullet list of dates, places, and times. "I'm having cosmetic surgery and you're my driver."

"Glancing at this itinerary, I'd say we're going to be seeing a lot of each other this Christmas season."

"Pre-surgery consultation, surgery, follow-up, and one week of recovery time. It's the best excuse we've had in years not to spend Christmas in San Bernardino."

I insisted in lining up at the crowded snack bar.

"Do you want anything?" I asked, knowing Rae never eats or drinks in the dark.

"Nah. I'll go get in our seats."

"A large buttered popcorn and diet Coke, please," I smiled in my post-surgical hijab.

"Would you like to use your membership points?" the snack bar attendant asked. "You have enough for a free large popcorn."

Wow, only five dollars will be spent today. The dream of owning a beach house may not be out of the realm of possibilities.

I settled into my soft burgundy chaise, and setting a bounty of napkins down, I whispered into my sister. "I'm in this one. I play a secretary in the FBI office."

"Please don't stand up and applaud when your fuzzed arm goes by," she commanded.

It was actually the bottom half of my pencil skirt in the fuzzed background that went by as it shuffled to the glass door. I obeyed her command and stayed silent in my seat, but I did toss a buttery kernel into her lap.

November rushed by into December. There were house keys that didn't fit door locks and open house signs to put out and pick up; there were cookies to frost and deliver, auditions to forget, and a little Scion to move in and out of tight parking spaces; there were twinkling lights to drape, a lonely Poinsettia flag to put out, and dozens of real estate forms with signatures missing. Hound's bowels had become increasingly loose, while mine continued to constrict.

To break things up a bit, a young man shouting "Allahu Akbar," an Arabic expletive soon to be admitted into the pages of the *Merriam-Webster Dictionary*, randomly released twenty rounds from a .40 caliber Smith & Wesson into passing cars at the intersection of Sunset and Vine, killing a music industry executive. An off-duty officer working security on a movie set location nearby and an L.A.P.D. detective confronted him, and when he wouldn't respond, they shot him. On my way to Trader Joe's for Two-Buck Chuck, hummus and pita chips, I had missed the excitement by a lucky ten minutes. The area cordoned off, I was forced to walk three blocks out of my way. The liberal and always politically correct *L.A. Times* reported that the reason for the rampage was the recent breakup with his girlfriend.

At the Vine Elementary School teachers' holiday soirée, held annually at a vintage second story duplex in prestigious Hancock Park, Mr. Bud Taylor, in a green and red Santa hat topped with a white fur shaft that erects when a string is pulled, introduces me proudly as his *roving reader*. Teachers will play when the kids are away and tonight, judging by the size of the rum punch bowl and the penis on Mr. Taylor's head, they will be letting their hair down.

I had dabbled in a bit of nuanced flirting with this rotund hyperenthusiastic, stifled creative since the new school year began with no response, my search for the glass slipper taking me into some unfamiliar, dubious shoe stores. I had warmed up to the gigantic 'ole bear, even as far as envisioning the two of us enjoying a road trip sing-a-long up the coast highway while slurping down gigantic sodas and searching for spilled orange Cheetos in between the seats.

Over an aluminum tray of mashed potatoes, he begins to share with me his living arrangements, a topic that has never come up in the three years of our partnership in the crippling of growing minds.

"My partner and I have been together for twenty years, but we don't live together."

"Because she snores?" I suggested, shrugging off my disappointment at the sordid news that Mr. Taylor already has a road trip companion to lick the orange dust from his chubby fingers.

"Because *he* snores."

Pulling my head out of my tight ass, I tried to show no sign of surprise.

"You didn't know I was gay?" Mr. Taylor cocked his head, the twinkle in his eye not missing a beat.

Why is it they are always so proud of it, underscored by a yearly frolicking in the streets almost naked in their *Gay Pride* parade? Reminiscent of the depraved decadence of *Mardis Gras*, gay men and lesbian women, transvestites, transsexuals, transgenders, and those who have not yet made up their minds, vainly sashay along the route saturated in sequined feathers or flaunting ripped luscious physiques to the cadence of "I Was Born This Way" and strut behind rainbow banners—*Out and Proud, God Made Me Queer*—in their attempts to shock the Christian community with their liberation. I was born female, without teeth and tethered to my mother's womb by a bloody rope, with a proclivity for the opposite sex, but I don't march down the street once a year swinging an umbilical cord in celebration. What possibly *would* I wear? Would anyone show up to wave their approval as I skipped on by?

Hell, no, I didn't know. Why would I assume an obese, animated school teacher, who just so happens to know the lyrics to every goddamned Broadway show tune, including each introduction, who MC's the annual Vine School Halloween costume contest dressed in Wilma Flintstone drag, who rules his kindergartners with an iron fist, and who if given the chance would flog each and every cringing child with metal coat hangers straight out of a *Mommy Dearest* closet, is a homosexual?

"Honestly, I never thought about it, " I shook my head.

"You look upset."

"Give me a moment," I hesitated and took in a cleansing breath. "I'm still reeling from Rock Hudson."

"Wanna pull my string?"

"Sure."

That night on *Facebook* I posted my first Christmas picture of the season: a smiling brunette jingling a sleigh bell from her new neck posed conspicuously close to a jolly man with a vulgar white furry penis protruding from the top of his Santa hat.

* * *

Following her pre-surgery consultation last week, today is the second day on my sister's Fountain of Youth itinerary. Up at 5:00 a.m. to meticulously prepare for my second meeting with her terribly handsome, previously hair-lipped, Middle Eastern surgeon of undisclosed religion, I'm off to fetch the cosmetic surgery guru of Glendale, Rae having exhaustively researched the medical community and, of course, the referrals of her face-lifted co-workers. Today we will drive once again west on the 134 to the I-5 north to Santa Clarita, a half hour's drive, to begin the first day of the rest of my sister's life.

Isn't what we're all hoping for from the fleeting pain and chargeable expense of cosmetic surgery—a simple slice, a tuck, a stitch, and a blepharoplasty—is to erase the perils of our past? *Poof!* We're not old anymore.

After my half-hour drive from Hollywood to Glendale, I find Rae in great anticipation out on the curb at six-thirty, the sun just coming up over the Armenian skyline. She leans in to ask the age-old question, "Do you need to use the restroom?"

"Nah, I'm good."

Rae is suitably and comfortably dressed in pre-surgery slob, a totally new look for her. No makeup, her blonde bobbed curls scrunched beneath a beige knit cap, and wearing Mr. Peabody black-rimmed coke bottle glasses. Looking very much like an intelligent beagle out for his morning constitutional, she is the picture of lens-corrected optimistic expectation.

Aware that Rae is uncomfortably strapped in my little booby trap of a car, I begin small talk to avert her nervous expectation that we are once again on an inevitable collision course with a concrete freeway barrier. "Stopping, starting, Nicorette fever, and starting again, but I refuse to buy another month's supply of fifty-dollar chewing gum. I haven't had a cigarette since December 12th. I haven't pooped either. I figured since I'm going to be your cell mate for a week, I'd be a good example. And you?"

"I quit last week. I can quit anytime I want."

In my faithful Scion XA hatchback, which rattles tumultuously when reaching the sixty-five mile an hour speed limit, two sisters in nicotine withdrawal denial twitched their way north on a barren highway, the bevy of traffic heading south into the city, not heading north away from it.

"I didn't want you to have to do any shopping for us, so I went crazy at the store last night. I brought home tubs of peanuts, red vines, and M&Ms. The fridge is maxed out with the essentials. Bags of freshly prepared salads, bok choy, tofu in teriyaki glaze, fruit juices, yogurt, gallons of wine, and enough cans of *Fancy Feast* to keep the cat fat and happy."

"And liter for his box too, I'm guessing. What's in the freezer?"

"Filet mignon, prawns, *Hungry Man* meatloaf and taters, crab Rangoon, and a dressed duck for Christmas dinner. I'm looking forward to being home in my robe all week and cooking."

"Not tonight you're not."

Using a slim Sharpie, the handsome doctor outlines Rae's face, neck, and eyelids where he will be slicing and dicing. I take pictures. Surreptitiously, I also take pictures of the unattractive scar on his upper lip left over from his childhood deformity. He's a cosmetic surgeon. Can't he get that removed?

Rae calls Mother. Big mistake. The drama has begun. She's on her way, she proclaims. "You can change your mind right now and walk out!"

"Well, that advice is a little late, Mom. Why didn't you tell me that thirty years ago on my wedding day?"

The drugs were kicking in. It's going to be a hell of a week.

While she's under the knife, I go to WalMart, where everything is marked down to coincide with the property values of the neighborhood. We don't have a WalMart in Hollywood. Greeted inside the automated glass doors by a cheerful old codger in blue, I am in suburbia heaven. Having four hours to kill, I push a blue plastic shopping cart up and down each tempting aisle in a one-story building as long and as wide as a football field. During hour no. 3, after a pepperoni pizza slice at the snack bar, I found Milk of Magnesia, the gentle, cramp-free laxative, on sale as a two-for-one. I put four bottles in my basket.

The car bulging with unnecessary impulse purchases of infomercial cleaning products and last-minute gifts, such as a pair of cotton bikini panties with reindeer and sleigh across the pink bottom—the perfect aloha Christmas gift for Alexandra and Benjamin—I am back at the Ear, Nose, Throat, and Facial Surgery Center. What I find slumped into a wheel chair and wrapped in a warm blanket is a mummified, drooling mystified woman, soon to be an unhappy prisoner in her own home, known as *The Woman in the Iron Mask*. From the top of her head to her collarbone, dotted with small holes for seeing, breathing, and eating, is band after band of cloth tape wrapped so tightly that the word *papier-mâché* suddenly comes to mind. The same encasement is wound about her skull, as if she'd volunteered for a lobotomy, at no extra charge of course. This is going to be a hell of a week.

On the drive home, the seat reclined as far back as it will go, she rests holding small pink ice pads to the holes where her eyes should be.

"Do you have my glasses? Do you?"

"Not to worry," I answered.

"I can't hear you with this thing on," she panicked.

"I've got them. Go to sleep."

"I can't stand not being able to see anything when you're driving."

On orders not to insert her contact lenses, she must wear her glasses over the mask. From the driver's seat, it's really fun to watch.

She is heavily medicated, and with my unsteady help, she barely makes it up the steep stairway to her second floor bedroom. "You're looking more like Daddy today," I jibe. My humor is lost on her as I remove her glasses and prop her up into two large pillows for the first of many, many naps. Her large black-on-white male cat *Spot* joins her.

During our childhood, Daddy was a fair, blue-eyed, tall and lean Marine. Always a Lucky Strike between his fingers, he was handsome in his dress blues. Somewhere along the way, by the time I began high school and my sister returned to junior high school, Dad retired from the corps and put away the blues. Putting on the pounds, he began wearing double knit old man pants and the accompanying baggy shirt flowered with yellow lilies and red poinsettias. He kept the crew cut and took to wearing large black-rimmed glasses over bloodshot blue eyes. These were the *divorce years*, when I was bounced around, first to Daddy, then to grandmother, and then back to Daddy and the new wife, while Rae was carted off to a nearby city to live with Mother and the new husband. These were the lost years of our teens, when a diabolical mother and a weak alcoholic father, unable to communicate civilly, separated two young women; each believing the other had abandoned her. We rarely speak of it, but it's always there.

The next morning while scooping out Spot's litter box, I hear a sudden whimpering of expletives coming from her bedroom. I rush upstairs to find an undisciplined, distraught mummy tugging violently at her cast.

"It's choking me. It's fucking choking me. Cut this thing off!"

"Calm down, King Tut. You know I can't do that. The doctor said you had to keep it on until *he* takes it off."

"Goddammit. Get the scissors from the bathroom drawer."

Straddling her chest and timidly aiming the scissors, I stall. She lengthens her neck and thrusts her chin at me. "Cut it!"

The thing is extremely tight at her neck; I can't get under it without a crowbar. Afraid I will draw blood, I ease my finger under and then attempt to take a squeeze with the scissors. Success. It felt as though I had let air out of a tire. "Hey, there's cotton under here," I discover. "Better?"

For the first three days she is in and out of consciousness, as I drive back and forth to Hollywood to check in with Hound and Brute. I dare not leave Rae alone overnight as yet, even though she is now sleeping on the living room couch, close to a bathroom and the refrigerator. She's chilled and groggy, awake and asleep, under her sarcophagus of quilts and fringed throws. I force her to eat Greek yogurt before giving her the little blue pills and green capsules, one each, enough to knock out a one hundred and sixty-five pound, sixty-year-old woman who just spent twelve-thousand dollars to have her skin cut, pulled, and sewn back together by an Egyptian.

"When does it stop hurting?" she agonizes.

"The Pyramids weren't built in a day, sweetie."

And she is asleep again.

At the bungalow, my antisocial neighbor Artemus abnormally hailed me from the other side of the fence. "Hey, Brute kept everyone, and I mean *everyone*, up all night. He stood on the back stoop and yipped until four this morning. Maureen and Randi came in my yard and tried to quiet him, but nobody's got a key."

"I'm so sorry. My sister had surgery and I'm her nurse, sort of."

Handing him a set of keys, it is arranged that Artemus will see that they are locked in each night. He recruits Maureen to walk them before bedtime. I am grateful for the help, though I see shit in my future, and I mean piles of it.

Coming up on four days without a shower, I find that the hot water in Rae's guest suite takes almost five minutes to heat up. What a waste of water. And I can't find a washcloth, not one washcloth in three bathrooms. I soak hand towels and use them to soothe the intermittent burning twinge in my neck. I am exhausted and I have no medication, having stupidly tossed out my Vicodin two weeks ago.

Just as they were leaving for the airport, I caught up with Alex and Benjamin outside her townhouse.

"I wrapped both your presents in one box so as not to take up room in your suitcases," I explained. "Just something to open Christmas morning in Kauai." I was sure his parents would get a big kick out of the holiday themed Fruit of the Loom, and as Mother would say, "Come on, keep your sense of humor."

"What is this?" I ask the fat and happy cat pitching bits of white fluff to and fro between his claws at the edge of Rae's bed. The evidence of when I'm away, the cat will play, is dotting her blue duvet. Apparently having defied the stairs, Rae has fallen asleep with a pair of scissors in her hand. "You've been cutting away at your mummy mask again. Naughty patient."

The drive to Santa Clarita today is treacherous, as my tiny Scion is whipped from lane to lane by gusts of suburban wind plummeting the I-5 freeway.

"Stay alongside a big truck," *The Joker* advises me from inside what is left of her super-villain costume. Rae hates having to be a passenger while her timid sister defensively controls the wheel. Admittedly, even heavily medicated she is a better driver than I am and a much more experienced drunk driver.

"What? Haven't you seen those movies where the little car is sucked up under the carriage of an eighteen-wheeler, the entire roof of the car sliced away? You want to take a chance on messing up your eye job? Go back to sleep."

The nurse gently cuts open the mold of bandages and the new neck is released.

I am awestruck. More so, I am jealous. Rae has no lumps, no bruising, and no redness. She is, however, puffed up like an exploded hard-boiled egg left too long in boiling water. The doctor pleased, she is re-wrapped in a more friendly fashion and sent home for her first shower. I stay close by her bathroom door. She seems very weak, where, although my neck is still burning, I'm as strong as a horse, having eaten every post-surgery treat I can get my nervous little hands on. And upon checking the refrigerator, it is time for me to replenish the wine.

Rae insists that I sleep at home tonight and I'm in complete agreement. She will sleep again safely on the ground floor, take her prescriptions, and see me in the morning for the final Santa Clarita turn around.

"I'll pick up supplies and be back to change your sheets by nine."

"Thanks. That would be great. Oh, and please don't write about this in any of your novels."

"Of course. This is your story."

Eager for my company, Hound and Brute gathered at my feet for a night of old movies, popcorn, and strips of beef jerky I toss to them in gratitude, having arrived home to an accident-free house. I slept wonderfully in my own bed surrounded by relieved creatures, which had surely given me up for dead. It was a two-dog night.

Christmas Day arrived and I returned to the condo once again; this time to the scent of roast duck in the air and an abnormally puffy Julia Child, all gussied up for the occasion.

"You look just wonderful. And your eyes! They're absolutely stunning, all big and baby blue."

"I hurt! Why did I do this?" Unable to blink back the tears, she bellowed and poured us each a glass of icy cold chardonnay. It's simply amazing how pain can melt away when there's a lot of wine to swallow it down and a commiserating sister to bitch to. "You didn't tell me it was going to hurt this much."

"If it makes you feel any better, I think I have nerve damage in my neck," I finally reported. "But thanks to your very generous Christmas gift of Botox and Restylane injections, I don't look worried about it anymore."

"Tommy called. That's the first phone call he's been allowed to make. He sounds so old."

And that's her story, too.

Within three years' time, as necks fell and wrinkles returned, Rae would be on the verge of suing her cosmetic surgeon, who would claim that her neck lift was not successful because of her skin type. Following a cascade of lawsuits complaining of inadequate results, as *Lifestyle Lift* fortunes began to sag, along with my jowls and neckline, the company would file for bankruptcy in March of 2015. My neck would still burn.

CHAPTER 38

Never On Sunday and Breakup Breadsticks

> ♪ Sleigh bells ring
> Are ya listening?
> In the lane
> Snow is glistnin' ♪
>
> *Winter Wonderland*
> Leroy Anderson 1908-1975

WAKING at Trudy and Ted's cottage, my head pounding from, perhaps, a bit too much champagne, rum, and wine during last night's redneck celebration of the New Year, I leaped from the bed in satin pajama bottoms and camisole and scurried two aging dogs out into the yard. The danger of a hungry coyote creeping through the clearing, I stayed close by, poop bags in hand.

"Brrrr." My filmy teeth chattering, I stood barefoot in the crusty snow left by yesterday evening's surprise flurry, a flurry that forced me to frantically dish out in perpetual gratitude forty-five dollars in cash and coin—all I had in my purse, the glove box, the coin tray, and under the seats of my car—to an entrepreneurial grizzly bear bundled up in an orange jumpsuit.

At midpoint up the mountain, having been cruelly diverted by the highway patrol to a turn-out off the slippery road, where on my knees, my mittens frozen to my fingertips, in the dark, in the fog, and in blowing snow, I had once again put my chains on inside out. *Ma'am, you get inside and stay warm.* Grizzly had rescued Julie, as he would many more a wet and dreary damsel in distress, by rectifying my incompetence with the speed and precision of a NASCAR pit crew. The dogs entertained and wildly amused by my frustration, I was sent on my klinkity-klink, klinkity-klink way up the mountainside.

"Hurry, hurry, boys. I have to pee too."

Trudy, still celebrating in a plastic *Happy New Year* jeweled crown and wrapped in my black and white feather boa, handed me a steaming hot cup of coffee with cream, of course.

"The plow came by, so we're going to Top Town for breakfast. Can you be ready in fifteen minutes?" she rushed my already mandated morning schedule.

"I promised my mother I'd stop by on my way home. She says she's going out of her way, giving up the daily newspaper crossword puzzle in bed, to prepare breakfast. She's promised me cold rubberized fried eggs, if I don't get there before ten."

"Okay. We'll miss you," Trudy said and hung the feathers over my neck.

"Are you guys watching the Rose Parade?"

"Ted says he can't find it, but he'd trade pancakes and sausages for flowers on floats anytime. And he needs your car keys."

Tossing her the keys from the doorway, I rushed back inside and warmed my hands at the wall heater. Wayne calls.

"I thought you'd be snuggling up next to the gold digger, watching the Rose Parade, and sipping Mimosas," I contemplated my friend Wayne's first day of 2012.

"She's in New York City with the kid and baby daddy. You know I don't drink and the Rose Parade is never held on Sunday, a religious tradition, apparently, brought about by the Catholics to keep the masses in church. A somewhat of a holy conspiratorial trade-off with God: no parade on Sundays; no rain on the parade."

"Are you available today? I need your opinion on something." My new neck and refreshed look had not been critiqued by Ted and Trudy, because they like me just the way I am. I needed an objective criticism.

"You're in town?"

"I'm in the mountains. I can leave the dogs with my mom and meet you for lunch?"

"Sure. Olive Garden at noon?"

I headed straight for the shower and a complete makeover, because even if you don't want to have sex with a man, you still want to be desirable, so that he'll want to have sex with you, even when you're not going to.

Just after hearing the rumble of the bridge as Trudy and Ted pulled out, Mother calls. Not a good sign and routinely expected.

"I've made a New Year's Resolution. I'm going to do one nice thing for someone everyday—starting with you. You can do whatever you want today. You don't have to come by. Don't worry about me, I'll be watching the annual Tournament of Roses Parade."

"The Rose Parade is postponed until tomorrow this year."

"How do you know? Get real, you don't even read the newspaper."

"It's a *Never On Sunday* thing. The Rose Bowl Parade committee promised God that they would never parade on a Sunday, if He would never rain on a Rose Bowl Parade."

"I suppose you read that on the Internet."

"No, your favorite criminal investigator, Wayne, told me."

"Well, then it's got to be true. When are you two ever going to get together?"

"After I leave your place today, Mother," I answered and continued on. "I'm meeting him for lunch."

"Well, then you won't be needing breakfast," she retorted, the jealous spite knifing its way up the icy road.

"I have gifts for you—from Rae and Alex too—and to be honest, I'm tired of carting bags of wrapped presents around in my car."

"Gifts? I said no gifts this year." I could see her blood red lips curling in anticipation of our trifling wares, as we all had ceased to purchase expensive gifts for her, because, as she boasts, she's got everything she needs or wants, and to top it off she's got *everything down to a science.*

My overnight bag and two dogs in the car, I locked up the cottage and hid the key under the mat. The sun had begun melting the snow and sweet Teddy had removed the snow chains from my front wheels. Sometimes having the right kind of man around is a very good thing.

First thing this morning, before fencing with the daily crossword puzzle, *en garde*, Mother has made up her pretty face, as she has for the sixty-three years I have known her. Her glamorous presentation, however, is that of a shrinking woman still in her pajamas, her malodorous silver hair pulled back into a ponytail. The scent of burnt toast is not wafting to the front porch. She has not made breakfast.

Mother insipidly and ungraciously opens each gift with tiring precision, purposely prolonging my extrication from her salon. Each curly ribbon and square of foil is salvaged, delicately folded and placed into a holiday gift bag to be sanctimoniously salvaged for the next commercialized Christmas. Thrilled and captivated by the throw-away Japanese cameras, the lilac hand soaps, a huge bottle of real bleu cheese salad dressing, a canister of Almond Roca, the traditional framed photo of the cousins, and a splendid cut glass decanter of chocolate mint liqueur, she insists at eleven o'clock that we pour a tad or two, which after two sips releases the venom from her tongue. The match was on.

"How is your sister doing?" The tongue is mightier than the sword.

"She hurts, but she looks great," I reassured her.

"Well, I hope it was worth it; the money, the pain, the time off from her important job. I really don't see much difference in your . . .what do you call it?

"A lift, just a bit of a lift."

"And Rae, I understand, also had her eyes done. Your eyes are holding up pretty well," she peered at my crow's feet. "It's because you have olive skin and brown eyes like your mother."

"No, they're hazel."

"Whatever. So how are you really?" she dramatized the question with a thrust of her small thin hand over mine. "You look, oh, I don't know, surprised."

To tell you the truth, I've been depressed, overwhelmed, and disgusted with myself what with all the drinking, the eating, the failed lookie-loo handholding, the wasted auditions, the continued mourning over my sociopathic lover, and the fact that my children hate me. Nobody likes me; everybody hates me; I'm going to go eat worms. So much so that throwing myself head first down a hilly ravine from the fifty-foot high *H* in the *Hollywood Sign* to my untimely death seems like a good idea. Or maybe I'll fly off from the **Y**, the letter restored by Hugh Hefner, the Playmate Philanthropist, in 1978—the sign previously crumbling and in disrepair— at the cost of twenty-eight thousand dollars. That might have more impact. Perhaps such a symbolic gesture would get someone's attention. Hell, it worked for poor little Peg Entwistle, a despondent young woman who, after a night of booze and depression, distraught that at the age of twenty-four she had not yet made it big in Hollywood, decided to end it in that same manner, which is, of course, where I got the idea. Some say she walks up there, at the end of Beachwood Canyon Drive, dressed in 1930's era clothing, still trim and attractive, her signature gardenia perfume permeating the air. After carting my mattress out to the corner, another farewell gesture, but before making the fatal jump, I'll be sure and drown myself in COCO Mademoiselle eau de parfum by Chanel, the only gift he ever gave me.

"I'm fine, Mom."

Reprising her doom treatise, she thrust out a three-pronged question in the hope of reliving in detail my continuing heartache. "Do you see him? Has he called? Have you taken another lover?"

"No, no, and no." I lunged right back.

Retreating, she poured us both a tad more of the syrupy chocolate. "I apologize for not having any gifts for you to open, dear. I was going to write you and your sister a big fat check, but I thought better of it."

"Mom, you've thought better of it for sixty-three years. Congratulations on continuing the tradition."

"Touché." She clinked her glass to mine. "Here's to Rae's recovery. It's too bad she couldn't be here to referee."

The dogs in Mother's care—she will cruelly lock them away in her screened patio as soon as I back out of her narrow driveway—I head down Arrowhead Avenue, leaving Mother's inherited Spanish house and the *Arrowhead* further behind. From Mother's front lawn, I've been able to see the wonder of the *Arrowhead* sitting in the foothills since playing sprinkler tag in the front yard with little Rae and Uncle Edwin. Looming above the valley is the unexplained natural geologic phenomenon, an imprint formed of light quartz and white sage replicating the flint of an Indian's arrow. Nestled between the bosoms of the hillside, the *Arrowhead* calls to you as it points the way to the hot springs below and the Arrowhead Springs Hotel, which drew the Hollywood stars of the "Golden Age" to the healing waters. Anyone entering the valley can't help but see it, if they ever looked up from their cell phones. Unlike the staked wood and metal *Hollywood Sign* on the hillside, its stark white presence promising that fairy tales do come true; the unexplained, mystical *Arrowhead* simply points the way, absolutely no promises made.

Coming upon the courthouse, I pull over and park across the street from what was my eight-to-five home for twenty years. New Year's day, the county offices are closed; there is no one around. Built in 1926, it's a grand stately old place of brown stone with gardens fronting the four-story building. Classical columns span the second and third floors. There are courtrooms on the first, second, third, and fourth floors. On the fourth floor are also holding cells where prisoners will await their arraignment or another day of trial. There's a stone fountain dividing the wide walkway leading to the glass front doors, the metal detectors, and the snack bar. During the twenty years I passed by that fountain, there was never any water in it, not that I can remember. During the first fifteen years of my assignment, there were no metal detector checkpoints, not until an angry father shot and killed his son-in-law outside the glass door of my office.

As you enter the foyer on the first floor, there's an elevator to the left, which will deliver you just a few feet from my glass door, or you can take the marble stairs. You can't miss my door. It's the one in the middle with the large cut-out manila paper star on it, a star Scotch Taped there by another court reporter the day after four-year-old Alexandra and I debuted as bathing beauty extras on the television show *Bay Watch*.

You can see my sash window on the third floor from the street. The yellowed shade is pulled down today and I can see that the unattractive tear caused by years of the San Bernardino sun beating down on it is still there.

I drive into the familiar crowded parking lot of the Olive Garden on Hospitality Row just east of the ghastly, distressed roadway of Waterman Avenue, which I have detoured my way around, not wanting to review sordid seedy hotel memories, golf course weddings, boarded up buildings, or dismal 7-Elevens. In khaki pants and an Oxford blue button down shirt, tucked in and belted, of course, Wayne lifts his tall cumbersome frame from his canary yellow Porsche as I park next to him.

His once black hair now thin and white, the gentleman opens my door and gives me his hand, helping me out of my seat. Squinting his glossed-over blue eyes, he thrusts his chin to his neck and backs away to put me in focus at the end of his nose. I too must back up for a clear view. It is the fate of the new old eyes to fuzz objects the closer I get to them. I would have to back up twenty feet to see the details of his face and the teeth in need of a complete redo, as I see all things clearly now from afar. I on my tiptoes, we both go in for a long-time-no-see hug and are stopped by the bang of the bulge.

"My goodness. We're both putting on the pounds, aren't we?" I self-effaced. My seductive preparations of the morning— the perfect hair, the perfect makeup, and the perfect duster flying over my midriff— weren't fooling anyone.

"Speak for yourself. I've lost ten pounds," Wayne began. "I just finished a twenty-mile bike ride. I showered, of course."

Finally seated at a table surrounded by white latticework wound with plastic greenery, I make the mistake of asking Wayne where he had biked this morning. Too soon I am on an arduous journey from his garage in the foothills of Redlands east through San Timoteo Canyon, where he chased a locomotive into Banning, flew north through Cherry Valley, pedaled south and west through the canyon to Loma Linda, reversed, returned to Redlands and hung the racing bike on a hook in his garage. Apparently, a trade wind of sorts had spirited him on his boring way.

"Notice anything different about me?" I interrupted the beginning of what surely would be another tedious tale of courtroom crime drama. I lifted my chin and wiggled my brows, which were no longer movable.

"I'll just say this. You look surprised."

"My mountain friends weren't impressed either."

"That's because we like you just the way you are."

Tonging my third helping of salad from the family-size plastic bowl and dipping a breadstick into marinara sauce, I set down my fork to give Wayne my full attention. Something big is happening. He unfolded and passed sheets of paper to my side of the table. Putting on my readers, I perused his work.

"Is this your breakup letter to the blonde gold digger? Three pages single-spaced? The size of the font looks like it might be eight? How many times do you mention that *I'll always love you*? No, wait, let me count. You're hurt because she takes vacations with the man who fathered her baby that is now a teenager. Of course, that was through artificial insemination. You still believe that? Wow! You're going to continue to pay her rent for six more months? Keep your hands off. Let me finish this paltry attempt to alienate a loathsome con artist you can't seem to live without, even though you only see her once a month. Christ, there, you said it again. *I'll always love you.* In bold? You've got to be kidding. No, you can't have it back. I'm still counting."

"Well, aren't you the one to be proselytizing on the merits of a clean break. You may not see him anymore, but you still love him. You of all people know how I'm hurting," he sulked.

"Yes, okay, but, you know, I've been thinking. Just maybe, I didn't so much love *him*, but I loved the tipsy shipwreck I became when he was around. It was a thrill to rock and sway, to have the chilled water slapped in my face, to sink deeper and deeper and then to buoy to the top again. Hell, it was a joy to just *feel*. And that is what you're experiencing. She makes you *feel,* you boorish intellectual cycling snob."

"Do you want the last breadstick?"

"No, you can have it. We both let it go too far . . . too far down. When I should have kept it here, here at my breasts, I let it go down, down to here, dangerously too far, indecently too far, to the place where life begins."

"Are you speaking of my balls?"

By Christmas of 2013, Wayne's total payout for his once-a-month fucking privilege would total well over one hundred thousand dollars and growing.

Returning to Mother's, the irritating yip of a sweet Maltese locked inside a screened porch rushes me to the front door. Bells are ringing, but no one is answering and, of course, the porch door is locked and I can't get the dogs out.

"Oh, there you are," she reproached my apparent tardiness. "I was taking my nap."

"How could you sleep with Brute barking like that?" I asked and sped by her to rescue my charges, which by now were surely in need of a trip to the front lawn.

"After you left, I remembered that yesterday the mailman had uncorked a bottle of champagne for me."

Home in time to catch the five o'clock showing of *We Bought a Zoo*, I treated myself to a New Year's Day movie alone in a crowded theatre. Apparently, every tourist on Christmas vacation in Hollywood has brought an entire menagerie of sticky-fingered children along. Sitting impatiently through a corny, sappy, kids and animals redemption movie, I'm wondering how Cameron Crowe could get this so wrong and why didn't I buy popcorn? Finally in the last eight minutes of the biopic, my wind-chilled right shoulder and bouncing brown curls *swipe* the camera. Matt Damon is adorable, but he never helps me up the trunk of a tree.

I climb into bed, sad that there will be no text message from my apathetic anguish, my Ali, wishing me a Happy New Year. He is gone and has forgotten me. But I am still here to remember.

CHAPTER 39

Shaken, But Not Stirred

> ♪ Can you read my mind?
> Do you know what it is you do to me? ♪
>
> The Love Theme-*Superman*
> Paul Williams

Now having to rely on Rite Aid at the Gower Gulch strip mall on Sunset to keep in stock my favorite shade of Egyptian Plum hair color, my disappointment in the buyer for beauty supplies at CVS Pharmacy having been registered as a formal complaint, it's time to walk the six blocks. I am also out of alcohol.

The box of dye clutched in my hand, I head to the liquor aisle. I am horrified to find that the cache of liquor has been locked into metal cabinets behind sliding glass doors, likened only to an alarmed jewel case at Tiffany's.

"Excuse me, sir. Do you work here?" I ask a young man in a blue polo shirt.

"Yes, ma'am."

"Just how do I go about purchasing a bottle of rum?" I faintly murmured.

"I don't have a key. I'll let the manager know." And off he went to the front of the store, leaving me to ponder my purchase. Looking curiously through my reflection in the glass, I am stunned. The same bottle of rum at CVS is one dollar less and here at the Rite Aid *Shame Center* I will get to pay one dollar more to grovel for it.

Suddenly over the loudspeaker came a deafening, judgmental screech. "Customer needs assistance in the liquor aisle."

The jig is up; the lady dressed in running pants and a ripped-out Hollywood souvenir t-shirt salivating uncontrollably in aisle no. 9 is a drunk.

My continued consternation between the imprisoned rum at one drug store, which stocks the perfect shade of mahogany-rouge, and the open bar at another, which refuses to yield to my hair color request, will have me walking an additional five miles per month for the next twenty years.

Leaving Trader Joe's with two bags of washed greens, my plastic bag swaying with rum and the salon in a box, the sun is down and the lights have come up. Strolling back down Vine Street passing Bed, Bath, and Beyond, an aspiring new nail salon, and the Verizon store, I look up to see that the billboard above *Fabiolus* Veronese restaurant on Sunset Boulevard is advertising itself.

BILLBOARD FOR LEASE
INQUIRE WITHIN
323-373-8766

Inspiration hits. What better way and at what better place to get myself arrested? The words *Sex With a Muslim in My Basement* stretched over canvas and standing fifteen feet high at the corner of Sunset and Vine would surely fan the fires of the American Civil Liberties Union, insight Mullahs to ordain fatwas ordering my immediate execution, and inspire writers to hammer out the screenplay overnight for instantaneous green lighting by Warner Bros or Paramount or Columbia or Universal or 20th Century Fox or Walt Disney Studios. And if they slam the door in our face, we'll take it to Lionsgate. They produce almost anything. We'll present the sordid screenplay to *DreamWorks* and keep them out of bankruptcy. Steven Spielberg himself will cause a front-page traffic jam at the famous intersection when he leaps from his limousine to capture a picture of my billboard. Maybe a sighting will bring Ali home, or at the very least he will send a process server to deliver my summons and complaint, beginning with the familiar love note, "Notice! You have been sued."

I stopped at the corner and dialed the number. The familiar La Dolce Vita accent answered.

"Fabi, this is Julie. I'm in there often with my daughter, Alex? Yes, the tall pretty brunette. I always order the house Chianti? Yes, that's me. I'm calling about the billboard. How much? Twenty-two hundred for thirty days? Does that include getting it up there? Okay. You have a designer? And how much does he charge? Around two thousand? I see. Yes, yes. I'll be right over."

Brimming with excitement, I answered Alexandra's text letting me know she was not available for lunch tomorrow.

> Thursday, January 5, 2012; 6:35p JULIE: I can't do lunch either now. Working background on movie, Seven Psychopaths. Walking on Sunset to Fabiolus.
> 6:36p ALEX: Don't get shot.
> 6:36p JULIE: Fabiolus is advertising the billboard overhead.
> 6:37p ALEX: How can you afford that?

Do I want to die not believing enough in *The Year I Learned to Text* to not put it up in lights? Crossing Sunset Boulevard at the urging of the *little green man walking* signal, I could be crushed by a left-hand-turn zealot, who, after the light turned red, would not give up his place in line. Simply walking to Trader Joe's for California Rolls, I could be gunned down on the spot by a Muslim extremist irritated that his girlfriend had deserted him. I could trip over little Brute; impale myself on the kitchen counter, slashing my head wide open, and bleed to death before anyone found me. In fact, my body would be in the rigor mortis stage before anyone even missed me. No. Decay would have begun, the worms crawling in and out, and I would decompose before the dogs would catch on and start barking.

Would I hold back from spending last year's interest earned on my IRA to appease the self-appointed czar of her mother's budget? No. The peeling paint on my windowsills could peel another year.

6:39p ALEX: I'm just curious. How much does it cost?
6:40p JULIE: Just about 4k. I am spending your inheritance.

On day no. 28 of no smoking, weighing in at a predictable one hundred and sixty-six pounds, munching on sourdough bread, I signed the contract with Mr. Fabiola Conti in the patio of his restaurant over a glass of Chianti. Being Italian and of the Catholic faith, he was not offended in the least by the fact that the words *Sex with a Muslim in My Basement* would soon be on a massive well-lit billboard soaring over his establishment.

***

Putting on a self-assured public presence, once inside the little Spanish house of Saltillo tile and rampant bougainvillea, I mourned privately and the self-sabotage raged. Even when I am well aware that I have to be up before dawn to drive to Santa Clarita to the set of implausible television shows such as *Switched at Birth;* even when I know the next day would have me driving from Sherman Oaks to Santa Monica to three auditions for varied pharmaceuticals replete with harmful side effects; even when I know my daily page count of *Jihad in Honeymoon* is dwindling, as I grow hard-pressed to find the funny—I continue to drink myself to sleep.

I wasn't always alone in my despicable self-indulgence, however. I spent one entire week in a wild sexually inebriated frenzy slumped in the big chair with my Netflix delivered soul mate, Pierce Brosnan. That first day I waited impatiently for the mailman to show up with my allotted thirty-minute disc from Season One of *Remington Steele*, circa 1982, but soon I began to chase him down, searching for him in and around the neighborhood to collect from his bag my every-other-night fix. When my thirty minutes of swooning came to a crashing end, I started the DVD again. Refilling my rum and Coke tumbler, I played it over and over again, lubricating the remote controls with warm popcorn butter, until the harmonious snoring of two dogs sent me to bed. I could have ordered two discs at a time for an additional cost, but as we know, my budget conscious daughter would not have approved. And during the lull times, without his subtle Irish intonations to flare up my libido, before hunting down the mailman, I *Googled* Pierce. I *liked* him on *Facebook*. I studied his every move. And in my stalking of Mr. Brosnan I learned a great deal. He is an environmentalist, who saves baby elephants, adores his plus-size wife, and enjoys vodka martinis, shaken not stirred.

My lust-transference marathon, however, has failed. As I return to writing *Jihad Honeymoon*, I am with my Muslim husband for hours and hours during the day, the writing day. Setting the clock timer at the stove, I force myself into the desk chair for four hours, knowing that as I flip through the pages of my diaries, I shall find him there, dark and mysterious, bored and brooding, pious and proud and pouting. The tears inevitably begin and I yearn to run to him, not knowing where to run; other times I am ashamed that I ever loved him, that I do love him. I realize that perhaps it is true that I never did love *him*, but fell in love with myself, the woman I became when I was around him; an adorable blithering idiot, the confused admirer of his contemptuous affections. Fuck, I looked so good in love.

Drowning myself in self-pity and filling my emptiness with strangers does not unlock the cage he has put me in. This mourning over a phantom romance must end, and boy, oh boy, do I want a cigarette.

And, indeed, in clarification to those that think I don't, I have begun saving money. On my bedroom chest of drawers I have placed a lovely pink and white box with a golden tassel as the pull handle. At the end of each successful day, I pull the tassel and place seven one-dollar bills inside. It's a cardboard memorial cache of sorts to my loss, to the death of my twenty daily companions; the little white sticks that fit so nicely between my fingers. I miss rinsing out the repugnant vestiges of my glorious habit from the glass tray, washing and drying it to a spotless shine with the kitchen dish towel, only to flick it full again with luscious, gray disgusting cinders. Now day no. 29 of no smoking, inside the coffin is enough money for twenty bottles of cheap rum.

Enthusiastic over my last Pap exam result of *no more HPV*—Ali's *STD* gift to me seems to come and go as mysteriously as the twinge in my neck—I returned the phone message, simply asking that I call, from one Clark Ghabal, a Match.com relationship that had gone no further than exchanging cell phone numbers in an online correspondence. No longer a card-carrying member of the dating site and, thus, unable to locate his profile, I had blindly listened to his calm, soothing ten-second message and tried to picture him. He must be good looking or I wouldn't have given him my number. The deep thinker crevice between my brows now useless, the Restylane injection doing its job, I was scrunching my eyes shut as far as I could, trying my best to recreate the man, when he answered the phone.

"Hello. Ghabal."

Candidate no. 5 certainly sounds important. He must be at work. Cell phones; you never know where the heck anyone really is.

"Hi, this is Julie returning your call?" I meekly replied.

"Julie? Oh, sure, Match.com. Thank you for calling. Nice good-bye note you left on the site. Broke a lot of hearts, including mine."

"I was medicated at the time, I think."

He chuckled and I sighed in relief. "I assure you I'm not one of the boys you directed your lash out to," Mr. Ghabal spoke gently, matter of fact and without disapproval. "I don't think I look like Antonio Banderas; I know I can't dance like John Travolta; and I have no idea how Johnny Depp kisses."

"Was I that harsh?"

"Charmingly so. And the three dates before sex thing put me over the top. I hate it when women expect thrills and chills on a first date."

Wow. He read and remembers all of your insulting remarks. He's a keeper. Don't fuck this up.

"I have to admit I don't remember your face, but I sure like your voice," our Julie swooned unable to restrain the warm cozy feelings beginning to stir somewhere between the safe spot right about *there* and the dangerous spot *down there*.

Good grief, you're a sixty-three year old woman, an experienced victim of the sex-too-soon moral ruination of this sordid world. A man speaks in a normal tone for one minute and you're ready to take a crotch-swooshing lavender bubble bath. He probably has a mouth full of small brown teeth. You know how you dislike bad teeth. Hold your horses; there's got to be a catch.

"Thank you. I like your voice too," Clark began to play. "You sound so young."

The *Lifestyle Lift* was working.

"Thank you. So do you," our Julie in total control refrained from throwing her underwear onto the stage. "So tell me about yourself, because I admit I didn't write it down," our Julie settled in, feigning the good listener posture as one on the edge of a pew transfixed by the beckoning sermon of salvation coming from the pulpit.

"Well, I'm a lawyer. I started out as criminal defense, but now I have my own civil litigation firm in Pasadena. I have a son in college, twenty-three, and I live in a one-bedroom, one-bath Spanish stucco house in Chatsworth," Mr. Ghabal recited as warmly and as innocently as a priest baptizing a baby.

"Me, too! I live in a one-bedroom, one-bath Spanish stucco house in Hollywood," our Julie infused the conversation with precise compatible details, her heart pounding; one hand wet with nervous anticipation gripped the phone, the other wrapped itself around a chilled Cuba Libre.

"How many kids and what do you do? I didn't write it down either. In fact, I canceled my Match subscription the end of December, a New Year's resolution, so . . . well, I found your number in my jacket pocket. I'm sorry I didn't call sooner."

"Well, three grown kids. I'm an actor trying to become a writer who drives lookie-loos around."

"Yes, I remember now. You're the retired court stenographer from San Bernardino."

"Yes, that was some time ago."

"So what do you like to do for fun?"

Yes, ma'am, he's going to ask you out on a real date. Don't fuck this up. "What do you like to do for fun?" Shaving your face, trimming the bushes, masturbating to Bill Nob *On The News*, frosting sugar cookies, bowling, and having sex in your basement are all off limits. And no long walks on the beach or anything that will irritate your bum knee.

"I'm pretty simple. Maybe a cocktail on the porch, a good movie, conversation over a nice meal."

"Well, how about if we try for all three this Friday? I don't drink, but I don't mind if you do," Father Ghabal answered our parishioner's every wish.

Our Julie is calm and cool as she gingerly sets the clinking glass of rum on the kitchen counter away from the phone. "Are you sure you want to venture out on a Friday the 13th?"

"I'm not superstitious. Are you?"

"I'm game. What time Friday?"

"I'm not sure. I have appointments on my calendar up until noon, but it could change. Text me your address and I'll let you know by one o'clock Friday, okay?" he promised her. And from miles away in the foothills of Los Angeles County he began to gently sprinkle Holy Water into her throbbing glass slipper.

The three-week-long Los Angeles Unified School District's exhausting holiday finally over and school back in session, I will now be reading to three classes. Mr. Taylor's gleaming recommendation of my jovial absurdities, wicked humor, and feigned love of children has enticed two of his female colleagues, a second grade teacher and a fifth grade teacher, to include my foolhardy volunteerism in their curriculum. They are looking forward to a weekly thirty-minute respite and a long potty break.

The second graders are quickly enamored with Grandma Julie. Leaping from their seats at my arrival, I am humbled by resounding applause for the lady who has come to give them a break from their daily routine. In *big hair* and performance makeup, my face I fear still a bit puffed from my mini-surgery, I begin to read an *Amelia Bedelia,* the comical maid who takes everything literally, when a curly headed seven-year-old boy blurts out, "You look like Snow White." Being called out as my favorite fairy tale heroine is the accomplishment of a lifetime.

♪ Someday my prince will come; someday I'll find my love . . . ♪

This little boy is no ordinary boy. His complexion is unusually fair, his cheeks pink as a winged cherub; yet he has dark feathered eyes in the shape of an almond, black and luminous. His nose is prominent and his black hair dances in curls about his sweet face. His lips are full and there is a slight suggestion of a dimple at his chin. I want to take him home with me. Could it be? Is this an inconvenient remnant left by Ali out on the town with one of the Mexican girls that he had once so brazenly spoken of?

> The clubs are full of Mexican girls now. They like Persian guys. Mexican girls are so horny. They grab your crotch the minute you walk in their house.

Ali, *The Year I Learned to Text*

Pleasant thoughts to have, Snow White, while being entrusted with the literary edification of small innocents sitting cross-legged on a rug of many colored squares. Yes, I am to keep looking for him, but not in the faces of adoring children.

"Thank you. That's a huge compliment. What's your name?"

"Jonathan."

I leaned in from my red plastic chair, "Well, Jonathan, you look like Aladdin," I smiled and all the little girls covered their mouths to stifle their flirtatious amusement. I do believe that Jonathan was the most popular boy on the playground that afternoon.

The fifth grade teacher was not prepared with a book for me, so I attempted to entertain twenty-five rambunctious children tingling on the edge of puberty, their regulating chemicals time warped and raging early on due to the injection of growth-promoting synthetic hormones into the beef of their burritos. Glancing around the rows of desks, I guesstimate the average bra size to be a whopping 36C. While the teacher took a cell phone call out into the hallway, I took charge.

"Let's sing! I'll start and you copy me, okay?"

Twenty-five boys and girls slumped into their polished wooden seats, their arms crossed and locked, stared me down. No one remarked on my similarity to Snow White. From somewhere tucked away in my repressed childhood memory came a song.

♪ Row, row, row your boat gently down the stream . . . ♪

♪ Row, row, row your boat gently down the street . . . ♪

"No, no. Not street. Streeeeeeeam! We're in a boat, not a car. Begin again. ♪ Row, row, row your boat gently down the—♪

And twenty-five mouths sang out ♪ Streeeeeeeam ♪

"Excellent. Ready? ♪ Merrily, merrily, merrily, merrily, life is but a dream ♪

Twenty-five throats sang out ♪ Marry me, marry me, marry me ♪

"Oh, for heaven's sake. No, no. It's a bit early for you to have that word on your mind. It is 'merrily,' as in Merry Christmas. You are happy to be rowing your boat! Let's start again."

Pleased with their abilities to sing the English nursery rhyme, I ventured into dangerous territory and divided the classroom into three sections; the first section beginning the song, the second section coming in with a resounding *row* on the word *boat*, and the third section coming in with a tentative *row* somewhere after the second section mumbled *boat*. My hands and arms conducting and my fingers pointing, very soon I had my attentive class singing *Row, Row, Row Your Boat* in the *round*, by golly, except for one spiteful fat fellow in the first row who insisted on singing along with section two and then section three, slamming a juggernaut into the joy of my orchestrated success. Regaining my composure, I started them up again, the lovely sound of young voices in the *round* being interrupted again by the stupid antics of a plump boy with only one oar in the water.

"Why do you keep singing when all your teammates have stopped?" I asked with painfully affected kindness. I had been previously instructed by Mr. Taylor, the new addition to my already auspicious entourage of gay men—who as of this publication have not yet filed suit demanding that the word *queer* be stripped entirely from the English language —that the use of the word *stupid*, even though the punishment may fit the crime, is taboo, even as far as the word *stupid* being viciously redacted by black mark-a-lots from children's books dating back to my immunized childhood of the fabulous fifties. The Los Angeles Unified School District had not yet, however, issued a politically correct replacement; *unintelligent, dull, slow-witted, feeble-minded,* and *asinine* vetoed as causing further damage. They have in their wisdom, however, put an end to the playground violence instigated by the game of *dodge ball*, a putative elementary school activity in which I received massive bruising, and in my clumsy inability to dodge the ball had been called out by my grade school colleagues as *stupid*.

"Because I want to sing it again," he stated, puffing up his enormous cheeks in belligerent protest.

"All right, of course. Now let's begin again."

His falsetto proudly spiraling an octave above all the rest, a choirboy was born.

Walking home from school after a quick dart into CVS, a heavy plastic bag swinging from my arm causing a bruise to form on my thinning epidermis, my cell phone alerted me. It was Beryl, my age-appropriate confidante and unfulfilled thespian.

"How are you doing with the cravings?"

"The what? I'm on Vine Street, a lot of traffic. Let me walk over a block." I settled myself in front of the cinema prop shop on Lillian Way. "Okay, try again."

"I'm calling with encouragement. As you know, I quit smoking and drinking cold turkey thirty years ago. Just hang in there. You can do it!"

Why does this startling advice make me want to go back into CVS for a carton of Virginia Slims?

"It's so hard for me to focus. I can't sit at the computer and write like I used to. I'm gnawing my fingers off."

"So you don't go crazy, go ahead and drink a bit. That, too, will go away, the craving for alcohol," she assured me, her timid voice reeking with sugarcoated wisdom and liberal optimism, which always grates my nerves.

"Thank you for the pep talk, Beryl. I'll keep at it. Day no. 31 now."

I rushed home and wrestled two bottles of chardonnay and a bottle of rum out of the plastic bag. I will heed the friendly advice of a self-imposed schizophrenic, an unfulfilled woman who today is three times the woman she was thirty years ago. I strapped myself into the writing chair, an iced wine at the wrist. At eleven-thirty in the morning, it is five o'clock somewhere.

At precisely one o'clock today, Friday having come at last, Mr. Clark Ghabal called in as promised with his estimated time of arrival. He shall depart his office in Pasadena by four o'clock and be at my behest no later than five o'clock. Careful to keep the clandestine clinking of ice chilling my cocktail away from the phone, I let him know how much I appreciated the phone call and that I very much looked forward to our meeting and a walk up to Sunset Boulevard. I spun around the kitchen sashaying gaily. I swept the kitchen floor, whistling while I worked, my expectations forecast onto another unsuspecting foot. Abandoning a perfect parking spot, I flew into *Pastel Nails & Spa* on Melrose Avenue.

"I'm sorry, but I'm in a hurry. Just a manicure, no pedicure," I disappointed the eager Korean manicurist, who in her normal posture bowed and scraped while repeating the only three English words she knows, *you pick color*. "I'm wearing boots this evening and they won't be coming off."

In a flurry, I shower, shave, and salivate over, what I have dubbed, my *lucky* first date of 2012, belying the myth of Friday the 13th as the unluckiest day of the year. After all, the day coming up to its seventeenth hour, I had not yet seen a black cat, walked under a ladder, or broken a mirror. Clothed in a soft purple, cowl neck sleeveless sweater, my flabby upper arms carefully concealed under a fringed, flowing long-sleeved black sweater, I zip up my boots over my skinny jeans. The cinched painful denim forcing the muffin top out should loosen up nicely if I sit in them during the trusting half hour wait for my soft-spoken redeemer.

Pleased with my presentation, I text my sister a picture of a future *Lifestyle Lift* infomercial model and she instantly texts back: *You look barely thirteen*. I am taken aback by her exaggerated compliment, but her kindness bolsters my confidence. Tonight I shall erase my past of failed and foolish escapades and reenter the dating life as the no-sex-until-the-third-date poster child. Restraining my friskiness, this I do for hopeful women everywhere, their time clocks ticking away another lonely Friday night as they languish in front of the flat screen drooling over the exploits of a handsome carpenter in a wife-beater t-shirt staple gunning a fixer-upper on an HGTV thirty-minute rehab makeover. I promise all of you that I shall be on my very best behavior: unassuming, shy, modest, and appropriately flirtatious. We don't want to turn him off completely.

I also text Rae my lucky date's name and phone number, just in case I go missing, after breaking my own new rule and end up in a one-bedroom, one-bath Spanish house in someone else's basement. I toss a few toothpicks into my bag in case there are popcorn kernels and spinach involved.

The dream date is a half hour late, according to my cryptic calculations and my cell phone. Where is my cat Morticia to encourage my wrath? I miss having her here, perched on the porch wall licking her privates precociously and mocking me. *Lock him out, leave a nasty note on the gate, hide in the kitchen*, she would insist. The traffic from Pasadena into Hollywood is always a sordid mess, Morticia.

The scoundrel is an hour late. Rather than calling him with "Just who do you think you are standing me up?" I choose to call with a concerned, calm, inquisitive message. Within one minute he calls me back.

"I'm on Highland near the Hollywood Bowl."

He's taken the wrong exit and has been dumped into the tourist trap at Hollywood and Highland, the Mecca for every out-of-towner looking to pick a fight with a cheaply costumed *Spider Man* insistent on five dollars for his snapshot taken in front of the celebrity footprints at Grauman's Chinese Theatre.

"It may take you another fifteen minutes to reach Fountain. After Hollywood Boulevard, after Sunset Boulevard, turn left there. It will take you to Cahuenga. Turn right and immediately look for a parking spot."

"At Hollywood Boulevard now. See you soon."

As I hung up, I prayed that this would be the very last time I would ever have to direct a man to my bungalow.

It's a bird; it's a plane; it's Clark at the gate.

♪ AVE MARIA ♪

In dark sleek jeans, a blue cotton dress shirt, deservedly tucked in, and a black suit jacket, he is powerful in posture and in stature, a stalwart of integrity; he's just the cutest thing. The only thing missing thus far is the white clergy collar. Behind his barely-there wire spectacles, his steel blue eyes twinkle. Full lips, a square jaw, black-blue hair trimmed at the ears with a bit of a flop at the brow, he resonates with a mature conservative presence, poised and utterly fearless. His clean, effortless features assure me that this man cannot tell a lie. And I haven't unlocked the gate yet.

Dog Test: Will he instantly befriend the boys with a playful ruffle to their ears, or will he reject them outright with an obsessive-compulsive hand gesture as germ-ridden, bothersome critters?

> ♪ Will you look at me quivering
> Like a little girl shivering? ♪

Opening the gate, my lucky dream date glides gently by me to sit down on the front porch and lands between two excited dogs feigning attention deprivation, starvation, and animal cruelty, their tails spinning round and round in unison, each with a *let's keep him* slobbering smile on their pitiful faces.

"These two need some scratching," he teased me and fluttered off a playful wink in my direction.

"Both of you stop with the *nobody loves me* routine. Brute, Hound, this is Clark."

"So it isn't true that you haven't fed them in weeks?"

"You speak *dog*? Good, I could use an interpreter."

Score: 10

> ♪ If you need a friend, I'm the one to fly to ♪

"You look very nice," he said rising to his softly leathered large feet.

"Thank you. So do you," I gushed, but controlled the rush in my cheeks to a sustained cotton candy shade of pink. Telltale Barbie pink should be saved until later.

"Great bungalow in a great location," he said and scanned the artifacts of my front porch. "I couldn't miss the Hollywood gate. Did you design it?"

"A Mr. Song and I stole the design from the hillside."

Clark laughed and sparkles flashed. His teeth are perfect. Large, white, and with the tiny ripples at the end of each front tooth still intact, which tells me my lucky dream date is not a night grinder.

"I'm sorry, but I left my phone in the car. Do you mind if we stop to get it?"

"Of course not. You'll need it in case I bore you." And I can check out your car.

"Pretty and funny too," he melted me with his smile, reassuring me that I would in no way bore him.

Car Test: Would the interior be crime-scene wiped clean? Or would his entire life spent as a recluse cruising the streets in search of prostitutes to capture and torture in chained bondage be laid out for me to dismiss? Would there be rolls of duct tape stacked on the back seat next to fetish fantasy silk coils of rope for me to explain away? Would the sweet and sickening odor from the trash bagged dead body in the trunk be waved away by my delusion? Would I give up a spaghetti dinner and a movie because of a few unfounded clues and speculative, circumstantial evidence? As Mother would encourage, *at least he's got a car.*

"I had to park over there a few blocks, beyond those apartments," he pointed and started to walk north to the intersection.

"We can cross here," I instructed.

"Wouldn't that be jaywalking?" he feared. Living on this busy street for eight noisy years, after watching my neighbors illegally cross the street and live to tell about it, I had quit walking the extra half block to the crosswalk sometime during week no. 2 of my life on Cahuenga Boulevard.

The light turned red at Fountain, the barreling traffic ceasing momentarily, he took my hand to guide me safely across the street. Not wanting to appear controlling or overly cautious, I let him take the lead without mentioning the car to our left making a rip-roaring turn in our direction from the side street. Without braking, the car swiped behind us, nipping at Clark's heels, I having wisely skipped ahead an arm's length.

Helping him to his feet, as he wiped the street from his knees and palms, I hurried him on. "Quick, here they come."

The light was green and the headlights raced forward. "All we need now is a black cat," he shouted over the thundering herd. Grabbing my hand, we landed on the sidewalk outside the senior apartment complex and continued around the corner to a black Mercedes Benz parked in front of the fenced fortress of secreted Craftsman bungalows of celebrity stylist Chaz Dean's salon, a salon I have never been to because I cannot afford two hundred dollar haircuts.

He reached in, and as the dome light flicked on inside his Benz, I looked quickly, not wanting to arouse suspicion. The interior was as naked as a newborn baby. The opulent scents of almond-mocha leather and *new car* wafted to my pulsating nostrils. As I leaned in to take a deeper whiff, he abruptly stood up and shut the door.

"I'm so sorry. I almost caught your hair in the door. Are you okay?"

"I'm fine, but could you move your car back to make room for a small car, perhaps?" I asked as kindly as anyone who is letting her date know he is a selfish jackass. "The way you're parked, you're taking up two spaces."

"You're right. I'm not used to parking on the street. I have a driveway."

Score: 10

♪ If you need to be loved,
Here I am ♪

Looking up at the white concrete three-story building with glass door frontage and the neon sign of *Stevenson Manor*, he comments, "This looks like a nice project."

"Government funded senior housing for foreigners only, it appears," I sadly recounted. "Imagine paying only eight-hundred a month for a one-bedroom apartment in Hollywood with underground parking," I drooled over the potential of moving across the street, my Scion parked in an assigned slot in the shade. "Never going to happen for me. The manager told me that unless I'm Russian and just arrived from the Social Security office, the first stop for immigrants, that I'll be dead before my name reaches the top of the waiting list."

Political test: Will he opine the liberal philosophy of global socialism, the need for more such glorious Big Government programs funded by the tax dollars of those who came before, believing that most of us are incapable of feeding ourselves, housing ourselves, or thinking for ourselves, and that the redistribution of wealth will cure all economic ills, even as far as handouts to non-citizens who show up late in life on our shores, whose Americanized children have learned the ropes?

"That doesn't seem fair or right," Mr. Conservative shook his head. "How does a foreigner, even though a senior, qualify for housing assistance?"

"The government calls it *Supplemental Security Income*, perhaps a stipend, but it qualifies one for low-income housing. All you need to be is at least sixty-five or blind or disabled, a legal resident of the State of California—or Texas, or Oregon, or any of the fifty states, including Washington, D.C.—and you don't need to have ever worked in the United States or paid into Social Security, because our government swears these handouts come from another pot. Of course, there are income and property limitations, but by the time they land at immigration, they have sold their real estate and given all the cash to their kids."

"Well, you're certainly full of information. I had no idea just how socialized our country has become, and with President Free Phone in the White House, it's going to get worse before it gets better."

"I *Googled* it when I was turned away without an application, the manager emphatically warning me that I'd never qualify for subsidized housing."

"Well, you're not sixty-five yet. So you've got, what?" my dream date hesitated, "at least ten more years before you need to worry about it?"

"Are you sure you didn't memorize my profile?" I asked while trying to remember my exact age as advertised previously on Match.com.

Score: 10

♪ Read my mind ♪

I can see nothing but goodness and honor in this tall hunk of possibility, but what do I have to offer in return? Stop the negative thinking, Julie. Remember the basics of *The Law of Attraction*: ask, believe, receive, and don't drink too much.

The luscious, rewarding evening turned chilly as we departed the boulevard legally by way of the crosswalk. Mr. Perfection offered me his suit coat, but I was satisfied with the fringed sweater and the warm arm about my shoulders. We made our way to Ivar on the sidewalk along the landscaped fencing of the undeveloped acreage extending east to Vine Street. Where once were two-story 1920 duplexes, editing companies, a sacred yoga sanctuary, a Kentucky Fried Chicken, and my one-block walk to cheap wine and toilet paper at Big Lots—properties purchased at over-market prices some time back—was now an eight-acre hub of potentiality.

"A group of celebrity investors in cahoots with the Academy of Arts and Sciences were going to build a fancy museum of Hollywood history here, but they've moved their big idea south to Fairfax and Wilshire in the old May Company building owned by the Los Angeles County Museum of Art."

"Not here in Hollywood? That's foolish. The tourists are right here, just walking around looking for something new to do."

I gazed out at the remaining buildings and the new-mown lawns beyond the fence. "I understand they'll be showing movies outdoors beginning in May with *Field of Dreams* . . .until they decide on what to do with the property."

"So instead of razing buildings and leaving behind a weed field, they are giving back to the community, huh?" He smiled that warm, understanding smile, the taunting smile that invites you to kiss not just the lips, but to flick your tongue on its remarkable teeth.

As we continued our walk, careful not to step on a crack or break our mothers' backs, the lamplight reflecting in his lenses, he looked down into my eyes, only to catapult head first onto the sidewalk, almost pulling me along with him. Simultaneously, there came a screeching yowling *meow* from underneath a parked car.

"What in the world? What did you trip on?" I asked in dire concern for my last love's health and physical safety.

In a withered slump on the concrete, he looked up at me with a fierce scowl on his shocked face. He had lost his charming calm control. "Black cat! I tripped over a goddamned black cat."

Holding back my instantaneous desire to cackle, picking up his glasses, I reached out my hand.

"What's so funny?" He, too, held back an instantaneous desire, his desire to run back to his car and lock the door. Damage control in effect, I knelt down on all fours for closer, more intimidating eye contact.

"I want to say 'I'm sorry, Clark,' but I had nothing to do with the black cat crossing your path, and I have a bad knee and now I can't get up without your help."

Blocking a sudden herd of pedestrians heading to Sunset Boulevard and causing a mini-spectacle as one by one cars made a foot-tapping California stop at the four-way alongside the ArcLight parking structure, Clark fell in with my stifled laughter and helped me to my feet.

"Where to now, my little witch?"

"Let's see what's playing at the ArcLight."

White earpieces in each ear, a trim, muscular twenty-something hipster crossed our path in multi-colored old school Puma running shoes and a sleeveless drenched gray t-shirt, which boasted highly of his workout at the 24 Hour Fitness facilities on the fourth floor of the complex. He listened intently to all the dire messages confronting his Friday night party schedule, which would not start until the stylish hour of ten o'clock, whereas we two fifty or sixty-somethings should be finished by ten o'clock. Arriving at his car, he lost his cool. The independent thinker swung open the windshield wiper on a heavily dented Honda Accord, plopped into the seat, and tossed another sixty-eight dollar parking ticket into his backseat.

"Why didn't he just park in the lot?" Practical Clark quizzed as the Honda skidded away full throttle through the four-way stop.

"With the gym parking validation, he'd have to pay two dollars and fifty cents."

"And you can just walk to the gym. Are you a member?"

"Long-standing, but I'm sure they don't know me by name, face, or workout outfit," I admitted. ♪ Da-da-da-daba daba da ♪ Skipping backwards and pulling him along by both hands, I sang gaily, a mischievous look on my face, remembering to keep smiling—my repaired marionette lines in training—so I would never look disappointed again.

"What are you singing?"

"The theme song from a very sexy 1966 French movie. ♪ Daba daba da ♪

"Daba daba doo, I'm familiar with, Mrs. Flintstone, but not the tune you're singing."

"*Un Homme et Une Femme.* Just the cover of the LP is enough to start sparks flying."

"I'm supposed to know how to speak French? Well, I do speak a little."

I spun around the corner at Sunset, leaving him to catch up with me.

"*A Man and A Woman!*" And as he caught me in a half twirl, face-to-face—well, all we needed was a bit of aesthetic rain and Gene Kelly dancing from the light pole to set the scene for our first kiss. Instead we got a whiplash from an irresponsible skateboarder that sent us hurling into a disheveled Randi, apparently frantic from a booze run into Rite Aid for overpriced, imprisoned vodka.

Dropping our handhold to make room for Randi's crisp brown paper bag, I was able to save the moment. "Bread and butter!"

"What?" Clark stood dumbfounded on the busy sidewalk. Clark did not repeat the phrase, which according to American folklore means that before the night is over we would have quite the quarrel.

"Can I use your shower?"
"Clark, this is my neighbor Miranda."
"Hi, Clark. As in Clark Kent?"
"No, last name Ghabal."
"Ghabal? What kind of a name is that?" Randi wagged her head back and forth, her matted violet auburn hair unable to shake in disdain, as she would have liked. "Are you American, as in White Anglo Saxon Protestant?"
"Actually, I'm Universal."

Turning into me, she pressed in a whisper. "I'll put the key in the mailbox. I'll be out of there in a half hour, I promise."

"We're still on for your birthday celebration at the races tomorrow?"

"Of course. Early to bed and on our way to Santa Anita by ten," she ordered.

I fished into my cross-body purse for the keys, a jangle of metal on a pink sequined ring, and scooped it into her open hand.

"Thanks. Here, I don't need the toothpicks." With an affectionate squeeze she folded my fingers over them and disappeared around the corner.

"Interesting character," Clark shared his immediately drawn opinion of my friend.

"Hey, she's a sweetheart, but for her drinking, her smoking, her inability to make a living as a car salesman or a set painter, and her infatuation with married men. Oh, and her broken water heater that she refuses to fix."

"Is she the type of person you should be allowing into your house, let alone be using your shower?"

You have no idea the type of people I've let use my shower.

"As long as she showers alone and hangs up the towels," I patronized his sanctimonious concerns, realizing that *but for the grace of God*, go I. Smugly, I continued my façade as the perfect match to my dream date, a dream that was slightly beginning to fade.

Passing by the water fixture raining down on the smooth gray river rocks at the entrance of the entertainment center, Clark once again bolted from my grasp.

"Oh, look a penny." The copper shining with tail's up, Clark bent down to fetch it.

"Stop, don't—" but it was too late to warn him of the impending doom of limitless bad luck that comes after picking up a penny on this Friday, the 13th.

"Julie, it's lucky to find a copper penny."

"Not when the tail's up, Clark."

"Gosh, I've never heard of that silly superstition."

"That's okay. You'll know soon enough whether it's an old wives tale or not. Just toss it for someone else and hopefully, it will land heads up."

Inside the grand foyer, Clark headed for the bookstore, which carries picture books, memorabilia, and collectables exclusively related to the grit and glamour of Hollywood.

"I have to admit, I've never been to the ArcLight. I hang out mostly in Pasadena. Looks like they have everything under one roof here: movies, a restaurant, and a high-end souvenir shop."

I checked out movie times on the marquis overhead while Clark amused himself. The movie I was hoping to see, *The Artist*, had already started and nothing else felt date-night worthy. I turned around to find Mr. Almost Wonderful spinning and tossing an umbrella like a majorette twirling a baton on fire.

"This is nice. A nude Marilyn Monroe umbrella."

"Stop, don't open that."

"Why not?" And whoosh with one click, the black and white nylon parasol opened, baring Ms. Monroe's flesh.

I quickly knocked on a wooden shelf.

The usual homeless enclave in front of the abandoned Wells Fargo building, *WF* having moved north to a more prestigious address on Vine Street, greeted us with outstretched empty coffee cups, an aura of ammonia, and pleading cardboard signs shaming anyone who passed by with *Bless You* scrawled in no. 2 lead pencil. Reverend Ghabal reached into his pants pocket.

"Please don't give them any change."

"Why not?"

"The same reason we're not to feed the pigeons," I answered with experienced retrospect, having witnessed first hand the violent attack of hungry birds in Piazza San Marco in Venice—Italy, not California.

Waiting for the little green man to allow us to cross Vine Street, I was taken aback. A half block east on Sunset, under the bright lights of Mr. Fabiola's billboard climbing the scaffolding is another little man.

"Clark, Clark! It's going up!"

"What's going up?"

Hand in hand we raced through the intersection dodging pedestrians, stolen grocery carts, and leashed pedigrees, reaching our destination after dismissing the fact we had taken a sidewalk shortcut under a twenty-four foot extension ladder with a frenetic crossing of the Trinity to our chests, just in case.

As usual, Fabi, his shaggy gray hair flying, is gregariously greeting diners inside his cochina Italiano.

"Is it going up tonight?" I asked out of breath from my excitement, Clark still holding the glass door.

"He's taking down the old sign and prepping for yours. It will be up soon," he controlled my enthusiasm.

"Clark, this is Fabi. He owns the joint."

"I love Italian. Let's eat here."

"Welcome, sir, right this way."

Familiar with my preference, Fabi placed us under the canvas in the garden patio. The maître d' quietly snuck up to our table and with his hands locked behind his back, he asked for our drink order.

"May I have that wonderful house Chianti you're always forcing on me?"

"Ah, yes, a bottle of Contemassi."

"Just one glass, I would think," Clark affirmed, as stoically as a priest inserting one crusty piece of the body of Christ into the mouth of a worshipping parishioner in a communion lineup.

"Of course," I agreed. It was my frugal routine to enjoy a single glass of wine when dining out. Only when my sister was in charge was a full bottle ordered. I'd never been on a date when an entire bottle of thirty-five dollar wine was ordered. I had been out with recovering alcoholics, teetotalers, and control freaks on a budget all of my life.

"What's all the excitement over a billboard?" he asked and spread his cloth napkin succinctly over his lap, smoothing it out ever so gently.

"I've written a novel and I'm spending my children's inheritance on advertising it."

"Not only an actress, but an artist. I'm impressed. What's it about?"

> Shaving your face, trimming the bushes, masturbating to Bill Nob *On The News*, frosting sugar cookies, bowling, and having sex in your basement are all off limits.

"The usual. Love gone terribly wrong."

"Well, I'm sure you won't ever have to write a sequel."

Smiling Alexandra's *I smell cookies* smile, my eyes at half moon, I exhaled what I hoped would be my final lonely lady breath. This fleeting moment of human connection was quickly brought back to the white tablecloth.

"I haven't eaten since dawn. I have a problem with low blood sugar. Let's order."

Enjoying the Ruspante insalate of spinach, roasted bell peppers, and smoked mozzarella, he discussed the desire for simplicity, peace, and a gentle sweetheart, while I controlled my desire to order another glass of wine.

"I find you glamorous and just a bit of an eccentric, someone I'd like to know a lot better."

"Well, I do live in Hollyweird. So what's your story, Clark? When do you rush out of the men's room in a tight blue t-shirt with a big red S on it?"

"And insightful, too," he parried, lifting one dark eyebrow. Superman gently wiped the corner of his lip with the napkin, and placing it back on his lap, he offered his hand across the table. Juggling a toothpick in my fingers, while sneaking an impolite peek at my teeth in the mirror of my compact, I set my tools down to meet his fingertips. Our eyes locked, and suddenly the saltshaker fell with a thud onto the pesto dipping plate, leaving a crystalline path on its way down.

"Oh, Judas," I blurted out, grabbing the glass shaker now green with oil. In my clumsy attempt to disrupt the ill luck of spilt salt by shaking salt into my palm and tossing it quickly over my shoulder, the shaker slipped from between my fingers and bounced with a bang off the small mirror of my *CoverGirl*. Like salt spillers before me, I somehow knew this would be our last supper.

"I know that one! Seven years bad luck," he warned me.

"Yes. May I have another glass of wine now?" I whimpered as I closed up the cracked glass.

"Save up. We're promenading to Musso and Frank's for a martini. I've always wanted to visit the esteemed eatery. Is it true that you have to pay extra for salad dressing? Is it far?"

"Yes and no."

We were in luck. We were seated at the only two remaining stools at the long polished mahogany bar, after we fibbed to the waiter dressed in a crisp red jacket that, yes, we were here for dinner and would spend the hour-long wait enjoying a cocktail. Over the clang of utensils onto chilled salad plates at the white linen clothed tables for eight behind us, stirring his pious Shirley Temple with two cherries, he began to quiz me on my whereabouts during the last fifty-some years. I glossed over four husbands and three children, hoping he wouldn't notice the lack of concise dates and ages.

"It's so fascinating, isn't it, what puts two people together at a certain time, when they mesh with *art*?"

I have no idea what he's talking about and the Beefeater-soaked olives aren't helping me to digest his intellectually contorted conversational flair.

"From the little you've shared, Julie, I can't help but think that you've simply had some bad luck along the way. Here in this very landmark, some of the world's greatest writers—Ernest Hemingway, F. Scott Fitzgerald, William Faulkner—discussed their works. And now I'm here with you, an artist, an actress, a retired court stenographer. If we had met at another time, in another place, in a courtroom, heaven forbid, we wouldn't be the same people that we are now."

"I suppose not."

"There are some things about me you need to know."

Here it comes.

"Yes, of course. I'm sorry. I've been monopolizing the conversation. Forgive me, Clark."

Here it comes.

"I've been holding back, waiting until I felt that we jelled, that you were understanding and kind, and that you, too, wanted a sweetheart."

"I think you're a very nice man, Mr. Ghabal. And by the way, what kind of name is that?"

Here it comes.

"It's Arabic," he answered and I swigged. "You won't believe this, but grandpa had nine wives over the course of his life and grandma was sad," he chuckled. "I have twenty-three siblings. Most of them are half-siblings, of course."

Where do they come from? And how do they find me?

"Waiter?"

"Yes, do have another," the Imam cynically encouraged me.

"So you're not Methodist?"

"I take a little from here, a little from there. In my home I keep the *Qur'an*, the *Bible*, and the *Torah*. I need to discuss with you—"

"What, no Dalai Lama's *Little Book of Buddhism*? Oh, thank you, Ruben, for the extra olives," I rose my perfectly sized glass to the legendary bartender, who in over forty-five years behind the bar has served some of the greatest drinkers in history, including Steve McQueen and Keith Richards.

"You see, legally, I'm married. My wife has cancer and needs to stay on my health insurance, and now that she's weaker and having long stays in the hospital, I'm in need of companionship."

"Whoa. That was a long sentence, Clark. Let me digest that and see if I've got the gist."

"Of course." He waited in awe of my patience, understanding, and limitless acceptance of skullduggery and chicanery.

"You're horny because your poor, sick bald wife is on her death bed," I shook a tooth-picked olive at his stunned face. "And the nurses advise against sexual activity in the ward, so you'd like me to suck your dick?"

"Keep it down, Julie," he whispered and grabbed my flaying hand, his rakish air caught off balance.

"Did ya bring a note from your wife? Wait! I guess it would be a prescription written by her oncologist, correct?"

I'd like to think it was that second vodka martini served over crushed ice that sent Lois Lane out of bounds furiously rifling unsuccessfully through her makeup bag for her stash of Kryptonite. I hadn't yet finished the chilled truth serum; there were two fingers left in the glass, and the excess liquor delivered in a miniature decanter glistened.

"Let's walk and talk and work this out. I'm not as bad as all that," my lucky first date of 2012 urged me with a tug to my elbow.

"It's early yet. And I've never tried Musso and Frank's famous creamed spinach," I smiled so I wouldn't look disappointed. "You go on home, wherever that is, and we can talk later." In perfunctory fashion, he jumped down from the stool and flew away. "Drinks are on me," I shouted after him, the din of diners covering my angry offering.

I skipped the spinach, but sipped a third one, stirred and not shaken. As I passed the lineup of scantily dressed girls and young men in black behind the gold rope at Lure nightclub and meat factory on Ivar, my phone vibrated. *Always look for him*, I was reminded by the blur of carefully tousled dark hair and neatly trimmed five o'clock shadows. Where would he be on this Friday night? Where is my one true unrequited love? He was my Johnny Depp, my Al Pacino, and my Pierce Brosnan. He was my made-up, make-believe soul mate; he was Johnny to my Frankie, homme to my femme, Superman to my Lois Lane, and unconscionable conqueror to my idiotic woman. If I kept sending my request out into the universe, asking to bring him home, believing that is what I truly wanted, I would surely get my wish. Watch what you wish for, Julie.

Checking my phone under a street lamp, I see that Clark has broken up with me by text message.

> Friday, January 13, 2012; 10:05pm CLARK: Thank you for the interesting evening, but I don't think we have a lot in common. Good luck.

"Vat an asshole."
"Are you out clubbing, Natasha?"

"I thought you'd appreciate a shoulder to lean on, because you're svaying all over zee sidewalk, dahlink."

"Why are you wearing my fake fur coat?"

"It eeze cold out and Boris forgot to peek up my meenk from the dry cleaner. I took the keys out of your mailbox and found this rag in your closet."

"Oh, okay."

"I'm so sorry, dahlink, that this evening turned out to be a vile embarrassment and an utter vaste of your precious time. After all, you may have only twenty years left, and only five of them worthy of catching a decent lover."

"It's okay. I was able to drop a lot of my personal opinions into this chapter."

"How could I know that Superman was another cheating moron?"

"You're a spy, Natasha. You have access to more than just a profile on. . . on. . .oh, shit, what is it?"

"Match.com. Dahlink, I cannot abuse my position in the National Clandestine Service of C.I.A. to vet men on the make. When he let you know he didn't drink alcohol, he vas vaving a red flag in your face."

"You're soooo right. Never trust a man that doesn't drink."

"You, me, and John Vayne, dahlink."

In 2014 the eight acres between Ivar and Vine would be purchased by Kilroy Realty Corporation for the proposed development of a one hundred million dollar glass and steel complex of towering apartments, sidewalk retail shops, overpriced restaurants, and upscale grocers, and I would be sitting pretty just two short blocks south awaiting a developer's knock at my gate.

Chapter 40

Green Boards and Hoping for a Miracle

♪ What a gripping,
Absolutely ripping moment ♪

Ascot Opening Day
Alan Jay Lerner and Frederick Lowe

My charming and unconventional friend rang the doorbell and I hustled on out. Somehow we have both dressed in purple and black with coordinating zip-up tall boots. "How did it go last night with Clark Kent?"

"He was deliciously debonair and almost perfect, except for the Middle Eastern lineage—"

"Where do they come from? And how do they find you?"

"And married, of course."

"Did you give him my phone number?"

"No. Not to change the subject, homewrecker, but how's your foot doing?"

"It's like brand new. Pedal to the metal, baby."

From her parking place in front of the Hollywood bungalows, Randi whizzed at treacherous speeds in and out of the Saturday morning 210 Freeway *Grand Prix* for a hair-raising thirty minutes. The race ended in Arcadia, an affluent small city nestled at the bottom of the San Gabriel Mountain range, its flora shimmering in winter blues and greens. When she crossed the finish line in the dusty parking lot of Santa Anita Park, the excited attendant feverishly waved us in with a checkered black and white flag. Apparently, she had broken all previous records.

"I suppose just because it's your fortieth birthday, I'm treating?" I teased Randi. Unleashing my frozen knuckles from the safety handle over my head, I reached across her chest and handed over my first fistful of cash to the valet.

"Hey, I drove," she deftly posited today's *win place and show* balancing act.

"I'm not staking you to any wagers. I couldn't bear it. If you were to lose, I'd probably rip that silly Kentucky Derby monstrosity of a hat right off your silly head. "

"You're just jealous because you didn't think to wear one."

Receiving our hand stamp at the gate, the newest members of Gamblers Anonymous headed to Clocker's Corner for a pre-lunch breakfast of pastries and a view of the ponies finishing up their pre-race exercise. Studying the daily racing form, I circled with indelible ink all the jockeys who would be saddling up in pink silks. I had inside information that any athlete caught dead in pastel pink had to have ferocious, unrelenting balls. These precisely chosen winners were tried and true speculations, having won an eighty-five dollar purse over twenty years ago when I placed a two-dollar bet *to show* on another shiny pink jockey.

Before the first race began, Randi in her felt feathered hat and I with a lighter purse, gathered with other professional risk-takers at the Paddock Gardens. Surrounded by thousands of flowers and tended greens, we painstakingly judged the parade of thoroughbreds for muscle tone, temperament, and the size of the bulge in the pants of their always-handsome riders.

Forty-eight dollars of draft Bud Light, hot dogs with onions and mustard, and warm jumbo pretzels later, the ninth and last race was announced by the bugler in red and gold with the call to post.

♪ ta-da-da, dat-tada, dat-tada, dat-ta-da-da ♪

"Which lame horse are you rooting for this time?" Randi reprimanded my previous eight losses.

"There's not a pink silk in the bunch, so I put two bucks on Teasing Bernie to show."

"I put all of my winnings, forty dollars total, on Mon Coeur, the favorite."

The crowd revved up as Mon Coeur in orange and yellow rounded the turn ahead of the pack. And here comes Teasing Bernie on the outside. The crowd's roar of "go, go, go," suddenly turned into one huge startled gasp when at fifty yards from the finish, Teasing Bernie running neck-to-neck with the leader was nipped by Mon Coeur, his jockey having drifted slightly to the right tangling Mon Coeur's hind legs with Bernie's left foreleg. Teasing Bernie fell head over hoofs onto the track and threw his jockey, who landed in a scraping thud. Teasing Bernie tried to stand up, but fell again.

"Oh, my God. Is he all right?" we both panted, our hands over our mouths in horror.

Faster than the horses had run from the starting gate, a large green board held by a dozen hands was rushed onto the track, hiding the gruesome scene before us.

"Are they going to shoot him?" Randi panicked.

"Oh, heavens, I hope not. He's gorgeous."

"The horse. Not the jockey."

"I know. I know," I comforted her and curled her up into my arms. My friend who would refuse to swat a fly away from the last available vodka tonic on earth, needless to say, was crying.

Men in coats disappeared behind the green board, while spectators in the stadium, the Club House, and the Turf Club stood in silence. The board was carried away and Teasing Bernie rose to his feet to thunderous applause by thousands of Saturday punters and one relieved tattooed and pierced forty-year-old lady in a funny hat.

Mon Coeur was disqualified and his jockey, the best looking one in the bunch, suspended. We returned home in Randi's Mini Cooper to rats, dogs, crickets, tarantulas and to the same parking place, because no other car had been able to fit into it.

Sleeping soundly after a long day of sun, suds, and salacious thoughts at the track, I am startled awake by whimpering and odd movements in the living room. I glance at the clock and switch on the lamp. At three in the morning, Hound is spinning in circles, slipping and sliding on the hardwood floor, his legs crumbling beneath him. I reach him too late. He lets go and we are both skidding through a puddle as I guide him by the collar to the back steps. Embarrassed and shaking, he leans into me down and into the garden, where he immediately upchucks into the ivy. He can barely stand and wobbles to and fro, side to side, and slams into the legs of the barbeque, bounces off and flops onto the brick walkway in a mess of pitiful bones and fur. He lifts up, his unsteady gate weaving from one obstacle to another. Ricocheting back and forth between the jasmine trellis, the yellow bell tree, the Rubbermaid storage shed, and the climbing rose trellis, Hound finally reaches his usual spot and unloads.

Heartbroken, I change into sweats, wipe down the living room floor, console Brute, who has not changed his position on my bed, and bring out Hound's bed and the caramel blanket and we both lay down behind the trashcans outside the kitchen windows. I've brought out his water bowl, and trying for a drink, he cannot control his head. I hold the bowl up close to his snout and his head shakes in a spasm. Side by side, I hold him, rubbing his joints as we cuddle up like an old married couple.

The sky still black and the morning not yet on its way, I sneak away and get back into bed, only to return to him when I hear him baying sorrowfully. My leg wrapped gently over his rump, the gal who would machine gun a fly diving at her vodka tonic cried. We spoon until the sun comes up.

By early day, he is able to lick water from his bowl. Nurse Julie, in her wisdom, knows that this is a good sign. Humans can survive for five weeks without food, but only five days without water. If Hound can drink, he can live.

Feeling that he would be accident free for a few more hours, I brought his bed and blanket back into the living room. While I whipped up a substantial breakfast for the three of us, he snuck out the back door and proudly began to maneuver the steps alone.

Drying my hands on a t-towel, I hurried the four steps to the back porch, where I found him collapsed on the second step, all four legs folded beneath him. "Stop, don't move."

I was too late. His limp body rolled onto the third step, convulsed onto the pavement and careened against the fence. He lay there on his back, his legs batting the air. I gingerly rushed to him—no sense in having both of us disabled—and helped him to his feet. While he somehow found his meandering tortuous way along the pathway obstacle course, I grabbed towels, bath rugs, and blankets to soften further crashes.

After sharing a meal of scrambled eggs and turkey bacon, feeding the old fellow as I would a bird fallen from a tree, his head jerking to stay on course, within ten minutes, Hound regurgitated all the water, the eggs, and the turkey in front of the laundry closet door. The liquid flowed down hill around and behind the entertainment center and passed the doorway of the kitchen, where the Mexican tile is higher than the living room floor. From there it pooled sumptuously in the corner under my cherry wood desk. Poor guy. The paper towels are going quickly.

Settled in the sun on the front porch, Hound regained his composure and took up his stealth duties as guard dog, his watch over the neighborhood renowned for its bark and never a bite. From the koffice, perched over another *Word* shamed grammatically incorrect fragment, my proclivity to dismiss it as literary license, I heard a few stammering barks, a gasping "Oh, my God" and a rattling thud. In white cotton socks—always trying to clean the floors when I can—I slid into the front porch scene.

Standing outside the gate is Michael, the bungalow's token gay hooker, walking his vicious yipping rat of a Chihuahua. Wedged between the final step and the bottom of the gate, Hound's twisted body lay in a jumbled heap.

"Is your dog okay? He took a mean fall."

Steadying Hound, I explained. "He's old and I think he had a stroke or a seizure last night."

"Well, you should get him to the vet."

"Today's Sunday. I'll see how he is tomorrow."

And off he piously went without a worry as to how I would pay the vet bill.

"Well, ole boy, you're this close to the sidewalk, so we might as well wander through the courtyard for a bit of rehab therapy."

At the sound of the lock turning in the metal gate, Brute made his way to the front door to see what the excitement was all about.

"Okay, you too." I slowly open the gate and Hound unrolls onto the sidewalk. "Well, are you coming?" And staring into his frightened eyes, I realize that Brute is not taking those stairs on his own. Is this a ploy to get my attention or a sympathetic illness to prove his loyalty to his roommate?

"The tandem leash was bad enough, Brute, but having to carry two dogs is going to send me to the emergency room."

Hound waited for me, because he couldn't move, while I carried his buddy down the steps, where Brute wrenched from my hold and toddled ahead. While he leaned into me, I controlled Hound's spastic movements as best I could by holding him by the collar. Going up the two lean steps into the grass was uneventful, neither one of us fell to the ground, so I let him free in the twelve-foot wide courtyard. He zigzagged from wall to wall, from fence to fence, from tree trunk to tree trunk, his sad handsome head bobbing at every turn. Marlene left her porch of cardboard boxes, yard sale artifacts, cat food supplies, and scattered unopened mail to meet us.

"What's happened? Can't he see?"

Interpretation: *What have you done to Hound?*

Marlene is not simply the self-appointed historian for everything Hollywood and our resident bungalow packrat—please do not throw a match anywhere near her front porch—but she is also a card-carrying member of PETA. Her love for the left and lonely, stranded and abandoned, abashedly uncontrolled, she has been fined by Code Enforcement for her excessive amount of felines, which run wild in and out of her open windows, the glass broken and not replaced, and out into the walkway to dump their thrice daily excrement, having somehow lost the genetic desire to bury it. This extraordinary need to save everything on four legs from wandering happily on the streets, unfortunately, extends to my pets.

"I think he had a stroke or a seizure late last night."

"He can hardly walk, Julie. Why isn't he at the vet?"

"It's Sunday. I'm waiting to see how he is in the morning."

And Hound plummeted at my feet.

"He keeps falling down. That's just cruel. You should put him down."

"He can drink water from his bowl. He's going to live!"

Everyone settled in, I reluctantly met Rae at the corner.

"You look harried. Everything okay?" she inquired and U-turned the Benz into traffic.

"Something's wrong with Hound. I think he had a stroke or a seizure last night. He can hardly walk straight and he's losing everything he eats."

Either to console me or to not disrupt our evening, she acknowledged,

"He's an old dog. Maybe you should put him down."

I turned violently to face her. "He's drinking water from his bowl. He's going to live!"

"You obviously need a cigarette," she affirmed and lit up. I was heading into the beginning of my second month smoke free.

Returning that evening from our previously arranged outing, a commitment to attend a disastrous one-woman showcase at a local theatre, after which my sister and I gorged ourselves at P. F. Chang's on calamari, egg rolls, and crab wonton, I am relieved to find that no one has relieved themselves inside the house. No throw up, no poop, and no pee. Upon further investigation, sadly I spend the rest of the evening mopping up drops of blood from the kitchen floor and helping two dogs down the steps for their final deluge of the day. In answer to the call of my *second wind*, I further indulge in buttered popcorn for sharing and watch once again *Driving Miss Daisy*. For these intimate moments of togetherness my friends are pleased and now satisfied, just as my children could not genuinely fall to sleep until I returned and read them a bedtime story, while we shared a scoop or two of vanilla ice milk.

> Bill Nob *On The News:* Mitt Romney just may be the man to beat Obama.

In groggy, early morning shock, I roll toward the clock radio. Is it true? That egotistical, two-faced irritant of my peaceful sleep is speaking up for my candidate, the former governor of Massachusetts, the financial wizard, the virile Mormon hottie, and the last great white hope to bring sanity back to this country? You've admitted voting for Obama. Have you come to your senses, you drooling old fool, you retired cocaine abuser, you gastric bypass slug? If there were one other station besides KFI to wake me up that came in without static, I would have turned the dial long ago. Beginning in 1922, *KFI AM 640* became one of the first 50,000 watt stations. It's not known as *Clear Channel* for nothing.

After lugging dogs in and out, I jump in and out of the shower in haste, my appointment with Dr. Hu scheduled for 10:00 am. Upon hearing the catastrophic news of Hound's seizure/stroke, Alexandra is on her way to visit *her* dog, a rare occasion spurned, apparently, by the smell of imminent death.

Sitting in the round on the kitchen floor, Alex hand feeds Hound from his bowl of kibble. "This is so frightening, to see them this way. Hound spastic, Brute stumbling around."

"Well, hopefully Brute is just stiff from sleeping too much."

"Although you're looking good for your age, you're going to end up the same way—and alone."

"Don't worry about me. I have a plan," I said stoically, holding Hound's head over his water bowl. "See? He can drink water. He's going to live!"

"What plan? I don't mean that I won't be around, but I can't be here all the time."

"A friend of mine, Captain Brainard, is going to buy one of the bungalows, as soon as someone dies. Probably Bunny will go first, as she's on a hospital bed inside her house. You should hear her complain about the Korean caretaker that picks at the Meals On Wheels tray before Bunny can drool into it. Brainard will be just a few steps away to watch over me, while he waits for me to die, because he really would prefer a house in the front."

"Stop. You sound morbid, like your mother. Who's Captain Brainard? Do I know him?"

"You haven't met him? That's odd. He's in and out of here like gangbusters. He's a retired Navy pilot, now an actor, and quite the ladies man."

"You're not dating him, are you?"

"Heavens no. I'm too fat."

Alex carries Hound and I carry Brute down the front steps and into the walkway for a spurt of exercise.

"He walks like he's drunk, Mother. How much weight has he lost?" she accuses.

"It's only been thirty-six hours since he lost control, but he does look rather spindly, doesn't he?"

"Can you get them back inside yourself? I have a casting in ten minutes."

"Sure, we can handle it."

"Let me know what happens at the vet."

Although I've lucked into a parking spot in front of the house, getting the invalid up into the backseat is a feat. When just three days ago, he would leap like a gazelle into the car, today he balks in trepidation, almost in fear of my guiding hands. It must be the towels I've strewn across the seat. He knows I'm up to no good.

"Need some help, ma'am?"

"Brainard, what are you doing here?"

"I have an audition down the street. Hey, old man, what's up with you?" Cupping Hound's head in his hands, Brainard studied his glossed-over golden eyes. "Stroke or seizure?"

"It happened early Sunday morning or late Saturday night. He's a mess. I'm taking him to the vet now."

The gate open and grumpy Brute impatiently waiting on the porch, Brainard coaxed him to join us on the sidewalk.

"Is he afraid to take the stairs?"

"Yes, the two of them are no longer ambulatory. I'm going to need a stroller for twins," I surmised.

"Okay, Brute, I'll carry you down," Brainard calmed the timid and cautious Maltese and placed him into the front seat of the Scion. "Okay, now up you go," and he lifted a shaking, confused German shepherd off the ground and into his favorite seat.

The passenger window rolled down, the captain leaned in, sharing the space with Brute's paws. "Let me know if you need anything. Oh, and how's Bunny doing? She's, what, ninety-four now?"

"She's not dead yet."

"Good news. What in the hell's keeping her alive? Martinis and cigarettes?"

"The thought of you moving in."

The drive to Laurel Pet by way of Santa Monica Boulevard was eerie. A two-and-a-half mile, twenty-minute trip like this would have Hound's head out the window sniffing and taking in all the sights, sounds, and smells of West Hollywood, where dogs are walked properly by neatly dressed stunning men in fashionable running attire daintily fingering pink leashes streaming from rhinestone studded collars. Today he lay in a heap on the towels. Not even the scent of grease bubbling on the grill as we passed Fatburger lifted him to the window.

The waiting room attendees shot me an unfavorable glance, as I trudged alongside a neurologically impaired old dog twitching, trembling, and sliding into a twisted lump onto the linoleum floor. If only I'd thought to bring a large green board to hide him under. I held a chubby ball of white hair in my left arm and signed Hound in at the counter.

I assured the onlookers, who clutched their pedigreed mongrels close to their Birkenstock sandaled feet, that I was well aware that my dog was ill, but not a harbinger of anything contagious. "He's had a stroke or a seizure."

An assistant calls for us, and inside the small room of white tile and stainless steel, Dr. Hu enters.

"How is everyone doing?"

The lovely young Asian veterinarian has been caring for my left-over pets for the last eight years, giving them their seasonal shots, shaking her head at their convivial conditioning, commenting on Brute's gradual weight gain, and sadly putting to sleep the household matriarch Morticia. She is a fine lady, who has commented more than once on how much my pets are loved.

"Hound can't control anything. Not his head, his feet, or his bladder. He woke up spinning and crying out very early Sunday morning."

"The assistant wasn't able to weigh him, I see. Let's take a look, Hound." Crouching by his side on the floor, she lifted his tail, which fortunately I had baby-wiped earlier, poked at his stomach, manipulated his legs, and peered into his glazed eyes.

"And he pooped a bit of blood. What's wrong with him?" I begged for a miracle cure, maybe one good shot from a long needle, because I'm not good at administering pills.

"Well, he either had a seizure or a stroke. There's really nothing we can do, but keep him comfortable. He is, after all, going on seventeen. He's enjoyed a long life. You might think about putting him down, if it gets too difficult for you," she calmly shot me in the foot.

"I'm paying how much for this medical advice?"

"No need to be rude."

"He's drinking water from a bowl. He's going to live!"

"And Brute's arthritis needs a pain reliever. I'd like to give him a Cortisone shot."

"I didn't bring him in for treatment. I think he's faking."

"Haven't you noticed how hard it is for him to walk?"

"I've only noticed that I don't have to chase him anymore."

Brute up on the examination tray, needle inserted, he gives me a *what for?* After all, it's Hound that's been causing all the trouble.

"Check back in a few weeks and let me know how Hound's doing. I can discuss with you the options and, perhaps, talk you down from the guilt feelings you're having."

I keep the backdoor open in the hope that Hound will take the back steps on his own, but he continues to awaken me during the night, resting his paws on my bedcovers before he slinks in a thud to the floor. I escort him down to the garden and leave him to his privacies. Brute comes along, too, as long as I carry him. Both are able to climb back up the stairs on their own. Hound continues to drink water from his bowl. He is trying his best to control his head jerks so that he can help himself to kibble until his caretaker gets off her duff and sits crossed legged on the tile floor, holding his jaw with one hand and placing Purina Beneful multi-colored veggie bits between his yellowed teeth with the other.

These are the days of our lives.

Chapter 41

Mikhail Baryshnikov and the Ugly Duckling

♪ Is your mouth a little weak?
When you open it to speak
Are you smart? ♪

My Funny Valentine
Lorenz Hart and Richard Rodgers

THE billboard is up in lights on January 19th. Rae joins me to celebrate at Fabiolus Italian Cucina, followed by an enchanting silent movie experience, *The Artist,* at the ArcLight. We both leave infatuated with the French lead, Monsieur Jean Dujardin, who is only heard speaking once and en Français, si'l vous plait, at the very end of the picture, proving that the less said the better when it comes to romancing the ladies.

By the end of January, I am not beheaded for blasphemy nor arrested for indecency nor sued for defamation of character, and not one hungry unemployed screenwriter has written to me on *Facebook*. The latter is of great disappointment, as I had fantasized that I would allow him to write the book-to-movie screenplay in my basement, while making mad love to me between scenes. Thrown out of his studio apartment at the Alto Nido at the top of Ivar, his car repossessed, he would be grateful that a punctilious paramour saved him from a miserable life on the streets. When I would eventually catch him cheating with a twenty-three-year-old hookup, I would march him the one block down to the Park and Recreation Olympic-size swimming pool, where I would shoot him in the back, his dream of making a big splash in Hollywood realized. When the police arrived soon after, I would be ready for my close up.

As luck would have it, Hound has begun chewing on the cancerous skin tag that's been hanging from his right-rear ankle for years, leaving trace amounts of blood on his bed and blanket. He's unable to eat without being handfed, yet the thrill of picking at the dangling sore with his teeth has his spastic head under control. Dr. Hu is notified and I bring him in to have the bloody thing removed. She is still dumbfounded as to a cure for Hound's neurological impairment. I return at five-thirty to fetch a disoriented dog that smells like a hospital ward doused with Iodoform antiseptic, his leg wrapped in a two hundred dollar bandage.

On Day no. 44 of no smoke, Hound and I whiz through the McDonald's drive thru leaving with an Angus cheeseburger combo and two dry hamburgers. Both orders come with fries and a diet Coke, which can only be tolerated when mixed with rum. Sitting on the living room floor, I share the bounty, while sobbing through tonight's DVD torture tool, *Chéri,* another lace-and-snuff period piece tragedy, which hits too close to home. I suffer along with the characters as I watch the destruction of the one perfect love, never to be found again, between two people born too many years apart; a beautiful older woman and her eighteen-year-old lover, who continually broods while obnoxiously calling her the pet name of *Nounoune* over and over again.

A bit tipsy, I put us all to bed, but not before tidying up the kitchen, the living room, and Windexing the bathroom mirror; I am a drunk, not a slob.

At Vine Elementary, after destroying another Dr. Seuss leftist morality tale, I share with Mr. Taylor my need and desire to quit drinking, because of the calories, of course.

"You must come with me to my AA meeting. Anytime! I have not had alcohol, drugs, nicotine—nothing for twenty-four years." Guessing his current weight at a hefty three hundred and some pounds, I am sure he's abusing something to calm his nerves.

The house smelling like the training ground for an infectious disease, I strap on the running shoes and boldly head up stream to the gym.

The top of my hair is held in a clip, the remainder bopping over and under a blue cotton kerchief wound tightly about my head to keep the forthcoming deluge of salty sweat from getting into my eyes. My prehistoric Walkman fearlessly strapped to my left upper arm, I set down the old lady bag that holds my phone and house keys, because I refuse to pay for a locker. Suspecting that one hundred and one youthful eyes are judging my every clumsy move, I place my feet on the gray rubber of the elliptical and with Cher screaming, "Baby, It's All or Nothing" into my ears from the tape cassette, I'm off. Three hundred calories burned and my toes inflamed, I move to the stationary bike for another miserable two-hundred-calorie Tour de France spectacle.

Over my head at each agonizing station is a screen bearing down on me tuned always to mainstream media, never Republican-friendly *Fox News*. President Obama is talking again, but thankfully there is no sound. A stenographer locked in a room somewhere is stroking out by way of computer-assisted transcription the closed captioning which runs across the bottom of the picture.

> An economy built to last, where hard work pays off and responsibility is rewarded.

Well, I can certainly agree with that. But what's the catch?

> We can either settle for a country where a shrinking number of people do really well, while a growing number of Americans barely get by.

Maybe they're not working hard enough.

> Or we can restore an economy where everyone gets a fair shot, everyone does their fair share, and everyone plays by the same set of rules.

Oops, *fair share*? Sounds like socialism to me. How much of what I earn must go to those that don't earn? Why can't they play torturous, violent sexually explicit rap music videos instead of *CNN*, so that I don't get riled up during my workout? I hate coming to the gym.

Marketing my first book, dressed as an author in a conservative black jacket, I bravely walk into Book Soup, a locally acclaimed, really cool bookstore on Sunset Boulevard way out in West, West Hollywood. I've brought with me a picture of the billboard in lights over Fabiola's Cuchina, several bookmarks, and two copies of *The Year I Learned to Text*. To my surprise, they take them, asking me to sign them. They are placed in the window under the designation of *Local Authors*. Waiting a respectable number of days, I send over two friends, one after the other, to purchase them in the hope that Book Soup, reeling from their instant popularity, will buy a dozen more. Book Soup never contacts me as to the sale of my complimentary novels. I am now out the wholesale cost of two books and the forty-two dollars I gave to my friends to buy them. In 2013, upon the publication of Part 2, Book Soup will order more books in the trilogy directly from Ingram, the wholesaler for book retailers. I am not involved and receive through my self-publisher four dollars in royalties. There is a means to my madness.

I continued the marketing madness by mailing copies of Part One to producers, actors, and to top literary agencies. I knew I had reached a level of success when Creative Artists Agency actually spent four dollars and ninety-seven cents to mail the book back to me in a very nicely padded manila envelope along with a letter. The letter implied that they did not accept unsolicited materials, that they had not read the book, and that any similar characters, plots, or subplots that might make their way onto the big screen any time soon would not be of their doing or of any of their associates.

Day no. 60 of no smoke, I sit down to write yet another love scene and I balk. I walk to the fridge and stare in. Dazed, nothing tantalizes me. I pour a drink. I sit back down. I cannot write. My concentration is muddled. My diagnosis is *ADHD*: Addled, Dumb, Horny, and Dopey. I can't take the depression one minute longer. I am like that old tree in the forest that falls when there's no one around to hear the thud. If Julie has a cigarette, will anyone really care?

Controlling my weakness, I walk quickly by the Smoke Shack conveniently located one block east at Fountain and Vine and pick up my pace almost into a staggering jog and head steadfast to Trader Joe's for sweet Moscato wine, knowing that if I make it passed the liquor store on my way back down, I will surely stop at the Smoke Shack, where, indeed, I do and discover that they are well-stocked with Virginia Slims, and the Armenian fellow gives me a free lighter.

By midnight, it's back in. I feel great. I smoked twelve cigarettes in four hours. I hit the pillow totally normal, satisfied, and at peace.

The following day I write three pages of hilarious chick-lit, visit the gym in a turquoise blue head scarf, pedal away four hundred and eighty-five calories, and strut the one mile to Trader Joe's, where I meet another candidate for post elective surgery, weight-loss coitus.

As the clerk fills a brown handled bag with two bottles of wine and two yogurt containers, in the checkout line immediately behind me a slight man with skinny bare legs bobs a full head of blond hair in my direction. I sneak a peek and quickly digest the statistics; fifty-something, clear blue eyes, broad shouldered, and square jawed. We make eye contact and he tosses me a quick *hello*. Still dripping from my Herculean efforts at 24 Hour Fitness and my stellar six-block speed walk, I disappear out the front door.

Heading home, I am stopped at a light on Vine, when I spy a man across the street walking in the same direction. Dressed in tailored black shorts and a freely flying black collared shirt, swinging two brown paper bags, he sets one down and he waves at me. Candidate no. 6 has caught up with me. I acknowledge him with a bit of a nod and continue on when the light turns green. My head high and my nose in the air, I glimpse his way while cautiously traversing glitches in the sidewalk, which may at any moment send me hurling to my death. The man seems to have an odd gate, his thin white legs descending into rather large black leather loafers. He's not wearing socks. My fourth husband did not wear socks with his loafers, although his loafers were half the size of this man's. But if I discount every man that dresses similarly to my ex-husbands, I'm not opening up; I'm never going to find him, the replacement and the perfect foot for my glass slipper.

Carefully descending another rise in the concrete path, sneaking another peek, I realize I have seen this guy before performing in the *Nutcracker* on PBS, fluttering in and out of positions in a mean brisé devant. Is it the world's only straight ballerina, Mikhail Baryshnikov? I walk faster and he—yes, he leaps into the air to keep up with me. This is Hollywood, so why not a celebrity sighting? Nah, this guy is not five-foot-six, Julie. He's at least five-foot-ten.

At the light at Fountain, I must cross over to get home. At the end of my plucky, yet casual, walk across Vine, he is there, his chassée halted in midair by the red light. He puts down his two bags. "Hi, I'm Carey Kowalski."

"Hi, I'm Julie."

Carey is too eager to tell me that he lives mostly at his spacious log cabin on the coastal plains of Carmel, but dabbles in flipping real estate here in Los Angeles, and since retiring from the Los Angeles Unified School District as an educator has kept a small apartment just a few blocks down the street on Lillian Way. He is surprised he has not seen me before, as his daily routine is to walk the neighborhood to accomplish mundane errands rather than to drive.

I share nothing, but do hand him my real estate card, which includes pertinent information, as in my cell phone number.

Studying my card, he compliments, "You're prettier in person. The tan and the heartiness."

"I have a tan? Shoot, I'm supposed to stay out of the sun."

Candidate no. 6 comes in at a close second, a photo finish, with what Mr. Baryshnikov might bring to the table: Cary has retirement income, investment income, a house, an apartment, a car, and he wears nothing on the ring finger of his left hand. Whether or not he can catch me as I leap from a pirouette is still up in the air. Mother is going to be thrilled.

I lead him off point and to stop his begging and whining, I allow him to walk me home, where he swoons over the bungalow's interesting Euro vive and the unpretentious gate, all from the sidewalk, of course. Pressuring me that he might need a cup of sugar some stormy night, he asks if it would be all right to call or text me.

"Certainly. Come by any time. The doorbell is inside the gate here on the wall."

"I'm here now."

"I have to write tonight, Cary."

"You're a writer. Wow."

"See you soon."

I have retirement income, two mortgages, a car, and I wear nothing on the ring finger of my left hand. Although I doubt my right knee is going to allow me to leap into his arms, it seems like everything is coming up roses for the both of us.

Too soon, the text messages began rolling in.

> Saturday, February 11, 2012; 6:40p CARY: You made today special with your beautiful smile. Thank you!
> 6:42p JULIE: Have a good night.
> 6:43p CARY: Glad you caught up with me! You are spectacular-What a beautiful lady!!!! So nice! ☺

Beware of men who use happy faces in the very beginning of a relationship or ever.

> 6:45p JULIE: I think ur pretty cute too.

I reviewed my checklist, copied and pasted below, from *Red Flags of Lovefraud*, a new book by Donna Anderson, which I had purchased to protect my fragile libido from falling for yet another sociopathic charmer. Let's see how smooth Cary fairs so far.

> If your new romantic interest exhibits all or most of the following behaviors, be careful. He or she might be a sociopath.
>
> 1. **Charisma and charm.** They're smooth talkers, always have an answer, never miss a beat. They seem to be very exciting.
> 2. **Enormous ego.** They act like the smartest, richest or most successful people around. They may actually come out and tell you that.

3. **Overly attentive.** They call, text and e-mail constantly. They want to be with you every moment. They resent time you spend with your family and friends.
4. **Jekyll and Hyde personality.** One minute they love you; the next minute they hate you. Their personality changes like flipping a switch.
5. **Blame others.** Nothing is ever their fault. They always have an excuse. Someone else causes their problems.
6. **Lies and gaps in the story.** You ask questions, and the answers are vague. They tell stupid lies. They tell outrageous lies. They lie when they'd make out better telling the truth.
7. **Intense eye contact.** Call it the predatory stare. If you get a chill down your spine when they look at you, pay attention.
8. **Move fast.** They quickly proclaim that you're their true love and soul mate. They want to move in together or get married quickly.
9. **Pity play.** They appeal to your sympathy. They want you to feel sorry for their abusive childhood, psychotic ex, incurable disease or financial setbacks.
10. **Sexual magnetism.** If you feel intense attraction, if your physical relationship is unbelievable, it may be their excess testosterone.

Donna Andersen, author of Love Fraud
@ lovefraud.com

Cary seems to have mastered no. 1, no. 2, and no. 3 on the list. I shall keep my eyes and ears wide open.

 7:45p CARY: Cute? How nice! You feel very nice to be next to. Would you like me to come visit you?

No, I want to be asked out on a date. Looking at the calendar, he has just three more days to play cupid and save me from eating an entire box of heart-shaped chocolates alone.

7:47p JULIE: Yes, sometime. That would be nice.
7:52p CARY: LET ME KNOW WHEN YOU'D LIKE COMPANY!!

The next day is floor duty at Overpriced Homes Realty, where I finish up my four hours signing up the Turkish Consulate to receive The Multi-Listing Service auto-notifications of inexpensive condos in pricy Westwood for his daughter, an impossible real estate venture. His stint on American soil is coming to an end, but he will be leaving one of his many Muslim children in attendance at U.C.L.A. to receive her American government-funded education. While he shares his pride in his politically active daughter's participation in the Muslim Student Association, I bite my lip until it bleeds.

I return home by way of CVS juggling a sixteen-pack of Charmin to find that a dozen roses in clear plastic tied with a red bow have been tossed over the gate and onto the porch. The phone immediately rings. It's Cary making sure I found the roses and have dutifully put them in water.

"I need to go to Rite Aid, so I thought I'd swing by," he suggests.

The poor guy is doing everything right, although I did notice that he seemed a bit hunched over last evening. We can work on our mutual slouched postures together, perhaps by sweating our way through the sexual acrobatics of the *Kama Sutra*, the ancient art of making love using mind and soul in the complete enjoyment of the five senses and, of course, exploring the mystique of the female clitoris.

"If you live on Lillian Way, the parking lot of CVS is certainly closer than Rite Aid. Why don't you go there?"

"I wanted to come by and see you."

Christ, be a grown up, Julie. Not every man that has a score of three out of ten on the *Red Flags* list is a nut case. "Okay, for a moment. I need to write tonight."

Cary must have been on his way already, because in two minutes he is ringing the doorbell while I'm on the toilet realizing I've left the paper supply on the porch. I shake off, Listerine my tobacco tongue, and check my lipstick in the mirror of the medicine chest.

I open the gate for him and with two ardent strides up the porch stairs, Cary is sweeping up the four-by-four pack of Charmin double rolls and heading into the house.

"No, please!" I stop him cold, retrieve the toilet paper and with one hand shuck the package onto the living room floor, pointing him to his seat on the porch with the other. It is six-thirty and dark. I light some candles, ask him if he wants something to drink, a glass of wine, a cocktail.

He sanctimoniously holds up his bottle of water. "I have my drink."

Never trust a man who turns down alcohol, unless he's performing open-heart surgery within the next two hours. Again, my fourth husband popped into my head, his irritating teetotaler expression, *I'll have a water shooter,* the laughing stock of every social occasion. Stop comparing apples to oranges and give this guy a chance. Okay, nothing for me either. It's always best to stay clear-headed during the initial psychoanalysis.

As this extremely intense blue-eyed blond leans into me as far as he can over the round glass-top table, I am uncomfortable. I counter attack with a delving and daring question. "Any kids?"

"No, but I was married once. I work part-time as an administrator in curriculum for LAUSD. I'm here for a symposium on troubled youth and street art."

"Don't you mean thugs and graffiti?"

"We don't use that kind of language at the school district."

Funny, on our first meeting, he was a right-wing capitalist here in L.A. flipping houses for profit and now he's touting liberal views on the ruination of underprivileged inner city gangsters. Cary was going through the *Red Flags of Lovefraud* faster than I could keep up. Sensing my uneasiness, he wisely rose to excuse himself. He, too, was out of toilet paper. He didn't inquire anything of me, but pulled me in for a hug without knowing I'd been happily married four times, gave birth to three children, did not vote for Obama, and was not currently up for the *Mother of the Year* award.

Cary stayed too long with his arms wrapped about my waist, my arms having automatically grasped his broad shoulders. I was glad to see him go.

> 6:51p CARY: It's all so beautiful! The simple way you live! The way you tenderly care for your little house! Thanks for the hugs!!

He is most definitely going to wear out that abused punctuation mark.

> 9:49p JULIE: Wrote an entire scene. The billboard for my novel @ Sunset & Vine over my fave Italian restaurant. Nice shoulders. Sweet dreams.
> Monday, February 13, 2012; 4:59am CARY: Which restaurant? Yes, strong shoulders to hold you ☺
> 9:06a JULIE: Fabiolus on Sunset. The Italian owner is from Verona. I am still in bed reading, as I was awakened by your text message at 5am and didn't fall back to sleep until 6am. Thank goodness I am parked in all day parking!
> 2:01p JULIE: My roses still scent-smell and I am cleaning out my desk drawer. Out with the old and in with the new.

And unlike Mother, who as a child lived through the scrimping years of *The Depression* only pretends to clean out her drawers, I spent the afternoon chucking out leaky pens, caked bottles of white correction fluid, and unhooking paperclips from each other. The underarm hair and the court steno *COPY* stamp are staying put.

> 5:50p CARY: Hi, love!! Reservation for dinner at Fabiolus 5:30 Tuesday. Can you make it? Let me know. Nice to see you!!!!!
> 5:54p JULIE: You're wonderful. Shall we walk to dinner?

I just wanted to be kind. Although this new friendship seemed to be ripening a bit early, no. 8 on the *Red Flags* list, Cary was doing all the right things.

6:35p   CARY: You're wonderful, too, and I am happy that you can go. Walking is good. See you 5:15, ok? Have a loving heart. I like you very much and feel happy in your arms. ☺ See you tomorrow. You are beautiful. PS: In meetings now, sorry can't call. Love and Hugs
6:38p   CARY: Glad I went to Trader Joe's and met you!!!!!!!!!!!!

Yee gads.

6:39p   CARY: Happy that you caught up to me. XOXO
10:23p JULIE: If it's raining, can you pick me up?

Today's schedule should keep me out of trouble: the weekly early-morning office meeting, a private showing of an elitist condominium at the Cahuenga Tennis Club, the usual Tuesday broker's caravan to view new million dollar listings, home for a cigarette and a bite, then a quick swing into a spa chair on Melrose just off Vine for a mani-pedi.

Today they're pushing a cherry red polish labeled *My Valentine*, which I okay for all twenty, even though ten will be buried in leather, and wish Ali would text me asking to "come by" so that I can end this novel. There are no tears today. Have I stopped crying in the nail parlor?

Home again, trying not to smudge a nail, I plug in the hot rollers and go to work on my hair. Applying a fresh swash of makeup, in the bathroom mirror I can see him just beyond the bathroom door resting his weary congested head on my bed pillows, watching me get ready for him, in this whirlwind of the nine-to-five working girl recovery. He is gone as I cross to slide open the closet.

Dressed in my go-to long, black and flirty double-knit pantsuit with its supple fake fur collar—a twenty dollar find from Ross Dress For Less—the flared pants falling over walk-about flat leather boots, I'm ready to be saintly seductive. A spray of COCO Mademoiselle by Chanel to my wrists, a pair of small rhinestone earrings inserted, I shoot innocent cupid in the foot by accessorizing with the red heart shaped *Kiss Me* pin. I am asking for it.

4:53p   CARY: Excited to see you in a few minutes!!!!!!!!

I am surprised his explanation point works at all.

4:54p JULIE: Me too.
4:55p CARY: Can I come now?
4:55p JULIE: Yes.
4:56p CARY: Five minutes.
4:57p JULIE: Slow down. Don't hurt yourself.

Here he comes ladies and gentlemen, the man I've been waiting for all of my life: Candidate no. 6.

Leading fervently with his stooped head, Cary slumps by passing the front gate, but quickly rebounds and spins around clumsily to return. I can see through the metal grating that his legs are bowed and his back is curved. Between those two masculine shoulders is a hump? I reflect on my first sighting of him as the striding dark figure with the dancer's legs gracefully gliding down Vine Street, the love theme from Tchaikovsky's *Swan Lake* playing in my head, and succumb to the fact that once again I have projected my needs and desires on an unsuspecting stranger. Julie, if it looks like a duck, walks like a duck, and quacks like a duck, let it be; it's a damned duck.

Has the poor man endured a neck injury of some kind? Is the poor man racked with osteoarthritis? Could this dreadful spell cast upon him of ill health and deformity be improved, if I am pure in heart and pledge to love him no matter how horribly buckled and bowed this ugly duckling may be? To whom can I turn to for substantive advice on these matters? Certainly not the good Dr. Hu, who is unable to cure the sudden onset of miniscule neurological deficiencies debilitating my own dog. Alone to reconnoiter the situation, I ponder. Obviously, I should be wearing the purity of white this evening to show my true colors of loving intent, but white would disclose my every bouncing bubble and rollicking roll, the corset having been dismissed to make room for pasta and polenta.

I lock the gate behind us. I'm on the street in the final hour of daylight with a man in a boxy over-sized tailored black shirt loosed over crisp blue jeans and pointed black leather boots. Taking him in now more closely, Cary really is quite handsome. He has a square jaw, light lovely blue eyes, healthy bold white teeth, and a full head of blond hair laced with gray. But he can hardly walk. What I had perceived from four lanes away as a man with a jaunty stride is now a man tripping over his own two feet. For the first time in my life, I slow down for a man, a hunched and bowlegged man, who knows exactly how to dress to minimize his deformities. During our short time together, Alexander's six-foot-five father had marched willfully ahead of me without any empathy for my high heels. The one time I demanded that he slow down and walk beside me, he cast off my sordid plea with a wave of his arm and instructed me to walk faster. The divorce came soon after.

Cary's curvature, taken as part of what might be a delightful package, does not offend me, as I, too, have begun to develop a bit of a postural defect, pronounced by the excess fat at the base of my neck, which is why I continue to grow my hair, its hopeful destination reaching below my shoulders. My pious acceptance of Cary's malformation put aside, he then begins to speak, undoubtedly as they all do.

"I've just returned from an exciting ski trip with friends in the Alps. We rented an awesome chalet. I had a marvelous time," he boasts. "Do you ski?" His intensity and the irritating throb in his forehead instantly beat me down into an admittedly withering frazzle of jetsetter athletic disappointment.

"Skied very little in my forties. Just up in Big Bear and once in Mammoth, and then gave it up. I have a tricky right knee now."

He stares in awe at each jewel of my unrehearsed words. It's as if his two piercing blue eyes have been captured, dilated, and secured by a phantom ophthalmologist into the death grip of a glaucoma testing apparatus, frozen in suspense awaiting the sudden poof of air, which will scare the bejeezus out of him.

"And that jump off the chair lift at the top is absolutely frightening," I remembered.

Without blinking, his eyebrows arched in awe. "You don't have to be afraid anymore. I can teach you. We could be wonderful together on the slopes, by the fireside, and cuddled under a down comforter."

I am weakened by his forward vision of our winter wonderland of togetherness somewhere in Switzerland. Unable to resist his forthcoming declaration of premature adulation, "You're simply lovely," I take his hand. He squeezes, smiles, and we continue as a couple to Vine Street. And then in front of the Mary Pickford Center for Motion Picture Study he whirls about, his arms thrust into the air triumphantly crossing the finish line, and reads aloud my silly holiday lapel pin to an elderly unwashed bag lady pushing her wheelchair, a cigar dangling from her curled lips. "Kiss Me!" he points out to her his license to slobber as she grumbles nonsensically away in horror.

He pulled me up and in and pressed his lips to mine, his arms caging me. Then he snuck out the slithering snake, flicking its curled venomous tongue. No fireworks here, ladies and gentlemen; not even a legal sparkler; a glowworm that won't light, perhaps. I stayed hinged to his wet, gurgling mouth, because it was Valentine's Day. I was being kind and pure of heart, although my hope of reinventing him as a total swan had been quashed; being that there is no cure for a bad kisser. My depth as a rescuer has become extremely shallow, yet sustainable for short periods of wasted precious time when Chianti, sour dough bread, and pesto dipping sauce are my rewards. But if he tickles my uvula, I'm going to vomit.

Coming up for a gasp of air, he continued his oration, as I discreetly wiped saliva from the corners of my mouth. "Oh, this is all so terrific. Meeting a pretty lady who is pleasant and open, and she's actually joining me for dinner...and on such a special day, a day reserved for lovers only."

"You know, when you caught my attention the other day on our walk down Vine, you seemed as light and gay as a professional dancer." If I can keep him talking and walking at the same time, I could get us to Fabiolus without another slobber attack.

"Oh, no, I can't dance. I have scoliosis, abnormal curvature of the spine. It doesn't affect my balance. I've just never had any rhythm whatsoever."

As if the Japanese had suddenly surrendered and he'd been let off the ship, he mauled me at the streetlight in front of the chain link construction fence protecting the empty lot of the demolished Kentucky

Fried Chicken. He tongue fucked me at the stoplight on Sunset and Vine outside the busy Bank of America ATM stations. In the crosswalk I let him kiss me over and over again. How could I not? The poor man has curvature of the spine. I would not be so cruel as to crush his spirited romantic reveling, not today of all days. As he lathered up and lay another one on me, the repeated sensation was reminiscent of the translucent sushi I was urged to taste, the snails I surrendered to only once after consuming large amounts of vodka, and the one slither of oysters on the half shell I succumbed to at Rae's urging, the sight alone initiating a gag reflex.

We walked past the Bodega Wine Bar, the dark lounge venue of our Islam-style wedding dinner celebration a lifetime ago, when a young Latina waitress remarked on how cute we were together, and then, of course, gave Ali her cell phone number under a ruse of some kind.

I pointed up to the billboard over Fabiolus. "The idea was to get me arrested or sued by the Muslim Brotherhood or at least the ACLU."

"How can you afford to put up a billboard? Maybe you should be paying for dinner."

"Cary, I don't allow anyone to talk to me in that way, except my youngest child."

When asked by the maître 'd under which name the reservation had been made, he answered, "Cary Christian." Kowalski, perhaps, was too difficult to spell out over the phone. When asked if we'd like something to drink, wine by the glass, coffee, Cary stared off into space. I answered brightly and stubbornly, "The house Chianti, please."

Cary arose from the arrogant silence of his deathbed. "Okay, yes. I'll have a little something too."

"Wine, sir?" asked the harried waiter, the restaurant filled to capacity with early diners eager to get the responsibility of a holiday dinner out of the way, their favorite television shows calling them home.

He tugged at his collar and winced.

"The Chianti is very nice," I assured my smug, anti-social former ballet dancer, who had gone from elated romantic idiot to indifferent diner the moment we entered the restaurant. Receiving no formal approval from Carey, I said, "He'll have a glass also," because I would most definitely be downing it.

At a patio table for four, he moved his wooden armchair awkwardly into my space, forcing my neck to painfully crook to the left. We toasted, but he didn't take one sip. Instead the Saint Valentine of *Public Displays of Affection* came in again and wet my lips with the slippery eel. How anyone surrounding us could enjoy his or her deep fried calamari under this circumstance is Italian Hollywood history. He talked about his ability to know a person by examining their habits, how women who smoke are not sexy and didn't I agree?

"My next trip is extreme white water rafting on the Corhu River in Turkey, when the snow melts in May. My die hard fanatical friends at it again."

Julie, you certainly must have something extreme to talk about. Pull something theatrical out of your hat.

"Did you see the movie *Valentine's Day*? I was in that movie."

"Yes, I did. Would I have seen you? Which part did you play?"

"A soccer mom. Just my right arm in a blue sweater made the cut."

"Oh."

"So, Cary, how long have you been divorced?" I asked gently, wiping my lips of white mushroom sauce.

"I'm NOT divorced!" he shrieked, pushing violently away from the table, as if I'd asked him how long he had been impotent. Apparently, a switch had been flipped, as in *Red Flag* no. 4.

"Oh, I see…" *I was married once*, he had said on the porch, never explaining his single status.

"She DIED," the widower exclaimed and swiftly rose from his chair, standing over me ready to strike. The audience silenced.

"Silenzioso. Control yourself, sir," Fabi rushed from out of nowhere to protect the dinner plates, his restaurant's reputation, and me.

"Please sit down, Cary." I reached out to touch his hand.

He slumped back down to pout, like a punished child. The clatter and chatter of diners began again.

Still determined to enjoy my free dinner, I kept cool and the actress took top billing with, "I'm so sorry. She must have been young. How long ago? How did it happen?"

"Five years now. Breast Cancer."

"What was her name?"

Oh, his body language was bad, very bad.

"Well, Cary, if we're going to be friends, it would be awkward not to know her name."

"Anne." I did not inquire as to one *N* or two.

"And she didn't smoke, drink, or eat badly. She wasn't anything like you. She was a vegetarian, an athlete. She was in the Olympics."

"Please pull yourself together," I suggested to the duck. "And how is it you know that I smoke?" I thought.

Draped over his spaghetti and Chicken Parmesan, he ate Euro-continental style, shoveling, stabbing, and forking, both elbows on the table. I ate like a baby bird of my polenta and cream sauce. I drained the two comforting glasses of wine. I finished with a bad taste in my mouth. Food tastes much better when you don't feel that you owe someone something for it.

"Come here, I want you to see something." After retrieving his charge card, he grabs my hand and leads me to the patio passageway connecting the boy and girl restrooms and catches me off guard with a darting marinara French kiss mixing violently with my residual wine and cream sauce. I rush ahead of him all the way home, delaying the final assault.

As I aim the key into the lock, he catches up. From behind his arms swirl about me. His crotch forcing my hips into the gate, he buries his nose into my furry neck. I push him off and quickly open the gate, banging his outstretched arms.

Unfazed, the switch toggles on and off. "Aren't we going in so we can kiss on your couch?"

"No, Cary, we're not," I confirmed and switched the deadbolt.

When the coast was clear, I took the dogs one by one down the front steps and into the courtyard, where I smoked a much-earned cigarette.

I changed into satin pajama bottoms and sweatshirt, poured a glass of wine, and with my family huddled at my feet, I sat down in front of the television and hoped for an HGTV renovation adventure in Tuscany.

8:17p   CARY: Sweet kisses. Sweet dreams.
8:22p   CARY: Kisses for you anytime. Text me anytime.

The only text I would be sending was to Alexander, who had wished me well today, her hope for a successful first date relieving her of Valentine's Day single-parent guilt. The excitement over a date with a stranger had kept me from calling my single Mother today. My own guilt would have to continue until tomorrow morning when I would call. It was late; she was probably soaking in her tub of three-day-old water.

> 8:07p   JULIE: Cary is a wacko who has been kissing me block after block. I had to peel him off me at the gate. Please bring my terrorist back to me!
>
> 8:46p   ALEXANDRA: The terrorist made you an emotional wreck…to the point where I barely recognized my own mother. Remember, anyone who makes you feel terrible, less than, or desperate isn't worth your time. Although you might have Oxytocin exploding like fireworks, the toll it takes on you and your daughter isn't worth it.

I'm thrilled to see that my first novel has had a lasting effect on her, but why is it always about her?

> 8:49p   JULIE: Cary is not a nice man nor is he any fun.
> 9:31p   ALEXANDRA: Cary sounds like a dick.
> 9:32p   JULIE: I don't think Cary has a dick, dear.
> 9:55p   ALEXANDRA: Which is why he overcompensates.
> 9:57p   JULIE: He became smarmy very quickly. He also ate slumped over a trough. And he's a bad kisser.
> 9:57p   ALEXANDRA: And we all know there's no cure for that.

Unfortunately, I had broken Romance Rule no. 1: never pee where you eat. I would continue to bump into Cary on the street and be treated to his extreme vacation tales for years to come. He never asked me out again.

Chapter 42

Dog Shit and Playing God

> ♪ Will you still love me
> When I'm 64? ♪
>
> *Sgt. Pepper's Lonely Heart Club Band*
> Lennon-McCartney

"Can you make it to dinner this Friday? Vivian is in town to visit her boys and Benjamin and I would like you to join the three of us for dinner."

Spinning my wheels in a slippery trough of real estate obligations that go nowhere, screaming obscenities at impolite imbeciles as I defensively drive to auditions in vain, handling two dogs that can barely walk, and now I'm going to meet Alexandra's new mother.

When Alex and I arrive at the Restaurante Ago on Melrose Place, Benjamin and Vivian are at the bar. She smiled and took my hand. "Oh, you're here. We've just ordered drinks and now our table is ready. We'll ask to have the drinks brought to the table."

She's a delicate woman, a brunette who could pass for my twin, but for her lack of excessive midriff bulge, ten years less wear and tear, and an apparent docile disposition.

Dining on the indoor patio under massive canvas tarps, the candles and heat lamps set our faces aglow, with the help of chilled dirty vodka martinis all around. Vivian orders extra ice, she explains to keep the drinks chilled and make them last longer. I cautiously sip, knowing this is not the time to become drunk and disorderly. The kids watch curiously the exchange.

How is your next book going? Ah, real estate? I dabbled at my husband's company until the late night calls wore me thin. Your neck lift? Oh, I had mine done in my forties and I'm still wincing from nerve damage. Love your outfit. I've spent the day shopping on Rodeo and couldn't find a thing. The designers don't have a clue.

"Mom shops at Ross Dress for Less. She finds the best pieces there."
"I've seen the ads, but I've never shopped there."
I fluffed up the fake fur on my black pantsuit. "Bought this suit eight years ago for twenty bucks."
"No, you did not."
"Yes, I did. But you have to go in weekly to catch the good stuff. I'm sure that even Santa Barbara has a Ross," and that you would run in horror from the nasty dressing rooms.
"So you really had sex with a Muslim?" Vivian delved with a sweet, sincere interest.
"Ah, I have a book mark for you and I'm sure Alex will lend you the first book. In Part Two, you'll learn a lot more about the Muslims, their desire to take us over, sort of an *Islam 101 for Dummies.*"
Suddenly Benjamin is up for a debate. "I really don't think Muslims are trying to take over anybody or anything."
"What about France, where the Muslims are all on welfare with four wives and twenty kids? And those twenty kids will each have twenty more. Why, in fifty years they will vote Sharia Law in and tear down the evil Eiffel Tower."
"Yes, I agree," came a quiet insertion from Vivian.
The menu arrives and I'm out of my element. Not one noodle is titled simply *spaghetti,* but intimidating choices such as *Spaghetti allo Scoglio* and *Spaghetti e Polpette.* I insist that Benjamin order for us. We began with appetizers of baby artichoke Frisée with shaved Parmesan and baked octopus with potatoes and cherry tomatoes in lemon dressing.
"These two have got me trying all kinds of weird stuff. You too?"
"I've never been out to dinner with them," I dropped the bomb.
Benjamin ordered another round.

Parked in front of Alexandra's townhouse to fetch my car, apparently the ice in the vodka hit me.

" Sorry that I brought it up."

"Mom, I've lost you. Ever since he came into your life, you've changed." Tears flowed during this conversation, which seems to be constantly repeating itself. "I don't want to lose you. I want to be close —not close friends, of course."

"Alex, you never return my texts unless it's to notify me when to drive you to the airport."

"I just can't be around you anymore."

"Wow! I'm glad I didn't catch cancer. What do you want me to say? How do you want me to *act*?"

"I'm sorry, but you wrote the book. Why isn't it over?"

"Because he did something to me. He *sociopathed* me."

"No. He *psychopathed* you."

"You feel guilty because I'm alone? I would have stayed with your father, but he didn't love me. How are the two love birds, anyway?"

Oops, my mother is in the car.

"They are not *together*. They just share a home."

"For twenty years?"

"Dad has gout. He doesn't take care of himself. He drinks milk and eats meat three times a day. Last week I met him in the emergency room whaling like a baby."

And as I pulled away from the curb, I had a big smile on my face.

Spring has sprung and today I'm sixty-four. Rae has planned a combined birthday celebration for her son Tommy and me, but today is mine to spend all alone and in any way I see fit. So I take in a movie in an empty theatre and sit in back below the projection room. Munching wet, salty popcorn, slurping an icy diet Coke, I remember again our first date—which is, of course, the reason I have come—when he massaged my hand, suggested a first kiss to relax me, and when I kindly refused, surprised me with a preview of his overblown, testosterone exploding sexuality by placing my buttered hand onto the hardness of his camel corduroy slacks.

Still miserably bonded to an immature man who became erect simply by watching Clint Eastwood pop a can of Pabst Blue Ribbon, I shivered at my irrational need to be desired that brought a charming sociopath into my home, into my life, and into my heart. Still sensing his presence, his unaltered body odor, during the previews I begin tearing up.

*　*　*

Washing the dogs once a week has become routine, as I can only afford the grooming fee of seventy-five dollars for two dogs in tandem every other month. Additionally, after eight years of customer loyalty, Hound has been blackballed by the Korean shop as an invalid dog that lets go without warning in the tub, is unable to stand up for the length of the trimming process, and should be put to sleep. Until the warmth of summer, when the cold water from the garden hose is refreshing, I must bathe Hound inside.

As his assisted-care nurse, I hike him over and into a drawn bathtub of warm frothy water, pull the curtain tight, aiming the shower spray and spurting the dog shampoo; I in shorts and an old t-shirt, Hound naked as a jaybird, his hair thinning and gray. Unable to get out on his own, I lift him up and over, his weight doubled when wet, onto the bathroom floor readied with hair dye stained towels to catch the after-bath shaky shakes and any surprise, uncontrollable accident. His thin legs trembling, he lies there in perfect submission while I enjoy treating him to a good old-fashioned rub down. He might not be able to walk straight, but he can be a well-groomed cripple.

Brute tolerates the kitchen sink hosing. I use the word *tolerates*, because the darling dog has never bit me during the ten-minute chore I've been successfully carrying out for over ten years. When one has a small breed dog, one must have a spray nozzle at the faucet. Through the entire ordeal of emasculating baby shampoo lathering, my insensitive attempts at drowning him, the spurting of hot water to his anus, and the use of waterboarding to clean out the gunk in his eyes, Brute snorts and tries his darnedest to wriggle free. Surely, President Obama will have me arrested for torture soon enough. Wrapped in soft terry cloth,

I carry him gently and securely to the bathroom sink to be blown dry. This is our bonding time, our cuddle time. This is the rare time given me to whisper sweet nothings into his agitated ears and sing ♪ How Much Is That Doggie in the Window? ♪ while I tickle a Q-tip into each pink canal, which has the wild one smiling.

And there's a smile on my face, too. Doggie doo-doo baby talk, my nose nuzzling his fluff, his paws fighting me off, this is our special time, when he can't wait to be on the floor and heading to a throw rug to scratch his ears and roll out his princely, aristocratic crown of glory.

Like a zookeeper, I spend the mornings and afternoons spraying down the brick pathway, sending massive globs of loose strangely yellow bowel movements into the ivy. And dear, sickly Hound continues to lose weight.

The big day arrives: Rae's not so secretively arranged *surprise* birthday gathering for me at her loft-style condo in Glendale. In an email she had asked for the contact information of a few people that liked me enough to drive out of Hollywood into the Armenian capitol of California for free artfully prepared food, a full array of spirits, and frivolity. I had sent her the short list: two gay male realtors, one a token African American and one a flaming Hispanic; Stephen, my gay actor, writer, and creative teammate; and my two steadfast girlfriends, Beryl and Randi. I would have enjoyed having Captain Brainard there, but the fear of my daughter Alex being trapped against the kitchen sink with tales of his F-14 *Tomcat* aircraft blowing up Muslims in *Desert Storm*, and how, after a grueling two hours and forty-five minutes, he had almost lost his wrist whipping a frigid woman into a clitoral climax stopped me from sharing his name or number.

Randi let the surprise cat out of the bag by texting me at dawn that she was too hung over to go anywhere, that she had lost her car saleswoman job, and that she would drop a card into my mailbox.

The female tenant at Le Petit Chalet d'Enchanté had called to complain of a constant chirping sound in the high ceiling of the bedroom loft. I killed two birds with one stone and took on the fortuitous angst of picking up Mother, a birthday party guest I had not put on my short list, after hauling a twelve-foot ladder up the steep, narrow staircase and replacing the battery in the fire alarm at the cabin. It would be a long, wet day.

Brute was excited to be along for the ride and quite smug to be road tripping without Hound. Hound was content to stay behind, a discarded futon mattress rescued from the sidewalk now placed at the bottom of the back stairs to soften his eventual somersault into the garden to politely and discreetly loose more undesirable, toxic fertilizer onto the pathway.

Mother was in the driveway when we pulled in.

"You're late."

"Brute may need to pee," I explained while opening the car door to fetch him.

"He can wait." And she was in, her seat belt snapped, her fervor for getting to her precious and favorite daughter's party quite apparent. I immediately backed out into the street and headed for the 210 Freeway on-ramp. The rain began with a tinkle on the windshield.

"Here's your birthday card. I saved a stamp."

"Thanks, Mom. Let's see, you've been sending me birthday checks for years and each year the check is equal to my age. Thirty-six more years to that C-note, huh?"

"Turn the wipers on," she demanded in her *I wear hearing aids* hissing whisper. "And don't pass San Fernando Road. It's coming up."

"Mom, it's at least another fifty miles," I calmly replied and switched on the wipers.

"Well, I've been this way before. It's not the first San Fernando, not the second, but the third San Fernando exit."

"Yes, you've been this way as a passenger, but I've been driving this freeway since 2007, when it finally opened."

The five-decade wait for the completion of a straight shot from upper Los Angeles by way of Burbank through Pasadena, Ontario, Pomona, and the scourge of the Fontana badlands to San Bernardino and the mountain communities of the National Forest was a deciding factor in purchasing my cabin, along with a straight shot to my aging mother, the thorn in my guilty side. Would my children drive more than seventy-five miles to visit me when I've shriveled into a snarly, nasty shadow of myself, my hair grossly overdue a thorough shampooing in hot water? Would I be of the mind to strike fear into them, always threatening expulsion from my last will and testament? Not becoming my mother is a life-long struggle.

"The government took our house, the entire neighborhood, and the community pool, when you were in high school. I don't know why it took them so damned long to finish the freeway."

"Well, the little house of my childhood wasn't *our* house anymore. Didn't you and dad let it go into foreclosure?"

"I didn't need it anymore. I moved to Redlands," she snooted. In the Inland Empire, Redlands has always been the go-to destination for anyone wanting the best for themselves and their children. In the mid 1990s, Redlands had been my home, a home for Alexandra.

"Yes, you escaped with your lover and my sister, leaving me to bounce from my father to my grandmother, back to my father and new stepmother, to marrying the first man that came along and who stayed just long enough to grant minimal respect to my new mother status," I thought.

I slid a Nat King Cole CD in the player. Perhaps she would enjoy music from her time.

"Turn that thing down," she commanded in her continual whisper, the infamous whisper that has me believing that I, too, am deaf.

The trickle turned into a slam-dunk down pour. The road filled with water quickly and the car planed. The woman next to me in cat hair infused, black see-through leggings ending in fringed black suede boots kept talking. I concentrated on the braking lights ahead and did not turn my head to acknowledge her re-re-recount of the man that always calls on Saturday mornings. She flicked her dainty vicious fingers at my arm. This was her irritating affliction, tapping at my skin for recognition, digging her nails into my wrist, or slapping my upper arm to reassure us both that I was listening.

I broke into the conversation with tales of Hound and how I was becoming impatient with him, how I was in the midst of making a morbid decision, not wanting to find him dead on the living room floor.

"I will make the appointment with the vet tomorrow," I concluded.

"And just how much is *that* going to cost you?"

Yet another person who is neither my financial advisor nor my forthcoming philanthropist is about to chastise me.

"The cat cost me one-fifty, so assuming they go by weight, it may cost me up to three hundred," I guessed. "He's lived a long happy life. He's almost seventeen. In dog years that's what? Seventeen times seven . . ."

"Surely, the Humane Society will do it for free. Get with it, Julie. You have a very sick dog, dear. They should just come and take him. He's much too big to just bury in the back yard."

"He's my responsibility and I doubt that they would do it for free."

"There's all kinds of free services for the elderly, anyone over sixty-two."

"Are you talking about me or the dog?"

"Remember when I totaled my Camaro and county services sent that adorable young black man once a week to take me shopping? It was free. Don't you just love it?"

"I remember he quit and refused to come back."

"Well, you keep me posted. I know you girls have your secrets."

"What the hell are you talking about? I am keeping you *posted*. I've just shared with you an intimate decision I'm not looking forward to making. Why do you insist on insinuating that I keep things from you? I write entire novels cataloging my failures for you to throw in my face. You have quite a selection to choose from. Don't get on me about my poor dog."

The wipers roared faster and faster. I had to concentrate to see the road in front of me. I was not driving a four-wheel drive Land Rover or *The Ultimate Driving Machine*. My lightweight, four-cylinder Toyota felt every swish and swerve and slip.

"Well, you know better than I do, dear. What do I know?" she provoked in her snide, cruel, deliberate way. "It's just too bad that your father passed away so soon, along with his wife. Just a week apart, can you believe it?"

"What's that got to do with euthanizing my dog?"

"It would be nice if you could ask his opinion, that's all."

"Since when have you ever encouraged me to seek the advice of my father? I didn't talk to Dad for ten years before he died. Stepmother made sure of that."

"And their deaths so close together and at home in the house, just makes you wonder, doesn't it?"

"Makes you wonder what? What are you saying? They were married for over forty years. Maybe they just wore each other out," I chuckled. "And that sort of thing happens a lot to couples that have been together for so long. She died instantly of a heart attack and he was already on his way out with hepatitis and liver problems and confined to bed."

"Well, alcoholism put him there. And don't forget her grown daughter was living with them at the time," she snooped. "Seems very suspicious to me."

"Mother, your sudden interest in the macabre is menacing. She had nothing to gain. Their wills left everything to the dogs, and I mean the Humane Society. You live only three blocks from their house. Maybe I should call in a forensic expert to open your suspected Cold Case with you as the number one suspect."

"I had no motive, but to outlive him, as I've outlived all three of the S.O.B.'s."

I was clutching the wheel when I let go and posted this.

"I don't want to hear another word from you until we park in Rae's gated garage. Do you understand me?"

"Whatever."

At the San Fernando off-ramp, the storm cleared. On her sunny patio, Rae waved us in from overhead, opening the gate with her remote control gadget. We slid into the parking place next to her Benz.

"I'm going to put Brute outside before going up," I said and headed for the front doors of the complex clutching my baby boy, abruptly awakened from a long nap.

"The elevator's here. You can do that later."

I stopped in my hasty tracks and jumped in behind Mother. One flight up and out onto the walkway, Brute wandered off to make circles and, as Mother hurried away—as fast as a decrepit, bent over octogenarian can hurry away—he straddled one stray weed in the concrete and emptied his bladder, the contents so abundant that it puddled at his paws. I walked through the door with him in my arms, shaking out his back feet.

The place is jumpin' with strangers, friends, and kin. Nephew Tommy is paired up in conversation with a young man unknown to me. The real estate guests sit together, paper plates balanced on their knees and plastic cups in their hands. Stephen is nowhere to be seen. The always-helpful Beryl is manning a silver tray of mini cantaloupe slices skewered with prosciutto. Scanning the horizon, I notice that Rae has filled the guest list with several of her personal friends, whose faces and names I am dumbfounded to remember, having never been on their guest lists.

Alexandra and Benjamin rush in behind me complaining of the long journey from Santa Barbara, their weekend celebrating his mother's birthday sadly shortened in order to make it to mine. Benjamin presents me with a pastel spring bouquet. Brute totters about arthritically on the polished art deco concrete floor, where surrounded by admiring dog lovers eager to give him a pet, he takes a flash dump.

Rae quickly pulled me aside. "Put that dog in my laundry room and lock the door."

"He'll yip," I answered and with my fingertips quickly removed the small brown turd from her embarrassment. "I'll just hold him."

Beryl magically slid up to me holding a plastic baggie. "Thanks, Beryl. Thank you for coming." She held the bag open and I dropped Brute's surprise inside.

"Please put that in the toilet and flush it away," Rae finalized her instructions and disappeared onto the patio deck for a cigarette with Tommy and his friend. The realtors followed, their new silver-haired coquette girlfriend between them.

"Mother, don't forget to powder your nose, okay?" I shouted out to her.

"Get real, dear. I'll be out on the patio with these nice gentlemen."

Secreted inside the bathroom, Brute shamelessly curled up on the cool tile, I dropped and Beryl flushed. "Did you know it was supposed to be a surprise party? I mean, nobody shouted 'surprise' when you walked in."

Not to shake her questionable sensibility, I answered, "Brute did it for them."

During a rip roaring game of Charades, Brute found a quiet place under the lime green mid-century chaise, a safe distance from Spot, the house cat, who is known for clandestine swatting, nails bared.

"How's Hound?" Alex leaned into me, as the circle of game players shouted out names of movies, all of them wrong, while Beryl timidly whispered the names of North American mountain ranges.

I leaned into Alex, "The vet is pushing for euthanasia. If I choose to play God, do you want to be there?"

As if I'd asked her to witness a beheading, she sharply responded with a decisive *No*.

The game wound down and Rae and I headed outside.

"I guess it's time to come clean. I'm smoking again," I hung my head and retrieved my nicotine paraphernalia from my purse.

"Thank God."

"Hound is wasting away. The vet suggests I put him down."

"Well, seeing the way Brute is waddling around, maybe you can get a twofer," and she lit my cigarette.

Alexandra popped her head out, "Mom! I thought you quit smoking."

And Mother peed all the way home.

My final decision was made upon my return to the bungalow after a grueling four-way turn around. Hound's quality of life has sunk to a new low; he hadn't been able to make it down into the garden.

Monday morning I place the call to Dr. Hu's office to set up the appointment.

"We like to do this kind of thing at the end of the day, when the office is quiet. Will seven-fifteen work for you?" a mild mannered, assisted-suicide expert asks.

"Tonight?" I pondered my question and gazed down at withered Hound asleep at my feet. "Yes, that's fine. I'd also like to get another cortisone shot for Brute."

I immediately sent a text to Alexander informing her that I am taking the dogs to the vet tonight at seven-fifteen. She does not respond.

Preparing steaks and a Caesar salad, Hound's last meal and his favorite, I am tiptoeing around pet pee pads strewn about the floor of my kitchen. After helping him chow down, the three of us wander together through the walkway one last time, Hound stumbling each step of the way. Randi has been notified of the grim news and has gathered the bungalow residents for a fond farewell to the gentle giant.

Greeting us along the way is my Goth Girl Randi in her regulation paint-spattered black t-shirt, Marianne the historian and PETA representative, and Michael in his typical female hysteria gripping a pink lace cotton handkerchief. Artemus stops reading his *Psychology Today* from his porch to nod as we precariously stroll solemnly by. Leaving their ladders and waving lavender paint soaked brushes, come the newlyweds, Earl and Carl Gaylord, who have purchased the crumbling house next door from the insane one-legged man. Waving at the window from her hospital bed are Bunny and Oscar, her neighbor across the walkway and lover of fifty years. The Korean caretaker leaned out the screen door and blew a kiss. Kandi is gone, not arrested, having sold her trap house and love shack to an unsuspecting new homeowner, a writer, actor, and Laundromat manager, who comes through his gate to see what's happening. Even the evil German Frau comes outside to stand on her rickety porch, as Hound lets go one more time in front of her house, but she does not shout at him today. Randi fetches her garden hose and quickly muddles the yellow sludge into the grass.

As arranged, Brainard arrives to lift the invalid into the back seat of my car. Brute is complicit in this family misfortune, as he lays low in the front seat, his paws covering his eyes, only taking a few peeks at me as if to ask *are we there yet?* For moral support, Brainard follows us in his white BMW to Laurel Pet Hospital. The only parking spot I find is three blocks south. Brainard catches up and carries Hound, while I wait in darkness at every tree trunk for Brute to do his business.

While Hound rests on the cold tile floor, Dr. Hu removes his collar and hands it to me. She then administers a calming medication to his rear end. Brute gets his shot and Hound sympathizes. The doctor leaves us to our final quiet time and Brainard starts talking.

"So I met this eighteen-year-old chick on the plane coming into LAX and she needed a ride into town. We made out in my car and she let me touch her breasts. So hot. She's a virgin! The next time she comes to L.A., I'm going to bang that right out of her and . . ."

"Not now, Brainard."

Waiting in the sterile room for what comes next, before turning my phone to *silent,* I text Alexandra that we'll wait for her, if she changes her mind and would like to be here.

> Monday, April 2, 2012; 7:53p ALEXANDRA: What? I thought you were taking them there because they needed to be boarded!

"Your daughter is on the phone at the front desk," I am alerted by a young woman in blue scrubs.

On the other end is another young woman screaming at me.

"Why didn't you tell me? What's wrong with you?"

"I asked you at my birthday party if you wanted to be here and you said *no.* You haven't come by to see Hound for months—"

"You're crazy. I never said that. You're deaf! How could you? You crazy bitch!"

How could I arrange a death without checking her schedule? Or how could I play God?

Alexandra continued her hysterics as I set the phone back on its cradle. I checked my silenced phone for text messages. She had been texting me.

> 7:59p ALEXANDRA: Are you still there?
> 8:08p JULIE: We're still here. My friend Brett Brainard is here. Brute too.
> 8:08p ALEXANDRA: Has he been put to sleep?
> 8:09p JULIE: No.

8:09p ALEXANDRA: You didn't tell me, mother. I would've been there.
8:10p JULIE: We'll wait for you.

"Heck, what's the matter with kids today? Sounds like you're going to have more than enough company, so I'll bow out," Brainard said, held Hound's head and kissed him on the snout. "See you soon, ole buddy."

"Ah, shucks, Brainard, you just don't want me to see you cry."

As he went out one door, through the other blew in the lovebirds.

Alexandra's face is mascara streaked down to her perfect six-thousand-dollar nose. Behind her is the boyfriend. My precious last moments alone with my companion have now been disrupted by a stranger.

Dr. Hu returns and Benjamin gently places Hound's now forty-eight pound suffering body onto the white towel on the silver tray. My tears are stayed. I am silent and speak not a prayer as the IV is inserted into Hound's leg. She injects the propofol. The sedative is quick. Hound is out. He is sleeping on his side. The doctor then injects the euthanasia solution and instantly his eyes open as his heart begins to slow. Holding Brute face to face with his buddy, I stroke Hound's face and try to close his eyes, but they won't close. He passes looking at me, his golden eyes at peace.

I wanted to be alone with my friend. I didn't want a circus. I wanted to cry, but the center stage was Alexandra, who kept a bit of tears going, while keeping her distance from the corpse. I wanted to lay my face against his and whisper a prayer. But I did not. I may have been seen as a cold, selfish woman who had tired of the responsibility of the care of an old man, his demands, and his petrification. And, perhaps, I am. Yet I had never been his caretaker; he had always been mine.

A heavy set Hispanic woman in blue scrubs enters, matter-of-factly wraps Hound in the towel, and silently carries him away. There would be no funeral or an urn of ashes to place on the fireplace shelf. I placed his collar dangling with silver dog tags—their clanging sound always a comfort to me as Hound wandered aimlessly through our little house —into my purse for safekeeping. Then I turned to Alexandra.

"Never talk to me that way again."

In the protection of her boyfriend and her new life beyond my reach, she answered. "We'll talk about this later."

When is it that the flip-flop occurs, that moment in your child's life when she takes on the role of parent? I can tell you when: the very first time you don't meet her expectations. In our case, perhaps it was when I drove ninety miles drunk with my fourteen-year-old daughter in the car and then smashed out the window of our back door to get into the house.

As I exit the corridor, Alex is at reception attempting to pay the bill.

"Your mother already paid it," the girl at the desk advises her.

Alexandra slammed her Gucci wallet into her Gucci purse and dashed out to her Prius.

Brute cuddled in my arms, I stepped out into the dark to walk three blocks to my car. Alexandra is parked in front, Benjamin at the wheel. I tapped on her car window and she rolled it down.

"Can we have a ride to my car, please?"

"Sure. Just scoot over the bags. Roy broke up with Lauren and she's given me the job of returning his stuff."

Brute and I fell into the back seat amidst bulging black plastic trash bags signaling another Hollywood romance gone awry.

In a trance, I bathed Brute in the kitchen sink and blew him dry in the bathroom sink, cooing and cuddling him every step of the way. After putting Brute's smaller bed on top of Hound's larger bed, the new King of the Bungalow waddled up and onto his throne. I fetched the collar from my purse and hung it on the key hook in the kitchen over Morticia's remembrance collar.

Today had been a big day: I was put on hold for a *Spike TV* promo; I registered for a new call-in background actor service; and I killed my dog. I finished off the day by drinking Jim Beam Red Cherry bourbon and smoking cigarettes while going through the mail. I sipped red wine and gorged myself on cheese melted over tortilla chips while *Googling* the subject of *sex with Muslim men* until my head spun. I collapsed at two a.m.

Juliet Montague

I slept in until ten, missing the office meeting and my promise to host the Broker's Open at a four million dollar listing on June Street in Hancock Park.

> Tuesday, April 3, 2012; 12:05p ALEXANDRA: Just wanted to see how you and Brute are doing today?
> 12:09p JULIE: I am staying close to him here at home. We're hanging out and having a bit of a pity party. Will walk over to the dollar store to get him new little bowls and soft mini bites, then work outside and trim.
> 12:11p JULIE: Hound is running in a field today.
> 12:11p ALEXANDRA: Hound has his balls back.
> 12:12p JULIE: He will be 17 on May 15, 119 years old.

In the darkness of early morning, the sirens spun red outside my bedroom window. Bunny was carried out on a stretcher to the ambulance. I waived her good-bye from the front porch. She was ninety-three years old. Within the month, Captain Brainard became the proud owner of her 1923 bungalow, a piece of history he immediately gutted after waiving the *death-in-the-house* disclosure. Very soon after, America's Oldest Teenager and the clean-cut host of *American Bandstand*, Dick Clark, died at eighty-two. Bunny's beau Oscar at eighty-five is still here at the bungalows maneuvering Monday's street cleaning day, returning precisely at one o'clock, his week's supply of groceries neatly stacked in the rear of his shiny new SUV. As I pull up right behind him in the lineup, he cuts a stately posture steadfastly filling his wire wheeled cart and heading into the walkway. On Tuesday at precisely one o'clock, Oscar will move his car to the other side of the street after returning from his weekly meeting with the San Fernando Valley Remote Control Airplane Club. In comparison, my mother rarely leaves the house, but for the monthly trip to the local grocery store and the car lot where she purchased her big, fat lemon, where the salesmen welcome her with donuts and coffee, while she waits for the gratuitous carwash to be completed. She is very sure they look forward to her visit.

CHAPTER 43

Crutches, a Stroller, and a Chair

> ♪ God Bless America, land that I love
> Stand beside her and guide her to
> the right with the light from above ♪
>
> *God Bless America*
> Irving Berlin, original lyrics of 1918

ONE of my clever solicitous realtor postcards, complete with a lovely picture of my bungalow and its *Hollywood* gate on the front, drew interest from a nearby homeowner, an elderly Iranian lady. I walked over in the hope of putting her house on the market. Instead, I spent four hours on her Persian living room rug drinking tea from a delicately engraved samovar kettle and listening to barely audible Islamic tales of woe emotionally delivered through her toothless mouth.

"I was married off at age thirteen. Ah, the pain. Muslim men are beasts. I came here to your wonderful America and have to leave my teenage son with nasty Iranians. I am now citizen and Christian, my son fifty-four and I am sixty-seven. I have cancer, glaucoma, neck injury, and carpal tunnel. I owned a beauty parlor on Fairfax for thirty years. I buy this house and buy their apartment in Tehran. But now he is free to leave, if I can get the paperwork done. I can't read, can't write. Can you help me?"

I took all her information, including her citizenship papers, and a packet of government forms home with me to digest. I returned with the necessary forms filled out for her, only to hear more about the screaming for help on her wedding day.

"They have sex with nine-year-olds," she moaned.

"Yes, I know."

Here I was aiding in the addition of yet another Muslim man, his Muslim wife and child to the burgeoning immigrant population, when all I'd wanted to do was to sell a three-bedroom, two-bedroom house just south of Sunset Boulevard. At the end of summer, I would receive a phone message. "Thank you for all your help. My son and family live here with me now. They receive food stamps, Medicaid, and my son paid eight hundred dollars a month to care for me. God bless you and God bless America."

I am released from the *Skype TV* hold. I was going to be filmed with my hair in curlers and a furry bathrobe, anyway.

A *Facebook* post further incited my day when my daughter Elizabeth celebrated her first date with her husband Manny by sharing this with the world:

> Twenty-five years ago I defied my mother and went out with a friend. By the end of the night he was my boyfriend. Two years later, my husband. It's not been perfect, but it's ours.

I was seething. Where are the Mark Zuckerberg *Facebook* Geek Police? While she's blurting out memorable moments, why not post this?

> Forty-three years ago my father abandoned me. Mother stuck around. She bought me my first horse when I was eight and rode him home holding me tightly in the saddle, when I know she was secretly scared to death. She made all my dresses, including a *Madonna-like* purple and black prom gown with matching fingerless gloves. When she didn't have much money, she made sure I had a wedding reception with round tables, white tablecloths, and a live country band. Thank you, Mom, for always being there.

I immediately deleted her as a friend.

I busied myself by spreading pastel powdered sugar frosting on bunnies, eggs, and chicks for two days. I delivered trays of resurrection good wishes to our commercial agency and to Alexandra's modeling agency. After dumping another tray off at Overpriced Homes Realty, I met Alex for lunch on trendy Larchmont Boulevard. She would be leaving for the Santa Barbara Easter hunt.

"Benjamin's mom is reading your book right now and can't put it down."

"Obviously, a woman with a great sense of humor."

"I'm glad you like her. I don't want to be spending so much time with someone you don't like."

"I like her as a social acquaintance, but not her morality. Aren't you uncomfortable living at their home pretending to be husband and wife?"

Silence.

"Honey, I'd just like to see a ring on your finger."

Silence.

It's a sure bet that if we were not sitting at a table on a sidewalk with the young and entitled shuffling passed in their Birkenstocks, there would not be silence. Are those tears I see behind her Fundi's?

"We're going to Coachella next week, you know, the music festival in the desert."

"Ah, yes, the *Woodstock* of the 21st century. How ghastly. The entire week?"

"No, just Friday through Sunday. We're staying in a nice house with friends."

"Don't you people ever go anywhere alone?" I thought.

"I don't want to go. I'm not a kid anymore. So I made him pay for the whole thing."

"You shouldn't be paying for anything. You know the old idiom, 'why pay for the cow when the milk's free?'"

On Friday Mother canceled Easter. She'd seen enough of all of us, I suppose. I had the weekend to myself. It had been quite a week. Three on a match: Hound, Bunny, and Jesus. Only one rose from the dead.

I fool hardily peeked at my *Yahoo! News*, and in my chenille burka stumbled into an article that sent necrophilia tremors up my lack-of-nookie va-jay-jay. In the new Democratic Islamic Egypt, since President Obama forced out Hosni Mubarak, the Muslim fanatics now controlling the country are introducing a new *farewell intercourse law*, which allows husbands to have sex with their dead wives up to six hours after death; a sort of après honor killing make-up sex. I posted the article to my *Facebook* book page and was seriously snipped at by Muslims around the world, none of which have ordered a book.

The Muslim from Bangladesh at the mini-market on Vine intrigues me. There he sits behind that cluttered counter day in and day out watching fútbol on *The Sports Channel*. He tells me he reads English much better than he can speak it, so I open a discussion on *Sex with a Muslim in My Basement*.

"Oh, no. Muslim cannot do that. He must be married."

"Well, we were, sort of. Would you like to read my books? I'm working on book two now. I could bring you the first one."

"My daughter goes to Pepperdine University in Malibu. She can read it to me."

"Well, that would be interesting for the both of you, maybe."

"Lottery ticket today?"

"Sure. Why not."

"*SuperLotto* Quick Pick? You still with the Muslim boyfriend?"

"No."

"Doesn't he miss you?"

"I wouldn't know, but I still miss him."

"He will come back. You will see."

It was passing by quickly, the year of 2012. My girls obliged me and shared Mother's Day here on my porch, enjoying tacos with all the fixings and stuffed walnut and goat cheese chili rellenos. My granddaughter inappropriately brought along her new beau that day, which may indeed have stilted any inner strife, as we in tongue and cheek fashion always attempt to appear in tune when in the company of strangers. Prompted by Alexandra, for almost forty-five seconds I was free to speak of my second novel and how nicely Elizabeth's poetry might fit into a scene. Mother was not there to stoke any fires.

My right knee soon gave way. Condemned by a meniscus tear, I succumbed to arthroscopic surgery, a cleaning away of debris or decrepit decay of some sort, followed by an injection of much needed artificial synovial fluid. Alexandra kindly delivered me, held my hand as I fell away under anesthesia, and helped me on my crutches back into the house. Randi dropped a funny get-well card into my mailbox. I was off the crutches in two days.

The City of San Bernardino has filed bankruptcy, the city's claims to fame being the home of the first McDonald's, the precursor to the adolescent muffin top, and the title of *Murder Capital of the United States,* when in 1993 there were eighty-four homicides, Julie reporting more than her share of the courtroom drama, the precursor to her damaged wrists. As of 2005, there was estimated to be one known gang member for every one hundred and fifty people. I suppose they have quit counting. Today this city, located at the end of a long, hot and ugly drive on the I-10 east out of Los Angeles, is one of the poorest, most violent cities in the United States. As her real estate equities continue to plummet, the granddame matriarch of the family is not fazed. Mother is not going anywhere any time soon; and like Julie, she receives her retirement checks from the County of San Bernardino and not from the City coffers.

August 27th, 2012, the icy martini shaker strained and drained, the Cheetos in a bowl on the TV tray, Brute and I sat down to watch the beginning hoopla of the Republican National Convention, of which Brute has little interest. My favorite senior citizen, actor Clint Eastwood, in a dapper suit and tie is the surprise speaker of the evening.

"Brute, he's talking about us! Right on, Clint. Yes, there are a lot of moderate people in Hollywood, not just the squawking left wingers."

Hey, how about opening that stick of salami you brought home today?

"Look, little buddy, he's got an empty chair and he's pretending to talk to Obama. Do you think he seems a bit shaky, unrehearsed, and nervous? Nah, he's just pulling this out of his concerned conservative ass."

Do I have to sit up on the couch with you? Please let me get on my bed.

"Okay, down you go. You tell 'em, Clint. Yes, Obama's broken a lot of promises. Why didn't someone slick down that cowlick at the back of your head? It's diminishing your credibility. Oh, hell, you look like an old man who just got out of bed."

You're lighting up again? Open a damned window. Thanks.

"Yes! The people should feel free to get rid of any politician who's not doing a good job. They work for us!"

I'm out of water and it's time to take me outside.

"What? Yes, say it, Clint! Make my day."

Mr. Eastwood would later summarize his comments on Obama. "President Obama is the greatest hoax ever perpetrated on the American people."

As Clint describes him, the *stellar businessman* Mitt Romney, Candidate no. 7 in my personal delegation, wins the nomination to run against the Muslim socialist as our next President of these United States.

I vow to put my money, my time, and my walking feet where my mouth is and head to Las Vegas on a bus without a bathroom to knock on the doors of undecided, wavering Republicans to whom I force *Romney*Ryan* bumper stickers into their hands before they can slam the screen door.

♪ For Once In My Life ♪ I have someone who needs me! I'm not alone anymore. And with two hundred flag waving conservatives on each of three buses, I'm not alone for an entire weekend.

I enlist as a volunteer at a call center and punch my fingertips down to mere nubs. My only complaint, "Why are they hanging up on me, when they're all registered Republicans?"

At a concert in Washington, D.C., Madonna, *The Material Girl*, endorsed the sitting president.

> "Ya'll better vote for fucking Obama, okay? For better or worse, all right? We have a fucking Black Muslim in the White House. Now, that's amazing shit. It means there is hope in this country."

After stripping down to her bra to reveal O-B-A-M-A scrawled across her taught fifty-four-year-old back, she warned that if he gets another term, she'll be taking it all off.

In the aftermath of the September 11, 2012 —an entirely coincidental date—terrorist attack on the American Embassy in Benghazi, which the White House Administration blames entirely on a cheaply produced anti-Muslim video starring Mohammed, Obama addresses the United Nations with a befuddled speech which includes this choice quote:

"The future must not belong to those who slander the prophet of Islam."

The prophet would, of course, be the *Pedophile of Peace*, Mohammed. I, therefore, have no future.

Ali had personally reprimanded me for inappropriately using in a text message the name of *Allah*, the main guy responsible for turning Mohammed on to writing the vile and merciless *Qur'an*. I remember how he scorned me.

> Thursday, October 28, 2010; 8:57p ALI: Because you said we were lovers and I can't do that. And you text a precious word, the name of Allah that should not be used out of context. It is blasphemy and worthy of death.
>
> Ali, *Jihad Honeymoon in Hollywood*

Intended to be my moving on "recovery tour" before wilting to a dried up, depressed damsel in distress, my sister and I began planning a trip to the Emerald Isle, believed to be the breeding ground of one fourth of our ancestry. Through my time share, having paid the yearly maintenance fee of eight hundred dollars and an additional trade fee of three hundred dollars, I booked us into a grand apartment and kitchenette, complete with a four-poster antique bed chamber, at Knocktopher Abbey. The abbey is a restored monastery built in 1356, twenty minutes from the bustling medieval city of Kilkenny in the southeastern countryside of Ireland. Rae, the consummate business traveler, would take on the job of acquiring round trip flights to Dublin for two sisters eager to visit Waterford, a short drive from the abbey, and return stateside with overpriced crystal shamrocks.

As time passed, the two of us cripples became more and more solitary. A walk on collar and leash through the grimy streets north to the ATM at Wells Fargo or south to CVS Pharmacy without his friend to torment along the way now an unthinkably cruel travail for the old dog, Brute and I spent bits of time in the bungalow walkway where he grazed, sniffed, and circled, taking a long pee break or a dump along the way. When my knee pain had become unbearable, Brute had empathized by becoming more and more arthritic and unstable. As my knee repaired, Brute's back legs and spine did not. He knew he was being left behind when I exited the front door to walk our old routes for cigarettes and booze. "I'm just going to the mailbox" never fooled him.

And then one day as we headed out to the walkway for Brute's morning scratch and sniff, there on the sidewalk lit by a ray of hope streaming down straight from heaven above, its front wheels sadly pushed into the dung of the gutter, was a child's stroller. As he padded away into the meager offering of closely mowed grass, weeds, and thorns, I inspected the classically designed khaki and black gift. Looking in all directions for its possible owner, I pulled the coincidental find up and out. Sturdy and clean, but for the mud on the tires, I've been given a *Free Stand, 1-Hand Fold, Jeep* brand child's stroller with large rubber tires in back and smaller double rubber tires in front. This isn't one of those newfangled umbrella strollers, the flimsy lightweight kind that the kid is mercilessly strapped into, his feet dangling. This is the real deal, complete with a tray and cup holder across the seat. There's a bonnet for shade that folds in or out, a footrest, and a good-sized net basket in the back large enough to bring home used vintage videos from The Goodwill store, paper plates and boxes of instant mashed potatoes from the Giant Dollar store, and hair dye, cigarettes, and bottles of rum from the drug store in one walkabout.

I'd never taken the dogs into stores. At CVS Pharmacy, I had tied their tandem leash to a tree and left them to pee and rest on the thick cool grass after a half-mile walk on hot sidewalks while I ran in for needed replenishment of my addictions. But an old cuddly Italian in a fancy buggy wouldn't possibly be turned away. I pictured us rolling down Sunset Boulevard to *Chic-Fil-A* and sharing a chicken sandwich under an umbrella on the patio, taking long uphill strolls into the Hollywood Hills, and traipsing through our favorite stores filling up the stroller's basket in complete togetherness once again. Brute wouldn't be getting much exercise, but pushing a heavy-duty stroller with a thirteen-pound old dog in it might be just what I need.

"Hey, Brute, come take a look at this," I hollered into the mews. From four houses down the walkway he shot me a confused look and continued his slow journey to his favorite spot in a creeping plant under the willow tree.

"I'll bring it to you," I said and spun the stroller into the sidewalk of the walkway. I waited for him to water the plant and then scooped him up, my hands gripping his tummy, his legs dangling. Without hesitation, I set him down back legs first in the seat. What happened next is a Hollywood Bungalow legend. He didn't slump down in the seat. He didn't scramble to get out. He put his front paws on the plastic tray and sat upright on his rump, his black nose pompously poised in wild anticipation of the sensory adventures that lie ahead.

I pushed our new transportation carefully through the walkway and called out to Randi, who came onto her porch in a Geisha girl kimono, her first morning cigarette between her teeth.

"It's eight o'clock in the morning. What's up?"

"I found this stroller on the sidewalk. Isn't this cool?"

"Yeah, the gal that bakes marijuana brownies in her kitchen put it out there last night. They got the kid a bike with training wheels, so they don't need it anymore."

"My good fortune."

"Did you put his feet like that?"

"No. He did it himself. Cutest thing ever, huh?"

I was utterly proud of my doggie, as proud as a new mother showing off her newborn baby, like she's the first woman to ever have one.

"I'm going to give him a bath and then take him shopping. Do you need anything?"

"Well, since I'm unemployed and a week away from my next unemployment check, can you stake me to a bottle of vodka and a couple packs of Marlboros?"

The two of us showered and fluffed, in high spirits I wheeled our Jeep on over to the Giant Dollar store for doggie treats, olive oil, instant mashed potatoes, and a bag of cobwebs to stretch over the black iron candelabra on the front porch. Halloween had crept up on me. Waiting for the light to turn green at Vine Street, a good-looking man in a shiny red Lamborghini waves at me. I immediately suck in my gut and smile big time.

"Is that a real dog? Mind if I take a picture?" and out his window came his cell phone.

The homeless man, who has taken over the bench at the bus stop, rises from his nap to flash a toothless grin as we pass by. "Well, if that's not the darnedest thing I ever seen."

The aging transvestite with flowing waist-length red hair and the most shapely legs in town, who always dresses to the nine's in varying shades of pink, pedals by on her pink bike in pink high heels. "Well, that just made my day, honey," she shouts back at us.

Flying down the concrete handicap ramp on a skateboard, an Asian boy with gold dreadlocks eats tuna salad from a mini can with a spoon. "That dog should be walking," he blurts out.

"Let's hope someone cares about you when you're old and arthritic, sonny," I rattle off and shake my head. Ah, youth, how foolish you are not to realize that the dog is not walking, because he can't.

I rushed right into the store passing the sign in the window, written in the usual Asian English:

NO PET
NO STROLLER
NO BACKPACK

Before finishing the pet supply aisle, a crowd of small brown children gathered, each eager to pet the century-old cuddle bunny. Their protective mothers quickly joined us. The gentleman Brute, his front feet poised, took to the affectionate attention like a duck to water as the children took their turn giving him a pat to the soft thinning white scruff between his ears.

At the register, I removed my few items from the basket at the back of the stroller, purposely having aimed Brute away from the clerk's view.

"He's so sweet. What's his name?" she asked as she tallied up the one-dollar items.

"Brute," I said and whirled the stroller around so she could get a better look. This is when they call the pet police, I fear.

"He's old, huh?"

"Yes, he's one hundred and two in dog years."

"You take good care of him. That's nice," she said and handed me the plastic bag and the receipt. "Miho, you've got a great mom."

Next stop is CVS south on Vine. Dogs are allowed in here. The greeter in her royal blue Polo shirt bends down and puts her hands over Brute's fluffy front feet. "Your mom's been coming in here for years without you. Where have you been keeping yourself, little guy?"

"He's my personal shopper now. His name is Brute."

"Well, that's a funny name for a gentle little boy like you."

"In his old age, he's lost a bit of his nip and growl, except when it comes to other dogs. He's a people person."

We left with vodka, cigarettes, and three bags of Halloween candy. Jogging gently behind the stroller, the bonnet pushed back, I smiled. The breeze lifted his ears. He was flying.

As a special outing, I began taking Brute to Vine Elementary on my Grandma Julie reading days: the first day of school to greet the new classes, the last day before the Christmas vacation, and the last day of school to say good-bye. I was reading to three classes for three different teachers now, and during each half hour, Brute quietly sits in his stroller, his paws on the tray, patiently listening to Grandma Julie's animated stories. Brute has become a bit of a celebrity around the neighborhood, the children calling out to him from passing cars, rushing to him in the aisles of the El Rancho market, and patiently waiting in line at the Giant Dollar store to gently touch his happy head. At Trader Joe's, we enter and pass right on by their huge colorful warning: *Service Dogs Only*. He's been unofficially named TJ's mascot by the night manager. Pavilions won't allow him in. In retribution, I only go there by car when skinless chicken breasts are on sale.

Finding that I have posted pictures of Brute in costume and sunglasses propped up in the Jeep on *Facebook,* Alexander is ashamed of me; she fears I'll be seen as a crazy homeless woman. She's got the *crazy* part right.

As in *The Story of Jesus,* what Christ was up to for the first thirty years is, apparently, irrelevant. His mother didn't keep a baby book or a family photo album revolving around the life of her son. As Jesus's apostles didn't start writing about their eyewitness relationship with him until after his death, because they didn't have time to write nor scrolls to etch upon during their travails with him, my friends and foes can write their own books filling in anything irrelevant that I'm about to leave out using their own *Word* program. They will discover that *Word* is complete with irritating grammatical corrections, spelling idiosyncrasies, a dictionary and a thesaurus.

* * *

Let's face it, readers, our Julie is rambling and has failed to get properly laid, as was promised somewhere back on page three. She has not found the proper replacement. Her Muslim lover spoiled her, somehow. The grass is not always greener, as we have witnessed. When God closed the trap door in her closet, he opened a window with bars? At her age, there aren't more fish in the sea. Before she can truly move on, she needs to forgive and forget, but she's sitting here sifting through each and every miserable moment of her *Jihad Honeymoon* succinctly chronicling Part Two of this sequel, which naturally, perpetuates the madness. I cannot take it anymore. The drinking, the whimpering, the orange chicken; all of it has to stop. I'm still here. I need you to be strong and sober and to keep me safe and healthy. I'm stickin' around, lady. With you at my back, the wind in my face, and my butt in the stroller, we're gonna take this town by storm. Innocent people are being shot up in dark movie theatres, so quit your whining, Cinderella. The fairy tale is over. Your carriage turned into a pumpkin years ago, and with that bum knee—surgery be damned; you can give up *The Lindy* right now— you're never wearing high-heeled glass slippers ever again.

Julie, you already know the ending to Part Two, so let's get to it, because you have Part Three to regurgitate, which in real time you are doing right now on the front porch. This is somewhat confusing, but puts the reader right inside the action where they're yearning to be, on a dirty street filled with unwashed cars blowing black exhaust fumes, their passengers the entertainment creators heading on down the Cahuenga Pass and back to work in the Hollywood *Media District*, while I pitifully beg for a toss of crispy burnt bacon.

✳ ✳ ✳

An adorable blonde, because all Republican women are adorable, I had met on the bus with no bathroom, invites me to write for her conservative website. I get a *PolitiChics* t-shirt and my first published angry article.

>PolitiChics.com
>After the Fall, Election Week, November 2012

>*Conviction Tested by Blood*

>Brother against brother; sister against sister, friend against friend, neighbor against neighbor—the divisive tactics of President Obama have spread civil unrest not seen since Hanoi Jane shook her aerobic fist at the troops in Vietnam. During this election season, I have been forced to delete more *friends* from *FaceBook* than I have scams, advertisements, and campaign donation requests from my e-mail account.

>My last check to my failed candidate, Mr. Romney, in the amount of one hundred dollars has not yet cleared. I am hoping that in fairness, it might be returned to me.

My liberal Hollywood neighbors here in the mews of bungalows —the socialist college math teacher; the lesbian marriage-family counselor and her three unwashed yipping dogs; the gay male couple who fly the stars and stripes on occasion from their porch; the mysterious film editor paying rent on the foreclosed house; the marijuana-brownie- baking mother of a five-year-old and two pit bulls; the writer who collects the coins from the Laundromat; the entitled tree-hugging hoarder and PETA representative who moves her three antiquated rusty cars in and out of parking slots about the crowded streets—have shunned me since I put the *Romney*Ryan* sticker on my little Scion.

Taking my little Maltese out to do his *thing* has turned into a sordid affair, during which I must be uplifting, cheerful, and nonchalant as they peer from behind their torn curtains at the war mongering, homophobic Christian actress who is so cruel and ignorant of the human condition that she voted for a wealthy Republican Mormon.

This new shame bestowed upon me, I can handle. With a smile on my face, I pick up my dog's daily droppings. I also pick up tossed cigarettes, discarded paper cups, and large crusted logs left carelessly by dog owners who take no responsibility.

What I can't handle is the cold silence, the condescending platitudes, and the mocking that has come from members of my own family. When my sibling learned of my sudden political activism, I was told, "The election is already over. You're wasting your time." This unsettling remark was delivered over Manhattans at her beach rental in June of this year. I did not inquire and she did not deliver up for whom she would be casting her vote, which was a dead giveaway hint.

My Republican mother got in the act over afternoon champagne when she pitied my resolve. "I'm voting for Romney, dear, but he's not going to win. It really doesn't matter. The president does not run the country." Her entire source of information is *The View* and her small town liberal newspaper. She has never heard of the *Fast and Furious* scandal, drones over Benghazi, or Islamic Ramadan feasts at the White House. My sister, unfortunately, has.

One daughter, the mother of my grandchildren, has refused to speak to me about politics since 2008, when I suggested that she read *Dreams From My Father*, Barack Hussein Obama's autobiography, before casting her vote. I had merely let out the words *communist* and *druggie*, before I was stopped from any further discussion with "Mom, you're such a racist."

My younger daughter has been in Hollywood too long. "Mother, I refuse to vote for anyone who won't allow me to have an abortion or takes away my contraception." I told her that I, too, believe in Pro-Choice: I chose not to kill any of my three unborn children, resulting in three live children who need to be told, "I brought you into this world and I can take you out," if I had the balls to speak to them in this manner.

The crowning glory came from my sibling on election night by way of a text in which she included a picture of me performing a stand-up routine at a comedy club:

> Stand up and be proud!
> Your passion is commendable.
> Proud of you, sisty!
> We are all in this TOGETHER.
> God Bless America.

> I replied: *And you voted for Obama.*

She has never answered my statement and has been off the radar since I canceled my appearance at the annual Thanksgiving feast, choosing instead to spend the day with right-wing rednecks in the forest watching reruns of *Hillbilly Handfishin'* and slugging down Cuba Libres. My younger daughter is now my sister's no. 1 *BFF.*

I have removed my makeshift Romney sign—two plastic *Romney*Ryan* yard signs sewn together and slipped over the flag pole —at the behest of my one Republican neighbor, who fears for my safety. The sticker is gone from the rear window of my hatchback. All that is left is the hole in my heart.

Mother called with her condolences and words of wisdom from one who has lived through eight decades of presidents, depressions, and wars. "This too shall pass, dear."

This time I'm not so sure she's right.

Chapter 44

DIY and Opportunity Knocks

♪ Hail, hail SB High
All hail to thee ♪

San Bernardino High School Hymn

"Oh, good, you're still here," Randi and her Kimono surprised me from outside the garden gate.

I pulled in the hose and began looping it neatly onto its rusty metal bed above the bib. "Where else would I be?"

"You threatened to leave the country if Obama won."

"I'm not letting that inept, corrupt, wasteful, subversive, destructive Muslim community agitator drive me away. I've lost my sister and my daughters because of his divisive routine. And I never said I was leaving my country; I was just going to move to the mountains, but I can't because my cabin is rented full time."

"Well, you've still got me. If it will make you feel any better, I slept through Election Day. I never made it to the polls."

"One less vote for King Obama. You know, he got ten million less votes than he did in the 2008 election. Randi, with forty-seven percent of registered voters in mourning this week, why do I feel so alone?"

"Want to go to Denney's for breakfast? I have a twofer coupon."

"Can't today. My friend Stephen and I are going to be contestants on *Let's Make a Deal*."

"Watcha dressing up as?"

"The usual, Ruby the Fortune Teller. Stephen's coming as a surgeon in scrubs."

"That's original."

"I suggested reprising Bette Davis from his original play *Bitch Slap*, but he said they'd never allow a drag queen to play the game."

"Have fun standing in line in the hot sun for four hours."

"Right. I should bring an umbrella."

The wait outside Sunset Bronson studios was long and hot before the production assistants guided three hundred outrageously costumed, perspiring wannabe contestants into the first interview or *casting exercise*. That is where Stephen is invisibly cut from the potential game player list, when he refuses to jump up and down like an idiot and answers their first question "tell us a little about yourself" with an arrogant response. "My name is Stephen and I'm an actor and a writer," he touts while simultaneously pulling out a surgical knife. I hold him back from slitting the throats of the pompous twenty-year-old game show casting directors while explaining that he really didn't want to come along anyway.

Jumping up and down like an idiot in my gypsy wig, I answer the question with dubious delivery, "I live close by, practically right around the corner, and I'm excited to report that I received my Medicare card in the mail yesterday! Apparently, they send it to you six months in advance of your sixty-fifth birthday!"

Neither one of us were called down stage to choose a curtain and make a deal. Out of three hundred contestants, Wayne Brady, the African-American host, played with only eight, two of which were of the Black race; a noticeably out-of-proportion percentage, considering there were only two Black contestants in the entire audience.

The switch that controls the back porch light has fallen off the job. I call Randi for advice. "Hey, do you know anything about changing a light switch? And, yes, I changed the light bulb."

"I'm a set painter. I paint around them. I don't change them. But I'll be right over."

Waving off the gregarious illegals running alongside my Scion, we entered the Home Depot parking lot on Sunset Boulevard rather than

OSH across the street, because I was stuck in the right-hand lane and couldn't get over. After successfully making our way through the towering maze, we left with soft water salt pellets and a new switch. We swooped into Rite Aid for alcohol and nicotine supplies. Spotting a parking place open in front of The Waffle restaurant across the street, I treated us to a sumptuous late breakfast of comfort foods. By sharing our load, we managed to get to the bottom of a Cornmeal Jalapeno waffle topped with chicken and gravy and one embarrassing plate of Smoked Salmon Scramble.

Laden with gaseous bulging tummies, we unloaded two bags of salt, a brown sack containing our fix-it project, and a plastic bag precariously protecting two bottles of liquor. Randi headed into the kitchen to inspect the DIY project, while I trudged two burdensome bags of salt down to the basement.

"Hey, where's the electrical box?" she asked from the bedroom.

"In the koffice. It's painted yellow to match the wall," I shouted up the ladder. Instantly, I was in the dark.

With a flat head screwdriver, Randi swiftly unscrewed the faceplate. "Hand me a Phillips," she said, thrusting the palm of her hand at me. She loosened three screws, pulled away the three wires, and slapped the old switch into my hand. I handed her the new switch. She leaned across the Spanish tiled counter to intently ponder the three eerie tentacles extruding from my kitchen wall.

"Hey, Dr. Randi, don't get all baffled on us now. It's going to get dark sometime today."

Suddenly dumbfounded, she stated the obvious, "There's two fucking black wires and one copper."

"We should have paid attention to what-was-what and what-goes-where before *you* took it all apart, Randi."

"Why don't these things come with instructions?" Shaking her head, she fetched her cigarettes and vodka from the plastic bag.

"Hey, traitor, where you going?"

"I have to take a shit and I want to do it alone."

She returned two pounds lighter pulling along a hot electrician she found wrangling with an old fuse box outside of Oscar's bungalow. "This is Jim, today's Godsend."

Jim worked swiftly spinning wires around screws like a champion crochet wizard, while I divided two hundred dollars per hour union scale by two minutes in my head. "That should do it, girls. Just have to screw the plate back in."

"Oh, I can do that. I unscrewed," Randi beamed.

"Well, all this screwing has me excited. How much do I owe you, Jim?"

"Ah, nothing. Glad to help. You can turn the power back on."

I took a cell phone shot of my handygirl surgeon screwing away, her big smile looking back at me. It would be the last picture I would take of my crazy, lazy, loving friend.

She flipped the switch and the light outside over the back door stoop lit up. While the sun went down, we celebrated *switchgate* on the front porch, slugging down iced coconut vodka while discussing the size of the bulge in Jim's Dockers and slapping ourselves for not getting his number.

Cost of one switch replacement outing: $92.66

Suffering from Post Traumatic Election Syndrome, I turn to the *Good Book* for answers.

> When the righteous triumph, there is great glory.
> But when the wicked prevail, people go into hiding.
>
> Wise Sayings of Solomon
> *Proverbs 28:12*

Hiding from those that at every turn were hell bent to steal my thunder, I would not speak to my sister for almost a year; correctly assuming that any plans to share a ten-day holiday in Éire had been discreetly flushed.

Dressed for a crisp mountain holiday in my new buckled camel boots and layered in beige, brown, and mahogany, I leave Hollywood sweating. Singing along to Christmas carols that have now taken over the airwaves ♫ Sleigh bells ring, are ya listenin'♫ and short one German shepherd, Brute and I return to Trudy and Ted and their two cottages on a gravel lot for the Thanksgiving feast and a good cry over the outcome of the election. Two out-of-the-home grown daughters, an illegitimate one-year-old grandson, and a heavily tattooed skinhead Baby Daddy, currently cohabitating with a single mother and her three toddlers, joined us mid-afternoon to give thanks and to dive gluttonously into a slow-barbequed *Butterball* turkey stuffed with cornbread, sausage, apples and walnuts. The guests departed in three separate cars as quickly as they had arrived, leaving us with the aftermath cleanup duties of a four-course dinner that had taken Trudy four days to prepare.

"Where's the Tupperware? I'll start packing up the leftovers," I said, realizing that it would take another four days before Trudy's kitchen was cleared, the dozens of pots and pans scoured and put away, and the deck swabbed.

"Could you make me a sandwich first before Trudy goes hiding the turkey away in the back of the fridge?"

"Ted, I heard that!"

"It's all right, Trudy. I'll make him a sandwich. Dressing, mashed potatoes, turkey on white, Ted?"

"And stick it all together with some Miracle Whip."

"Ted, we have company. Take it outside."

Being a good guest, I ignored the sounds and the sudden smell wafting from Ted's resting place in front of the television.

"Julie, we're real sorry about Hound. How old was he?" Trudy asked.

"Seventeen."

"You must miss him terribly."

"Sometimes I swear I hear his dog tags jingling through the house."

"Isn't that the same age your cat went?"

"Well, yes it is. How do you remember that, Trudy? My second book isn't even out yet," I pondered.

"She's got some memory, unfortunately. And how old's little Brute now? He's getting on."

"He's twelve-and-a-half."

"Four-and-a-half years to go, old boy." Ted straightened up in his recliner and held up the weekly local rag. "The county will be taking applications come January 1st."

"Applications for what?" I was interested.

"Public Service Employee at the regional park. Didn't you say you always wanted to work at the lake?"

"Well, yes, I did. I've always wanted to be the gate lady, welcoming people in, but I can't afford to boot out my tenant for three months. I can't apply. I have no place to stay up here."

"What about your mom's cabin in Valley of the Moon?" Ted asked.

"Ted, why open up that can of worms?" Trudy poured more grease into a coffee can.

"What about your neighbor next door to your cabin, the one flying the *Don't Tread On Me* flag? Looks like he's got plenty of room," Ted suggested.

"Oh, heavens no. Cole is a friend, yes, but he doesn't want me living with him."

"Well, he keeps his place up real nice. I seen him out there shoveling snow before it even sticks to the ground. I don't know how he does it with missing those fingers and all."

Grabbing a t-towel, Trudy wiped her hands. "Goodness sakes. You can stay right here."

Rednecks, paddleboards, teenage lifeguards in red bathing trunks, sand, and green water; for the three months of summer, I'd be in hillbilly heaven.

"But I'd pay you, of course."

"Just paint that peeling wooden fence around the cottage. I can't get Tom Sawyer here to do it. Looks like shit."

"Sure, sure. I love to paint. I'll sand, prime, and paint. I'll bring up my power sander."

Teddy Bear shook the newspaper and folded it into his big, cuddly lap. "And you'll kick in five hundred for utilities. There's no air conditioning, so maybe we'll make a profit. You'll be making eight dollars an hour part-time, Miss Moneybags. Now get back to that sandwich."

"Oh, thank you. You two are the best," and as I hugged them both, the lump in my throat caught me off guard. Could it be that I was coming home?

Brute in his gently-used child's car seat—a treasure from Trudy I whipped out twenty bucks for—his sniffing view now even to the open passenger window, we returned in time to walk with my neighbor Barry, another male friend who wouldn't want me living with him, the three blocks up Ivar to Sunset Boulevard to catch the eighty-first annual Hollywood Christmas Parade; Joe Mantegna, the star of *Criminal Minds*, this year's Grand Marshall.

"Doesn't Hugo want to go?" I inquired as to his roommate, who has stayed too long in the illegal addition with no bathroom in Barry's garage.

"He's boiling more chicken and I'm sure a watered down red sauce to pour over it. Said he couldn't leave it unattended to pulverize alone. My kitchen is going to be a slimy mess by nine o'clock. I don't know what cooking skills he picked up at the French Cordon Bleu this past year, but Hugo is not giving up his Hungarian heritage any time soon."

In my furry Santa hat dancing with holiday pins and Brute in reindeer ears and a jingle bell scrunchie 'round his neck, I parked the stroller on the sidewalk outside the glass doors of Boho, the neighborhood gastro pub. Barry and I bought sausage dogs smothered in roasted green bell peppers and yellow onions from a roving street cart. Spectators lined both sides of the street four chairs deep. Plastic bullhorn sales were doing well. Sponsored by the Marine Corps' *Toys for Tots* charity, the parade's highlight for me is the honor guard in dress blues, just like my daddy used to wear, which marches by at the very beginning.

"The red, white and blue comes by and we're the only patriots standing with our hand over our heart." Barry made note.

"Maybe when the green, white and red comes by they'll all stand up and shout *olé*," I made note.

"It's shameful."

"Well, the best part's over and my dog is done. Can we go home now?"

"Brute's tired? He looks like he's ready to rock 'n roll."

"I meant my hot dog." My cocktail alarm clock had rung.

"There's supposed to be real movie stars this year. Let's stay. Don't you want to see Santa and his sleigh?"

"Christ, that'll be in two hours."

"You don't want to miss the L. Ron Hubbard Scientology Christmas balloon, do you?"

"Gosh, how do they choose which cult members get to drag it down the parade route?"

"For sure, they're not letting anyone out of the basement to run free. I think it's an Operating Thetan level thing. Maybe we'll see John Travolta."

"Okay, we'll stay."

Marching bands, movie muscle cars, convertibles with waving unknown adolescent television stars, and horses dumping dung as they strutted by, the children were more amazed by a funny little white dog wiggling his black nose sitting up in his stroller. He was sweetly mauled by parade goers strolling on the boulevard; his picture now on the *Facebook* pages of his innumerable new fans. John Travolta did not show up.

Up and down the scale I go. Weighing in at a solid one hundred and sixty-eight pounds, the seriousness of the situation has me listing my daily food intake.

Toast lathered with peanut butter	300 calories
Coffee with hazelnut cream x 2	50 calories
Tuna sandwich and Fritos	700 calories
Green salad wet with Bleu Cheese	400 calories
Four vodka martinis	800 calories
Tortilla chips and cheese	500 calories
Ben & Jerry's Cherry Garcia	1200 calories
Twenty cigarettes	0 calories

I don't need a calculator to realize that if I keep up this unconscious consumption of feel-good remedies forked, sloshed, and spooned in front of the television, by the first of January I will be forced to endure the dreaded corset day and night, under my sweats and under my sleeping camisole, as punishment for my undoing.

Hope, my high school friend and *Lifestyle Lift* nurse, took precious time out from her weekly trips with her grandkids down memory lane to her once upon a time employer Disneyland Park to spread the word through social media that a San Bernardino High School alumnus from the class of '66 had written a novel. Out of the woodwork and onto *Facebook* came new friends posting *Impeach Obama* banners, cat videos, and pictures of their last meal. Amongst them were high school mates who swore I had been in drill team with them and posted a picture taken in a photo booth to prove it.

In rain, sleet, and the threat of snow at the Village in Lake Arrowhead, I met up with one such stranger for a late lunch, because she had read Part One of the trilogy and was excited to catch up after forty-six years. Leighanne graduated one year ahead of me and married her high school sweetheart upon his return from the Vietnam War. They raised two sons in the San Bernardino Mountains. Two years ago, lying next to her in their bed on a cold winter's night, he passed away, having suffered a massive heart attack.

Awaiting me at Papagayo's Cantina, her thin gray hairs teased into a severe helmet and her shocking light blue eyes sparkling, Leighanne stepped from the booth overlooking the lake and met me with a robust hug, from a robust gal. I could only assume that the last two years as an accidental widow had lead her to the comforting jaws of many late-night Ben & Jerry sniveling pity parties.

"I thought your photos on *Facebook* were photoshopped, but you haven't got one wrinkle on your face," I complimented her.

"It's my Norwegian heritage. Blonde, blue-eyed, and a big round face with pink cheeks."

How does one bounce back from the death of a husband you've shared a bed with for over forty years? I was ill equipped to relate. My first instinct to foolishly compare her great loss to my trivial romantic folly was immediately quashed and humbled by her talkative gentle spirit. Apparently, during her two-year mourning period, she had fallen to pieces.

After Leighanne cheerfully shared her forthcoming shoulder surgery, her future neck surgery, her eventual back surgery, her failed attempts at weight loss due to her inability to exercise in any way, shape, or form, her fight with fibromyalgia, and the constant burning in her feet, we ordered another set of margaritas and our second basket of tortilla chips.

"Do you ever see your high school sweetheart?" she asked with her slight lisp, seemingly brought on by temporomandibular joint problems, which she had explained in excruciating detail. "What was his name?"

"Peter. You know, they say a man reaches his sexual prowess at age seventeen, so I missed his by four years. I hoped to run into him last year at the forty-fifth high school reunion, but he didn't show up."

"Did he marry? Does he have kids? Is he still in Berdoo?"

"No, never married, no kids, as far as I know, and he lives in a little cracker box Craftsman in the dregs of north San Bernardino. He's lived there since his parents died, when he had to move out of their house, almost twenty-five years ago now."

"How do you know where he lives?"

"He's in the phone book. You know, I've sent him a birthday card every year, but he's never responded. Some fellas at the reunion think that maybe he's gay. I have that effect on men."

"Maybe he's the one you should have married in the beginning. You know, I loved reading in your book about high school and San Bernardino and the mountains and all and about your relationships, especially with Peter. I couldn't help but think that if things had worked out for you two—"

"So anyway, on the night of the reunion we were all given lanyards with our senior yearbook faces dangling from them. I left the country club around midnight pretty tipsy, and on my way back to my mom's to spend the night, I spun on by the big guy's house. The lights were out, but his old white pickup truck was in the driveway. The chain link fence was locked up tight, so I hung the lanyard over the gate post."

"And he didn't respond to it? He has your address, right? And he didn't write to you or try to contact you?" Leighanne took an anticipatory breath.

"Peter quit talking to me in 1971. I have that effect on men. Years later, in between husband no. 2 and husband no. 3, he did come to the farmhouse in Cherry Valley and played his guitar for Elizabeth, just like he did back when she was a toddler. But he left in an old white pickup truck after making out with me in the downstairs bathroom—he tasted exactly the same—with a final good-bye, telling me to find a doctor or a lawyer, not a guy who puts *For Sale* signs up and down on front lawns."

"Oh, that's sad."

"Particularly, the fact that he still drives an old white pickup truck."

"You should put that in a novel."

"I just did."

"Oh, okay. I brought the 1965 *TYRO*," Leighanne said and began turning the paper clipped shiny pages of the leather-bound high school annual. "See, there we are in drill team together."

Her finger pointed to a row of miniature soldiers dressed in white short-skirted uniforms.

"Oh, my. We were so skinny, weren't we?" I was shocked. I hadn't looked at this book from my junior year since it floated away in a mudslide in Crestline, way back in 1978. There I was in white tasseled marching boots, my thighs thin and taut. I couldn't have weighed more than one hundred and thirty pounds.

The waitress returned and we ordered combination plates of prodigious proportion.

"And there's Rory," she pointed to another blonde stick of a girl. "She's a widow now too. Actually, twice widowed. You know, she had three boys early on and practically abandoned them when they were all under six years old. Well, you know, she didn't actually just *abandon* them. She left them in the care of their father and his new wife, of course. Very difficult to judge, you know, unless you've walked in someone else's shoes. Rory has a relationship with all her boys now, of course. She's extremely generous to them. I don't think any of them even speak to their father."

"Isn't that always the way?"

"What is?"

"The evil parent that disciplined them, sacrificed for them, and put up with their shit ends up getting the short end of the stick."

"Oh, I see. You know, she has more grandkids than I do."
"I'm sorry, Leighanne. I don't remember either one of you."
"Well, we all remember you, football queen and all."
"I'm a bit ashamed of my lack of jolly high school memories."
"It's okay. After reading your book, I've gotten to know you a lot better. I didn't realize what the most popular girl in school was going through with so much family turmoil. I mean, I remember the talk about the coach and the affair with your mother and all. They got married, right? I just never . . .well, at that age, you just don't put two and two together. I'm sure nobody gossiped about you personally, you know. I guess knowing about your pain now—"
"Whoa. Stop. Ready for another margarita?"

I headed back to Hollywood, before the chain requirement would pull me over into a forced highway patrol snowdrift, determined to inspire Leighanne to grow out her hair and to color it the ultimate *Merry Widow* blonde. I wouldn't be advising anyone on the healthful attributes of weight loss until I had put down the fork myself.

Part Two, *Jihad Honeymoon in Hollywood*, had come to its cryptic ending and I was into the editing process, which consists of printing up almost five hundred pages, setting up the cardboard table in the living room, and with a yellow marker searching for each and every incorrect spelling of names, places, and things—italics or no italics, quotation marks or no quotation marks, one word or two words—grammatical insults to my native language; inconsistent time warps; and just downright boring boondoggles. Then it's back into the *Word* file to make the corrections marked in yellow, their irascible replacements scribbled incoherently in the margins. Corrections done, it's time to print it all up again and begin the process all over. Hiring an editor at the least expensive cost of five dollars per page is inconceivable. I'd be paying out twenty-five hundred dollars for a baboon to turn the pages, leaving fecal matter and lice in the margins and gutters, a primate who cares nothing about politics or religion, disruptive sexual relationships, the *Qur'an's* stand on masturbation, or the details of *Female Genital Mutilation*. I called Leighanne, my new fan.

"Say, you enjoyed my first novel so much, how would you like to be the first one to read Part Two?"

Her work was stellar. Each evening she coursed through a chapter and found what she thought might be a spelling error or a passage needing some correction. I frequently disagreed with her, but thanked her for being my extra set of eyes. She accepted my explanation for the use of *past* versus *passed; past* being yesterday and *passed* being as in gas. Her nightly email to me always began with: "Holy cow, girlfriend, please tell me none of this is true."

Leighanne will not allow me to add her name to the *acknowledgment* section of *Jihad Honeymoon in Hollywood*, fearing for her life and the lives of her family, including her cruel and meddling ex-daughter-in-law.

During the editing process, I finally booked another pharmaceutical commercial advertising the *Novolog Flex Pen*, a new and less disgusting device for injecting insulin. I arrived at base camp, an amphitheater in Pasadena surrounded by grassy knolls, and was quickly swift away into the horrors of the makeup and hair trailer.

While I pretended to be the *Plain Jane*, kind and loving wife picnicking with her diabetic husband who shoots insulin willy-nilly into his thigh with an orange pen, on the other side of the country in a small Connecticut town, a young psycho, who began his shooting rampage at home playing video games in the basement and killing his mother, entered classrooms at Sandy Hook Elementary school with an arsenal, leaving twenty-eight dead, including twenty children. President Obama immediately began harping on gun control rather than behavioral control. Watching the news footage later, I couldn't help but notice that, perhaps, the interviewees—the teachers and parents—had been subjected to the same hairstyling conspiracy that had ruined my day on the *Novolog* location shoot.

Christmas week was uneventful, but for a wild surprise of a check for one thousand dollars delivered in a Christmas card from Mother. I immediately put in a frightened text to Alex asking if she knew whether or not my estranged sister had also received this mysterious gift from Mrs.

Scrooge. She returned my text in record time and alerted me that Rae was also reeling from her mysterious matching gift and isn't it sad that because of my love of politics over family, there would be no Christmas this year. She has made plans to share in the joy of the season with Benjamin, his brother, and the parents. I could drop off any gifts at her townhouse, because I have a key.

Suspicious of Mother's sudden stroke of generosity, I called in shock to thank her, but she cut me off and headed the conversation straight into left field dementia, which ended with my agreeing to spend the holy day with her and a frozen turkey dinner. Before Christmas Day, I received a card from Alexandra. I waited four suspicious hours to open it only to find something trite written in cursive about hoping that in 2013 we could begin anew, turn a new leaf.

Kid, I'm not an oak tree. I'm your mother. You are stuck.

Christmas morning just after dawn, Brute and I left Hollywood in the little blue hatchback sleigh weighted down with offerings in red and green gift bags and headed east to the horse country of Cherry Valley. My eight a.m. surprise visit to Elizabeth and her pajama-clad family was not well received. After downing one mimosa and opening one unwrapped gift box with no tag containing a bejeweled navy blue chiffon scarf—a scarf to this day I swear I gave to my daughter many years ago—I was sent on my way by eight-thirty.

At the Spanish hacienda, Mother tired of me quickly and, as previously arranged and discussed, at four o'clock I excused myself and with Brute in his new peekaboo car seat, we drove to an old friend's gathering a half hour away in the foothills of Redlands. I would return to spend the night and be out of Mother's testy hair before ten o'clock the next morning to leave for my new best friend Leighanne's second home in the wine country of Temecula.

Enjoying lively conservative, Christian Obama-bashing conversation and on my third, fourth, or fifth glass of Merlot, Mother called the cell.

"I think it would be better if you went on home to Hollywood rather than coming back here."

"What? I'm sleeping at your house and then heading south first thing in the morning."

"Do you have any idea what time it is? Get with it, Julie."

"Mom, I'll be there in thirty minutes. It's not even nine o'clock."

"I'm locking the door. It's passed my bedtime."

And, of course, I do not have the key. Rae, of course, does.

As fate would have it, I had not removed my overnight bag from the car. I slept on the bottom bunk in a pre-teen's black and purple wallpapered room. Brute crashed on a black fuzzy bean chair beside me. I slept like a baby.

Meeting up with Leighanne in Temecula, an hour's drive from San Bernardino, the drama I would soon come to expect began. Rory, whom I don't remember from drill team, is talking to Leighanne from her car as she is driving in the opposite direction back up to her mountain home in Big Bear City after picking up her forty-year-old son from Riverside County Jail.

"Well, Julie's in the car with me right now. We're going to Old Town for lunch. I'd love for you to meet up with us. Yes, I understand, that's out of your way. Oh, you're moving your son into your house? Did you have to pay his bail? Is he out on parole? Oh, probation. Yes, well, okay. We'll meet up soon. Yes, let's get together before you take down your Christmas decorations. Love you, too."

Just maybe, there's a very good reason why I don't remember them. Or would this indissoluble bond of growing up in the 50s in a once-lovely green valley at the bottom of the National Forest fill a need for compatible friendships that I had been unable to nurture while living in a town brimming with thirty-somethings who have no concept of the simple joy playing in the front yard with your neighborhood pals until the street lights come on can bring.

January 3rd of the New Year at precisely eight in the chilly morning, I am at the Lake Gregory Boat House to hand deliver my application, resume, and theatrical head shot, which I'm sure is not required and entirely unexpected. Snow crackling under my boots, I climb down the familiar stone steps to the landing. The park ranger on duty is an albino man in a green uniform, who looks nothing at all like Smokey the

Bear. He calmly tells me that all applications will be reviewed and that the office will get back to me if my application is tentatively accepted.

"Will I get to wear a ranger outfit?"

"If you're hired, you'll wear forest green walking shorts and a khaki polo shirt . . . with a Regional Parks patch over your heart."

"Awesome," and I never use that ridiculously immature word.

After setting Brute on a frozen patch of pine needles to do his thing, in my excitement I foolishly call Mother from the car before making the drive to Leighanne's and on to my first visit to her friend Rory's cabin by way of Highway 18 and the long and winding Arctic Circle around Big Bear Lake.

"Why would they hire you? And don't even hint at living at my cabin. I'm going to be using it myself come summertime."

"Gosh, Mother, please don't be subtle with me."

"Get with it, Julie. You've got your own damned cabin."

"Mom, why do you love Rae more than you love me and why does she have the key to your cabin and I don't?"

"Because she needs to be loved more than you do. She was married for thirty years. I let them use the cabin all the time. You don't have a key because in between your array of husbands, you may have brought up to my cabin all sorts of untoward strangers, tramps, and misfits of a suspicious nature."

"A mother should not be jealous of her own daughter."

"Why in the hell would I be jealous of you?"

I suspend the urge to slam down the receiver, because I am on a cell phone. It seems that Mother's scheduled Dr. Pepper and whiskey cocktail hours of ten-two-and-four may be starting a bit earlier.

"I've already arranged for housing, but thank you for offering."

"You're retired. Can't you just relax and enjoy it? I don't get all of this running around trying to be an actor, trying to be a realtor, and writing blasphemous tirades. And now you want to rent out pedal boats? Why do you always have to be doing something?"

"I've always wanted to be the gate lady at the north entrance, next to the hamburger stand. I have such sweet memories of summers on the lake and getting my hand stamped so that I could come back in without paying."

"You were five. How do you remember that?"

"I was five, six, and seven. I was eight, nine, and ten. I was fifteen, sixteen, and seventeen. And then I was twenty-three, twenty-four and twenty-five, a mom with two small kids."

"Do Elizabeth and Glen have the same silly childhood memories?"

"I don't think they even remember being children and having a mother. Getting that stamp was so cool. But when we left for the day, you never let me go back in just to flash my stamp."

"They were closed."

"That's the excuse you and grandma always gave me."

CHAPTER 45

Miss Manners, Drawing Blood, and Cruel Intentions

♪ Some people get their kicks by steppin' on a dream ♪

That's Life
Dean Kay and Kelly Gordon

Rory is a superlative hostess. She is the comfort-food cooking czar. Heavily wrinkled from a lifetime of smoking, a pack-a-day habit she matter-of-factly states she hung up one morning a few years back and never took it off the hook again, she seems generous to a fault. Her cabin of high-end finishes and alder wood is spotted here and there with the iconic black bear statuettes as in most Big Bear homes. The sparkling man-made lake, a summer haven for kayaking, jet skiing, water skiing, fishing and picnicking along its shores, is not outside the front door, but a short ride into town, where the ski slopes of *Snow Summit* rise above the quaint village of shops and eateries. Christmas décor has been ritually placed big time all about Rory's place. From the plastic deer in the front yard to the poinsettia guest towels in each of the three bathrooms, there is no way in hell you're going to mistake her for a Jew.

With the exception of her son, the toothless, prison tattooed meth-head that skulks in and out of the kitchen, whom I am alerted sleeps sitting up in a wooden shed in the backyard, Brute and I are comfortable sleeping in her second bedroom. A brash Clairol bleached blonde in great shape, whose cultural entertainment is the constant running and re-running of *Lifetime* movies from four eighty-five-inch LCD screens installed about the house, Rory is in bed by seven o'clock with her three dogs that will insist on their morning feeding at five a.m., when she will wake her guests with the running of the vacuum. Her second deceased husband left her sitting pretty; her home is mortgage free. I do not remember her from drill team. To be honest, I don't remember marching in one parade with anyone.

In celebration of Rory's sixty-fourth, Leighanne and I treated her to dinner at the Captain's Anchorage, where we ate from the old fashioned salad bar, knifed through thick steaks, and shared two bottles of red.

"You've got to read Julie's novel. She holds nothing back, and I mean *nothing*," Leighanne exuberantly broke in as my proud publicist.

"I don't read," Rory barked.

"Why not?" Leighanne asked.

"It hurts my eyes."

"But you're going to miss out on learning all about Muslims and the truth about Obama."

"Let's get the check. I don't talk religion or politics and it's passed my bedtime."

"Let's talk sex, then," I smiled and leaned in to whisper. "Do you guys use a vibrator?"

"Well, that's personal," Rory flatly responded, tossing her wadded cloth napkin onto her plate, a disgusting habit. "But, yes. Don't you?" I twitched, controlling the impulse to remove the napkin lounging in her mushroom gravy.

Stifling the comment, *someone in the kitchen will be forced to touch that thing*; I admitted to my sexual unsophistication, "I've never bought one, online or otherwise, although it's been suggested . . ."

"I have two, you know, in case the battery quits in one," Leighanne spurted and then cupped her hand over Rory's ear. "Julie uses her fingers."

"Yuck. How do you know that?"

"I read her novel."

With my fingers, I neatly placed my napkin to the appropriate left under the rim of my plate in the hope that my *Ms. Manners'* proper etiquette would catch on.

When I carried Brute out for his last pee and my final outdoor cigarette of the evening, the snow was falling steadily. No problem. Leighanne drives a heavy four-wheel drive SUV, as does Rory. Both of their cars could eat my Scion, which is parked in Leighanne's Running Springs driveway a treacherous seventeen-miles down the hill. Standing in pajamas on bare feet watching the white stuff remove any semblance of a roadway, hopefully, tomorrow afternoon my little car will not be buried under two feet of snow.

Passing by Rory's guilt trip, the toothless recidivist, on his trek from the downstairs bathroom in the guest suite to the backyard, a cold jagged knife in his hand, I went to bed with the desk chair against the locked door. Brute safely settled below me, from my plush queen-sized bed I watched *Death Wish II*, in which street thugs repeatedly sexually assault the Hispanic maid and the daughter before bludgeoning them to death. Spinning mildly from an abundance of holiday cheer, a nightmare followed in *Helter Skelter* fashion. I awakened before dawn to the hum of a vacuum cleaner, Rory's vibrator ostensibly out of power, relieved to find that the four dogs had not been disemboweled, Leighanne nor I hog tied and raped, and Rory still in one piece.

Safely home, I am despondent to see that the construction crew at Artemus' house on the other side of the wooden fence and eight feet from my back door has begun excavating under the foundation in order to stabilize the project for the addition of another story and a rooftop deck. Aware of my upcoming insanity over the ruination of an historical 1923 Spanish bungalow, Artemus flashed a three-finger salute to me as he passed through the walkway and left for the six-month duration of his city-approved project for an apartment near the junior college where he teaches subgrade delinquents.

Non-stop Mariachi music from a transistor radio, Latino grumbling, the rat-tat-tat of staple guns, the scent of fresh tortillas fired up on a grill, and dirt and dust floating over and under the fence began each of my previously serene mornings. The saddest part was that as the project rose above me, the sun no longer burst through the stained glass window showering light of turquoise blue and maize onto my bathroom walls.

Rising from the luxurious comfort of my morning bed, I was dismayed to find in its place the grizzly shadow of an illegal immigrant in a wife-beater t-shirt hammering long nails into four by fours. As the weeks went by, his early morning silhouette rose higher and higher.

When the additions were completed in June, this was not a *McMansion*, an irritably expensive re-do, but a replica of a Benghazi whorehouse with what appeared to be gun turrets pointing down at my roof, no back-up artillery on its way to save me. Upon his return to his personal enhancement to neighborhood blight, Artemus would top off the lime-green stucco monstrosity by flying a black and white, skull and crossbones *Jolly Roger* pirate flag from a homemade wooden pole tied to the skimpy wrought iron railing surrounding the roof deck. This flag will rage an evil shadow whipping violently onto my innocent stucco walls.

He continues to roll his sweet tobacco cigarettes on his front porch, never venturing up the spiral staircase inside the living room to sit on the upper deck. He's built a tall wooden fence in front of his porch to hide behind. He no longer pays the five dollars per month for lawn care. The tons of dirt removed from under the house during construction, only hastily and meagerly removed by the crew, continue to seep under our shared fence and into my walkway below the back stoop. Artemus is a total asshole.

* * *

I have been tentatively accepted as a seasonal Public Service Employee applicant. The Regional Parks office has mailed to me three appointment cards for the regimen of tests I must endure: blood testing for sexually transmitted diseases—my interloping HPV not a disqualifying factor—drug testing for illegal substances and abuse of alcohol—so I'm sobering up—and a health evaluation—to be sure I'm strong enough to stamp the hands of excited little children, I suppose. All these tests force me to maneuver the painful hour-and-a-half drive into San Bernardino on three separate occasions, which brings forth a guilt-ridden need to have lunch with my mother, which I successfully squelch. If I pass these tests, I will be interviewed by the Lake Gregory officials lauding over the PSEs who will be serving summer visitors and locals at my childhood play land of Lake Gregory.

On my final trip in, and with absolutely no plan to even let Mother know I am within fifteen minutes of her adobe, I am surprised to see Wayne calling from his investigator's office in the courthouse annex.

"Wayne, what's up?"

"Just thought I'd check in and remind you to send me a birthday card this month."

"It's already in the mail. I'm having blood drawn on Rialto Avenue. Then I'm off to the sheriff for fingerprinting."

"You're in town?"

"I want to be the gate lady at Lake Gregory this summer. I've begun the employment process."

"It's official then."

"Not yet. There's a final interview."

"No, that you're nuts. Won't hauling paddle boards up and down the beach hurt those crippled wrists of yours?" Wayne asked.

"Ah, they won't have me doing any heavy lifting. I'll just be pushing buttons at the register, maybe helping kids into pedal boats, and patrolling the shore for bullies knocking down sand castles. I get to wear a mini-ranger outfit."

"Very sexy. How was your holiday?"

"I dropped off presents at Alexandra's apartment, but I guess she opened them all by herself after returning from her holiday. Haven't heard a peep. Mom sent me a thousand dollars, which I'm using to publish Part Two of the trilogy, but she locked me out on Christmas day. Elizabeth and family are officially out of the will. My son lost my number, obviously, and I haven't had sex for—"

"Am I supposed to be writing all this down?"

"Nah. How did you do? Did Santa come?"

"No, but I did."

"How is the tramp?"

"In pre-payment for sex, she forced me to attend a family Christmas dinner with her parents, the kid, the kid's Baby Daddy, his parents, a bloated turkey, slimy sweet pineapple ham, and the new dog, after which I could hardly get it up."

"How much did the little doggie cost you?"

"Twelve hundred. He's a monster, a Standard poodle with an embarrassing set of balls on him," he went on. "Are you still there?"

"I'm not saying a word."

The warm weather turned with a cold and vicious wind, finishing off with days of rain. I thought of Ali and how he loved the rain. Of course, I think of him when each new full moon traverses over the bungalow, when during the monthly mani-pedi my calves moan with pleasure under the Mongolian manicurist's gentle massage, and when the *TMZ* double-decker tour bus stops in front of my house, the comedic guide bellowing from the loudspeaker.

> "To your right behind the blue unlicensed and unauthorized Hollywood gate is the *House of Shame*, where in her basement a foolish old woman once believed a young Persian hypochondriac actually loved her. Get your cameras ready! Those three clean and polished trashcans on the sidewalk—the neatly placed black, green, and blue—belong to Ms. Julie, so we might be able to catch her coming out in her robe to fetch them. But if you want to get down into her basement, you'll need to arrange a viewing with Dearly Departed Tours.
>
> They specialize in the macabre tales, the deaths, and the scandals of Hollywood—as in *The Black Dahlia, Janis Joplin, Hugh Grant, Michael Jackson, Bela Lugosi, Sharon Tate,* and *John Belushi*. Included are tours of the actual crime scenes. We're not exactly sure of the crime that took place here, but she's been given a life sentence without parole."

In her attempt to *turn a new leaf*, Alexandra has not communicated since her holiday card, never thanking me for the gifts I left under her tree, a tree which in the past I had helped to choose, heroically erect, and meticulously string lights about its boughs. The tree was left behind this year to wilt alone in her townhouse while she savored the two weeks of the holiday with a steadfast family, the parents married forever and to each other, not one divorce in the lineage.

In a panic, Stephen called from his triplex in the Hollywood Hills, where he lives in the main house with his spouse Chuck, a Libertarian previously married to a woman, an employed music director and composer.

"My friend Joel—he's a gay nurse and married to Donovan. Donovan is a nurse, too, who writes music. We've been perfecting a script for over five years. We finally have the cast and a table read this Saturday, but the lead actress is out of town or something. Please, can I borrow you for a few hours?"

"Are wine, chips and dip involved?"

"For you, anything. I'll send you an email with the script attached. Look for *What's My Intention?* It's a web series taking potshots at miserable acting coaches and the bad actors that pay them large sums of money in the hope they'll turn them into James Dean."

"And what part am I reading?"

"Stella, the acting coach, an out-of-work, famous old school movie star. She's a mix of Uta Hagen and Stella Adler, Elizabeth Taylor and Jane Fonda. She's demanding, intoxicating, and usually intoxicated. You won't have to dig too deep."

"Sure, Stephen. I have great respect for your writing. I can't wait to read it."

"In case you can't tell by the subtext, it's a comedy."

"Right up my alley. See you Saturday."

Arriving at Stephen's a bit tardy; the sagging L-shaped couch is stuffed with young actors, not my favorite people. The co-writer Joel, who is also cast as a wannabe future theatrical idol, is here. He appears to be a gentle soul, a steel-blue eyed, forever consuming and granting child, a Lord Fauntleroy, with the cut of *Blue Boy*, but definitely never with a *Pinkie*, his homosexuality flaunted by the diamond studs in both of his pointed ears, which resemble those of a forest fairy.

I am simply here to read the part of Stella, to fill in for the actress that has other obligations today. Having devoured months before Stephen's book, *Awakening the Actor Within*, after two glasses of pinot noir and a basket of Doritos, I found my "vein of gold," as he had instructed in his tutorial. That evening Stephen calls and I am given the leading role, a gratuitous position that promises instant *YouTube* fame and absolutely no fortune.

During the three-weekend filming of the web series, directed by C. Stephen Foster behind a mini-cam and shot on location under screens and lighting in Joel and Donovan's Silver Lake living room, dining room, and kitchen, I cultivated a new family of friends who would grow to love the Republican who loved the sinner, although admitting to disliking the sin. They accepted my stubborn political views, were charmed by my first novel, and encouraged me to continue writing my truth. They were shocked and sniggered by Julie's heterosexual misadventures, becoming ruthless in their attempts to make me one of the *boys*, while secreting their handholding antics under the kitchen table. Upon my entrance and my aristocratic "I'm here now," any conversational reference to man-on-man was gentlemanly squelched; although, as a writer, I was more than interested in the unnatural phenomena and in learning the inside scoop.

All corrections to the manuscript of *Jihad Honeymoon in Hollywood* hopefully made, I email the file to Abbott Press, my new choice of publisher, as I tire of dealing with Xlibris and the lovely high-pressure Filipinos that speak to me with their hands over their mouths in uninterruptable, indistinguishable sentences from thatched huts. The self-publishing company with offices within the United States will return my second novel in *galley* format, a trial print run, a mirror of exactly what the pages in the book will look like, with my name on the left page and the name of the book on the right. The final work begins soon after when new mistakes will appear, when the formatting will be a jumbled mess, and when I pull my hair out.

I spent an evening enthralled in the movie *The Holiday*, a story centered around two women living across the pond from each other, one a producer in Hollywood; one a working girl in the English countryside;

both in the midst of break-up sorrow, each swapping houses through a website. I had rented the movie by mail delivery on *Netflix* to watch the scene I had been in as a stand-in for a Team One passenger on an airplane cabin heading for America. Of course, a stand-in is never shot by the camera, but I wanted to relive the moment.

As the credits rolled by, I fetched the computer and searched through IMDB, the *Internet Movie Data Base*, and found that the director, Nancy Meyers, had written the script after learning about *Home Exchange*, an Internet site where homeowners can share their homes by moving into the homes of other members, while they move into theirs.

My need, however, was of a different nature. If I booked the lake job, I would benefit only by renting out the Hollywood bungalow for the summer, not exchanging it. Thus, I spent the next two hours posting pictures of my house on another website that had popped up, www.airbnb.com, an international hosting site charging a three percent commission, boasting a million dollar insurance coverage. *Airbnb*, the name a play on the standard bed and breakfast, took care of everything, but the window washing, the cleanup, and the laundry. I had no idea what I was getting into, but to recoup the total cost of my monthly mortgage and the cost of utilities by renting out my cherished bungalow to total strangers from around the world was intriguing: visitors eager to see the *Hollywood Sign* (you can see it from the corner across the street); visitors excited to traipse over the urine-stained stars in the sidewalks of the *Walk of Fame*; visitors enthusiastic to spot movie stars from an open-air tourist bus and happy to stand in line for hours at *Pink's* for a famous hot dog. My bungalow was sitting at just the right spot.

February and the Cupid flag flying, the pink night-blooming jasmine are beginning to peep as the vines creep up and over the trellis outside my bedroom window. Soon the scent of lovely times when he let me love him will permeate my sweet little home. Tearing up, as the staple gun rat-a-tatting next door brings me back to reality, I wonder, "When is this sorrow going away?"

"Dahlink, it's never going away as long as you keep pining over dat Islamic idiot," Natasha answered me from behind the closed door. "You're out of toilet paper."

"There's more on the metal spindle behind you to the right."

"Ah, very good."

"Natasha, why are you still hanging around? I've given up espionage. I just want to welcome rug rats to the lake, stamp the back of their chubby little hands, and smell the red onions toasting on the grill at the hamburger shack."

"We all miss you. Rocky, Bullwinkle, even Boris. If you evah need us, dahlink, just remember the good ole days before Edward Snowden let the cat out of the bag, when being a spy was an exemplar vocation, and we'll meet you in the bathroom for old times sake."

I waited for the flush and the tank to refill before opening the door, and she was gone.

Playing Russian roulette with my living space, not yet having an appointment for the mini-ranger interview, I received my first request on *Airbnb* to book the bungalow. Along with a picture of a heavyset American woman and her daughter, an operatic protégé, both residing in Liverpool, England, was a sweet note asking for a two months' stay beginning the first of June. Nervously, I clicked *reservation accepted* and crossed my fingers that whoever would be interviewing me would see in me what I saw in myself: the finest greeter that would ever grace the north gate entrance of the green and slimy shores of the Lake Gregory swim beach.

By the end of March and without an interview, I would book two more guests: an African-American soap opera producer/writer living in Dublin, Ireland; and a young married couple, recent graduates of NYU, driving across the continent to search for their dream jobs in Los Angeles, along with their two cats in two cages. I am off to Target to shop for new bed pillows, a super-duper mattress cover, and holiday cards.

Against my true inner feelings, I mailed out humorous V-Day cards to Elizabeth and the grandkids. All three cards were void of cash.

* * *

Rory and Leighanne were persistently insistent that I not spend the most romantic day of the year alone. On my list of things to do in order to grow and to successfully *move on* was the absolute, non-negotiable acceptance of any and all invitations from the few people still out there who yearned for my jovial company, unless, of course, it was an invitation from Mother.

I met up with my two new heterosexual best friends at The Macaroni Grill in Redlands at a shopping center that teased at my shopping glands. As I glanced at the storefronts, one after another after another, I began to drool. Right here surrounding one gigantic parking lot were the seeds of a shopping frenzy. In my neighborhood there are no shopping centers or shopping malls. Target is two miles away and its horrific underground parking lot is not for sissies. Kmart is three miles away in an unpleasant strip mall across from The Grove, its anchor store the overpriced and snooty Nordstrom's department store. Bed, Bath, and Beyond is a decent stroller walk on the way to Wells Fargo, but to bring home anything larger than a teapot, I'd have to drive and park the car in the garage, and if I were to forget to have my ticket validated, I'd be handing over four bucks for the privilege.

Here I am in a *free* parking lot the size of a small town. My head is spinning. I had forgotten how the squalor of south Redlands had matured into Citrus Plaza—so named because it sits where the orange groves once scented the San Bernardino Valley. Here you can shop until you drop—without having to move your car—through Pier 1 Imports, Michael's, Kohl's, Bed, Bath, and Beyond, BevMo!, the Barnes and Noble Bookstore, Cost Plus World Market, Sports Chalet, Tilly's, and Target; then get up from your credit card swiping lethargy to eat and drink your way through Red Robin, Magic Wok, Café Rio, Niko Niko Sushi, Starbucks, Chick-fil-A, Macaroni Grill. You can put gas in your tank at the 76 station on your way out, your car not having been towed for overstaying your visit.

Leighanne waved me to a table in the back. Without coordinating a gift exchange, all three of us had brought along Valentine gift bags sprouting with red glitter tissue paper and filled with wrapped chocolates and powder pink candy hearts. I passed out pink and red mini feather boas.

"You three ladies got the right idea," the waitress commented as she set down *Mama's Trio,* a platter of tidy servings of manicotti, chicken Parmesan, and lasagna, all dripping with cheese.

"We're sharing that, so just scoot it in the middle," Leighanne instructed.

"Yes, scoot it far enough away, so that Rory won't be tossing her napkin onto that gooey red mess," I thought.

"So you all are single?" the waitress inquired while popping the cork on a bottle of decent Chianti.

"Yes. I'm the gay divorcée."

"Four times, you know."

"Thank you, Leighanne for clarifying that. And lovely Rory is our infamous Black Widow—"

"The what?" Rory protested. "You're strange."

"You'll get used to it," I assured her.

"So sad. Rory's lost two husbands in less than ten years."

"Thank you again, Leighanne."

"You're welcome. I've been a widow for two years. He was a strapping, virile man, you know. You know, he drank too much and had a heart attack in his sleep one night."

"You must miss him a lot," the young waitress said. "And what do they call you?"

"The Grieving Widow," I answered for her.

"No, no wine for me. I'm the driver," Rory put her hand over the top of her glass.

"What? Have some wine. The Shrimp Portofino will sop it up and you'll be fine," I encouraged.

"Don't be a party pooper, Rory," Leighanne added. Rory handed her stemmed glass to the waitress.

"Fine. More for us," I smiled, knowing that Leighanne being a lightweight, I'd be finishing off the bottle before burning my alcohol level down to zero skipping aisle by tantalizing aisle through Michael's craft store.

Checking my emails for an audition notification from my agent, as Leighanne and Rory answered text messages from holiday well-wishers,

I was delighted to see my daughter Elizabeth had thanked me for the empty cards. The next sentence sobered up my cupid day with girlfriends, when she shot me straight in the heart.

> I did not give you permission to put my poem in your book. You asked for a copy because you did not have one, then you followed up with this e-mail in 2011.

She's attached an email sent a year ago? She's not deleted emails for over a year? Or does she save mine in a lust for vengeance? I scrolled down for more uplifting Valentine's Day prose from the poet.

> The point is that I do not want my poetry or my name in your book, so please do whatever you have to and have it removed.

"Are you crying?" Rory asked.
"No, actually I'm seething," and I passed the phone to her.
"Well, that's cold," she passed the phone to Leighanne.
"Well, what a bitch. Has she even read your book?"
"She's never told me that she has, but maybe this is her way of saying that she has."

I skipped the shopping excursion and headed straight home to the MacBook. My reply to Elizabeth was simple: *Deleted.*

I forwarded the revision to the publisher and poured myself three inches of bourbon over ice and lit up. Clicking my jaw, I blew a few smoke rings out the koffice window. I didn't know I could do that. I'm learning something new every day, as in approval of my work is not needed and neither is the poem.

> *My own experience has been that the tools I need for my trade are paper, tobacco, food, and a little whiskey.*
>
> William Faulkner, Author, Dead at 62

Chapter 46

Honey, Don't You Have a Dream?

♪ I've made up my mind,
I'm keeping my baby ♪

Papa, Don't Preach
Stephen Bray, Brian Elliot, Madonna

BEFORE Ali, no one had addressed me as *darling* or *babe*, trite expressions of anonymity, yet sweet little tokens dropped obscurely on pillowcases with the intention of manipulating my affections. Wiping away all the presumptive cobwebs, I'm such a simple creature. I turn my attentions to amicable Brute. So precious, so perfect, there is much pleasure in watching him sleep, which he spends twenty-two hours of each day in cuddled repose, undisturbed by my tickling affections. Ah, but I've a different standard applied to my sleeping dog than I do to a significant other sleeping in after eight in the morning unless there is group activity involved.

Besmirching the esteemed office of the President of the United States, from the Governor's Dinner at the White House, First Lady Michelle Obama stoops to a new low, when from an overhead screen at the 2013 Academy Awards ceremonies, she turns the evening into a political event by announcing the winner for best picture: *Argo*, my pick, the story of Tony Mendez, the C.I.A. agent who rescued six Americans and flew them out of Tehran during the United States hostage crisis of 1980 in Iran. The star and director, Ben Affleck, accepts the award and thanks his wife for *working* so hard on their marriage, work she may tire of sooner than later.

I finally found an open spot in Alexandra's busy schedule. We take a six-block walk from her townhouse to Lulu's Cafe on the corner of Detroit Street and Beverly Boulevard. Enjoying a pleasant, sunny day, while scooting to single file on the sidewalk to make room for the Hasidic Jew mothers in appropriate modesty wigs hurriedly pushing their children to temple in designer strollers, we have a one-sided conversation. She advises me that because her sister Elizabeth is no longer speaking to me, Mother's Day celebrations can be added to the holidays I have ruined. She is decisively cold. Walking carefully on the recognizable eggshells set carefully in my path, I decide to offer up no explanation for the sudden dispute over a poem; my *deleted* must have touched her sister's poetic nerve.

"Benjamin and I are taking a much-needed vacation to New York. Of course, Christmas we'll be off to Hawaii with his parents and his brother, who is currently without a boyfriend."

At Lulu's we take a table outside. "I've been off the pill for a year. I couldn't manage the weight gain any longer. And as you like to remind me, I need to stay thin to earn a living."

Let that one go.

"What protection are you using?" I asked, controlling the urge to remind her that Obama now in his second irritating term, no one is taking away her contraception.

"Condoms."

The look on my face was that of the overly arched eyebrows, which when held for long periods is a remarkable wrinkle eraser and much cheaper than Botox.

"Don't worry and don't preach. At my age, if I get pregnant I'm keeping my baby. I'll just move into his parents' home. They've got plenty of room."

"Hasn't being my daughter all these years weaned you away from wanting to be a mother?" I thought.

"Well, they've been putting you in Benjamin's bedroom for, what, two-and-a-half years now. What did they think might happen?"

"His mother would be thrilled."

"Yes, Benjamin is her only option for a no-explanation-necessary grandchild," I thought.

My eyebrows leaped to my hairline; such facial expression causing the lips to seal. Yep, I won't need any costly poisonous injections for quite some time.

***

Waiting for Brute to do his thing, I wander through the bungalow walkway and catch Randi sitting on her worn wooden porch holding a royal blue metal tube between her yellowed fingers, the skulls and skeletons of her forever Halloween holiday dangling overhead.

"I know that's not a lipstick," I surmise. "Are you smoking a miniature hookah pipe? And are you staying in your robe all day?"

"It's an E-cig, an electronic cigarette. It has all the benefits of nicotine without the stink of smoke, the arsenic, the carbon monoxide, the urethane, the toluene, and the acetone—all the carcinogens that will kill us sooner or later. Look, you just hold down this button on the battery and it heats up the liquid." She sucked in long and hard and released a billow of white air. "They call it *vaping*."

The scent was sweet and exotic. "Raspberry Essence," she explained. "All the oils have fancy names. There's even bubblegum flavor. No more ashtrays, yellow nails, or foul breath."

"Sold. Where do I get mine?"

Brute and I strolled down Cahuenga beyond Santa Monica Boulevard and over to Vine Street, passing the elementary school, the busy car wash, and CVS Pharmacy, Liquor, Photo, and Beauty—and anything else I would ever need, including bug bombs. Sitting front paws up, Brute began to quiver and cock his head my way. In his frightened black eyes I could see the threat of a scramble out of the stroller and onto the pavement, his avenue of escape north to the Hollywood Hills.

"Don't have a panic attack. On those legs you wouldn't make it ten feet. Calm down. No one is cutting your toenails today."

On his better days, when taking an occasional walk on the tandem leash to the pet groomer, after passing CVS, Brute would bolt in reverse gear, spinning Hound off his feet. For the remaining four blocks, I untangled them from fire hydrants, telephone poles, and bus benches until carrying the rebel into the bathhouse. Brute may be losing his eyesight and his hearing, but he still knows where he's at and where he's headed. From the front seat of the car, he can tell you when the 134 turns into the 210 East.

Continuing on our way, we passed the Professional Musicians Union Hall Local 47, the pink Roadway Motel with its white columns and white barred windows, and crossed at the light outside of Pavilion's parking lot.

He let out a sigh of relief when we entered the Armenian smoke shop next to the pet groomer next to the dry cleaners next to the nail parlor in the Hancock Park Plaza strip mall on Melrose. Inside the tidy shop with glass cases displaying colorful glass water pipes and ornate hookahs, I uncomfortably let the proprietor know I was here to purchase a legal piece of non-smoking equipment and certainly not something I could be arrested for sucking on. I laid down fifty bucks for an electronic cigarette *kit*: a battery charger and one slim royal blue battery screwed into a clear shaft ending at a glass tip. Added to the bill was twelve dollars for a week's supply of Raspberry Essence nicotine oil.

"Depending on your vaping habit, this should last a week. But some people puff all day, so you may want to buy two or three. With six you get one free," he haggled.

"Oh, no, not me, I promise. This one will do."

At seven dollars for a pack of cigarettes, my initial investment of an e-cig and a bottle of nicotine oil versus my pack-a-day habit should save me well over thirty-five dollars a week and increase my life expectancy by a few dreary years or so. By the time we returned to Randi's porch, she was frantically tearing the plastic off her pack of Marlboros.

"What? You're off the wagon already?"

"It's not doing it for me. I'll trade this thing for any cigarettes you want to get rid of."

"But you don't smoke Virginia Slims."

"I do now."

The Arab Sprung

Even though my e-cig experience was nearly sabotaged by an exploding battery while descending a mountain road, tempting me to drive directly into the nearest 7-Eleven for a carton of Virginia Slims, I've never smoked another cigarette. My initial investment has ballooned. My house is exploding with long, thin tubular batteries screwed into chargers, which are plugged into various wall sockets about the house, for to not have a charged battery at the ready is tantamount to the sweating nausea of a heroin addict unable to reach his connection. I keep a flavorful selection of oils in a kitchen drawer; with six you get one free. Bubblegum and Cappuccino are my favorites. The first week into my newly acquired vice, I spent hours up and down the ladder, rag and water bucket close at hand, swabbing the walls of the bungalow to remove the acrid smell of cigarette smoke. My entire bungalow now greets you with the aura of fruit oils filming the windows, the scene reminiscent of a Chinese dragon lady lounging on her big chair in a cloudy opium den.

* * *

Here it comes, ladies and gentlemen, my sixty-fifth birthday!

I prepared the bungalow for my sleepover guests. Spit shined, the bungalow is dusted and polished, the scents of lemon Pledge and bubblegum mixing together nicely. Dressed to comfortably walk Hollywood Boulevard, I greet two gals who have driven from a mountain top through suburbia hell, through valley after valley, to reach me. Curbside, after a short training session on how to parallel park while traffic dispassionately whizzed by Rory's four-wheel-drive truck and Leighanne feverishly kept one eye out for knife-thrusting vagrants, the Mountain Widows stepped for their first time on the grungy sunny sidewalks of Hollywood.

"Oh, you didn't have to!" I hugged them both and set their gift bags on the porch table.

"Put it on," Leighanne insists and I press the pink and silver glistening H-A-P-P-Y-B-I-R-T-H-D-A-Y plastic crown into my curls. As Rory and I waited patiently for an opening, Leighanne talking nonstop during margaritas, chips and salsa on the porch, Captain Brainard stops by on his way to his newly acquired fixer-upper in the mews.

"I told them they'd meet an actor—so here's Brent. Brent, this is Rory and Leighanne."

"Good day, ladies. And the crown is for?"

"My sixty-fifth birthday that apparently you forgot about along with Alexandra. Not even a card from her. Isn't reaching sixty-five equal to the first, the fifth, the thirteenth, the sixteenth, the twenty-first, the thirtieth, the dreaded fortieth, and the fiftieth? And my mother sent a card without a sixty-five dollar check in it. But these two gals have come all the way from the San Bernardino Mountains to spend the weekend with me."

♪ Ain't no mountain high enough. Nothing can keep me, keep me from you ♪ Leighanne sang out, the margaritas hitting a high note.

"Text me later. Maybe I'll catch up."

After a sneak-in view of the grand foyer of the Pantages Theatre and being asked to leave immediately, we lined up on the barstools at the Frolic Room next door. I soon learned that keeping Rory entertained was easy enough: simply slide a barstool under her bootie and a shiny bar under her elbows. She had spent most of her adult life working on the other side, bartending in stilettos. We were surprised that free drinks were available to a sixty-five-year-old woman wearing a delightful plastic deco crown, not only at the forever happy hour at the Frolic Room, but all the way up and down Hollywood Boulevard, where I *vaped* my way in and out of bars, bars that did not allow smoking. This memorable experience would soon be shunned and eventually banned from all public places by the liberal city fathers of Los Angeles in their constant attempt to control what I eat, smoke, and drink, while allowing the trail of second-hand marijuana fumes from passing pedestrian punks to fill my lungs.

By the time we settled into a crowded bistro for dinner, the free drinks abruptly ended when the stiff manager, muttering something about excessive alcohol consumption, refused to serve me. The crown has become a birthday celebration essential, which we three share.

Later that evening at Hemingway's Lounge on Hollywood Boulevard, we caught up with Brainard, who, after treating us to thick red wine as a rock band bellowed over our tired heads, walked three old ladies home. Leighanne bellyached each dreadfully painful step of the way before passing out on the big chair pullout bed. As her sanctuary from Leighanne's horrendous snoring just six feet from my queen bed, Rory chose the quilts and pillows of the basement, unaware of what glorious sexual ghosts played down there.

Ambushing the three-women-in-one-bathroom curse, by six o'clock the next morning, she was showered, blown dry, and impatiently waiting for Leighanne to join us on a drive to the Santa Monica Pier and Bubba Gump's for a bucket of shrimp; a surface street adventure down Pico Boulevard interrupted by an L.A.P.D. pedestrian-crossing sting operation yielding Rory a ticket, online traffic school, and another complaint about cops that would serve her for years to come.

President Obama, responsible for racking the national debt up to sixteen trillion, has named April *National Financial Capability Month*, calling on all Americans to handle their money more responsibly.

Central Casting booked me directly to work on *The Big Bang Theory*, a total waste of two days, the director not having the good sense to call me out of the background lineup to star in the sitcom.

On my little plantation, I dust and mop, I climb up and down a ladder to prune, I take the three trashcans in and out, and I wonder out loud, "The Republicans freed the slaves; what in the world were we thinking?"

This week three celebrities pass on into the forever after: Jonathan Winters, eighty-seven; Margaret Thatcher, eighty-eight; and my favorite Mouseketeer Annette Funicello, seventy. My mother doesn't even have a cold.

Screening of *Midnight's Children* at the ArcLight Cinema and the book signing by Salman Rushdie, the author of *Satanic Verses*, a controversial novel blaspheming Muslims written before its time. Assuming at present Mr. Rushdie is no longer in fear of the fatwa placed on him in 1989 by the Ayatollah Khomeini, the then Supreme Leader of Iran, he signs and returns my copy of his book-to-movie and I plop a

Muslim Romance Trilogy bookmark into his hand. I'm still waiting for an email exalting my writing technique and requesting a meeting with his publisher.

> Bill Nob *On the News*: Julie, wake up. Your Muslim lover may have completed his mission in pressure cooker style, beyond disturbing the last good years of your life. And I'm talking body parts here. Two Muslim brothers—and one of them looks just like the scoundrel. Watertown, Massachusetts, is closed down due to an intense manhunt for the Boston Marathon bombers, another instance of homegrown terrorism, perhaps. It's an incredible sight and a no-fly zone. One suspect is held at bay inside a house.
>
> The older brother was shot dead last night after an attempted 7-Eleven robbery? Hey, ho, or was he then run over by his own brother, good golly, after fleeing some Middle Eastern shit hole for freedom in America? Whoa, Nelly. Now I have to learn to pronounce more tongue twisting Arabic names, which I'm getting pretty good at.

I knew I should have changed that station. I grabbed the phone, the dog, and my reading glasses and headed for the basement. Is this why Ali insisted that I put locks on the underside of the door in the floor?

Stepping backwards and half the way down to my safe house, Brute cradled under my arm, the cell phone is sounding. It's not a text, but an actual phone call and it's Brainard.

"I just want you to know that those two lunatics in Boston are not the brothers Ali and Ghali."

"You know where Ali is?"

"No, we don't. We've lost him," Brainard said and waited for me to respond. "No worries, Julie. Go back to sleep."

I turned off the phone, shut off the radio, and sat trembling on the edge of the bed. *No worries.* How had one innocent and curious movie date with a sociopath taken me this far?

***

The Arab Sprung

At the Lake Gregory boathouse, after climbing a tight and dirty flight of wooden stairs, I am told to sit. The interviewers, a brunette, acne scared overweight gal teamed up with an attractive blonde dyke, both in ranger costumes behind a long dusty table, begin their interrogation.

"The North Beach bathroom is all tile and metal. How would you clean it?"

"How will I have time to clean a bathroom when I'm stamping the sandy hands of innocent children?" I thought. "I grew up using that disgusting bathroom," I foolishly share. "With a fire hose?"

"If a train carrying twenty tons of coal leaves Chicago at five in the morning traveling west at one hundred and twenty miles per hour . . ."

"What? Can you repeat that?"

"We're just playing with you."

"Oh."

"A guest gives you two ten dollar bills. The cost of admittance is five dollars, but they want an all-day water slide bracelet, which is ten dollars. What do you give them back?"

The stale room is spinning, my palms are sweating, just me alone with two angry minimum wage earners trying to twiddle me down to racking sobs. The slanted roof in this attic is scrunching me into the knotty pine floor.

"Five dollars and a bracelet?"

"Excellent. You wouldn't believe how many applicants get that one wrong. Do you have any questions for us?"

"Yes. I do get to wear a ranger uniform with a patch, right? And do you still have those cute little hand stamps?"

"Yes and yes."

Not at all sure I would be passing out any all-day water slide bracelets, I forged ahead in the preparation for my *Airbnb* guests. In and out of the walk-in closet and up and down the basement stairs I go hauling embarrassing personal items, offensive books, and a cumbersome collection of family videotapes. I apologized to Jesus on the bedroom wall and, not wanting to offend anyone, exchanged him for the black and white Audrey Hepburn. Taking a walk-down-memory-lane break, I popped in a tape marked *Cherry Valley* into the ancient TV/VCR combo in the basement. There we were dancing to Bruce Springsteen's *Born in the USA* on the old and tired forest green carpet in the 1908 farmhouse dining room. My pubescent, chubby son strummed maniacally on a broom handle, while I in my bathrobe dipped and swayed my new baby girl. Ah, there's teenage Elizabeth, too, wandering through the kitchen in her bathrobe and waving off Alexandra's young, strapping proud father, who couldn't seem to stop taking movies with the new Panasonic. Closing the door in the floor, I wondered if I would ever again retrieve my life's treasures.

Realizing I would have to store the clothing from half a full-length closet and from four of the drawers, I called in a locksmith to install a deadbolt on the walk-in closet door, where inside I would erect a garment rack. Being an *Airbnb* host is not for sissies and there was still so much more to do: clean three fan lights; wash all the windows inside and out; and scrub and shine and empty out the fridge, leaving the condiments in the shelves of the door in sparkling order. The Hollywood vacation bungalow was taking shape; uncluttered, bright and cheery, even I would pay eighteen hundred dollars a month to stay here. Actually, I do.

Today I have an audition to which I will arrive wearing no makeup and my coffee-stained beige sweatshirt. It's my third day without a shower. My drab, greasy hair delicately brushed through with a streak or two of Ben Nye theatrical grade silver-gray paint, I am ripe for the role of *Winner Woman 2* in a **MoneyGram** commercial, as described in the email from L.A. Casting by way of my agent.

> Female-looks to be a middle-aged woman, looks to be in her mid-50s. Slightly shabby. Desperate looking. She may have some subtle signs that she has bad motives-rings under her eyes, interesting look, missing tooth, quirky, shifty, hinky, etc. NOT THE CLICHÉ, I.E. drug addict. MUST BE ABLE to show a wide range of talent.

Casting directors are not required to display a wide range of knowledge of grammar, editing, or the proper use of a *hyphen* versus an *em dash*.

Requested wardrobe: slightly shabby and desperate, without being over the top.

The attached script was wordy, thirty-seconds worth. Obviously, I was to be a scam artist trying to persuade someone on a city bus to mail a check to a certain address so they could claim the five million dollars that was waiting for them. The *button* I would add on to the written lines: "Honey, don't ya have a dream?"

Upon entering the waiting room, I am not surprised to see that my competition have showered, shaved, and dressed ritualistically in their twinset sweaters and pressed khaki pants; their eyes done up, their hair painstakingly coifed, their lips gleaming with gloss. I, on the other hand, while waiting my turn at the SAG sign in sheet, am asked by the assistant if I have, perhaps, wandered in, having taken a wrong turn somewhere.

"This is the MoneyGram audition, isn't it?" I ask flashing my few expertly blacked out front teeth and hacking up a wad into a tissue retrieved from my pocket. "Sorry about that. I quit smoking and it's all coming up."

"Yes. Sorry. Go ahead and sign in."

I booked the commercial to shoot the night of May 1st and I booked the lake job to begin the end of May on Memorial Day weekend—both surprises came in on the same day. I was in Hand-Stamping-*Airbnb*-SAG-Union-Rate Heaven.

Chapter 47

Cobwebs, Coconut Vodka, and Cocktails at Six

♪ There ain't no cure for the
Summertime Blues ♪

Eddie Cochran
1938-1960

Mother has been avoiding me. The last time I stopped by her house uninvited, her front porch had been taken over by cobwebs stretching from the front door across to the front windows, where they had somehow mingled with the mound of moist bird poop on the windowsill. When she finally came to the door in a stained sweatshirt circa 1972, her hair in a ponytail, she peaked out, slipped through the crack in the doorway, carefully ducked under the disgusting display and ordered me not to touch anything.

She described these naturally recurring phenomena as part of the *Circle of Life* and as such were not to be disturbed. Mother did not allow me into the house, where I know from past observance she's protecting the spiders that she insists will kill the ants that march around the bathtub that is never drained of tepid water and plastic water lilies.

♫ Hakuna Matata ♫ It's time for a phone call and invite.

"Hello," Mother answered in her singsong breathless way, always hoping to find a John Thomas on the other end. Her rotary phones do not have caller I.D.

"Good morning, Mother. How are you?"

"The same as I was a minute ago," she snapped. "Did you forget to tell me something?"

"It's Julie, your first born with the hazel eyes," I explained.

"Oh. I keep getting you two confused. You both sound so much alike. When I tell you something, I think I've told Rae or that you've passed it on to her, but since you're not speaking to her, I guess I'll have to repeat myself."

Now I'm confused. "You want to tell me something?"

"I know you're calling about Mother's Day."

"Yes. Alexandra is taking me to lunch and a movie on Saturday before leaving for Santa Barbara, and I have to be on the mountain for some life saving certification class on the Monday after, so I thought we'd—"

"You're really taking that job?"

"I already told you that." Oops, I've just insinuated that she has forgotten our last conversation. I'm going to bed without supper again.

"Listen to me! Don't you know where I'm coming from?"

"Are we talking about brunch next Sunday?"

"I want you to spend Mother's Day with your children. I told Rae the same thing. I told her to spend it with her son, like she did last year," she recounted calmly. Switching gears, she began to scream hysterically. "Last year you had your girls with you and I was all alone and that's just the way I like it!"

"The first time in sixty-four Mother's Days—" I shouted back.

"You little shit, why don't you make up with your sister?"

"So that's it. You don't want to see me unless Rae comes along," I easily surmise.

"Are you so sure that at your age you want to take orders from part-time county employees? You were a professional court reporter. You're retired. And just who are these people that are letting you stay with them all summer? Why would they do that? You'd better wise up and ask yourself why a married couple would want you hanging around."

"I'm hanging up, Mother," I spoke softly and gently put the house phone into the cradle.

She immediately left a syrupy message on my cell phone. "Enjoy your Mother's Day. I know I will."

Good grief.

The Time Warner cable box has been coming in and out and in and out again. Today the basic cable is in, another *Airbnb* hosting expense. Guests will also have Wi-Fi and the password. Not staying to the end of the school year, I wave an early good-bye to Vine Elementary for the summer. Mr. Taylor is saddened that I will miss the annual Volunteer Appreciation Day breakfast of chorizo, potato, egg and cheese burritos. I returned home with a large handmade *Thank You, Grandma Julie* card signed in print by my rug-rat fans, a drawing of Brute in his stroller on the front.

Mopping down the front porch steps, I hailed Randi, as she passed by the gate. "Grab your smokes! I've got coconut vodka in the freezer and lots to tell you."

"Be there within the half hour. It's feeding time at the zoo."

"Say hello to the rats and tarantulas for me and good-bye to the crickets."

Carrying two icy glasses and tripping over the open suitcase on the living room floor, I rushed down the front steps to let her in.

"Mmmm, you can actually taste the coconut," she laughed and lit a cigarette.

"Oh, I'll get you an ashtray. I hid them away."

"So you're still on the e-cig?" Randi shouted after me. I returned with the black and white Hollywood souvenir ashtray, a rhinestone-studded pink e-cig, and a small bottle of oil.

"Yes, 'tis true. They're wonderful. I'm saving money and my breath smells like bubblegum."

"Coconut bubblegum. So what's up?"

"Remember the lake job I applied for? Well, I booked it and I'm leaving tomorrow for the whole summer," I answered and blew out a hefty cloud.

"You bitch. You're leaving me?"

"Oh, don't be sad. You can come up and visit. There's a pullout in the living room. You'll love it up there in the idyllic lake village of Crestline," I urged her.

"The Mini Cooper will take those mountain roads like a jaguar in the wilds of Africa," she envisioned. "Are there jaguars in Africa?"

"I don't know. Probably. We'll kayak, sunbathe on paddleboards, hike, and have steaks at the Stockade Grub & Whiskey. And you're going to love Ted and Trudy."

"Who are they? I don't want to intrude."

"Intrude? They're the salt of the earth. I'm staying at their guest cottage."

"Because you can't use your cabin."

"Yep. And heads up, I've rented this one too. I am officially an *Airbnb* host. I've printed a list for you with their phone numbers, their pictures, and the dates. The boys next door will have one too in case."

"In case what? Hey, I can handle it. So you're a landlord guru now? Am I supposed to entertain them?"

"No, just make yourself known and report any suspicious activity."

"What if he shows up when someone else is here?"

"If who shows up?"

"You're into Chapter 47 of Part Three of *The Muslim Romance Trilogy* and you don't know who *he* is?"

"Time for a refill."

The sun finally made way for the May moon, which by midnight hung in crescent shape in the background over the quiet boulevard. The vintage iron streetlights clicked on up and down the block. The vodka bottle empty, Bogie's Liquor delivered another within twenty minutes. Brute wandered out to sniff the night air and to remind me that he needed assistance.

The three of us visited the walkway lit by my string of white lights looped over the branches in the old snarly tree.

"When did you put the pink and red streaks in your hair?"

"Valentine's Day."

"Sorry, I just noticed."

"That's okay. I just noticed your neck. I put the green streaks in for Saint Paddy's Day."

"Sorry, I didn't notice that either."

"Like your holiday flag rotation, I changed my clit ring from a red ruby to a green emerald. Red goes back in on the Fourth of July."

"Doesn't it rub a hole into the crotch of your panties?"

"I never wear panties."

"Less laundry for you and quick access for your future husband."

"I always thought someday I'd marry, but I was too busy sowing wild oats everywhere. Everyone should sow their wild oats before they marry."

"Randi, I married all my oats. I'm the link to a great marriage. After me, the only way is up."

"I'll drink to that."

"All of my husbands enjoyed a great sex life. I just wish I'd been a part of it."

"Are you doing a stand-up routine right now?"

"When I was having my babies, the world was a much nicer place."

"That's 'cause they kept all the bad stuff secret. I need to use the toilet."

"You know, I didn't tell my sister I was pregnant with Alex 'cause I didn't want to piss her off."

"Hold that thought," she said as I closed the gate behind us.

"Be careful when you stand up, sweetie. Thank goodness for the Internet. No excuse for ignorance anymore."

"What were we talking about?"

"The Internet. No excuses anymore for dating a crazy one. Google the asshole and this time believe what you read."

"What about being pregnant and your sister?"

"Oh, yeah. I'd had two kids already, years before, and my sister finally got pregnant. So I wanted to wait until she was three months along before I let her know I was having a third at the age of thirty-seven."

"I'm getting old, Julie. I'll never have any children. And now that one little abortion is haunting me."

"Fuck, Randi, you've had more than one, which is why you had a hysterectomy. Anyway, there's more to life than recreating yourself. Old? You're only forty. But I'll tell you this, getting old ain't for sissies."

"You stole that."

"Bette Davis would be proud of my unlicensed quotes."

"Which kid aren't you speaking to today?"

"Actually, all of them, and I have a theory. Three husbands and one kid each, half siblings all, but I never thought of them as half of or parts of anything. But now they've taken their respective halves and given greater credence to the half that they don't share."

"Okay, I'm losing you."

"Father-daughter, father-son, father-daughter; mother-daughter, mother-son, mother-daughter; sister-brother, brother-sister; sister-sister, brother-sister-sister. That's ten relationships to nurture, mangle, and disrupt. And, shit, three's a crowd. Maybe I need a pen and paper to figure this out, but I'm too drunk to get up and get it."

"Not to change this interesting mathematical subject, but are you afraid to die?"

"Well, that's morbid. No, I'm not. I'm going to be run over by a Prius."

"What?"

"They're everywhere and they make no sound. It will be a silent death."

"Maybe this summer you'll be carried away by a redneck in a big red truck."

"I want my cabin back. You never went with me. You've never seen it. It's so pretty."

"Maybe I can see it when I come up."

"Please don't sleep all day and drink all night when I'm gone. Promise me."

"Oh, sure. While you're babysitting fat kids on the beach, I'm going to a horror-night campout next week in the wilds of Griffith Park."

"Please don't scare yourself to death."

"But before I go to bed, 'cause it's fucking one o'clock in the morning, I leave you with these fucking drunk words of wisdom. Make up with your daughter, the one who's married to the Indian/Italian/Mexican? Bury the hatchet. Smoke the peace pipe. Call your son. And remember to live each day as if it's your last."

"You're so full of shit. Get the hell out of here."

***

The little car-that-could rolled over the wooden bridge and onto the dirt and gravel drive fronting my summer home.

"My God, girl, whatcha got in there?" Teddy bent down and peered into my open window.

"I'm staying for three months. Did you forget?"

"Nah, been looking forward to it. Got ya a couple sturdy brushes and two gallons of primer and paint."

"And I brought my Craftsman sander. I'm here and ready to go to work. I start orientation at the lake on Wednesday."

"Well, today's Monday, so I figure you can plug that little sucker in right now," he smiled.

"That little sucker is at the bottom of the pile," I pointed to the mound behind me. "Under the stroller, the suitcase, the box of reference materials, the fold-up table, the garment bag, the beach bag, Brute's two beds, and the three-month supply of dog food."

"Cocktails on the back porch every night at six. Trudy be coming up the mountain from work pretty soon or I'd offer ya a Cuban Libra right now. Best not to do any partying until the wife pulls in."

The rules had been set.

"I'm worried that Brute will bark when I leave for work," I said and reached over to the car seat to ruffle his ears.

"He'll probably need to relieve himself some time, too. Can't have the little guy just wandering around the place like coyote bait. Don't you worry about it. I'll enjoy the company."

"Thanks, Ted."

"Gotta get back inside to my office. I'm the trusty truck dispatcher, ya know, for another half hour."

"I'll be busy writing on my days off. You won't even know I'm here."

"Except for the sound of sandpaper on peeling paint. Oh, here's your key."

Weeks before I had purchased a post office box here in Crestline to which my Cahuenga Boulevard mail would be forwarded. I added another key to the ring.

My first *Airbnb* guests, a plump mother and her daughter, arrived in Hollywood and were successful at opening the push-button lock box secured onto the wrought iron fence. Within three days, *Airbnb* deposited the first month's rent into my checking account. Within four days, the complaints came in: there are homeless people here, there is traffic noise, we can't find a parking place after eight o'clock, and the bed leans to the left.

There would be no refund.

Cheerfully excited and dressed to oversee in green shorts with many pockets and my regulation khaki polo shirt—with the Park and Recreation embroidery patch of sunshine and evergreens—I slipped on my new olive green canvas shoes from the Rite Aid summer footwear collection, removed the pink foam overnight rollers, brushed out my curls, plopped on a green African safari hat, and said good-by to Brute, who had no idea why we were here and where I was going.

Driving down the swift turn into the north parking lot hidden below rows of pine trees, my heart sank. I understood that this year the Lake Gregory swim beaches had been dredged of the green slime and mud which made the lake bottom slippery and creepy, but I didn't expect to find thousands of cubic feet of moist silt, murky debris, slimy dead fish, and an old rubber tire or two piled two stories high rising up from the asphalt. Blocked by a small tractor and backhoe, the north gate admittance booth, my cherished little hand stamps inside, was behind padlocked chain link gates. The driver waived me away as he lifted a miniscule load from the *Close Encounters of the Third Kind* frightening mound. Had the rangers been waiting all spring for the Mother Ship to arrive, the aliens a peaceful tribe tooting John Williams' tunes through tubas for all to enjoy? Not making a dent in the disgusting pile, he headed up and out to the street to dump the drop in his bucket someplace far from humanity. At this rate, I thought, the lot won't be cleared until Labor Day, the last day of summer. I circled up to the street and parked behind a long line of cars above the boathouse driveway. My childhood dream of greeting sunbathers on opening day was beginning to shrivel.

Initiation day proved to be a cliquish event, with more returning mini-rangers than newbies. In a group of twenty seated at picnic tables on the outdoor pavilion above the freshly raked sandy beach, the only PSE anywhere near my age was a frail man in his seventies, John. He couldn't and wouldn't hear a word I said, as I tried my best to explain the orders being given by the grumpy brunette, now distinguished as Tina, the heterosexual women who had interviewed me. The orientation vague, apparently a secret joke played on the new troops, there was not one word from the pulpit on how to fill out a time sheet, how to work a register, or how to refill the automated paper towel machines.

"Where are all the people?" the old man blurted out, drawing unneeded attention to the senior citizens huddled together on the bench in the back row.

"There's nobody here but the crew, because the lake doesn't open until Saturday," I quieted him. "Our first duty is to move all the paddle boards from the wooden stands over there on the sand down to the water."

"I'm just here to check bags for alcohol and glass containers at the gates. They promised."

"And what qualifies you for that prized position, John?"

"I'm a retired prison guard, State of California."

"You should come in handy."

All of the Public Service Employees, including buoyant teenage lifeguards in red shorts or red razor back swimsuits, were dispersed to the sand on the north beach, where John succumbed to helping me lift one hundred and fifty pound antiquated boards painted red or yellow and carry them twenty-five yards to the shore. After ten hauls under a blazing sun, we agreed that we had done our share.

Exhausted, John and I are hoisted into the bed of a Regional Parks truck along with two teenage boys and driven with Tina at the wheel to the San Moritz Lodge at the cove on the other side of the lake.

The lodge on the southeast shore, and nowhere near the Alps of Switzerland, was built in 1950 in Tyrolean style as a members-only club with a private beach for swimming and sailing. At the age of eight I knew of its existence hidden round a bend beyond the towering trees, but would never sunbathe there. During visits to my grandparents' Swiss chalet, a compact and efficient cabin at the edge of the National Forest, one swooping drive down from Crestline's Top Town, I had once heard my grandmother whisper over a game of Canasta while she sipped ginger ale and bourbon that *only the very rich are allowed at the San Moritz Lodge*. Now owned and operated by the county park service, today the only remaining buildings are the restaurant—a massive two-hundred and fifty capacity dining room for gatherings and receptions—a stage and flagstone fireplace, a stainless steel industrial kitchen, and a separate red leather and polished wood bar area reminiscent of days gone by. The remodeled bathhouse, which sits on the other side of the cove, is now a senior center. Built using gigantic stripped and polished tree trunks as beams supporting the grand pitched roof, the beams extend out to and over the patio, where the windows span the length of the frontage from floor to ceiling. An inexpensive, rustic venue, the lodge also offers setups for wedding ceremonies, which are held on a patch of lawn overlooking the once private bay.

Parked alongside the side entrance, Tina began barking orders before opening the tailgate.

"You clean the ladies bathroom," she pointed an insistent finger at me. "You three follow me."

"I'm not supposed to be here," John murmured while holding steadfast to the truck bed. "I'm just supposed to check for alcohol and glass containers at the gates."

Waiting for the two young men to assist me down from the truck seemed to further infuriate her. "We can't waste the day waiting on you. Maybe you should have stayed retired. You're a retired court stenographer? That's what you call it, right?"

"Yes, ma'am," I answered in humble military form. Where are the little hand stamps and why would a woman so out of shape tuck her brown shirt in, I thought.

"Do you know where the bathrooms are or do I have to show you?"

"Yes, ma'am. I've been here before. I even taught a Syrian how to do the chicken dance at Oktoberfest. I can find the bathroom."

But what do I clean it with?

Back at the cottages, the six o'clock cocktail hour couldn't have come any sooner.

"So tell us about your first day on the job," Trudy asked and settled into her plastic Adirondack. Ted handed me my first of many Cuba Libres.

"Well, after the disappointment of finding the bottom of the lake piled high in the north parking lot, a skimpy orientation and carrying paddle boards up and down the sand, I cleaned the ladies bathroom at the San Moritz Club," I smiled, insinuating a pleasant day at the beach. Brute left my lap and stumbled away to sleep under the patio table.

"That place is always dirty. I'm glad you're there to spruce it up," Trudy gave me a fist bump.

"Spider webs decorating the windows, blood stains on the personal female items box, strands of hair caked into what just might be fecal matter behind the toilets. But not so fast, let me get to the good part. This bitch, my boss Tina, orders me to clean the bathroom, where I stand stupid for fifteen minutes without even a bottle of Windex. I don't know where the cleaning supplies are. I've been to the lodge to eat, drink, and be merry, not to scrub it. So she whizzes in and slams a can of industrial grade Ajax onto the Formica dressing shelf and poof, white dust settles into the grime on this big fuckin' mirror. Then she points to this door locked with a Master lock, grumbles through her jailhouse keys and opens it. She storms away leaving me to navigate this dank, dark closet to find the moldiest, filthiest, most disgusting sponge, broom, mop, and bucket ever conceived. Lucky for me, there was a fresh pair of long green rubber gloves in its original packaging on the shelf."

"Wait, I'm conjuring up an image," Ted raised a hand and closed his eyes. "Were they over your elbows?"

"Yes."

"Very sexy. Continue."

"It took me fifteen minutes to clean the mop in the toilet bowl, dunk it, back out of the stall and squeeze the dirty water into another toilet bowl. I returned to bowl no. 1, flushed it, and retraced my steps over and over again, before I could swab the tile floor with it. I bravely set forth where no one has gone before, and on my hands and knees wiped with the sponge behind the toilets in the four stalls."

"How long did it take you to clean the sponge?" Ted inquired.

"Is that really important, Ted?" Trudy asked.

"Here's the best part. Tina returns on her broomstick and reprimands me for not cleaning the men's room yet. Jeez."

"More drinks, ladies?"

"How long did that take you?" Trudy inquired.

"Tina called in the troops to 'finish my job,' as she shamed me in front of the boys and the old prison guard. I was mortified. She moved me to vacuum duties in the ballroom, after making me fold up and roll out dozens of round dinner tables into another room. The vacuum is an icon from 1950 with a cord the length of a football field. I'm sure the bag has not been emptied since President Eisenhower left office. I was still recoiling when Tina ordered me outside to push a rack of folding chairs to the lawn and unfold them."

"Shouldn't the men be doing that kind of work?" Trudy asked.

"Apparently, there is no gender discrimination at Parks and Rec."

"No age discrimination either, huh?" Ted set down another round of drinks. "You sure are blowing a lot of smoke there."

"It's vapor. Your cottage is gonna smell like blueberry cheesecake tonight."

In the darkness the brown bear cub, hopefully abandoned by its mother, snuck up to raid the trashcans, his evening ritual. Finding the tops locked and chained, once again he knocked all three down and sulked away on all fours back down the ravine.

"Ted, maybe we should call the forestry service. He's getting bigger every day."

"Sweetie, the bears were here first. As far as the wildlife is concerned, live and let live and keep the rifle loaded."

"Are you going back tomorrow?" Trudy inquired.

"Of course I am. That miserable miscreant is not messing up my summer vacation."

"What does *mis-cre-ant* mean?" Trudy inquired.

"A villain, a scoundrel, a troublemaker. You know, like King Obama," Ted surprised us both with his definition skills.

"Well, aren't you the know-it-all," Trudy said. "Next thing you know, you'll be picking up a book and reading it."

"Seems like. Oh, that reminds me. A big box was delivered for you today."

"My books are here already?"

"Good thing 'cause you got a book signing at McCabe's in July," Trudy smiled.

"Two novels down and one to go."

"And a fence to paint," Ted grumbled. "And in case you're wondering, Brute only yipped for an excruciating half an hour after you left this morning."

"Ted, your vocabulary is giving me chills," Trudy signaled that it was time for me to go.

As I parked my car on Lake Drive just above the boathouse, I received an unexpected phone call from one of Randi's aborted baby daddies, a musician and wild child of the 60s, whom I had met only once years ago as he passed through the walkway. He apologized for the rasp in his voice; he had been calling everyone on Randi's cell phone contact list for the past twenty-four hours.

"Randi passed away in her sleep. Her mother has requested an autopsy, because the cause of death is unknown."

Later it was determined that Randi died of congestive heart failure. Her mother drove the red Mini Cooper home to Las Vegas and left Randi's pet tarantulas and rats with Marlene, the bungalow mews packrat and PETA representative. Baby Daddy took possession of Randi's sex toys and her collection of body jewelry. On the anniversary of her passing, with the permission of the new tenant, we neighbors gather on her porch to share bottles of wine, vanilla vodka, and vivid stories of our short time spent with the Goth Girl.

Taking Randi's cue to live each day as if it's my last, at the end of the next two weeks, I had sanded and primed the long rugged wooden fence, removed the weeds and landscaped the sandy front yard of my cottage with layers of redwood bark scattered with pathway bricks and planted a row of red geraniums outside the fence. I brought home a used plastic patio set from an antique store in town, so that I could enjoy the great outdoors. Trudy was pleased; she threatened Ted that if their yard wasn't fixed up soon, she would be leaving him and moving in with me.

Assigned to the boathouse, my shift began at seven in the morning four days a week. Having no defined responsibilities, but to jump when Tina said *jump*, I saw what needed to be done and took the initiative to do it. While PSE alumni manned the two cash registers, I found a broom hidden away in a forgotten closet and swept the cobwebs from the boathouse windows; I swept and mopped the floors, sanitized the upstairs employee washroom, shined up the scummy windows, emptied trash cans on the dock before they toppled over, wiped down counters, organized the live worm bait section in the glass cabinet, and baled out pedal boats with a Styrofoam cup. When the mound was cleared from the North Beach entrance, I patiently waited to be trained for an assignment as gate lady. During my half-hour lunch break, the misanthrope I had become launched a pedal boat, hummed ♪ sail on silver girl ♪ while enjoying a sack lunch away from the skeptical eyes of my evil nemesis, who hoped for me to fail, and with a net skimmed the rocking water of floating, belly-up slithery silver fish.

During that first month, I learned through trial, error, shame, and threats how to operate the registers and to balance the cash drawers. I was over two dollars just one time. I was right on the money from then on. My boathouse duties included renting out fifteen pedal boats and twenty fishing boats, with or without a motor—fifty-pound motors I was ordered by Tina to carry from the garage, down the boat dock, and to place onto the boats—and chaining all vessels one to the other at the five o'clock closing time.

I became expert at blowing up frozen corn dogs on a stick in the microwave and pouring smoldering molten nacho cheese sauce over tortilla chips while making change, never flinching as Tina made it her daily chore to swoop in and berate me in front of other PSE's. Being included in the rescue of a wayward row boat battling the current on a windy day was something to look forward to; it was my only chance to board the official speed boat and toss a life buoy at some damn fool, toting a wife and three frightened children, who had refused to pay the cost of a motor nor heed my warning not to get close to the dam.

There is no radio talk show host to roust me from sleep with more carnage, because there is no radio at the cottage, and I enjoy the quiet and the escape from the ruination of my once innocent world. But I couldn't seem to get into Part Three of *The Muslim Romance Trilogy*. My best bungalow mate had passed into the forevermore and I had yet to grieve. The proposed endeavor of returning to Christmas of 2010 and continuing on without an ending in sight became overwhelming. What would be the recurring motif: familial relationship struggles; the end of my America, the land of the free, and the beginning of Islamic imposed Sharia Law; the fear of the bougainvillea taking over my front porch? There was too much turmoil to devour and regurgitate, too many failed attempts on my part to connect intimately with the perfect foot for my glass slipper to revisit, too many challenging visits to Mother, too many Obama scandals and controversies to decipher and unclutter, such as whether the force-feeding of terrorist prisoners on a hunger strike at Guantanamo Bay is tantamount to torture. Hell, what mother has not force-fed her toddler while he's strapped in a high chair? Was the American Consulate compound in Benghazi attacked in protest of an obscure anti-Muslim video or to cover up the CIA secret gunrunning operation for the Muslim Brotherhood and other insurgents fighting in Syria and beyond? It was all too much for me to compartmentalize, organize, and then spew out onto my *Word* program in stand-up comedy format. And as former Secretary of State Hillary Clinton has said, "What difference at this point does it make?"

On my days off, at the fold out table smothered in reference notebooks, diaries, *Googled* information printouts, and the hair pulled from my head, I sat bug eyed in front of the Mac without a word to say. Instead of knocking out the next *Great American Novel*, I had painted the fence, strolled Brute through the pathway surrounding the lake, joined the Wednesday night bowling league, and devoured in a drunken stupor Trudy's nightly comfort food casserole.

Although in hindsight, a trip abroad on my own may have been a superb, noble idea—and a slick maneuver to send my sister a *what for* from five thousand miles away—I opted through a group email to invite Alexandra, Leighanne, and Rory to join me on my search for a wealthy Irish potato farmer, a winsome widower in need of a good massage living in County Kilkenny, in the hope not all three would answer in the affirmative. Alexandra did not respond. Leighanne explained in a two-page email that she had another surgery coming up and sadly would be unable to travel such an exhausting distance; that the prospect of applying for her first U.S. passport had sent her into a paperwork morass, from which she would never recover.

Rory accepted. Having never been out of the country, she hurriedly expedited her very first United States citizen passport. Together, having different *frequent flyer miles* earned from purchasing exuberant amounts of unnecessary forgotten items, while enjoying wine at her cabin, we booked online two separate airplane tickets from two separate carriers, leaving from two separate airports, and arriving in Dublin at two separate times on the same day. The cost of my round trip tickets a surprising three hundred and thirty six dollars. This October, Rory and I would be trick-or-treating on the streets of Dublin. Immediately after our wet kayaking adventure and a tour of Big Bear Lake while sipping cans of beer off the bow of *Miss Liberty*, an 1880s replica of the grand riverboats of the Mississippi, I begin shopping with my American Airlines Citibank charge card for all things green and warm.

At the boathouse, while the teenage PSE's would begin and end their phone conversations with potential guests calling for information with *I don't knows,* my conversations with inquiring guests would be chock-full of interesting facts, tidbits, and encouragement.

> "You've never been up here? Oh, my. You've been missing out. Crestline used to be known as the swingingest town in America. When I was a little kid there were seven bars in Top Town—that's the stop sign where State Highway 138 meets Crest Forest Drive. Back then there was drinking, prostitution, and two penny arcades.

Nah, sorry, you missed all that. Now there are antique stores, the senior citizen thrift shop, a great breakfast café, a Mexican cantina of sorts, and two real estate offices up there. Down here on Lake Gregory, we've got fishing boats, pedal boats, aqua cycles, paddleboards, a water slide, and scrumptious messy hamburgers. Why, I can smell the onions on the grill right now.

"Your teenage daughter is in a monthly way? A what? Oh, of course. No, she won't get wet on a pedal boat, unless it fills with water in the wind. What? You live right down the hill in San Bernardino and you've never been up here? It's a man-made lake. Its water comes in from a dam or something. When it was completed in 1937, everyone thought it would take three years to fill it up. They even left construction equipment on the lakebed and, surprise, that year the rains were so heavy, it filled up in three days. The urban legend is that way down below is a backhoe. Maybe if you swim deep enough, you can find it. Nah, there's no Loch Ness Monster here.

"Hiking? Yes, there's a one-mile walk along a creek bed through the forest to Heart Rock, where the rushing water has carved out an actual shape of a heart in a big old craggy rock. Your kids will love it. That's over in the Valley of Enchantment, just five miles from the lake. Here at the lake, there's a hiking trail that will take you along the water's edge most of the way around."

Calls came in from frantic brides-to-be as to why Tina, the Brown Shirt Nazi in charge of booking weddings and making the reception arrangements, had not returned their last three calls. I filled out the message forms smudged with nacho cheese sauce and walked them up the dusty staircase one by one to put them on her computer keyboard, for which Tina reprimanded me for going outside the scope of my employment.

As an employee of the lake, my close family members are allowed to enjoy all amenities free of charge. I text my grandchildren, who both have cars and live forty-five minutes away, an invite to meet me at the lake—any day, any time—for an all day blowout of paddle boards, fishing boats, pedal boats, and water slide bracelets. As of the final edit of this book in 2016, there has yet to be a response. Mother has turned down my every invitation for breakfast, lunch, or dinner. The fact she has a vacation cabin on the other side of the lake or that I have taken residence in a mountain cottage, a twenty-minute drive to her home in the valley, has exploded in her a feverish need to clean out another drawer, which she explains will be taking up all her time this summer. Because I am not speaking to my sister, my daughter Alex is not speaking to me, and consequently will not be coming up. My gay male troupe of three drove up for a day of frivolous frolic. I passed them off at the north gate as my wild and crazy sons. Even fifty-something Donovan slipped by without investigation, his husband Joel and little Stephen eagerly skipping in behind him. Each was given an all-day water slide bracelet. I declined.

As part of a transitional two-man mini-ranger team assigned to set up the lawn for wedding ceremonies, to prepare the ballroom for two hundred party-hardy diners, and to clean up the aftermath of the reception brawl, I found myself at the San Moritz Lodge with its murky, webbed windows and dying rose garden every weekend, Saturdays and Sundays until after midnight. The cleansing and beautification of the lodge became my pet project. When the weather forecast rain and the boathouse visitors dwindled down to a few early morning fishermen, after explaining to Tina the need to remove the unrestrained amount of cobwebs, clean all the windows and rejuvenate the garden, I was given permission to drive over to the lodge on my own only to prune and rake. I found a hose on a carrier in a stock room behind the old red leather bar, but was told by Tina that I could not turn on the water without permission. Tina refused to give me permission to spray and wipe down the massive windows. She thwarted my efforts at every turn.

A benefit of being a PSE, I am given privileged access to the boathouse parking lot and the dock for the July 4th Independence Day fireworks extravaganza over the lake. Trudy and Ted are thrilled to join me, the yearly ordeal of finding a parking place in a tourist destination lifted from their weary shoulders. While we "ooh and aah" and drink wine through straws secreted in plastic sippers, another Arab is sprung.

In Egypt, a country that receives one-and-a-half billion dollars from the United States each year, the natives have become restless after just one year of the democratically elected Mohamed Morsi, who replaced the ousted Muslim President Hosni Mubarak in 2011 at the beginning of the so-called *Arab Spring*. While Mubarak had insisted that his draconian regime was a necessary evil to combat Islamist terrorism, which disrupted Egypt's lucrative tourism sector, Morsi brought in his own terrorists in the form of the Muslim Brotherhood to rewrite the Egyptian constitution, granting Morsi unlimited powers, including the power to legislate without judicial oversight. Apparently, the citizenry composed of Christians and Muslims alike feel that too much Islamic pride is not always a good thing. At the end of a four-day violent protest, the military removed Morsi, with fireworks bursting in air over Cairo's Tahrir Square.

Brute and I returned to Hollywood for an overnighter to change the sheets, scour the toilet, and tidy up for our next guest, the soap opera guy from Dublin. I had seen his picture on the *Airbnb* website, but when he arrived in the flesh the next morning dressed in a white dress shirt and a slim black suit, I was thrilled and excited to see that he looked more like President Obama than President Obama himself. His presence would definitely boost my credibility as a non-discriminating *Airbnb* host; there would be no complaints from my liberal neighbors about my short-term rental, at least not this week.

Back on the mountain, the big day has arrived. I am assigned to the north gate of the swimming beach, which opens at ten a.m.

At nine forty-five I am in place and itching to begin. I've counted my cash drawer twice. The sky is clear with a projected high of eighty-seven. The return stamp of the day is a teeny giraffe. I line up the water slide bracelets, which must be accounted for at the end of my shift, ending at five-thirty, with a half hour lunch. Outside the gate is a lineup of families with small children, ice chests, umbrellas, and brightly colored beach bags stuffed with sand toys and towels. John is outside the window of my little booth to inspect the ice chests for glass containers and alcohol. Glass is not allowed on the beach, because broken glass can cut little bare feet; alcohol is not allowed anywhere near water in California, because no one can be trusted to recognize their drowning limit.

I unlock the gates and guests in groups of two to twenty-two loaded down with beach chairs, sand umbrellas, and illegal blow-up rafts impatiently wait to pass through.

"Welcome to the lake. Oh, you're going to have such a good time. Sorry, no alcoholic beverages. John will put it aside for you. We do have a snack bar or you can have lunch across the street at Toni's. They have wine margaritas. I can stamp your hand on your way out and you can come back in today free of charge. Would you like an all-day water slide wristband? No, of course not. I can relate. Senior rate? Oh, you're not sixty-five? Oh, my, that's such an adorable bikini on such a sweet little girl. The paddleboards are just three dollars for a half an hour. You can tan your backside while drifting on the water. When I was your age, I used to come here with my sister, grandma, mom, and my uncle, who was only three years older than me. We used to bring our own floats. We had a huge Charlie Tuna blow-up. Sorry, sweetie, but you can't bring yours in. Oh, those down the beach? They're aqua bike thingies. They're hard to peddle, so your mom or dad will have to go along with you. My goodness, I've never seen so many tattoos on one body before and I live in Hollywood!"

After five hours at the gate, no one has come to break me for lunch and I am famished. Knowing that eating in the booth is forbidden, I weaken and take a bite from the apple in my sack lunch. Within five minutes, Tina arrives.

"We've had two complaints about your treatment of guests, that you were rude and offensive, and even suggested to a guest to get loaded on margaritas at Toni's across the street. It's also been reported that you ate during your shift," the Gestapo sergeant spoke.

"No one was around when I snuck a bite of my apple. Who complained?"

"Who complained doesn't matter. I am removing you."

"From the gate or the park?"

"The gate."

"There's a camera watching me," I point to the chrome ball over my head. "Can we review the tape?"

"No."

"I have two more hours to work. Can I go to the lodge and wash the windows? It's a nice day for it." I cross my fingers behind my back.

"You can go to the lodge, but you can't use the water. There's a ceremony on the lawn tomorrow. You can put out the chairs by yourself."

Late afternoon the following day, the bride and her decorating entourage arrived. My assigned teammate did not. I helped the wedding party put the flower arrangements into the refrigerators until the caterers arrived, a no-no according to the OSHA rules taped on the stainless steel door. I dragged out the two worn and wooden sixteen-foot ladders from a back room and two giggling young ladies hung their bohemian décor of dried flowers from a rope tied column to column. The news given to me by the Mother of the Bride struck a familiar ring: there would be no need for the ceremony on the grass knoll; the marriage had taken place in Las Vegas a week before because the Father of the Bride was dying of cancer and they didn't want him to miss it, just in case, and could she be refunded the six-hundred dollar outdoor ceremony setup charge. This change of plan I had written down on a telephone message form and placed on Tina's computer keyboard twice in one week.

I began sweeping away the cobwebs from the patio windows when Tina blew through the restaurant and caught up with me after a short conversation with the bride.

"So, you want to wash the windows? Today you have permission."

"The reception is starting in two hours. I don't think I'll be able to wash and dry in time."

"Before you wash your precious windows, I need you to remove the chairs from the ceremonial lawn."

"I hate to admit it, but doing it alone will take me over an hour."

"Oh, poor little court reporter. Get your ass out there and get moving."

"*And* wash the windows?"

"Yes. Stop your whining. You finally get your wish," she finished with her hands on her fat green hips.

I clutched the broom handle. I would not cry in front of her. I held my head high, leaned the broom against the window and headed for the lawn. On my way, I turned a quick left into the old bar, where I fetched my purse hidden in a cubby behind the stacks of folded linen napkins. Rushing through the gaiety of the preparation of the wedding reception, I headed straight for my car, straight to Goodwin's Market for booze, and straight to a personal, self-indulgent tearful deluge at the cottage.

You only live once, but if you do it right, once is enough.

Mae West
1893-1980

Forcibly cuddling my best friend and dousing my anger with a third rum and Coke, I wrote a three-page email to the Director of the San Bernardino County Parks and Recreation informing him that I had walked off the job. I attached my theatrical head shot for him to throw darts at. Using, I thought, humor and an interesting plot, I informed Mr. Keith Lee in sordid detail of my thwarted summer vacation and my resultant bruised ego. Believing that the County immediately lawyered up in fear I would sue for some kind of employee abuse, I understand why I have never received a reply from Mr. Lee or a phone call from anyone at the boathouse investigating my whereabouts. I did, however, receive my final paycheck.

The book signing and release party at McCabe's Books was a success, as mountain readers of Part One, all three Juliet fans strangers to me, returned to purchase a signed copy of Part Two. This was the greatest compliment I could have ever wished for. In creative supportive style, Ted and Trudy, the Mountain Widows, and the Fag Hag Heroes, all showed up to buy a copy; thus leading me to believe I was truly an author, a self-published paperback writer.

Chapter 48

Looking For Closure in the Kimchi

♪ Oh, Danny Boy,
the pipes, the pipes are calling . . . ♪

Danny Boy
Frederic Weatherly

When the final *Airbnb* guests and their two cats vacated the Hollywood bungalow, Trudy and Ted waved me their relieved goodbye from the wooden bridge. The burly brown bear joined in the farewell by laying a dump down below in front of his cave on the fern thicket shore of the dry creek bed. I returned at precisely one o'clock on street cleaning day from my storybook *Snow White and the Seven Dwarfs* summer in the forest turned *Sleeping Beauty*, complete with my own personal wicked Maleficent, and parked smack dab in front of my gate. Artemus's lime green, gun-turret phallic symbol spiraling over my roof, I rushed Brute to the walkway before emptying the Scion. Up and down the front steps, I carried in my *work in progress* thrown haphazardly into a large cardboard box, a bulging suitcase, a toppling beach bag, the stroller and doggie beds, the chunky garment bag bottom heavy with canvas shoes, sandals, and sun hats.

Balking at the drudgery facing me of moving a rack of clothes that no longer fit me from the walk-in closet back into the main closet and returning the piles of unorganized and unused reference materials back to their cluttered places on top of the neat and empty desktop, I lose it. Unfortunately, my two token gay friends, Joel and Stephen, stop by while I'm throwing a tantrum.

"What are you doing?" they asked in unison, twanging their watered-down effeminate *Bible Belt* southern accents.

"I'm trashing it all, Mutt and Jeff," I stated flatly as I raged back and forth on the Mexican tile in my kitchen, slamming paperwork into the trashcan.

"Mutt and Jeff? I'm Joel and he's Stephen. You ... you ... you've been gone too long."

"*Mutt and Jeff* was a cartoon strip. Mutt is tall and dimwitted and Jeff is a half-pint."

"Well, Julie, which one am I?"

"You're a foot taller than Stephen. You figure it out." With no apology, I continued my tizzy fit. "The three-ring binders of *Google* printouts, the painstakingly detailed diaries, the offensive post-it notes I stupidly left taped on the koffice walls for my guests to see—what was I thinking—it's all going, all of it. If I can't write *story* without having to refer to another Muslim terrorist attack or another of Obama's ridiculous quotes, I have no business writing. And my recounting of it all will not change a thing."

"What did he ever say that was rid ... rid ... ridiculous?"

"Joel, I don't think having a political debate with our beloved Republican is what she needs right now," Stephen stopped the pending argument and began smoothing out crumpled sheets of paperwork taken from the trashcan.

"Wow, Julie. When ... when...when you're famous, those journals and diaries and post-it notes will be worth millions. Even more than the books."

"I love you, Joel. But you're such an idiot," I shook my head.

"I agree. We can sell them on *eBay* after you're dead," Stephen smiled.

"Stephen, do you agree that I'm an idiot?"

"Of course not. But you have a childlike, buoyant tolerance about you, Joel. You seem to just bounce up and down without much thought."

"Gosh, how do you keep your white cabinets so clean?" Joel ran a pinkie along the triple trim molding on a spit-shined fiberboard door.

"I clean them, Joel."

"Oh." Joel gushed, "We all love your books, Julie."

"When are you sending them to the protagonist?"

"The what?" Joel winced.

"The hero, the main character, her lover."

"Don't you mean my antagonist, Stephen?"

"She doesn't even know where he lives."

"Actually, I do. At least I have an idea."

"No, no. I don't want you ever going near that creep again," Joel protected me.

"I think you need closure. You need to get back together, just to see how it turns out."

"Stephen, no! There isn't enough ink left in the world."

"What do you call a trilogy with a fourth volume?"

"Joel, you both know I can't ever contact him."

"We do?"

"Joel, you just finished reading Part Two, didn't you?"

"Yes. So it's true, you being a spy?" Joel gulped.

"That's between me and my publisher."

"But you self-published."

"So?" I pulled out the shredder from under the desk.

"Put that away. You're just … you're just—"

"Frustrated as hell," I finished Joel's sentence, which I often do, and slid the shredder back. "Unfortunately, you're right; I need all of this stuff, including the binders and books and bullshit on the shelf in my closet waiting to topple down and knock me unconscious. But once the third book is done, we're having a bonfire."

"You need closure. Besides, I think he must miss you by now," Stephen romanticized. "Where do you think Ali is?"

"I did a public records search using his name and found that he purchased a two-bedroom condo in Korea Town."

"And he didn't even use you as his realtor. What a user and after all the houses you showed him," Joel sympathized.

"He quit claimed the property to his brother, Ghali, but my guess is he's living there too."

"That's it!" Stephen threw his little arms in the air and sat down at the butcher-block table. "We'll take the books to him. After he reads them, he'll come running back to you."

"Or he'll hire a lawyer and sue me."

"Or . . . or . . . or he'll have you stoned."

"Joel, I don't think he'd be that upset. She glorifies the bastard in her novels. His narcissistic self will get a big kick out of it."

"His what?"

"No, no, boys. We are not going to Korea Town."

The road to closure in Korea Town was crowded. Upon hearing of Stephen's plan, Leighanne immediately offered up her four-wheel drive SUV as our stakeout mobile. Rory brought down from the mountain a mac and cheese casserole, paper plates, plastic forks, and a bottle of Jameson. Nurses Donovan and Joel brought along Jose Cuervo, a plastic bag of split limes, a can of mixed nuts, and a first-aid kit. Stephen showed up, as usual, without a thing but his positive-thinking rhetoric straight out of *The Secret* and a pair of binoculars. I arrived at Joel and Donovan's Silver Lake home, the meet-up destination, with an angel corkscrew and two bottles of cabernet, a bottle of Vanilla Vodka, and a cooler with melting ice. As the sun began to slink away, we piled into the SUV and stopped at Albertson's for plastic cups and paper towels.

After four tours around the block of Harvard Boulevard from 6th Street to 5th Street, Leighanne lucked into a parking spot with an excellent view of the underground parking garage driveway and the glass entrance door of the least appealing building in the neighborhood of apartment houses turned condominiums. I had shown foreclosed properties in that linoleum infused dump. My clients were offended that I thought for one moment that walls flanked with flaking black and gold etched wall-to-ceiling mirrors were to their liking. When the nauseous scent of boiling red pepper cabbage kimche hit their Caucasian nostrils, they fled by way of three flights of stairs into the street. It was fitting that Ali and Ghali had ended up here, a one-mile walk to their mosque, the Islamic Center of Southern California, at 4th and Vermont.

As Stephen is excited over the proposed reuniting of his favorite cougar with her cub, the remainder of the surveillance team is resolute in their decision that if, by chance, we catch the Islamic womanizer exiting the building, he will be tarred, feathered, and kicked all the way back to his Bedouin ancestry to spend the remainder of his miserable life pillaging donkeys in the deserts of Iran.

STEPHEN: Where are the books?

JULIE: In the brown paper bag at my feet.

JOEL: I brought my graphic novel, *NURSING HELL*o. It's about me and Madonna changing out bedpans and penile catheters. We can drop this off too.

STEPHEN: You think a backwards-thinking, Western civilization hating wannabe terrorist, who wants to kill you, will be interested in a comic book about drawing blood cultures and a nurse named Madonna?"

JOEL: Everybody likes Madonna.

RORY: Can we do this? Spy?"

LEIGHANNE: Sure we can. We can spy under the Patriot Act. The President collected every American citizen's phone records to purportedly find terrorists. I don't think he'll mind if we sneak up on one measly Muslim.

JULIE: Here's his picture. Pass it around back there. He drives a black BMW SUV with blacked out windows. It's old. Got to be twelve years old by now.

LEIGHANNE: Exactly as you described him. He's awfully cute.

STEPHEN: Stay focused, everyone. What's the license plate number?

JULIE: I foolishly never wrote that down.

STEPHEN: Probably a personalized plate, because he's such a narcissist.

JOEL: Something like 'Hit Me and You're Dead'?

STEPHEN: No, too many letters.

RORY: Explain again what we're doing here? I've never read the books. I started, but got bored after the first few pages.

STEPHEN: You're one of those, huh? Julie, let me say this one more time. Don't be willing to give up your dreams, your ideas, your passion based on the opinion of people who are indifferent, confused, and downright mean. You go for it, girl. You do it.

RORY: What did I say to deserve that?

JULIE: How about this one: 911HAHA. Nah, I would have remembered that one.

JOEL: Or MARTYR?

STEPHEN: We're here so that the A-Hole can relive over and over again the years he stole from Julie.

LEIGHANNE: Oh, my God. There it is, a big black BMW SUV pulling into the garage. Give me the binoculars. Thanks. The license plate frame says *Hooman Motors*. That's got to be him.

STEPHEN: Here I go.

Stephen rushed to the driver's side of the BMW as the gate to the garage slowly rolled open. Too soon he was back in the car clutching the brown paperback.

STEPHEN: False alarm. Just an Asian man bringing home Korean takeout. God, that car smelled to high heaven of putrefied cabbage.

DONOVAN: Well, I don't think that all Koreans eat cabbage or that all Muslims should be lumped together. After all, the Christians started it. Don't forget *The Crusades* when the Christians attacked the Muslims.

LEIGHANNE: My feet hurt. The doctor says one more surgery on my back may cure it.

JULIE: We aren't walking, Leighanne. We're sitting and drinking.

DONOVAN: How many surgeries have you had?

RORY: Too many. She's now the Bionic Woman. And I'm missing my Lifetime movie.

JULIE: What? Close your eyes and review the last six movies you've fallen asleep in front of. You have the Lifetime Movie Network, one repeat excruciatingly after another. And Donovan, *The Crusades* were in retaliation of Muslim raids, where they massacred, raped, and took over entire countries. Have another drink and don't be such an uninformed bully.

JOEL: My mom loves Donovan.

DONOVAN: Maybe you should control the amount of tequila you're inhaling, Julie.

JOEL: My mom just loves Donovan.

DONOVAN: Yeah, she does, but she thinks we're both going to homosexual hell. And Julie does, too, don't ya?

RORY: Anybody want a plate of mac and cheese?

JULIE: I'd love some.

STEPHEN: A moment on the lips, forever on the hips. Remember, Karen Carpenter dieted for our sins. You don't want to end up like her, do you?

JULIE: You lost me. Are you telling me to eat mac and cheese or to not eat mac and cheese?

DONOVAN: The far-right Koch Brothers have all the money and the big corporations cheat and steal through their tax exemptions. The poor Hispanics are starving on the streets.

JOEL: Why do you always get like this when you drink?

JULIE: When was the last time you had to walk over a dead Mexican on the street, Donovan? And they're all on food stamps and welfare, so they're not starving.

DONOVAN: No, the Mexicans are not on welfare. You have to be a citizen to receive welfare benefits, Medicaid, or food stamps. Clinton fixed all that in 1995.

JULIE: No, Donovan, you're so uninformed. You don't have to be a citizen; just your baby has to be born here, your anchor baby.

DONOVAN: Well, let's rip them off their mother's tit.

JOEL: Donovan, you're getting really loud and cruel and your anger is directed toward Julie just because she's a Tea Bag lady.

JULIE: Tea Party, Joel.

DONOVAN: Yeah, the Bible thumping, right wing nut who wants to deport all the brown babies.

JULIE: Well, I'm drinking Spic tequila with you, so I couldn't be all that bad.

LEIGHANNE: Julie didn't say that . . . well, she never said that the Mexican children should go hungry.

JOEL: What's Spic tequila?

JULIE: When was the last time you spent time with a Mexican child, read to them, took them to a movie?

DONOVAN: I take care of Mexicans all day long at the hospital.

JOEL: Donovan, you know most of our patients are on Medicaid, don't you?

DONOVAN: We work at the county hospital, Joel. Yes, I realize that.

LEIGHANNE: Did you hear Obama's speech at Knox College?

DONOVAN: I don't watch the news.

LEIGHANNE: Of course you don't. "If I don't get my way, social tensions will rise." Your buddy ended it with "The American Dream. No matter what you look like; no matter where you came from; no matter who you love."

JOEL: He's such a great speaker.

JULIE: Oh, please. He's a phony and a liar.

JOEL: But everyone tells lies, Julie. You just don't like him because he's black.

JULIE: He quit telling anyone his mother was white so that he could ride the wave of the poor black boy.

JOEL: His mother was white?

DONOVAN: What should I know about this Ali character other than he's cute?

STEPHEN: If you haven't read her novels, you really shouldn't be in this car. Ali is a forty-year-old radical Muslim, a graduate of U.C.L.A. who believes all homos should be killed by dropping walls on them. The only plus on his side is that he's a Democrat, Donovan.

DONOVAN: If he's a Democrat, I'm on his side.

JOEL: No matter what?

DONOVAN: No matter what.

JOEL: Well, being a Democrat should not be the deciding factor in . . . in . . . in whether someone is a good person or not.

JULIE: He's forty-three and he doesn't vote. No paper trail. He says this is California, the lefty candidates will always win, so no reason to get out of bed on Election Day.

LEIGHANNE: How can you be such a staunch, ignorant supporter of Obama, Donovan? The only thing he's done worthwhile is made Jimmy Carter happy because now Jimmy is no longer the worst president we've ever had.

RORY: That's enough. Don't talk politics or religion. Can we get out of here? It's passed my bedtime and I need to get home and feed my dogs.

LEIGHANNE: You told me you fed the dogs before you left the house.

RORY: Well, I need to feed them again.

LEIGHANNE: We're staying at Julie's tonight.

DONOVAN: I have to pee.

STEPHEN: All I see going in there are squinty-eyed Asians.

LEIGHANNE: The front door is locked, but you have the apartment number, so go in behind one of the gooks and leave the sack in front of Ali's door.

JOEL: What's a gook?

LEIGHANNE: Oh, sorry. It's a not so nice word for the Japanese.

STEPHEN: These are all Koreans. That's why it's called Korea Town.

LEIGHANNE: Well, you know, my dad served in World War II and, you know, he brought home some colorful language.

STEPHEN: Did he fight in Korea, too? What word you got for them?

LEIGHANNE: Chink?

JULIE: No, that's Chinese.

JOEL: Was there a war in Korea?

STEPHEN: Here comes one now. You go, Joel.

JULIE: Oh my God, he's following that tiny old lady in.

LEIGHANNE: No, he's running from the door.

JOEL: I can't breath! Let me in. What was that smell?

JULIE: Cabbage slow cooked for weeks with some kind of chili seasoning. It's a Korean staple.

LEIGHANNE: I thought you guys were worldly and all forgiving. Get your ass back in there.

JOEL: I'm just gay, not Ghandi."

DONOVAN: Why did you ever waste your time on this guy?

JULIE: ♪ I fell in love ♪

LEIGHANNE and RORY: ♫ Whatcha wanna do that for? ♫

JULIE: ♪ I never knew what hit me. I fell in love ♪

LEIGHANNE and RORY: ♫ Whatcha wanna do that for? ♫

DONOVAN: It's ten o'clock and I have to pee. Let's head over to Masa in Echo Park for pizza.

STEPHEN: Take a piss behind that bush and let's order pizza.

JOEL: They don't deliver outside of Silver Lake and Echo Park.

LEIGHANNE: A racist pizza parlor in your neighborhood, Donovan?

JULIE: Great idea, Donovan. Here I am skulking over an unemployed terrorist. I'm lurking outside the greasy, hairball apartment of a Muslim sociopath, staining my shirt with red wine and my girlfriend Randi died. For God's sake, she died. She just fuckin' died in her sleep. People, she was only forty. She always said to live each day as if it were my last. If this is my last day, what a waste I'm making of it. Christ, I'm wasting more time on this idiot, more wasted time.

RORY: I'll toast to that.

LEIGHANNE: Rory, please, she's upset.

JOEL: Gosh, Julie, we're enjoying your company. You're not … you're not … you're not wasting your time.

JULIE: Oh, Joel, lay some innocence on me. Can I sit on your lap?

* * *

It's time to put sex in, even if Julie is by herself. ♪ In the wee small hours of the morning, when the whole wide world is fast asleep … ♪ I am a fantasy sex addict.

The aftermath of gorging on boathouse corn dogs followed by evening meals of comfort dishes served up in blue and white Corning Ware prepared by my doting cottage hostess has left me robustly *Rubenesque*, perilously plump and vilely voluptuous, which in this age of *you can never be too rich or too thin,* certainly cannot be denoted as complimentary.

It would appear that I have obviously booked a large, a very large part in a big, big movie. I liken myself to Robert De Niro, a true method actor, who gained sixty pounds for his role as boxer-turned nightclub owner Jake La Motta in Martin Scorsese's *Raging Bull.* I see myself as Renee Zellweger who gained twenty-eight pounds by eating pizza and doughnuts for her role as the weight-battling heroine in *Bridget Jones's Diary.*

Cuddling with the covers before the sun enters, I am on my back answering the buzz that creeps upon us, some of you—me maybe once a month now—rising up between my legs at the same time as the phantom menstrual cycle, which is now dormant, my eggs flushed away, leaving me without purpose. Yet my body aches with purpose, the desire to love and quench this nagging thirst and have him here to cover me.

The fantasy takes a bit to get going, as I remove my ghastly self from the scene. It is Ali, Ali rising up and then down over me, taunting me, his hair flying. Simply thinking of him floods my brain with the chemicals of love. The dimple or the cleft in his chin—doesn't matter which—is so damned wonderful. His black wide eyes stare at me in sociopathic pose. My eyes watching his eyes, I use his magic wand to soothe the sparks, to put out the fire; it is my decision when he will enter me. Gently now, gently get the boat rocking, and I have learned how to relax to the movement of the oars, so relaxed that without a warning, air escapes causing me embarrassment; my only witness a sleeping dog a foot away, his hearing questionable. Is this what true intimacy is: a letting go, a complete surrender?

Mortified by the thought of doing so, my fingers do not penetrate. Will not exercising the vagina result in Atrophic Vaginitis? If I did not use one crinkled, sagging arm for three years, what would happen to it? Waste away, lessen in its abilities, weaken, wither, shrivel, degenerate, and deteriorate? Would it disappear?

I am taken far away, tipping on white-capped waves in an ocean storm with no rain, yet the hint of danger sends me rushing to safety as pulsing waves hit the ship and water fills the deck. Sinking and rising, rising and sinking, the buoyancy of the craft is pure amazement.

How does this all happen: the rush, the explosion, the crying out, and that burning in my gut, a nauseous, yet frightening splendid spasm? His presence brings forth an explosion of oxytocin, which begins the intense utero contractions and the first twinge of labor pains, for I am truly bringing forth life. There's a luxurious peace, a throbbing bliss and a pure release, which begins and ends with no one else in the room. He has given this to me.

Yes, I must have booked a very big part in a very big movie, where the contract states that I must gain thirty pounds to portray the role of a miserable, loathsome, obese woman who can't get a date. Will she triumph in the reveal, as a trimmed up fashionista? Or will *he* appear out of nowhere—certainly not at the gym—the man who loves her *just the way she is?* This guy, of course, would have to be another porker. Together, they can spill Cheetos between the seats in his car.

I'm back to work as a *featured extra* playing the silent role of the wife of a police chief on a television show titled *Rake*, starring Greg Kinnear as Keegan Deane, a disheveled criminal defense attorney. Sitting in the front pew of the gallery, I am to pensively watch my husband being torn to shreds on cross-examination by Mr. Deane, who chips away at the integrity of my honest and loving husband by accusing him of forcing his innocent serial killer client to sign a fake confession.

As a retired court stenographer, I am appalled by the courtroom setup. The jury box is short one juror, the alternate; there is no bailiff; there is no court clerk; and the court reporter sitting in the well in front of the judge has no idea how to stroke the machine properly, causing me to cringe in disbelief. They can't afford to hire a professional? At the grueling end of a dozen takes, because Mr. Kinnear can't remember his lines, but has mastered the "line, please" request to the script supervisor, I am twitching to grab the suit sleeve of the director, Sam Rami, and set him straight on the correct arrangement of a trial courtroom.

After six grueling hours of *reset to one*—my medieval corset becoming unbearable under my go-to-set royal blue suit—and sitting on a cruel wooden bench surrounded by extras dressed as a Los Angeles Police Department S.W.A.T. team, lunch is called. The principals sneak off to the privacy of their trailers, while the background actors and crew queue up outside at the catering wagon, the crew taking nourishment first ahead of the twelve jurors, the pudgy wife, the inane court stenographer, the courtroom audience, and the S.W.A.T. team.

After finishing off a mushroom and gravy pork chop, I check my phone for messages. I have a voice mail from Alexandra, a desperate plea informing me that *Auntie Rae*, Alexandra's newly coined phrase, misses me, has a tumor of some sordid kind and wants to see me. Would I come to Rae's new digs for a pool party, where, apparently, Alexandra has been spending her summer soaking up sun and chlorine, while I skimmed a green, slimy lake of bottomed up trout during my *Big Fat Summer*. This message, its obvious intent to melt my heart and butter me up for a family reunification, puts a lid on my itching desire to educate the court reporter on computer-assisted transcription and the fashion news that highly-paid stenographers with the responsibility of keeping the record do not wear black running shoes, but dress appropriately for a court of law in red stiletto heels. I sneak far away from the crowd with my e-cig to answer her call.

It's another sizzling September day when I pull into Rae's driveway next to Alexandra's Prius, soon to be referred to as the *most unattractive* car ever made. I'm jealous immediately as I follow Rae in a silk flowing caftan through the front door of this charming home decorated in mid-century modern style as only my *Architectural Digest* fanatic sister can do. From the living room spills a large patio with canvas and wicker outdoor seating, pieces brought from her condo, and a dining table for large gatherings. Spotted here and there are orange, green, and ocean blue sun umbrellas. The inviting swimming pool sparkles turquoise with Spanish tiles trimming the edge of its interior. Set around the pool are opulent ceramic pots brimming with exotic plants, none of which I know the names of.

Languishing on a posh pink rubber mat, my bathing beauty floats by. "Thank you for coming, Mommy," she says.

"Did you bring your swimsuit?" Rae asks.

"Of course, I did," I smiled and the ice was broken.

Holding glasses of white wine poured over ice cubes to keep them chilled and to dilute the alcohol, we girls stand in the shallow end for sun and conversation.

"So show me this lump."

"It's this grotesque swelling on my neck," she said and lifted her chin.

"Maybe it's an infection from the neck lift."

"That would be great. I'll sue the bastard. When they cut it open, we'll find out. But if it is cancer, I refuse to wear anything pink and you're not running in any pink ribbon marathons."

"I'll raise my glass to that!"

"Mother, you'll raise your glass to anything."

"Is it true that my granddaughter's moved in with her boyfriend?" I inquired of Alex, who has become notably protective of all estranged family members who have chosen not to communicate with me. She is a *friend* to all of them on *Facebook*.

"Yes, with her father's blessing. They're renting a house just a few blocks from Elizabeth," Alex let me know.

"And Elizabeth is okay with this arrangement?"

"She doesn't want to lose her daughter."

"It's just that . . . from her parent's house straight to shacking up is never what I expected of her."

"Yes, I know. She should have gotten her own place first."

"She's going to miss out on being a single gal with her own job and her own money," Rae acknowledged. "She's doing so well as a hairdresser."

"How do you know that?" I winced.

"We're friends on *Facebook*."

Facebook: The cruelest invention of all time, where jealousies rage with one click of the mouse, where self-pity is rampant, and where you can pick fights with strangers.

"And without even an engagement ring in sight, I suppose?" I continued.

"He has a ring for her, but he's waiting until—"

I broke in, "What? Waiting for what, Alex? Shouldn't the 'may I have your hand in marriage' on one knee with a ring in tow come before cohabitating?"

"God, Mother, you're so old fashioned and judgmental."

"That's news," my sister added.

"Hey, you don't have a daughter. You have a son. You're on the side of the enemy. Young women these days, giving it away for free, destroying the values that made our country great . . . and, by the way, values that made boys into men."

"Well, Benjamin is his own man. He doesn't want me moving in with him and has no plans to give me a ring," Alex boasted.

"But you've been steady for three years now," Rae blurted out and followed her judgmental *oops* with a wink in my direction.

"I respect him for that. And by the way, he's taking me to the Aces Hotel in Palm Springs for my twenty-eighth birthday weekend."

"That's so very chic and pricey," Rae cooed. "And mid-century cool."

"And in December we're traveling with his family to Hawaii to spend the Christmas holidays."

"Again? La-dee-da. Doesn't pretending to be a daughter-in-law get boring?" I thought an *oops*, but saved myself from speaking it out loud by diving to Alexandra's feet and toppling her four feet under water, along with her glass of chardonnay.

During the small talk over a late lunch of buttermilk pesto dressing drizzled over iceberg lettuce, bell peppers, and pan fried garlic shrimp, there is no spoken apology given to me for her dastardly text on Election Night 2, a day that will go down in infamy. My sister smokes the peace pipe by presenting to me a necklace engraved with this sentiment: *Sisters from the same garden, but different flowers*. While smoking Virginia Slim menthols one after the other, she mocks me for vaping. She asks and I agree to take her to her upcoming appointment, where she will be put under while the biopsy is performed on her neck. Previously informed by Alex of my upcoming trip to Ireland, Rae insists that I take home her new black wool pea coat and a sophisticated black trunk on wheels.

"I know I can trust you to get me to a neck surgery on time. See you next Wednesday at five a.m."

***

My dear aunt and uncle, my mother's brother, have offered to babysit little Brute. I make the one hundred and eighty mile turnaround to their gated community in the windy desert outside of Palm Springs. On my return home to continue packing for Ireland, a daunting exercise, with my plane leaving for JFK in eight hours, Rae calls with the results of her biopsy. I leave for Ireland, the trip we had originally planned to take together, with the news that my sister may have less than five years to live.

Following my inexpensive two five-hour layover stops of a twenty-four hour flight from LAX, I am upset when I realize my cell phone is useless; the Verizon international plan Rory and I had signed up for had failed us. After a frustrating search for Rory in the terminal and a rollicking bus ride through Dublin to the very modern Ashling Hotel across from the main train station, I found the blonde half of our duo peacefully napping in our room, where we would bunk in separate single beds for the first three days and two nights before heading to Knocktopher Abbey. We spent the first few hours in the city purchasing small, throwaway phones so that we could call each other if one of us wandered off with a potato farmer.

Halloween being an international affair, we dressed in black and orange sparkling t-shirts. Huddling in jackets against a cold wind, we walked down the bustling street along the River Liffey, marveling at its lit bridges connecting the north bank to the south bank. Tempted by a flyer, we took in a tourist trap dinner where cloggers clicked their heels and their toes, on a black wooden floor over our heads.

As previously arranged through correspondence on *Facebook,* bright and early the next morning, we gratuitously drop off Part One and Part Two of *The Muslim Romance Trilogy* at the independent Gutter Book Store across the river on Cow's Lane in Temple Bar on the South Bank. Gutter Book Store is so named after Oscar Wilde's quote "We are all in the gutter, but some of us are looking at the stars." As the Muslim population begins to grow in Dublin, the proprietor is in agreement that, perhaps, someone ought to be reading them, even if Rory is not.

We quickly learn that not all the Irish speak the Queen's English, but warble out a delectable accent stemming from the original Gaelic, a Celtic language of the British Isles, which at times we need a translator to dissect. We also quickly learn how to jump on a bus, an attribute we would take home with us and later employ when bar hopping in Big Bear. Rory encouraged me to sing along at a piano bar, where I captivated the audience of three vacationing Americans with my rendition of "Danny Boy," although I may have trilled out a verse incorrectly here and there.

During the day, in between searching in vain for the painted doors of Dublin, scurrying in and out of churches, and chasing down our fish and chips with brown beer, we shopped; I for refrigerator magnets; Rory for flat-heeled leather boots to add to her collection.

The second afternoon after wincing through my first taste of mushy peas, which at first blush I assumed was a spoonful of guacamole, and before reaching the O'Connell Street Bridge and being dragged into another shoe store, I bump into my summer house guest, the soap opera writer/producer of *Fair City*, Ireland's most popular and only soap opera, on his way to meet his wife for lunch. He invites us to their home for a dinner party that night, along with other writers and producers, but the look on Rory's face tells me that a bus ride thirty miles into the countryside in the opposite direction of Knocktopher, our final destination, is not on her itinerary. The miracle of meeting him there on the street—it truly is a small, small world—still haunts me. Would I have become a member of the *Fair City* cast? Would I have met my Irish lover? Would I have been forced to politely spoon down more mushy peas? Would I now be living in a frickin' castle?

We take in the zoo—why, we're not sure—just a steep walk up and away from the hotel. It's a lovely, expansive zoo, brimming with young wild noisy animals, the sort neither Rory nor I are especially fond. In my case, I adore them for short intervals and only when they are seated on a rug of colored squares in a controlled environment. The sun is out and the air is still. Rory and I deduce by the enormous attendance of parents hauling their noisy, but well-dressed, children through the trails of the Kazaranga Forest, through the pathways of the African Plains, and through the walkways of the Fringes of the Arctic that, apparently, Halloween in Dublin is a week-long national holiday.

At the bus stop in front of the hotel, Rory, nervously perspiring under her unnecessary coat, is feverishly folding and unfolding an extensive bus schedule to determine which route number to take to the car rental office on the other side of town, when two nice-looking on-duty *Guardians of the Peace* come to our rescue. They offer us a ride in their patrol car, lest we lose it, begin to cry uncontrollably, and spend the rest of the day lost and drunk on the dignified streets of Dublin.

Rory rents the car sight unseen that will take us eighty-five miles to our destination at Knocktopher Abbey, plus an additional daily charge to add me as a driver in case of an emergency, of course. We catch a bus heading to the quay and bound off at first sightings of another pub.

The following morning, we vote unanimously to return to the car rental lot by taxi without a police escort. A sexy spit of a do-it-yourselfer, an oil-changing Tom Boy, she takes control of a mid-sized compact automatic with the steering wheel on the wrong side, drives it out of the rent-a-car parking garage, makes a brave tight left turn into the nearest lane onto a two-lane street, where everyone is driving on the wrong side of the road. We fill up at the first petrol station and leave unharmed.

She takes us to the highway, wide open and easygoing, and into Kilkenny, where after bolstering ourselves with a shot of whiskey at the first pub of polished wood and etched mirrors of the day, we walk to a cathedral along the North Bank of the River Nore in pouring rain, the wind turning our umbrellas inside out. After Rory purchases her first cable knit sweater from a shop across the way, where she learns begrudgingly a sweater is now to be known as a *jumper*, we quickly dry out in the next pub. There's always a pub within ten paces to the left or the right, a charming shop with a green or red door in between.

The small village of Knocktopher consists of one pub, a hotel / restaurant / bar, and a petrol station next to a curious old-fashioned general store. The Manor House of the Abbey stands behind six foot gray walls on a large grassy field on seventeen acres of tranquil parkland. The manager greets us in the foyer at the bottom of a grand and steep staircase carpeted in royal red velvet.

"This is one night you're not turning me out, Scarlett," I whispered to Rory.

"What? You're strange. You know that?"

"Frankly, my dear, I don't give a damn."

The registration process complete, realizing that we had been placed on the third floor, we stood dumbfounded once again at the bottom of the stairs, no bellman in sight.

"Should we take the elevator?" we implored, each of us toting a strap-over purse, a carry-on, and dragging a large case on wheels behind us.

"There is no elevator," the pompous manager proudly announced.

"Well, that's a fret," I countered.

"Are you going to be speaking Irish slang the entire week?" Rory voiced her disfavor with my *Googled* Gaelic phraseology.

"Welcome to the year 1356, ladies. We have minimal modern conveniences here. We do, however, have Wi-Fi in the downstairs billiard room."

We each lugged eighty pounds up three opulent flights of carpeted stairs, down a wide hallway to a hidden set of wooden steps, and into the long golden oak paneled hall of a secreted apartment in the attic.

"Why am I thinking that this was once upon a time the maids' quarters?" I remark after plunking my suitcase on the white duvet in the only bedroom, which is void of the advertised antique four-poster.

"Do monks have maids?"

"They're men, aren't they?" I reasoned.

The living area is ample with a long comfy tweed couch which doubles as a pull out, a loveseat, a good-sized flat screen television, and a round wooden dining table with four chairs.

"There's a lot of light coming in at the table. We can do our makeup in here," I suggested, the bathroom not having enough counter space to set out the tools of daily beautification.

"I'll take the couch," Rory let me know and I didn't argue with my guest. Although there would not be one *Lifetime* movie airing, she would be able to fall asleep in front of the TV, which she admits is her one indulgence.

In the efficient, tidy kitchen, I immediately plugged in the American-to-United Kingdom adaptor and three e-cigarette batteries. We unpacked and neatly arranged our jumpers and jeans in the many drawers and hung our skirts, shirts, and coats in the living room closet, placing our walking boots of black and brown leather on the closet floor. I set out my toiletries neatly on the toilet lid; COCO Mademoiselle by Chanel *eau de parfum* vaporizer spray the focal point of the arrangement. I had brought this reminder of Ali, he who had watered my sensuality into one out-of-control petal blossom, only to tear it fiercely from its stem and toss it to the wind; he who had given to me my first bottle of the fragrance as a birthday present, sharing in diabolical form that his last girlfriend always wore it.

"Rory, there's no shower in here, just a hand-held spray thing. The hose is so short, we're going to have to sit down in the tub to wash our hair," I shouted from behind the bathroom door.

"Next you'll be telling me there's no heat," she hollered back at me from the kitchen off the hallway. "Where's the coffee? There's no coffee maker."

On the back of the door, I hung my plastic pocketed fold-out containing mini travel bottles of shampoo, cream rinse, and mouth wash, pouches of Q-Tips and cotton balls, a manicure kit with nail polish and remover, and a catch-all zip lock baggie. The view from the window settled me, as an Irish mist crossed over the tops of the stone carriage houses below.

"Are you done in the bathroom yet?"

"Yes, sure. Your turn," and we passed each other in the tiny hallway separating the kitchenette from the living room. "When we're out and about, get used to asking for the public *toilet* or we'll be directed to a room in somebody's house."

"I hate having to use public restrooms," and she closed the door behind her.

"Ireland is the cleanest place in the world. You can drink the water and you don't have to tip, because it's not expected." I had done my homework.

"I'm only drinking Jameson whiskey," she exclaimed.

"They've put out cute little packets of instant coffee, tea, and hot chocolate. I think this plug-in kettle boils water," I discovered.

Suddenly from behind the closed bathroom door, "You brought condoms?" Rory shrieked.

"I only brought three."

"You're strange."

Yes, the perfect slipcover for the perfect foot to fit my glass slipper: Trojan latex *THINTENSITY* with *UltraSmooth* lubricant, another reminder of my overblown opinion of my sensuality. I had not given up. I was going to get laid on this trip, *sure look it*, in a wealthy potato farmer's haystack. Whilst shucking my bloomers and ravishing my plentiful inner thighs with his orange prickly beard, he will declare, "Whatever it tis you're wearin', lassie, the scent is drivin' me mad!"

Not wanting to drive or walk the street surrounding the monastery in the dark, we are directed to a mown pathway winding its way through the green field to the gray stone pub with the red door and red shutters, the light from its flower box windows guiding us. The proprietor and bartender, a talkative gray-haired married gentleman—a strike out for me—Eamon welcomes us each night upon our return from our daily jaunts about the countryside. Jolly, red-faced men who frequent the bar smile at the American ladies through decayed yellow, brown, and black teeth and often the gaping hole where a tooth should be. My glass held high, puffing on my e-cig, I announce from the stool in a Jameson stupor, "I'm going home to Hollywood to become a dentist, but I shall return to set up shop in the apartment above Eamon's Irish bar." And the crowd went wild.

Voyaging about on road trips to towns nearby, as Rory whizzes the passenger side of the car frightfully close to the gray stone wall barriers on my side of the car, we leave purses on pub chairs and on hooks below bar counters and return in a panic to find them still there.

Rory lets me drive once, but her sordid accusation that I was surely going to graze the river rock on her side of the car brought the car to a screeching halt. I relinquished control of the car. Her night vision impaired, we returned before dark each day, freshened up, and headed through the grassy path first to the small hotel for our supper of meat and potatoes and then next door to Eamon's pub to prattle away the evening entertained by local strummers and the happy, formidable middle-class of County Kilkenny.

Rory continued to rattle about at a dreadfully early hour, perhaps looking for a vacuum, while I hid in my room sipping tea and devouring a novel until the light of day.

The mist rolled in and an early morning rain left a rainbow as bright as I'd never seen arched half circle over the stone carriage house below and splashed into the moist sparkling green mowed lawn. This perfect picture taken from the window in the dining room of the maids' quarters would be my coveted personal moment, a cherished souvenir to be printed on canvas and wrapped over a small frame.

We road on horseback in traditional English riding boots and helmets at Mount Juliet Equestrian Center in nearby Thomastown for a group trail ride about the private grounds, my embarrassment of having to be heaved from a large rock onto my tall horse thankfully not recorded.

In Waterford we missed meeting a marauding Viking by eleven hundred years, but ran into Alexandra modeling in a print ad for *Bare Essentials* lip gloss at the cosmetics counter in Debenham's Department Store. While Rory was being treated to an Irish makeover, I pulled out the phone and caused quite a stir showing off pictures of my daughter to the excited salesgirls, who immediately tweeted "Look who I met in Waterford, Ireland, today!"

Rather than continuing through Waterford and adventurously discovering the seashore—my plea to watch foaming waves beat on rocky cliffs—we never ventured further; Debenham's Department Store became our home away from the monastery.

Dreading our return flights departing at dawn, using the computer in the billiard room, we booked a hotel in Dublin, which we mistakenly believed was close to the airport. From the hotel, we ventured out on one final outing, a double-deck bus on-and-off tour through the streets of Dublin, ending at the Guinness Factory, where we learned to sip a pint with our eyes looking up, not to disturb the foam.

The only entry in my journal related to the Ireland trip:

Never go on vacation with a headstrong, easily bored woman who thinks rising at five-thirty is sleeping in and who would rather shop for another cable knit jumper than slow down and take in the Irish life, while helping me to find an extinct potato farmer—except to warm up all the barstools across the Emerald Isle from Dublin to Waterford, where after a tour of the crystal factory, I purchased a heavy shamrock paperweight, but did not buy one for my sister. And never stay in a monastery if you want your condoms put to good use. Well, then again, if you're in several bars each day, isn't your tour mate helping you to find an Irish hookup?

Eamon, the owner of Irish's Bar, is now our *Facebook* friend. He posts pictures of tulips blooming in the flower boxes and smiling toothless patrons raising their pints, beckoning us back to Knocktopher.

CHAPTER 49

Fan Letters and Tow Trucks

> You see things and you say *why?*
> But I dream things that never were;
> And I say *why not?*
>
> George Bernard Shaw (1856-1950)
> *Back to Methuselah, Act I*

Heading to my laptop securely hidden in the koffice pullout drawer, the opened suitcase on the living room floor flashed at me like the red ball on a cop car. Abruptly pulling me over were green sweaters, green hats, the beaded black scarf, and the raccoon collar, circa 1967, its ends collected under a pearl and rhinestone fashion pin, nestled atop an untidy bundle of sleepwear, pants and skirts, boots, and black underwear. There wasn't one wealthy potato farmer to be found in the disarray. I am the world's worst luggage organizer.

What would be less taxing: beginning my third novel or sorting, washing, and putting away my Ireland vacation?

By noon, load no. 2 was dried, folded, and stacked high on the top shelf of my bedroom closet with other winter wear items, because it's never winter in Hollywood. Stepping down from the small plastic step bench, I spied through the window my neighbor Earl plucking a tomato from his box garden brimming with flowers and fruit alongside the walkway.

I unlatched the window and called out to him.

"I'm home! May I come over and get my mail?"

Underwear and pajamas in the washer, I met Earl on the sidewalk.

"You sure do get a lot of junk mail," he teased and handed me a cardboard box. "How was the trip?"

"I think it's the type of adventure that needs to sink in a bit. Thanks so much for collecting my mail. And thank Carl, too, please."

"We didn't peek at any of it, but we couldn't help but notice the envelope with the foreign postage on it. And we're sure it's not from Ireland."

I hurried up the porch stairs and settled on the loveseat, the box of mail on my lap and a small trashcan at my feet.

The Republican Party needed more money. Pavilion's weekly sale rag had expired. A Closet World colorful ad enticed me. I would love to *organize*, but cannot afford it. These I tossed into the trashcan. The sanitation bill for the cabin, a CVS Pharmacy twenty-five percent off coupon, the Los Angeles Department of Water and Power bimonthly fright bill—all these I stacked on the wooden TV tray.

Writers' Digest reminded me that I had not renewed my subscription. I pondered the need for the magazine. In the two years I had been receiving it, the *how-to-write* articles had begun repeating themselves, the majority of them blurting out, "Julie, you are doing it all wrong. There must be a beginning, middle, and end. There must be a character arc! The protagonist must learn something and come out having changed and grown!" I trashed the postcard.

There were colorful, tempting coupons from Jack in the Box, Carl's Jr., and Subway. I could smell the cheese melting over the buns.

And in the contender's corner, weighing in at one hundred and seventy-eight pounds, our lethargic, despondent, and depressed rejected lover, Julie.

Shouting, "No more fast food!" I trashed them all. On the Isle I hadn't seen one drive-thru. The Irish sit down civilly in pubs to dine, always a pint of ale in hand to wash down the mushy peas.

And then there was a handwritten white envelope, letter-size, my address penned in black ink. Many hands had touched it on its journey to me. The postage stamps were varied with one of a spotted leopard curled up in the right-hand corner. The words *Postes Afghanes* were visible under the smudge of a hand stamp, round, black, and posted *Kabul* October 11, 2013. There was no return address.

I held the letter to my gut. Perhaps an American soldier has read my novels, somehow found me, and has written to me. Excited, yet wary, I rushed to the fridge for ice, a frozen tumbler, and a splash or two of Red Stag by Jim Beam, a Kentucky Straight Bourbon Whiskey infused with natural flavors of black cherry. Cocktail hour midday, I am still on Dublin time.

At the kitchen counter I refilled an e-cig with blueberry oil and settled back on the couch. The silver letter opener in hand and comforted by two selections from one of the basic food groups—fruit of blueberry and fruit of black cherry—I settled back into my big chair. What if this letter is not from a boots-on-the-ground Marine requesting to be my naughty author's pen pal, but instead hate mail from a sexually frustrated Taliban soldier assigned to camel herding duty without a ladder?

Folded precisely in three turns is the word-processed, neatly typed three-page reply to my break-up email of November 4, 2010. In his usual callous tardiness, it is three years late.

Kabul, Afghanistan

Dear Julie,

I hope you don't mind, but I had my good friend, a lawyer, go by your house to be sure of the address. You may remember, he texted me one night when you and I were out and asked what a blowjob was going for in Hollywood. He says that you have a fine blue wrought iron gate with the word "Hollywood" set above leafed filigree. The old wooden gate was in need of replacement. I am glad you were able to upgrade.

I have moved about often since leaving L.A.; first to Taliban training in Virginia and then abroad to Yemen. Alas, it seems that the freedom fighters are made up of younger men and that my services in that arena are not taken seriously. You and I know differently. My inability to master the Arabic language has held me back to some extent, whereas my father's past reputation as an officer in the Iranian Revolutionary Guard has opened many doors for me.

Under the leadership of the Quds Force, I was, therefore, assigned to global Jihad duties of a more sedentary and administrative nature. My last assignment in the USA was Boston, Massachusetts. Realizing that you keep up on these things, you are aware of our success there. Allahu Akbar. Our God is Greater.

My brother, Ghali, is still very ill. I bought him a foreclosed condo in Korea Town, not that far from you. As a realtor, you may already be aware of this. My mother now lives there, too, although we had to drag her kicking and screaming out of Westwood to put her there.

My obligations have taken me to Kabul, Afghanistan, where I have another desk job in Internet and social media recruitment for the Caliphate. I do not live in a cave here, as I had hoped. I do now wear a white long-sleeved shirt and a tie, as you had hoped. FYI, my tick has disappeared and I am no longer sneezing. Dogs are not kept as pets here.

After receiving your break-up email, I glorified myself with chastity. I cleansed my soul with it. Here I have now taken a wife, a widow with three young sons. In Afghanistan I can no longer get away with the "casual sex thing," as I did in America, but properly married her in the mosque with the entire tribe in attendance.

Nina—the girl child I wish for—is still a glimmer in my eye. Good fortune has fallen on me, as my new wife has a younger cousin, who is also a widow, but childless, whom I shall marry on Norooz, the Persian New Year and the beginning of our spring. Perhaps by Christmas, Inshalla, I can write to you in celebration of Nina's birth.

My work here is not with a rebel group, as your papers write about, but Allah's (Peace Be Upon Him) fight for the good of all people. President Obama may be a Muslim brother, but he is not the Messiah of Change. Your President will put forth a patriotic face and attempt to keep the war against what the Western World believes to be terrorists neatly in Syria, Iraq, and Afghanistan. But the war will be on your soil and on the soil of all countries welcoming multiculturalism. New and old Muslims will rise up from every continent and take out the non-believers without fear, for it is their duty to become martyrs for Allah. They won't be stopped, as believers have already been placed in high positions in the current administration. Through social media, we will use your freedom of speech, your freedom of religion, and your misguided tolerance to end your freedoms.

The leaders in the Middle East will not join forces to protect themselves from the new Islamic State. We Muslims have never been good at cooperating with each other. We are taught from birth to distrust even our own brothers.

It is my hope that you took my advice and installed locks on the inside of the door in the floor. The basement will be the perfect safe house for you in the beginning.

Before leaving for Afghanistan, I ordered on Amazon, received, and read your book. Like you, it is funny and sexy. I didn't realize I had traumatized you to such a degree. My friend saw the billboard on Sunset at Vine some time ago and alerted me to it.

I told you from our beginning that we would be good for five years, when I would have to marry and start a family. I cared for you, but you were unable to have any more children. I just want you to know that I use your pretty face to excite me. You will always be my personal Hollywood fantasy, my Jasmine.

Your Personal Aladdin,
Ali

PS. Alibaba and the Two Thieves miss you.

"Brainard here. Yes, Julie, what's up?"

"I just received a letter from Ali. Apparently, he's in Afghanistan, but there's no return address."

"Don't open it," Captain Brainard gasped. "I'll be right there."

"I already did. No white powder or poof-poof."

"You little fool. You're damned lucky you didn't get your head blown off."

"I thought it might be a fan letter. I couldn't help myself."

"Well, did he admit to any particular crimes here in the United States?"

"Not directly, of course. He mentioned Boston and babbled on about a Muslim take over. Nothing new. Just that he may have broken my heart."

"The department can't begin a global search for a heartbreaker, Julie."

It was time to make the long drive into the desert to pick up the dog, return by the cocktail hour, and to call Mother.

"Have you spoken to your sister? She never calls me back. You two have no idea what this cancer thing is doing to me."

"I've only been back home for twenty-four hours, Mother."

"You're keeping me out of the loop. I don't know what's going on."

"I happen to know," I slowed down and spoke loudly and succinctly. "I happen to know that Rae has sent you all the information on the upcoming procedure. She has the best doctors in the world. She's informed."

"I'm going to give Rae her inheritance so she can do all the things she's ever wanted to do."

"Christ, Mother, don't be so positive. Ireland was lovely, by the way."

"Rae just didn't take care of herself; smoking, drinking, the divorce, and working so hard. Are you taking care of your health?" she accused me.

"I'm glad you asked. Yes. Now that I'm receiving Medicare, I switched to the Kaiser Permanente healthcare system. It's a city within a city on both sides of Sunset Boulevard with five-dollar copays. In one day I had blood drawn for a myriad of possible ailments followed by a mammogram, vaginal and rectal swabbing, a radiology bone density x-ray, and a visit to audiology. By late afternoon I was notified by email that I have a lump in my breast, syphilis, diabetes, the bones of a thirty year old, I'm pregnant and—you're going to love this—I'm deaf."

"How can you make jokes when your sister is contagious with cancer and has only a few years to live? Don't you care?"

"Try to keep your sense of humor, Mom. I'm helping with her care. We're going wig shopping tomorrow."

"She's dying and you're going shopping?"

"Her idea. Her hair is falling out."

* * *

By Christmas season, Clint Eastwood is a single man again at the age of eighty-four and Alexandra, without an engagement ring on her hopeful slender finger, is moving in with Benjamin, who has sent his roommates scrambling to find new digs. The large items having been transported by truck in bubble wrap, I arrived at her townhouse to load into the Scion a half dozen garment bags, boxes of clothing from her chests of drawers, loose kitchen items, black plastic bags of *I don't know what's*, and long plastic keepsake boxes from her garage, keepsakes which would end up in the rafters of Aunt Rae's garage. The rejected roommate enjoyed her view of Alex's *movin' on out* from the comfort of the couch while clicking on her laptop, never taking her eyes away from my decade-old, fifty-four inch tube television, her consolation prize. After many trips up and down the steep marble staircase to and from her bedroom, and too many trips passing by the roommate, Alexandra and I caravanned across town with the final haul.

The 1920s two-bedroom, one-bath Craftsman home has not been properly cleaned in preparation for her arrival. The few closets are full of men's clothing. Together we fall in a giggling heap onto the layers of designer clothes strewn onto her mattress and box spring, now the guestroom bed.

Warn out and frustrated after two days and multiple excursions to and from West Hollywood to Silver Lake, a half hour drive one way through stop and go traffic, her weary tears hidden behind laughter, my arm under her head, she admits, "It's shameful how much stuff I've accumulated since coming to Hollywood as an eighteen-year-old kid."

"May I suggest, that we throw everything in here and sort it out later, so that when Benjamin comes home tonight, his life will not be disrupted. There will be plenty of time for that later."

"Great idea, Mom. Thanks."

I had let her go. I had my daughter back.

On the island of Maui with Benjamin and his family, Alex sends a text:

> 3:40p ALEXANDRA: There have been shark attacks close to shore, so I'm not allowed to go in the water this year above my knees, because I started my period.

I am relieved to know that the condoms are working.

> 5:45p JULIE: A new year and new beginning for you and Benjamin. Koonis-a-noo.

I like using silly, invented cuddly terms from their childhood. It reminds them that I used to be their mother.

> 5:50p ALEXANDRA: Love you. I was just talking here about how great this past year has been with you. See you next week. Happy New Year.

I must have behaved myself this year. Walking on eggshells will get you accolades.

My girlfriend Beryl is moving home to Dallas, Texas, where her married daughter has rented her a one-bedroom apartment. In celebration of my 66th we meet up at our usual gabfest spot, Denny's at the Gower Gulch strip mall on Sunset.

"Brute is not sleeping with me anymore."

"Typical male behavior. He's probably just afraid of the height. Don't get your feelings hurt."

"I miss smelling his breath in the morning. But you're the one with news. You're going to have fun shopping for furniture in Dallas."

"I'm being put in a furnished apartment, furnished by my daughter."

"Last step before assisted living."

"I brought a card. No present this year, so eat up. I'm treating."

"My mother sent me a birthday card without the sixty-six dollar check in it."

"She's very old. She probably just forgot."

"She's punishing me because I haven't come down with my sister's cancer yet. Hey, let's walk up to the Frolic Room next to the Pantages for a gin and tonic. It's Happy Hour."

"It's okay to leave my car here?"

"Sure."

We returned an hour later to the Denny's parking lot from which Beryl's Toyota Corolla had been towed in violation of overstaying the posted *one-hour limit*, a sort of going away present from the City of L. A. Outside the gate of the city tow yard, we said our good-byes. I still feel guilty for not splitting the two hundred and seventy-five dollar fine with her, because I'm the one that insisted on gin and tonic no. 2, while she had sipped her Shirley Temple.

To stay on top of the development boom, I have volunteered to be a board member of the Central Hollywood Planning, Land Use and Management Committee for District 13. We meet once a month, when the developers parade before us their plans for retail shops and skyscraping metal and glass multi-residential units soon to be towering over my little orange and blue bungalow. My question to them is always: Where is everyone going to park?

As cranes rise high into the sky all over Hollywood, I foresee that I shall never move my car again in fear that I would return to find absolutely no parking space within a square mile radius. I begin *Googling* mass transit routes and the cost of a senior citizen annual bus pass.

Poof! I'm old.

Chapter 50

Potato Flakes and the Death of Butterflies

♪ Well, you can tell by the way I use my walk
I'm a woman's man; no time to talk ♪

Stayin' Alive
The Bee Gees

Monday, April 7, 2014
Another *April's Fool Day* has come and gone. The paint on the bungalow's wooden window trim continues to peel away, unlike my burgeoning girth which clings pathetically to my upper back and drapes in a disgusting ripple over the sides of my brazier. I am moving on, but have turned in my quest for revenge in exchange for melted American cheddar cheese on greasy burgers, melted American cheddar cheese on tortilla chips, and melted American cheddar cheese on anything that will stay still long enough to be heated up in the microwave.

It's hot this morning and due to the drought, I am not allowed to water until Tuesday and again on Thursday and Sunday, which I forgot to do yesterday. When I went out to move the car from the Tuesday side back to the Monday side, the car was hot, almost San Bernardino hot, even though I had placed the sunshade inside the windshield on Saturday when I moved the car over. This is my rudimentary, stale life chore, lining up five minutes before one o'clock on Monday afternoon to secure a parking space at the end of street cleaning. I need an eight-to-five job, but I just love not having one. Everything happens for a reason, and for now moving my car is my career.

As witness to its sustained viability, when I finished off the grueling thirty minutes of Richard Simmon's 1988 videotape *Sweatin' to the Oldies*, my headscarf was soaking wet. The low-impact repertoire of dance tunes from my younger days, including "It's My Party" *(and I'll Cry If I Want to)*, *(Let's Do)* "The Twist," and *(Vroom-Vroom)* "The Leader of the Pack," along with Richard's enthusiasm for all things fat, had shamed my tired body into staying the course.

I contemplated going out au natural, but then fixed my face. The brown spots are growing larger. I'm in the sun too much. I'll need to purchase another tube of concealer soon. The hair is longer, but it's unhappy. I pulled the sides up into a tortoiseshell clip. My style choices for the afternoon: a burgundy t-shirt shouting out *Don't Talk to Me; I'm Only Talking to My Dog Today*, a birthday gift from Leighanne; a white sleeveless knit zip-up vest left unzipped; over-the-knee black Lycra exercise pants, and white *Champion* tennis shoes purchased at Payless. In need of toilet paper, I am prepared to meet my Prince Charmin' today.

Brute and I are in sync with our increasing old age, when silent farts may turn to surprise turds. He is so unbelievably in tune with me, he knows that we're down to one roll of toilet paper and two cans of O'Doul's non-alcoholic brew and yips at the front door in anticipation of his daily parade down and up Cahuenga Boulevard or up and down Vine Street. A twenty-five percent off coupon securely positioned into my purse pocket, we are off to CVS Pharmacy, Liquor, Photo, and Beauty once more.

"What? Why can't I use this coupon on these items?"

"You can't use coupons on sale items," Magda reminds me from behind the counter. I think that maybe I've been told this a dozen times in the last ten years.

"Then stop sending me these teases. You know I never buy anything unless it's on sale."

And that's what I did. Balanced on the stroller bonnet is a packaged sixteen roll bundle of Charmin'—'cause I'm worth it—and crammed halfway into the bottom basket is a twelve pack of O'Doul's non-alcoholic beer—'cause I'm cleaning up my act. If Rae is being forced to *go on the wagon*, I will do my darnedest to take the same ride.

I am now my sister's official cancer caretaker. Apparently, the health management Gestapo won't allow Rae to leave the City of Hope's experimental T-cell Immunotherapy Treatment sessions unless I'm the one to drive her away. I proudly am now the rattletrap Scion chauffeur; the go-to Gunga Din water boy for her poolside plants; the cat box bungler for her Spot; the rain, sleet, and snow mailman; the Chinese laundry fluff 'n fold service; the bedside Scrabble sidekick; the status update uplifting email messenger to Rae's best friends unknown to me; and the picture-taking historian to keep Mother informed and far away from the hospital. My new job is the best thing to come along since spending all night on a city bus shooting the MONEYGRAM scammer alert spot.

I've Googled all things *BMT*—bone marrow transplantation. My bald once golden-haired sister is going in for a month-long stay at the City of Hope; a cancer campus nestled below the 210 Freeway in the City of Duarte, a forty-five minute drive from Hollywood. From what I understand, they will drop her white blood count to zero, infuse more chemotherapy, and proceed with reintroduction of her very own harvested blood—frozen, cleaned, thawed, and ready for the IV drip. When her blood count reaches a certain level, she will be released. Rae is not a happy camper. Realizing that for four weeks while she is tethered to a rolling I.V. cart and no longer in control, I will be in charge of washing her bras and folding her clean underpanties has her in a bit of a wad.

"How's little Brute today? It's awfully hot out there for the little guy," Magda informed me and handed me the receipt.

"Please stop panting, Brute." Someone is always going to call the Animal Control officer on me. "He's fine. There's a breeze if I walk really fast, and it's my sister you should be worrying about."

By ten a.m. the sun is beating down. I can't seem to pick up speed on the half-mile stroller crawl up Cahuenga. I am flushed. I should have worn a hat. What is wrong with me? I slept last night without alcohol, week no. 2. It was unbelievably difficult to fall asleep, but I did it without getting up for a snack. But I'm so very tired. My sister is the one with cancer, not me. No, I'm the one with the potential cervical cancer caused by the sexually transmitted disease that's come back, and I have to undergo the microscope-up-the-vagina-biopsy thing again next week. I'm just hot.

The newly acquired three hundred dollar remote control thermostat tells me it is a hefty eighty degrees in the house. Using the newly acquired three hundred dollar remote-control thermostat, I turn on the newly installed eight thousand dollar unit on my roof to *cool* at seventy degrees. I finish up the tuna with a bagged American green salad topped with a sprinkle of grated cheddar cheese and a side of crumbled tortilla chips drowning in melted cheese. Indebted for life to Home Depot, I washed it all down with a frothy glass of fake beer. At ten cents per minute, the hums of cool air shower over us.

I'm watching again *The Great Deception*, a Muslim takeover documentary produced by Steven Emerson, who very kindly endorsed my first two books. My hope is that the frightening information will anger me to write once more the warning I have been destined to shout out in the dark from my little desk in my safe kitchen, "They're here and Sharia Law is coming!" Muslim women punished by acid thrown into their faces, a brutal stoning here and there, honor killings that have found their way to American soil, while our tax dollars go to support terrorism around the world. Why is no one listening?

I set the oven timer to go off in four hours and push myself to sit at the desk and open up the diary dating from December 2010 and on into February 2011, knowing Ali will not be making an appearance —not on one scrawled, single-spaced lined page. It's time to stop the devastating misery and to spill my guts once again. I begin to type into Microsoft Word a sort of outline for Part Three, but I am overwhelmed. I've waited too long. I've procrastinated beyond my initial knee-jerk inspiration. Is it true that Ali himself wrote the first two books for me? It is true. He was my silent partner, my ghostwriter, my unknowing cheerleader and companion through the days and nights of misgivings, fear of failure, and indescribable loneliness.

I glance through the scribbled pages: still in misery over the Muslim, my gradual weight gain, my depression, and my lack of any kind of discipline; the rain, Obama's new America, the Israeli roofer, the rain, Islam and honor killings, the Crucifix chained Armenian buttslapper, Mom's continual crazed cruelty, washing Alexandra's laundry on Christmas Day with a dryer that is not drying, the dryer vent men. Men, men, men, but—where is the story?

I hammer out a prologue, whip up a vague outline, and make notes of a plausible ending, all the while sipping O'Doul's and puffing cappuccino-flavored nicotine oil.

The buzzer goes off. It's already seven-thirty.

"Wake up, Brute, old man, let's go for another walk."

He cocked his head, shook out his ears, and stumbled over the kitchen floor toward the front door.

"I want sautéed spinach and instant mashed potatoes for dinner."

Out on the sidewalk, the streetlights have blinked on. It is still desert hot, or is it just me? At Sunset, the boulevard is cheery with couples hand in hand, groups of guys in black hoodies peddling passed on skateboards, old women pulling two-wheeled cloth grocery carts, and smiling pedestrians cooing over Brute.

I stop at Bank of America and slide my card in at the ATM. The account is empty; still no deposit from the unemployment department due to its confusion over my reported thirty-two cent check from The American Broadcasting Company for those residual-stimulating nine lines on *General Hospital* way back when.

Rolling over stars in the sidewalk, I stopped to peek through the green net construction fence at the historical corner of Selma and Vine, where an unattractive parking lot serving the restaurants, the nightclubs, and the Pantages Theatre had been just weeks before. It was here in 1913 Cecil B. DeMille and Jesse Laskey rented a barn and the first feature film, *The Sqaw Man*, was produced. The construction boys and their toys have begun excavating the site. Soon to emerge over my head, shading the street, and blocking the view of the famous sign on the hill, will be three-hundred-plus high-end apartments atop a ground level retail strip mall and a massive underground parking structure. Each time I pass by, the yellow dump trucks become smaller and farther away. China must be their destination.

The billboard stretching the length of the 1600 Vine luxury apartment building towering above Trader Joe's warns me of another premiering cable show: *Deadbeat.* A pudgy guy with facial hair in a knitted ski cap is grinning down at me. Something about how he helps ghosts, but can't help himself, a *Hulu* original. Looming behind him, as my neck gets a good stretch, is Disney's attempt to destroy another classic: a scathing sky-scraping billboard for *Maleficent*, a cruel spin off of *Sleeping Beauty.* Angelina Jolie is winged enormously in black and blue feathers and horned in a most frightening way; her traditionally wet and bloated beet red lips prepped to cast a vicious spell over the unsuspecting survey takers attacking tourists on the sidewalk outside of Trader Joe's.

Unscathed, we wheel in through the glass and steel frontage and pass by the art deco caricature of Charlie Chaplin and the welcome slogan: *Trader Joe's Production With You As Our Stars.* Traversing the cleanest floors in Hollywood, we grab a fresh bag of baby spinach and check out the dry foods aisle. Enlisting my reading glasses, I am dismayed to discover there are no instant mashed potatoes, just instant mac and cheese, couscous, quinoa pasta, and organic brown rice. In this day of gluten-free hysteria, the cult grocer has outlawed my spiraling downfall into white, coagulating yumminess. The arrogant assumption is that only fat people eat mashed potatoes made from chemically preserved instant flakes; therefore, this naughty unnatural nutrient is not allowed on a pious Trader Joe shelf.

Laying down rubber wheeled skid marks, I slide into the fast lane. I've got to get to the Giant Dollar before it closes. There I won't be shunned for buying a little box of dried carbohydrates. Here in urban trendy territory, the clerks are always irritatingly cheerful until you stop the flow of traffic with a simple question. "Why don't you carry instant mashed potatoes?"

"Nobody ever bought 'em."

Arrogant and smug, he can't wait to move me along. "Next person in line!" As usual, the next person in line is up my ass before I can toss the spinach into the stroller.

I hurry down Vine to Brute's favorite pee spot on the lawn at the driveway of Chase Bank. The resident stinky street beggar bids me good evening with a tip of his top hat. Brute wanders in an irritating circle on the infected grass to find just the right spot.

"Do your thing. Hurry up now."

We fly by the steps of Chase Bank and its poor man's Trevi fountain at Sunset and continue down Vine to the liquor store for a lottery ticket. Ahmed is staring blankly at a soccer game on the big screen on the wall.

"This job must make you crazy, just sitting here all day," I interrupted the play-by-play.

Handing me my ticket, he speaks. "Tonight you lucky."

"These numbers are for Tuesday, tomorrow night."

"You have nice makeup on tonight. Tonight you lucky."

"Thanks, Ahmed."

I push on to get to Giant Dollar before it closes. What time is it? When do they close?

As I rush by the red neon lights of Winchell's Donuts, a ghost passes through me. I'm caught unaware. I had stopped looking for him on the streets months ago. I had even quit searching the news for his name to appear in connection with the bombing of any local synagogues. I shake the déjà vu off, the scent of an evening long ago, a two-block drive at midnight when Ali bought us something sweet, because he needed sugar. He's probably dying of untreated diabetes in Afghanistan, where I put him.

I have written the prologue, totaling five pages, scratched out a rough, incomplete outline, and envisioned an ending to Part Three of the trilogy. I'm excited to write the entire book and be done with it. Then I'll hysterically throw out all the research notebooks, the post-it notes, and all of the Islam info books. I'll have a bonfire in the barbeque, tossing the *Qur'an* in first. I'll take a break to garden, to paint the trim on the house, to sweat at the gym until they beg me to leave, and then begin to write Nobel Peace Prize worthy romance novels, beginning with the winsome tale of a lovely lady who falls rapturously in love with her shaggy, white Italian dog—a Maltese who turns into a handsome, virile, wealthy monarch each time she rubs his belly. The conflict: her children want to commit the dog lover to an insane asylum and confiscate her bank accounts and property, because they're never around long enough to see the little dog do his magic.

I skip behind the stroller, Brute's bunny ears flying.

The intersection at Fountain is busy. Brute receives more adoration from pedestrians in the crosswalk. Through the windows of El Pollo Loco, I see a long line of fire-roasted chicken lovers. I just want my mashed taters.

The clip in my hair has become loose. I pull it out, shake my head, and wheel into the parking lot under the new brightly lit Goodwill store signage at the strip mall shared with the Giant Dollar store.

"Oh, boy, it's still open," I exclaim.

The transvestite bicyclist pedals by, her candy cane pink stiletto heels hitting the pavement, and shoots me an arrogant eye roll to which I respond, "I have a dog I'm talking to here!"

The lot is lined with parked cars, an unusual amount of cars for this time of night. It's been too hot for everyone, I suppose. Shoppers have waited for the cool of evening to venture out. I bump the stroller over the threshold, passing by the sign in the window that reads:

NO PET
NO STROLLER
NO BACKPACK

Mario, the constant unarmed security guard, greets us with a welcome swath of his hand and a hum; a hum that has been known to bellow into a full aria while he double duties as a shelf stocker.

Over the dirtiest linoleum floors in Hollywood, we head straight to aisle no. 5 to grab a box of instant potatoes and slide into the checkout line, where the Latina clerk leans over the counter with a kind "Hola, Brute." Exactly one dollar and I'm pushing the stroller down the little ramp to make a left into the well-lit parking lot, when I catch a glimpse of man-boy in shades of gray looking at me as if he's about to raise his arm and wave a *hello*. He has a nose too wide for his face. His hair is ink black, thin, and sparse. Clean-shaven, he is truly gray in the face.

He's wearing a long-sleeved V-neck gray sweater over a dark gray t-shirt over dark gray jeans. It's hot out and he's dressed for a cold wind.

He saunters, yet moves closer with a determined swagger. Continuing on my way, my head down, I hear the clap of wood to asphalt as he moves closer. Is he wearing boots with well-worn heels? Somehow I know I should know him. Is he an extra I worked with, a carwash jockey, someone I chatted with on an Internet dating site and then blocked?

I am walking behind parked cars toward the sidewalk and still wondering who he could have been, as he has obviously reached the inside of the store, when I hear a frantic, "Julie? Julie?"

A breathless second passes and I hear it again, "Julie!" I am caught in an empty parking space under the bright lights of the lot. I spin the stroller around and he's standing there. Exhausted at the end of a ten-yard sprint up and over the craggy rocks of the moors, his arms heavy with freshly gathered heather, in desperation Heathcliff speaks.

> Didn't you recognize me? I thought it was
> a baby in there. Where's the big one?

He passed away a few years ago.

> I'm sorry.

♫ At first I was afraid, I was petrified, kept thinkin'
I couldn't live without you by my side ♫

My head cocked in shock, I study his face. Who is this man? Is this the lost love I've been whining over? Is this my masturbatory fantasy? I must have totally dreamed up my Muslim lover, because this guy isn't worth writing about. Sir Lawrence Olivier he is not. Shame on me; this guy isn't worth a trip to the manicurist or one lavender bubble bath.

> How have you been? Are you still acting?

♫ And so you're back from outer space ♫

I book a job now and then. You look like shit.
What the hell are you doing at my dollar store?

He no longer looks like Johnny Depp—on crack, maybe—if he ever did. His full boyish beautiful face I cherished is now gaunt, the pores in need of a good scrubbing. He is truly dismal.

>I drove in to get some candy.
>My bloodsugar's low. I feel sick.

You always feel sick.

>I have a friend, a doctor, and he's had
>me hiking and running and I'm too
>old and out of shape. I can't do it.

You're going to be only forty-four next week.

>I feel much older. You remember my—

I remember you getting out of a day with me
by way of the 'Persians don't hike' excuse.
Do you even remember how old I am?

>You know that never made any difference.

Mario has emerged, and in anticipation of a parking lot scuffle, he leans protectively on the entrance railing. "Everything okay, miss?" I nod and Mario serenades, his hum now at full throttle.

>♪ Will you still need me?
>Will you still feed me?
>When I'm sixty-four? ♪

Sixty-six. I'm sixty-six!

"I never would have guessed that," Mario complimented.
Brute gazed up at me with his *I wanna go home now* look.

Juliet Montague

Why are you in my neighborhood?

> I go to L.A. Fitness up on El Centro
> just below Hollywood Boulevard.

You were just there?

> I go by your house all the time.

♪ I have often walked down this street before, but the pavement always stayed beneath my feet before ♪

Why?

> Because I go to L.A. Fitness.

He doesn't look like he's ever lifted a five-pound dumbbell.

> I thought maybe you'd be outside someday
> and then maybe I'd come by.

♪ All at once am I several stories high knowing I'm on the street where you live! ♪

Do you like the new gate?

> Sure. The old gate was a mess. Looks
> expensive. Did you design it yourself?

With the help of the wrought iron man.

> Nice. What's he singing?

He's serenading me with a song from *My Fair Lady*.

> Never heard of it.

Of course you haven't. You traumatized me.

> I think you were afraid of me
> because of my good looks.

What?

> Oh, Julie. How long has it been?

Three years and five months!
You didn't even answer my breakup letter.

He's taller. No, he's got those heeled snake boots on.

> You sent me a letter?

No. An email. I didn't have an address.
Where do you live?

> I'm sort of a hippy. No place really.
> I don't remember an email.

I do. I can see it as if I were holding it in my hand.

> Dear Ali,
>
> Just wanted to check in.
> November 4, 2010: Day no. 22 of no smoke!
> Day no. 3 of no alcohol! Day no. 17 of **NO HUSBAND**!
> My head is clear and my face looks fabulous!
> Today: Day no. 1 of the end of cruelty, oppression, and
> manipulation by an immature, insecure, selfish sociopath.
> Do not contact me again.
>   The Lady in Red
>
>   P.S. If I am kicking you when you are down, try standing up.

So out of the blue, for no reason, you just quit coming over?

> I don't remember.

♪ What kind of fool am I, who never fell in love? ♪

You just quit texting me for no reason?

                              I don't remember.

♪ What kind of lips are these that lied with every kiss? ♪

You didn't know I'd blocked your number from my cell phone? Which, by the way, cost me $4.95 a month.

                              I just don't remember.

♪ That whispered empty words of love
that left me alone like this? ♪

You didn't even know I broke up with you or why?

                              I don't remember. I think you
                              were just getting—

♪ Why can't I fall in love like any other man? ♪

    "Mario, please, you have to stop singing. I don't have the rights to any of those lyrics."
    "Okay, miss. Yell out if you need me," and he hummed away into the lights of aisle no. 3: pesticide, pet supply, candles, auto supply, hardware, and home décor.

I was asking too many questions. Like, why can't you love me?

                                Yeah, maybe.

That extraordinary dimple in his chin...

Why aren't you in Afghanistan working for the Taliban? I thought you were going to save the widows and all the children of Palestine! Why are you standing in the parking lot of my dollar store—and my Goodwill store?

> It's L.A. It's so comfortable, you
> never leave and do those things—
> things that take a bit of energy.

Not to mention you are on the No-Fly list.

So you didn't write me a letter from Afghanistan?

> I don't remember.

You don't remember being in Afghanistan or you don't remember writing me a letter from Afghanistan?

> I don't remember.

Let's add amnesia to the list of his illnesses.

So you're working for Hamas right here in L.A.

> I won't have anything to do
> with those Muslim gangsters.

Apparently, the terrorists won't have anything to do with you either.

He's dreary. There is a gloomy doom settled upon him. Was it always there and I didn't see it? He is absolutely ashen. I'm not letting this guy's foot anywhere near my glass slipper.

You're missing a tooth.

> Yes. I'm going to get a real tooth.

So a plug and not a partial. A partial can be icky.

There is no way in hell I'm putting my tongue in that hole.

Juliet Montague

> Yes, I have a good dentist. He'll
> take good care of me.

It was that little brown tooth,
the one you hid with a half smile.

> I didn't hide it.

Yes, you did. You tried to hide it by not smiling
all the way, like you're doing right now.

> Well, right now there's a hole there.

What color are my eyes?

> Brown.

They're hazel.

> It was dark in the basement.

How's your brother?

> He's still in treatment.

I know you purchased a
one-bedroom condo in Korea Town.

> You *Google* me?

I *Googled* you and found the
information on public records.

> Two bedrooms. I bought it for Ghali.

You quit-claimed it to him,
but don't you live there?

Nah.

A bank foreclosure; $230k cash

I keep studying his face. His eyes are no longer mesmerizing me, turning me into a wanton slut. His lips are still appealing, full, yet I have no desire to kiss them.

Since you, I've really been examining my life, my attitudes toward women, girls. Too much sex—you know I don't do one-night stands—but too many relationships outside of marriage is not good, especially for a Muslim.

You said the same thing five years ago.
So you've been chaste for how long?

Been what?

Celibate. Not having intercourse.

Oh, like chastity.

If he's not getting any, it's easy to see why. His hair is dirty. A few long greased strands are spun across the receded hairline. He keeps tossing his head back to keep them from falling in his eyes. He's dying it black, because at the temples are the telltale blotches of gray. No, not gray, but white. How did I ever compare him to the beauty of Olivier Martinez? Olivier still has hair.

He reaches into his pants pocket to pull out his phone and dips his head to do so. Yes, the genetically approved bald spot, shining like a Middle Eastern stamp of authenticity, is now the size of softball.

Give me your number and maybe we can hang out.

> *Urban Dictionary: 1.* **hang out**
> *Less serious than getting together or dating.*
> *Spending time with someone in the context*
> *of casually exploring whether you like*
> *someone as just a friend or maybe more*
> *than a friend.*

You didn't keep my number?

> I lost a lot of numbers. Long story. All my other girlfriends call me, so I still have their numbers. Want to hang out?

The CIA ran over your phone after you tossed it out the car window during a high-speed chase.

The computer programming, how's it going? Your company?

> I let the computer geeks go and shut it down.

You never paid them anyway.

Why?

> My eyes were hurting.

You're wearing your contact lenses.

> Right now I am.

Can he see the Lifestyle Lift scars in front of my earlobes?

What are you doing for work?

> Ah, this and that. Not much. Taking some time off.

Daddy's money from Iran is endless.

You're a broken record.

> Why do you say that?

You were on vacation when we first met.
You told me you were living off your savings.
Much later you let me know all the money
was in your brother's name and in Iran.

> I told you that?

Yes, when you had me
house hunting for you.

> I was messing with you.

Yes, the art of taqiyya, Allah's given right to all Muslims to lie unabashedly to all non-Muslims.

You stopped kissing me.

> No, I always kissed you.

No. You told me that men didn't like to kiss,
that the only reason you kissed me was to get me
excited, but that I was wet the minute you parked
your car on my street.

> We had a connection. We really did.

And you were mean to me, telling
me I should be happy that a stud like
you bothers to see an old woman.

> I may have been mentally ill when
> we were seeing each other.

No, that was your brother.

> We really had a connection, a spiritual
> connection. You really look good.

Tell me that you're sorry.

No, I don't. I've gained a lot of
weight since you last saw me.

> You always had a pretty face. And I like
> you heavier. Come on, babe. Give me
> your number. We'll hang out.

He likes you just the way you are.

I'm not giving you my number.

He didn't ever write them down? My cell number? My landline?

My sister has cancer. She's still drinking
and smoking and fighting. I'm going to be
busy helping her.

> I love Americans. You're all so
> positive and resilient.

You don't even know my sister.
You never met her.

> Are you still smoking?

I quit several times. I smoke e-cigs now.

That's still tobacco.

Not tobacco, just nicotine in delightful flavors.
And why did you leave me crying in the basement?

I quit smoking by just asking god.
Just ask him to help you. Why do you
remember all this stuff anyway?

I have over nine hundred
pages of notes.

But why? You're just upsetting yourself.
You wrote a book?

Don't even nod. Change the subject. Two can play at this game.

I just had a new air conditioning
system put in. New vents, coils, ducts,
the whole deal.

You're tempting me.

And I have HPV again. Apparently it comes
back on its own—without any physical contact.

Hey, and I didn't give you that 'cause
no one else has it. It was someone
else, some guy before me.

Five years before you,
a sixty-seven-year-old Dutchman?

Who? Yes.

Don't you always wear a condom?

Not when I'm in a relationship.

This answer put the nail in the coffin. I shall never forget its unapologetic ignorant grandiosity, which assured that I would never again open the gate to him.

Have you marched every girl you've been with into the gynecologist?

Ah, Julie, Julie.

His arms reached out and pulled me into his chest. My arms automatically wrapped themselves around his spindly shoulders, because I'm made that way, I guess. My lips were too close to his neck. I searched for a memory scent, but the scent that bonded me to him and opened up my insides to him was gone.

Has he taken to wearing deodorant? Turn away. Move back. I stayed. He was so close, yet so out of reach. Then his small, thin fingers were uncharacteristically at the base of my neck tickling through my hair, like awkward, newborn fluttering butterflies unaware they had but a short time to live. But tonight there were no butterflies churning in my stomach. They had somehow found their way into the world.

Brute let out a screeching yip. I reached down and brought him out of the stroller and cradled him in my arms.

He wants to go home.

He's again pulled out the womanizing weapon from his pocket.

No, you'll just start texting me again.

Ali slid the phone back into his jeans, and with his head down he backed away from me. For a moment, his foot made a gesture, as if it were kicking a stone across a playground. He looked up and dealt himself the pity card. The power of his cunning persuasion lost on me, I took in a final glance of someone I used to love.

> You're right. No phone calls.
> I shall surprise you one day
> and ring the doorbell.

♫ You can ring my be-e-ell, ring my bell ♫

Oh, how I miss disco. Where are my girls? Anita Ward, Gloria Gaynor, Donna Summer, Diana Ross, Irene Cara?

I set my best friend in the stroller, his two fluffy front paws proudly propping him up, and spun toward the exit. Without a glance back, we hurried home to write the true and final ending, culminating in my shame of allowing a pretender to hold my heart for so very long, an ending that would free me to write a new beginning.

Traffic had thinned out on Vine Street. It must be almost nine o'clock. At the signal, not to miss my chance to leave the scene before the light turned red, my bum knee be damned, I swiftly put my traveling feet into high gear. My grungy Payless Champion brand tennis shoes would be, perhaps, the most comfortable and trustworthy glass slippers I'd ever need, and my own feet fit them very well indeed.

Hitting the opposite curve at record-breaking speed, I passed the Armenian Church driveway and realized I had forgotten to ask him if we were still married.

The End

Juliet Montague

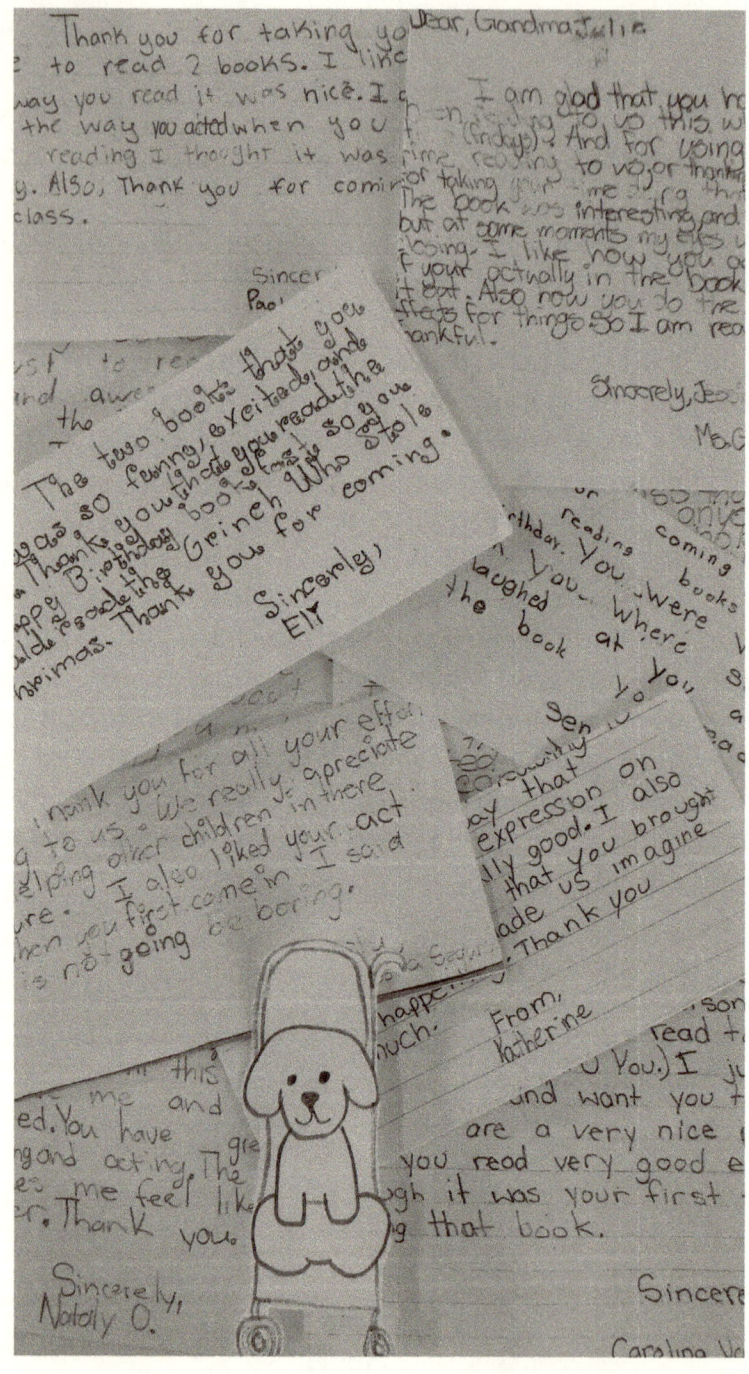

Epilogue

♪ I wouldn't have missed it for the world,
Wouldn't have missed lovin' you . . . ♪

I Wouldn't Have Missed It for the World
Rhonda Kye Fleming, Dennis W. Morgan, Charles Quillen

The only good parts of a book are the explanations that are left out.

Charles Baudelaire, French poet and critic
1821-1867

Alexandra and Benjamin are engaged and I am on *The Mother of the Bride* diet from hell.

Rae is in remission and retired. She has alerted me that she never voted for President Obama, currently a popular trend. We're having fun being sisters.

Mother, her cat, her spiders, and her ants are all doing well.

The City of Los Angeles has approved the architectural plans for Captain Brainard's bungalow remodel. He will be adding another story to Bunny's little house. We're going to grow old together.

Wayne stopped paying Blondie's rent and hasn't seen her since.

A retail chain, Dollar Tree, has replaced my Dollar Store. Mario no longer sings there.

Brute snores the day away in his bed behind me under the butcher-block table until rousted and forced to join the living. He insists on at least one stroller adventure per day.

On December 2nd, 2015 my hometown was put on the map, when two devout Muslims, a husband and wife, wearing ski masks and black tactical gear gunned down employees at a holiday get-together at the San Bernardino County Inland Regional Center on Waterman Avenue. Leaving twenty-two injured and fourteen dead, it was the largest loss of life on American soil in a terrorist attack since 9/11/2001. Subsequent to the vehicle pursuit later that day, both Jihadists initiated a gun battle exchange and were killed by police.

The Soundtrack

Song	Composer
Addicted to Love	Robert Palmer
What'll I do?	Irving Berlin
Summer in the City	The Lovin' Spoonful
California Girls	Brian Wilson and Mike Love
I Couldn't Live Without Your Love	Tony Hatch and Jackie Trent
You Can't Hurry Love	The Supremes
The Lady is a Tramp	Rogers and Hart
I'm Amazed	Paul McCartney
Rockin' Around the Christmas Tree	Brenda Lee
All I want for Christmas is You	Carey and Walter Afanasieff
Happy Birthday to You	Patty and Mildred Hill
Shut up and Drive	Rivers Rutherford
It's Raining Men	Paul Jabara and Paul Shaffer
Smoke, Smoke, Smoke That Cigarette	Merle Davis and Tex Williams
We're Off to See the Wizard	Harold Arlen and E.Y. Harburg
Stormy Weather	Harold Arlen and Ted Koehler
Tonight/Westside Story	Leonard Bernstein and Stephen Sondheim
Raindrops Keep Falling on My Head	Burt Bacharach and Hal David
Officer Krupke/Westside Story	Harold Arlen and E.Y. Harburg
Lemonade/Babes in Toyland	Mel Leven and George Bruns
America/Westside Story	Leonard Bernstein and Stephen Sondheim
I Have a Love/Westside Story	Leonard Bernstein and Stephen Sondheim
Somewhere/Westside Story	Leonard Bernstein and Stephen Sondheim

Jet Song/Westside Story	Leonard Bernstein and Stephen Sondheim
Unchained Melody	Alex North and Hy Zaret
Matchmaker/Fiddler on the Roof	Jerry Bock and Sheldon Harnick
Hot Stuff	Fahey, Billotte, Blanchard, Faltermeyer, Forsey, Gallifent, and Kenny
I'm in the Mood for Love	Jimmy McHugh and Dorothy Fields
Sway	Luis Demetrio and Pablo Beltran Ruiz
Come Fly with Me	Jimmy Van Heusen and Sammy Cahn
Have You Ever Really Loved a Woman?	Bryan Adams, Robert Lange, Michael Kamen
There's No Business Like Show Business	Irving Berlin
That's Amore	Henry Warren and Jack Brooks
Let It Snow	Sammy Cahn and Jule Styne
The Best Song Ever	Amanda Flynn, Katie Armiger, Bruce Wallace
A Whole New World/Aladdin	Alan Menken and Tim Rice
It's Gonna Take a Miracle	Teddy Randazzo, Bob Weinstein, Lou Stallman
I'm Too Sexy (For My Shirt)	Right Said Fred
Under the Sea/The Little Mermaid	Alan Menken and Howard Ashman
When Irish Eyes Are Smiling	Chauncy Olcott, Ernest R. Ball, George Graff, Jr.
Danny Boy	Frederic Weatherly
After Loving You	Charles Aznavour
Surfin' Safari	Brian Wilson and Mike Love
Will You Still Love Me Tomorrow?	Gerry Goffin and Carole King
Crazy	Seal and Guy Sigsworth
I Hate to See October Go	Johnny Mercer, Barry Manilow
Rockin' the Kasbah	The Clash
Winter Wonderland	Leroy Anderson

The Love Theme from Superman	Paul Williams
Ascot Opening Day/My Fair Lady	Alan Jay Lerner and Frederick Lowe
My Funny Valentine	Lorenz Hart, Richard Rodgers
When I'm 64	Lennon-McCartney
How Much is That Doggie in the Window?	Bob Merrill
God Bless America	Irving Berlin
For Once in My Life	Ron Miller, Orlando Murden
That's Life	Dean Kay, Kelly Gordon
Papa, Don't Preach	Stephen Bray, Brian Elliot, Madonna
Ain't No Mountain High Enough	Nickolas Ashford and Valerie Simpson
Summertime Blues	Eddie Cochran
Hakuna Matata/The Lion King	Elton John and Tim Rice
Bridge Over Troubled Water	Paul Simon
I Fell in Love	Benmont Tench, Carlene Carter, Howie Epstein, Perry M. Lameck
Stayin' Alive/Saturday Night Fever	Barry Gibb, Robin Gibb, Maurice Gibb
I Will Survive	Dino Fekaris, Freddie Perren
On the Street Where You Live/My Fair Lady	Alan J. Lerner and Frederick Lowe
What Kind of Fool Am I?	Leslie Bricusse and Anthony Newley
Ring My Bell	Frederick Knight
I Wouldn't Have Missed it for the World	Rhonda Kye Fleming, Dennis W. Morgan, Charles Quillen, Ronnie Milsap

Juliet's Recommended Reading

American Jihad; The Terrorists Living Among Us; Steven Emerson

A Time to Betray; The Astonishing Double Life of a CIA Agent inside the Revolutionary Guards of Iran; Reza Kahlili

Miss Webster and Chérif ; Patricia Dunker

The Ayatollah Begs to Differ; The Paradox of Modern Iran; Hooman Majd

The Final Move Beyond Iraq; The Final Solution While the World Sleeps; Mike Evans

They Must Be Stoppped; Why We Must Defeat Radical Islam and How We Can Do It; Brigitte Gabriel

Thirty-Three Secrets Arab Men Never Tell American Women; A Dissection of How Muslims Treat Women and Infidels; Cassandra

Understanding Muhammad, A Psychobiography; Ali Sina

Dreams from My Father, copyright 1995 and 2004, Barack Obama

Awakening the Actor Within; C. Stephen Foster

NURSING HELLo; a graphic novel by Joel Craig

About the Author

In her sincere desire to contribute to World Peace, Juliet is no longer dating. She continues to audition for commercials touting disreputable pharmaceuticals, but refuses to show one more blood-sucking lookie-loo a fixer-upper. She and Brute are happy at home in Hollywood, where Juliet begins to pen her next roman à clef; true names will again be changed to protect the *not-so* innocent and to nip in the bud any frivolous lawsuits.

In April of 2016, all three volumes of *THE MUSLIM ROMANCE TRILOGY* were scrutinized and eventually banned from print-on-demand services by Ms. Montague's own self-publisher, Abbott Press, an arm of Author Solutions Corporation, when she refused to be censored. Her website was also taken down.

www.facebook.com/muslimromance
www.amazon.com/author/julietmontague
www.youtube.com/whatsmyintention

www.ingramcontent.com/pod-product-compliance
Lightning Source LLC
Chambersburg PA
CBHW020726160426
43192CB00006B/129